P9-CRB-940

OBJECT-ORIENTED DATA STRUCTURES

USING

JAVA™ THIRD EDITION

NELL DALE
University of Texas, Austin

DANIEL T. JOYCE
Villanova University

CHIP WEEMS
University of Massachusetts, Amherst

JONES & BARTLETT
LEARNING

World Headquarters

Jones & Bartlett Learning
40 Tall Pine Drive
Sudbury, MA 01776
978-443-5000
info@jblearning.com
www.jblearning.com

Jones & Bartlett Learning Canada
6339 Ormindale Way
Mississauga, Ontario L5V 1J2
Canada

Jones & Bartlett Learning International
Barb House, Barb Mews
London W6 7PA
United Kingdom

Jones & Bartlett Learning books and products are available through most bookstores and online booksellers. To contact Jones & Bartlett Learning directly, call 800-832-0034, fax 978-443-8000, or visit our website, www.jblearning.com.

Substantial discounts on bulk quantities of Jones & Bartlett Learning publications are available to corporations, professional associations, and other qualified organizations. For details and specific discount information, contact the special sales department at Jones & Bartlett Learning via the above contact information or send an email to specialsales@jblearning.com.

Copyright © 2012 by Jones & Bartlett Learning, LLC

All rights reserved. No part of the material protected by this copyright may be reproduced or utilized in any form, electronic or mechanical, including photocopying, recording, or by any information storage and retrieval system, without written permission from the copyright owner.

Production Credits
Publisher: Cathleen Sether
Senior Acquisitions Editor: Timothy Anderson
Senior Editorial Assistant: Stephanie Sguigna
Production Director: Amy Rose
Associate Production Editor: Tiffany Sliter
Associate Marketing Manager: Lindsay White
V.P., Manufacturing and Inventory Control: Therese Connell
Cover and Title Page Design: Kristin E. Parker
Composition: Northeast Compositors, Inc.
Cover Image: © Image Source/age fotostock
Chapter opener image courtesy of Earth Sciences and Image Analysis Laboratory, NASA Johnson Space Center [ref #STS026-41-86], http://eol.jsc.nasa.gov
Printing and Binding: Malloy, Inc.
Cover Printing: Malloy, Inc.

Library of Congress Cataloging-in-Publication Data

Dale, Nell.
  Object-oriented data structures using Java / Nell Dale, Daniel T.
Joyce, and Chip Weems. — [3rd ed.].
       p. cm.
  Includes index.
  ISBN-13: 978-1-4496-1354-9 (casebound)
  ISBN-10: 1-4496-1354-3 (casebound)
  1. Object-oriented programming (Computer science) 2. Data structures
(Computer science) 3. Java (Computer program language) I. Joyce,
Daniel T. II. Weems, Chip. III. Title.
  QA76.64.D35 2012
  005.1'17—dc22
                                    2010043038
6048

Printed in the United States of America
15 14 13 12 11   10 9 8 7 6 5 4 3 2 1

To Alfred G. Dale.

–ND

To Kathy, Tom, and Julie, thanks for the love and support.

–DJ

To Lisa, Charlie, and Abby, thank you for tolerating all of the hours that I have not been able to spend with you, while working on this.

–CW

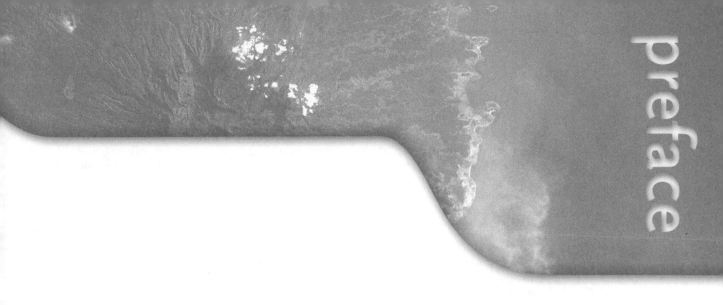

Welcome to the third edition of *Object-Oriented Data Structures Using Java™*. This book presents the algorithmic, programming, and structuring techniques of a traditional data structures course in an object-oriented context. You'll find the familiar topics of stacks, queues, lists, trees, graphs, sorting, searching, Big-O complexity analysis, and recursion, all covered from an object-oriented point of view using Java. We stress software engineering principles throughout, including modularization, information hiding, data abstraction, stepwise refinement, the use of visual aids, the analysis of algorithms, and software verification methods.

To the Student

At this point you have completed at least one semester of computer science coursework. You know that an algorithm is a sequence of unambiguous instructions for solving a problem. You can take a problem of moderate complexity, design a small set of classes/objects that work together to solve the problem, code the method algorithms needed to make the objects work, and demonstrate the correctness of your solution.

Algorithms describe actions. These actions manipulate data. For most interesting problems that are solved using computers, the structure of the data is just as important as the structure of the algorithms used to manipulate the data. Using this textbook you will discover that the way you structure data affects how efficiently you can use the data; you will see how the nature of the problem you are attempting to solve dictates your structuring decisions; and you will learn about the data structures that computer scientists have developed over the years to help solve problems.

Abstract Data Types

Over the last 20 years the focus of the data structures course has broadened considerably. The topic of data structures now has been subsumed under the broader topic of *abstract data types* (*ADTs*)—the study of classes of objects whose logical behavior is defined by a set of values and a set of operations. The term *abstract data type* represents a domain of values and a set of operations on those values that are specified independently of any particular implementation. The shift in emphasis is representative of the move toward more abstraction in computing education. We are interested in the abstract properties of classes of data objects in addition to how the objects might be represented in a program.

In this textbook we view our data structures from three different perspectives: their specification, their application, and their implementation. The specification describes the logical or abstract level—*what* the logical relationships among the data elements are and *what* operations can be performed on the structure. The application level, sometimes called the user level, is concerned with how the data structure is used to solve a problem—*why* the operations do what they do. The implementation level involves the coding details—*how* the structures and operations are implemented.

Object-Oriented Programming with Java

Our primary goal is to present the traditional data structure topics with an emphasis on problem solving and software design. Using the Java programming language as a vehicle for problem solutions, however, presents an opportunity for students to expand their familiarity with a modern programming language and the object-oriented paradigm. As our data structure coverage unfolds, we introduce and use the appropriate Java constructs that support our primary goals. Starting early and continuing throughout the text, we introduce and expand on the use of many Java features such as classes, objects, generics, packages, interfaces, library classes, inheritance, and exceptions. Our case studies demonstrate how to identify and filter candidate classes and how to organize modular solutions to interesting problems. We use Universal Modeling Language (UML) class diagrams throughout to help us model and visualize our classes and their interrelationships.

Second Edition Improvements Retained

The second edition of this textbook included many significant changes to the first edition. This third edition retains and builds on all of those improvements. We maintain the early introduction to the heart of the textbook material, introducing data structures and the use of references (pointers, links) as a structuring mechanism in Chapter 1. We have retained the popular Chapter 2, which was added to the second edition, where we introduce a simple yet interesting ADT (a StringLog). Our development of this ADT, including both array-based and reference-based implementations, acts as a gentle introduction to the approaches used for the more complicated ADTs throughout the rest of the text.

In the second edition we also rearranged our coverage of the classic data structures, starting with the simpler stack and queue structures and then moving to the more complicated lists, trees, and graphs. We continue to follow that approach, as well as introducing recursion much earlier (Chapter 4 rather than Chapter 7), immediately after our coverage of the related Stack ADT. This rearrangement of topics from the second edition allows our List ADT coverage in Chapter 6 to include both traditional and recursive implementations of list operations, and to include a presentation of an indexed list ADT.

In addition to the major structural changes in the second edition, we streamlined our presentation of concepts throughout, added even more exercises, and included many additional example applications. We took advantage of several of the new features of Java 5.0, including autoboxing and the Scanner class, to simplify our problem solutions. Two new appendices that rounded out our second edition improvements have been retained—one devoted to Java 5.0's new generics mechanism and one providing Application Programmer Interfaces (APIs) for the Java library classes used throughout the textbook.

New to the Third Edition

When we published the second edition we chose to omit generics for reasons outlined in Section 3.2 of that edition. We believe that was a reasonable decision at the time—but since then, Java generics have become a mature technology. Therefore, we now include their use throughout the textbook, providing the dual benefits of allowing for a type-safe use of data structures while exposing students to modern approaches.

With this edition we are pleased to be among the first data structures textbooks to address the topics of concurrency and synchronization, which are growing in importance as computer systems move to using more cores and threads to obtain additional performance with each new generation. We introduce the topic in the new Section 5.7 where we start with the basics of Java threads, continue through examples of thread interference and synchronization, and culminate in a discussion of efficiency concerns.

In addition to the two major changes described above, we have improved the book in many smaller ways. We have included more code examples, added programming exercises including several project-type exercises, rearranged the order of presentation of topics in several chapters, simplified the list architecture used in Chapter 6, and clarified many tables and figures. In the robust set of exercises at the end of each chapter, you will still find the familiar computer icon indicating an exercise involving programming—but now you will see two such icons beside those problems with a "significant" programming component, indicating exercises that might be used for major class projects.

We hope that you enjoy this updated, modern approach to the data structures course.

Prerequisite Assumptions

In this book, we assume that readers are familiar with the following Java constructs:

- Built-in simple data types and the array type
- Control structures *while*, *do*, *for*, *if*, and *switch*
- Creating and instantiating objects
- Basic user-defined classes
  - variables and methods
  - constructors, method parameters, and the *return* statement
  - visibility modifiers

Throughout the text we use several of the support classes from the Java Class Library, such as *String, Scanner* (new in Java 5.0), *System, Random*, and *Math*. Appendix E provides an introduction to these classes.

Input/Output

It is difficult to know what background the students using a data structures textbook will have in Java I/O. Some may have learned Java in an environment where the Java input/output statements were "hidden" behind a package provided with their introductory textbook. Others may have learned graphical input/output techniques, but never learned how to do file input/output. Some have learned how to create graphical interfaces using the Java AWT; others have learned Swing; others have learned neither. To allow all the students using our textbook to concentrate on the primary topic of data structures, we use the simplest I/O approach we can, namely console I/O. For input we use the *Scanner* class, a class introduced in Java 5.0 that greatly simplifies the input task. Output is accomplished using the simple *System.out.print* command.

To support those teachers and students who prefer to work with graphical user interfaces (GUIs), we provide GUIs for many of our case studies (in addition to the console-based solutions). In this way they have a code base to support instruction and additional work using GUIs. At the conclusion of each case study we discuss the GUI-based solution, include some screenshots of the program in action, and provide some related exercises.

Content and Organization

Chapter 1 is all about **Getting Organized**. It introduces ways of organizing software development and software solutions. An overview of object orientation stresses mechanisms for organizing objects and classes of objects. Our primary topic of data structures starts with a look at the classic structures and the two fundamental language constructs that are used to implement those structures: the array and the reference (link/pointer). The chapter concludes with a study of Big-O analysis—how we evaluate algorithms that provide access to, or otherwise use, our data structures.

Chapter 2 introduces **Abstract Data Types** (ADTs). We view data from three different levels: the logical, application, and implementation levels. We introduce the Java *interface* mechanism as a means of supporting this three-tiered view. As a simple example of an ADT we present a collection of strings and show how it is handled at each of the three levels. For the implementation level we include both array-based and reference-based approaches. To support the reference-based approach we introduce the linked list structure. We also address ways of verifying the correctness of our work. Finally, in a case study, we see how the use of abstraction simplifies the task of implementing a trivia game system.

Chapter 3 presents **The Stack ADT**. The stack is first considered from its abstract perspective, and the idea of recording the logical abstraction in an ADT specification as a Java *interface* is reinforced. Sub-interfacing allows us to define both bounded and unbounded stack abstractions. We investigate the kinds of elements we should store in our collection ADTs, such as the stack, to make them generally usable. We also study ways of handling exceptional situations that might arise when using our ADTs. We show how stacks are used to determine if a set of grouping symbols is well formed and to support evaluation of mathematical expressions. We investigate the implementation of stacks using the two basic implementation approaches introduced previously in the text: arrays and references. We also investigate an approach using the Java Library class *ArrayList.*

Chapter 4 discusses **Recursion**, first providing an intuitive view of the concept, and then showing how recursion can be used to solve programming problems. Guidelines for writing recursive methods are illustrated with many examples. After demonstrating that a by-hand simulation of a recursive routine can be very tedious, a simple three-question technique is introduced for verifying the correctness of recursive methods. A more detailed discussion of how recursion works leads to an understanding of how recursion can be replaced with iteration and stacks. Our sample applications include the classic Towers of Hanoi and Blob Counting (image analysis).

Chapter 5 presents **The Queue ADT**. As with the stack, the queue ADT is first considered from its abstract perspective, followed by a formal specification, and then implemented using both array-based and reference-based approaches. We include an array-based approach to implementing an unbounded queue. Example applications for the queue involve checking for palindromes, simulating the card game War, and simulating a system of real-world queues. Finally, we look at Java's concurrency and synchronization mechanisms, explaining issues of interference and efficiency.

Chapter 6 introduces **The List ADT**. Because list management requires us to directly compare objects, the chapter begins with a review of that topic. This is followed by a general discussion of lists and then a formal specification of a list framework, supporting unsorted, sorted, and indexed lists. We use inheritance to take advantage of the commonalities among our list variations for both our array-based and reference-based implementations. Three interesting applications, involving poker, golf, and music, demonstrate how each of the list variations can be used to help solve problems. This chapter includes a study of the binary search algorithm, which is useful when searching for an element in an array-based sorted list. The chapter concludes with a section on the practical topic of storing and retrieving data structures using files.

Chapter 7 looks at **More Lists**: circular linked lists, doubly linked lists, and lists with headers and trailers. An alternative representation of a linked structure, using static allocation (an array of nodes), is designed. The case study uses a list ADT developed specifically to support the implementation of large integers.

Chapter 8 introduces **Binary Search Trees** as a way to arrange data, giving the flexibility of a linked structure with efficient insertion and deletion time. We exploit the inherent recursive nature of binary trees by presenting recursive algorithms for many of the operations. We also address the problems of balancing binary search trees and implementing them with an array. The case study discusses the process of building an index for a manuscript and implements the first phase of the process.

Chapter 9 presents a collection of other ADTs: **Priority Queues, Heaps, and Graphs**. The graph algorithms make use of stacks, queues, and priority queues, thus both reinforcing earlier material and demonstrating the general usability of these structures.

Chapter 10 presents a number of **Sorting and Searching Algorithms**. The sorting algorithms that are illustrated, implemented, and compared include straight selection sort, two versions of bubble sort, insertion sort, quick sort, heap sort, and merge sort. The sorting algorithms are compared using Big-O notation. The discussion of algorithm analysis continues in the context of searching. Previously presented searching algorithms are reviewed and new ones are described. Hashing techniques are discussed in some detail.

Additional Features

Chapter Goals   Sets of knowledge and skill goals are presented at the beginning of each chapter to help the students assess what they have learned.

Sample Programs   Numerous sample programs and program segments illustrate the abstract concepts throughout the text.

Case Studies   Each of the five major case studies includes a problem description, an analysis of the problem, the identification of a set of support classes to use in solving the problem, the development of the code for the support classes and the driving application, and a discussion of testing the solution. The class identification stage includes descriptions of brainstorming, filtering, and scenario analysis techniques as needed.

Chapter Summaries   Each chapter concludes with a summary section that reviews the most important topics of the chapter and ties together related topics.

Chapter Exercises   We average more than 40 exercises per chapter. The exercises are organized by chapter sections to make them easier for you to manage. They vary in levels of difficulty, including short and long programming problems (marked with "programming-required" icons—one icon to indicate short exercises and two icons for projects), the analysis of algorithms, and problems to test students' understanding of abstract concepts.

Appendices   The appendices summarize the Java reserved word set, operator precedence, primitive data types, the ASCII subset of Unicode, and the Java library classes used in the textbook.

Website   http://www.jblearning/catalog/9781449613549/
This website provides access to the textbook's source code files, presentation slides for each chapter, and a glossary of terms. Additionally, registered instructors are able to access answers to most of the textbook's exercises and a test item file. Please contact the authors if you have material related to the text that you would like to share with others.

Acknowledgments

We would like to thank the following people who took the time to review this textbook: Mark Llewellyn at the University of Central Florida, Chenglie Hu at Carroll College, Val Tannen at the University of Pennsylvania, Chris Dovolis at the University of Minnesota, Mike Coe at Plano Senior High School, Mikel Petty at University of Alabama in Huntsville, Gene Sheppard at Georgia Perimeter College, Noni Bohonak at the University of South Carolina–Lancaster, Jose Cordova at the University of Louisiana–Monroe, and Judy Gurka at the Metropolitan State College of Denver. A special thanks to Christine Shannon at Centre College, to Phil LaMastra at Fairfield University, and to Kristen Obermyer and Tara Srihara, both at Villanova University, for specific comments leading to improvements to this edition.

A virtual bouquet of roses to the people at Jones & Bartlett Learning who contributed so much, especially Tim Anderson, Amy Rose, Tiffany Sliter, Melissa Potter, and Stephanie Sguigna.

ND
DJ
CW

1 Getting Organized 1

Getting Organized

Knowledge Goals

You should be able to
- describe software life-cycle activities
- describe several differences between the classic approach to software development and agile methods of software development
- describe the goals for "quality" software
- define the following terms: software engineering, software requirements, software specifications, methodology
- describe some benefits of object-oriented programming
- describe the genesis of the Unified Method
- explain the relationships among classes, objects, and inheritance
- explain how method calls are bound to method implementations with respect to inheritance
- describe, at a high level, the following structures: array, linked list, stack, queue, list, tree, graph
- identify which structures are implementation dependent and which are implementation independent
- explain the subtle ramifications of using references/pointers
- explain the use of Big-O notation to describe the amount of work done by an algorithm

Skill Goals

You should be able to
- interpret a basic UML class diagram
- design and implement a Java class that uses primitive data types for its instance variables
- create a Java application that uses the Java class
- use packages to organize Java compilation units
- predict the output of short segments of Java code that exhibit aliasing
- declare, initialize, and use one- and two-dimensional arrays in Java, including both arrays of a primitive type and arrays of objects
- given an algorithm, identify an appropriate size representation and determine its Big-O complexity
- given a section of code, determine its Big-O complexity

Before embarking on any new project, it is a good idea to prepare carefully—to "get organized." In this first chapter that is exactly what we do. A careful study of the topics of this chapter will prepare you for the material on data structures and algorithms covered in the remainder of the book. The chapter topics themselves are all about organization. Section 1.1, "Software Engineering," discusses ways of organizing software development. Section 1.2, "Object Orientation," reviews the primary benefits of the object approach. Java's object-oriented support constructs that are used to organize our programs are treated in Section 1.3, "Classes, Objects, and Applications," and Section 1.4, "Organizing Classes." Structures that computer scientists have created to organize data are introduced in Section 1.5, "Data Structures." Section 1.6, "Basic Structuring Mechanisms," looks at the two fundamental language constructs that are used to implement those structures. Finally, Section 1.7, "Comparing Algorithms: Big-O Analysis," describes how we can evaluate algorithms that provide access to or otherwise use our data structures.

1.1 Software Engineering

When we consider computer programming, we immediately think of writing code in some computer language. As a beginning student of computer science, you wrote programs that solved relatively simple problems. Much of your effort went into learning the syntax of a programming language such as Java: the language's reserved words, its data types, its modularization constructs, its constructs for selection and looping, and its input/output mechanisms.

You learned a programming methodology that takes you from a problem description all the way through the delivery of a software solution. There are many design techniques, coding standards, and testing methods that programmers use to develop high-quality software. Why bother with all that methodology? Why not just sit down at a computer and enter code? Aren't we wasting a lot of time and effort, when we could just get started on the "real" job?

If the degree of our programming sophistication never had to rise above the level of trivial programs (such as summing a list of prices or averaging grades), we might get away with such a code-first technique. Some new programmers work this way, hacking away at the code until the program works more or less correctly—usually less!

As your programs grow larger and more complex, you must pay attention to other software issues in addition to coding. If you become a software professional, you may work as part of a team that develops a system containing tens of thousands, or even millions, of lines of code. The successful creation of complex programs requires an organized approach. We use the term software engineering to refer to the field concerned with all aspects of the development of high-quality, complex software sys-

> **Software engineering**   The field devoted to the specification, design, production, and maintenance of computer programs that are developed to meet specifications on time and within cost estimates, using tools that help to manage the size and complexity of the resulting software products

tems. It encompasses *all* variations of tasks required during software development including supporting activities such as documentation and teamwork.

Software engineering is a broad field. Most computing education programs devote one or more advanced courses to the topic. In fact, several schools offer degrees in the discipline. This section provides a brief introduction to this important field.

Software Life Cycles

The term "software engineering" was coined in the 1960s to emphasize that engineering-like discipline is required when creating software. At that time software development was characterized by haphazard approaches with little organization. The primary early contribution of software engineering was the identification and study of the various activities involved in developing successful systems. These activities make up the "life cycle" of a software project:

- *Problem analysis*   Understanding the nature of the problem to be solved
- *Requirements elicitation*   Determining exactly what the program must do
- *Requirements specification*   Specifying what the program must do (the functional requirements) and the constraints on the solution approach (nonfunctional requirements, such as which language to use)
- *Architectural and detailed design*   Recording how the program meets the requirements, from the "big picture" overview to the detailed design
- *Implementation of the design*   Coding a program in a computer language
- *Testing and verification*   Detecting and fixing errors and demonstrating the correctness of the program
- *Delivery*   Turning over the tested program to the customer or user (or instructor!)
- *Operation*   Actually using the program
- *Maintenance*   Making changes to fix operational errors and to add or modify the function of the program

Classically, these activities were performed in the sequence shown above. Each stage would culminate in the creation of structured documentation, which would provide the foundation upon which to build the following stage. This became known as the "waterfall" life cycle, because its graphical depiction resembled a cascading waterfall, as shown in Figure 1.1(a). Each stage's documented output would be fed into the following stage, like water flowing down a waterfall.

The waterfall approach was widely used for a number of years and was instrumental in organizing software development. However, software projects differ from one another in many important ways—for example, size, duration, scope, required reliability, and application area. It is not reasonable to expect that the same life-cycle approach will be appropriate for all projects. The waterfall model's inflexible partitioning of projects into separate stages and its heavy emphasis on documentation caused it to lose popularity. It is still useful when requirements are well understood and unlikely to change, but that is rarely the case for modern software development.

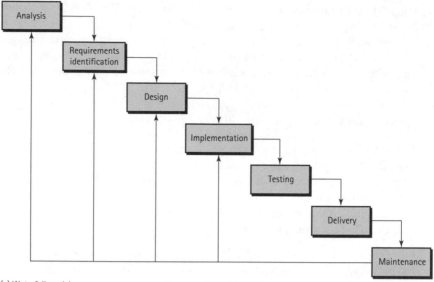

(a) Waterfall model

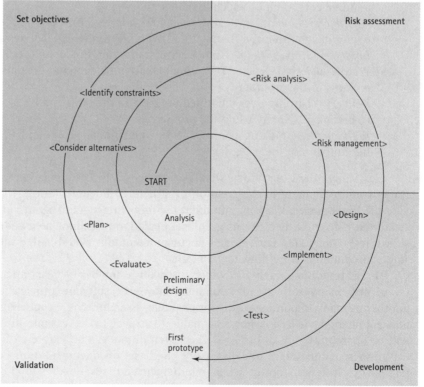

(b) Spiral model

Figure 1.1 *Life-cycle models*

Alternative life-cycle approaches evolved. For example, the spiral model depicted in Figure 1.1(b) directly addresses major risks inherent in software development, such as the risk of creating an unneeded product, the risk of including unnecessary features, and the risk of creating a confusing interface. Important activities, such as objective setting, risk assessment, development, and validation, are repeated over and over in a spiral manner as the project moves from its original concept to its final form. The spiral model emphasizes continual assessment and adjustment of goals.

Many other models of the software development process have been defined. There are models that emphasize prototyping, models for real-time systems development, and models that encourage creative problem solving. In one sense, as many models exist as organizations that develop software. Each organization, if it has wise management, pulls those ideas from the various standard approaches that best fit with its goals and creates its own version of the life cycle, one that works best for its particular situation. The top organizations constantly measure how well their approaches are working and attempt to continually improve their processes. Software development in the real world is not easy and requires good organization, flexibility, and vigilant management.

Agile Methods

The formal software engineering methods that emerged prior to the 1990s emphasized careful planning, detailed specifications, controlled development, and rigorous testing. These approaches remain useful for developing large software systems that are intended to be used for many years. However, a large percentage of current software does not fall into this category.

Today it is often important from a business standpoint for software to be developed quickly so as to meet a pressing need or to provide leverage in a rapidly changing world. In such cases the carefully controlled, document-heavy, classic approaches do not work well. A collection of methods, often called "agile" or "lightweight" methods, has been identified to help in such situations.

Specific agile methods include, but are not limited to, the following:

- *Heavy customer involvement in all stages of the project* Agile approaches encourage having a customer representative become a member of the development team. This representative takes an active role in the development of the product, ensuring that the communication lines between the developers and the customer remain open throughout the project.
- *Incremental delivery of the product* Rather than delivering the final product to a customer in one large package at the end of the project, agile approaches favor incremental development and delivery.
- *An openness to change in the specifications of the system* No matter how carefully requirements are specified, they still tend to change as the project unfolds.

Agile methods embrace this change, emphasizing that customer satisfaction is the primary goal, not conforming to original plans.

- *Developers working in pairs in a supportive, collaborative manner*   Pair programming is an approach to coding in which two programmers sit side by side, designing and coding, at a single workstation. Studies have confirmed that such an approach results in fewer code defects than programmers working by themselves.

The common purposes of agile methods are to produce software that can be changed quickly, to satisfy the customer, and to increase the morale of the development team. Your instructor may have you practice some of these approaches as you study data structures.

Goals of Quality Software

No matter which approach is used, our objective is to develop quality software. Quality software is much more than a program that runs without run-time errors or without locking up the computer. Specific quality objectives for a software system vary from project to project. The overall purpose of each project will usually help developers derive these specific goals, goals related to cost, efficiency, reliability, and robustness.

Here are four quality goals that all software should meet to some degree:

1. It works.
2. It can be modified without excessive time and effort.
3. It is reusable.
4. It is completed on time and within budget.

Let's wrap up this short introduction to software engineering by looking at each of these goals a little more closely.

Goal 1: Quality Software Works

A program must accomplish its job, and it must do so correctly and completely. Thus an important task is to determine the program's requirements. For students, requirements often are included in the instructor's problem description. For programmers on a government contract, a requirements document may be hundreds of pages long. For "agile" programmers, the requirements might be embodied in the person of a customer representative.

We develop programs that meet requirements by fulfilling their software specifications. The specifications indicate the format of the input and output, details about processing, performance measures (How fast? How big? How accurate?), actions to take in case of errors, and so on. The specifications tell *what* the program does, but not *how* it is done. Sometimes your instructor will provide detailed specifications; at other times you will have to determine them yourself, based on a partial problem description, conversations with your instructor, or intuition.

Requirements   Requirements capture what is to be provided by a computer system or software product

Software specification   A detailed description of the function, inputs, processing, outputs, and other requirements of a software product

How do you know when the program works? A typical program has to be

- *complete:* It should "do everything" needed.
- *correct:* It should "do it right."
- *usable:* Its user interface should be "easy to work with."
- *efficient:* It should finish in a "reasonable amount of time" considering the complexity and size of the task.

Goal 2: Quality Software Can Be Modified

Software changes often and in all phases of its life cycle. Recognizing this fact, experienced software engineers try to develop programs that are easy to modify. Modifications to programs often are not made by the original authors but rather by subsequent maintenance programmers. Someday you may be the one making the modifications to someone else's program.

What makes a program easy to modify? First, it should be readable and understandable to humans. Before it can be changed, it must be understood.

Second, it should be well designed. Before a change can be made, the maintenance programmer must locate the place or places to make the change. When a program is well designed, it is usually easy to determine where the changes must take place.

Finally, it should be able to withstand small changes easily. The key idea is to partition your programs into manageable pieces that work together to solve the problem, yet are relatively independent.

Goal 3: Quality Software Is Reusable

It takes time and effort to create quality software. Therefore, it is important to wring as much value from the software as possible.

One way to save time and effort when building a software solution is to reuse programs, classes, methods, and so on, from previous projects. By using previously designed and tested code, you arrive at your solution sooner and with less effort.

Creating reusable software does not happen automatically. It requires extra effort during the specification and design of the software. Reusable software is well documented and easy to read. It usually has a simple interface so that it can easily be plugged into another system. It is modifiable (Goal 2), in case a small change is needed to adapt it to the new system.

When creating software to fulfill a narrow, specific function, you can sometimes make the software more generally usable with a minimal amount of extra effort. For example, if you are creating a routine that sorts a list of integers, you might generalize the routine so that it can also sort other types of data.

Goal 4: Quality Software Is Completed on Time and Within Budget

You know what happens in school when you turn your program in late. Although the consequences of tardiness sometimes are minimal in the academic world, they often are significant in the business world. A program that meets its functional requirements is not useful if it isn't ready when needed.

If the program is part of a contract with a customer, there may be monetary penalties for missed deadlines. If it is being developed for commercial sales, delayed completion may mean being beaten to the market by a competitor and being forced out of business.

1.2 Object Orientation

Software design was originally driven by an emphasis on actions. Programs were modularized by breaking them into subprograms or procedures. A subprogram performs some calculations and returns information to the calling program, but it doesn't "remember" anything. It is like an old-fashioned bathroom scale that simply shows your weight when you step onto it. In the late 1960s, researchers argued that this approach was too limiting and did not allow us to successfully represent the constructs needed to build complex systems.

Two Norwegians, Kristen Nygaard and Ole-Johan Dahl, created Simula 67 in 1967. It was the first language to support object-oriented programming. Object-oriented languages promote the object as the prime modularization mechanism. Objects represent both information and behavior and can "remember" internal information from one use to the next. They are like modern bathroom scales that show your weight and then cheerfully report: "You have gained three pounds." This crucial difference allows them to be used in many versatile ways. In 2001, Nygaard and Dahl received the Turing Award, sometimes referred to as the Nobel Prize of computing, for their work.

The capability of objects to represent both information (the objects have *attributes*) and behavior (the objects have *responsibilities*) allows them to be used to represent "real-world" entities as varied as bank accounts, genomes, and hobbits. The self-contained nature of objects makes them easier to implement, modify, and test for correctness.

Object-oriented classes, when designed properly, are very easy to reuse. Additionally, the inheritance mechanism, which is a key facet of the object-oriented approach, makes it easy to incrementally change the definitions of classes so that they can be reused in new situations.

The Unified Method

> **Methodology** A collection of specific procedures for creating a software system to meet a user's needs

The object-oriented approach to programming is based on implementing models of reality. But how do you go about this? Where do you start? How do you proceed? The best plan is to follow an organized approach called a methodology.

In the late 1980s, many people proposed object-oriented methodologies. By the mid-1990s, three proposals stood out: the Object Modeling Technique, the Objectory Process, and the Booch Method. Between 1994 and 1997, the primary authors of these proposals got together and consolidated their ideas. The resulting methodology was dubbed the Unified Method. It is now, by far, the most popular organized approach to creating object-oriented systems.

The Unified Method features three key elements:

1. It is use-case driven. A use-case is a description of a sequence of actions performed by a user within the system to accomplish some task. The term "user" here should be interpreted in a broad sense and could represent another system.

2. It is architecture-centric. The word "architecture" refers to the overall structure of the target system; the way in which its components interact.

3. It is iterative and incremental. Like the spiral life-cycle model described in Section 1.1, the Unified Method involves a series of cycles, with each one building upon the foundation established by its predecessors.

One of the main benefits of the Unified Method is improved communication among the people involved in the project. The Unified Method includes a set of diagrams for this purpose, called the Unified Modeling Language (UML).[1] UML diagrams have become a de facto industry standard for modeling software. They are used to specify, visualize, construct, and document the components of a software system. We use UML *class diagrams* throughout this text, starting in Section 1.3, to model our classes and their interrelationships.

1.3 Classes, Objects, and Applications

Object orientation is centered on classes and objects. Objects are the basic run-time entities used by applications. An object is an instantiation of a class; alternatively, a class defines the structure of its objects. In this section we review these object-oriented programming constructs, which we use to organize our programs.

Java-reserved words (when used as such), user-defined identifiers, class and file names, and so on, appear in `this font` throughout the entire textbook.

Classes

A class defines the structure of an object or a set of objects. A class definition includes variables (data) and methods (actions) that determine the behavior of an object. The following Java code defines a `Date` class that can be used to create and manipulate `Date` objects—for example, within a school course-scheduling application. The `Date` class can be used to create `Date` objects and to learn about the year, month, or day of any particular `Date` object.[2] The class also provides methods that return the Lilian Day Number of

---

1. The official definition of the UML is maintained by the Object Management Group. Detailed information can be found at http://www.uml.org/.

2. The Java library includes a `Date` class, `java.util.Date`. However, the familiar properties of dates make them a natural example to use in explaining object-oriented concepts. Here we ignore the existence of the library class, as if we must design our own `Date` class.

the date (the code details have been omitted—see the feature section on Lilian Day Numbers for more information) and return a string[3] representation of the date. Note that within comments the word "this" represents the current object.

```java
//-----------------------------------------------------------------
// Date.java              by Dale/Joyce/Weems            Chapter 1
//
// Supports date objects with year, month, and day attributes.
//-----------------------------------------------------------------

public class Date
{
  protected int year;
  protected int month;
  protected int day;
  public static final int MINYEAR = 1583;

  // Constructor
  public Date(int newMonth, int newDay, int newYear)
  {
    month = newMonth;
    day = newDay;
    year = newYear;
  }

  // Observers
  public int getYear()
  {
    return year;
  }

  public int getMonth()
  {
    return month;
  }

  public int getDay()
  {
    return day;
  }
```

---

3. Appendix E includes information concerning the Java String class.

```
public int lilian()
{
  // Returns the Lilian Day Number of this date.

  // Algorithm goes here.
  // See Lilian Day Numbers feature section for details.
}

public String toString()
// Returns this date as a String.
{
  return(month + "/" + day + "/" + year);
}
}
```

The `Date` class demonstrates two kinds of variables: instance variables and class variables. The instance variables of this class are `year`, `month`, and `day` declared as

```
protected int year;
protected int month;
protected int day;
```

Their values vary for each different instance of an object of the class. Instance variables represent the *attributes* of an object. `MINYEAR` is declared as

```
public static final int MINYEAR = 1593;
```

It is a class variable because it is defined to be `static`. It is associated directly with the `Date` class, instead of with objects of the class. A single copy of a class variable is maintained for all objects of the class.

Remember that the `final` modifier states that a variable is in its final form and cannot be modified; thus `MINYEAR` is a constant. By convention, we use only capital letters when naming constants. It is standard procedure to declare constants as class variables. Because the value of the variable cannot change, there is no need to force every object of a class to carry around its own version of the value. In addition to holding shared constants, class variables can be used to maintain information that is common to an entire class. For example, a `BankAccount` class may have a class variable that holds the number of current accounts.

In the `Date` class example, the `MINYEAR` constant represents the first full year that the widely used Gregorian calendar was in effect. The idea here is that programmers should not use the class to represent dates that predate that year. We look at ways to enforce this rule in Section 3.3, where we discuss handling exceptional situations.

Constructor An operation that creates a new instance of a class

Observer An operation that allows us to observe the state of an object without changing it

Transformer An operation that changes the internal state of an object

The methods of the class are `Date`, `getYear`, `getMonth`, `getDay`, `lilian`, and `toString`. Note that the `Date` method has the same name as the class. Recall that this means it is a special type of method, called a class constructor. Constructors are used to create new instances of a class—that is, to instantiate objects of a class. The other five methods are classified as observer methods, because they "observe" and return information based on the instance variable values. Other names for observer methods are "accessor" methods and "getters," as in accessing or getting information. In addition to constructors and observers, there is one other general category of method, called a transformer. As you probably recall, transformers change the object in some way; for example, a method that changes the year of a `Date` object would be classified as a transformer.

You have undoubtedly noticed the use of the access modifiers `protected` and `public` within the `Date` class. Let's review the purpose and use of access modifiers. This discussion assumes you recall the basic ideas behind inheritance and packages. Inheritance supports the extension of one class, called the superclass, by another class, called the subclass. The subclass "inherits" properties (data and actions) from the superclass. We say that the subclass is derived from the superclass. Packages let us group related classes together into a single unit. Inheritance and packages are both discussed more extensively in the next section.

Java allows a wide spectrum of access control, as summarized in Table 1.1. The `public` access modifier used with the methods of `Date` makes them "publicly" available; any code that can "see" an object of the class can use its public methods. We say that these methods are "exported" from the class. Additionally, any class that is derived from the `Date` class using inheritance inherits its public parts.

Table 1.1 *Java Access Control Modifiers*

	Access Is Allowed			
	Within the Class	Within Subclasses in the Same Package	Within Subclasses in Other Packages	Everywhere
`public`	X	X	X	X
`protected`	X	X	X	
`package`	X	X		
`private`	X			

Public access sits at one end of the access spectrum, allowing open access. At the other end of the spectrum is private access. When you declare a class's variables and methods as `private`, they can be used only inside the class itself and are not inherited by subclasses. You should routinely use private access within your classes to hide their data. You do not want the data values to be changed by code that is outside the class. However, if you plan to extend your classes using inheritance, you may want to use protected or package access instead.

An exception to this guideline of hiding data within a class is shown in the `Date` example. Notice that the `MINYEAR` constant is publicly accessible. It can be accessed directly by client code. For example, a client could include the statement

```
if (myYear <= Date.MINYEAR) ...
```

Because `MINYEAR` is a final variable, its value cannot be changed by the client. Thus, even though it is publicly accessible, no other code can change its value. It is not necessary to hide it. The client code above also shows how to access a public class variable from outside the class. Because `MINYEAR` is a class variable, it is accessed through the class name, `Date`, rather than through an object of the class.

The `protected` access modifier used in `Date` provides visibility similar to private access, only slightly less rigid. It "protects" its data from outside access, but allows the data to be accessed from within its own class *or* from any class derived from its class. Therefore, the methods within the `Date` class can access `year`, `month`, and `day`, and if, as we will show in Section 1.4, the `Date` class is extended, the methods in the extended class can also access those variables.

The remaining type of access is called package access. A variable or method of a class defaults to package access if none of the other three modifiers are used. Package access means that the variable or method is accessible to any other class in the same package; also, the variable or method is inherited by any of its subclasses that are in the same package.

A diagram representing the `Date` class is shown in Figure 1.2. The diagram follows the standard UML class notation approach. The name of the class appears in the top section of

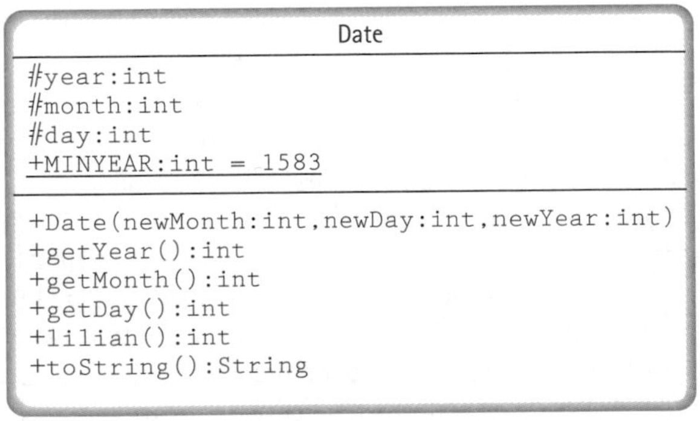

```
┌─────────────────────────────────────────────────┐
│                      Date                         │
├─────────────────────────────────────────────────┤
│ #year:int                                         │
│ #month:int                                        │
│ #day:int                                          │
│ +MINYEAR:int = 1583                               │
├─────────────────────────────────────────────────┤
│ +Date(newMonth:int,newDay:int,newYear:int)        │
│ +getYear():int                                    │
│ +getMonth():int                                   │
│ +getDay():int                                     │
│ +lilian():int                                     │
│ +toString():String                                │
└─────────────────────────────────────────────────┘
```

Figure 1.2 *Class diagram for the* `Date` *class*

the diagram, the variables (attributes) appear in the next section, and the methods (operations) appear in the final section. The diagram includes information about the nature of the variables and method parameters; for example, we can see at a glance that `year`, `month`, and `day` are all of type `int`. Note that the variable `MINYEAR` is underlined; this indicates that it is a class variable rather than an instance variable. The diagram also indicates the visibility or protection associated with each part of the class (+ = public, # = protected).

Lilian Day Numbers

Various approaches to numbering days have been proposed. The idea is to choose a particular day in history as day 1, and then to number the actual sequence of days from that day forward with the numbers 2, 3, and so on. The Lilian Day Number (LDN) system uses October 15, 1582, as day 1, or LDN 1.

Our current calendar is called the Gregorian calendar. It was established in 1582 by Pope Gregory XIII. At that time 10 days were dropped from the month of October, to make up for small errors that had accumulated throughout the years.

Thus, the day following October 4, 1582, in the Gregorian calendar is October 15, 1582, also known as LDN 1 in the Lilian day numbering scheme. The scheme is named after Aloysius Lilius, an advisor to Pope Gregory and one of the principal instigators of the calendar reform.

Originally, Catholic European countries adopted the Gregorian calendar. Many Protestant nations, such as England and its colonies, did not adopt the Gregorian calendar until 1752, at which time they also "lost" 11 days. Today, most countries use the Gregorian calendar, at least for official international business. When comparing historical dates, one must be careful about which calendars are being used.

In our `Date` class implementation, `MINYEAR` is 1583, representing the first full year during which the Gregorian calendar was in operation. We assume that programmers will not use the `Date` class to represent dates before that time, although this rule is not enforced by the class. This assumption simplifies calculation of LDNs, as we do not have to worry about the phantom 10 days of October 1582.

To calculate LDNs we must understand how the Gregorian calendar works. Years are usually 365 days long. However, every year evenly divisible by 4 is a leap year, 366 days long. This aligns the calendar closer to astronomical reality. To fine-tune the adjustment, if a year is evenly divisible by 100, it is not a leap year but, if it is also evenly divisible by 400, it is still a leap year. Thus 2000 was a leap year, but 1900 was not.

Given a date, the `lilian` method of the `Date` class counts the number of days between that date and the hypothetical date 1/1/0—that is, January 1 of the year 0. This count is made under the assumption that the Gregorian reforms were in place during that entire time period. In other words, it uses the rules described in the previous paragraph. Let's call this number the Relative Day Number (RDN). To transform a given RDN to its corresponding LDN, we just need to subtract the RDN of October 14, 1582, from it. For example, to calculate the LDN of July 4,

1776, the method first calculates its RDN (648,856) and then subtracts from it the RDN of October 14, 1582 (578,100), giving the result of 70,756.

Here is the code of the `lilian` method:

```java
public int lilian()
{
  // Returns the Lilian Day Number of this date.
  // Precondition⁴:  This date is a valid date after 10/14/1582.
  //
  // Computes the number of days between 1/1/0 and this date as if
  // no calendar reforms took place, then subtracts 578,100 so that
  // October 15, 1582, is day 1.

  final int SUBDAYS = 578100;   // number of calculated days
                                // from 1/1/0 to 10/14/1582

  int numDays = 0;

  // Add days in years.
  numDays = year * 365;

  // Add days in the months.
  if (month <= 2)
    numDays = numDays + (month - 1) * 31;
  else
    numDays = numDays + ((month - 1) * 31)
                      - ((4 * (month-1) + 27) / 10);

  // Add days in the days.
  numDays = numDays + day;

  // Take care of leap years.
  numDays = numDays + (year / 4) - (year / 100) + (year / 400);

  // Handle special case of leap year but not yet leap day.
  if (month < 3)
  {
    if ((year % 4) == 0)    numDays = numDays - 1;
    if ((year % 100) == 0) numDays = numDays + 1;
    if ((year % 400) == 0) numDays = numDays - 1;
  }
```

---

4. The use of preconditions is covered in Section 2.1.

```
// Subtract extra days up to 10/14/1582.
numDays = numDays - SUBDAYS;

return numDays;
}
```

Objects

Objects are created from classes at run time. They can contain and manipulate data. Multiple objects can be created from the same class definition. Once a class such as Date has been defined, a program can create and use objects of that class. The effect is similar to expanding the language's set of standard types to include a Date type. To create an object in Java we use the new operator, along with the class constructor, as follows:

```
Date myDate = new Date(6, 24, 1951);
Date yourDate = new Date(10, 11, 1953);
Date ourDate = new Date(6, 15, 1985);
```

We say that the variables myDate, yourDate, and ourDate reference "objects of the class Date" or simply "objects of type Date." We could also refer to them as "Date objects."

In Figure 1.3 we have extended our previous diagram (shown in Figure 1.2) to show the relationship between the instantiated Date objects and the Date class. As you can

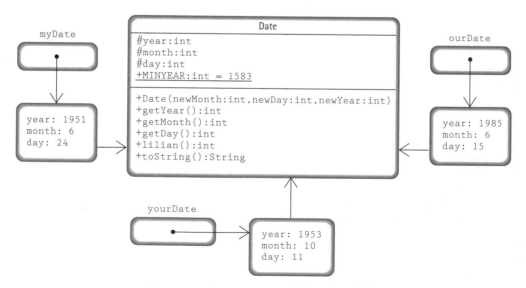

Figure 1.3   *Class diagram showing* Date *objects*

see, the objects are concrete instantiations of the class, as represented by arrows in the figure. Notice that the `myDate`, `yourDate`, and `ourDate` variables are not objects, but actually hold references to the objects. The references are shown by the pointers from the variable boxes to the objects. In reality, references are memory addresses. The memory address of the instantiated object is stored in the memory location assigned to the variable. If no object has been instantiated for a particular variable, then its memory location holds a `null` reference.

Object methods are invoked through the object upon which they are to act. For example, to assign the value of the `year` attribute of the `ourDate` object to the integer variable `theYear`, a programmer would code

```
theYear = ourDate.getYear();
```

Recall that the `toString` method is invoked in a special way. Just as Java automatically changes an integer value, such as that returned by `getDay`, to a string in the statement[5]

```
System.out.println("The big day is " + ourDate.getDay());
```

it automatically changes an object, such as `ourDate`, to a string in the statement

```
System.out.println("The party will be on " + ourDate);
```

The output from these statements would be

The big day is 15

The party will be on 6/15/1985

To determine how to change the object to a string, the Java compiler automatically looks for a `toString` method for that object, such as the `toString` method we defined for `Date` objects in our `Date` class.

Applications

You should view an object-oriented program as a set of objects working together, by sending one another messages, to solve a problem. But where does it all begin? How are the objects created in the first place?

A Java program typically begins running when the user executes the Java Virtual Machine and passes it the program. How you begin executing the Java Virtual Machine depends on your environment. You may simply use the command "java" if you are working in a command line environment. Or, you may click a "run" icon if you are working within an integrated development environment. In any case, you indicate the name of a class that contains a `main` method. The Java Virtual Machine loads that class and starts executing that method. The class that contains the `main` method is called a Java application.

---

5. Appendix E includes information concerning the `System` class.

Let's consider an example. Suppose we want to write a program named `DaysBe-tween` that provides information about the number of days between two dates. The idea is for the program to prompt the user for two dates, calculate the number of days between them, and report this information back to the user.

In object-oriented programming a key step is identifying classes that can be used to help solve a problem. Our `Date` class is a perfect fit for the days-between problem. It allows us to create and access date objects. Plus, its `lilian` method returns a value that can help us determine the number of days between two dates. We simply subtract the two Lilian Day Numbers.

The design of our application is

```
display instructions
prompt for and read in information about the first date
create the date1 object
prompt for and read in information about the second date
create the date2 object
if dates entered are too early
    print an error message
else
    use the date.lilian method to obtain the Lilian Day Numbers
    compute and print the number of days between the dates
```

The application code is shown below. Some items to note:

- The program imports the `util` package from the Java class library. The `util` package contains Java's `Scanner` class,[6] which the program uses for input. We call our `Scanner` object `conIn` because it represents console input.
- The `DaysBetween` class contains just a single method, the `main` method. It is possible to define other methods within an application and to invoke them from the `main` method. Such functional modularization can be used if the `main` method becomes long and complicated. However, because we are emphasizing an object-oriented approach, our applications rarely subdivide a solution in that manner. Rather, we will use the `main` method to instantiate objects that help us solve our problems. Classes and objects are our primary modularization mechanisms, not application methods.

---

6. Appendix E includes information concerning the Java `Scanner` class.

- Although the program checks to ensure the entered years of the dates are "modern," it does not do any other input correctness checking. This issue is addressed in Exercise 23.

```
//------------------------------------------------------------
// DaysBetween.java          by Dale/Joyce/Weems         Chapter 1
//
// Asks the user to enter two "modern" dates and then reports
// the number of days between the two dates.
//------------------------------------------------------------

import java.util.Scanner;

public class DaysBetween
{
  public static void main(String[] args)
  {
    Scanner conIn = new Scanner(System.in);
    int day, month, year;

    System.out.println("Enter two 'modern' dates: month day year");
    System.out.println("For example, January 12, 1954, would be: 1 12 1954");
    System.out.println();
    System.out.println("Modern dates occur after " + Date.MINYEAR + ".");
    System.out.println();
    System.out.println("Enter the first date:");
    month = conIn.nextInt();
    day = conIn.nextInt();
    year = conIn.nextInt();
    Date date1 = new Date(month, day, year);
    System.out.println("Enter the second date:");
    month = conIn.nextInt();
    day = conIn.nextInt();
    year = conIn.nextInt();
    Date date2 = new Date(month, day, year);
    if ((date1.getYear() <= Date.MINYEAR)
        ||
        (date2.getYear() <= Date.MINYEAR))
      System.out.println("You entered a 'pre-modern' date.");
    else
    {
      System.out.println("The number of days between");
      System.out.print(date1);
      System.out.print(" and ");
      System.out.print(date2);
```

```
      System.out.print(" is ");
      System.out.println(Math.abs(date1.lilian() - date2.lilian()));
   }
 }
}
```

Here's the result of a sample run of the application. User input is shown in this color. We'll use the birth date of a friend and the date this chapter was last modified.

Enter two 'modern' dates: month day year
For example, January 12, 1954, would be: 1 12 1954
Modern dates occur after 1583.

Enter the first date:
 1 12 1954
Enter the second date:
 5 25 2010

The number of days between
1/12/1954 and 5/25/2010 is 20587

Wow. That's a lot of days!

1.4 Organizing Classes

During object-oriented development dozens—even hundreds—of classes can be generated or reused to help build a system. The task of keeping track of all of these classes would be impossible without some type of organizational structure. In this section we review two of the most important ways of organizing Java classes: inheritance and packages. As you will see, both of these approaches are used "simultaneously" for most projects.

Inheritance

Inheritance is much more than just an organizational mechanism. It is, in fact, a powerful reuse mechanism. Inheritance allows programmers to create a new class that is a specialization of an existing class. We say that the new class is a subclass of the existing class, which in turn is the superclass of the new class.

A subclass "inherits" features from its superclass. It adds new features, as needed, related to its specialization. It can also redefine inherited features as necessary. "Super" and "sub" refer to the relative positions of the classes in a hierarchy. A subclass is below its superclass and a superclass is above its subclasses.

Suppose we already have a Date class as defined previously, and we are creating a new application to manipulate Date objects. Suppose also that in the new application we are often required to "increment" a Date object—that is, to change a Date object so that it represents the next day. For example, if the Date object represents 7/31/2001, it would represent 8/1/2001 after being incremented. The algorithm for incrementing the date is not trivial, especially when you consider leap year rules. But in addition to developing the algorithm, another question that must be addressed is where to put that algorithm. There are several options:

- Implement the algorithm within the new application. The code would need to obtain the month, day, and year from the Date object using the observer methods; calculate the new month, day, and year; instantiate a new Date object to hold the updated month, day, and year; and assign the new object to all the variables currently referencing the original Date object. This might be a complex task. Besides, if future applications also need this functionality, their programmers would have to reimplement the solution for themselves. This approach does not support reusability and possibly requires complex tracking of object aliases.
- Add a new method, called increment, to the Date class. This method would update the value of the current object. Such an approach allows future programs to use the new functionality. However, in some cases, a programmer may want a Date class with protection against any changes to its objects. Such objects are said to be immutable. Adding increment to the Date class undermines this protection.
- Use inheritance. Create a new class, called IncDate, which inherits all the features of the current Date class, but that also provides the increment method. This approach resolves the drawbacks of the previous two approaches.

We now look at how to implement the last approach, that is, to use inheritance to solve our problem. We often call the inheritance relationship an *is a* relationship. In this case we would say that an object of the class IncDate is also a Date object, because it can do anything that a Date object can do—and more. This idea can be clarified by remembering that inheritance typically means specialization. IncDate is a special case of Date, but not the other way around. To create IncDate in Java we would code:

```
public class IncDate extends Date
{
  public IncDate(int newMonth, int newDay, int newYear)
  {
    super(newMonth, newDay, newYear);
  }

  public void increment()
  // Increments this IncDate to represent the next day.
  // For example, if this = 6/30/2005, then this becomes 7/1/2005.
  {
    // Increment algorithm goes here.
  }
}
```

Note that sometimes in code listings in this textbook we emphasize the sections of code most pertinent to the current discussion by underlining them.

Inheritance is indicated by the keyword `extends`, which shows that `IncDate` inherits from `Date`. It is not possible in Java to inherit constructors, so `IncDate` must supply its own. In this case, the `IncDate` constructor simply takes the month, day, and year arguments and passes them to the constructor of its superclass (that is, to the `Date` class constructor) using the `super` reserved word.

The other part of the `IncDate` class is the new `increment` method, which is classified as a transformer because it changes the internal state of the object. The `increment` method changes the object's `day` and possibly the `month` and `year` values. The method is invoked through the object that it is to transform. For example, the statement

```
ourDate.increment();
```

transforms the `ourDate` object.

Note that we have left out the details of the `increment` method because they are not crucial to our current discussion (see Exercise 30).

A program with access to each of the date classes can now declare and use both `Date` and `IncDate` objects. Consider the following program segment:

```
Date myDate = new Date(6, 24, 1951);
IncDate aDate = new IncDate(1, 11, 2001);

System.out.println("mydate day is:    " + myDate.getDay());
System.out.println("aDate day is:    " + aDate.getDay());

aDate.increment();
System.out.println("the day after is: " + aDate.getDay());
```

This program segment instantiates and initializes `myDate` and `aDate`, outputs the values of their days, increments `aDate`, and finally outputs the new day value of `aDate`. You might ask, "How does the system resolve the use of the `getDay` method by an `IncDate` object when `getDay` is defined in the `Date` class?" Understanding how inheritance is supported by Java provides the answer to this question. The extended class diagram in Figure 1.4, which shows the inheritance relationships and captures the state of the system after the `aDate` object has been incremented, helps us investigate the situation. As is standard with UML class diagrams, inheritance is indicated by a solid arrow with an open arrow head (a triangle). Note that the arrow points from the subclass to the superclass.

The compiler has available to it all the declaration information captured in the extended class diagram. Consider the `getDay` method call in the statement

```
System.out.println("aDate day is:    " + aDate.getDay());
```

To resolve this method call, the compiler follows the reference from the `aDate` variable to the `IncDate` class. It does not find a definition for a `getDay` method in the `IncDate` class, so it follows the inheritance link to the superclass `Date`. There it finds, and uses, the `getDay` method. In this case, the `getDay` method returns an `int` value that repre-

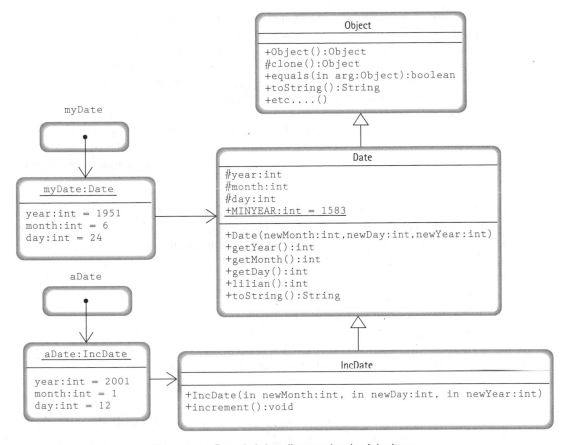

Figure 1.4 *Extended class diagram showing inheritance*

sents the day value of the aDate object. During execution, the system changes the int value to a String, concatenates it to the string "aDate day is: ", and prints it to System.out.

The Inheritance Tree
Java supports single inheritance only. This means that a class can extend only one other class. Therefore, in Java, the inheritance relationships define an inheritance tree.

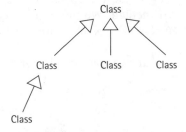

Figure 1.4 shows one branch of the overall system inheritance tree. Note that because of the way method calls are resolved, by searching *up* the inheritance tree, only objects of the class `IncDate` can use the `increment` method—if you try to use the `increment` method on an object of the class `Date`, such as the `myDate` object, no definition is available in either the `Date` class or any of the classes above `Date` in the inheritance tree. The compiler would report a syntax error in this situation.

Notice the `Object` class in Figure 1.4. Where did it come from? In Java, any class that does not explicitly extend another class implicitly extends the predefined `Object` class. Because `Date` does not explicitly extend any other class, it inherits directly from `Object`.`Date` as a subclass of `Object`. The solid arrows with the open arrowheads indicate inheritance in the diagram.

All Java classes can be traced back to the `Object` class. We say that the `Object` class is the root of the inheritance tree. The `Object` class defines several basic methods: comparison for equality (`equals`), conversion to a string (`toString`), and so on. Therefore, for example, any object in any Java program supports the method `toString` because it is inherited from the `Object` class. Let's consider the `toString` example more carefully.

As discussed previously, just as Java automatically changes an integer value to a string in the statement

```
System.out.println("aDate day is:     " + aDate.getDay());
```

so it automatically changes an object to a string in the statement

```
System.out.println("tomorrow: " + aDate);
```

If you use an object as a string anywhere in a Java program, the Java compiler automatically looks for a `toString` method for that object. In this case the `toString` method is not found in the `IncDate` class, but it is found in its superclass, the `Date` class. However, if it was not defined in the `Date` class, the compiler would continue looking up the inheritance hierarchy and would find the `toString` method in the `Object` class. Given that all classes trace their roots back to `Object`, the compiler is always guaranteed to find a `toString` method eventually.

But wait a minute. What does it mean to "change an object to a string"? Well, that depends on the definition of the `toString` method that is associated with the object. The `toString` method of the `Object` class returns a string representing some of the internal system implementation details about the object. This information is somewhat cryptic and generally not useful to us. This situation is an example of where it is useful to redefine an inherited method. We generally override the default `toString` method when creating our own classes so as to return a more relevant string, as we did with the `Date` class.

Table 1.2 shows the output from the following program segment:

```
Date myDate = new Date(6, 24, 1951);
IncDate currDate = new IncDate(1, 11, 2001);
```

Table 1.2   *Output from Program Segment*

Object Class *toString* Used		*Date* Class *toString* Used	
mydate:	Date@256a7c	mydate:	6/24/1951
today:	IncDate@720eeb	today:	1/11/2001
tomorrow:	IncDate@720eeb	tomorrow:	1/12/2001

```
System.out.println("mydate:   " + myDate);
System.out.println("today:    " + currDate);

currDate.increment();
System.out.println("tomorrow: " + currDate);
```

The results on the left show an example of the output generated if the `toString` method of the `Object` class is used by default; the results on the right show the outcome if the `toString` method of our `Date` class is used.

One last note: Remember that subclasses are assignment compatible with the superclasses above them in the inheritance hierarchy. Therefore, in our example, the statement

```
myDate = currDate;
```

would be legal, but the statement

```
currDate = myDate;
```

would cause an "incompatible-type" syntax error.

Packages

Java lets us group related classes together into a unit called a package. Packages provide several advantages:

- They let us organize our files.
- They can be compiled separately and imported into our programs.
- They make it easier for programs to use common class files.
- They help us avoid naming conflicts (two classes can have the same name if they are in different packages).

Package Syntax

The syntax for a package is extremely simple. All we have to do is to specify the package name at the start of the file containing the class. The first noncomment, nonblank line of the file must contain the keyword `package` followed by an identifier and a semi-colon. By convention, Java programmers start a package identifier with a lowercase letter to distinguish package names from class names:

```
package someName;
```

Following the package name specification in the file, we can write import declarations, so as to make the contents of other packages available to the classes inside the package we are defining, and then one or more declarations of classes. Java calls this file a *compilation unit*. The classes defined in the file are members of the package. The imported classes are not members of the package.

The name of the file containing the compilation unit must match the name of the public class within the unit. Therefore, although we can declare multiple classes in a compilation unit, only one of them can be declared public. All nonpublic classes in the file are hidden from the world outside the package. If a compilation unit can hold at most one public class, how do we create packages with multiple public classes? We have to use multiple compilation units, as described next.

Packages with Multiple Compilation Units

Each Java compilation unit is stored in its own file. The Java system identifies the file using a combination of the package name and the name of the public class in the compilation unit. Java restricts us to having a single public class in a file so that it can use file names to locate all public classes. Thus a package with multiple public classes must be implemented with multiple compilation units, each in a separate file.

Using multiple compilation units has the further advantage of providing us with greater flexibility in developing the classes of a package. Team programming projects would be more cumbersome if Java made multiple programmers share a single package file.

We split a package among multiple files simply by placing its members into separate compilation units with the same package name. For example, we can create one file containing the following code (the ... between the braces represents the code for each class):

```
package gamma;
public class One{ ... }
class Two{ ... }
```

A second file could contain this code:

```
package gamma;
class Three{ ... }
public class Four{ ... }
```

The result: The package `gamma` contains four classes. Two of the classes, `One` and `Four`, are public, so they are available to be imported by application code. The two file names must match the two public class names; that is, the files must be named `One.java` and `Four.java`, respectively.

Many programmers place every class in its own compilation unit. Others gather the nonpublic classes into one unit, separate from the public classes. How you organize your packages is up to you, but you should be consistent, to make it easy to find a specific member of a package among all of its files.

How does the Java compiler manage to find these pieces and put them together? The answer is that it requires that all compilation unit files for a package be kept in a single directory or folder that matches the name of the package. For our preceding example, a Java system would store the source code in files called `One.java` and `Four.java`, both in a directory called gamma.

The Import Statement

To access the contents of a package from within a program, you must import it into your program. You can use either of the following forms of import statements:

```
import packagename.*;
import packagename.Classname;
```

An import declaration begins with the keyword `import`, the name of a package, and a dot (period). Following the dot you can write either the name of a class in the package or an asterisk (*). The declaration ends with a semicolon. If you want to use exactly one class in a particular package, then you can simply give its name in the import declaration. More often, however, you want to use more than one of the classes in a package. In this case the asterisk is a shorthand notation to the compiler that says, "Import whatever classes from this package that this program uses."

Packages and Subdirectories

Many computer platforms use a hierarchical file system. The Java package rules are defined to work seamlessly with such systems. Java package names may also be hierarchical; they may contain "periods" separating different parts of the name—for example, `ch03.stacks`. In such a case, the package files must be placed underneath a set of subdirectories that match the separate parts of the package name. Continuing the same example, the package files should be placed in a directory named `stacks` that is a subdirectory of a directory named `ch03`. You can then import the entire package into your program with the following statement:

```
import ch03.stacks.*;
```

As long as the directory that contains the `ch03` directory is on the `ClassPath` of your system, the compiler will be able to find the package you requested. The compiler automatically looks in all directories listed in `ClassPath`. Most programming environments provide a command to specify the directories to be included in the `ClassPath`. You will need to consult the documentation for your particular system to see how to do this. In our example, the compiler will search all `ClassPath` directories for a subdirectory named `ch03` that contains a subdirectory named `stacks`; upon finding such a subdirectory, it will import all of the members of the `ch03.stacks` package that it finds there.

The Textbook Program Files

Many of the files created to support this textbook are organized into packages. They are organized exactly as described above and are available at the book's website, www.jblearning.com/catalog/9781449613549/. All of the files are found in a directory named `bookFiles`. It contains a separate subdirectory for each chapter of the book: `ch01`, `ch02`, ... Where packages are used, you will find the corresponding subdirectories underneath the chapter subdirectories. For example, the `ch03` subdirectory does, indeed, contain a subdirectory named `stacks`, which in turn contains files that define Java classes related to a Stack ADT. Each of the class files begins with the statement

```
package ch03.stacks;
```

Thus they are all in the `ch03.stacks` package. If you write a program that needs to use these files, you can simply import the package into your program and make sure the parent directory of the `ch03` directory (that is, the `bookFiles` directory), is included in your computer's `ClassPath`.

We suggest that you copy the entire `bookFiles` directory to your computer's hard drive, ensuring easy access to all of the book's files and maintaining the crucial subdirectory structure required by the packages. Also, make sure you extend your computer's `ClassPath` to include your new `bookFiles` directory.

1.5 Data Structures

You are already familiar with various ways of organizing data. When you look up a number in a telephone directory or a word in a dictionary, you are using an ordered list of words. When you take a number at a delicatessen or barbershop, you become part of a line of people awaiting service. When you study the pairings in a sports tournament and try to predict which team or player will advance through all the rounds and become champion, you create a treelike list of predicted results.

Just as we use many approaches to organize data to deal with everyday problems, programmers use a wide variety of approaches to organize data when solving problems using computers. When programming, the way you view and structure the data that your programs manipulate greatly influences your success. A language's set of primitive types (Java's are `byte`, `char`, `short`, `int`, `long`, `float`, `double`, and `boolean`) can be very useful if we need a counter, a sum, or an index in a program. Generally, however, we must also deal with large amounts of data that have complex interrelationships.

Computer scientists have devised many organizational structures to represent data relationships. These structures act as a unifying theme for this textbook. In this section we introduce the topic in an informal way, by briefly describing some of the classic approaches.

Implementation-Dependent Structures

The underlying implementation of the first two structures we present is an inherent part of their definition. These structures act as building blocks for many of the other structures.

Array

[0]	x
[1]	x
[2]	x
[3]	x
[4]	x
[5]	x

You have studied and used arrays in your previous work. An array's components are accessed by using their positions in the structure. Arrays are one of the most important organizational structures. They are available as a basic language construct in most high-level programming languages. Additionally, they are one of the basic building blocks for implementing other structures. We look at arrays more closely in Section 1.6, "Basic Structuring Mechanisms."

Linked List

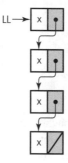

A linked list is a collection of separate elements, with each element linked to the one that follows it in the list. We can think of a linked list as a chain of elements. The linked list is a versatile, powerful, basic implementation structure and, like the array, it is one of the primary building blocks for the more complicated structures. Teaching you how to work with links and linked lists is one of the important goals of this textbook. We look at Java's link mechanism in Section 1.6, "Basic Structuring Mechanisms." Additionally, throughout the rest of the textbook we study how to use links and linked lists to implement other structures.

Implementation-Independent Structures

Unlike the array and the linked list, the organizational structures presented in this subsection are not tied to a particular implementation approach. They are more abstract.

The structures presented here display different kinds of relationships among their constituent elements. For stacks and queues, the organization is based on when the elements were placed into the structure; for sorted lists, it is related to the values of the elements; and for trees and graphs, it reflects some feature of the problem domain that is captured in the relative positions of the elements.

Each of these structures is treated separately later in the textbook, when we describe them in more detail, investigate ways of using them, and look at several possible implementations.

Stack

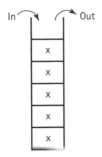

The defining feature of a stack is that whenever you access or remove an element, you work with the element that was most recently inserted. Stacks are "last in, first out" (LIFO) structures. To see how they work, think about a stack of dishes or trays. Note that the concept of a stack is completely defined by the relationship between its accessing operations, the operations for inserting something into it or removing something from it. No matter what the underlying implementation is, as long as the LIFO relationship holds, we have a stack.

Queue

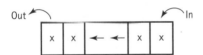

Queues are, in one sense, the opposite of stacks. They are "first in, first out" (FIFO) structures. The defining feature of a queue is that whenever you access or remove an element from a queue, you work with the element that was in the queue for the longest time. Think about an orderly line of people waiting to board a bus or a group of people, holding onto their service numbers, at a delicatessen. In both cases, the people will be served in the order in which they arrived. In fact, this is a good example of how the abstract organizational construct, the queue, can have more than one implementation approach—an orderly line or service numbers.

Sorted List

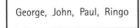

George, John, Paul, Ringo

Both the telephone directory and the dictionary are examples of sorted lists. The elements of such a list display a linear relationship. Each element (except the first) has a predecessor, and each element (except the last) has a successor. In a sorted list, the relationship also reflects an ordering of the elements, from "smallest" to "largest," or vice versa.

You might be thinking that an array whose elements are sorted is a sorted list—and you would be correct! As we said earlier, arrays are one of the basic building blocks for constructing other structures. But that is not the only way to implement a sorted list. We will cover several other approaches.

Tree

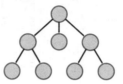

Stacks, queues, and lists are all linear structures. Their elements can be drawn in a line because each element has at most one element preceding it and one following it.

Trees and graphs are nonlinear. Each element of a tree is capable of having many successor elements, called its *children*. A child element can have only one *parent*. Thus, a tree is a branching structure. Every tree has a special beginning element called the *root*. The root is the only element that does not have a parent.

Trees are useful for representing hierarchical relationships among data elements. For example, they can be used to classify the members of the animal kingdom or to organize a set of tasks into subtasks. Trees can even be used to reflect an *is a* relationship among Java classes, as defined by the Java inheritance mechanism.

Graph

A graph is made up of a set of elements, usually called *nodes* or *vertices*, and a set of *edges* that connect the vertices. Unlike with trees, there are no restrictions on the connections between the elements. Typically, the connections, or edges, describe relationships among the vertices. In some cases, values, also called weights, are associated with the edges to represent some feature of the relationship. For example, the vertices may represent cities and the edges may represent pairs of cities that are connected by airplane routes. Values of the edges could represent the distances or travel times between cities.

Throughout the years, dozens of ways to organize data have been identified, with hundreds of variations. In this textbook we explore all of the ones introduced in this section, plus a few more. This will provide you with a diverse set of structures to help solve problems with computers and give you the background needed to continue your exploration of the many available advanced structures on your own.

What Is a Data Structure?

We have divided our examples of structures into implementation-dependent and implementation-independent categories. Originally, in the infancy of computing, such a distinction was not made. Most of the emphasis on the study of structures at that time dealt with their implementation. The term "data structure" was associated with the details of coding lists, stacks, trees, and so on. As our approaches to problem solving have evolved, we have recognized the importance of separating our study of such structures into both abstract and implementation levels.

As is true for many terms in the discipline of computing, you can find varied uses of the term "data structure" throughout the literature. One approach is to say that a data structure is the implementation of organized data. With this approach, of the structures described in this section, only the implementation-dependent structures, the array and the linked list, are considered data structures. Another approach is to consider any view of organizing data as a data structure. With this second approach, the implementation-independent structures, such as the stack and the graph, are also considered data structures.

No matter how you label them, all of the structures described here are important tools for solving problems with programs. In this textbook we will explore all of these data structures, plus many additional structures, from several perspectives.

1.6 Basic Structuring Mechanisms

All of the structures described in Section 1.5 can be implemented using some combination of two basic structuring mechanisms, the reference and the array. Most general-purpose high-level languages provide these two mechanisms. In this section we review Java's versions of them. In Chapter 2 we will begin to use references and arrays to build organizational structures.

To help present the concepts of this section, we assume access to a `Circle` class. The `Circle` class defines circular objects of different diameters. It provides a constructor that accepts an integer value that represents the diameter of the circle. The `Circle` class provides a convenient example, allowing us to graphically represent objects in our figures—we simply use actual circles of various diameters to represent the `Circle` objects.

References

As discussed in Section 1.3, "Classes, Objects, and Applications," variables of an object class hold references to objects. Consider the effects of the following Java statements:

```
Circle circleA;
Circle circleB = new Circle(8);
```

The first statement reserves memory space for a variable of class `Circle`. The second statement does the same thing, but also creates an object of class `Circle` and places a reference to that object in the `circleB` variable.

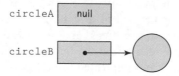

The reference is indicated by an arrow. In reality, the reference is a memory address. References are sometimes referred to as *links*, *addresses*, or *pointers*. The memory address of the `Circle` object is stored in the memory location assigned to the `circleB` variable. Note how we are representing the `Circle` object with an actual circle. In reality it would consist of a section of memory allocated to the object.

Because no object has been instantiated or assigned to the `circleA` variable, its memory location holds a `null` reference. Java uses the reserved word `null` to indicate an "absence of reference." If a reference variable is declared without being assigned an instantiated object, it is automatically initialized to the value `null`. You can also explicitly assign `null` to a variable:

```
circleB = null;
```

In addition, you can use `null` in a comparison:

```
if (circleA == null)
  System.out.println("The Circle does not exist");
```

Reference Types Versus Primitive Types

It is important to understand the differences in how primitive and nonprimitive types are handled in Java. Primitive types, such as the `int` type, are handled "by value." Nonprimitive types, such as arrays and classes, are handled "by reference." Whereas the variable of a primitive type holds the value of the variable, the variable of a nonprimitive type holds a *reference* to the value of the variable. That is, the variable holds the address where the system can find the value associated with the variable.

The differences in how "by value" and "by reference" variables are handled are seen dramatically in the result of a simple assignment statement. Figure 1.5 shows the result of the assignment of one `int` variable to another `int` variable, and the result of the assignment of one `Circle` variable to another `Circle` variable.

When we assign a variable of a primitive type to another variable of the same type, the latter becomes a copy of the former. But, as you can see from Figure 1.5, this is not the case with reference types. When we assign `Circle c2` to `Circle c1`, `c1` does *not* become a copy of `c2`. Instead, the reference associated with `c1` becomes a copy of the reference associated with `c2`. As a consequence, both `c1` and `c2` now reference the same object. The ramifications of this difference are discussed in the next four subsections.

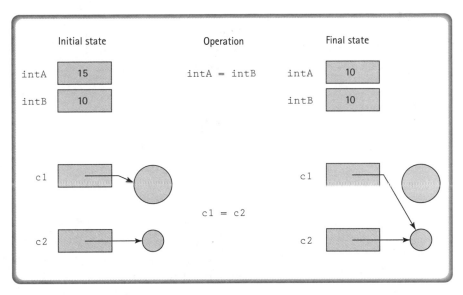

Figure 1.5   *Results of assignment statements*

Aliases

The assignment of one object to another object, as shown in Figure 1.5, results in both object variables referring to the same object. Thus we have two "names" for the same object. In this case we have an "alias" of the object. Good programmers avoid aliases because they make programs difficult to understand. An object's state can change, even though it appears that the program did not access the object, when the object is accessed through the alias. For example, consider the IncDate class that was defined in Section 1.4. If date1 and date2 are aliases for the same IncDate object, then the code

```
System.out.println(date1);
date2.increment();
System.out.println(date1);
```

would print out two different dates, even though at first glance it would appear that it should print out the same date twice (see Figure 1.6). This behavior can be very confusing for a maintenance programmer and lead to hours of frustrating testing and debugging.

Garbage

It would be fair to ask in the situation depicted in the lower half of Figure 1.5, "What happens to the space being used by the larger circle?" After the assignment statement the program has lost its reference to the large circle, so it can no longer be accessed. This kind of memory space, which has been allocated to a program but can no longer be

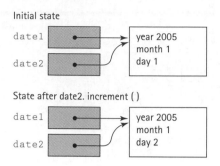

Figure 1.6 *Aliases can be confusing*

Garbage   The set of currently unreachable objects

accessed by a program, is called garbage. Garbage can be created in several other ways in a Java program. For example, the following code would create 100 objects of class Circle, but only one of them can be accessed through the c1 variable after the loop finishes executing:

```
Circle c1;
for (n = 1; n <= 100; n++)
{
    Circle c1 = new Circle(n);
    // Code to initialize and use c1 goes here.
}
```

The other 99 objects cannot be reached by the program. They are garbage.

When an object is unreachable, the Java run-time system marks it as garbage. The system regularly performs an operation known as garbage collection, in which it identifies unreachable objects and deallocates their storage space, returning the space to the free pool for the creation of new objects.

Garbage collection   The process of finding all unreachable objects and deallocating their storage space

Deallocate   To return the storage space for an object to the pool of free memory so that it can be reallocated to new objects

Dynamic memory management   The allocation and deallocation of storage space as needed while an application is executing

This approach—creating and destroying objects at different points in the application by allocating and deallocating space in the free pool—is called dynamic memory management. Without it, the computer would be much more likely to run out of storage space for data.

Comparing Objects

The fact that nonprimitive types are handled by reference affects the results returned by the == comparison operator. Two variables of a nonprimitive type

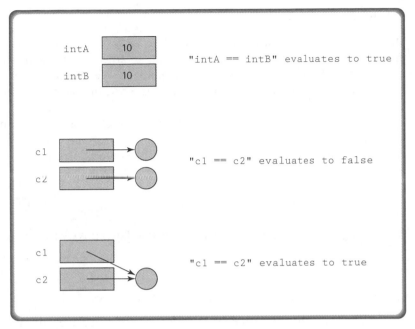

Figure 1.7   *Comparing primitive and nonprimitive variables*

are considered identical, in terms of the == operator, only if they are aliases for each other. This makes sense when you consider that the system compares the contents of the two variables; that is, it compares the two references that those variables contain. So even if two variables of type Circle reference circles with the same diameter, they are not considered equal in terms of the comparison operator. Figure 1.7 shows the results of using the comparison operator in various situations.

Parameters

When methods are invoked, they are often passed information (arguments) through parameters. Some programming languages allow the programmer to control whether arguments are passed by value (a copy of the argument's value is used) or by reference (a copy of the argument's address is used). Java does not allow such control. Whenever a variable is passed as an argument, the value stored in that variable is copied into the method's corresponding parameter variable. In other words, all Java arguments are passed by value. Therefore, if the argument is of a primitive type, the actual value (int, double, and so on) is passed to the method. However, if the argument is a reference type, an object, or an array, then the value passed to the method is the value of the reference—it is the address of the object or the array.

As a consequence, passing an object variable as an argument causes the receiving method to create an alias of the object. If the method uses the alias to make changes to the object, then when the method returns, an access via the original variable finds the object in its modified state.

Arrays

The second basic structuring construct is the array. Whereas a reference provides the programmer with a direct address mechanism, an array allows the programmer to access a sequence of locations using an indexed approach. We assume you are already familiar with the basic use of arrays from your previous work. In this subsection we review some of the subtle aspects of using arrays in Java.

Arrays in Java are a nonprimitive type and, therefore, are handled by reference, just like objects. Thus they need to be treated carefully, just like objects, in terms of aliases, comparison, and their use as arguments. And like objects, in addition to being declared, arrays must be instantiated. At instantiation you specify how large the array will be:

```
numbers = new int[10];
```

As with objects, you can both declare and instantiate arrays with a single command:

```
int[] numbers = new int[10];
```

Let's discuss a few questions you may have about arrays:

- What are the initial values in an array instantiated by using `new`? If the array components are primitive types, they are set to their default value. If the array components are reference types, such as arrays or classes, the components are set to `null`.
- Can you provide initial values for an array? Yes. An alternative way to create an array is with an initializer list. For example, the following line of code declares, instantiates, and initializes the array `numbers`:

```
int numbers[] = {5, 32, -23, 57, 1, 0, 27, 13, 32, 32};
```

- What happens if we try to execute the statement

```
numbers[n] = value;
```

when `n` is less than 0 or when `n` is greater than 9? A memory location outside the array would be accessed, which causes an out-of-bounds error. Some languages—C++, for instance—do not check for this error, but Java does. If your program attempts to use an index that is not within the bounds of the array, an `ArrayIndexOutOfBoundsException`[7] is thrown.

In addition to component selection, one other "operation" is available for our arrays. In Java, each array that is instantiated has a public instance variable, called

---

7. Appendix E includes information concerning the Java `Exception` class.

`length`, associated with it that contains the number of components in the array. You access this variable using the same syntax you use to invoke object methods—you use the name of the object followed by a period, followed by the name of the instance variable. For the `numbers` example, the expression

```
numbers.length
```

would have the value 10.

Arrays of Objects

Although arrays with primitive-type components are very common, many applications require a collection of objects. In such a case we can simply define an array whose components are objects.

Let's define an array of `Circle` objects. Declaring and creating the array of objects are exactly like declaring and creating an array where the components are primitive types:

```
Circle[] allCircles = new Circle[10];
```

This means `allCircles` is an array that can hold 10 references to `Circle` objects. What are the diameters of the circles? We don't know yet. The array of circles has been instantiated, but the `Circle` objects themselves have not. Another way of saying this is that `allCircles` is an array of references to `Circle` objects, which are set to `null` when the array is instantiated. The objects must be instantiated separately. The following code segment initializes the first and second circles. We'll assume that a `Circle` object `myCircle` has already been instantiated and initialized to have a diameter of 8.

```
Circle[] allCircles = new Circle[10];
allCircles[0] = myCircle;
allCircles[1] = new Circle(4);
```

Normally, such an array would be initialized using a "for loop" and a constructor method, but we used the above approach so that we could demonstrate several of the subtleties of the construct. Figure 1.8 provides a visual representation of the array.

Two-Dimensional Arrays

A one-dimensional array is used to represent elements in a list or a sequence of values. A two-dimensional array is used to represent elements in a table with rows and columns.

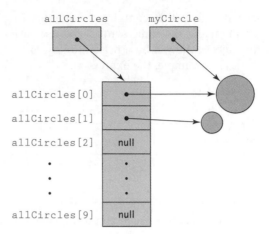

Figure 1.8   *The* `allCircles` *array*

Figure 1.9 shows a two-dimensional array with 100 rows and 9 columns. The rows are accessed by an integer ranging from 0 through 99; the columns are accessed by an integer ranging from 0 through 8. Each component is accessed by a row–column pair—for example, [0][5].

A two-dimensional array variable is declared in exactly the same way as a one-dimensional array variable, except that there are two pairs of brackets. A two-dimensional array object is instantiated in exactly the same way, except that sizes must be specified for two dimensions.

The following code fragment would create the array shown in Figure 1.9, where the data in the table are of type `double`.

```
double[][] alpha;
alpha = new double[100][9];
```

The first dimension specifies the number of rows, and the second dimension specifies the number of columns.

To access an individual component of the `alpha` array, two expressions (one for each dimension) are used to specify its position. We place each expression in its own pair of brackets next to the name of the array:

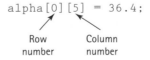

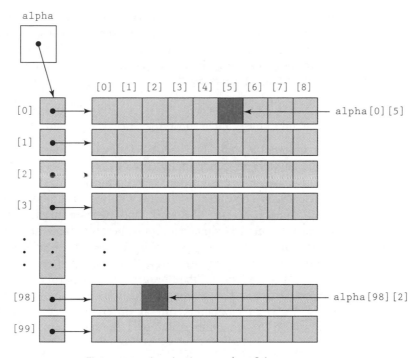

Figure 1.9 *Java implementation of the* `alpha` *array*

Note that `alpha.length` would give the number of rows in the array. To obtain the number of columns in a row of an array, we access the `length` field for the specific row. For example, the statement

```
rowLength = alpha[30].length;
```

stores the length of row 30 of the array `alpha`, which is 9, into the `int` variable `rowLength`.

Remember that in Java each row of a two-dimensional array is itself a one-dimensional array. Many programming languages directly support two-dimensional arrays; Java doesn't. In Java, a two-dimensional array is an array of references to array objects.

1.7 Comparing Algorithms: Big-O Analysis

The analysis of algorithms is an important area of theoretical computer science. In this section we introduce this topic to an extent that will allow you to determine which of two algorithms requires less work to accomplish a particular task. The efficiency of algorithms and the code that implements them can be studied in terms of both time (the number of statements executed) and space (the amount of memory required). When appropriate throughout this textbook we point out space considerations, but usually we concentrate on the time aspect—how fast the algorithm is as opposed to how much space it uses.

As you already know, there is more than one way to solve most problems. If you were asked for directions to Joe's Diner (see Figure 1.10), for example, you could give either of two equally correct answers:

1. "Go east on the Big Highway to the Y'all Come Inn, and turn left."
2. "Take the Winding Country Road to Honeysuckle Lodge, and turn right."

The two answers are not the same, but because following either route gets the traveler to Joe's Diner, both answers are functionally correct.

How we choose between two algorithms that do the same task often comes down to a question of efficiency. Which one does the job with the least amount of work?

How do programmers measure the work that two algorithms perform? The first approach that comes to mind is simply to code the algorithms and then compare the execution times for running the two programs. The one with the shorter execution time is clearly the better algorithm. Or is it? Using this technique, we really can determine only that program A is more efficient than program B on a particular computer at a particular time using a particular set of input. Execution times are specific to a particular computer, because different computers run at different speeds. Sometimes they are dependent on what else the computer is doing in the background. For example, if the

Figure 1.10   *Map to Joe's Diner*

Java run-time engine is performing garbage collection, it can affect the execution time of the program. Of course, we could test the algorithms on many possible computers at various times, but that would be unrealistic and too specific (new computers become available all the time). We want a more general measure.

A second possibility is to count the number of instructions or statements executed. This measure, however, varies with the programming language used as well as with the style of the individual programmer.

A standard approach, and the one we use in this text, is to isolate a particular operation fundamental to the algorithm and count the number of times that this operation is performed. Suppose, for example, that we are iteratively summing the elements in an integer array. To measure the amount of work required, we could count the integer addition operations. For an array holding 100 integers, there are 99 addition operations. Note, however, that we do not actually have to count the number of addition operations; it is some function of the number of elements (N) in the array. Therefore, we can express the number of addition operations in terms of N: For an array of N elements, there are $N - 1$ addition operations. Now we can compare the algorithms for the general case, not just for a specific number of integers.

Big-O Notation

We have been talking about work as a function of the size of the input to the operation (for instance, the number of integers in the array to be summed). We can express an approximation of this function using a mathematical notation called order of magnitude, or Big-O notation. (This is a letter O, not a zero.) The order of magnitude of a function is identified with the term in the function that increases fastest relative to the size of the function input. For instance, if

> **Big-O notation**   A notation that expresses computing time (complexity) as the term in a function that increases most rapidly relative to the size of a problem

$$f(N) = N^4 + 100N^2 + 500,$$

then $f(N)$ is of order N^4–or, in Big-O notation, $O(N^4)$. That is, some multiple of N^4 dominates the function for sufficiently large values of N.

How is it that we can just drop the low-order terms? Consider Table 1.3, which shows the amounts and percentage contributed to the total by each of the terms of $f(N)$.

As you can see, for large values of N, N^4 is so much larger than 500, or even $100N^2$, that we can ignore these other terms if we are approximating the value of $f(N)$. This doesn't mean that the other terms do not contribute to the computing time; it merely indicates that they are not significant in our approximation when N is "large."

What is this value N? N represents the size of the problem. Most of the problems in this book involve data structures—stacks, queues, lists, trees, and graphs. Each structure is composed of elements. We develop algorithms to add an element to the structure and to modify or remove an element from the structure. We can describe the work done by these operations in terms of N, where N is the number of elements in the structure.

Table 1.3

N	N^4		$100N^2$		500		$f(N)$
1	1	00.17%	100	16.64%	500	83.19%	601
10	10,000	48.78%	10,000	48.78%	500	02.44%	20,500
100	100,000,000	99.01%	1,000,000	00.99%	500	00.00%	101,000,500
1,000	1,000,000,000,000	99.99%	100,000,000	00.01%	500	00.00%	1,000,100,000,500

Let us look at a variation of our example of summing the integers in an array. Suppose that we have an array called Numbers that is full of integers. We want to create a method that returns true if the sum of the integers in Numbers is greater than 0, and false otherwise. How much work is that? The answer depends on how many integers are in the array. Our algorithm is as follows:

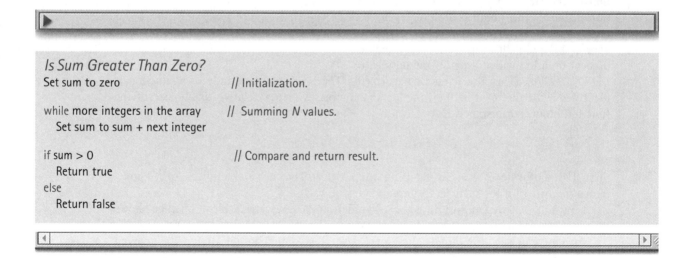

Is Sum Greater Than Zero?
Set sum to zero   // Initialization.

while **more integers in the array**   // Summing N values.
   Set sum to sum + next integer

if sum > 0   // Compare and return result.
   Return true
else
   Return false

If N is the number of integers in the array, the "time" required to do this task is

```
   time-to-set-sum-to-zero
 + (N * time-to-do-an-addition)
 + time-to-compare-sum-to-zero
 + time-to-return-Boolean-value
```

This algorithm is $O(N)$ because the time required to perform the task is proportional to the number of elements (N)–plus a little time to do a set, a compare, and a return. How can we ignore the set, compare, and return times when determining the Big-O approximation? If the array has only a few integers, the time needed to set, compare, and return may be significant. For large values of N, however, adding the integers accounts for most of the algorithm's time.

Common Orders of Magnitude

$O(1)$ is called bounded time. The amount of work is bounded by a constant and is not dependent on the size of the problem. Initializing a sum to 0 is $O(1)$. Although bounded time is often called constant time, the amount of work is not necessarily constant. It is, however, bounded by a constant.

$O(\log_2 N)$ is called logarithmic time. The amount of work depends on the logarithm, in base 2, of the size of the problem (Table 1.4 shows some values of $\log_2 N$). Algorithms that successively cut the amount of data to be processed in half at each step typically fall into this category. Note that in the world of computing we often just say "log N" when we mean $\log_2 N$. The base 2 is assumed.

$O(N)$ is called linear time. The amount of work is some constant times the size of the problem. Printing all the elements in a list of N elements is $O(N)$.

$O(N \log_2 N)$ is called (for lack of a better term) N log N time. Algorithms of this type typically involve applying a logarithmic algorithm N times. The better sorting algorithms,

Table 1.4   *Comparison of Rates of Growth*

N	$\log_2 N$	$N \log_2 N$	N^2	N^3	2^N
1	0	1	1	1	2
2	1	2	4	8	4
4	2	8	16	64	16
8	3	24	64	512	256
16	4	64	256	4,096	65,536
32	5	160	1,024	32,768	4,294,967,296
64	6	384	4,096	262,144	About 1 month's worth of instructions on a supercomputer
128	7	896	16,384	2,097,152	About 10^{12} times greater than the age of the universe in nanoseconds (for a 6-billion-year estimate)
256	8	2,048	65,536	16,777,216	Don't ask!

such as Quicksort, Heapsort, and Mergesort presented in Chapter 10, have $N \log N$ complexity. That is, these algorithms can transform an unsorted array of size N into a sorted array in $O(N \log_2 N)$ time.

$O(N^2)$ is called quadratic time. Algorithms of this type typically involve applying a linear algorithm N times. Most simple sorting algorithms are $O(N^2)$ algorithms.

$O(2^N)$ is called exponential time. These algorithms are extremely slow. An example of a problem for which the best-known solution is exponential is the traveling salesperson problem—given a set of cities and a set of roads that connect some of them, plus the lengths of the roads, find a route that visits every city exactly once and minimizes total travel distance. As you can see in Table 1.4, exponential times increase dramatically in relation to the size of N.

Example 1: Sum of Consecutive Integers

Let's look at two different algorithms that calculate the sum of the integers from 1 to N. Algorithm Sum1 is a simple *for* loop that adds successive integers to keep a running total.

```
Algorithm Sum1
sum = 0;
for (count = 1; count <= n; count++)
    sum = sum + count;
```

That seems simple enough. The second algorithm calculates the sum by using a formula. To understand the formula, consider writing two arithmetic expressions of the sum, one "forward" and one "backward," and then adding together each of the columns as shown:

```
    sum =        1   +       2 +       3 + . . . + (N - 1)  +        N
  + sum =        N   + (N - 1) + (N - 2) + . . . +       2  +        1
-------    -------   -------   -------   -------           -------  -------
2 X sum =  (N + 1)   + (N + 1) + (N + 1) + . . . + (N + 1)  + (N + 1)
```

We pair up each number from 1 to N with another, such that each pair adds up to $N + 1$. There are N such pairs, giving us a total of $(N + 1) * N$. Now, because each number is included twice, we divide the product by 2. This gives us the formula sum = $(N \times (N - 1))/2$. Now we have a second algorithm:

Algorithm Sum2
sum = (N * (N + 1))/2;

The descriptions of both algorithms are short. Let's compare the algorithms using Big-O notation. The size of the problem is *N*, which represents how many numbers are included in the sum. The basic operation performed by Sum1 is the addition operation that takes place within the *for* loop. This operation occurs once, each time through the loop. It is easy to see that the loop is executed *N* times. Therefore, the Sum1 algorithm is O(*N*). As *N* gets larger, the amount of work grows proportionally. If *N* is 50, Sum1 works 10 times as hard as when *N* is 5.

Sum1 Algorithm

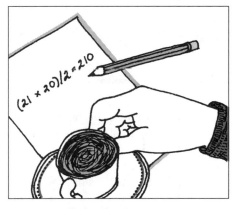

Sum2 Algorithm

Sum2 is even easier to analyze. It always consists of an addition, a multiplication, and a division. No matter whether *N* = 5 or *N* = 50, it still requires only those three operations. In fact, whatever value we assign to *N*, the algorithm does the same amount of work to solve the problem. Algorithm Sum2, therefore, takes a constant amount of time. We say it is O(1). Sum2 is more efficient than Sum1.

Does this mean that Sum2 is always faster? Is it always a better choice than Sum1? That depends. Sum2 might seem to do more "work," because the formula involves multiplication and division, whereas Sum1 is a simple running total. In fact, for very small values of *N*, Sum2 actually might do more work than Sum1. So the choice between the algorithms depends in part on whether they are used for small or large values of *N*.

Another issue is the fact that Sum2 is not as obvious as Sum1, and thus it is harder for the programmer (a human) to understand. Sometimes a more efficient solution to a problem is more complicated; we may save computer time at the expense of the programmer's time.

So, what's the verdict? As usual in the design of computer programs, there are trade-offs. We must look at our program's requirements and then decide which solution is better.

Example 2: Finding a Number in a Phone Book

Suppose you need to look up a friend's number in a phone book. How would you go about finding the number? To keep matters simple, assume that the name you are searching for is in the book—you won't come up empty. Here is a straightforward approach.

Algorithm Lookup1
Check the first name in the book
while (have not yet found the name)
    Check the next name in the book

Even though this algorithm is inefficient, it is correct and does work.

What is the Big-O efficiency rating of this algorithm? How many steps does it take to find someone's name? Clearly the answers to these questions depend on the size of the phone book and the name that you are searching for. If you are looking for your friend Aaron Aardvark, it probably takes you only one or two steps. If your friend's name is Zina Zyne, you are not so lucky.

The Lookup1 algorithm displays different efficiency ratings under different input conditions. This is not unusual. To handle this situation, analysts define three complexity cases: best case, worst case, and average case. Best case complexity tells us the complexity when we are very lucky; it represents the smallest number of steps that an algorithm can take. In general, best case complexity is not very useful as a complexity measure. Worst case complexity, by contrast, represents the greatest number of steps that an algorithm would require. Average case complexity represents the average number of steps required, considering all possible inputs.

Let's evaluate Lookup1 in each of these cases. Following our previous convention we label the size of our phone book N. Our fundamental operation is "checking a name."

Best case complexity   Related to the minimum number of steps required by an algorithm, given an ideal set of input values in terms of efficiency

Worst case complexity   Related to the maximum number of steps required by an algorithm, given the worst possible set of input values in terms of efficiency

Average case complexity   Related to the average number of steps required by an algorithm, calculated across all possible sets of input values

- *Best case*   The name we are looking for is the first name in the phone book, so it takes us only one step to find the name. The best case Big-O complexity of the algorithm is constant or O(1).
- *Worst case*   The name we are looking for is the last name in the phone book, so it takes us *N* steps to find the name. The worst case Big-O complexity of the algorithm is O(*N*).
- *Average case*   Assuming that each name in the phone book is equally likely to be the name we are searching for, the average number of steps required is *N*/2. Sometimes the name is toward the front of the book, and sometimes it is toward the back of the book. On the average, it is in the middle of the book—thus *N*/2 steps. The average case Big-O complexity of the algorithm is also O(*N*).

The average case analysis is usually the most difficult. Often, as in this example, it evaluates to the same Big-O efficiency class as the worst case. For our purposes we will typically use worst case analysis.

Let's look at a more efficient algorithm for finding a name in a phone book.

Algorithm Lookup2

```
Set the search area to the entire book
Check the middle name in the search area
while (have not yet found the name)
    if the middle name is greater than the target name
        Set the search area to the first half of the search area
    else
        Set the search area to the second half of the search area
    Check the middle name in the search area
```

With this algorithm we eliminate half of the remaining phone book from consideration each time we check a name. What is the worst case complexity? Another way of asking this is to say, "How many times can you reduce *N* by half, before you get down to 1?" This is essentially the definition of $\log_2 N$. Thus the worst case complexity of Lookup2 is $O(\log_2 N)$. This is significantly better than the worst case for Lookup1. For example, if each of New York City's 22 million people were listed in your phone book, then in the worst case Lookup1 would take you 22,000,000 steps, but Lookup2 would require only 25 steps.

Note that the successful use of the Lookup2 algorithm depends on the fact that the phone book organizes names in alphabetical order. This is a good example of a situation in which the way the data are structured and organized affects the efficiency of our use of the data.

Goal: Find "Smith, John"

Algorithm Lookup1

Algorithm Lookup2

And so on?

Done!

Summary

This chapter is all about organization.

When studying data structures from an academic point of view, it is easy to forget how software is developed in the real world to solve real problems. Complex problems often require teamwork, and using an organized approach is necessary to handle both the complexity of the problem and the complex interactions among the team members. Software engineering is the field devoted to these issues. We begin the book with an introduction to this field to emphasize its importance in the overall scheme of software development.

Object orientation is one approach to software analysis and design. It allows developers to organize their solutions around models of reality, accruing benefits of understandability, reusability, and maintainability. The primary construct for creating systems using this approach is the class. Classes are used to create objects that work together to provide solutions to problems. Java's inheritance mechanism and package construct help us organize our classes.

Programs operate on data, so how the data are organized is of prime importance. Data structures deal with this organization. Several classical organizational structures have been identified through the years to help programmers create correct and efficient solutions to problems. The Java language provides basic structuring mechanisms for creating these structures—namely, the array and the reference mechanisms. Big-O notation is an approach for classifying the efficiency of algorithms that we will use when studying the algorithms for implementing and using our data structures.

Programmers are problem solvers. Software engineering provides proven approaches to working in teams to identify the problems and design the solutions. Object orientation allows seamless integration of problem analysis and design, resulting in problem solutions that are maintainable and reusable. Data structures provide ways of organizing the data of the problem domain so that solutions are correct and efficient. Staying organized is the key to solving difficult problems!

Exercises

1.1 Software Engineering

1. Explain what we mean by "software engineering."

2. Which of these statements is always true?

   a. All of the program requirements must be completely defined before design begins.

   b. All of the program design must be complete before any coding begins.

   c. All of the coding must be complete before any testing can begin.

   d. Different development activities often take place concurrently, overlapping in the software life cycle.

3. Create your own software "process." In other words, write a description of the steps you follow when working on a programming project. This is a good exercise for students to work on together, in small teams. Perhaps the teams that create the most interesting processes could present their results to the class.

4. Research Question: Locate information about agile software development methods. Identify one particular agile approach that you find intriguing. Write a paragraph describing the approach and explain which aspect of that approach intrigues you.

5. Research Question: Locate the Agile Manifesto on the Web. Browse through the list of hundreds of signatories and see what they have to say about agile approaches. Select two interesting statements to share with your classmates.

6. List the four goals for quality software described in this section. Note that these are broad, general goals. Now create your own list of more specific goals. This is

a good exercise for students to work on together, brainstorming a list of specific goals that software projects might aspire to.

7. Explain why software might need to be modified

    a. In the design phase

    b. In the coding phase

    c. In the testing phase

    d. In the maintenance phase

8. Goal 4 says, "Quality software is completed on time and within budget."

    a. Explain some of the consequences of not meeting this goal for a student preparing a class programming assignment.

    b. Explain some of the consequences of not meeting this goal for a team developing a highly competitive new software product.

1.2 Object Orientation

9. Research Question: The Turing Award has been awarded annually since 1966 to a person or persons for making contributions of lasting and major technical importance to the computer field. Locate information about this award on the Web. Study the list of award winners and their contributions. Identify those winners whose contributions dealt directly with programming. Then identify those winners whose contributions dealt directly with object orientation.

10. Explain how object-oriented approaches support each of the four goals for software quality.

11. Research Question: List and briefly describe the UML's 12 main diagramming types.

1.3 Classes, Objects, and Applications

12. Find a tool that you can use to create UML class diagrams and re-create the diagram of the Date class shown in Figure 1.2.

13. What is the difference between an object and a class? Give some examples.

14. Describe each of the four levels of visibility provided by Java's access modifiers.

15. A common use of an object is to "keep track" of something. The object is fed data through its transformer methods and returns information through its observer methods. Define (no coding necessary) a reasonable set of instance variables, class variables, and methods for each of the following classes. Indicate the access level for each construct. Note that each of these class descriptions are somewhat fuzzy and allow multiple "correct" answers.

    a. A time counter—this will keep track of total time; it will be fed discrete time amounts (in either minutes and seconds or just in seconds); it should provide information about the total time in several "formats," the number of discrete time units, and the average time per unit. Think of this class as a tool that could be used to keep track of the total time of a collection of music, given the time for each song.

b. Basketball statistics tracker—this will keep track of the score and shooting statistics for a basketball team (not for each player, but for the team as a unit); it should be fed data each time a shot is taken; it should provide information about shooting percentages and the total score when requested.

c. Tic-tac-toe game tracker—this will keep track of a tic-tac-toe game; it should be fed moves and return an indication of whether a move was legal; it should provide information about the status of the game (Is it over? Who won?) when requested.

16. For one or more of the classes described in the previous exercise

a. Implement the class.

b. Design and implement an application that uses the class.

c. Use your application to help verify the correctness of your class implementation.

17. Modify the `Date` class so that

a. Its `toString` method returns a string of the form "month number, number"— for example, "May 13, 1919."

b. It provides a public class `mjd` (standing for Modified Julian Day) that returns the number of days since November 17, 1858.

c. It provides a public class `djd` (standing for Dublin Julian Day) that returns the number of days since January 1, 1900.

18. Think about how you might test the `DaysBetween` application. What type of input should give a result of 0? Of 1? Of 7? Of 365? Of 366? Try out the test cases that you identified.

19. According to the `DaysBetween` application, how many days are between 1/1/1900 and 1/1/2000? How many leap years are there between those dates? What about between 1/1/2000 and 1/1/2100? Explain the difference in these answers.

20. Use the `DaysBetween` application to answer the following:

a. How old are you, in days?

b. How many days has it been since the United States adopted the Declaration of Independence on July 4, 1776?

c. How many days between the day that Jean-François Pilâtre de Rozier and François Laurent became the first human pilots, traveling 10 kilometers in a hot-air balloon on November 21, 1783, and the day Neil Armstrong took one small step onto the moon at the Sea of Tranquility on July 20, 1969?

21. Based on the range of the Java `int` type (see Appendix C), what is the latest date that can be "handled" by the `Date` class?

22. Modify the `DaysBetween` application so that after it displays the information about the number of days between the two dates, it prompts the user to see

whether he or she wants to continue. If the answer is "yes," it repeats the sequence of interactions with the user, again prompting for two dates, and so on.

23. The `DaysBetween` application is not very robust. That is, it does not gracefully handle erroneous input. This exercise asks you to revise the application so that it is more robust.

  a. When a user is prompted to enter a date, the program does not check whether the user entered an integer. If the user does not enter an integer, the program will "bomb" due to an input mismatch error. Revise the program so that it uses the `Scanner` class's `hasNextInt` method to check that the next input value is an integer before reading it. If it is not, the program should display the message "Illegal input was entered" and exit. Note that you can exit the program using Java's `return` statement.

  b. Users can enter any combination of three integers to represent a date, even those that do not make any sense. For example, 15 37 2006 would represent the thirty-seventh day of the fifteenth month of 2006. To remedy this potential problem, you should first add a public instance method `valid` to the `Date` class. The method should return `true` if the date represented by the object is a valid date and `false` otherwise. Valid dates are "real" dates that occur after October 14, 1582. Don't forget about leap years. After creating and testing the `valid` method, use it to check dates from within the `DaysBetween` program. If an invalid date is entered, display the message "That is not a valid date" and exit.

24. You will create a class that keeps track of the total cost, average cost, and number of items in a shopping bag.

  a. Create a class called `ShoppingBag`. Objects of this class represent a single shopping bag. Attributes of such an object include the number of items in the bag and the total retail cost of those items. Provide a constructor that accepts a tax rate as a `float` parameter. Provide a transformer method called `place` that accepts an `int` parameter indicating the number of the particular items that are being placed in the bag and a `float` parameter that indicates the cost of each of the items. For example, `myBag.place(5, 10.5);` represents placing 5 items that cost $10.50 each into `myBag`. Provide getter methods for the number of items in the bag and their total retail cost. Provide a `total-Cost` method that returns the total cost with tax included. Provide a `toString` method that returns a nicely formatted string that summarizes the current status of the shopping bag. Finally, provide a program, a "test driver," that demonstrates that your `ShoppingBag` class performs correctly.

  b. Create an application that repeatedly prompts the user for a number of items to put in the bag, followed by a prompt for the cost of those items. Use a 0 for the number of items to indicate that there are no more items. The program then displays a summary of the status of the shopping bag. Assume the tax rate is 6%. A short sample run might look something like this:

Enter count (use 0 to stop): 5

Enter cost: 10.50
Enter count (use 0 to stop): 2
Enter cost: 2.07
Enter count (use 0 to stop): 0

The bag contains 7 items. The retail cost of the items is $161.64.

The total cost of the items is $171.34.

25. You will create a class that keeps track of some statistics, including the score, of a bowling game. If you do not understand bowling terminology or how points are earned in bowling you should research the game or talk to someone who does understand . . . or both!

a. Create a class called BowlingGame. Objects of this class represent a single game of bowling. Attributes of such an object include the name of the bowler, the current score and frame, and the number of strikes, spares, and gutter balls rolled so far in the game. Provide

- A constructor that accepts the name of the bowler as a String parameter.
- A transformer method called shot that accepts an int parameter indicating the number of pins knocked down on the next "shot." The shot method should return a boolean indicating whether the current frame is over for the bowler. You can assume that the shot method will only be passed integers that "make sense" within the current bowling game (e.g., it will not be passed a negative, it will not be passed a 5 if there are only 3 pins currently standing).
- Getter methods for the various attributes
- A toString method that returns a nicely formatted string that summarizes the current status of the game
- A "test driver" program that demonstrates that your BowlingGame class performs correctly

b. Create an application that prompts the user for his or her name and instantiates a BowlingGame object using his or her name. The program should then repeatedly prompt the user for the number of pins knocked over by the next ball rolled, reporting the status of the game after each frame, until the game is over. You can assume that the user provides numbers that "make sense." A partial sample run might look something like this:

Your name: Fred
Pins knocked over : 5
Pins knocked over : 0
Fred's game after frame 1: Score is 5, Strikes 0, Spares 0, Gutter Balls 1
Pins knocked over : 10
Fred's game after frame 2: Score is 15, Strikes 1, Spares 0, Gutter Balls 1
Pins knocked over : 5
Pins knocked over : 5
Fred's game after frame 3: Score is 35, Strikes 1, Spares 1, Gutter Balls 1
And so on.

26. You will create a class that represents a polynomial; for example, it could represent $5x^3 + 2x - 3$ or $x^2 - 1$.

    a. Create a class called `Polynomial`. Objects of this class represent a single polynomial. Attributes of such an object include its degree and the coefficients of each of its terms. Provide a constructor that accepts the degree of the polynomial as an `int` parameter. Provide a transformer method called `setCoefficient` that accepts as `int` parameters the degree of the term it is setting and the coefficient to which it should be set. For example, the polynomial $5x^3 + 2x - 3$ could be created by the sequence of statements:

    ```
    Polynomial myPoly = new Polynomial(3);
    myPoly.setCoefficient(3,5);
    myPoly.setCoefficient(1,2);
    myPoly.setCoefficient(0,-3);
    ```

    Provide an `evaluate` method that accepts a `float` parameter and returns the value of the polynomial, as a `float`, as evaluated at the parameter value. For example, given the previous code the following sequence of code would print -3.0, 4.0, and -1.375.

    ```
    System.out.println(myPoly.evaluate(0));
    System.out.println(myPoly.evaluate(1));
    System.out.println(myPoly.evaluate(0.5));
    ```

    Finally, provide a program, a "test driver," that demonstrates that your `Polynomial` class performs correctly.

    b. Create an application that accepts the degree of a polynomial and the coefficients of the polynomial, from highest degree to lowest, as a command line parameter and then creates the corresponding `Polynomial` object. For example, the polynomial $5x^3 + 2x - 3$ would be represented by the command line parameter "3   5 0 2 –3." The program should then repeatedly prompt the user for a float value at which to evaluate the polynomial and report the result of the evaluation. A sample run, assuming the previously stated command line parameter, might look something like this:

    ```
    Enter a value>  0
    The result is -3.0
    Continue?> Yes
    Enter a value>  1
    The result is 4.0
    Continue?> Yes
    Enter a value>  0.5
    The result is -1.375
    Continue?> No
    ```

    c. Create an application that accepts the degree of a polynomial and the coefficients of the polynomial as a command line parameter as in part b. The program should then prompt the user for two float values that will represent the end points of an interval on which the polynomial is defined. Your program should then calculate and output the approximation of the definite integral of the polynomial on the indicated interval, using 1000 bounded rectangles.

1.4 Organizing Classes

27. Describe the concept of inheritance, and explain how the inheritance tree is traversed to bind method calls with method implementations in an object-oriented system.

28. Given the definitions of the `Date` and `IncDate` classes in this chapter, and the following declarations

```
int temp;
Date date1 = new Date(10,2,1989);
Date date2 = new Date(4,2,1992);
IncDate date3 = new IncDate(12,25,2001);
```

indicate which of the following statements are illegal, and which are legal. Explain your answers.

a. `temp = date1.getDay();`

b. `temp = date3.getYear();`

c. `date1.increment();`

d. `date3.increment();`

e. `date2 = date1;`

f. `date2 = date3;`

g. `date3 = date2;`

29. Create a `Date` class and an `IncDate` class as described in this chapter (or copy them from the website). In the `IncDate` class you must create the code for the `increment` method, as that was left undefined in the chapter. Remember to follow the rules of the Gregorian calendar: A year is a leap year if either (1) it is divisible by 4 but not by 100, or (2) it is divisible by 400. Create an application that uses these classes.

30. Modify your `IncDate` class from Exercise 29 so that it also provides an `increment` method that accepts an argument `numDays` of type `int` and modifies the date so that it is `numDays` later. For example, if the date represents December 31, 2002, then after an invocation of `increment(3)` the date would represent January 3, 2003. *Hint:* You may consider creating an "inverse" `lilian` method that takes an LDN and converts it to a date to help you solve this problem.

31. You will extend your `BowlingGame` class from Exercise 25 with a new class called `RBowlingGame` ("Robust Bowling Game").

a. The `RBowlingGame` class provides a new `shot` method for which the assumption that the integral parameter "makes sense" is dropped. If the parameter is less than 0, the method will act as if the parameter was 0. If the parameter indicates a number of pins that is more than the current number of pins standing, then the method will act as if the parameter was equal to the number of pins standing. Also create a test driver that shows that your `RBowlingGame` class works correctly.

b. Create an application that instantiates two bowling game objects, one for the bowler "Steady Freddy" using the `BowlingGame` class and one for the bowler "Wild Child" using the `RBowlingGame` class. When Steady Freddy bowls he knocks down either 4 or 5 pins with each ball. About half the time he knocks down 4 pins and about half the time he knocks down 5 pins. Therefore, for the number of pins he knocks down with any particular ball you can generate a random integer in the range 4 to 5. Wild Child, on the other hand, is not so predictable. For the number of pins she knocks down with any particular ball you can generate a random integer in the range -3 to 15. Your application should simulate a bowling match between these two bowlers, showing the results frame by frame. Who do you think will win?

32. Explain how packages are used to organize Java files.

33. Suppose file 1 contains   and file 2 contains

```
package media.records;        package media.records;
public class Labels{ ... }     public class Length{ ... }
class Check {...}              class Review { ... }
```

a. Are the `Check` class and the `Review` class in the same package?
b. What is the name of file 1?
c. What is the name of file 2?
d. What is the name of the directory that contains the two files?
e. What is the directory in part d a subdirectory of?

34. Organize the files you created to solve Exercise 29 with a package called `dates`.

1.5 Data Structures

35. Research Question: On the Web find two distinct definitions of the term "data structure." Compare and contrast them.

36. Identify things in the following story that remind you of the various data structures described in this section. Be imaginative. How many can you find? What are they? (*Note:* We can find nine!)

Sally arrives at the train station with just a few minutes to spare. This weekend is shaping up to be a disaster. She studies the electronic map on the wall for a few seconds in confusion. She then realizes she just needs to select her destination from the alphabetized list of buttons on the right. When she presses Gloucester, a path on the map lights up—so, she should take the Blue train to Birmingham, where she can connect to the Red train that will take her to Gloucester. The wait in line to buy her ticket doesn't take long. She hurries to the platform and approaches the fourth car of the train. Double-checking that her ticket says "car 4," she boards the train and finds a seat. Whew, just in time, as a few seconds later the train pulls out of the station. About an hour into the journey Sally decides it's time for lunch. She walks through cars 5, 6, and 7 to arrive at car 8, the dining car. She grabs the top tray (it's still warm from the tray dryer) and heads for the candy machine, thinking to herself, "May as well figure out what to have for dessert first, as usual. Hmmm, that's an interesting Pez dispenser in slot F4." She presses the button contentedly, and thinks, "Looks like this is going to be a nice weekend after all. Thank goodness for data structures."

37. Describe three uses of the tree structure as a way of organizing information that you are familiar with.

38. Some aspect of each of the following can be modeled with a graph structure. Describe, in each case, what the nodes would represent and what the edges would represent.

   a. Travel routes available through an airline

   b. Countries and their borders

   c. A collection of research articles about data structures

   d. Actors (research the "six degrees of Kevin Bacon")

   e. The computers at a university

   f. The Web

1.6 Basic Structuring Mechanisms

39. What is an alias? Show an example of how it is created by a Java program. Explain the dangers of aliases.

40. Assume that date1 and date2 are objects of class IncDate as defined in Section 1.4. What would be the output of the following code?

```
date1 = new IncDate(5, 5, 2000);
date2 = date1;
System.out.println(date1);
System.out.println(date2);
date1.increment();
System.out.println(date1);
System.out.println(date2);
```

41. What is garbage? Show an example of how it is created by a Java program.

42. Assume that date1 and date2 are objects of class IncDate as defined in Section 1.4. What would be the output of the following code?

```
date1 = new IncDate(5, 5, 2000);
date2 = new IncDate(5, 5, 2000);
```

```
if (date1 == date2)
  System.out.println("equal");
else
  System.out.println("not equal");
date1 = date2;
if (date1 == date2)
  System.out.println("equal");
else
  System.out.println("not equal");
date1.increment();
if (date1 == date2)
  System.out.println("equal");
else
  System.out.println("not equal");
```

43. Write a program that declares a 10-element array of `int`, uses a loop to initialize each element to the value of its index squared, and then uses another loop to print the contents of the array, one integer per line.

44. Write a program that declares a 10-element array of `Date`, uses a loop to initialize the elements to December 1 through 10 of 2005, and then uses another loop to print the contents of the array, one date per line.

45. Create an application that instantiates a 20 × 20 two-dimensional array of integers, populates it with random integers drawn from the range 1 to 100, and then outputs the index of the row with the highest sum among all the rows and the index of the column with the highest sum among all the columns.

1.7   Comparing Algorithms: Big-O Analysis

46. Describe the order of magnitude of each of the following functions using Big-O notation:

   a. $N^2 + 3N$

   b. $3N^2 + N$

   c. $N^5 + 100N^3 + 245$

   d. $3N\log_2 N + N^2$

   e. $1 + N + N^2 + N^3 + N^4$

   f. $(N * (N - 1)) / 2$

47. Give an example of an algorithm (other than the examples discussed in the chapter) that is

   a. O(1)

   b. O(N)

   c. O(N^2)

48. Describe the order of magnitude of each of the following code sections, using Big-O notation:

a.
```
count = 0;
for (i = 1; i <= N; i++)
   count++;
```

b.
```
count = 0;
for (i = 1; i <= N; i++)
    for (j = 1; j <= N; j++)
       count++;
```

c.
```
value = N;
count = 0;
while (value > 1)
 {
   value = value / 2;
   count++;
 }
```

d.
```
count = 0;
value = N;
value = N * (N - 1);
count = count + value;
```

e.
```
count = 0;
for (i = 1; i <= N; i++)
   count++;
for (i = N; i >= 0; i--)
   count++;
```

49. Assume that numbers is a large array of integers, currently holding N values in locations 0 through $N-1$. Describe the order of magnitude of each of the following operations, using Big-O notation:

a. Insert the number 17 into location N of numbers.

b. Shift all values in the numbers array to the "right" one location to make room at location 0 for a new number without disrupting the order of the current values; insert the number 17 into location 0.

c. Randomly choose a location L from 0 to $N-1$; shift all the values in the numbers array, from location L to location $N-1$, to the right one location to make room at location L for a new number; insert the number 17 into location L.

50. Consider the following two algorithms that initialize every element in an N-element array to zero.

```
Algorithm Init1                    Algorithm Init2
elements[0] = 0;                   for (index = 0; index < N; index++)
elements[1] = 0;                       elements[index] = 0;
elements[2] = 0;
elements[3] = 0;

    .

    .

    .

elements[N–1] = 0;
```

What is the Big-O efficiency of the first algorithm? Of the second algorithm? Explain.

51. Algorithm 1 does a particular task in a "time" of N^3, where N is the number of elements processed. Algorithm 2 does the same task in a "time" of $3N + 1000$.

a. What is the Big-O efficiency of each algorithm?

b. Which algorithm is more efficient by Big-O standards?

c. Under what conditions, if any, would the "less efficient" algorithm execute more quickly than the "more efficient" algorithm?

Abstract Data Types

Knowledge Goals

You should be able to
- explain the following terms and their relationships: abstraction, information hiding, data abstraction, data encapsulation, abstract data type (ADT)
- describe the benefits of using an abstract data type
- define, for the Java programming language, the meanings of *abstract method* and *interface*
- describe the benefits of using a Java `interface` to specify an ADT
- describe the StringLog ADT from three perspectives: logical level, application level, and implementation level
- classify StringLog operations into the categories of constructor, observer, and transformer
- describe two variations of stepwise refinement
- describe strategies to avoid software errors

Skill Goals

You should be able to
- use the Java `interface` construct to formally specify an ADT
- use stepwise refinement to transform a high-level algorithm into code
- specify the preconditions and postconditions (effects) of a public method
- design a reasonable test plan for an ADT
- create a test driver for an ADT
- define and use a self-referential class to build a chain of objects (a linked structure)
- draw figures representing a sequence of operations on a linked list
- implement the StringLog ADT as an array-based structure
- implement the StringLog ADT as a linked structure
- determine the Big-O efficiency of each of the StringLog implementation methods
- use the StringLog ADT as a component of a solution to an application problem

This chapter focuses on the use of abstraction in program design. Here you begin to learn how to deal with the complexity of your data using abstraction and how to use the Java language mechanisms that support this approach.

We review the related concepts of abstraction and information hiding and show how these approaches encourage us to view our data at three different "levels"—the application, logical, and implementation levels. We introduce the Java `interface` mechanism as a means of supporting this three-tiered perspective. As an example of the abstraction of data, we present a collection of strings and show how it is handled at each of the three levels. For the implementation level, we include both array-based and reference-based approaches. To support the reference-based approach, we introduce the linked list structure. We also address ways of verifying the correctness of our work. Finally, in a case study, we see how the use of abstraction simplifies the task of implementing a trivia game system.

2.1 Abstraction

The universe is filled with complex systems. We learn about such systems through *models*. A model may be mathematical, like equations describing the motion of satellites around the earth. A physical object such as a model airplane used in wind-tunnel tests is another form of model. Typically, only the relevant characteristics of the system being studied are modeled; irrelevant details are ignored. For example, in-flight movies are not included in the model airplanes used to study aerodynamics.

Abstraction   A model of a system that includes only the details essential to the perspective of the viewer of the system

An abstraction is a simplifying model of an object or process that includes only the essential details. What does abstraction have to do with software development? Writing software is difficult because both the systems we model and the processes we use to develop the software are complex. Abstractions are the fundamental way that we manage complexity. In every chapter of this textbook we make use of abstractions to simplify our work.

Information Hiding

Many software design methods are based on decomposing a problem's solution into modules. By "module" we mean a cohesive system subunit that performs a share of the work. In Java, the primary module mechanism is the *class*. Decomposing a system into modules helps us handle complexity.

Modules act as an abstraction tool. The complexity of their internal structure can be hidden from the rest of the system. As a consequence, the details involved in implementing a module are isolated from the details of the rest of the system. Why is hiding the details desirable? Shouldn't the programmer know everything? *No!* Information hiding helps manage the complexity of a system because a programmer can safely concentrate on different parts of a system at different times.

Information hiding   The practice of hiding details within a module with the goal of controlling access to the details from the rest of the system

Of course, a program's modules are interrelated—they work together to solve the problem. Modules provide services to one another through carefully defined interfaces. The interface in Java is usually provided by the public methods of a class. Programmers of one module do not need to know the internal details of the modules it interacts with, but they do need to know the interfaces. Consider a driving analogy—you can start a car without knowing how many cylinders are in the engine. You just have to understand the interface; that is, you only need to know how to turn the key.

Data Abstraction

Any data, such as a value of type `int`, processed by a computer is just a collection of bits that can be turned on or off. The computer manipulates data in this form. People, however, tend to think of data in terms of more abstract units such as numbers and lists, and thus we want our programs to refer to data in a way that makes sense to us. To hide the irrelevant details of the computer's view of data from our own, we use data abstraction to create another view.

Let's take a closer look at the very concrete—and very abstract—integer you've been
using since you wrote your earliest programs.
Just what is an integer? Integers are physically represented in different ways on different computers. However, knowing exactly
how integers are represented on your computer is not a prerequisite for using integers in
a high-level language. With a high-level lan-

> **Data abstraction** The separation of a data type's log-
> ical properties from its implementation
>
> **Data encapsulation** The separation of the represen-
> tation of data from the applications that use the data
> at a logical level; a programming language feature that
> enforces information hiding

guage you use an abstraction of an integer. This is one of the reasons it's called a "high"-level language.

The Java language encapsulates integers for us. Data encapsulation means that the physical representation of the data remains hidden. The programmer using the data doesn't see the underlying implementation but deals with the data only in terms of its logical picture—its abstraction.

But if the data are encapsulated, how can the programmer get to them? Simple—the language provides operations that allow the programmer to create, access, and change the data. As an example, let's look at the operations Java provides for the encapsulated data type `int`. First, you can create variables of type `int` using declarations in your program. Then you can assign values to these integer variables by using the assignment operator and perform arithmetic operations on them by using the +, -, *, /, and % oper-ators. Figure 2.1 shows how Java has encapsulated the type `int` in a nice, neat black box.

The point of this discussion is that you have already been dealing with a logical data abstraction of integers. The advantages of doing so are clear: You can think of the data and the operations in a logical sense and can consider their use without having to worry about implementation details. The lower levels are still there—they're just hidden from you.

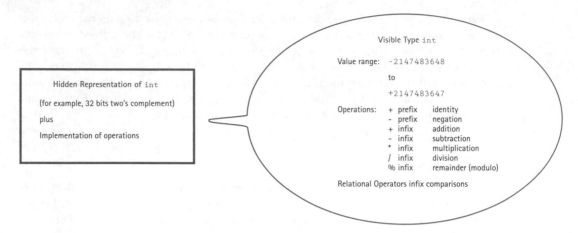

Figure 2.1 *A black box representing an integer*

Abstract data type (ADT) A data type whose properties (domain and operations) are specified independently of any particular implementation

We refer to the set of all possible values (the domain) of an encapsulated data "object," plus the specifications of the operations that are provided to create and manipulate the data, as an abstract data type (ADT for short).

In effect, all of Java's built-in types, such as int, are ADTs. A Java programmer can declare variables of those types without understanding the underlying implementation. The programmer can initialize, modify, and access the information held by the variables via the provided operations.

In addition to the built-in ADTs, Java programmers can use the Java *class* mechanism to create their own ADTs. For example, the Date class defined in Chapter 1 can be viewed as an ADT. Yes, it is true that the programmers who created it needed to know about its underlying implementation; for example, they needed to know that a Date is composed of three int instance variables, and they needed to know the names of the instance variables. The application programmers who use the Date class, however, do not need this information. They simply need to know how to create a Date object and how to invoke its exported methods so as to use the object.

Data Levels

In this textbook we define, create, and use ADTs. We say that we deal with ADTs from three different perspectives, or levels:

1. *Application (or user or client) level* As the application programmer, we use the ADT to solve a problem. When working at this level we simply need to know what program statements to use to create instances of the ADT and invoke its operations. That is, our application is a *client* of the ADT. There can be many different applications that use the same ADT.

2. *Logical (or abstract) level* This level provides an abstract view of the data values (the domain) and the set of operations to manipulate them. At this level, we deal with the *what* questions: What is the ADT? What does it model? What are its responsibilities? What is its interface? At this level we provide a specification of the properties of the ADT independent of its implementation.

3. *Implementation (or concrete) level* At this level we provide a specific representation of the structure to hold the data as well as the implementation (coding) of the operations. Here we deal with the *how* questions: How do we represent and manipulate the data in memory? How do we fulfill the responsibilities of the ADT? There can be many different answers to these questions.

When you write a program, you often deal with data at each of these three levels. In this section, which features abstraction, we concentrate on the logical level. In one sense, the ADT approach centers on the logical level. The logical level provides an abstraction of the implementation level for use at the application level. Its description acts as a contract created by the designer of the ADT, relied upon by the application programmers who use the ADT, and fulfilled by the programmers who implement the ADT.

For the most part the logical level provides independence between the application and implementation levels. Keep in mind, however, that there is one way that the implementation details can affect the applications that use the ADT—in terms of efficiency. The decisions we make about the way data are structured affect how efficiently we can implement the various operations on that data. The efficiency of operations can be important to the users of the data.

Preconditions and Postconditions

Suppose we want to design an ADT to provide a service. Access to the ADT is provided through its exported methods. To ensure that an ADT is usable at the application level, we must clarify how to use these methods. To be able to invoke a method, an application programmer must know its exact interface: its name, the types of its expected parameters, and its return type. But this information isn't enough: The programmer also needs to know any assumptions that must be true for the method to work correctly and the effects of invoking the method.

> **Preconditions** Assumptions that must be true on entry into a method for it to work correctly

We call the assumptions that must be true when invoking a method preconditions. The preconditions are like a product disclaimer:

WARNING
If you try to execute this operation when the preconditions are not true, the results are not guaranteed.

For example, the `increment` method of the `IncDate` class, described in Chapter 1, could have preconditions related to legal date values and the start of the Gregorian calendar. The preconditions should be listed at the beginning of the method declaration as a comment:

```
public void increment()
// Preconditions: Values of day, month, and year represent
//                a valid date.
//                The value of year is not less than MINYEAR.
```

Establishing the preconditions for a method creates a contract between the programmer who creates the method and the programmers who use the method. The contract says that the method meets its specifications if the preconditions are satisfied. It is up to the programmers who use the method to ensure that the preconditions are true whenever the method is invoked. This approach is sometimes called "programming by contract."

> **Postconditions (effects)** The results expected at the exit of a method, assuming that the preconditions are true

We must also specify which conditions are true when the method is finished. The postconditions are statements that describe the effects of the method. The postconditions do not tell us *how* these results are accomplished; they merely tell us *what* the results should be. We use the convention of stating the main effects—that is, the postconditions—within the opening comment of a method, immediately after any preconditions that are listed. For example,

```
public void increment()
// Preconditions: Values of day, month, and year represent
//                a valid date.
//                The value of year is not less than MINYEAR.
//
// Increments this IncDate to represent the next day.
```

Java Interfaces

Java provides a construct, the `interface`, which we can use to formally specify the logical level of our ADTs.

The word "interface" means a common boundary shared by two interacting systems. We use the term in many ways in computer science. For example, the user interface of a program is the part of the program that interacts with the user, and the interface of an object's method is its set of parameters and the return value it provides.

In Java, the word "interface" has a very specific meaning. In fact, `interface` is a Java keyword. It represents a specific type of program unit. A Java interface looks very similar to a Java class. It can include variable declarations and methods. However, all variables declared in an interface must be constants and all the methods must be abstract. An abstract method includes only a

> **Abstract method** A method declared in a class or an interface without a method body

description of its parameters; no method bodies or implementations are allowed. In other words, only the *interface* of the method is included.

Unlike a class, a Java interface cannot be instantiated. What purpose can a Java interface serve if it can only hold abstract methods and cannot be instantiated? It provides a template for classes to fit. To make an interface useful, a separate class must "implement" it. That is, a class must be created that supplies the bodies for the method headings specified by the interface. In essence, Java interfaces are used to describe requirements for classes.

Here is an example of an interface with one constant (`PI`) and four abstract methods (`perimeter`, `area`, `setScale`, and `weight`):

```
public interface FigureGeometry
{
  final float PI = 3.14f;

  float perimeter();
  // Returns perimeter of this figure.

  float area();
  // Returns area of this figure.

  void setScale(int scale);
  // Scale of this figure is set to "scale."

  float weight();
  // Precondition: Scale of this figure has been set.
  //
  // Returns weight of this figure. Weight = area × scale.
}
```

Although Java provides the keyword `abstract` that we can use when declaring an abstract method, we should not use it when defining the methods in an interface. Its use is redundant, because all methods of an interface must be abstract. Similarly, we can omit the keyword `public` from the method signatures, because interface methods are public by default. It is best not to use these unnecessary modifiers when defining an interface, as future versions of Java may not support their use.

Interfaces are compiled, just like classes and applications. Each of our interfaces is kept in a separate file. The name of the file must match the name of the interface. For example, the interface shown above must reside in a file called `FigureGeometry.java`. The compiler checks the interface code for errors; if there are none, it generates a Java byte code file for the interface. In our example, that file would be called `FigureGeometry.class`.

To use this interface a programmer could, for example, create a `Circle` class that implements the interface.

When a class implements an interface, it receives access to all of the constants defined in the interface and it must provide an implementation—that is, a body—for all of the abstract methods declared in the interface. Thus the `Circle` class, and any other class that implements the `FigureGeometry` interface, would be required to repeat the declarations of the four methods and provide code for their bodies.

```
public class Circle implements FigureGeometry
{
  protected float radius;
  protected int scale;

  public Circle(float radius)
  {
    this.radius = radius;
  }

  public float perimeter()
  // Returns perimeter of this figure.
  {
    return(2 * PI * radius);
  }

  public float area()
  // Returns area of this figure.
  {
    return(PI * radius * radius);
  }

  public void setScale(int scale)
  // Scale of this figure is set to "scale."
  {
    this.scale = scale;
  }

  public float weight()
  // Precondition: Scale of this figure has been set.
  //
  // Returns weight of this figure. Weight = area × scale.
  {
    return(this.area() * scale);
  }
}
```

Note that many different classes can all implement the same interface. For example, you can imagine the classes `Rectangle`, `Square`, and `Parallelogram`, all of which

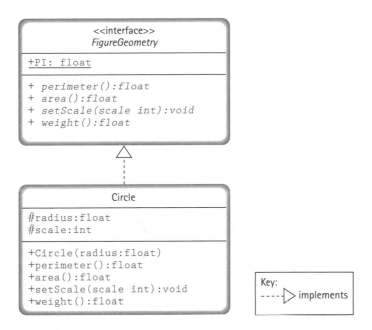

Figure 2.2   *The* `Circle` *class implements the* `FigureGeometry` *interface*

implement the `FigureGeometry` interface. A programmer who knows that these classes implement the `FigureGeometry` interface can be guaranteed that each provides implementations for the `perimeter`, `area`, `setScale`, and `weight` methods.

The UML class diagram in Figure 2.2 shows the relationship between the `Figure-Geometry` interface and the `Circle` class. The dotted arrow with the open arrowhead indicates a class implementing an interface. Classes that implement an interface are not constrained to implementing the abstract methods of the interface as in this example; they can also add data fields and methods of their own.

Interfaces are a versatile and powerful programming construct. Among other things, they can be used to specify the logical view of an ADT. Within the interface we define abstract methods that correspond to the exported methods of the ADT implementation. We use comments to describe the preconditions and postconditions of each abstract method. An implementation programmer, who intends to create a class that implements the ADT, knows that he or she must fulfill the contract spelled out by the interface. An application programmer, who wants to use the ADT, can use any class that implements the interface.

Using the Java interface construct in this way for our ADT specifications produces several benefits:

1. We can formally check the syntax of our specification. When we compile the interface, the compiler uncovers any syntactical errors in the method interface definitions.

2. We can formally verify that the interface "contract" is satisfied by the implementation. When we compile the implementation, the compiler ensures that the method names, parameters, and return types match those defined in the interface.

3. We can provide a consistent interface to applications from among alternative implementations of the ADT. Some implementations may optimize the use of memory space; others may emphasize speed. An implementation may also provide extra functionality beyond that defined in the interface. Yet all of the implementations will have the specified interface in common.

In the next section we use a Java interface to specify an ADT that provides a collection of strings.

2.2   The StringLog ADT Specification

In this section we specify an ADT that we will use throughout the rest of this chapter—the StringLog ADT. You are already familiar with the concept of a "log." For example, a ship's captain keeps a log of a voyage to record its progress, and students log into a science laboratory to show that they attended a help session. The name of the former log might be "The Nautilus," while the latter might be called "Intermediate Chemistry Lab."

A *log* is used to record entries and allow someone to access those entries at a later time. Our StringLog ADT provides similar functionality. The primary responsibility of the StringLog ADT is to remember all the strings that have been inserted into it and, when presented with any given string, indicate whether an identical string has already been inserted. A StringLog client uses a StringLog to record strings and later check whether a particular string has been recorded.

In this section we address the logical level, so we do not have to worry about how the strings will be stored. Recall that at this level we deal with the *what* questions—in particular, "What services should a StringLog provide?"

Constructors

A constructor creates a new instance of the ADT. Users of the StringLog instantiate a StringLog object by invoking the `new` command on a constructor. It is up to the implementer of the StringLog to decide how many, and what kind of, constructors to provide.

Every StringLog must have a name. The implementer of a StringLog might decide to provide a default name within the implementation. However, that means that every time a StringLog is created it will have the same name. A more flexible approach is to allow the user to pass a name to a constructor when instantiating the StringLog:

```
shipLog = new StringLogImplementation("The Nautilus");
```

We use this approach in our implementations later in the chapter.

Another question facing the implementer is "How many strings can be held in a StringLog?" There are several possible answers—for example, design an unbounded

StringLog with no limits on size, or a bounded StringLog of a default size, or a bounded StringLog where the maximum size is indicated by a constructor parameter. Using the third approach, the instantiation of a new StringLog might look like this:

```
classLog = new StringLogImplementation("Physics", 100);
```

Later in this chapter we study both bounded and unbounded implementations.

Transformers

Transformers change the content of the StringLog in some way. We include two transformers:

- insert   This operation requires a parameter representing the string to be inserted. It adds that string to the log of strings. Note that this operation does not specify any relationship among the strings in the log; there is no implicit ordering of the log's contents. As part of the "contract" for using the StringLog, we disallow insertion of a string if the StringLog is already full. The application programmer can use the isFull operation (see the "Observers" subsection) to check whether the log is full before attempting to insert another string.
- clear   This operation resets the StringLog to the empty state; the StringLog retains its name.

Observers

We specify five operations that observe something about a StringLog object and return the observed information:

- contains   This operation embodies the prime functionality of a StringLog. It requires a string as a parameter to search for and returns whether the StringLog contains that string. We ignore case when comparing the strings. For example, "JoHn" and "john" are considered equal.
- size   This operation returns the number of elements currently held in the StringLog.
- isFull   This operation returns whether the StringLog is full. If full, the client should no longer invoke the insert operation.
- getName   This operation returns the name attribute of the StringLog.
- toString   This operation returns a nicely formatted string that represents the entire contents of the StringLog.

The StringLogInterface

It is possible to identify many more potential operations for a StringLog. However, our goal in this chapter is to illustrate defining, implementing, and using ADTs, for which our minimal set of operations is sufficient.

So far we have specified the StringLog ADT only informally. We have not yet carefully defined the interface, preconditions, or effects of the operations. This detailed information is required by both the programmer who implements the StringLog and any programmers who intend to use the StringLog.

Our next step is to use Java's `interface` construct to formally capture our specification. The method interfaces are listed as Java code. All other parts of the specification are presented as comments. Here is the interface of the StringLog:

```java
//-------------------------------------------------------------------
// StringLogInterface.java       by Dale/Joyce/Weems        Chapter 2
//
// Interface for a class that implements a log of strings.
// A log "remembers" the elements placed into it.
//
// A log must have a "name."
//-------------------------------------------------------------------

package ch02.stringLogs;

public interface StringLogInterface
{
  void insert(String element);
  // Precondition:    This StringLog is not full.
  //
  // Places element into this StringLog.

  boolean isFull();
  // Returns true if this StringLog is full, otherwise returns false.

  int size();
  // Returns the number of strings in this StringLog.

  boolean contains(String element);
  // Returns true if element is in this StringLog,
  // otherwise returns false.
  // Ignores case differences when doing a string comparison.

  void clear();
  // Makes this StringLog empty.

  String getName();
  // Returns the name of this StringLog.

  String toString();
  // Returns a nicely formatted string representing this StringLog.
}
```

We call the interface `StringLogInterface`. Note that it includes a `package` statement. This interface is the first of several units we develop to specify and implement our StringLog ADT. To help keep our files organized, we collect them in a single package called `ch02.stringLogs`.[1]

An interface does not include constructors. Because you cannot instantiate objects of an interface, it does not make sense to define constructors. In fact, Java syntax rules do not allow it. The class that implements the interface provides the appropriate constructors.

Only one of our operations, `insert`, has a precondition. What happens if this operation is invoked and the precondition is not satisfied? In this specification, the responsibility of checking for error conditions is borne by the programmer who is using the class. The effect of the `insert` method, if invoked when the StringLog is full, is unspecified. Anything could happen! Recall that we call this approach programming "by contract." We have provided the `isFull` operation, so the user of the StringLog can verify that the precondition is met before invoking `insert`.

Using the StringLogInterface

Here is a simple example of an application program that uses the `StringLogInterface` and creates and uses a StringLog. It imports the `ch02.stringLogs` package so that it has access to the interface and the associated implementation.

```
//------------------------------------------------------------------
// UseStringLog.java          by Dale/Joyce/Weems          Chapter 2
//
// Simple example of the use of a StringLog.
//------------------------------------------------------------------

import ch02.stringLogs.*;

public class UseStringLog
{
  public static void main(String[] args)
  {
    StringLogInterface sample;
    sample = new ArrayStringLog("Example Use");
    sample.insert("Elvis");
    sample.insert("King Louis XII");
    sample.insert("Captain Kirk");
```

1. The files can be found in the `stringLogs` subdirectory of the `ch02` subdirectory of the `bookFiles` directory that contains the program files associated with the textbook.

```
System.out.println(sample);
System.out.println("The size of the log is " + sample.size());
System.out.println("Elvis is in the log: " + sample.contains("Elvis"));
System.out.println("Santa is in the log: " + sample.contains("Santa"));
    }
}
```

We have <u>emphasized</u> the code that uses `StringLogInterface`. Note, however, that the `new` command is applied through the `ArrayStringLog` class (this is also emphasized). This class, which is developed in Section 2.3, is an implementation of the `StringLogInterface`. It is good practice for a client program to declare the ADT at as abstract a level as possible. This approach makes it easier to change the choice of implementation later. Thus `sample` is declared to be the more abstract `StringLogInterface` rather than the more concrete `ArrayStringLog`.

The output from the `UseStringLog` program follows:

Log: Example Use

1. Elvis
2. King Louis XII
3. Captain Kirk

The size of the log is 3
Elvis is in the log: true
Santa is in the log: false

To review, for the StringLog ADT, we deal with three different perspectives or levels:

1. *Application level* The `UseStringLog` program is the application. It declares a variable `sample` of type `StringLogInterface`. It uses the `ArrayStringLog` implementation of the `StringLogInterface` to perform some simple tasks.

2. *Logical level* The `StringLogInterface` interface provides an abstract view of the StringLog ADT. It is used by the `UseStringLog` application and implemented by the `ArrayStringLog` class.

3. *Implementation level* The `ArrayStringLog` class (see Section 2.3) provides a specific implementation of the StringLog ADT, fulfilling the contract presented by the `StringLogInterface`. It can be used by applications such as `UseStringLog`. Likewise, the `LinkedStringLog` class (see Section 2.6) provides an implementation.

The UML diagram in Figure 2.3 shows the relationships among `StringLogInterface`, `ArrayStringLog`, `LinkedStringLog`, and `UseStringLog`. The exported method and instance variable name details have been omitted from the figure.

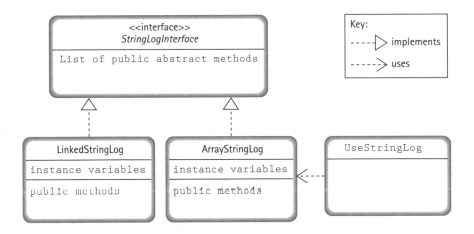

Figure 2.3 *UML diagram showing relationship among StringLog classes*

2.3 Array–Based StringLog ADT Implementation

In this section we look at an array-based StringLog implementation. The distinguishing feature of this implementation is that the strings are stored sequentially, in adjacent slots in an array. We call the class `ArrayStringLog` to show that it implements the StringLog interface using an array and to differentiate it from the reference-based implementation studied later. Like the `StringLogInterface`, it is placed in the `ch02.stringLogs` package. `ArrayStringLog` is an example of a bounded implementation.

Instance Variables

In this implementation, the elements of a StringLog are stored in an array of `String` objects named `log`.

```
String[] log;       // array that holds strings
```

Originally the array is empty. Each time the `insert` command is invoked, another string is added to the array. A straightforward approach for handling this task is to use a variable that tracks the index of the "last" string inserted into the array. This way we know how far to search in the array when looking for a string and where to store the next string that is inserted. We call this variable `lastIndex`. Because our language is Java, we must remember that the first slot of the array is indexed by 0. Because initially there are no strings in the array, we initialize `lastIndex` to -1.

```
int lastIndex = -1;      // index of last string in array
```

With this implementation of a bounded StringLog, there is another size-related attribute of the StringLog: capacity. The *capacity* of a StringLog is the maximum number of elements that can be stored in the StringLog. We do not need an instance variable to hold the capacity of the StringLog—we can use the array attribute `length` to determine the capacity of the StringLog at any point within our implementation. In other words, the capacity of our StringLog is the length of the underlying array: `log.length`.

A review of the specification for StringLog in Section 2.2 reveals one additional instance variable that we must declare. Can you think of what it is? We must declare a variable to hold the *name* attribute of the StringLog. Recall that every StringLog must have a *name*. We call the needed variable `name`.

```
String name;            // name of this log
```

Here is the beginning of the class file, which includes the instance variable declarations. Note that it also includes the `package` statement, an introductory comment, and descriptive comments for each of the variables.

```
//-----------------------------------------------------------------------
// ArrayStringLog.java            by Dale/Joyce/Weems            Chapter 2
//
// Implements StringLogInterface using an array to hold the log strings.
//-----------------------------------------------------------------------

package ch02.stringLogs;

public class ArrayStringLog implements StringLogInterface
{
  protected String name;            // name of this log
  protected String[] log;           // array that holds log strings
  protected int lastIndex = -1;     // index of last string in array
  .
  .
  .
```

Notice that we follow the principle of information hiding and use the `protected` visibility modifier for each of the variables. Recall that this form of access means that the variables can be "seen" by subclasses of the `ArrayStringLog` class. It is not unusual to extend an ADT class to create a related ADT. Using `protected` allows us to easily extend the class, yet still provides a reasonable degree of information hiding.

Constructors

Now let's look at the operations for the StringLog ADT. The first things we need are constructors that create empty StringLogs. Recall that a class constructor is a method having the same name as the class but no return type. A constructor instantiates and returns an object of the class. If necessary, it initializes variables and allocates resources (usually memory) for the object being constructed. Like any other method, a constructor has access to all the variables and methods of the class.

Our constructor requires two parameters: a string that indicates the name of the StringLog and a positive integer parameter that indicates the maximum size. We use this size value to create the array that holds the strings.

```
public ArrayStringLog(String name, int maxSize)
// Precondition:   maxSize > 0
//
// Instantiates and returns a reference to an empty ArrayStringLog
// object with name "name" and room for maxSize strings.
{
  log = new String[maxSize];
  this.name = name;
}
```

The code for this constructor is straightforward and requires little explanation. When it creates the array of capacity maxSize, it must set the value in each of the array slots to null.[2] Therefore the efficiency of this constructor is O(N), where N is maxSize.

Note the use of the Java keyword this, which is used to access the name instance variable as opposed to the name parameter. The instance variable name is set equal to the argument represented by the parameter name.

Figure 2.4 shows both the internal and abstract views of a StringLog implemented as an ArrayStringLog as it goes through various stages of use. The first two stages show a StringLog object called strLog after it has been declared and instantiated using the above constructor.

We decide to include a second constructor, one that does not have a size parameter. In this case, we make the default size of the underlying array 100, and note that decision within the introductory comment.

```
public ArrayStringLog(String name)
// Instantiates and returns a reference to an empty ArrayStringLog
// object with name "name" and room for 100 strings.
{
  log = new String[100];
  this.name = name;
}
```

2. Setting the array slots to null occurs automatically. We do not have to explicitly code it.

Overloading of Names

Notice that the two constructors have the same name: `ArrayStringLog`. How is this possible? Recall that in the case of methods, Java uses more than just the name to identify them; it also uses the parameter list. A method's name, the number and type of parameters that are passed to it, and the ordering of the different parameter types within the list combine to form what Java calls the signature of the method.

Signature The distinguishing features of a method heading; the combination of a method name with the number and type(s) of its parameters in their given order

Overloading The repeated use of a method name with a different signature

Java allows us to use the name of a method as many times as we wish as long as each method has a different signature. When we use a method name more than once, we are overloading its identifier. The Java compiler needs to be able to look at a method call and determine which version of the method to invoke. The two constructors in the class `ArrayStringLog` have different signatures: One takes a string argument and an integer argument; the other takes only a string argument. Java decides which version to call based on the arguments in the statement that invokes `ArrayStringLog`.

Transformers

We have two transformer operations: `insert` and `clear`. Let's start with `insert`—after all, to use a StringLog you must first insert something into it. As we explained earlier, the plan is to place a new string into the next available array slot. Because `lastIndex` indicates the highest array slot being used, we just increment it to access the next slot.

```
public void insert(String element)
// Precondition:   This StringLog is not full.
//
// Places element into this StringLog.
{
  lastIndex++;
  log[lastIndex] = element;
}
```

Note that in addition to inserting the new string into the array, we have changed the value of `lastIndex` so that it continues to indicate the highest array slot being used. The precondition permits us to assume that we do not increase this value inappropriately—that is, to an index past the end of the array. Because the `insert` method always executes just two statements, its execution efficiency is O(1).

You can now study the rest of Figure 2.4, which shows both the internal (implementation) view and the abstract view of a StringLog object called `strLog` after it has

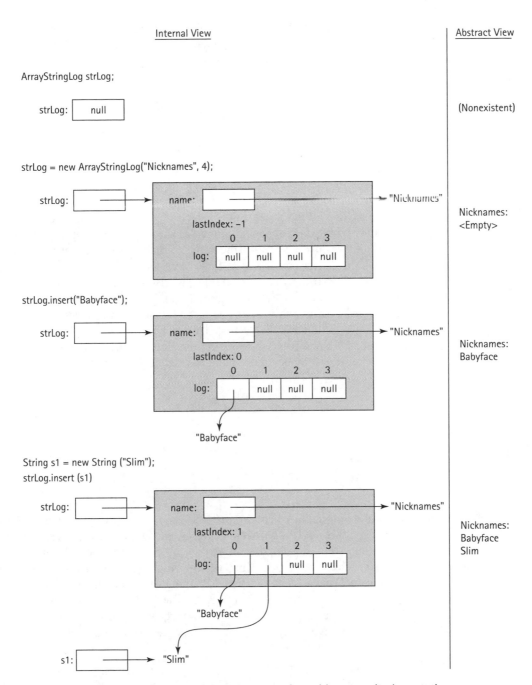

Figure 2.4 *Results of* StringLog *operations with an array implementation*

been declared, instantiated, and received several `insert` messages. In one invocation of `insert` a string literal is passed as the argument; in the other invocation a string variable is passed. Here is the application code represented in the figure:

```
ArrayStringLog strLog;
strLog = new ArrayStringLog("Nicknames", 4);
strLog.insert("Babyface");
String s1 = new String("Slim");
strLog.insert(s1);
```

Figure 2.4 shows the strings as existing outside of the `strLog` object. Although these strings are referenced by the `log` array, they exist independently of the `strLog` object. This is most obvious in the case of the string "Slim," which is referenced by another variable, `s1`.

The remaining transformation operation is `clear`. At first glance, this operation might appear simple. We just have to set the value of the `lastIndex` variable back to its original value, −1. Of course, by resetting that value we are saying that we no longer need to access any of the strings that were previously inserted into the array. Yet the array still references those strings, as shown in Figure 2.5(a). To allow the garbage collector to reclaim the space used by those strings, it is better to set each of the array slots to `null`, as shown in Figure 2.5(b). Otherwise, the garbage collector assumes the strings are still being used, as they are still being referenced. Resetting the slots requires using a *for* loop to step through the section of the array being used and to reset all string references to `null`.

```
public void clear()
// Makes this StringLog empty.
{
  for (int i = 0; i <= lastIndex; i++)
    log[i] = null;
  lastIndex = -1;
}
```

The "lazy" clear approach, where we just set `lastIndex` to −1, has a Big-O complexity of O(1). The "thorough" approach, represented by the code above, has an efficiency of O(*N*), where *N* is the number of strings in the StringLog. Although the lazy approach is more efficient in terms of time, the thorough approach allows unused memory locations to be reclaimed for future use. For many problems the differences between these two approaches would have little effect on the performance of your system; in those situations where it is important, your decision regarding which approach to follow should be guided by the overall system goals with respect to resource use.

Observers

We continue by looking at the implementations of the simple observer operations `isFull`, `size`, `getName`, and `toString`. For the Big-O analysis of these operations we assume the StringLog contains *N* strings. The `isFull` operation just compares the

(a) Internal view after "lazy" strLog.clear();

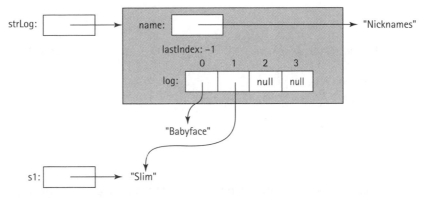

(b) Internal view after "thorough" strLog.clear();

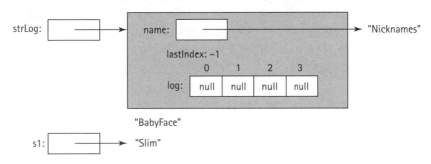

Figure 2.5   *(a) A StringLog after a poorly designed clear operation, and*
            (b) A StringLog after a well-designed clear operation

current value of `lastIndex` to the length of the array. Because array indexing begins at 0, the comparison is actually made to the length of the array minus 1.

```
public boolean isFull()
// Returns true if this StringLog is full, otherwise returns false.
{
  if (lastIndex == (log.length - 1))
    return true;
  else
    return false;
}
```

The body of the observer method `size` is just one statement.

```
public int size()
// Returns the number of strings in this StringLog.
```

```
{
  return (lastIndex + 1);
}
```

Likewise, the `getName` method is simple, as getter methods usually are.

```
public String getName()
// Returns the name of this StringLog.
{
  return name;
}
```

It is easy to see that each of these operations is O(1).

The `toString` method is intended to create a nicely formatted string that represents the information in the StringLog. There are many ways to design such a string. We implement `toString` so that it first displays the name of the StringLog and then provides a numbered list of the current contents. For example, if the StringLog is named "Three Stooges" and contains the strings "Larry," "Moe," and "Curly Joe," then the result of displaying the string returned by `toString` would be

> Log: Three Stooges
>
> 1. Larry
> 2. Moe
> 3. Curly Joe

The implementation of `toString` is O(N), as it must handle each of the strings:

```
public String toString()
// Returns a nicely formatted string representing this StringLog.
{
  String logString = "Log: " + name + "\n\n";

  for (int i = 0; i <= lastIndex; i++)
    logString = logString + (i+1) + ". " + log[i] + "\n";

  return logString;
}
```

The final observer operation, `contains`, is the most complicated method of `ArrayStringLog`. The `contains` operation allows the application programmer to provide an argument string and discover whether an identical string already exists in the StringLog. A `boolean` value is returned by the method—if the argument string matches a string in the StringLog, `true` is returned; otherwise, `false` is returned.

As described in the specification, we ignore case distinctions between strings when comparing them. Several methods for comparing strings are available from the Java library's `String` class. Given that we wish to ignore case, a good choice for us is the `equalsIgnoreCase` method. It returns `true` if the string passed to it as an argument is equal, ignoring case, to the string upon which it is invoked, and `false` otherwise. For example, if the `String` object `name` contains the string "Rumplestiltskin," then

```
name.equalsIgnoreCase("rumpleSTILTskin")
```

returns `true`, while

```
name.equalsIgnoreCase("Rumplestiltskinny")
```

returns `false`.

The overall approach we should use is obvious: traverse the array one location after another, comparing the array contents with the parameter string `element` until we either find a match or reach the end of the stored elements. If `element` is not in the array, this algorithm requires *N* steps, as it must compare `element` to each of the *N* strings in the StringLog. In the worst case, the efficiency of this approach is O(*N*).

Although the implementation of our algorithm is not overly difficult, neither is it trivial. Stepwise refinement is a technique we can use to help us design nontrivial methods. The feature section on "Stepwise Refinement" introduces this technique and presents as an example the development of the code for `contains`.

This concludes our implementation of the `ArrayStringLog` class. The code in its entirety is listed below. Of course, our work is not finished. We still need to test our implementation. In the next section we discuss software testing issues in general. At the end of the section we explicitly address testing of our `ArrayStringLog` class and develop a test driver for it.

```java
//------------------------------------------------------------------
// ArrayStringLog.java        by Dale/Joyce/Weems        Chapter 2
//
// Implements StringLogInterface using an array to hold the strings.
//------------------------------------------------------------------

package ch02.stringLogs;

public class ArrayStringLog implements StringLogInterface
{
  protected String name;              // name of this StringLog
  protected String[] log;             // array that holds strings
  protected int lastIndex = -1;       // index of last string in array
```

```
public ArrayStringLog(String name, int maxSize)
// Precondition:   maxSize > 0
//
// Instantiates and returns a reference to an empty StringLog object
// with name "name" and room for maxSize strings.
{
  log = new String[maxSize];
  this.name = name;
}

public ArrayStringLog(String name)
// Instantiates and returns a reference to an empty StringLog object
// with name "name" and room for 100 strings.
{
  log = new String[100];
  this.name = name;
}

public void insert(String element)
// Precondition:   This StringLog is not full.
//
// Places element into this StringLog.
{
  lastIndex++;
  log[lastIndex] = element;
}

public boolean isFull()
// Returns true if this StringLog is full, otherwise returns false.
{
  if (lastIndex == (log.length - 1))
    return true;
  else
    return false;
}

public int size()
// Returns the number of strings in this StringLog.
{
  return (lastIndex + 1);
}
```

```java
public boolean contains(String element)
// Returns true if element is in this StringLog,
// otherwise returns false.
// Ignores case differences when doing string comparison.
{
  int location = 0;

  while (location <= lastIndex)
  {
    if (element.equalsIgnoreCase(log[location]))  // if they match
      return true;
    else
      location++;
  }

 return false;
}

public void clear()
// Makes this StringLog empty.
{
  for (int i = 0; i <= lastIndex; i++)
    log[i] = null;
  lastIndex = -1;
}

public String getName()
// Returns the name of this StringLog.
{
  return name;
}

public String toString()
// Returns a nicely formatted string representing this StringLog.
{
  String logString = "Log: " + name + "\n\n";

  for (int i = 0; i <= lastIndex; i++)
    logString = logString + (i+1) + ". " + log[i] + "\n";

  return logString;
}
}
```

Stepwise Refinement

In addition to concepts such as abstraction and information hiding, software developers need practical approaches to conquer complexity. Stepwise refinement is a widely applicable approach. Undoubtedly you have learned a variation of stepwise refinement in your studies, because it is a standard method for organizing and writing essays, term papers, and books. For example, to write a book an author first determines the main theme and the major subthemes. Next, the chapter topics can be identified, followed by section and subsection topics. Outlines can be produced and further refined for each subsection. At some point the author is ready to add detail—to actually begin writing sentences.

In general, with stepwise refinement, a problem is approached in stages. Similar steps are followed during each stage, with the only difference being the level of detail involved. The completion of each stage brings us closer to solving our problem. There are two standard variations of stepwise refinement:

- *Top-down*   First the problem is broken into several large parts. Each of these parts is, in turn, divided into sections, then the sections are subdivided, and so on. The important feature is that *details are deferred as long as possible* as we move from a general solution to a specific solution. The outline approach to writing a book is a form of top-down stepwise refinement.
- *Bottom-up*   As you might guess, with this approach the details come first. It is the opposite of the top-down approach. After the detailed components are identified and designed, they are brought together into increasingly higher-level components. This strategy could be used, for example, by the author of a cookbook who first writes all the recipes and then decides how to organize them into sections and chapters. In the world of programming, the bottom-up approach is useful if you can identify previously created program components to reuse in creating your system.

The top-down approach is often used for the design of nontrivial methods. Let's apply this approach to the development of the `contains` method for the `ArrayStringLog` class. The idea is to start with an abstract solution and to add detail as we refine the solution in successive steps.

In the early and middle steps, we express our solution using a mixture of Java and English. We use Java to structure our solution, and we use English to describe our solution in an abstract way. A combination of a programming language with a natural language, such as we use here, is called *pseudocode* and is a convenient means for expressing algorithms. As we refine our solution we will use increasingly more Java and increasingly less English until we arrive at our final solution, which is expressed completely in Java. Our pseudocode will evolve into real code!

We've already identified an overall approach: traverse the array one location after another, comparing the array contents with the string element until we either find a match or reach the end of the stored elements. Capturing this approach in pseudocode we get

```
public boolean contains(String element)
{
   Set variables
   while (we still need to search)
   {
      Check the next value
   }
   return (whether we found the element)
}
```

Assuming that we correctly "refine" this solution, it looks good. Which part of it should we refine first? Let's work on finding the element as that is the central focus of the operation.

When we "Check the next value," if it matches the argument element, we can immediately return true. Recall that a return statement terminates the execution of the method, so upon finding the element we end execution and return true.

But what if we do not find the element? By the time the *while* loop is exited, if we have not found the element, then it is not in the StringLog. Therefore, if we exit the *while* loop, we can properly return false. The second refinement captures these decisions:

```
public boolean contains(String element)
{
   Set variables;
   while (we still need to search)
   {
      if (the next value equals element)
         return true;
   }
   return false;
}
```

Our algorithm is beginning to look more like Java code. Next we tackle the issue of "next value." What exactly does that mean? Upon reflection we realize that we really need to keep track of the current array location we are checking. If we don't have a match to element, we need to increment that location to the next location in the array.

We use a variable location to represent the current location of the array that we need to check. We initialize location to 0 so that we begin checking at the beginning of the array, as we planned. At this point we can add the string comparison detail, using the equalsIgnore-Case operation provided by the String class. Putting all of this together, we get

```
public boolean contains(String element)
{
   int location = 0;
   while (we still need to search)
   {
     if (element.equalsIgnoreCase(log[location]))
        return true;
     else
        location++;
   }
   return false;
}
```

The only part of the solution left to address is how to determine when "there are more values to search." Recall that the object variable lastIndex holds the index of the rightmost string in the array. Therefore there are more values to search as long as the current value of location is less than or equal to the value of lastIndex. Incorporating this idea, plus adding a few explanatory comments, completes our development of the contains method:

```
public boolean contains(String element)
 // Returns true if element is in this StringLog,
 // otherwise returns false.
 // Ignores case differences when doing string comparison.
{
   int location = 0;
   while (location <= lastIndex)
   {
```

```
    if (element.equalsIgnoreCase(log[location]))  // if they match
      return true;
    else
      location++;
  }
  return false;

}
```

2.4 Software Testing

In Chapter 1 we discussed some characteristics of good programs. The first of these criteria was that a good program works—it accomplishes its intended function. How do you know when your program meets that goal? The simple answer is, *test it*. Of course, software testing is only one facet of software verification. Verification activities don't need to start when the program is completely coded; they can be incorporated into the whole software development process, from the requirements phase on. See the feature section "Validation and Verification" for a discussion of this topic. In this section we concentrate on testing.

> **Software testing** The process of executing a program with data sets designed to discover errors
>
> **Unit testing** Testing a class or method by itself

The software testing process requires us to devise a set of test cases that, taken together, allow us to claim that a program works correctly. The goal of each test case is to verify a particular program feature. For instance, we may design several test cases to demonstrate that the program correctly handles various classes of input errors. Or we may design cases to check the processing when a data structure (such as an array) is empty or when it contains the maximum number of elements.

For each test case, we must perform the following tasks:

- Identify inputs that represent the test case.
- Determine the expected behavior of the program for the given input.
- Run the program and observe the resulting behavior.
- Compare the expected behavior and the actual behavior of the program.

For now we are talking about test cases at a class, or method, level. It's much easier to test and debug modules of a program one at a time, rather than trying to get the entire program solution to work all at once. Testing at this level is called unit testing.

How do we know which kinds of unit test cases are appropriate and how many are needed? Identifying the set of test cases that is sufficient to validate a unit of a program is in itself a difficult task.

Identifying Test Cases

Functional domain The set of valid input data for a program or method

Black-box testing Testing a program or method based on the possible input values, treating the code as a "black box"

In those limited cases where the set of valid inputs, or the functional domain, is extremely small, we can verify a program unit by testing it against every possible input element. This approach, known as *exhaustive testing*, can prove conclusively that the software meets its specifications. In most cases, however, the functional domain is very large, so exhaustive testing is almost always impractical or impossible.

You can attempt program testing in a haphazard way, entering data randomly until you cause the program to fail. Guessing doesn't hurt, but it may not help much either. The random approach is likely to uncover some bugs in a program, but it is very unlikely to find them all. Fortunately there are strategies for detecting errors in a systematic way.

One goal-oriented approach is to cover general dimensions of data. Within each dimension you identify categories of inputs and expected results. You then test at least one instance of each combination of categories across dimensions. For example, the following dimensions and categories could be identified for the `contains` method of the StringLog ADT:

- Expected result: true, false
- Size of StringLog: empty, small, large, full
- Properties of element: no blanks, contains blanks
- Properties of match: perfect match, imperfect match where character cases differ
- Position of match: first string placed in StringLog, last string placed in StringLog, "middle" string placed in StringLog

From this list we can identify dozens of test cases—for example, a test where the expected result is true, the StringLog is full, the element contains blanks, it's an imperfect match, and the string being matched was the "middle" string placed into the StringLog.

Note that some combinations across dimensions do not make sense. For example, we cannot construct a test case where the expected result is false and the match is perfect. By carefully identifying dimensions and categories, and by ensuring that all feasible combinations of categories across dimensions are tested, we can arrive at a reasonably sized set of test cases that provide a good representation of the functional domain.

Testing like this, based on data coverage, is called black-box testing. The tester must understand the external interface to the module—its inputs and expected outputs—but does not need to consider what is happening inside the module (the inside of the black box).

Validation and Verification

Software validation and verification activities span the entire software life cycle. These activities address separate, albeit related, concerns. Software validation activities help ensure that the delivered software actually fits the needs of the intended user. There have been countless times when a programmer finishes a large project and delivers the software, only to be told, "Well, that's what I asked for, but it's not what I need." Software verification activities help ensure that each stage of software development succeeds in terms of its stated goals. In other words, validation asks, "Are we doing the right job?" and verification asks, "Are we doing the job right?"[3]

> **Software validation** The process of determining the degree to which software fulfills its intended purpose
>
> **Software verification** The process of determining the degree to which a software product fulfills its specifications

Design Review Activities

When an individual programmer is designing and implementing a program, he or she can find many software errors with old-fashioned pencil and paper. Deskchecking the design solution is a widely used method of manually verifying a program. The programmer writes down essential data (variables, input values, parameters, and so on) and walks through the design, marking changes in the data on the paper. Known trouble spots in the design or code should be double-checked. A checklist of typical errors (such as loops that do not terminate, variables that are used before they are initialized, and parameters that are given in incorrect order on method calls) can be used to make the deskcheck more effective. A few minutes spent deskchecking your designs can save lots of time and eliminate difficult problems that would otherwise surface later in the life cycle (or even worse, would not surface until after delivery).

> **Deskchecking** Tracing an execution of a design or program on paper
>
> **Walk-through** A verification method in which a team performs a manual simulation of the program or design
>
> **Inspection** A verification method in which one member of a team reads the program or design line by line and the others point out errors

Most sizable computer programs are developed by *teams* of programmers. Two extensions of deskchecking that are effectively used by programming teams are design or code walk-throughs and inspections. These formal team activities are intended to move the responsibility for uncovering bugs from the individual programmer to the group. Because testing is time-consuming and errors cost more the later they are discovered, the goal is to identify errors before testing begins.

In a *walk-through*, the team performs a manual simulation of the design or program with sample test inputs, keeping track of the program's data by hand on paper or a blackboard. Unlike

---

3. B. W. Boehm, *Software Engineering Economics* (Englewood Cliffs, NJ: Prentice Hall, 1981).

thorough program testing, the walk-through is not intended to simulate all possible test cases. Instead, its purpose is to stimulate discussion about the way the programmer chose to design or implement the program's requirements.

At an *inspection*, a reader (never the program's author) goes through the requirements, design, or code line by line. The inspection participants are given the material in advance and are expected to have reviewed it carefully. During the inspection, the participants point out errors that are recorded on an inspection report. Many of the errors may have been noted by team members during their preinspection preparation. Other errors are uncovered just by the process of reading aloud.

As with the walk-through, the chief benefit of the team meeting is the discussion that takes place among team members. This interaction among programmers, testers, and other team members can uncover many program errors long before the testing stage begins.

Test Plans

The organization of all the test cases for a class or system is called a test plan. Some test plans are very informal—for example, a list of test cases, written by hand on a piece of paper. Even this type of test plan may be more than you have ever been required to write for a class programming project. Other test plans (particularly those submitted to management or to a customer for approval) are very formal, containing the details of each test case in a standardized format.

Test plan   A document showing the test cases planned for a program or module, along with their purposes, inputs, expected outputs, and criteria for success

For program testing to be effective, *it must be planned.* You must design your testing in an organized way, and you must put your design in writing. You should determine the required or desired level of testing, and plan your general strategy and test cases before testing begins. *In fact, it's advantageous to start planning for testing before writing a single line of code.*

Testing ADT Implementations

The major focus of this textbook is data structures: what they are, how we use them, and how we implement them as ADTs using Java. It seems appropriate to end this section about software testing with a look at how we can test the ADTs we implement in Java.

A General Approach

Test driver   A program that calls operations exported from a class, allowing us to test the results of the operations

Every ADT that we implement supports a set of operations. For each ADT, we can create an interactive test driver program that allows us to test the operations in a variety of sequences. How can we write a single test driver that allows us to test numerous operation sequences? The solution is to create a test driver that repeatedly presents the user—that is, the tester—with a choice of operations representing the exported methods of the ADT. In this way the tester can test any sequence of operations he or she chooses. When the tester chooses an operation that requires one or more arguments, then the test driver must prompt the tester to supply the arguments.

Our interactive test drivers all follow the same basic algorithm. Here is a pseudocode description:

Interactive Test Driver for ADT Implementation

```
Prompt for, read, and display test name
Determine which constructor to use, obtain any needed parameters, and instantiate a new instance of the ADT
while (testing continues)
{
  Display a menu of operation choices, one choice for each
    method exported by the ADT implementation, plus a "show
    contents" choice, plus a "stop testing" choice
  Get the user's choice and obtain any needed parameters
  Perform the chosen operation
}
```

The interactive test driver program obtains the operation requests from the user one at a time, performs the operation by invoking the methods of the class being tested, and reports the results to an output stream. In addition to requesting one of the ADT operations, the user can request a display of the contents of the ADT instance or indicate that he or she is finished with the program. This approach provides us with maximum flexibility for minimum extra work when we are testing our ADTs.

Notice that the first step prompts for, reads, and displays the name of the test case. This step might seem unnecessary for an interactive program given that the name of the test is reported directly back to the user who enters it. However, the programmer performing the test may want to save a record of the interactive dialogue for later study or as archival test documentation, so establishing a name for the interactive dialogue can prove useful.

A Test Driver for the ArrayStringLog Class

Here we present an interactive test driver for our `ArrayStringLog` class. The implementation is fairly straightforward and is based on our pseudocode. We call the program `ITDArrayStringLog`, with the "ITD" standing for "Interactive Test Driver."

```java
//--------------------------------------------------------------------------
// ITDArrayStringLog.java          by Dale/Joyce/Weems        Chapter 2
//
// Interactive Test Driver for the ArrayStringLog class.
//--------------------------------------------------------------------------

import java.util.*;
import ch02.stringLogs.*;

public class ITDArrayStringLog
{
  public static void main(String[] args)
  {
    ArrayStringLog test = new ArrayStringLog("Testing");
    Scanner conIn = new Scanner(System.in);

    String skip;        // skip end of line after reading an integer
    boolean keepGoing;  // flag for "choose operation" loop
    int constructor;    // indicates user's choice of constructor
    int operation;      // indicates user's choice of operation

    System.out.println("What is the name of this test?");
    String testName = conIn.nextLine();
    System.out.println("\nThis is test " + testName + "\n");

    System.out.println("Choose a constructor:");
    System.out.println("1: ArrayStringLog(String name)");
    System.out.println("2: ArrayStringLog(String name, int maxSize)");
    if (conIn.hasNextInt())
      constructor = conIn.nextInt();
    else
    {
      System.out.println("Error: you must enter an integer.");
      System.out.println("Terminating test.");
      return;
    }
    skip = conIn.nextLine();

    switch (constructor)
    {
      case 1:
      test = new ArrayStringLog(testName);
      break;
```

```
    case 2:
    System.out.println("Enter a maximum size:");
    int maxSize;
    if (conIn.hasNextInt())
      maxSize = conIn.nextInt();
    else
    {
      System.out.println("Error: you must enter an integer.");
      System.out.println("Terminating test.");
      return;
    }
    skip = conIn.nextLine();
    test = new ArrayStringLog(testName, maxSize);
    break;

    default:
    System.out.println("Error in constructor choice. Terminating test.");
    return;
}

keepGoing = true;
while (keepGoing)
{
  System.out.println("\nChoose an operation:");
  System.out.println("1: insert(String element)");
  System.out.println("2: clear()");
  System.out.println("3: contains(String element)");
  System.out.println("4: isFull()");
  System.out.println("5: size()");
  System.out.println("6: getName()");
  System.out.println("7: show contents");
  System.out.println("8: stop testing");
  if (conIn.hasNextInt())
    operation = conIn.nextInt();
  else
  {
    System.out.println("Error: you must enter an integer.");
    System.out.println("Terminating test.");
    return;
  }
  skip = conIn.nextLine();
```

```java
        switch (operation)
        {
          case 1:  // insert
          System.out.println("Enter string to insert:");
          String insertString = conIn.nextLine();
          test.insert(insertString);
          break;

          case 2:  // clear
          test.clear();
          break;

          case 3:  // contains
          System.out.println("Enter string to search for:");
          String searchString = conIn.nextLine();
          System.out.println("Result: " + test.contains(searchString));
          break;

          case 4:  // isFull
          System.out.println("Result: " + test.isFull());
          break;

          case 5:  // size
          System.out.println("Result: " + test.size());
          break;

          case 6:  // getName
          System.out.println("Result: " + test.getName());
          break;

          case 7:  // show contents
          System.out.println(test.toString());
          break;

          case 8:  // stop testing
          keepGoing = false;
          break;

          default:
          System.out.println("Error in operation choice. Terminating test.");
          return;
        }
      }
    System.out.println("End of Interactive Test Driver");
    }
}
```

Study the test driver program. You should be able to follow the control logic and recognize that it is a refinement of the pseudocode presented earlier. You should also understand the purpose of each statement. Although the program is straightforward, a few points require further explanation:

- The program starts by using `new` to instantiate `test`, an `ArrayStringLog` variable. It then proceeds to ask the user to select one of the two available constructors and, under the control of the first `switch` statement, instantiates `test` again. It does not appear that the first use of the `new` command, in the opening statement of the `main` method, is necessary. It seems to be redundant. However, some Java compilers require that statement. Without it they report an error such as "variable `test` might not have been initialized" because the later `new` commands are embedded within a decision structure (the `switch` statement) that includes a branch without a `new` command (the `default` branch). These compilers conclude that `new` may not be executed. Including the `new` command in the opening statement resolves the problem.
- This test driver does some error checking to ensure that user inputs are valid, but it does not represent a completely robust program. For instance, it doesn't verify that the size provided for the second constructor is a positive number, and it doesn't prevent the user from inserting too many elements into a StringLog. Although both of these situations are disallowed by the contract of `ArrayStringLog`, based on the stated preconditions, they should not be prevented by our test driver program. The user of the test driver, who is testing the `ArrayStringLog`, might wish to determine what happens when preconditions are not met and, therefore, needs the ability to violate the preconditions during a test run.

Using the Test Driver

The subsection "Identifying Test Cases" gave an example that dealt with the `contains` method of the `ArrayStringLog` class. The specific test case involved the following conditions:

- The expected result is true,
- The StringLog is full,
- The element contains blanks,
- It's an imperfect match, and
- The string being matched is the "middle" string placed into the StringLog.

Here's the result of a run of the test driver where this test is administered. User input is shown in green. The repeated display of the operation menu has been replaced with . . . in most places.

```
What is the name of this test?
Textbook Example


This is test Textbook Example
```

```
Choose a constructor:
1: ArrayStringLog(String name)
2: ArrayStringLog(String name, int maxSize)
2
Enter a maximum size:
3

Choose an operation:
1: insert(String element)
2: clear()
3: contains(String element)
4: isFull()
5: size()
6: getName()
7: show contents
8: stop testing
1
Enter string to insert:
trouble in the fields

Choose an operation:
...
1
Enter string to insert:
love at the five and dime

Choose an operation:
...
1
Enter string to insert:
once in a very blue moon

Choose an operation:
...
4
Result: true
```

```
Choose an operation:

...

3

Enter string to search for:

Love at the Five and Dime

Result: true


Choose an operation:

...

8

End of Interactive Test Driver
```

Our `ArrayStringLog` class passed the test. Note that if desired a single execution of our test driver could be used to run several tests. It would have been easy to continue the preceding test and test for exact matches in the middle, matches at the beginning or end, and so on. A carefully designed test plan can help minimize the number of test runs needed.

Professional Testing

The interactive testing approach described in this section provides several benefits:

- It allows us to easily change our test case—we just have to change the sequence of operations requested or the argument values supplied.
- Pedagogically it provides an example of a program that "uses" our ADT, and it allows a student to experiment interactively with the ADT.

However, in a production environment where hundreds or even thousands of test cases need to be performed, an interactive approach can be unwieldy to use. Instead, automated test drivers are created to run in batch mode.

For example, a software engineer constructing a test case equivalent to the one addressed in the "Using the Test Driver" subsection might create the following program (let's assume this is test case number 34):

```java
public class Test034

import ch02.stringLogs.*;

{
  public static void main(String[] args)
  {
```

```
ArrayStringLog test = new ArrayStringLog("Test 34", 3);
test.insert("trouble in the fields");
test.insert("love at the five and dime");
test.insert("once in a very blue moon");
if (test.contains("Love at the Five and Dime"))
    System.out.println("Test 34 passed");
else
    System.out.println("Test 34 failed");
    }
}
```

This program can run without user intervention and will report whether the test case has been passed. By developing an entire suite of such programs, software engineers can automate the testing process. A prime benefit of such an approach is that the same set of test programs can be used over and over again, throughout the development and maintenance stages of the software process. Frameworks exist that simplify the creation, management, and use of batch test suites. For example, you can find information about JUnit, a popular Java-based testing framework, at www.junit.org.

Exercise 39 asks you to construct a batch test program.

2.5 Introduction to Linked Lists

Recall from Section 1.5, "Data Structures," that the array and the linked list are the two primary building blocks for the more complex data structures. In this section we discuss linked lists in more detail, show how to create linked lists using Java, and introduce operations on linked lists. We use linked lists of strings in our examples to support the ongoing example of an ADT in this chapter, the StringLog ADT.

Arrays Versus Linked Lists

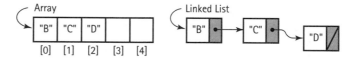

The figure depicts abstract views of an array of strings and a linked list of strings. An important difference between the two approaches is the underlying layout of the data in memory and the way in which we access the individual elements. With an array, we view all the elements as being grouped together, sitting in one block of memory. With a linked list, each element sits separately in its own block of memory. We call this small separate block of memory a "node."

An array is a built-in structure in Java and most other programming languages. In contrast, although a few languages provide built-in linked lists (e.g., Lisp and Scheme), most do not. Java supports common types of linked lists through a part of its Class Library called the Collections Framework. Even though the linked lists in the library are sufficient for many applications, software engineers need to understand how they work, both to appreciate their limitations, and also to be able to build custom linked list classes when the need arises. In the next subsection we show you how to create a linked list class using Java references.

As you know, the array structure allows us to access any element directly via its index. In comparison, the linked list structure seems very limited, as its nodes can only be accessed in a sequential manner, starting at the beginning of the list and following the links. So why should we bother to use a linked list in the first place? There are several potential reasons:

- The size of an array is fixed. It is provided as an argument to the new command when the array is instantiated. The size of a linked list varies. The nodes of a linked list can be allocated on an "as needed" basis. When no longer needed, the nodes can be returned to the memory manager.
- For some operations a linked list is a more efficient implementation approach than an array. For example, to place an element into the front of a collection of elements with an array you must shift all elements by one place toward the back of the array. This task requires many steps. With a linked list you simply allocate a new node and link it to the front of the list. This task requires only two steps.

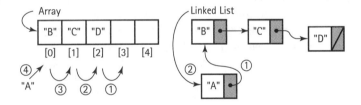

- For some applications you never have to directly access a node that is deep within the list without first accessing the nodes that precede it on the list. In those cases the fact that nodes of a linked list must be accessed sequentially doesn't adversely affect performance.

The LLStringNode Class

To create a linked list we need to know how to do two things: allocate space for a node dynamically and allow a node to link to, or reference, another node. Java supplies an operation for dynamically allocating space, an operation we have been using for all of our objects—the new operation. Clearly, that part is easy. But how can we allow a node to reference another node? Essentially a node in a linked list is an object that holds some important information, such as a string, plus a link to another node. That other node is the exact same type of object—it is also a node in the linked list.

When we define the node class, we must allow the objects created from it to reference node class objects. We call this type of class a self-referential class. We include in its

> **Self-referential class** A class that includes an instance variable or variables that can hold a reference to an object of the same class

definition two instance variables: one that holds the important information that the linked list is maintaining and one that is a reference to an object of its same class. As an example, let's design a self-referential class that provides nodes for use within a linked list of strings. We call our class LLStringNode. Because we use it only to support a link or reference-based implementation of the StringLog ADT, we make its instance variables private and place it in the ch02.stringLogs package. Its declarations include the self-referential code, which is <u>emphasized</u> here:

```
public class LLStringNode

package ch02.stringLogs;

{
  private String info;        // information stored in list
  private LLStringNode link;  // reference to a node
  . . .
```

The LLStringNode class defines an instance variable info to hold a reference to the string represented by the node and an instance variable link to reference another LLStringNode object. That next LLStringNode can hold a reference to a string and a reference to another LLStringNode object, which in turn holds a reference to a string and a reference to another LLStringNode object, and so on. The chain ends when the LLStringNode holds the value null in its link, indicating the end of the linked list. As an example, here is a linked list with three nodes, referenced by the LLStringNode variable letters. Given that we know how the nodes of our linked list are implemented, we now use a more concrete view in our figures.

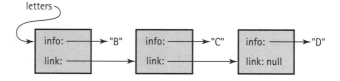

We define one constructor for the LLStringNode class:

```
public LLStringNode(String info)
{
  this.info = info;
  link = null;
}
```

The constructor accepts a string as an argument and sets the info variable to that string. For example,

```
LLStringNode sNode1 = new LLStringNode("basketball");
```

results in the structure

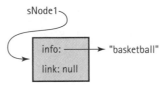

We could have created other constructors, such as one that accepts an LLStringNode reference as an argument and sets the link variable. We do not think they would add much to the usability of the class.

Note that our constructor essentially creates a linked list with a single element. How, then, can you represent an empty linked list? You do so by declaring a variable of class LLStringNode but not instantiating it with the new operation. In that case, the value held in the string node variable is null.

```
LLStringNode theList;
```

theList: null

Completing the class are the definitions of the setters and getters. Their code is standard and straightforward. The setLink method is used to link nodes together into a list. For example, the following code

```
LLStringNode sNode1 = new LLStringNode("basketball");
LLStringNode sNode2 = new LLStringNode("baseball");
sNode1.setLink(sNode2);
```

results in the structure

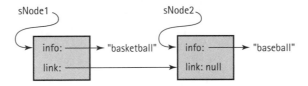

The complete LLStringNode class is shown next. It is used in Section 2.6 to create a reference-based implementation of the StringLog ADT. Before seeing how that is accomplished, we introduce the standard operations on linked lists.

```
//-------------------------------------------------------------------------
// LLStringNode.java          by Dale/Joyce/Weems          Chapter 2
//
// Implements String nodes for a Linked List.
//-------------------------------------------------------------------------

package ch02.stringLogs;

public class LLStringNode
{
  private String info;
  private LLStringNode link;

  public LLStringNode(String info)
  {
    this.info = info;
    link = null;
  }

  public void setInfo(String info)
  // Sets info string of this LLStringNode.
  {
    this.info = info;
  }

  public String getInfo()
  // Returns info string of this LLStringNode.
  {
    return info;
  }

  public void setLink(LLStringNode link)
  // Sets link of this LLStringNode.
  {
    this.link = link;
  }

  public LLStringNode getLink()
  // Returns link of this LLStringNode.
  {
    return link;
  }
}
```

Operations on Linked Lists

Node classes, such as LLStringNode, provide a set of building blocks for linked lists. It is up to us to use these building blocks to create and manipulate linked lists.

Three basic operations are performed on linked lists: A linked list can be traversed to obtain information from it, a node can be added to a linked list, and a node can be removed from a linked list. Let's look more carefully at each of these categories. To help simplify our presentation, we assume the existence of this linked list of LLStringNode objects referenced by the variable letters:

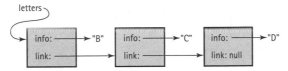

Traversal

Information held in a linked list is retrieved by traversing the list. There are many potential reasons for traversing a list—for the purposes of this discussion we assume that we want to display the information contained in the letters linked list one line at a time, starting at the beginning of the list and finishing at the end of the list.

To traverse the linked list we need some way to keep track of our current position in the list. With an array we use an index variable. That approach will not work with a linked list because it is not indexed. Instead we need to use a variable that can reference the current node of the list. Let's call it currNode. The traversal algorithm is

```
Set currNode to first node on the list
while (currNode is not pointing off the end of the list)
    display the information at currNode
    change currNode to point to the next node on the list
```

Let's refine this algorithm, transforming it into Java code as we go. Our letters list is a linked list of LLStringNode objects. Therefore currNode must be an LLStringNode variable. We initialize currNode to point to the beginning of the list:

```
LLStringNode currNode = letters;
while (currNode is not pointing off the end of the list)
    display the information at currNode
    change currNode to point to the next node on the list
```

Next let's turn our attention to the body of the *while* loop. Displaying the information at `currNode` is achieved using the `getInfo` method. That part is easy:

```
System.out.println(currNode.getInfo());
```

But how do we "change currNode to point to the next node on the list"? Consider the situation after `currNode` has been initialized to the beginning of the linked list:

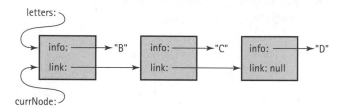

We want to change `currNode` to point to the next node, the node where the `info` variable points to the string "C." In the preceding figure notice what points to that node—the `link` variable of the node currently referenced by `currNode`. Therefore we use the `getLink` method of the `LLStringNode` class to return that value and set the new value of `currNode`:

```
currNode = currNode.getLink();
```

Putting this all together we now have the following pseudocode:

```
LLStringNode currNode = letters;
while (currNode is not pointing off the end of the list)
{
    System.out.println(currNode.getInfo());
    currNode = currNode.getLink();
}
```

The only thing left to do is determine when `currNode` is pointing off the end of the list. The value of `currNode` is repeatedly set to the value in the `link` variable of the next node. When we reach the end of the list, the value in this variable is `null`. So, as long as the value of `currNode` is not `null`, it "is not pointing off the end of the list." Our final code segment is

```
LLStringNode currNode = letters;
while (currNode != null)
```

```
{
    System.out.println(currNode.getInfo());
    currNode = currNode.getLink();
}
```

Figure 2.6 traces through this code, graphically depicting what occurs using our example linked list.

Before leaving this example we should see how our code handles the case of the empty linked list. The empty linked list is an important boundary condition. Whenever you are dealing with linked lists, you should always double-check that your approach works for this oft-encountered special case.

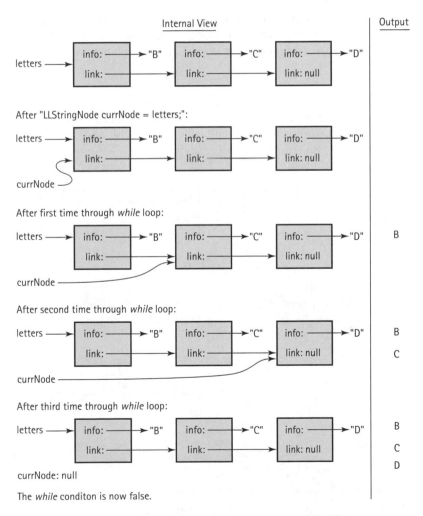

Figure 2.6 *Trace of traversal code on* `letters` *linked list*

Recall that an empty linked list is one in which the value in the variable that represents the list is `null`:

letters: null

What does our traversal code do in this case? The `currNode` variable is initially set to the value held in the `letters` variable, which is `null`. Therefore `currNode` starts out `null`, the *while* loop condition

```
(currNode != null)
```

is immediately false, and the *while* loop body is not entered. Essentially, nothing happens—exactly what we would like to happen when traversing an empty list! Our code passes this deskcheck. We should also remember to check this case with a test program.

Insertion

Three general cases of insertion into a linked list must be considered: insertion at the beginning of the list, insertion in the middle of the list, and insertion at the end of the list.

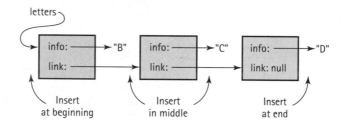

Let's consider the case where we want to insert a node into the beginning of the list. Suppose we have the node `newNode` to insert into the beginning of the `letters` linked list:

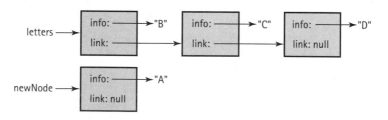

Our first step is to set the `link` variable of the `newNode` node to point to the beginning of the list:

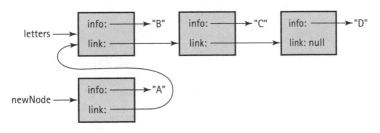

To finish the insertion we set the `letters` variable to point to the `newNode`, making it the new beginning of the list:

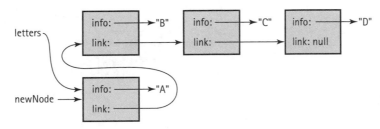

The insertion code corresponding to these two steps is

```
newNode.setLink(letters);
letters = newNode;
```

Note that the order of these statements is critical. If we reversed the order of the statements, we would end up with this:

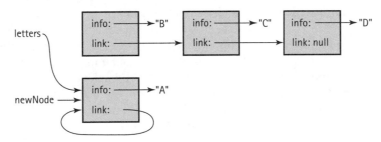

You must be very careful when manipulating references. Drawing figures to help you follow what is going on is usually a good idea.

As we did for the traverse operation, we should ask what happens if our insertion code is called when the linked list is empty. Figure 2.7 depicts this situation graphically. Does the method correctly link the new node to the beginning of the empty linked list? In other words, does it correctly create a list with a single node? First, the `link` of the new node is assigned the value of `letters`. What is this value when the list is empty? It is `null`, which is exactly what we want to put into the `link` of the only node of a

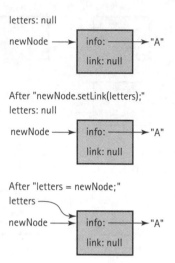

Figure 2.7 *Results of insertion code on an empty linked list*

linked list. Then `letters` is reset to point to the new node. The new node becomes the first, and only, node on the list. Thus this method works for an empty linked list as well as a linked list that contains elements.

Implementation of the other two kinds of insertion operations requires similar careful manipulation of references.

Remaining Operations

So far in this section we have developed Java code that performs a traversal of a linked list and an insertion into the beginning of a linked list. We provided these examples to give you an idea of how you can work with linked lists at the code level.

Our purpose in introducing linked lists was to enable us to use them later for implementing ADTs. We defer development of the remaining linked list operations, including deletions, until they are needed to support the implementation of a specific ADT. For now, we will simply say that, as with insertion, there are three general cases of deletion of nodes from a linked list: deletion at the beginning of the list, deletion in the middle of the list, and deletion at the end of the list.

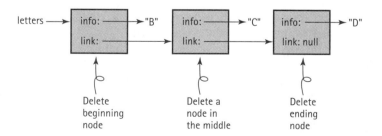

In this chapter our ongoing example is the StringLog ADT. The next section presents an implementation that uses a linked list as the underlying construct to hold the collection of strings. It only requires a traversal operation and an insertion into the beginning of the list operation, which just happen to be the two operations we have already covered! In Chapters 3 (stacks), 5 (queues), and 6 (lists), we will encounter ADTs encapsulating other classic linear data structures. The following table shows which operations are an inherent part of the linked implementation of each structure. By the time you finish Chapter 6, you will have encountered all of the basic operations.

Chapt	Structure	Traversal	Insertion			Deletion		
			Beginning	Middle	End	Beginning	Middle	End
2	StringLog	✔	✔					
3	Stack		✔			✔		
5	Queue				✔	✔		
6	List	✔	✔	✔	✔	✔	✔	✔

2.6 Linked List StringLog ADT Implementation

You have already seen an implementation of the StringLog ADT using an array. In this section we show how you can implement a StringLog using a linked list. Note that we do not plan to use a linked list directly at the application level to store strings. Rather, we hide the linked list within our ADT implementation. A StringLog is *not* an array and it is *not* a linked list. It is an abstract entity—a container that holds strings, has a name, and provides the operations insert, isFull, size, contains, clear, getName, and toString.

We call our new StringLog class the LinkedStringLog class to differentiate it from the array-based class of Section 2.3. We also refer to this approach as a reference-based approach. Determining names for our classes is important and not always easy. See the feature "Naming Constructs" for more discussion of this topic.

Like the ArrayStringLog class, our LinkedStringLog class is part of the ch02.stringLogs package, fulfills the StringLog specification, and implements the StringLogInterface interface. Recall that when we developed the specification and created the interface, our purpose was to provide a definition of a StringLog ADT that did not depend on the underlying implementation. Unlike the ArrayStringLog, the LinkedStringLog will implement an unbounded StringLog. In other words, there is no limit on how many strings it can hold. This criterion is a natural choice when using a linked list to implement an ADT. Of course, we are not required to use this approach.

Naming Constructs

Choosing appropriate names for programmer-defined constructs is an important task. In this sidebar, we discuss this task and explain some of the naming conventions used in this textbook.

Java is very lenient in terms of its rules for programmer-defined names. We have been following standard conventions when naming the constructs created for this text. Our class and interface names all begin with an uppercase letter, such as `ArrayStringLog` and `StringLogInterface`. Our method and variable names all begin with a lowercase letter, such as `insert` and `log`. If a name contains more than one word, we capitalize the start of each additional word, such as `getLink` and `lastIndex`. Finally, when naming constants such as `MINYEAR`, we use all capital letters.

The name assigned to a construct should provide useful information to someone who is working with that construct. For example, if you declare a variable within a method that should hold the maximum value of a set of numbers, you should name it based on its use—name it `maximum` or `maxValue` instead of `X`. The same is true for class, interface, and method names.

Because classes tend to represent objects, we typically name them using nouns—for example, `Date` and `ArrayStringLog`. Because methods tend to represent actions, we generally name them using verbs—for example, `insert` and `contains`.

When we use interfaces to specify ADTs, we use the name of the ADT plus the term "interface" within the name of our interface—for example, `StringLogInterface`. Although this nomenclature is a bit redundant, it is the approach favored by the Java library creators. Note that the name of the interface does not imply any implementation detail. Classes that implement the `StringLogInterface` interface can use arrays, vectors, array lists, or references—the interface itself does not restrict implementation options and its name does not imply anything about implementation details. The name does help us identify the purpose of the construct; thus `StringLogInterface` defines the interface required by the StringLog ADT.

Implementation-Based Class Names

We must confess that we were hesitant to use names such as `ArrayStringLog` and `LinkedStringLog` for our classes. Can you guess why? Recall our goal of information hiding: We want to hide the implementation used to support our ADTs. When we use terms such as "`Array`" and "`Linked`" in the names of our ADTs, we reveal clues about the very information we are trying to hide. However, we finally settled on using implementation-dependent terms within our class names. There are several reasons why we took this approach:

1. It is the same approach used by the Java library—for example, the `ArrayList` class.
2. Although information hiding is important, some information about the implementation is valuable to the client programmer, because it affects the space used by objects of the class and the execution efficiency of the methods of the class. Using "array" and "linked" in the class names does help convey this information.
3. We already have a construct associated with our ADTs whose name is independent of implementation: the interface.
4. In this textbook we create multiple implementations of many different ADTs; this multiplicity is fundamental to the way we study ADTs. Using implementation-dependent names makes it easier to distinguish among these different implementations.

If we desired, we could implement a bounded StringLog using links or, alternatively, an unbounded StringLog using arrays. Such approaches require extra work but are possible, as we will see later in the text.

In this section we follow the same basic outline that we employed when describing the array-based implementation, making it easy to compare and contrast the two implementation approaches.

Instance Variables

In this implementation, the elements of a StringLog are stored in a linked list of LLStringNode objects. The LLStringNode class was defined in Section 2.5. As we did in the array-based approach, we call the instance variable that we use to access the strings log. It will reference the first node on the linked list, so it is a reference to an object of the class LLStringNode.

As with the array approach, we use a string variable called name to hold the name of the StringLog. For the array-based approach we needed one additional instance variable to keep track of the last position in the array that was being used. We do not need to track that information for the linked approach, as we do not use indexes. The beginning of the class definition looks like this:

```
//---------------------------------------------------------------------
// LinkedStringLog.java        by Dale/Joyce/Weems          Chapter 2
//
// Implements StringLogInterface using a linked list
// of LLStringNode to hold the log strings.
//---------------------------------------------------------------------

package ch02.stringLogs;

public class LinkedStringLog implements StringLogInterface
{
  protected LLStringNode log;  // reference to first node of linked
                               // list that holds the StringLog strings
  protected String name;       // name of this StringLog
  . . .
```

Constructors

For the array-based approach we included two constructors: one in which the capacity of the array was specified as an argument and one in which it wasn't. Because a linked list is a dynamic structure that grows as we add elements to it, we do not need to worry about a size parameter. We need only a single constructor.

Our constructor requires one parameter: a string that indicates the name attribute of the StringLog. A new StringLog is created empty; that is, the number of strings in it is 0. Therefore, when we instantiate an object of class `LinkedStringLog`, we set the `log` variable to `null`. The code for this constructor is straightforward. Its efficiency is O(1), as it requires only two steps.

```
public LinkedStringLog(String name)
// Instantiates and returns a reference to an empty
// StringLog object with name "name."
{
  log = null;
  this.name = name;
}
```

The first two stages of Figure 2.8 show both the internal or implementation view and the abstract view of a StringLog object called `strLog` after it has been declared and instantiated using this constructor.

Transformers

We have two transformer operations: `insert` and `clear`. Each time the `insert` command is invoked, another string is added to the linked list. The best approach for handling this task is to insert the new string at the beginning of the linked list. It is the most efficient approach because we already have a reference to the beginning of the list in the form of the variable `log`. In Section 2.5 we developed an approach for insertion of a node into the front of a linked list. In this case we must first create the node so that it holds the string passed to the method in the `element` parameter, and then insert the node into the linked list. This operation has an efficiency of O(1).

```
public void insert(String element)
// Precondition:   This StringLog is not full.
//
// Places element into this StringLog.
{
  LLStringNode newNode = new LLStringNode(element);
  newNode.setLink(log);
  log = newNode;
}
```

Figure 2.8 shows a StringLog object called `strLog` after it has been declared, instantiated, and received several `insert` messages, as shown in the following code:

```
LinkedStringLog strLog;
strLog = new LinkedStringLog("Nicknames");
strLog.insert("Babyface");
```

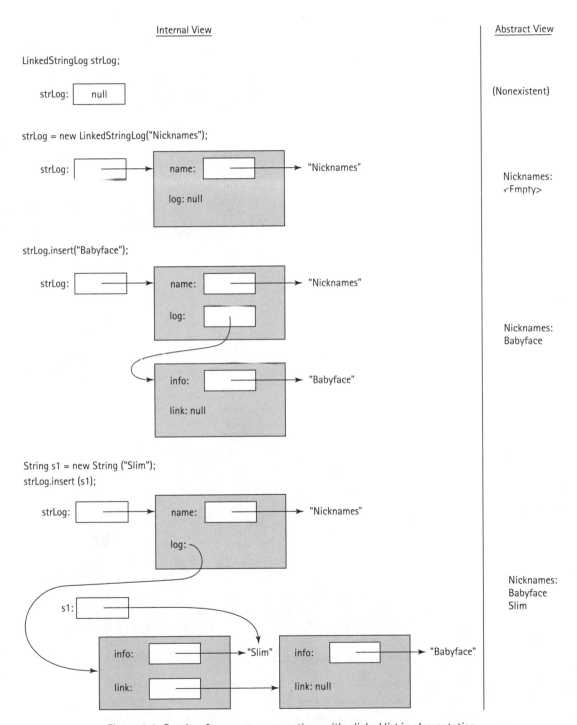

Figure 2.8 *Results of* `StringLog` *operations with a linked list implementation*

```
String s1 = new String("Slim");
strLog.insert(s1);
```

In one invocation of insert a string literal is passed as the argument; in the other invocation a string variable is passed. You might like to compare this figure with Figure 2.4, which displays the results of a similar sequence of operations for the array-based approach.

Recall that for the clear operation in the array-based approach we set the array slots that weren't being used to null, allowing the garbage collector to reclaim the space used by those strings if appropriate. We do not have to worry about this issue with the linked list approach. If we set the instance variable log to null, in effect unlinking the list from the StringLog object, the garbage collector is able to reclaim the space used by the LLStringNode objects and any unreachable strings.

```
public void clear()
// Makes this StringLog empty.
{
   log = null;
}
```

Figure 2.9 continues the example from Figure 2.8, showing the result of the clear method. Although the Big-O complexity of this clear operation is apparently O(1), which

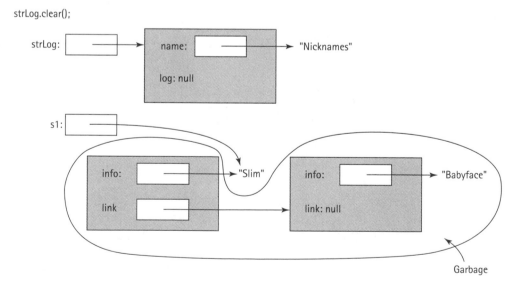

Figure 2.9 *A StringLog after the clear operation*

is more efficient than the O(*N*) operation we used with the array-based implementation, the difference between these operations is misleading. With the linked list approach, the garbage collector still takes *N* steps to reclaim the cleared nodes. The job of clearing and reclaiming is still O(*N*).

Observers

First let's look at the observer operation `isFull`. Given that we are implementing an unbounded StringLog, we do not have an explicit limit on the StringLog size. As a consequence, we always return `false` for the `isFull` method. The only way the log could be full is if the program runs out of system space. In this rare case the Java run-time system causes an error anyway.

```
public boolean isFull()
// Returns true if this StringLog is full, false otherwise.
{
   return false;
}
```

The `getName` method is also simple. In fact, it is unchanged from the array-based approach.

```
public String getName()
// Returns the name of this StringLog.
{
   return name;
}
```

Both of these methods, `isFull` and `getName`, are O(1).

The `size` method was easy to write for the array-based approach. We just returned the value of `lastIndex + 1`. However, we do not have any indexes in the linked list approach. To determine the number of strings in the StringLog we must traverse the linked list, counting the strings. In Section 2.5 we developed an approach for traversing a linked list. Now we simply modify that approach to count list elements. That is easy—we just start our count at 0 and increment it by 1 each time we visit another node.

```
public int size()
// Returns the number of strings in this StringLog.
{
   int count = 0;
   LLStringNode node;
   node = log;
```

```
   while (node != null)
   {
     count++;
     node = node.getLink();
   }
   return count;
}
```

This method has Big-O complexity of O(N). An alternative approach to handle this operation is to declare another instance variable, of type int, and use it to keep track of the size of the StringLog as changes are made to it. This approach would simplify the implementation of size but adds an extra step to the insert method, as each time a string is inserted we need to increment the value of the variable. Whether we realize an efficiency savings depends on the relative number of times our application invokes the insert and size methods. We ask you to investigate this alternative approach in Exercise 52.

The implementation of the toString method is also just a simple modification of our traversal approach. We told you that traversing a linked list was a common operation! Like size, the toString method has an efficiency of O(N).

```
public String toString()
// Returns a nicely formatted string representing this StringLog.
{
   String logString = "Log: " + name + "\n\n";
   LLStringNode node;
   node = log;
   int count = 0;

   while (node != null)
   {
     count++;
     logString = logString + count + ". " + node.getInfo() + "\n";
     node = node.getLink();
   }

   return logString;
}
```

Because our insert method always inserts strings at the front of the linked list, the toString method displays the strings in the opposite order of their insertion. We have not assumed that insertion order is important for our StringLogs, so this behavior is acceptable.

The final observer operation, contains, is yet another variation of a list traversal. Recall that in the array-based approach we used stepwise refinement to design our code for this operation. We can now reuse our design of the array-based `contains` method, replacing the array-related statements with their linked list counterparts.

The overall approach is the same: traverse the structure containing the log strings one element after another, comparing the strings with the parameter string `element` until we either find a match or reach the end of the list. Here is the second stage of refinement from our array-based approach:

```
public boolean contains(String element)
{
    Set variables;
    while (we still need to search)
    {
        if (the next value equals element)
            return true;
    }
    return false;
}
```

None of this pseudocode depends on using an array. We already understand how to encode the required operations using a linked list, so it is easy to create the code. This method is O(N), just like its array-based counterpart.

```java
public boolean contains(String element)
// Returns true if element is in this StringLog,
// otherwise returns false.
// Ignores case difference when doing string comparison.
{
    LLStringNode node;
    node = log;

    while (node != null)
    {
        if (element.equalsIgnoreCase(node.getInfo()))  // if they match
            return true;
        else
            node = node.getLink();
    }
```

```
    return false;
  }
```

The LinkedStringLog class is now complete. We list the class in its entirety below. Exercise 53 asks you to create and use a test driver for this class.

```
//--------------------------------------------------------------------------
// LinkedStringLog.java         by Dale/Joyce/Weems           Chapter 2
//
// Implements StringLogInterface using a linked list
// of LLStringNodes to hold the log strings.
//--------------------------------------------------------------------------

package ch02.stringLogs;

public class LinkedStringLog implements StringLogInterface
{
  protected LLStringNode log; // reference to first node of linked
                              // list that holds the StringLog strings
  protected String name;      // name of this StringLog

  public LinkedStringLog(String name)
  // Instantiates and returns a reference to an empty StringLog object
  // with name "name."
  {
    log = null;
    this.name = name;
  }

  public void insert(String element)
  // Precondition:   This StringLog is not full.
  //
  // Places element into this StringLog.
  {
    LLStringNode newNode = new LLStringNode(element);
    newNode.setLink(log);
    log = newNode;
  }

  public boolean isFull()
  // Returns true if this StringLog is full, false otherwise.
  {
    return false;
  }
```

```
public int size()
// Returns the number of strings in this StringLog.
{
  int count = 0;
  LLStringNode node;
  node = log;
  while (node != null)
  {
    count++;
    node = node.getLink();
  }
  return count;
}

public boolean contains(String element)
// Returns true if element is in this StringLog,
// otherwise returns false.
// Ignores case difference when doing string comparison.
{
  LLStringNode node;
  node = log;

  while (node != null)
  {
    if (element.equalsIgnoreCase(node.getInfo()))   // if they match
      return true;
    else
      node = node.getLink();
  }

  return false;
}

public void clear()
// Makes this StringLog empty.
{
  log = null;
}

public String getName()
// Returns the name of this StringLog.
```

```
  {
    return name;
  }

  public String toString()
  // Returns a nicely formatted string representing this StringLog.
  {
    String logString = "Log: " + name + "\n\n";
    LLStringNode node;
    node = log;
    int count = 0;

    while (node != null)
    {
      count++;
      logString = logString + count + ". " + node.getInfo() + "\n";
      node = node.getLink();
    }

    return logString;
  }
}
```

2.7 Software Design: Identification of Classes

In this section we take a brief look at the object-oriented design approach we use in our case studies throughout the text. We then apply this approach to design and create a trivia game in Section 2.8.

Brainstorm

The key task in solving a problem with an object-oriented program is identifying classes to use within the solution. There is no foolproof technique for doing this. One approach is to just start brainstorming ideas. A large program is typically written by a team of programmers, so the brainstorming process often occurs in a team setting. Team members identify whatever objects they see in the problem and then propose classes to represent them. The proposed classes and their responsibilities are all written on a board. None of the ideas for classes are discussed or rejected in this first stage.

Filter

After brainstorming, the team goes through a process of filtering the classes. First they eliminate duplicates. Then they discuss whether each class really represents objects in the problem. (It's easy to get carried away and include classes, such as "the user," that are beyond the scope of the problem.) The team next looks for classes that seem to be related. Perhaps they aren't duplicates but have much in common, so they are grouped together on the board. Such classes might potentially be merged or organized with inheritance. At the same time, the discussion may reveal some classes that were overlooked.

Scenario Analysis

Usually it is not difficult to identify an initial set of classes. In most problems we naturally find entities that we wish to represent as class objects. For example, in designing a program that manages a checking account, we might identify checks, deposits, an account balance, and account statements as objects. These objects interact with one another through messages (invoking methods). For example, we might decide that a check object should send a message to a balance object that tells it to deduct an amount object from itself. If we didn't originally list an amount class in our initial set of classes, we have now identified another class that we need to represent.

Our example illustrates a common approach to object-oriented design. We begin by identifying a set of classes that we think are important in a problem. Then we consider some scenarios in which objects of these classes interact to accomplish a task. In the process of envisioning how a scenario plays out, we identify additional classes, objects, and messages. We keep creating new scenarios until we feel that our set of classes, objects, and messages is sufficient to accomplish any task that the problem requires. This "scenario analysis" is similar to the more formal "use-case analysis" briefly described in Chapter 1.

Nouns and Verbs

A standard technique for identifying classes and their attributes and responsibilities is to look for objects in the problem statement. Candidate objects and their attributes are sometimes found in the nouns. For example, suppose the problem statement includes these sentences: "The student averages must be sorted from best to worst before being output. The output should list the names and averages of each student." A potential class is "student." Potential attributes of objects of this class are "name" and "average." A potential responsibility is to maintain the correct value of the average.

If you have a printed copy of your requirements, you can circle the nouns. The set of circled nouns then represents your candidate classes. Of course, you have to filter this list, but at least it provides a good starting point for design. You might also highlight the verbs some way, perhaps by underlining—the verbs are often associated with responsibilities and actions for the classes.

The (student) averages must be sorted from best to worst before being

output. The output should list the (names) and (averages) of each student.

Cohesive Designs

Elegant designs are easy to understand. One property that helps distinguish an elegant design from an inelegant one is the cohesiveness of the classes. A cohesive class exhibits a single purpose or identity, and it "sticks" together well. A good way to validate the cohesiveness of an identified class is to try to describe its primary responsibility in a single coherent phrase. If you cannot do so, then you should reconsider your design. Some examples of cohesive responsibilities follow:

- Maintain a list of integers
- Handle file interaction
- Represent a date

Examples of "poor" responsibilities include these two:

- Maintain a list of integers and provide special integer output routines
- Handle file interaction and draw graphs on the screen

Summation of Our Approach

In summation, we have developed the following approach to identifying classes for our systems. We present it here as an algorithm.

Identification of Classes

repeat
  Brainstorm ideas, perhaps using the nouns in the problem statement to help identify potential object classes
  Filter the classes into a set that appears to help solve the problem
  Consider problem scenarios where the classes carry out the activities of the scenario
until the set of classes provides an elegant design that successfully supports the collection of scenarios

---

This simple approach works well for the types and sizes of problems we encounter in this textbook. More complicated approaches are required to solve more complicated problems, but they are beyond the scope of this book.

Sources for Classes

Java programs are built using a combination of the basic language and preexisting classes. In effect, the preexisting classes act as extensions to the basic language; this extended Java language is large, complex, robust, powerful, and ever changing. Java programmers should never stop learning about the nuances of the extended language—an exciting prospect for those who like an intellectual challenge.

When designing a Java-based system to solve a problem, we first determine which classes are needed. Next we determine whether any of these classes already exist. If not, we try to discover classes that do exist that can be used to build the needed classes. Additionally, we often create our own classes, "helper" classes that are used to build the needed classes.

Programmer

Off-the-Shelf Components

Java Class Library

Basic Java Language

Where do the classes come from? There are three sources:

1. *The Java Class Library*   The Java language is bundled with a class library that includes hundreds of useful classes. The library classes that we use throughout the text are introduced in Appendix E.

2. *Build your own*   Suppose you determine that a certain class would be useful in solving your programming problem, but the class does not exist. You then create the needed class, possibly using preexisting classes in the process. The new class becomes part of the extended language and can be used on future projects. Our ADT implementations are examples of such classes.

3. *Off the shelf*   Software components, such as classes or packages of classes, that are obtained from third-party sources are called off-the-shelf components. When they are bought, we call them "commercial off-the-shelf" components (COTS). Java components can be bought from software shops or even found free on the Web. When you obtain software, or anything else, from the Web for your own use, you should make sure you are not violating a copyright. You also need to use care in determining that free components work correctly and do not contain viruses or other code that could cause problems on your system.

Design Choices

When working on a design, keep in mind that many different correct solutions are possible for most problems. The design techniques we use to create our programs may seem imprecise, especially compared with the precision that is demanded by the computer. But the computer merely demands that we express a particular solution precisely. The process of deciding which particular solution to use is far less precise. It is our human ability to make choices without having complete information that enables us to solve problems. Different choices naturally lead to different solutions to a problem.

For example, in developing a simulation of an air traffic control system, we might decide that airplanes and control towers are objects that communicate with each other. Alternatively, we might decide that pilots and controllers are the objects that communicate. This choice affects how we subsequently view the problem and which responsibilities we assign to the objects. Either choice can lead to a working application. We may simply prefer the one with which we are most familiar.

Some of our choices may lead to designs that are more or less efficient than others. For example, keeping a list of names in alphabetical rather than random order makes it possible for a program to find a particular name much faster. However, choosing to leave the list randomly ordered still produces a valid (but slower) solution, and it may even be the best solution if you do not need to search the list very often.

The point is this: Don't hesitate to begin solving a problem because you are waiting for some flash of genius that leads you to the perfect solution. There is no such thing. It is better to jump in and try something, step back, see if you like the result, and then either proceed onward or make changes. Designing successful software solutions to problems is a challenging, yet rewarding, task.

2.8 Case Study: A Trivia Game

Our task for this case study is to create an interactive trivia game for a single user. The user is told the name of the game, the number of questions, and the number of chances he or she will have to answer the questions. As is typical for trivia games, to provide context each question has an associated category that is presented along with the question. The program cycles through the questions until they are all answered correctly or there are no more chances remaining.

After responding to a question the user is told whether the answer is correct. Answers entered by the user will be compared to a set of acceptable answers using case-insensitive comparison.

Here's an example of how a game played through the console might appear. User input is shown in blue.

Welcome to the General Trivia 1 trivia quiz.

You will have 6 chances to answer 4 questions.

Rock and Roll: Give the first name of one of The Beatles.
Pete
Incorrect

Math: What is 5 + 2?
7
Correct!

History: Who was the second president of the United States?
Ford
Incorrect

Vegetables: What color are carrots?
orange
Correct!

Rock and Roll: Give the first name of one of The Beatles.
ringo
Correct!

History: Who was the second president of the United States?
Smith
Incorrect

Game Over

Results:
    Chances used: 6   Number Correct: 3

Thank you.

The Source of the Trivia Game

Before we start development, let's discuss where to obtain information about a specific game. For example, how many questions are there? What are their categories? What are the questions? What are the acceptable answers? The game information might come from several possible sources: It might come from a database of trivia questions, it might come from a structured file, or it could even be generated by another program.

We will design the program to be easily adapted to any of these sources. For practical reasons, we limit our actual code example to a single approach, in which the information is in a text file in a specific format. With this approach, to make a different quiz we just create a new text file of information.

We assume all the data about the trivia quiz is located in a text file named `game.txt`. The system reads the quiz information from the file and then presents the quiz to the user.

The information in the file should be organized as follows:

- Line 1: the quiz name
- Line 2: the number of questions
- Line 3: the number of chances allowed
- For each question:
    - Line a: the category
    - Line b: the question
    - Line c: the number of acceptable answers
    - For each acceptable answer:
        - The answer

For example, the sample run we saw previously was based on the following file:

```
General Trivia 1
4
6
Rock and Roll
Give the first name of one of The Beatles.
5
John
Paul
George
Ringo
Richard
Math
What is 5 + 2?
2
7
seven
History
Who was the second president of the United States?
2
Adams
```

John Adams

Vegetables

What color are carrots?

1

orange

Note that our approach permits a great deal of freedom—the author of a quiz can include as many questions, chances, and acceptable answers as he or she chooses.

Identifying Support Classes

Let's use the design approach introduced in Section 2.7.

Brainstorm

We said that nouns in the problem statement represent potential classes/objects/attributes. Let's identify the nouns in the problem statement.

> Our task is to create an interactive trivia game for a single user. The user is told the name of the game, the number of questions, and the number of chances he or she will have to answer the questions. As is typical for trivia games, to provide context, each question has an associated category that is presented along with the question. The program cycles through the questions until they are all answered correctly or there are no more chances remaining.

> After responding to a question the user is told whether the answer is correct. Answers entered by the user will be compared to a **set of** acceptable answers using case-insensitive comparison.

The relevant nouns are trivia game, name of the game, questions, associated category, number of questions, number of questions answered correctly, number of chances, number of chances left, answers, and set of acceptable answers. Let's examine these nouns and see what insights they give us into the solution of this problem.

Filter

First let's group together those nouns that "go together"—for example, *question* and *answer* are obviously related to each other. It doesn't take long to reorganize our nouns into two sets:

- Trivia game
  - Name of the game
  - Number of questions
  - Number of chances
  - Number of questions answered correctly
  - Number of chances remaining
- Question
  - Associated category
  - Answer
  - Set of acceptable answers

We have identified two candidate classes: a trivia game and a question. The other nouns in the problem statement can all be considered attributes of objects of one of these two classes. Let's call our candidate classes `TriviaGame` and `TriviaQuestion`.

Scenario Analysis

We decide the `TriviaGame` class should hold the current state of the trivia game. Initially it will hold all the information contained in the text file that represents the game (or whatever source representation is used), but as the game progresses it must be updated to capture the ongoing changes in the state of the game. The objects of the `TriviaQuestion` class should represent the different questions associated with the trivia game. We imagine a scenario where the game information is read from its source (file, database, or whatever) to create the original `TriviaGame` object; the program then repeatedly retrieves a `TriviaQuestion` object from the game object, uses it to present the question to the user, and checks if the provided answer is correct, with the state of the `TriviaGame` object being updated accordingly. This entire process repeats until the game is over.

Based on our brief scenario analysis we are content that we are following a reasonable approach, so we continue with a bottom-up development of our system. First we consider the `TriviaQuestion` class. What are the responsibilities of this class? The prime responsibility is to represent a trivia question—its category, the text of the question, and a set of acceptable answers. The class must allow this information to be set appropriately and to be observed at a later time. Also, because the relevant information includes the set of acceptable answers, we decide to make the class responsible for determining whether a given answer is in that set.

Given that we intend to use the `TriviaQuestion` class to support a trivia game, it is tempting to assign it the responsibility of remembering whether a question has been answered correctly.[4] We could initialize a `boolean` instance variable to `false`, set it to `true` when the question is answered correctly, and provide an observer method to return its value. But does such information really belong in the `TriviaQuestion` object? The "correctly answered" status of a question is an aspect of a particular instance of a trivia game. Recall from our previous scenario analysis that maintaining such information is the responsibility of the `TriviaGame` object—the object that represents the game, not the `TriviaQuestion` object that represents the question. Therefore we do not include this responsibility for the `TriviaQuestion` class.

Table 2.1 captures the abstract view of our `TriviaQuestion` class. This type of view can be created during the design stage, used to help with scenario analysis, and later consulted to help determine implementation needs.

Next we consider the `TriviaGame` class. An object of this class represents an entire trivia game, including static information such as the list of questions and dynamic

---

4. Originally this was the approach we used. But as the design evolved it didn't feel right, so we had to back up and redesign. Sometimes during design you'll make poor decisions—be open to recognizing such situations, regrouping, and redesigning.

Table 2.1   *Abstract View of* `TriviaQuestion` *Class*

Class Name: TriviaQuestion
Primary Responsibility: Model a question for the trivia game problem
Responsibilities:
    Provide ways of setting the question information
    Provide ways of getting the question information
    Inform whether an attempted answer is correct

Table 2.2   *Abstract View of* `TriviaGame` *Class*

Class Name: TriviaGame
Primary Responsibility: Maintain a representation of a trivia game in a consistent state
Responsibilities:
    Provide ways of setting game information
    Provide ways of getting game information
    Keep track of whether a question has already been answered correctly
    Keep track of the number of remaining chances and the number of correct and incorrect answers
    Determine whether the game is over

information such as which questions have already been answered correctly and whether the game is over.

Of course, in addition to holding game information the class provides ways for a client to access and update the information as needed. We decide that it is the responsibility of the `TriviaGame` class to keep itself in a consistent state that represents the current status of the game. In contrast, it is the responsibility of the client program to send appropriate messages to the `TriviaGame` class as the game unfolds—for example, to indicate that the user has answered a question correctly or incorrectly.

Putting all of this together, we arrive at the abstract view of the `TriviaGame` class shown in Table 2.2.

Implementing the Support Classes

Next we continue with the detailed design of these classes.

The TriviaQuestion Class

An object of this class represents a single question. It will support attributes representing the category, the text of the question, and the set of acceptable answers. Both the category and text can be strings. But what about the set of answers?

We could hold the answers in an array, but we have a more suitable structure. What do you think it is? Consider what we need to do with the set of answers. We need to initialize the set by inserting the answers into it as we read them from the file. Also, we need to see whether a user's answer is in the set of acceptable answers. Thus, we need a class that supports insertion of strings and allows us to see whether a given string has been previously inserted. That does sound familiar, doesn't it? Our StringLog ADT is a perfect choice!

We have two StringLog ADT implementations: the `ArrayStringLog` and the `LinkedStringLog`. Which should we use to hold the trivia question answers? One of the key differences between the two implementations is that the former implements a bounded StringLog, while the latter implements an unbounded StringLog. Recall that our input text file includes, for each question, the number of its acceptable answers. Therefore we know exactly how many answers are associated with a trivia question as we are initializing the trivia game. We decide to use the bounded StringLog implementation, the `ArrayStringLog`.

The code for the `TriviaQuestion` class is shown below. It includes a constructor that takes arguments containing the category, the text of the question, and an integer indicating the maximum number of acceptable answers. The last argument allows it to instantiate the `StringLog` object to hold the answers. A `storeAnswer` method allows the client to repeatedly store the acceptable answers. The class also provides getter operations so a client can retrieve information about the question. In addition, it provides the `tryAnswer` method that identifies whether a given answer is correct.

The implementation of the class is very straightforward, thanks mostly to the fact that the StringLog ADT is doing all the hard work for us. Note that the `answers` object is declared to be of type `StringLogInterface` but instantiated as an object of class `ArrayStringLog`. We have <u>emphasized</u> the code that directly involves a StringLog.

```
//------------------------------------------------------------------
// TriviaQuestion.java        by Dale/Joyce/Weems        Chapter 2
//
// Provides trivia question objects.
//------------------------------------------------------------------

import ch02.stringLogs.*;

public class TriviaQuestion
{
  private String category;              // category of question
  private String question;              // the question
  private StringLogInterface answers;   // acceptable answers

  public TriviaQuestion(String category, String question,
                        int maxNumAnswers)
  // Precondition:  maxNumAnswers > 0
```

```
{
  this.category = category;
  this.question = question;
  answers = new ArrayStringLog("trivia", maxNumAnswers);
}

public String getCategory()
{
  return category;
}

public String getQuestion()
{
  return question;
}

public boolean tryAnswer(String answer)
{
  return answers.contains(answer);
}

public void storeAnswer(String answer)
// Precondition:   answers is not full
{
  answers.insert(answer);
}
}
```

Of course, before continuing with the design of other classes, the TriviaQuestion class should be thoroughly tested. A test driver for the class should allow a tester to create trivia question objects and exercise the various observer methods.

The TriviaGame Class
The code for the TriviaGame class is shown below. Most of the game information is initially set through the constructor. After instantiation, insertQuestion is used to add TriviaQuestion objects to the game. TriviaQuestion objects are added to the private questions array. Note that the class transforms the provided question numbers, which start at one, into array indexes, which start at zero.

The TriviaGame class also keeps track of which questions have been answered correctly. To support this task, we include a boolean array correct. Each time insertQuestion is called, the corresponding element of the correct array is set to false. We also provide a method, called correctAnswer, that the client program calls when a particular question has been answered correctly. When invoked, correctAnswer sets the corresponding element of the correct array to true, increments numCorrect, and decrements remainingChances. Similarly, an invocation of incorrectAnswer increments numIncorrect and decrements remainingChances.

```java
//-------------------------------------------------------------------------
// TriviaGame.java          by Dale/Joyce/Weems          Chapter 2
//
// Provides trivia game objects.
//-------------------------------------------------------------------------

public class TriviaGame
{
  private String quizName;
  private int maxNumQuestions;
  private int numChances;
  private int remainingChances;
  private int numCorrect = 0;
  private int numIncorrect = 0;
  private TriviaQuestion[] questions;  // the set of questions
  private boolean[] correct;           // true if corresponding
                                       // question answered correctly
  private int currNumQuestions = 0;

  public TriviaGame(String quizName, int maxNumQuestions, int numChances)
  // Precondition:  maxNumQuestions > 0 and numChances > 0
  {
    this.quizName = quizName;
    this.maxNumQuestions = maxNumQuestions;
    this.numChances = numChances;
    remainingChances = numChances;
    questions = new TriviaQuestion[maxNumQuestions];
    correct = new boolean[maxNumQuestions];
  }

  public String getQuizName()
  {
    return quizName;
  }

  public int getNumChances()
  {
    return numChances;
  }
```

```java
public int getRemainingChances()
{
  return remainingChances;
}

public int getNumCorrect()
{
  return numCorrect;
}

public int getNumIncorrect()
{
  return numIncorrect;
}

public int getCurrNumQuestions()
{
  return currNumQuestions;
}

public TriviaQuestion getTriviaQuestion(int questionNumber)
// Precondition:    0 < questionNumber <= currNumQuestions
{
  return questions[questionNumber - 1];
}

public boolean isAnswered(int questionNumber)
// Precondition:    0 < questionNumber <= currNumQuestions
{
  return correct[questionNumber - 1];
}

public boolean isOver()
// Returns true if this game is over, false otherwise.
{
  return (numCorrect == currNumQuestions)
          ||
          (remainingChances <= 0);
}

public void insertQuestion(TriviaQuestion question)
// Precondition:  currNumQuestions < maxNumQuestions
//
// Adds question to this TriviaGame.
```

```
  {
    questions[currNumQuestions] = question;
    correct[currNumQuestions] = false;
    currNumQuestions = currNumQuestions + 1;
  }

  public void correctAnswer(int questionNumber)
  // Preconditions: 0 < questionNumber < maxNumQuestions
  //
  // Updates game status to indicate that question number
  // questionNumber was answered correctly.
  {
    correct[questionNumber - 1] = true;
    numCorrect = numCorrect + 1;
    remainingChances = remainingChances - 1;
  }

  public void incorrectAnswer()
  // Updates game status to indicate that a question
  // was answered incorrectly.
  {
    numIncorrect = numIncorrect + 1;
    remainingChances = remainingChances - 1;
  }
}
```

The GetTriviaGame Class

How do we initialize our TriviaGame objects? Recall that the game information sits in the file game.txt. We need a way to transform that information into a game object. One approach is to allow a TriviaGame object to extract the information from the text file and initialize itself. However, so that our system is easily adaptable to alternative game sources in the future, we decide to decouple this task from the TriviaGame class. We create a separate class, GetTriviaGame, whose responsibility is to obtain trivia game information from a source and manufacture a TriviaGame object.

For this case study we handle only a single game source in our GetTriviaGame class, the text file described previously. However, the class could be expanded to handle alternative sources.

The code for the class appears below. It uses a Scanner object to read the information from the specified file. After constructing the TriviaGame object, it repeatedly scans the input source for each question, constructs a corresponding TriviaQuestion object, and inserts it into the trivia game.

Consider how abstraction has simplified our task. Although we know that ArrayStringLog objects are being created and used to support this system, all of the details of their use—in fact, their very existence—remain hidden from us. At this level we need not worry about them. We can concentrate on higher-level constructs, such as the trivia game itself.

```java
//------------------------------------------------------------------
// GetTriviaGame.java          by Dale/Joyce/Weems          Chapter 2
//
// Provides methods that obtain information about a trivia game,
// create and return TriviaGame objects.
//
// Note: Currently only option is to obtain a game from a text file,
// but other options could be added later.
//------------------------------------------------------------------

import java.util.*;
import java.io.*;

public class GetTriviaGame
{
  public static TriviaGame useTextFile(String textfile)
    throws IOException⁵
  // Precondition:  The textfile exists and contains a correctly
  //                formatted game.
  {
    TriviaGame game;

    String quizName;
    int numQuestions;
    int numChances;

    // for a specific trivia question
    TriviaQuestion tq;
    String category;
    String question;
    String answer;
    int numAnswers;

    FileReader fin = new FileReader(textfile);
    Scanner triviaIn = new Scanner(fin);
    String skip;          // skip end of line after reading integer

    // Scan in basic trivia quiz information and set variables.
    quizName = triviaIn.nextLine();
```

---

5. The `FileReader` constructor throws an `IOException` if its argument does not indicate an appropriate file.

```
numQuestions = triviaIn.nextInt();
numChances = triviaIn.nextInt();
skip = triviaIn.nextLine();

// Instantiate the TriviaGame.
game = new TriviaGame(quizName, numQuestions, numChances);

// Scan in and set up the questions and answers.
for (int i = 1; i <= numQuestions; i++)
{
  category = triviaIn.nextLine();
  question = triviaIn.nextLine();
  numAnswers = triviaIn.nextInt();
  skip = triviaIn.nextLine();
  tq = new TriviaQuestion(category, question, numAnswers);
  for (int j = 1; j <= numAnswers; j++)
  {
    answer = triviaIn.nextLine();
    tq.storeAnswer(answer);
  }
  game.insertQuestion(tq);
}

return game;
}
}
```

Some testing of the `TriviaGame` and `GetTriviaGame` classes should be performed using a simple test driver. However, because the functionality of the class is intimately tied to the functionality of our trivia game playing system, it can be most thoroughly tested after we have completed a working version of the entire system.

We have now developed classes to represent trivia questions and games. Although this wasn't trivial, it also wasn't difficult. We were helped by the availability of preexisting classes, most notably the `String` class from the Java library and the `ArrayStringLog` class developed earlier in this chapter. We took advantage of abstraction in that we just used these classes based on their external interfaces, without worrying about their internal details. As we move forward, we can use our two new classes, `TriviaQuestion` and `TriviaGame`, in the same way to simplify the rest of our job.

The Trivia Game Application

Our approach to program design in this textbook is to separate, as best we can, the user interface code from the rest of the program. We design classes, such as `TriviaQuestion` and `TriviaGame`, that use our ADTs to solve some type of problem. We then design an application class that interacts with the user, taking advantage of the previously defined classes. In our examples and case studies we present console-based application programs. For the case studies we also create GUI-based applications and provide a few screenshots of the program in action. The GUI-based application is always presented briefly in a feature section, at the conclusion of the case study, for those readers who are interested. Here we describe the console-based application in some detail.

The TriviaConsole Class

Our basic algorithm for the console approach is as follows:

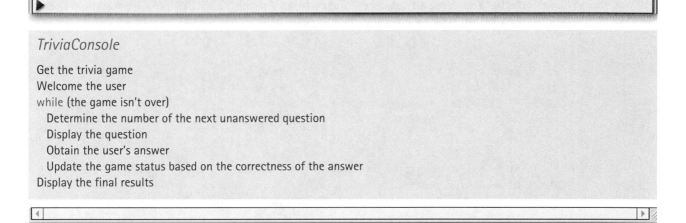

TriviaConsole

Get the trivia game
Welcome the user
while (the game isn't over)
  Determine the number of the next unanswered question
  Display the question
  Obtain the user's answer
  Update the game status based on the correctness of the answer
Display the final results

Implementing this algorithm turns out to be incredibly easy, thanks to the work we accomplished earlier. Let's look at it line by line:

- *Get the trivia game* The GetTriviaGame class provides this functionality.
- *Welcome the user* This is done with println statements. We access game information with the getter methods from the TriviaGame class and then print it.
- *While (the game isn't over)* We use the TriviaGame isOver method.
- *Determine the number of the next unanswered question* We know there is at least one unanswered question; otherwise the game would be over. We continually increment the current question number until we find a question that is unanswered. When incrementing the question number, we must remember to "wrap around" to question number 1 if we reach the end of the questions.
- *Display the question* We use the TriviaGame getTriviaQuestion method, followed by the TriviaQuestion getQuestion method to obtain the question, and then display it with a println statement.
- *Obtain the user's answer* We use the Scanner nextLine method.
- *Update the game status based on the correctness of the answer* We use the TriviaQuestion tryAnswer method to determine whether the provided answer is correct. Based on the result we report either "correct" or "incorrect" to the user and call the

appropriate method of the TriviaGame class, either correctAnswer or incorrectAnswer, to update the status of the game. Note that when we call correctAnswer we must pass it the number of the question, as the TriviaGame class is responsible for keeping track of which questions have been answered correctly.

- *Display the final results* We use some of the getter methods of TriviaGame and display the results.

The program can be tested by constructing a variety of trivia games and playing them. In particular, boundary conditions should be tested, such as a game with only a single question or a particular instance of a game when no questions are answered correctly. You have already seen a sample run of the TriviaConsole program earlier in this section. The code for the class appears below.

```
//-------------------------------------------------------------------
// TriviaConsole.java        by Dale/Joyce/Weems            Chapter 2
//
// Allows the user to play a trivia game.
// Uses a console interface.
//-------------------------------------------------------------------

import java.io.*;
import java.util.Scanner;

public class TriviaConsole
{
  public static void main(String[] args) throws IOException
  {
    Scanner conIn = new Scanner(System.in);

    TriviaGame game;     // the trivia game

    int questNum;        // current question number
    TriviaQuestion tq;   // current question
    String answer;       // answer provided by user

    // Initialize the game.
    game = GetTriviaGame.useTextFile("game.txt");

    // Greet the user.
    System.out.println("Welcome to the " + game.getQuizName()
                       + " trivia quiz.");
```

```
    System.out.print("You will have " + game.getNumChances()
                        + " chances ");
    System.out.println("to answer " + game.getCurrNumQuestions()
                        + " questions.\n");

    questNum = 0;
    while (!game.isOver())
    {
      // Get number of next unanswered question.
      do
        if (questNum == game.getCurrNumQuestions())
          questNum = 1;
        else
          questNum = questNum + 1;
      while (game.isAnswered(questNum));

      // Ask question and handle user's response.
      tq = game.getTriviaQuestion(questNum);
      System.out.println(tq.getCategory() + ": " + tq.getQuestion());
      answer = conIn.nextLine();
      if (tq.tryAnswer(answer))
      {
        System.out.println("Correct!\n");
        game.correctAnswer(questNum);
      }
      else
      {
        System.out.println("Incorrect\n");
        game.incorrectAnswer();
      }
    }

    System.out.println("\nGame Over");
    System.out.println("\nResults:");
    System.out.print("  Chances used: " + (game.getNumChances()
                                    - game.getRemainingChances()));
    System.out.println("   Number Correct: " + game.getNumCorrect());
    System.out.println("\nThank you.\n");
  }
}
```

The GUI Approach

As promised, we include here a GUI-based implementation of this case study. First is an example of the opening screen. For this game the user gets nine chances to answer seven questions. With our GUI approach, we allow the user to specify the category of the next question.

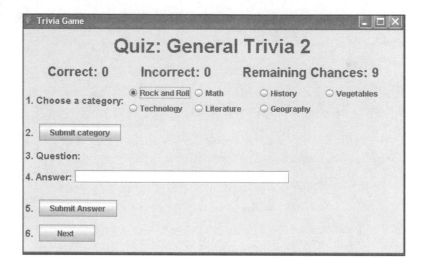

Here is a screen capture taken during the game. Note that when the user answers a category question correctly, that category is grayed out on the interface and can no longer be chosen.

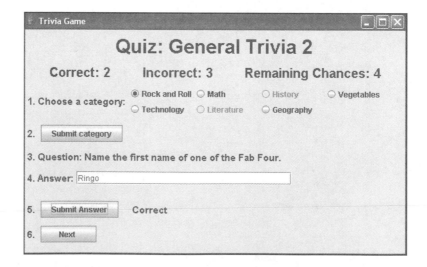

The GUI application is contained in the `TriviaGUI` class. We do not list the code for that class here, but you can find it with the rest of the textbook code on the website. A look at that code reveals a straightforward implementation:

- Panels, labels, buttons, and textfields are declared globally so that the various methods all have access to them.
- In separate sections of the class, the layouts of the panels are set, label fonts are defined and set, label text is set, buttons are initialized, constructs are added to eight main panels, and finally those panels are added, one after another using the box layout scheme, to the interface.
- A separate method, `setGameValues`, sets the appropriate labels and buttons so that the current state of the `TriviaGame` object is reflected in the interface.
- The remaining methods implement the actions to take when the user clicks an interface button.

Exercises

1. As the game is being played, the first "available" category button is always selected until the user clicks a different category. Explain where and how the program selects the first "available" button.
2. Explain why the value 1 is consistently added to the `selectedIndex` before it is passed to `TriviaGame` methods—for example, in the `submitButton` class's `actionPerformed` method in the statement

   ```
   game.correctAnswer(selectedIndex + 1);
   ```

3. [Class project] Create your own GUI for the trivia game system. Demonstrate your GUI to your class. Constructively criticize one another's approaches and award a prize to the overall best approach.

Case Study Summation

We have created a trivia game that is versatile enough to support alternative data sources, although we implemented only one of the approaches with the `useTextFile` method. We implemented two user-interaction approaches: one for console-based play and one that uses a GUI. Our development efforts were simplified through the use of abstraction and bottom-up refinement, as we used Java library classes such as `String` and `Scanner` as well as some classes of our own design: `ArrayStringLog`, `Trivia-Question`, and `TriviaGame`.

Summary

Data can be viewed from multiple perspectives. As we have seen, Java encapsulates the implementations of its predefined types and allows us to encapsulate our own class implementations.

In this chapter we specified a StringLog ADT and saw how to formalize our StringLog concept using the Java `interface` construct. We created two implementations of the StringLog ADT: one based on arrays and one based on references. To support our reference-based approach, we first learned how to create and manipulate a reference-based linked list. We also discussed software verification in general and we saw how we can test the implementation of an ADT in particular. Finally, we developed an application that administers a trivia quiz to a user, as an example of using the StringLog ADT.

When we use data abstraction to work with data structures such as a log of strings, there are three levels or views from which we can consider our structures. The logical or abstract level describes *what* the ADT provides to us. This view includes the domain of what the ADT represents and what it can do, as specified by its interface. At the application level, we decide *when* to use the ADT to solve problems. Finally, the implementation level provides the specific details of *how* we represent our structure and the code that supports the operations. The logical level acts as a contract between the application level "above" it and the implementation level "below" it.

What do we gain by separating these views of the data? First, we reduce complexity at the higher levels of the design, making the client program easier to understand. Second, we make the program more readily modifiable: The implementation can be changed without affecting the program that uses the data structure. Third, we develop software that is *reusable*: The structure and its accessing operations can be used by other programs, for completely different applications, as long as the correct interfaces are maintained.

Exercises

2.1   Abstraction

1. Describe four ways you use abstraction in your everyday life.
2. Explain what we mean by *data abstraction*.
3. What is data encapsulation? Explain the programming goal, "to protect our data abstraction through encapsulation."
4. Name three different perspectives from which we can view data. Using the logical data structure "a list of student academic records," give examples of how we might view the data from each perspective.
5. Describe one way that the implementation details can affect the applications that use an ADT, despite the use of data abstraction.

6. What is an abstract method?

7. What kinds of constructs can be declared in a Java interface?

8. What happens if a Java interface specifies a particular method signature, and a class that implements the interface provides a different signature for that method? For example, suppose interface `SampleInterface` is defined as

```
public interface SampleInterface
{
   public int sampleMethod();
}
```

and the class `SampleClass` is

```
public class SampleClass implements SampleInterface
{
   public boolean sampleMethod()
   {
      return true;
   }
}
```

9. True or False? Explain your answers.

   a. You can define constructors for a Java interface.

   b. Classes implement interfaces.

   c. Classes extend interfaces.

   d. A class that implements an interface can include methods that are not required by the interface.

   e. A class that implements an interface can leave out methods that are required by an interface.

   f. You can instantiate objects of an interface.

   g. An interface definition can include concrete methods.

10. Create Java classes `Circle` and `Rectangle` that implement the `FigureGeometry` interface defined in the "Java Interfaces" subsection. The `Circle` class should include a constructor that accepts a `float` value as an argument representing the radius of the circle. The `Rectangle` class should include a constructor that accepts two `float` values as arguments representing the length and width of the rectangle. Given access to your classes, the following application program should produce the output shown below:

```
public class UseFigs
{
   public static void main(String[] args)
   {
      Circle myCircle = new Circle(5);
```

```
      System.out.println(myCircle.perimeter());
      System.out.println(myCircle.area());

      Rectangle myRectangle = new Rectangle(7, 8);
      System.out.println(myRectangle.perimeter());
      System.out.println(myRectangle.area());
   }
}
```

Output:

31.400002

78.5

30.0

56.0

11. Consider an ADT called `SquareMatrix`. (The matrix can be represented by a two-dimensional array of integers with n rows and n columns.)

   a. Write the specification for the ADT as a Java interface. Include the following operations (parameters are already listed for the first two operations; for the remaining operations you must determine which parameters to use yourself, as part of the exercise):

   `MakeEmpty(n)`, which sets the first n rows and columns to zero

   `StoreValue(i, j, value)`, which stores `value` into the position at row i, column j

   `Add`, which adds two matrices together

   `Subtract`, which subtracts one matrix from another

   `Copy`, which copies one matrix into another

   b. Create a Java class that implements the interface. Assume a maximum size of 50 rows and columns.

   c. Create a small application that uses the class.

2.2 The StringLog ADT Specification

12. The StringLog interface represents a contract between the implementer of a StringLog ADT and the programmer who uses the ADT. List the main points of the contract.

13. `StringLogInterface` defines seven abstract methods. Describe four other operations that might be useful to export from a StringLog ADT.

14. Suppose instead of a log of strings we wish to have a log of variables of type `int`. Create an `IntLogInterface` file that is similar to the `StringLogInterface` file.

15. A friend of yours is having trouble instantiating an object of type StringLogInterface. His code includes the statement

```
StringLogInterface myLog = new StringLogInterface();
```

What do you tell your friend?

2.3 Array-Based StringLog ADT Implementation

16. Design and implement a constructor for `ArrayStringLog` that does not accept a name parameter. Note that the constructor should still assign a name to the StringLog it creates.

17. For each of the methods exported from `ArrayStringLog` (both constructors, insert, isFull, size, contains, clear, getName, toString) identify what type of operation it is (constructor, observer, or transformer) and its Big-O efficiency.

18. Describe the ramifications of each of the following changes to the code for `ArrayStringLog`:

a. Constructors: reverse the order of the two statements within one of the constructors

b. `insert`: reverse the order of its two statements

c. `isFull`: change `(lastIndex == (log.length - 1))` to `(lastIndex > log.length)`

d. `contains`: change `int location = 0` to `int location = 1`

e. `contains`: change `(location <= lastIndex)` to `(location < lastIndex)` in both places

19. Explain the difference between the "lazy" and "thorough" approaches to the `clear` operation for the `ArrayStringLog` class.

20. What is the functional difference between these two portions of code?

```
StringLogInterface log;
log = new ArrayStringLog("Exer 20");
log.insert("what is the difference");
log.clear();

StringLogInterface log;
log = new ArrayStringLog("Exer 20");
log.insert("what is the difference");
log = new ArrayStringLog(log.getName());
```

21. Design and code a new method to be exported from `ArrayStringLog` called `isEmpty`, with the following signature:

```
public boolean isEmpty()
```

The method returns `true` if the StringLog is empty and `false` otherwise.

For Exercises 22–25, use case-insensitive string comparisons.

22. Design and code a new method to be exported from `ArrayStringLog` called `howMany`, with the following signature:

    `public int howMany(String element)`

    The method returns an `int` value indicating how many times `element` occurs in the StringLog.

23. Design and code a new method to be exported from `ArrayStringLog` called `uniqInsert`, with the following signature:

    `public boolean uniqInsert(String element)`

    The method inserts `element` into the StringLog unless an identical string already exists in the StringLog, in which case it has no effect on the StringLog. If it does insert the string, it returns `true`; otherwise, it returns `false`.

24. Design and code a new method to be exported from `ArrayStringLog` called `delete`, with the following signature:

    `public boolean delete(String element)`

    The method deletes one occurrence of `element` from the StringLog, if possible. It returns `true` if a deletion is made and `false` otherwise.

25. Design and code a new method to be exported from `ArrayStringLog` called `deleteAll`, with the following signature:

    `public int deleteAll(String element)`

    The method deletes all occurrences of `element` from the StringLog. It returns the number of deletions that occurred.

26. Design and code a new method to be exported from `ArrayStringLog` called `smallest`, with the following signature:

    `public String smallest()`

    The method returns the smallest string in the StringLog. By "smallest," we mean in terms of the lexicographic ordering supported by the `String` class's `compareTo` method. As a precondition you should assume that the StringLog is not empty.

27. Create a new implementation of the StringLog ADT using the Java library's `ArrayList` class instead of an array to hold the strings. Call your new class `ALStringLog`. You may create a case-sensitive `contains` method.

28. In Exercise 14 you were asked to design and create an `IntLogInterface`.
    a. Using the same approaches developed in the text for the `ArrayStringLog`, create an `ArrayIntLog` class that implements the `IntLogInterface`.
    b. Create an application called `TestLuck` that repeatedly generates random numbers between 1 and 10,000 until it generates the same number twice. The program should report how many numbers it had to generate before it matched a

previously generated number. Your application should store generated numbers in an `ArrayIntLog` and use its `contains` method to test for matches.

c. Run your program 10 times and record the results. What is the average result? Is this about what you expected? Explain.

29. A `StringBag` ADT is similar to a `StringLog` ADT. Clients can insert strings into it, clear it, use its `toString`, and check to see if it is full. However, for a bag rather than checking to see if it contains a given string, the client can only remove a random string (as if the client is blindly reaching into a bag of candy and taking one piece). The `remove` method randomly selects a string from the bag, "deletes" it from the bag, and returns it to the client. The number of copies of a string that are put into the bag IS important—if three "lollypop" strings are inserted, then three "lollypop" strings can be removed. We can assume that `remove` is not called if the bag is empty—therefore a bag should include an `isEmpty` method that returns whether or not the bag is empty, for the client's use. For example, the client code here might produce the output shown below it:

```
StringBag b = new StringBag(5);
b.insert("Jeannine");
b.insert("Dora");
b.insert("Dora");
b.insert("Jo-Anne");
while (!b.isEmpty())
{
   System.out.println(b.remove());
}

   Dora
   Dora
   Jo-Anne
   Jeannine
```

Design a StringBag ADT, define it with a `StringBag` interface, and then implement it using a private array to hold the inserted strings. Design a test driver that shows that your `StringBag.java` class works correctly. Create a report that documents your design decisions, lists your interface, class, and driver code, shows the results of using the driver, and describes your experience with this project (what went well, what went wrong, etc.).

30. This is a three-part exercise:

a. Create a `Card` class that represents a typical playing card. It should hide two attributes: rank (1 through 13 representing Ace through King, respectively) and suit (1 through 4 representing clubs, diamonds, hearts, spades, respectively). A constructor accepts rank and suit as `int` parameters. Provide the standard getter methods and a `toString` method. For example, the client code here might produce the output shown below it:

```
Card c = new Card(1,4);
System.out.println(c.getSuit());
System.out.println(c);

   4
   Ace of Spades
```

Create a driver program that demonstrates the functionality of the `Card` class.

b. Design a `DeckofCards` class that represents a typical deck of 52 playing cards using a private array of `Card`. The constructor of the class should initialize the hidden array to contain the standard deck of cards. The class should implement the following interface

```
public interface DeckofCardsInterface
{
    public void shuffle();
    // shuffles the deck of cards and resets deal
    // to beginning of deck

    public int cardsLeft();
    // returns number of undealt cards

    public Card dealCard();
    // if all cards dealt, shuffles cards
    // returns next card

    public String toString();
    // returns a string representing the entire deck of cards
}
```

Design a test driver that shows that your `DeckofCards.java` class works correctly. Create a report that documents your design decisions, lists your interface, class, and driver code, shows the results of using the driver, and describes your experience with this project (what went well, what went wrong, etc.).

c. Design a card game that uses your deck of cards. Make the game as complicated as you like. A straightforward game is "in-between" where the player is dealt two cards and then must predict, possibly through betting, whether the next card dealt will be "in-between" the first two cards, based on its rank. Submit a report about your game.

2.4 Software Testing

31. Explain the difference between program verification and program validation.

32. Describe the similarities and differences among deskchecking, walk-throughs, and inspections.

33. The following program has two separate errors, each of which would cause an infinite loop. As a member of the inspection team, you could save the programmer a lot of testing time by finding the errors during the inspection. Can you help?

```
public class TryIncrement
{
  public static void main(String[] args) throws IOException
  {
    int count = 1;
    while(count < 10)
      System.out.println(" The number after " + count);  /* Now we will
      count = count + 1;                                     add 1 to count */
      output.println(" is " + count);
  }
}
```

34. When is it appropriate to start planning a program's testing?

   a. During design or even earlier

   b. While coding

   c. As soon as the coding is complete

35. Devise a black-box-based test plan to test the `increment` method of the `IncDate` class from Chapter 1.

36. A programmer has created a module `sameSign` that accepts two `int` arguments and returns `true` if they are both the same sign—that is, if they are both positive, both negative, or both zero. Otherwise, it returns `false`. Identify a reasonable set of test cases for this module.

37. A program is to read in a numeric score (0 to 100) as an integer and display an appropriate letter grade (A, B, C, D, or F).

   a. What is the functional domain of this program?

   b. Is exhaustive data coverage possible for this program?

38. Devise a black-box test plan for testing the `isFull` method of the `ArrayStringLog` class. Enumerate the test cases within the plan. Use the `ITDArrayStringLog` program to carry out the plan.

39. Design a noninteractive program that carries out the test plan you identified for Exercise 38. Call the program `TestIsFull`. It should run without input and report whether all test cases were passed successfully. If any test cases are not passed, it should report their test numbers.

2.5 Introduction to Linked Lists

40. What is a self-referential class?

41. What changes would need to be made to the `LLStringNode` class to allow it to support linked lists of integers instead of linked lists of strings?

42. Draw figures representing our abstract view of the structures created by each of the following code sequences.

   a.
   ```java
   LLStringNode node1 = new LLStringNode("alpha");
   LLStringNode node2 = new LLStringNode("beta");
   LLStringNode node3 = new LLStringNode("gamma");
   node1.setLink(node3);
   node2.setLink(node3);
   ```

   b.
   ```java
   LLStringNode node1 = new LLStringNode("alpha");
   LLStringNode node2 = new LLStringNode("beta");
   LLStringNode node3 = new LLStringNode("gamma");
   node1.setLink(node2);
   node2.setLink(node3);
   node3.setLink(node1);
   ```

   c.
   ```java
   LLStringNode node1 = new LLStringNode("alpha");
   LLStringNode node2 = new LLStringNode("beta");
   LLStringNode node3 = new LLStringNode("gamma");
   node1.setLink(node3);
   node2.setLink(node1.getLink());
   ```

   d.
   ```java
   LLStringNode nodeList = new LLStringNode("alpha");
   LLStringNode node = new LLStringNode("beta");
   node.setLink(nodeList);
   nodeList = node;
   LLStringNode node = new LLStringNode("gamma");
   node.setLink(nodeList);
   nodeList = node;
   ```

43. In this section we developed Java code for traversing a linked list. Here are several alternate, possibly flawed, approaches for traversal of the linked list accessed through `letters`. Critique each of them:

   a.
   ```java
   LLStringNode currNode = letters;
   while (currNode != null)
   {
      System.out.println(currNode.getInfo());
      currNode = currNode.getLink();
   }
   ```

   b.
   ```java
   LLStringNode currNode = letters;
   while (currNode != null)
   {
      currNode = currNode.getLink();
      System.out.println(currNode.getInfo());
   }
   ```

c.
```
LLStringNode currNode = letters;
while (currNode != null)
{
    System.out.println(currNode.getInfo());
    if currNode.getLink() != null
        currNode = currNode.getLink();
    else
        currNode = null;
}
```

2.6 Linked List StringLog ADT Implementation

44. What is the main difference, in terms of memory allocation, between using an array-based StringLog and a reference-based StringLog?

45. Compare our array- and reference-based StringLog implementations in terms of the Big-O efficiency of their methods.

46. Trace the following code segment and show its expected output. Normally when tracing application code that uses an ADT you need not worry about the details of the code implementation. But for this exercise we want you to "wear the hat" of the implementer and carry your tracing down to the implementation level so that you can see exactly what is returned by the `toString` methods. Explain why the two StringLogs are not displayed in exactly the same way.

```
StringLogInterface info1;
StringLogInterface info2;
info1 = new ArrayStringLog("Information 1");
info2 = new LinkedStringLog("Information 2");
info1.insert("Tom");
info2.insert("Tom");
info1.insert("Julie");
info2.insert("Julie");
System.out.println(info1.toString());
System.out.println(info2.toString());
```

47. Describe the ramifications of each of the following changes to the code for `LinkedStringLog`:

a. Constructor: reverse the order of the two statements

b. `insert`: reverse the order of the last two statements

c. `size`: change `int count = 0;` to `int count = 1;` and change `node = log;` to `node = log.getLink();`

d. `contains`: reverse the order of the two statements in the *else* statement

e. `toString`: change `int count = 0;` to `int count = 1;` and move the increment of the count variable from the first statement of the *while* loop to the last statement of the *while* loop

48. Design and code a new method to be exported from `LinkedStringLog` called `isEmpty`, with the following signature:

    ```
    public boolean isEmpty()
    ```

    The method returns `true` if the StringLog is empty and `false` otherwise.

For Exercises 49–50 use case-insensitive string comparisons.

49. Design and code a new method to be exported from `LinkedStringLog` called `howMany`, with the following signature:

    ```
    public int howMany(String element)
    ```

    The method returns an `int` value indicating how many times `element` occurs in the StringLog.

50. Design and code a new method to be exported from `LinkedStringLog` called `uniqInsert`, with the following signature:

    ```
    public boolean uniqInsert(String element)
    ```

    The method inserts `element` into the StringLog unless an identical string already exists in the StringLog, in which case it has no effect on the StringLog. If it does insert the string, it returns `true`; otherwise, it returns `false`.

51. Design and code a new method to be exported from `LinkedStringLog` called `smallest`, with the following signature:

    ```
    public String smallest()
    ```

    The method returns the smallest string in the StringLog. By "smallest," we mean in terms of the lexicographic ordering supported by the `String` class's `compareTo` method. As a precondition you should assume that the StringLog is not empty.

52. An alternative design for the `LinkedStringLog` class is to include an instance variable `size` that represents the number of strings contained in the StringLog.

    a. Describe the changes you would make to the `LinkedStringLog` implementation presented in the text as a result of this new approach.

    b. Create a new class, `LinkedStringLog2`, that uses this approach.

    c. Test the `LinkedStringLog2` class.

    d. How would this change affect an application program that uses a StringLog?

53. Design, code, and use an interactive test driver for the `LinkedStringLog` class. (*Hint:* You could proceed by making a copy of the `ITDArrayStringLog` class and then implementing the appropriate changes.)

54. Design a StringBag ADT (see Exercise 29), define it with a `StringBag` interface, and then implement it using a private linked list to hold the inserted strings. Design a test driver that shows that your `StringBag.java` class works correctly. Create a report that documents your design decisions, lists your interface, class, and driver code, shows the results of using the driver, and describes your experience with this project (what went well, what went wrong, etc.).

2.7 Software Design: Identification of Classes

55. Make a list of potential classes that you might design to help create the following programs:

    a. A screen saver that looks like an aquarium

    b. An interactive version of the card game Blackjack

    c. A traffic simulation for modeling the effects of new highway proposals

    d. A fantasy role-playing game based on the *Lord of the Rings* mythology

56. Explain how to use the nouns and verbs in a problem description to help identify candidate classes and methods for a design.

2.8 Case Study: A Trivia Game

57. Create your own trivia `game.txt` file containing a trivia game of your devising. Exchange files with classmates and see who does the best job answering trivia questions, using our trivia game application.

58. Explain why and how the StringLog ADT is used to support the `TriviaQuestion` class.

59. Describe how you would change the code of the `TriviaQuestion` class so that it uses the reference-based implementation of the StringLog ADT rather than the array-based implementation.

60. Describe the ramifications of each of the following changes to the code for the trivia game system:

    a. In the constructor for `TriviaQuestion` reverse the order of the first two statements.

    b. In the `insertQuestion` method of `TriviaGame` reverse the order of the first two statements.

    c. In the `isOver` method of `TriviaGame` change the `||` operation to `&&`.

61. Several of the methods of the `TriviaGame` class have preconditions. What happens if those preconditions are not met?

62. Describe what changes you would make to the `TriviaGame` class so that it constantly keeps track of the "game over" status in an instance variable, rather than calculating that status whenever the `isOver` method is called.

63. Change our trivia game playing system so that it keeps track, and reports to the user in an appropriate fashion, how many times the user attempts to answer each of the various questions.

The Stack ADT

Knowledge Goals

You should be able to
- describe a stack and its operations at a logical level
- list three options for making a collection ADT generally usable
- explain three ways to "handle" exceptional situations when defining an ADT
- explain the difference between the formal definitions of bounded and unbounded stacks
- describe an algorithm for determining whether grouping symbols (such as parentheses) within a string are balanced using a stack
- describe algorithms for implementing stack operations using an array
- describe algorithms for implementing stack operations using an `ArrayList`
- describe algorithms for implementing stack operations using a linked list
- use Big-O analysis to describe and compare the efficiency of algorithms for implementing stack operations using various data structuring mechanisms
- define inheritance of interfaces and multiple inheritance of interfaces
- describe an algorithm for evaluating postfix expressions, using a stack

Skill Goals

You should be able to
- use the Java generics mechanism when designing/implementing a collections ADT
- implement the Stack ADT using an array
- implement the Stack ADT using the Java library's `ArrayList` class
- implement the Stack ADT using a linked list
- draw diagrams showing the effect of stack operations for a particular implementation of a stack
- create a Java exception class
- throw Java exceptions from within an ADT and catch them within an application that uses the ADT
- use a Stack ADT as a component of an application
- evaluate a postfix expression "by hand"

In this chapter we investigate the stack, an important data structure. As we described in Chapter 1, a stack is a "last in, first out" structure. We study the stack as an ADT, looking at it from the logical, application, and implementation levels. At the logical level we formally define our Stack ADT using a Java `interface`. We discuss many applications of stacks and look in particular at how stacks are used to determine whether a set of grouping symbols is well formed and to support evaluation of mathematical expressions. We investigate the implementation of stacks using our two basic approaches: arrays and linked lists. We also investigate an approach using the Java library's `ArrayList` class.

This chapter will also expand your understanding of ADTs and your practical knowledge of the Java language. Early in the chapter we look at ways to make an ADT generally usable and options for addressing exceptional situations. Java topics in this chapter include a closer look at the exception mechanism and the introduction of generics and the inheritance of interfaces.

3.1   Stacks

Consider the items pictured in Figure 3.1. Although the objects are all different, each illustrates a common concept—the stack. At the logical level, a stack is an ordered group of homogeneous elements. The removal of existing elements and the addition of new ones can take place only at the top of the stack. For instance, if your favorite blue shirt is underneath a faded, old, red one in a stack of shirts, you first take the red shirt from the top of the stack. Then you remove the blue shirt, which is now at the top of the stack. The red shirt may then be put back on the top of the stack. Or it could be thrown away!

> **Stack**   A structure in which elements are added and removed from only one end; a "last in, first out" (LIFO) structure

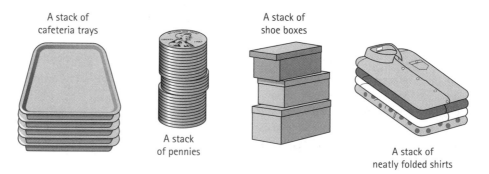

A stack of cafeteria trays

A stack of pennies

A stack of shoe boxes

A stack of neatly folded shirts

Figure 3.1 *Real-life stacks*

A stack may be considered "ordered" because elements occur in sequence according to how long they've been in the stack. The elements that have been in the stack the longest are at the bottom; the most recent are at the top. At any time, given any two elements in a stack, one is higher than the other. (For instance, the red shirt was higher in the stack than the blue shirt.)

Because elements are added and removed only from the top of the stack, the last element to be added is the first to be removed. There is a handy mnemonic to help you remember this rule of stack behavior: A stack is a LIFO ("last in, first out") structure.

The accessing protocol for a stack is summarized as follows: Both to retrieve elements and to store new elements, access only the top of the stack.

Operations on Stacks

The logical picture of the structure is only half the definition of an abstract data type. The other half is a set of operations that allows the user to access and manipulate the elements stored in the structure. What operations do we need to use a stack?

When we begin using a stack, it should be empty. Thus we assume that our stack has at least one class constructor that sets it to the empty state.

The operation that adds an element to the top of a stack is usually called *push*, and the operation that removes the top element off the stack is referred to as *pop*. Classically, the *pop* operation has both removed the top element of the stack and returned the top element to the client program that invoked *pop*. More recently, programmers have been defining two separate operations to perform these actions because operations that combine observations and transformation can result in confusing programs.

We follow modern convention and define a *pop* operation that removes the top element from a stack and a *top* operation that returns the top element of a stack.[1] Our *push* and *pop* operations are strictly transformers, and our *top* operation is strictly an observer. Figure 3.2 shows how a stack, envisioned as a stack of building blocks, is modified by several *push* and *pop* operations.

Using Stacks

Stacks are very useful ADTs, especially in the field of computing system software. They are most often used in situations in which we must process nested components. For example, programming language systems typically use a stack to keep track of operation calls. The main program calls operation A, which in turn calls operation B, which in turn calls operation C. When C finishes, control returns to B; when B finishes, control returns to A; and so on. The call and return sequence is essentially a last in, first out sequence, so a stack is the perfect structure for tracking it, as shown in Figure 3.3.

---

1. Another common approach is to define a pop operation in the classical way—that is, it removes and returns the top element—and to define another operation, often called peek, that simply returns the top element.

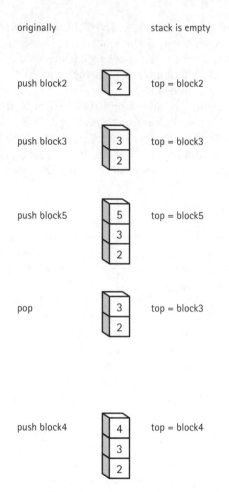

originally		stack is empty
push block2		top = block2
push block3		top = block3
push block5		top = block5
pop		top = block3
push block4		top = block4

Figure 3.2 *The effects of* `push` *and* `pop` *operations*

You may have encountered a case where a Java exception has produced an error message that mentions "a system stack trace." This trace shows the nested sequence of method calls that ultimately led to the exception being thrown. These calls were saved on the "system stack."

Compilers use stacks to analyze language statements. A program often consists of nested components—for example, a *for* loop containing an *if-then* statement that contains a *while* loop. As a compiler is working through such nested constructs, it "saves" information about what it is currently working on in a stack; when it finishes its work on the innermost construct, it can "retrieve" its previous status from the stack and pick up where it left off.

	Stack contains
main running	Top: <empty>

	Stack contains
main calls method A	
method A running	Top: main

	Stack contains
method A calls method B	
method B running	Top: A
	main

	Stack contains
method B calls method C	
method C running	Top: B
	A
	main

	Stack contains
method C returns	
method B running	Top: A
	main

	Stack contains
method B returns	
method A running	Top: main

	Stack contains
method A returns	
main running	Top: <empty>

Figure 3.3 *Call-return stack*

Similarly, an operating system sometimes saves information about the current executing process on a stack so that it can work on a higher-priority, interrupting process. If that process is interrupted by an even higher-priority process, its information can also be pushed on the process stack. When the operating system finishes its work on the highest-priority process, it retrieves the information about the most recently stacked process and continues working on it.

3.2 Collection Elements

A stack is an example of a collection ADT. A stack *collects* together elements for future use, while maintaining a first in, last out ordering among the elements. Before continuing our coverage of stacks, we examine the question of which types of elements can be stored in a collection. We look at several variations that are possible when structuring collections of elements and describe the approaches we adopt for use throughout this text. It is important to understand the various options, along with their strengths and weaknesses, so that you can make informed decisions about which approach to use based on your particular situation.

> **Collection** An object that holds other objects. Typically we are interested in inserting, removing, and iterating through the contents of a collection.

Generally Usable Collections

The StringLog ADT we constructed in Chapter 2 is also a collection ADT. It was constrained to holding data of one specific type—namely, strings. Based on the approach used in that chapter, if we wanted to have a log of something else—say, integers or programmer-defined bank account objects—we would have to design and code additional ADTs. (See Figure 3.4a.)

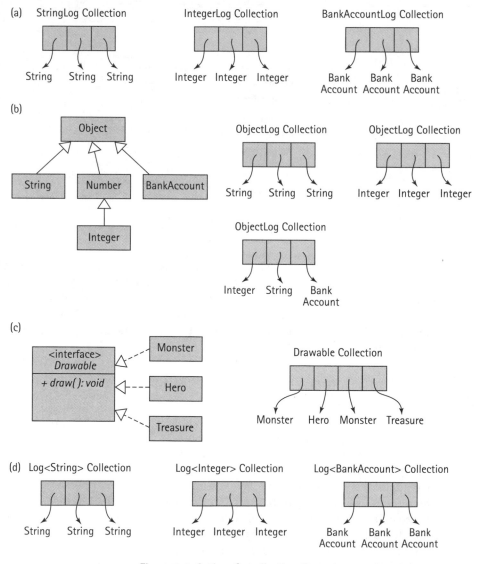

Figure 3.4 *Options for collection elements*

Although the StringLog ADT is handy, a Log ADT would be much more useful if it could hold any kind of information. In Chapter 2 our goal was to present basic ADT concepts using a simple example, so we were content to create an ADT restricted to a single type of element. In this section we present several ways to design our collections so that they hold different types of information, making them more generally usable.

Collections of Class Object

One approach to creating generally usable collections is to have the collection ADT hold variables of class `Object`. Because all Java classes ultimately inherit from `Object`, such an ADT is able to hold a variable of any class. (See Figure 3.4b.) This approach works well, especially when the elements of the collection don't have any special properties—for example, if the elements don't have to be sorted.

Although this approach is simple, it is not without problems. One drawback: Whenever an element is removed from the collection, it can be referenced only as an `Object`. If you intend to use it as something else, you must cast it into the type that you intend to use. For example, suppose you place a string into a collection and then retrieve it. To use the retrieved object as a `String` object you must cast it, as <u>emphasized</u> here:

```
collection.push("E. E. Cummings");      // push string on a stack
String poet = (String) collection.top(); // cast top to String
System.out.println(poet.toLowerCase());  // use the string
```

Without the cast you will get a compile error, because Java is a strongly typed language and will not allow you to assign a variable of type `Object` to a variable of type `String`. The `cast` operation tells the compiler that you, the programmer, are guaranteeing that the `Object` is, indeed, a `String`.

The `Object` approach works by converting every class of object into class `Object` as it is stored in the collection. Users of the collection must remember what kinds of objects have been stored in it, and then explicitly cast those objects back into their original classes when they are removed from the collection.

As shown by the third `ObjectLog` collection in Figure 3.4(b), this approach allows a program to mix the types of elements in a single collection. That collection holds an `Integer`, a `String`, and a `BankAccount`. In general, such mixing is *not* considered to be a good idea, and it should be used only in rare cases under careful control. Its use can easily lead to a program that retrieves one type of object—say, an `Integer`—and tries to cast it as another type of object—say, a `String`. This, of course, is an error.

Collections of a Class That Implements a Particular Interface

Sometimes we may want to ensure that all of the objects in a collection support a particular operation or set of operations. As an example, suppose the objects represent elements of a video game. Many different types of elements exist, such as monsters, heroes, and treasure. When an element is removed from the collection it is drawn on the screen, using a `draw` operation. In this case, we would like to ensure that only objects that support the `draw` operation can be placed in the collection.

Recall from Chapter 2 that a Java interface can include only abstract methods—that is, methods without bodies. Once an interface is defined we can create classes that implement the interface by supplying the missing method bodies. For our video game example we could create an interface with an abstract `draw` method. A good name for the interface might be `Drawable`, as classes that implement this interface provide objects that can be drawn. The various types of video game elements that can be drawn on the screen should all be defined as implementing the `Drawable` interface.

Now we can ensure that the elements in our example collection are all "legal" by designing it as a collection of `Drawable` objects—in other words, objects that implement the `Drawable` interface. In this way we ensure that only objects that support a `draw` operation are allowed in the collection. (See Figure 3.4c.)

Later in the text we present two data structures, the sorted list and the binary search tree, whose elements are organized in a sorted order. Every element that is inserted into one of these collections must provide an operation that allows us to compare it to other objects in its class. That is, objects inserted into the collection must support a `compareTo` operation. To enforce this requirement we define our sorted list and binary search ADTs as collections of `Comparable` objects. The `Comparable` interface is defined within the `java.lang` package and includes exactly one abstract method: `compareTo`.

Generic Collections

Beginning with version 5.0, the Java language supports generics. Generics allow us to define a set of operations that manipulate objects of a particular class, without specifying the class of the objects being manipulated until a later time. Generics represented one of the most significant changes to the language in this version of Java.

In a nutshell, generics are *parameterized types.* Of course, you are already familiar with the concept of a parameter. For example, in our `StringLog` class the `insert` method has a `String` parameter named `element`. When we invoke that method we must pass it a `String` argument, such as "Elvis":

```
log.insert("Elvis");
```

Generics allow us to pass type names such as `Integer`, `String`, or `BankAccount` as arguments. Notice the subtle difference—with generics we actually pass a *type*, for example, `String`, instead of a *value* of a particular type, for example, "Elvis."

With this capability, we can define a collection class, such as `Log`, as containing elements of a type T, where T is a placeholder for the name of a type. We indicate the name of the placeholder (convention tells us to use T) within braces; that is, <T>, in the header of the class.

```
public class Log<T>
{
  private T[] log;              // array that holds objects of class T
```

```
private int lastIndex = -1; // index of last T in the array
...
```

In a subsequent application we can supply the actual type, such as `Integer`, `String`, or `BankAccount`, when the collection is instantiated.

```
Log<Integer> numbers;
Log<BankAccount> investments;
Log<String> answers;
```

If we pass `BankAccount` as the argument, we get a `BankAccount` log; if we pass `String`, we get a `String` log; and so on.

In place of passing a type when instantiating a generic collection we have the option of passing a java `interface`, for example

```
Log<Drawable> avatars;
```

As discussed in the previous subsection, this could then allow us to include any object that implements the interface in the collection—the `avatars` log could contain humans, elves, and ogres, as long as each of their respective classes implements the `Drawable` interface.

Generics provide the flexibility to design generally usable collections yet retain the benefit of Java's strong type checking. They are an excellent solution and we will use this approach throughout most of the remainder of this textbook.

3.3 Exceptional Situations

There is one more topic to cover before formally specifying our Stack ADT. In this section we take a look at various methods of handling exceptional situations that might arise when running a program. For example, what should happen if a stack is empty and the *pop* operation is invoked? There is nothing to pop! As part of formally specifying a stack, or any ADT, we must determine how such exceptional situations will be addressed.

Handling Exceptional Situations

Many different types of exceptional situations can occur when a program is running. Exceptional situations alter the flow of control of the program, sometimes resulting in a crash. Some examples follow:

> **Exceptional situation** Associated with an unusual, sometimes unpredictable event, detectable by software or hardware, which requires special processing. The event may or may not be erroneous.

- A user enters an input value of the wrong type.
- While reading information from a file, the end of the file is reached.

- A user presses a control key combination.
- An illegal mathematical operation occurs, such as divide-by-zero.
- An impossible operation is requested of an ADT, such as an attempt to *pop* an empty stack.

Working with these kinds of exceptional situations begins at the design phase, when several questions arise: What are the unusual situations that the program should recognize? Where in the program can the situations be detected? How should the situations be handled if they occur?

Java (along with some other languages) provides built-in mechanisms to manage exceptional situations. In Java an exceptional situation is referred to simply as an *exception*. The Java exception mechanism has three major parts:

- *Defining the exception*   Usually as a subclass of Java's Exception class
- *Generating (raising) the exception*   By recognizing the exceptional situation and then using Java's throw statement to "announce" that the exception has occurred
- *Handling the exception*   Using Java's try-catch statement to discover that an exception has been thrown and then take the appropriate action

Java also includes numerous predefined built-in exceptions that are raised automatically under certain situations.

From this point on we use the Java term "exception," instead of the more general phrase *exceptional situation*. Here are some general guidelines for using exceptions:

- An exception may be handled anywhere in the software hierarchy—from the place in the program module where it is first detected through the top level of the program.
- Unhandled built-in exceptions carry the penalty of program termination.
- Where in an application an exception is handled is a design decision; however, exceptions should always be handled at a level that knows what the exception means.
- An exception need not be fatal.
- For nonfatal exceptions, the thread of execution can continue from various points in the program, but execution should continue from the lowest level that can recover from the exception.

Exceptions and ADTs: An Example

When creating our own ADTs we identify exceptions that require special processing. If the special processing is application dependent, we use the Java exception mechanism to throw the problem out of the ADT and force the application programmers to handle it. Conversely, if the exception handling can be hidden within the ADT, then there is no need to burden the application programmers with the task.

For an example of an exception created to support a programmer-defined ADT, let's return to our Date class from Chapter 1.

```
public class Date
{
  protected int year;
  protected int month;
  protected int day;
  public static final int MINYEAR = 1583;

  public Date(int newMonth, int newDay, int newYear)
  {
    month = newMonth;
    day = newDay;
    year = newYear;
  }

  public int getYear()
  {
    return year;
  }

  public int getMonth()
  {
    return month;
  }

  public int getDay()
  {
    return day;
  }

  public int lilian()
  {
    // Returns the Lilian Day Number of this date.
    // Algorithm goes here.
    // See "Lilian Day Numbers" feature, Chapter 1, for details.
  }

  public String toString()
  {
    return(month + "/" + day + "/" + year);
  }
}
```

As currently defined, an application could invoke the Date constructor with an impossible date—for example, 25/15/2000. We can avoid the creation of such dates by checking the legality of the month argument passed to the constructor. But what should our constructor do if it discovers an illegal argument? Here are some options:

- Write a warning message to the output stream. This is not a good option because within the `Date` ADT we don't really know which output stream is used by the application.
- Instantiate the new `Date` object to some default date, perhaps 0/0/0. The problem with this approach is that the application program may just continue processing as if nothing is wrong and produce erroneous results. In general it is better for a program to "bomb" than to produce erroneous results that may be used to make bad decisions.
- Throw an exception. This way, normal processing is interrupted and the constructor does not have to return a new object; instead, the application program is forced to acknowledge the problem (catch the exception) and either handle it or throw it to the next level.

Once we have decided to handle the situation with an exception, we must decide whether to use one of the Java library's predefined exceptions or to create one of our own. A study of the library in this case reveals a candidate exception called `DataFormatException`, to be used to signal data format errors. We could use that exception but we decide it doesn't really fit: It's not the format of the data that is the problem in this case, it's the value of the data.

We decide to create our own exception, `DateOutOfBounds`. We could call it "MonthOutOfBounds" but we decide that we want to use the exception to indicate other potential problems with dates, not just problems with the month value.

We create our `DateOutOfBounds` exception by extending the library's `Exception` class. It is customary when creating your own exceptions to define two constructors, mirroring the two constructors of the `Exception` class. In fact, the easiest thing to do is define the constructors so that they just call the corresponding constructors of the superclass:

```
public class DateOutOfBoundsException extends Exception
{
  public DateOutOfBoundsException()
  {
    super();
  }
  public DateOutOfBoundsException(String message)
  {
    super(message);
  }
}
```

The first constructor creates an exception without an associated message. The second constructor creates an exception with a message equal to the string argument passed to the constructor.

Next we need to consider where, within our Date ADT, we throw the exception. All places within our ADT where a date value is created or changed should be examined to see if the resultant value could be an illegal date. If so, we should create an object of our exception class with an appropriate message and throw the exception.

Here is how we might write a Date constructor to check for legal months and years:

```java
public Date(int newMonth, int newDay, int newYear)
                            throws DateOutOfBoundsException
{
  if ((newMonth <= 0) || (newMonth > 12))
    throw new DateOutOfBoundsException("month " + newMonth + "out of range");
  else
    month = newMonth;

  day = newDay;

  if (newYear < MINYEAR)
    throw new DateOutOfBoundsException("year " + newYear + " is too early");
  else
    year = newYear;
}
```

Notice that the message defined for each throw statement pertains to the problem discovered at that point in the code. This should help the application program that is handling the exception, or at least provide pertinent information to the user of the program if the exception is propagated all the way to the user level.

Finally, let's see how an application program might use the revised Date class. Consider a program called UseDates that prompts the user for a month, day, and year and creates a Date object based on the user's responses. In the following code we hide the details of how the prompt and response are handled, by replacing those statements with comments. This way we can emphasize the code related to our current discussion:

```java
public class UseDates
{
  public static void main(String[] args)
                            throws DateOutOfBoundsException
  {
    Date theDate;

    // Program prompts user for a date.
    // M is set equal to user's month.
    // D is set equal to user's day.
    // Y is set equal to user's year.
```

```
      theDate = new Date(M, D, Y);

    // Program continues ...
  }
}
```

When this program runs, if the user responds with an illegal value—for example, a year of 1051—the `DateOutOfBoundsException` is thrown by the `Date` constructor; because it is not caught and handled within the program, it is thrown to the interpreter as indicated by the emphasized `throws` clause. The interpreter stops the program and displays a message like this:

```
Exception in thread "main" DateOutOfBoundsException: year 1051 is too
early
        at Date.<init>(Date.java:18)
        at UseDates.main(UseDates.java:57)
```

The interpreter's message includes the name and message string of the exception as well as a trace of calls leading up to the exception (the system stack trace mentioned in Section 3.1.)

Alternatively, the `UseDates` class could catch and handle the exception itself, rather than throwing it to the interpreter. The application could ask for a new date when the exception occurs. Here is how `UseDates` can be written to do this (again we ignore user interface details and emphasize code related to exceptions):

```
public class UseDates
{
  public static void main(String[] args)
  {
    Date theDate;
    boolean DateOK = false;

    while (!DateOK)
    {
      // Program prompts user for a date.
      // M is set equal to user's month.
      // D is set equal to user's day.
      // Y is set equal to user's year.
      try
      {
        theDate = new Date(M, D, Y);
        DateOK = true;
      }
      catch(DateOutOfBoundsException DateOBExcept)
      {
```

```
      output.println(DateOBExcept.getMessage());
   }
  }


  // Program continues ...
 }
}
```

If the `new` statement executes without any trouble, meaning the `Date` constructor did not throw an exception, then the `DateOK` variable is set to `true` and the *while* loop terminates. However, if the `DateOutOfBounds` exception is thrown by the `Date` constructor, it is caught by the `catch` statement. This, in turn, prints the message from the exception and the `while` loop is reexecuted, again prompting the user for a date. The program repeatedly prompts for date information until it is given a legal date. Notice that the `main` method no longer throws `DateOutOfBoundsException`, as it handles the exception itself.

One last important note about exceptions. The `java.lang.RunTimeException` class is treated uniquely by the Java environment. Exceptions of this class are thrown when a standard run-time program error occurs. Examples of run-time errors include division-by-zero and array-index-out-of-bounds. Because run-time exceptions can happen in virtually any method or segment of code, we are not required to explicitly handle these exceptions. Otherwise, our programs would become unreadable because of so many `try`, `catch`, and `throw` statements. These errors are classified as unchecked exceptions. The exceptions we create later in this chapter to support our Stack ADT are extensions of the Java `RunTimeException` class and, therefore, are unchecked.

> **Unchecked exception** An exception of the `RunTimeException` class. It does not have to be explicitly handled by the method within which it might be raised.

Error Situations and ADTs

When dealing with error situations within our ADT methods, we have several options.

First, we can detect and handle the error within the method itself. This is the best approach if the error can be handled internally and if it does not greatly complicate the design. For example, if an illegal value is passed to a method, we may be able to replace it with a useful default value. Suppose we have a method used to set the employee discount for an online store. Passing it a negative number might be construed as an error—it might be reasonable in such a case to set the value to zero and continue processing. When handling a problem internally in this way, it may be possible to pass information about the situation from the method to the caller through a return value. For example, we could design a *push* operation for a stack that returns a `boolean` value of `true` if the operation is successful and the argument is pushed onto the stack, and a value of `false` if the operation fails for some reason (e.g., because the stack is full). As another example, consider a *top* operation that returns the object from the top of the stack. Instead of terminating the program if the stack is empty, the operation could return the value `null`, indicating that the operation "failed." In these examples the caller is responsible for checking the returned value and acting appropriately if failure is indicated.

Second, we can detect the error within the method, throw an exception related to the error, and thereby force the calling method to deal with the exception. If it is not clear how to handle a particular error situation, this approach might be best—throw it to a level where it can be handled. For example, if an application passes a nonsensical date to the `Date` class constructor, it is best to throw an exception—the constructor doesn't "know" what the ramifications of the impossible date are, but the application should. Another example is when an application attempts to *pop* something from an empty stack. The Stack ADT doesn't "know" what this erroneous situation means, but the application should. Of course, if the caller does not catch and handle the thrown exception, it will continue to be thrown until it is either handled or thrown all the way to the interpreter, causing program termination.

Third, we can ignore the error situation. Recall the "programming by contract" discussion related to preconditions in Chapter 2. With this approach, if the preconditions of a method are not met, the method is not responsible for the consequences. For example, suppose a method requires a prime number as an argument. If this is a precondition, then the method assumes that the argument is prime—it does not test the primality of the number. If the number is not prime, then the results are undefined. It is the responsibility of the calling code to ensure that the precondition is met. See the feature "Programming by Contract" for more information.

When we define an ADT, we partition error situations into three sets: those to be handled internally, those to be thrown back to the calling process, and those that are assumed not to occur. We document this third approach in the preconditions of the appropriate methods. Our goal is to strike a balance between the complexity required to handle every error situation internally and the lack of safety resulting from handling everything by contract.

Programming by Contract

Let's revisit briefly our "programming by contract" approach. We want to emphasize the way we handle method preconditions, because some programmers use a different methodology: They test preconditions within a method and throw exceptions when preconditions aren't met. They treat unmet preconditions as errors. We don't.

We don't believe in unmet preconditions. If a condition might not be true when a method is called, then it shouldn't be listed as a precondition. It should be listed as an error condition. The point of a precondition is to simplify our code and make it more efficient, not to complicate things with extra levels of unneeded testing.

Why is our approach more efficient? Preconditions are always supposed to be true. Thus testing them each time a method is called is a waste of time.

Consider the example of the method that requires a prime number as an argument. Suppose `methodA` obtains a prime number and passes it to `methodB`. It guarantees that the number is prime. If we require `methodB` to test the primality of the number (a nontrivial task), we are unnecessarily complicating `methodB` and slowing down our program. Instead, we simply state within our preconditions that the argument is prime and no longer worry about it:

```
public void methodB(int primenumber)
// Precondition:   primenumber is prime.
. . .
```

On the other hand, if we cannot assume that the number passed to `methodB` is prime, then we document this possibility as a potential error condition, test for it, and handle it if needed:

```
public void methodB(int primenumber) throws NotPrimeException
// Throws NotPrimeException if primenumber is not prime,
// otherwise ...
```

For any specific condition we use one or the other of these approaches, but not both!

3.4 Formal Specification

In this section we use the Java interface construct to create a formal specification of our Stack ADT. To specify any collection ADT we must determine which types of elements it will hold, which operations it will export, and how exceptional situations will be handled. Some of these decisions have already been documented.

Recall from Section 3.1 that a stack is a "last in, first out" structure, with three primary operations:

- `push` Adds an element to the top of the stack.
- `pop` Removes the top element off the stack.
- `top` Returns the top element of a stack.

In addition to these operations we need a constructor that creates an empty stack.

As noted in Section 3.2, our Stack ADT will be a generic stack. The class of elements that a stack stores will be specified by the client code at the time the stack is instantiated. Following the common Java coding convention, we use <T> to represent the class of objects stored in our stack.

Now we look at exceptional situations. As you'll see, this exploration can lead to the identification of additional operations.

Exceptional Situations

Are there any exceptional situations that require handling? The constructor simply initializes a new empty stack. This action, in itself, cannot cause an error—assuming, of course, that it is coded correctly.

The remaining operations all present potential problem situations. The descriptions of the `pop` and `top` operations both refer to manipulating the "top element of the stack." But what if the stack is empty? Then there is no top element to manipulate. We know that there are three ways to deal with this scenario. Can we handle the problem within the methods themselves? Should we detect the situation and throw an exception? Is it reasonable to state, as a precondition, that the stack be nonempty?

How might the problem be handled within the methods themselves? Given that the `pop` method is strictly a transformer, it could simply do nothing when it is invoked on an empty stack. In effect, it could perform a vacuous transformation. For `top`, which must return an `Object` reference, the response might be to return `null`. For some applications this might be a reasonable approach, but for most cases it would merely complicate the application code.

What if we state a precondition that a stack must not be empty before calling `top` or `pop`? Then we do not have to worry about handling the situation within the ADT. Of course, we can't expect every application that uses our stack to keep track of whether it is empty; that should be the responsibility of the Stack ADT itself. To address this requirement we define an observer called `isEmpty`, which returns a `boolean` value of `true` if the stack is empty. Then the application can prevent misuse of the `pop` and `top` operations.

```
if !myStack.isEmpty()
  myObject = myStack.top();
```

This approach appears promising but can place an unwanted burden on the application. If an application must perform a guarding test before every stack operation, its code might become inefficient and difficult to read.

It is also a good idea to provide an exception related to accessing an empty stack. Consider the situation where a large number of stack calls take place within a section of code. If we define an exception—for example, `StackUnderflowException`—to be thrown by both `pop` and `top` if they are called when the stack is empty, then such a section of code could be surrounded by a single *try-catch* statement, rather than use multiple calls to the `isEmpty` operation.

We decide to use this last approach. That is, we define a `StackUnderflowException`, to be thrown by both `pop` and `top` if they are called when the stack is empty. To provide flexibility to the application programmer, we also include the `isEmpty` operation in our ADT. Now the application programmer can decide either to prevent popping or accessing an empty stack by using the `isEmpty` operation as a guard or, as shown next, to "try" the operations on the stack and "catch and handle" the raised exception, if the stack is empty.

```
try
{
  myObject = myStack.top();
  myStack.pop();
  myOtherObject = myStack.top();
  myStack.pop();
}
catch (StackUnderflowException underflow)
{
  System.out.println("There was a problem in the ABC routine.");
  System.out.println("Please inform System Control.");
  System.out.println("Exception: " + underflow.getMessage());
  System.exit(1);
}
```

We define `StackUnderflowException` to extend the Java `RuntimeException`, as it represents a situation that a programmer can avoid by using the stack properly. The `RuntimeException` class is typically used in such situations. Recall that such exceptions are unchecked; in other words, they do not have to be explicitly caught by a program.

Here is the code for our `StackUnderflowException` class. Note that it includes a `package` statement. This class is the first of several classes and interfaces we develop related to the stack data structure. We collect all of these together into a single package called `ch03.stacks`.[2]

```
package ch03.stacks;

public class StackUnderflowException extends RuntimeException
{
  public StackUnderflowException()
  {
    super();
  }

  public StackUnderflowException(String message)
  {
    super(message);
  }
}
```

2. The files can be found in the `stacks` subdirectory of the `ch03` subdirectory of the `bookFiles` directory that contains the program files associated with the textbook.

Because `StackUnderflowException` is an unchecked exception, if it is raised and not caught it is eventually thrown to the run-time environment, which displays an error message and halts. An example of such a message follows:

Exception in thread "main" ch03.stacks.StackUnderflowException: Top attempted on an empty stack.

at ch03.stacks.ArrayStack.top(ArrayStack.java:78)

at MyTestStack.main(MyTestStack.java:25)

On the other hand, if the programmer explicitly catches the exception, as we showed in the `try-catch` example, the error message can be tailored more closely to the specific problem:

There was a problem in the ABC routine.

Please inform System Control.

Exception: top attempted on an empty stack.

A consideration of the `push` operation reveals another potential problem: What if we try to push something onto a stack and there is no room for it? In an abstract sense, a stack is never conceptually "full." Sometimes, however, it is useful to specify an upper bound on the size of a stack. We might know that memory is in short supply or problem-related constraints may dictate a limit on the number of `push` operations that can occur without corresponding `pop` operations.

We can address this problem in a way analogous to the stack underflow problem. First, we provide an additional `boolean` observer operation called `isFull`, which returns `true` if the stack is full. The application programmer can use this operation to prevent misuse of the `push` operation. Second, we define `StackOverflowException`, which is thrown by the `push` operation if it is called when the stack is full. Here is the code for the `StackOverflowException` class:

```
package ch03.stacks;

public class StackOverflowException extends RuntimeException
{
  public StackOverflowException()
  {
    super();
  }

  public StackOverflowException(String message)
  {
    super(message);
  }
}
```

As with the underflow situation, the application programmer can decide either to prevent pushing information onto a full stack through use of the `isFull` operation or to "try" the operation on a stack and "catch and handle" any raised exception. The `StackOverflowException` is also an unchecked exception.

The Interfaces

We are now ready to formally specify our Stack ADT. As we planned, we use the Java `interface` construct. But how do we handle the fact that sometimes we may want to use a stack with an upper bound on its size and sometimes we want an unbounded stack?

We were faced with this same situation in developing our `StringLog` ADT in Chapter 2. In that case we decided to include the `isFull` operation as part of the single interface, even though its existence did not make sense for some implementations of the `StringLog`. Recall that in the linked-list-based implementation, `isFull` *always* returned `false`. For the Stack ADT we use a different approach: We define separate interfaces for the bounded and unbounded versions of the stack. In fact, we define three interfaces.

Whether a stack is bounded in size affects only the `push` operation and the need for an `isFull` operation. It has no effect on the `pop`, `top`, or `isEmpty` operations. First, we define a general stack interface, `StackInterface`, that contains the signatures of those three operations:

```
//--------------------------------------------------------------------------
// StackInterface.java          by Dale/Joyce/Weems          Chapter 3
//
// Interface for a class that implements a stack of T.
// A stack is a last in, first out structure.
//--------------------------------------------------------------------------

package ch03.stacks;

public interface StackInterface<T>

{
  void pop() throws StackUnderflowException³;
  // Throws StackUnderflowException if this stack is empty,
  // otherwise removes top element from this stack.

  T top() throws StackUnderflowException;
  // Throws StackUnderflowException if this stack is empty,
  // otherwise returns top element from this stack.
```

---

3. Because our stack exceptions are unchecked exceptions, including them in the interface actually has no effect on anything from a syntactic or run-time error-checking point of view. They aren't checked. However, we still list them as being thrown because we are also trying to communicate our requirements to the implementation programmer.

```
    boolean isEmpty();
    // Returns true if this stack is empty, otherwise returns false.


}
```

In Section 3.2 we presented our intention to create generic collection ADTs. This means that in addition to implementing our ADTs as generic classes—that is, classes that accept a parameter type upon instantiation—we also will define generic interfaces for those classes. Note the use of <T> in the header of StackInterface. As with generic classes, ⟨T⟩ used in this way indicates that T is a placeholder for a type provided by the client code. T represents the class of objects held by the specified stack. Since the top method returns one of those objects, in the interface it is listed as returning T. This same approach is used for ADT interfaces throughout the remainder of the textbook.

Note that we document the effects of the operations, the postconditions, as comments. For this ADT there are no preconditions because we have elected to throw exceptions for all error situations.

Next, we turn our attention to the bounded version of the stack, for which we create a second interface, BoundedStackInterface. A stack that is bounded in size must support all of the operations of a "regular" stack plus the isFull operation. It must also provide a push operation that throws an exception if the operation is invoked when the stack is full.

Java supports inheritance of interfaces. That is, one interface can extend another interface. (In fact, the language supports multiple inheritance of interfaces so that a single interface can extend any number of other interfaces.) The fact that the new interface requires all of the operations of our current StackInterface makes this a perfect place to use inheritance. We define our BoundedStackInterface as a new interface that extends StackInterface and adds isFull and push methods. Here is the code for the new interface (note the extends clause):

Inheritance of interfaces   A Java interface can extend another Java interface, inheriting its requirements. If interface B extends interface A, then classes that implement interface B must also implement interface A. Usually, interface B adds abstract methods to those required by interface A.

Multiple inheritance of interfaces   A Java interface may extend more than one interface.[4] If interface C extends both interface A and interface B, then classes that implement interface C must also implement both interface A and interface B. Sometimes multiple inheritance of interfaces is used simply to combine the requirements of two interfaces, without adding any more methods.

```
//--------------------------------------------------------------------------------
// BoundedStackInterface.java         by Dale/Joyce/Weems          Chapter 3
//
// Interface for a class that implements a stack of T with a bound
// on the size of the stack. A stack is a last in, first out structure.
//--------------------------------------------------------------------------------

package ch03.stacks;
```

---

4. In contrast, a Java class can extend only one other class.

```
public interface BoundedStackInterface<T> extends StackInterface<T>

{

  void push(T element) throws StackOverflowException;
  // Throws StackOverflowException if this stack is full,
  // otherwise places element at the top of this stack.

  boolean isFull();
  // Returns true if this stack is full, otherwise returns false.

}
```

Finally, we create an interface for the unbounded case. An unbounded stack need not support an `isFull` operation, because it will "never" be full.[5] For this same reason, the `push` operation need not throw an exception.

```
//-------------------------------------------------------------------------
// UnboundedStackInterface.java      by Dale/Joyce/Weems        Chapter 3
//
// Interface for a class that implements a stack of T with no bound
// on the size of the stack. A stack is a last in, first out structure.
//-------------------------------------------------------------------------

package ch03.stacks;

public interface UnboundedStackInterface<T> extends StackInterface<T>

{
  void push(T element);
  // Places element at the top of this stack.

}
```

We have now defined our three interfaces, along with two exception classes. Their relationship is shown in the UML diagram in Figure 3.5. A specific implementation of a stack would `implement` either the `BoundedStackInterface` or the `UnboundedStack-Interface`. By virtue of the interface inheritance rules, it must also implement the `StackInterface`.

---

5. The only way it could be full is if the system runs out of space. In this rare case the Java run-time system raises an exception anyway.

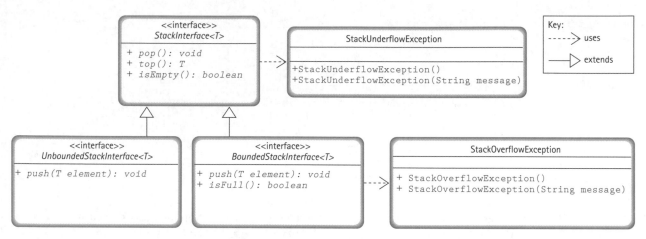

Figure 3.5   *UML diagram of our Stack ADT interfaces*

Note that our Stack ADT interfaces are not an example of multiple inheritance of interfaces. That occurs when one interface inherits from more than one other interface. Here we have defined two interfaces that inherit from the same interface, just as in a normal class hierarchy. We discussed multiple inheritance in this section simply because it is an aspect of the Java syntax for interface inheritance that you should be aware of.

Example Use

The simple `ReverseStrings` example shows how we can use a stack to store strings provided by a user and then to output the strings in the opposite order from which they were entered. The code uses the array-based implementation of a stack we develop in the following section. The parts of the code directly related to the creation and use of the stack are emphasized. We declare the stack to be of type `BoundedStackInter-face<String>` and then instantiate it as an `ArrayStack<String>`. Within the *for* loop, three strings provided by the user are pushed onto the stack. The *while* loop repeatedly removes and prints the top string from the stack until the stack is empty. If we try to push any type of object other than a `String` onto the stack, we will receive a compile time error message saying that the `push` method cannot be applied to that type of object.

```
//-----------------------------------------------------------------------------
// ReverseStrings.java          by Dale/Joyce/Weems          Chapter 3
//
// Sample use of stack. Outputs strings in reverse order of entry.
//-----------------------------------------------------------------------------
```

```
import ch03.stacks.*;
import java.util.Scanner;

public class ReverseStrings
{
  public static void main(String[] args)
  {
    Scanner conIn = new Scanner(System.in);

    BoundedStackInterface<String> stack;
    stack = new ArrayStack<String>(3);

    String line;

    for (int i = 1; i <= 3; i++)
    {
      System.out.print("Enter a line of text > ");
      line = conIn.nextLine();
      stack.push(line);
    }

    System.out.println("\nReverse is:\n");
    while (!stack.isEmpty())
    {
      line = stack.top();
      stack.pop();
      System.out.println(line);
    }
  }
}
```

Here is the output from a sample run:

```
Enter a line of text > the beginning of a story
Enter a line of text > is often different than
Enter a line of text > the end of a story

Reverse is:

the end of a story
is often different than
the beginning of a story
```

The Java Stack Class and the Collections Framework

The Java library provides classes that implement ADTs that are based on common data structures—stacks, queues, lists, maps, sets, and more. The library's `Stack` class is similar to the Stack ADT we develop in this chapter in that it provides a LIFO structure. However, in addition to our `push`, `top`, and `isEmpty`[6] operations, it includes two other operations:

- `pop`   Removes and returns the top element from the stack.
- `search(Object o)`   Returns the position of object o on the stack.

Because the library `Stack` class extends the library `Vector` class, it also inherits the many operations defined for `Vector` and its ancestors.

Here is how you might implement the reverse strings application using the `Stack` class from the Java library. The minimal differences between this application and the one using our Stack ADT are emphasized.

```
//---------------------------------------------------------------------
// ReverseStrings2.java          by Dale/Joyce/Weems          Chapter 3
//
// Sample use of the library Stack.
// Outputs strings in reverse order of entry.
//---------------------------------------------------------------------

import java.util.Stack;
import java.util.Scanner;

public class ReverseStrings2
{
  public static void main(String[] args)
  {
    Scanner conIn = new Scanner(System.in);

    Stack<String> stack = new Stack<String>();

    String line;

    for (int i = 1; i <= 3; i++)
    {
      System.out.print("Enter a line of text > ");
      line = conIn.nextLine();
      stack.push(line);
    }
```

---

6. In the library `isEmpty` is called `empty`, and `top` is called `peek`.

```
    System.out.println("\nReverse is:\n");
    while (!stack.empty())
    {
      line = stack.peek();
      stack.pop();
      System.out.println(line);
    }
  }
}
```

As discussed in Section 3.2, another term for a data structure is collection. The Java developers refer to the set of library classes, such as `Stack`, that support data structures as the *Collections Framework*. This framework includes both interfaces and classes. It also includes documentation that explains how the developers intend for us to use them. As of Java 5.0 all the structures in the Collections Framework support generics (see the subsection Generic Collections in Section 3.2).

The Collections Framework comprises an extensive set of tools. It does more than just provide implementations of data structures; it provides a unified architecture for working with collections. In this textbook we do not cover the framework in great detail. This textbook is meant to teach you about the fundamental nature of data structures and to demonstrate how we define, implement, and use them. It is not an exploration of how to use Java's specific library architecture of similar structures.

Before you become a professional Java programmer, you should carefully study the Collections Framework and learn how to use it productively. This textbook prepares you to do this not just for Java, but for other languages and libraries as well. Nevertheless, when we discuss a data structure that has a counterpart in the Java library, we will briefly describe the similarities and differences between our approach and the library's approach, as we did here for stacks.

If you are interested in learning more about the Java Collections Framework, you can study the extensive documentation available at Oracle's website.

3.5 Array-Based Implementations

In this section we study an array-based implementation of the Stack ADT. Additionally, in a feature section, we look at an alternative implementation that uses the Java library's `ArrayList` class.

Note that Figure 3.17, in the Summary on page 230, shows the relationships among the primary classes and interfaces created to support our Stack ADT, including those developed in this section.

The ArrayStack Class

First we develop a Java class that implements the `BoundedStackInterface`. We call this class `ArrayStack`, in recognition of the fact that it uses an array as the underlying structure. An array is a reasonable structure to contain elements of a stack. We can put elements into sequential slots in the array, placing the first element pushed onto the stack into the first array position, the second element pushed into the second array position, and so on. The floating "high-water" mark is the top element in the stack. Given that stacks grow and shrink from only one end, we do not have to worry about inserting an element into the middle of the elements already stored in the array.

What instance variables does our implementation need? We need the stack elements themselves and a variable indicating the top of the stack. We hold the stack elements in a protected array called `stack`. We use a protected integer variable called `topIndex` to indicate which element of the array is the top. We initialize `topIndex` to −1, as nothing is stored on the stack when it is first created.

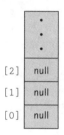

As we push and pop elements, respectively, we increment and decrement the value of `topIndex`. For example, starting with an empty stack and pushing "A," "B," and "C" we would have

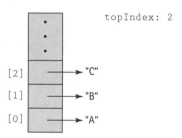

We provide two constructors for use by clients of the `ArrayStack` class: One allows the client to specify the maximum expected size of the stack, and the other assumes a default maximum size of 100 elements. To facilitate the latter constructor, we define a constant `DEFCAP` (default capacity) set to 100.

The beginning of the `ArrayStack.java` file is shown here:

```
//------------------------------------------------------------
// ArrayStack.java          by Dale/Joyce/Weems          Chapter 3
//
// Implements BoundedStackInterface using an array to hold the
// stack elements.
//
```

```
// Two constructors are provided: one that creates an array of a
// default size and one that allows the calling program to
// specify the size.
//-------------------------------------------------------------

package ch03.stacks;

public class ArrayStack<T> implements BoundedStackInterface<T>
{
  protected final int DEFCAP = 100; // default capacity
  protected T[] stack;              // holds stack elements
  protected int topIndex = -1;      // index of top element in stack

  public ArrayStack()
  {
    stack = (T[]) new Object[DEFCAP];⁶
  }

  public ArrayStack(int maxSize)
  {
    stack = (T[]) new Object[maxSize];⁶
  }
```

We can see that this class accepts a generic parameter `<T>` as listed in the class header. The `stack` variable is declared to be of type `T[]`, that is, an array of class `T`. This class implements a stack of `T`'s—the class of `T` is not yet determined. It will be specified by the client class that uses the bounded stack. Because the Java translator will not generate references to a generic type, our code must specify `Object` along with the *new* statement within our constructors. Thus, although we declare our array to be an array of class `T`, we must instantiate it to be an array of class `Object`. Then, to ensure that the desired type checking takes place, we cast array elements into class `T`, as shown here:

```
stack = (T[]) new Object[DEFCAP];
```

Even though this approach is somewhat awkward and typically generates a compiler warning, it is how we must create generic collections using arrays in Java. We could use the Java library's generic `ArrayList` to rectify the problem (see the feature *The*

---

6. An unchecked cast warning is generated because the compiler cannot ensure that the array contains objects of class T—the warning can safely be ignored.

`ArrayListStack` Class at the end of this section), but we prefer to use the more basic array structure for pedagogic reasons. The compiler warning can safely be ignored.

Definitions of Stack Operations

As we are now implementing the `BoundedStackInterface`, we must provide a concrete implementation of the `isFull` method. For the array-based approach, the implementations of `isFull` and its counterpart, `isEmpty`, are both very simple. The stack is empty if the top index is equal to –1, and the stack is full if the top index is equal to one less than the size of the array.

```
public boolean isEmpty()
// Returns true if this stack is empty, otherwise returns false.
{
  if (topIndex == -1)
    return true;
  else
    return false;
}

public boolean isFull()
// Returns true if this stack is full, otherwise returns false.
{
  if (topIndex == (stack.length - 1))
    return true;
  else
    return false;
}
```

Now let's write the method to push an element of type `T` onto the top of the stack. If the stack is already full when we invoke `push`, there is nowhere to put the element. Recall that this condition is called stack overflow. Our formal specifications state that the method should throw the `StackOverflowException` in this case. We include a pertinent error message when the exception is thrown. If the stack is not full, `push` must increment `topIndex` and store the new element into `stack[topIndex]`. The implementation of this method is straightforward.

```
public void push(T element)
// Throws StackOverflowException if this stack is full,
// otherwise places element at the top of this stack.
{
  if (!isFull())
  {
```

```
      topIndex++;
      stack[topIndex] = element;
  }
  else
      throw new StackOverflowException("Push attempted on a full stack.");
}
```

The pop method is essentially the reverse of push: Instead of putting an element onto the top of the stack, we remove the top element from the stack by decrementing topIndex. It is good practice to also "null out" the array location associated with the current top. Setting the array value to null removes the physical reference. Figure 3.6 shows the difference between the "lazy" approach to coding pop and the "proper" approach.

If the stack is empty when we invoke pop, there is no top element to remove and we have stack underflow. As with the push method, the specifications say to throw an exception.

```
public void pop()
// Throws StackUnderflowException if this stack is empty,
// otherwise removes top element from this stack.
{
  if (!isEmpty())
  {
    stack[topIndex] = null;
    topIndex--;
  }
  else
    throw new StackUnderflowException("Pop attempted on an empty stack.");
}
```

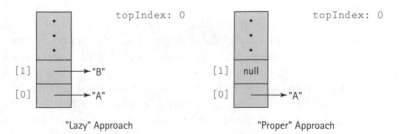

Figure 3.6 *Lazy versus proper* pop *approaches for an array-based stack after* push("A"), push("B"), *and* pop()

Finally, the `top` operation simply returns the top element of the stack, the element indexed by `topIndex`. Consistent with our generic approach, the `top` method shows type `T` as its return type. As with the `pop` operation, if we attempt to perform the `top` operation on an empty stack, a stack underflow results.

```
public T top()
// Throws StackUnderflowException if this stack is empty,
// otherwise returns top element from this stack.
{
  T topOfStack = null;
  if (!isEmpty())
    topOfStack = stack[topIndex];
  else
    throw new StackUnderflowException("Top attempted on an empty stack.");
  return topOfStack;
}
```

Test Plan

Our `ArrayStack` implementation can be tested using the general ADT testing approach described in Section 2.4, "Software Testing," where we presented an example based on the StringLog ADT. Unlike the StringLog ADT, our Stack ADT does not include a `toString` operation. Therefore it is not as easy to check the contents of a stack during testing. There are several ways we can address this problem. For instance, we could add a `toString` operation to our stack implementations. (See Exercise 29.) Alternatively, we could create an application-level method that is passed a stack; uses `top`, `pop`, and `push` to take the stack apart and display its contents; and then uses the same operations to put the stack back together. This approach requires a second stack to hold the contents of the original stack under investigation, while it is being "taken apart." (See Exercise 30d.)

Once the problem of viewing the contents of a stack has been solved, we can create an interactive test driver, as we did for the `ArrayStringLog` in Chapter 2. Such a driver helps us carry out our test plans.

Page 191 shows a short test plan for the `ArrayStack`. The test plan tests a stack of `Integer`. The type of data stored in the stack has no effect on the operations that manipulate the stack, so testing an `Integer` stack suffices. We set the stack size to 5, to keep our test cases manageable.

One final note about using an array to implement a stack. We implemented the `BoundedStackInterface` using an array because the size of an array is fixed. We can also use arrays to implement the `UnboundedStackInterface`. One approach is to instantiate increasingly larger arrays, as needed during processing, copying the current array into the larger, newly instantiated array. We investigate this approach when we implement the Queue ADT in Chapter 5.

Operation to be Tested and Description of Action	Input Values	Expected Output
`ArrayStack`	5	
apply isEmpty immediately		Stack is empty
`push`, `pop`, and `top`		
push 4 items, top/pop and print	5,7,6,9	9,6,7,5
push with duplicates and		
top/pop and print	2,3,3,4	4,3,3,2
interlace operations		
push	5	
pop		
push	3	
push	7	
pop		
top and print		3
`isEmpty`		
invoke when empty		Stack is empty
push and invoke		Stack is not empty
pop and invoke		Stack is empty
`isFull`		
push 4 items and invoke		Stack is not full
push 1 item and invoke		Stack is full
throw `StackOverflowException`		Outputs string:
push 5 items then		"Push attempted on a full stack."
push another item		Program terminates
throw `StackUnderflowException`		Outputs string:
when stack is empty		"Pop attempted on an empty stack."
attempt to pop		Program terminates
when stack is empty		Outputs string:
attempt to top		"Top attempted on an empty stack."
		Program terminates

The ArrayListStack Class

There are often many ways to implement an ADT. In this feature, we present an alternate implementation for the Stack ADT based on the `ArrayList`[7] class of the Java class library. The `ArrayList` is part of the Java Collections Framework discussed at the end of Section 3.4.

The defining quality of the `ArrayList` class is that it can grow and shrink in response to the program's needs. As a consequence, when we use the `ArrayList` approach we do not have to worry about our stacks being bounded. Instead of implementing the `BoundedStackInterface`, we implement the `UnboundedStackInterface`. Our constructor no longer needs to declare a stack size. We do not implement an `isFull` operation. We do not have to handle stack overflows.

One could argue that if a program runs completely out of memory, then the stack could be considered full and should throw `StackOverflowException`. However, in that case the run-time environment throws an "out of memory" exception anyway; we do not have to worry about the situation going unnoticed. Furthermore, running out of system memory is a serious problem (and ideally a rare event) and cannot be handled in the same way as a Stack ADT overflow.

The fact that an `ArrayList` automatically grows as needed makes it a good choice for implementing our unbounded Stack ADT. Additionally, it provides a `size` method that we can use to keep track of the top of our stack. The index of the top of the stack is always the `size` minus one.

Study the following code. Compare this implementation to the previous implementation. They are similar, yet different. One is based directly on arrays, whereas the other uses arrays indirectly through the `ArrayList` class. One nice benefit of using the `ArrayList` approach is we no longer receive the annoying unchecked cast warning from the compiler. This is because an `ArrayList` object, unlike the basic array, is a first-class object in Java and fully supports the use of generics. Despite the obvious benefits of using `ArrayList` we will continue to use arrays as one of our basic ADT implementation structures throughout most of the rest of the book. Learning to use the standard array is important for future professional software developers.

```
//----------------------------------------------------------------
// ArrayListStack.java        by Dale/Joyce/Weems        Chapter 3
//
// Implements UnboundedStackInterface using an ArrayList to
// hold the stack elements.
//----------------------------------------------------------------

package ch03.stacks;

import java.util.*;
```

---

7. Appendix E contains information concerning the Java `ArrayList` class.

```
public class ArrayListStack<T> implements UnboundedStackInterface<T>
{
  protected ArrayList<T> stack;              // ArrayList that holds stack
                                             // elements

  public ArrayListStack()
  {
    stack = new ArrayList<T>();
  }

  public void push(T element)
  // Places element at the top of this stack.
  {
    stack.add(element);
  }

  public void pop()
  // Throws StackUnderflowException if this stack is empty,
  // otherwise removes top element from this stack.
  {
    if (!isEmpty())
    {
      stack.remove(stack.size() - 1);
    }
    else
      throw new StackUnderflowException("Pop attempted on an empty " +
                                        "stack.");
  }

  public T top()
  // Throws StackUnderflowException if this stack is empty,
  // otherwise returns top element from this stack.
  {
    T topOfStack = null;
    if (!isEmpty())
      topOfStack = stack.get(stack.size() - 1);
    else
      throw new StackUnderflowException("Top attempted on an empty " +
                                        "stack.");
    return topOfStack;
  }

  public boolean isEmpty()
  // Returns true if this stack is empty, otherwise returns false.
  {
    if (stack.size() == 0)
      return true;
    else
      return false;
  }
}
```

3.6   Application: Well–Formed Expressions

Stacks are great for "remembering" things that have to be "taken care of" at a later time. In this sample application we tackle a problem that perplexes many beginning programmers: matching parentheses, brackets, and braces in writing code. Matching *grouping symbols* is an important problem in the world of computing. For example, it is related to the legality of arithmetic equations, the syntactical correctness of computer programs, and the validity of XHTML tags used to define web pages. This problem is a classic situation for using a stack, because we must "remember" an open symbol (e.g., (, [, or {) until it is "taken care of" later by matching a corresponding close symbol (e.g.,),], or }, respectively). When the grouping symbols in an expression are properly matched, computer scientists say that the expression is *well formed* and that the grouping symbols are *balanced*.

Given a set of grouping symbols, our problem is to determine whether the open and close versions of each symbol are matched correctly. We'll focus on the normal pairs: (), [], and {}. In theory, of course, we could define any pair of symbols (e.g., <> or /\) as grouping symbols. Any number of other characters may appear in the input expression before, between, or after a grouping pair, and an expression may contain nested groupings. Each close symbol must match the last unmatched open grouping symbol, and each open grouping symbol must have a matching close symbol. Thus, matching symbols can be unbalanced for two reasons: There is a mismatching close symbol (e.g., {]) or there is a missing close symbol (e.g., {{[]}). Figure 3.7 shows examples of both well-formed and ill-formed expressions.

The Balanced Class

To help solve our problem we create a class called `Balanced`, with a single exported method `test` that takes an expression as a string argument and checks whether the grouping symbols in the expression are balanced. As there are two ways that an expression can fail the balance test, there are three possible results. We use an integer to indicate the result of the test:

0 means the symbols are balanced, such as (([xx])xx)

1 means the expression has unbalanced symbols, such as (([xx}xx))

2 means the expression came to an end prematurely, such as (([xxx])xx

Well-Formed Expressions	Ill-Formed Expressions
(xx (xx ( )) xx)	(xx (xx ( )) xxx) xxx)
[ ] ( ) { }	] [
([ ] { xxx } xxx ( ) xxx)	(xx [xxx) xx]
([{[(([{x}])x)]}x])	([{[(([{x}])x)]}x})
xxxxxxxxxxxxxxxxxxxxxxxx	xxxxxxxxxxxxxxxxxxxxx {

Figure 3.7 *Well-formed and ill-formed expressions*

We include a single constructor for the `Balanced` class. To make the class more generally usable, we allow the application to specify the open and close symbols. We thus define two string parameters for the constructor, `openSet` and `closeSet`, through which the user can pass the symbols. The symbols in the two sets match up by position. For our specific problem the two arguments could be "`([{`" and "`)]}`."

It is important that each symbol in the combined open and close sets is unique and that the sets be the same size. Otherwise, it is impossible to determine matching criteria. We use programming by contract and state these criteria in a precondition of the constructor.

```
public Balanced(String openSet, String closeSet)
// Preconditions: No character is contained more than once in the
//                combined openSet and closeSet strings.
//                The size of openSet = the size of closeSet.
{
  this.openSet = openSet;
  this.closeSet = closeSet;
}
```

Now we turn our attention to the `test` method. It is passed a `String` argument through its `subject` parameter and must determine, based on the characters in `openSet` and `closeSet`, whether the symbols in `subject` are balanced. The method processes the characters in `subject` one at a time. For each character, it performs one of three tasks:

- If the character is an open symbol, it is pushed on the stack.
- If the character is a close symbol, it is checked against the last open symbol, which is obtained from the top of the stack. If they match, processing continues with the next character. If the close symbol does not match the top of the stack or if the stack is empty, then the expression is ill formed.
- If the character is not a special symbol, it is skipped.

The stack is the appropriate data structure in which to save the open symbols because we always need to examine the most recent one. When all of the characters have been processed, the stack should be empty—otherwise, there are open symbols left over.

Now we are ready to write the main algorithm for `test`. We assume an instance of a Stack ADT as defined by `BoundedStackInterface`. We use a bounded stack because we know the stack cannot contain more elements than the number of characters in the expression. We also declare a `boolean` variable `stillBalanced`, initialized to `true`, to record whether the expression, as processed so far, is balanced.

Test for Well-Formed Expression Algorithm (String subject)

Create a new stack of size equal to the length of subject
Set stillBalanced to true
Get the first character from subject

while (the expression is still balanced AND there are still more characters to process)
  Process the current character
  Get the next character from subject

if (!stillBalanced)
  return 1
else if (stack is not empty)
  return 2
else
  return 0

The part of this algorithm that requires expansion before moving on to the coding stage is the "Process the current character" command. We previously described how to handle each type of character. Here are those steps in algorithmic form:

if (the character is an open symbol)
  Push the open symbol character onto the stack
else if (the character is a close symbol)
  if (the stack is empty)
    Set stillBalanced to false
  else
    Set open symbol character to the value at the top of the stack
    Pop the stack
    if the close symbol character does not "match" the open symbol character
      Set stillBalanced to false
else
  Skip the character

The code for the `Balanced` class is listed next. Because the focus of this chapter is stacks, we have <u>emphasized</u> the calls to the stack operations in the code listing. There are several interesting things to note about the `Balanced` class:

1. We declare our stack to be of type `BoundedStackInterface`, but instantiate it as class `ArrayStack`, following the convention suggested in "Using the StringLogInterface" at the end of Section 2.2.

2. We use a shortcut for determining whether a close symbol matches an open symbol. According to our rules, the symbols match if they share the same relative position in their respective sets. This means that when we encounter an open special symbol, rather than save the actual character on the stack, we can push its *position* in the `openSet` string onto the stack. Later in the processing, when we encounter a close symbol, we can just compare its position with the position value on the stack. Thus, rather than push a character value onto the stack, we push an integer value.

3. We instantiate our stacks to hold elements of type `Integer`. But, as just mentioned, in the `test` method we push elements of the primitive type `int` onto our stack. How can this be? As of Java 5.0, Java includes a feature called *Autoboxing*. If a programmer uses a value of a primitive type as an `Object`, it is automatically converted (boxed) into an object of its corresponding wrapper class. So when the `test` method says

    ```
    stack.push(openIndex);
    ```

    the integer value of `openIndex` is automatically converted to an `Integer` object before being stored on the stack. In previous versions of Java we would have needed to state the conversion explicitly:

    ```
    Integer openIndexObject = new Integer(openIndex);
    stack.push(openIndexObject);
    ```

4. A corresponding feature, introduced with Java 5.0, called *Unboxing*, reverses the effect of the *Autoboxing*. When we access the top of the stack with the statement

    ```
    openIndex = stack.top();
    ```

    the `Integer` object at the top of the stack is automatically converted to an integer value. In previous versions of Java we would have needed to write

    ```
    openIndex = stack.top().intValue();
    ```

5. In processing a closing symbol, we access the stack to see if its top holds the corresponding opening symbol. If the stack is empty, it indicates an unbalanced expression. We have two ways to check whether the stack is empty: We can use the `isEmpty` method or we can try to access the stack and catch a `StackUnderflowException`. We choose the latter approach. It seems to fit the spirit of the algorithm, because we expect to find the open symbol and finding the stack empty is the "exceptional" case.

6.   In contrast, we use `isEmpty` to check for an empty stack at the end of processing the expression. Here, we don't want to extract an element from the stack—we just need to know whether it is empty.

Here is the code for the entire class:

```
//---------------------------------------------------------------
// Balanced.java          by Dale/Joyce/Weems          Chapter 3
//
// Checks for balanced expressions using standard rules.
//
// Matching pairs of open and close symbols are provided to the
// constructor through two string parameters.
//---------------------------------------------------------------

import ch03.stacks.*;

public class Balanced
{
  private String openSet;
  private String closeSet;

  public Balanced(String openSet, String closeSet)
  // Preconditions: No character is contained more than once in the
  //                combined openSet and closeSet strings.
  //                The size of openSet = the size of closeSet.
  {
    this.openSet = openSet;
    this.closeSet = closeSet;
  }

  public int test(String expression)
  // Returns 0 if expression is balanced.
  // Returns 1 if expression has unbalanced symbols.
  // Returns 2 if expression came to end prematurely.
  {
    char currChar;          // current expression character being studied
    int  currCharIndex;     // index of current character
    int  lastCharIndex;     // index of last character in the expression

    int openIndex;          // index of current character in openSet
    int closeIndex;         // index of current character in closeSet

    boolean stillBalanced = true;   // true as long as expression is balanced
```

```
// holds unmatched open symbols
BoundedStackInterface<Integer> stack;
stack = new ArrayStack<Integer>(expression.length());

currCharIndex = 0;
lastCharIndex = expression.length() - 1;

while (stillBalanced && (currCharIndex <= lastCharIndex))
// while expression still balanced and not at end of expression
{
  currChar = expression.charAt(currCharIndex);
  openIndex = openSet.indexOf(currChar);

  if(openIndex != -1)    // if the current character is in the openSet
  {
    // Push the index onto the stack.
    stack.push(openIndex);
  }
    else
    {
      closeIndex = closeSet.indexOf(currChar);
      if(closeIndex != -1) // if the current character is in the closeSet
      {
        try                       // try to pop an index off the stack
        {
          openIndex = stack.top();
          stack.pop();

          if (openIndex != closeIndex)   // if popped index doesn't match
          {
            stillBalanced = false;        // then expression not balanced
          }
        }
        catch(StackUnderflowException e) // if stack was empty
        {
          stillBalanced = false;          // then expression not balanced
        }
      }
    }
  currCharIndex++;                 // set up processing of next character
}

if (!stillBalanced)
  return 1;              // unbalanced symbols
else
```

```
      if (!stack.isEmpty())
        return 2;              // premature end of expression
      else
        return 0;             // expression is balanced
    }
  }
```

The Application

Now that we have the `Balanced` class, it is not difficult to finish our application. Of course, we should carefully test the class first—but in this case we can use our application as a test driver.

Because the `Balanced` class is responsible for determining whether grouping symbols are balanced, all that remains is to implement the user input and output. Rather than processing just one expression, we allow the user to enter a series of expressions, asking whether he or she wishes to continue after each result is output. Following our standard approach, we implement a console-based system. It is straightforward to convert this application to a GUI, if you are familiar with Java's Swing classes. We call our program `BalancedApp`. Note that when the `Balanced` class is instantiated, the constructor is passed the strings "({ [" ")]}" so that it corresponds to our specific problem.

```
//--------------------------------------------------------------------------
// BalancedApp.java          by Dale/Joyce/Weems               Chapter 3
//
// Checks for balanced grouping symbols.
// Input consists of a sequence of expressions, one per line.
// Special symbol types are (), [], and {}.
//--------------------------------------------------------------------------

import java.util.Scanner;

public class BalancedApp
{
  public static void main(String[] args)
  {
    Scanner conIn = new Scanner(System.in);

    // Instantiate new Balanced class with grouping symbols.
    Balanced bal = new Balanced("([{", ")]}");

    int result;                  // 0 = balanced, 1 = unbalanced,
                                 // 2 = premature end

    String expression = null;    // expression to be evaluated
    String more = null;          // used to stop or continue processing
```

```
  do
  {
    // Get next expression to be processed.
    System.out.println("Enter an expression to be evaluated: ");
    expression = conIn.nextLine();

    // Obtain and output result of balanced testing.
    result = bal.test(expression);
    if (result == 1)
      System.out.println("Unbalanced symbols ");
    else
    if (result == 2)
      System.out.println("Premature end of expression");
    else
      System.out.println("The symbols are balanced.");

    // Determine if there is another expression to process.
    System.out.println();
    System.out.print("Evaluate another expression? (Y=Yes): ");
    more = conIn.nextLine();
    System.out.println();
  }
  while (more.equalsIgnoreCase("y"));
}
}
```

Here is the output from a sample run:

```
Enter an expression to be evaluated:
(xx[yy]{ttt})
The symbols are balanced.

Evaluate another expression? (Y=Yes): Y

Enter an expression to be evaluated:
((()
Premature end of expression

Evaluate another expression? (Y=Yes): Y

Enter an expression to be evaluated:
(ttttttt]
```

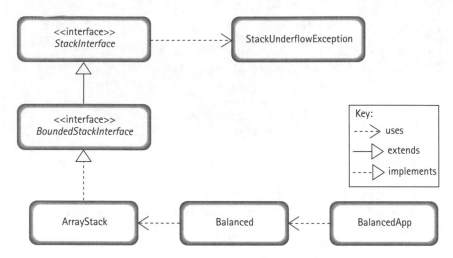

Figure 3.8 *Program architecture*

Unbalanced symbols

Evaluate another expression? (Y=Yes): Y

Enter an expression to be evaluated:
(){}[]({{[{({})}]}})]
The symbols are balanced.

Evaluate another expression? (Y=Yes): n

Figure 3.8 is a UML diagram showing the relationships among our interfaces and classes used in this program. The intent is to show the general architecture, so we do not include details about attributes and operations.

3.7 Link–Based Implementation

In Chapter 2 we introduced linked lists and explained how they provide an alternative to arrays when implementing collections. It is important for you to learn both approaches. Recall that a "link" is the same thing as a "reference." The Stack ADT implementation presented in this section is therefore referred to as a reference- or link-based implementation.

Figure 3.17, in the Summary on page 230, shows the relationships among the primary classes and interfaces created to support our Stack ADT, including those developed in this section.

The LLNode Class

Recall from Chapter 2 that to create a linked list we needed to define a self-referential class to act as the nodes of the list. Our approach there was to define the `LLStringNode` class that allowed us to create a linked list of strings. If we merely needed to create stacks of strings, we could reuse the `LLStringNode` class to support our link-based implementation of stacks. However, the class of objects held by our stacks must be parametizable—it will be specified by the client whenever a stack is instantiated. Therefore we define a class that is analogous to the `LLStringNode` class called `LLNode`. Figure 3.9 shows the corresponding UML class diagram. The self-referential nature of the class is evident from the fact that an `LLNode` has an instance variable, `link`, of class `LLNode`. Because we plan to use this class to support our development of several data structures, we place it in a package named `support`.[8]

The implementation of the `LLNode` class is essentially the same as that of the `LLStringNode` class. The `info` variable contains a reference to the object of class `T` representing the information held by the node, and the `link` variable holds a reference to the next `LLNode` on the list. The code includes a constructor that accepts an object of class `T` as an argument and constructs a node that references that object. An abstract view of a single `LLNode` is pictured in Figure 3.10. The code also includes setters and getters for both the `info` and `link` attributes so that we can create, manipulate, and traverse the linked list of `T` nodes.

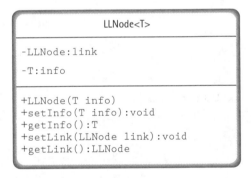

```
LLNode<T>

-LLNode:link
-T:info

+LLNode(T info)
+setInfo(T info):void
+getInfo():T
+setLink(LLNode link):void
+getLink():LLNode
```

Figure 3.9 *UML class diagram of* `LLNode`

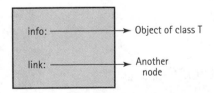

info: ⟶ Object of class T

link: ⟶ Another node

Figure 3.10 *A single node*

---

8. The `LLNode` class file can be found in the `support` subdirectory of the `bookFiles` directory that contains the program files associated with the textbook.

```
//------------------------------------------------------------------
// LLNode.java                  by Dale/Joyce/Weems            Chapter 3
//
// Implements <T> nodes for a linked list.
//------------------------------------------------------------------

package support;

public class LLNode<T>
{
  private LLNode link;
  private T info;

  public LLNode(T info)
  {
    this.info = info;
    link = null;
  }

  public void setInfo(T info)
  // Sets info of this LLNode.
  {
    this.info = info;
  }

  public T getInfo()
  // Returns info of this LLNode.
  {
    return info;
  }

  public void setLink(LLNode link)
  // Sets link of this LLNode.
  {
    this.link = link;
  }

  public LLNode getLink()
  // Returns link of this LLNode.
  {
    return link;
  }
}
```

The LinkedStack Class

We call our new stack class LinkedStack, to differentiate it from the array-based classes of the previous section. LinkedStack implements the UnboundedStackInterface.

We need to define only one instance variable in the LinkedStack class, to hold a reference to the linked list of objects that represents the stack. Because we just need quick access to the top of the stack, we maintain a reference to the node representing the most recent element pushed onto the stack. That node will, in turn, hold a reference to the node representing the next most recent element. That pattern continues until a particular node holds a null reference in its `link` attribute, signifying the bottom of the stack. We call the original reference variable `top`, as it will always reference the top of the stack. It is a reference to a `LLNode`. When we instantiate an object of class `Linked-Stack`, we create an empty stack by setting `top` to `null`. The beginning of the class definition is shown here. Note the `import` statement that allows us to use the `LLNode` class.

```
//-------------------------------------------------------------
// LinkedStack.java        by Dale/Joyce/Weems        Chapter 3
//
// Implements UnboundedStackInterface using a linked list
// to hold the stack elements.
//-------------------------------------------------------------

package ch03.stacks;

import support.LLNode;

public class LinkedStack<T> implements UnboundedStackInterface<T>
{
  protected LLNode<T> top; // reference to the top of this stack

  public LinkedStack()
  {
    top = null;
  }
. . .
```

Now, let's see how we implement our link-based stack operations.

The push Operation

Pushing an element onto the stack means creating a new node and linking it to the current chain of nodes. Figure 3.11 shows the result of the sequence of operations listed here. It graphically demonstrates the dynamic allocation of space for the references to the stack elements. Assume A, B, and C represent objects of class `String`.

```
UnboundedStackInterface<String> myStack;
myStack = new LinkedStack<String>();
myStack.push(A);
myStack.push(B);
myStack.push(C);
```

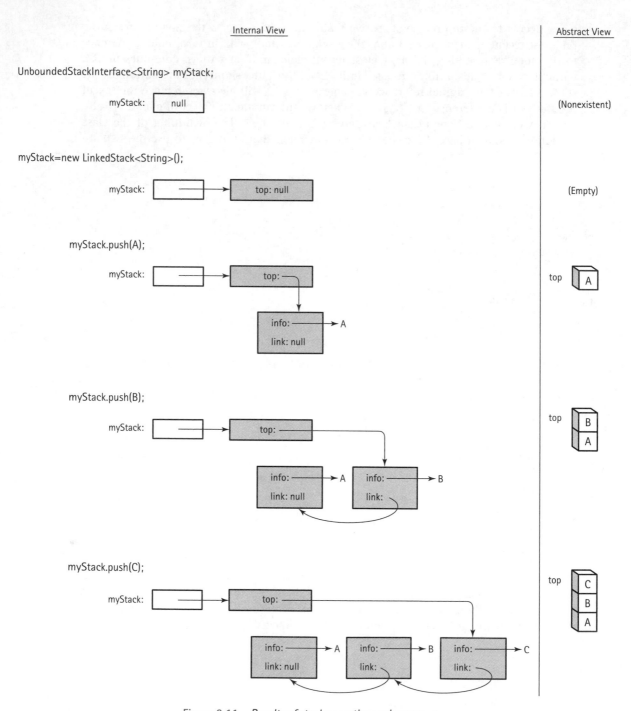

Figure 3.11 *Results of stack operations using* `LLNode`

When performing the `push` operation we must allocate space for each new node dynamically. Here is the general algorithm:

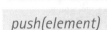

push(element)

Allocate space for the next stack node
    and set the node info to element
Set the node link to the previous top of stack
Set the top of stack to the new stack node

Figure 3.12 graphically displays the effect of each step of the algorithm, starting with a stack that already contains A and B and showing what happens when C is pushed onto it. This is the same algorithm we studied previously in Section 2.5 for insertion into the beginning of a linked list. We have arranged the node boxes visually to emphasize the last in, first out nature of a stack.

Let's look at the algorithm line by line, creating our code as we go. Follow our progress through both the algorithm and Figure 3.12 during this discussion. We begin by allocating space for a new stack node and setting its `info` attribute to the `element`:

```
LLNode<T> newNode = new LLNode<T>(element);
```

Thus, `newNode` is a reference to an object that contains two attributes: `info` of class `T` and `link` of the class `LLNode`. The constructor has set the `info` attribute to reference `element`, as required. Next we need to set the value of the `link` attribute:

```
newNode.setLink(top);
```

Now `info` references the `element` pushed onto the stack, and `link` references the previous top of stack. Finally, we need to reset the top of the stack to reference the new node:

```
top = newNode;
```

Putting it all together, the code for the `push` method is

```
public void push(T element)
// Places element at the top of this stack.
{
  LLNode<T> newNode = new LLNode<T>(element);
  newNode.setLink(top);
  top = newNode;
}
```

Allocate space for the next stack node and set the node info to element

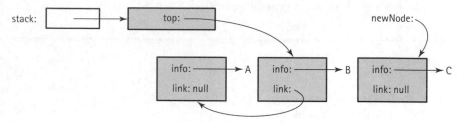

Set the node link to the previous top of stack

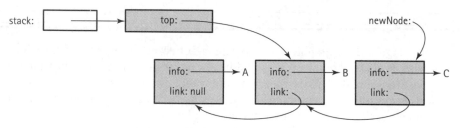

Set the top of stack to the new stack node

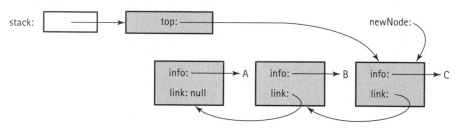

Figure 3.12 *Results of* push *operation*

Note that the order of these tasks is critical. If we reset the top variable before setting the link of the new node, we would lose access to the stack nodes! This situation is generally true when we are dealing with a linked structure: You must be very careful to change the references in the correct order, so that you do not lose access to any of the data.

You have seen how the algorithm works on a stack that contains elements. What happens if the stack is empty? Although we verified in Section 2.5 that our approach works in this case, let's trace through it again. Figure 3.13 shows graphically what occurs.

Space is allocated for the new node and the node's info attribute is set to reference element. Now we need to correctly set the various links. The link of the new node is assigned the value of top. What is this value when the stack is empty? It is null, which is exactly what we want to put into the link of the last (bottom) node of a linked stack. Then top is reset to point to the new node, making the new node the top of the stack. The result is exactly what we would expect—the new node is the only node on the linked list and it is the current top of the stack.

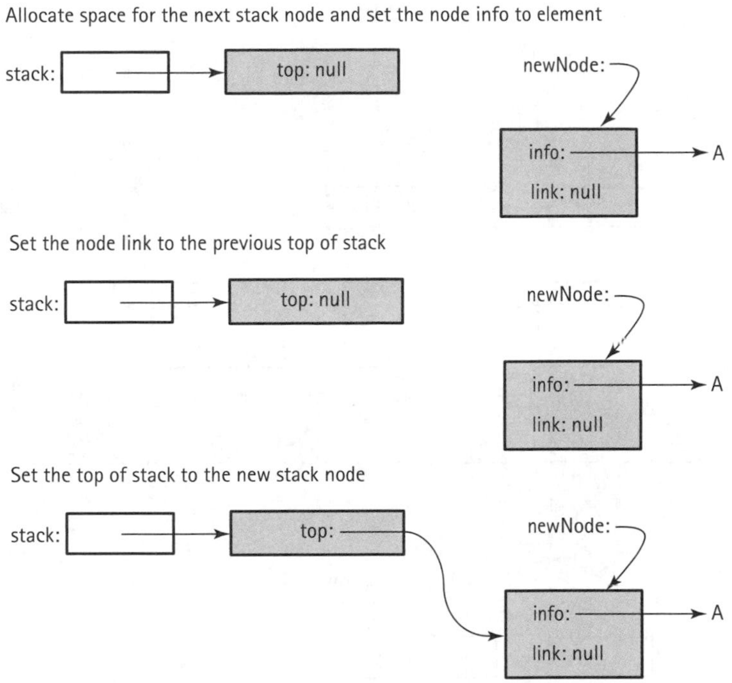

Allocate space for the next stack node and set the node info to element

Set the node link to the previous top of stack

Set the top of stack to the new stack node

Figure 3.13 *Results of push operation on an empty stack*

The pop Operation

The pop operation is equivalent to deleting the first node of a linked list. It is essentially the reverse of the push operation.

To accomplish it we simply reset the stack's top variable to reference the node that represents the next element. That is all we really have to do. Resetting top to the next stack node effectively removes the top element from the stack. See Figure 3.14. This requires only a single line of code:

```
top = top.getLink();
```

The assignment copies the reference from the link attribute of the top stack node into the variable top. After this code is executed, top refers to the LLNode object just below the prior top of the stack. We can no longer use top to reference the previous top object, because we overwrote our only reference to it.

As indicated in Figure 3.14, the former top of the stack is labeled as garbage; the system garbage collector will eventually reclaim the space. If the info attribute of this object is the only reference to the data object labeled C in the figure, it, too, is garbage and its space will be reclaimed.

Internal View   Abstract View

Original

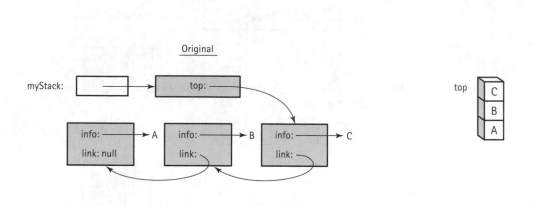

After   myStack.pop();

which equals: top = top.getLink();

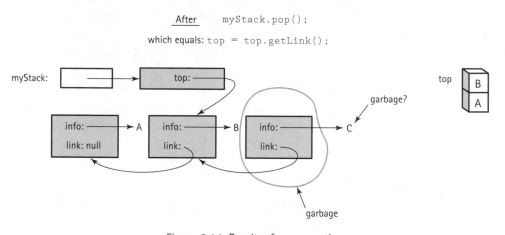

Figure 3.14 *Results of* pop *operation*

Are there any special cases to consider? Given that we are removing an element from the stack, we should be concerned with empty stack situations. What happens if we try to pop an empty stack? In this case the top variable contains null and the assignment statement "top = top.getLink;" results in a run-time error: Null-PointerException. To control this problem ourselves, we protect the assignment statement using the Stack ADT's isEmpty operation. The code for our pop method is shown next.

```
public void pop()
// Throws StackUnderflowException if this stack is empty,
// otherwise removes top element from this stack.
{
  if (!isEmpty())
  {
    top = top.getLink();
  }
  else
    throw new StackUnderflowException("Pop attempted on an empty stack.");
}
```

We use the same `StackUnderflowException` we used in our array-based approaches.

There is one more special case—popping from a stack with only one element. We need to make sure that this operation results in an empty stack. Let's see if it does. When our stack is instantiated, `top` is set to `null`. When an element is pushed onto the stack, the `link` of the node that represents the element is set to the current `top` variable; therefore, when the first element is pushed onto our stack, the `link` of its node is set to `null`. Of course, the first element pushed onto the stack is the last element popped off. This means that the last element popped off the stack has an associated `link` value of `null`. Because the `pop` method sets `top` to the value of this `link` attribute, after the last value is popped `top` again has the value `null`, just as it did when the stack was first instantiated. We conclude that the `pop` method works for a stack of one element. Figure 3.15 graphically depicts pushing a single element onto a stack and then popping it off.

The Other Stack Operations

Recall that the `top` operation simply returns a reference to the top element of the stack. At first glance this might seem very straightforward. Simply code

```
return top;
```

as `top` references the element on the top of the stack. However, remember that `top` references an `LLNode` object. Whatever program is using the Stack ADT is not concerned about `LLNode` objects. The client program is only interested in the object that is referenced by the `info` variable of the `LLNode` object.

Let's try again. To return the `info` of the top `LLNode` object we code

```
return top.getInfo();
```

That's better, but we still need to do a little more work. What about the special case when the stack is empty? In that situation we need to throw an exception instead of returning an object. The final code for the `top` method is shown next.

Empty Stack:

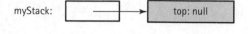

After   myStack.push(A):

And then   myStack.pop();

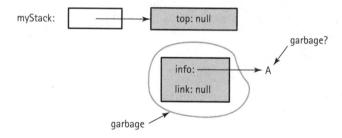

Figure 3.15 *Results of push, then pop on an empty stack*

```java
public T top()
// Throws StackUnderflowException if this stack is empty,
// otherwise returns top element from this stack.
{
  if (!isEmpty())
    return top.getInfo();
  else
    throw new StackUnderflowException("Top attempted on an empty stack.");
}
```

That wasn't bad, but the `isEmpty` method is even easier. If we initialize an empty stack by setting the `top` variable to `null`, then we can detect an empty stack by checking for the value `null`.

```
public boolean isEmpty()
// Returns true if this stack is empty, otherwise returns false.
{
  if (top == null)
    return true;
  else
    return false;
}
```

An even simpler way of writing this is

```
return (top == null);
```

The linked implementation of the Stack ADT can be tested using the same test plan that was presented for the array-based version, except we would not have to test an `isFull` operation.

Comparing Stack Implementations

Let's compare our two classic implementations of the Stack ADT, `ArrayStack` and `LinkedStack`, in terms of storage requirements and efficiency of the algorithms. First we consider the storage requirements. An array that is instantiated to match the maximum stack size takes the same amount of memory, no matter how many array slots are actually used. The linked implementation, using dynamically allocated storage, requires space only for the number of elements actually on the stack at run time. Note, however, that the elements are larger because we must store the reference to the next element as well as the reference to the user's data.

We now compare the relative execution "efficiency" of the two implementations in terms of Big-O notation. The implementations of `isFull` and `isEmpty`, where required, are clearly O(1); they always take a constant amount of work. What about `push`, `pop`, and `top`? Does the number of elements in the stack affect the amount of work required by these operations? No, it does not. In both implementations, we directly access the top of the stack, so these operations also take a constant amount of work. They, too, have O(1) complexity.

Only the class constructor differs from one implementation to the other in terms of the Big-O efficiency. In the array-based implementation, when the array is instantiated, the system creates and initializes each of the array locations. As it is an array of objects, each array slot is initialized to `null`. The number of array slots is equal to the maximum number of possible stack elements. We call this number N and say that the array-based constructor is O(N). For the linked approach, the constructor simply sets the `top` variable to `null`, so it is only O(1).

Overall the two stack implementations are roughly equivalent in terms of the amount of work they do.

So, which is better? The answer, as usual, is "It depends." The linked implementation does not have space limitations, and in applications where the number of stack elements can vary greatly, it wastes less space when the stack is small. Why would we ever want to use the array-based implementation? Because it's short, simple, and efficient. If pushing occurs frequently, the array-based implementation executes faster than the link-based implementation because it does not incur the run-time overhead of repeatedly invoking the `new` operation. When the maximum size is small and we know the maximum size with certainty, the array-based implementation is a good choice.

3.8 Case Study: Postfix Expression Evaluator

Postfix notation[9] is a notation for writing arithmetic expressions in which the operators appear after their operands. For example, instead of writing

$$(2 + 14) \times 23$$

we write

$$2 \ 14 + \ 23 \times$$

With postfix notation, there are no precedence rules to learn, and parentheses are never needed. Because of this simplicity, some popular handheld calculators of the 1980s used postfix notation to avoid the complications of the multiple parentheses required in traditional algebraic notation. Postfix notation is also used by compilers for generating nonambiguous expressions.

In this case study, we create a computer program that evaluates postfix expressions.

Discussion

In elementary school you learned how to evaluate simple expressions that involve the basic binary operators: addition, subtraction, multiplication, and division. These are called *binary operators* because they each operate on two operands. It is easy to see how a child would solve the following problem:

$$2 + 5 = ?$$

---

9. Postfix notation is also known as reverse Polish notation (RPN), so named after the Polish logician Jan Lukasiewicz (1875–1956) who developed it.

As expressions become more complicated, the pencil-and-paper solutions require a little more work. Multiple tasks must be performed to solve the following problem:

$$(((13 - 1) / 2) \times (3 + 5)) = ?$$

These expressions are written using a format known as *infix* notation, which is the same notation used for expressions in Java. The operator in an infix expression is written *in* between its operands. When an expression contains multiple operators such as

$$3 + 5 \times 2$$

we need a set of rules to determine which operation to carry out first. You learned in your mathematics classes that multiplication is done before addition. You learned Java's operator-precedence rules[10] in your first Java programming course. We can use parentheses to override the normal ordering rules. Still, it is easy to make a mistake when writing or interpreting an infix expression containing multiple operations.

Evaluating Postfix Expressions

Postfix notation is another format for writing arithmetic expressions. In this notation, the operator is written after (*post*) the two operands. Here are some simple postfix expressions and their results:

Postfix Expression	Result
4 5 +	9
9 3 /	3
17 8 −	9

The rules for evaluating postfix expressions with multiple operators are much simpler than those for evaluating infix expressions; simply perform the operations from left to right. Now, let's look at a postfix expression containing two operators.

$$6 \; 2 / 5 +$$

We evaluate the expression by scanning from left to right. The first item, 6, is an operand, so we go on. The second item, 2, is also an operand, so again we continue. The third item is the division operator. We now apply this operator to the two previous operands. Which of the two saved operands is the divisor? The one we saw most

---

10. See Appendix B, Java Operator Precedence.

recently. We divide 6 by 2 and substitute 3 back into the expression, replacing 6 2 /.
Our expression now looks like this:

$$3\ 5\ +$$

We continue our scanning. The next item is an operand, 5, so we go on. The next
(and last) item is the operator +. We apply this operator to the two previous operands,
obtaining a result of 8.

Here's another example:

$$5\ 7\ +\ 6\ 2\ -\ \times$$

As we scan from left to right, the first operator we encounter is +. Applying this to the
two preceding operands (5 and 7), we obtain the expression

$$12\ 6\ 2\ -\ \times$$

The next operator we encounter is −, so we subtract 2 from 6, obtaining

$$12\ 4\ \times$$

We apply the last operator, ×, to its two preceding operands and obtain our final
answer: 48.

Here are some more examples of postfix expressions containing multiple operators,
equivalent expressions in infix notation, and the results of evaluating them. See if you
get the same results when you evaluate the postfix expressions.

Postfix Expression	Infix Equivalent	Result
4 5 7 2 + − ×	4 × (5 − (7 + 2))	−16
3 4 + 2 × 7 /	((3 + 4) × 2)/7	2
5 7 + 6 2 − ×	(5 + 7) × (6 − 2)	48
4 2 3 5 1 − + × + ×	?×(4 + (2 × (3 + (5 − 1))))	not enough operands
4 2 + 3 5 1 − × +	(4 + 2) + (3 × (5 − 1))	18

Our task is to write a program that evaluates postfix expressions entered interactively
from the keyboard. In addition to computing and displaying the value of an expression, our
program must display error messages when appropriate ("not enough operands," "too many
operands," and "illegal symbol"). Before we describe our specific requirements, let's look at
the data structure and algorithm involved in postfix expression evaluation.

Postfix Expression Evaluation Algorithm

As so often happens, our by-hand algorithm can serve as a guideline for our computer
algorithm. From the previous discussion, we see that there are two basic items in a post-

fix expression: operands (numbers) and operators. We access items (an operand or an operator) from left to right, one at a time. When the item we get is an operator, we apply it to the preceding two operands.

We must save previously scanned operands in a collection object of some kind. A stack is the ideal place to store the previous operands, because the top item is always the most recent operand and the next item on the stack is always the second most recent operand—just the two operands required when we find an operator. The following algorithm uses a stack to evaluate a postfix expression:

Evaluate Expression

```
while more items exist
    Get an item
  if item is an operand
    stack.push(item)
  else
    operand2 = stack.top()
    stack.pop()
    operand1 = stack.top()
    stack.pop()
    Set result to (apply operation corresponding to item to operand1 and operand2)
    stack.push(result)
result = stack.top()
stack.pop()
return result
```

Each iteration of the *while* loop processes one operator or one operand from the expression. When an operand is found, there is nothing to do with it (we haven't yet found the operator to apply to it), so we save it on the stack until later. When an operator is found, we get the two topmost operands from the stack, perform the operation, and put the result back on the stack; the result may be an operand for a future operator.

Let's trace this algorithm. Before we enter the loop, the input remaining to be processed and the stack look like this:

5 7 + 6 2 - *

After one iteration of the loop, we have processed the first operand and pushed it onto the stack.

```
5 7 + 6 2 - *  |     |
               |     |
               |     |
               |_____|
                  5
```

After the second iteration of the loop, the stack contains two operands.

```
5 7 + 6 2 - *  |     |
               |     |
               |     |
               |  7  |
               |__5__|
```

We encounter the + operator in the third iteration. We remove the two operands from the stack, perform the operation, and push the result onto the stack.

```
5 7 + 6 2 - *  |     |
               |     |
               |     |
               |     |
               |_12__|
```

In the next two iterations of the loop, we push two operands onto the stack.

```
5 7 + 6 2 - *  |     |
               |     |
               |  2  |
               |  6  |
               |_12__|
```

When we find the − operator, we remove the top two operands, subtract, and push the result onto the stack.

```
5 7 + 6 2 - *  |     |
               |     |
               |     |
               |  4  |
               |_12__|
```

When we find the * operator, we remove the top two operands, multiply, and push the result onto the stack.

Now that we have processed all of the items on the input line, we exit the loop. We remove the result, 48, from the stack.

Of course, we have glossed over a few "minor" details, such as how we recognize an operator and how we know when we are finished. All of the input values in this example were one-digit numbers. Clearly, this is too restrictive. We also need to handle invalid input. We discuss these challenges as we continue to evolve the solution to our problem.

Specification: Program Postfix Evaluation

Here is a more formal specification of our problem.

Function
The program evaluates postfix arithmetic expressions containing integers and the binary operators +, -, *, and /.

Interface
Following our established conventions, we are not specifying which type of interface the program should provide. We develop a console-based solution but also provide a GUI solution for your study. In either case, the program must allow the user to enter a postfix expression, have it evaluated, and see the results of the evaluation. The user should then have the option of entering additional expressions or ending the program.

Input
The input is a series of arithmetic postfix expressions, entered interactively from the keyboard. An expression is made up of operators (the characters +, -, *, and /) and integers (the operands). Operators and operands must be separated by at least one blank.

Data

All numbers input, manipulated, and output by the program are integers.

Output

After the evaluation of each expression, the results are displayed:

"Result = value"

Error Processing

The program should recognize illegal postfix expressions. Instead of displaying an integer result when the expression is entered, in such a case it should display error messages as follows:

Type of Illegal Expression	Error Message
An expression contains a symbol that is not an integer or not one of "+", "-", "*", and "/"	Illegal symbol
An expression requires more than 50 stack items	Too many operands—stack overflow
There is more than one operand left on the stack after the expression is processed; for example, the expression 5 6 7 + has too many operands	Too many operands—operands left over
There are not enough operands on the stack when it is time to perform an operation; for example, 6 7 + + +; and, for example, 5 + 5	Not enough operands—stack underflow

Assumptions

1. The operations in expressions are valid at run time. This means that we do not try to divide by zero. Also, we do not generate numbers outside of the range of the Java `int` type.
2. A postfix expression has a maximum of 50 operands.

Brainstorming and Filtering

A study of the specifications provides the following list of nouns that appear to be possibilities for classes: postfix arithmetic expressions, operators, result, operands, and error messages. Let's look at each in turn.

- The *postfix arithmetic expressions* are entered by the user and consist of both numbers and other characters. We conclude that an expression should be represented by a string.
- This means we can probably represent *operators* as strings, too. Another possibility is to hold the operators in an ADT that provides a "set" of characters. How-

ever, upon reflection, we realize that all we really have to do is recognize the operator character, and the built-in string and character operations we already have at our disposal should be sufficient.

- The *result* of an evaluation is an interesting case. Where does the result come from? We propose the creation of a separate class `PostFixEvaluator` that provides an `evaluate` method that accepts a postfix expression as a string and returns the value of the expression. Our main program will use this class (and a few others) to solve the problem.
- The *operands* are integers.
- The *error messages* we need to generate are all related to the evaluation of the postfix expression. Because the `PostFixEvaluator` class evaluates the postfix expression, it will discover the errors. Therefore, to communicate the error messages between `PostFixEvaluator` and the main program, we propose the creation of an exception class called `PostFixException`.

From our knowledge of the postfix expression evaluation algorithm we know we also need a stack. We decide to use our `ArrayStack` class, which implements the `BoundedStackInterface`, because the problem description places an upper bound of 50 on the size of the stack. Additionally, we intend to use our standard approach and create a main program that provides interaction with the user.

Let's look at a short scenario describing how these classes can be used to solve our problem. The main program will prompt the user for an expression and read it into a string variable. It can then pass this string to the `evaluate` method of the `PostFix-Evaluator` class, which will use an `ArrayStack` object to help determine the value of the expression, assuming it is a legal expression. The `evaluate` method is used within a *try-catch* statement that allows the main program to determine whether any `PostFix-Exception` exceptions have been thrown. In either case it reports the result to the user and prompts for another expression. We can proceed with confidence that our set of classes seems sufficient to solve the problem.

We now move on to the design, implementation, and testing of the classes. Note that we can test the classes together, once they have all been created, by evaluating a number of postfix expressions (both legal and illegal) with the application.

Evolving a Program

We present our case studies in an idealized fashion. We make a general problem statement; discuss it; define formal specifications; identify classes; design and code the classes; and then test the system. In reality, however, such an application would probably evolve gradually, with small unit tests performed along the way. Especially during design and coding, it is sometimes helpful to take smaller steps and to evolve your program rather than trying to create it all at once. For example, for this case study you could take the following steps:

1. Build a prototype of the main program that just provides input/output activity—it would not support any processing. Its purpose is to test the usability of the user interface and provide a driver for further development.
2. Build a small part of `PostFixEvaluator` and see if you can pass it a string from the interface at the appropriate time.
3. See if you can pass back some information—any information—about the string from `PostFixEvaluator` to the main program and have it display on the user interface. For example, you could display the number of tokens in the string.
4. Upgrade `PostFixEvaluator` so that it recognizes operands and transforms them into integers. Have it obtain an operand from the expression string, transform it, push the integer onto a stack, retrieve it, and pass it back for display.
5. Upgrade `PostFixEvaluator` to recognize operators and process expressions that are more complicated. Test some legal expressions.
6. Add the error trapping and reporting portion. Test using illegal expressions.

Devising a good program evolution plan is often the key to successful programming.

The PostFixEvaluator Class

The purpose of this class is to provide an `evaluate` method that accepts a postfix expression as a string and returns the value of the expression. We do not need any objects of the class, so we implement `evaluate` as a `public static` method. This means that it is invoked through the class itself, rather than through an object of the class.

The `evaluate` method must take a postfix expression as a string argument and return the value of the expression. The code for the class is listed below. It follows the basic postfix expression algorithm that we developed earlier, using an `ArrayStack` object to hold operands of class `Integer` until they are needed. Note that it instantiates a `Scanner` object to "read" the string argument and break it into tokens.

Let's consider error message generation. Look through the code for the lines that throw `PostFixException` exceptions. You should be able to see that we cover all of the error conditions required by the problem specification. As would be expected, the error messages directly related to the stack processing are all protected by *if* statements that check whether the stack is empty (not enough operands) or full (too many operands). The only other error trapping occurs if the string stored in operator does not match any of the legal operators, in which case we throw an exception with the message "Illegal symbol."

```
//-------------------------------------------------------------------
// PostFixEvaluator.java        by Dale/Joyce/Weems          Chapter 3
//
// Provides a postfix expression evaluation.
//-------------------------------------------------------------------

package ch03.postfix;
```

```java
import ch03.stacks.*;
import java.util.Scanner;

public class PostFixEvaluator
{
  public static int evaluate(String expression)
  {
    BoundedStackInterface<Integer> stack = new ArrayStack<Integer>(50);

    int value;
    String operator;

    int operand1;
    int operand2;

    int result = 0;

    Scanner tokenizer = new Scanner(expression);

    while (tokenizer.hasNext())
    {
      if (tokenizer.hasNextInt())
      {
        // Process operand.
        value = tokenizer.nextInt();
        if (stack.isFull())
          throw new PostFixException("Too many operands - stack overflow");
        stack.push(value);
      }
      else
      {
        // Process operator.
        operator = tokenizer.next();

        // Obtain second operand from stack.
        if (stack.isEmpty())
          throw new PostFixException("Not enough operands - stack " +
                                     "underflow");
        operand2 = stack.top();
        stack.pop();

        // Obtain first operand from stack.
        if (stack.isEmpty())
          throw new PostFixException("Not enough operands - stack " +
                                     "underflow");
```

```
        operand1 = stack.top();
        stack.pop();

        // Perform operation.
        if (operator.equals("/"))
          result = operand1 / operand2;
        else
        if(operator.equals("*"))
          result = operand1 * operand2;
        else
        if(operator.equals("+"))
          result = operand1 + operand2;
        else
        if(operator.equals("-"))
          result = operand1 - operand2;
        else
          throw new PostFixException("Illegal symbol: " + operator);

        // Push result of operation onto stack.
        stack.push(result);
      }
    }

    // Obtain final result from stack.
    if (stack.isEmpty())
      throw new PostFixException("Not enough operands - stack underflow");
    result = stack.top();
    stack.pop();

    // Stack should now be empty.
    if (!stack.isEmpty())
      throw new PostFixException("Too many operands - operands left over");

    // Return the final result.
    return result;
  }
}
```

The PFixConsole Class

This class is the main driver for our console-based application. Using the PostFixEvalu-ator and PostFixException classes, it is easy to design our program. We follow the same basic approach we used for BalancedApp earlier in the chapter—namely, prompt the user for an expression, evaluate it, return the results to the user, and ask the user if he or she would like to continue. Note that the main program does not directly use `ArrayStack`; it is used strictly by the `PostFixEvaluator` class when evaluating an expression.

```java
//---------------------------------------------------------------------------
// PFixConsole.java            by Dale/Joyce/Weems              Chapter 3
//
// Evaluates postfix expressions entered by the user.
// Uses a console interface.
//---------------------------------------------------------------------------

import java.util.Scanner;
import ch03.postfix.*;

public class PFixConsole
{
  public static void main(String[] args)
  {
    Scanner conIn = new Scanner(System.in);

    String line = null;            // string to be evaluated
    String more = null;            // used to stop or continue processing

    int result;                    // result of evaluation

    do
    {
      // Get next expression to be processed.
      System.out.println("Enter a postfix expression to be evaluated: ");
      line = conIn.nextLine();

      // Obtain and output result of expression evaluation.
      try
      {
        result = PostFixEvaluator.evaluate(line);

        // Output result.
        System.out.println();
        System.out.println("Result = " + result);
      }
      catch (PostFixException error)
      {
        // Output error message.
        System.out.println();
        System.out.println("Error in expression - " + error.getMessage());
      }
```

```
      // Determine if there is another expression to process.
      System.out.println();
      System.out.print("Evaluate another expression? (Y = Yes): ");
      more = conIn.nextLine();
      System.out.println();
    }
    while (more.equalsIgnoreCase("y"));

    System.out.println("Program completed.");
  }
}
```

Here is a sample run of our console-based application:

Enter a postfix expression to be evaluated:
5 7 + 6 2 - *

Result = 48

Evaluate another expression? (Y = Yes): y

Enter a postfix expression to be evaluated:
4 2 3 5 1 - + * + *

Error in expression - Not enough operands - stack underflow

Evaluate another expression? (Y = Yes): n

Program completed.

Testing the Postfix Evaluator

As mentioned earlier, we can test all of the classes created for this case study by simply running the postfix evaluator program and entering postfix expressions. We should test expressions that contain only additions, subtractions, multiplications, and divisions, as well as expressions that contain a mixture of operations. We should test expressions where the operators all come last and expressions where the operators are intermingled with the operands. Of course, we must evaluate all test expressions "by hand" to verify the correctness of the program's results. Finally, we must test that illegal expressions are correctly handled, as defined in the specifications. This includes a test of stack overflow, which requires at least 51 operands.

The GUI Approach

Most of the code in the `PFixConsole` program is responsible for presenting a console-based interface to the user. Just as that program used the `PostFixEvaluator` and `PostFixException` classes to do its primary processing, so can a program that presents a graphical user interface. Our `PFixGUI` program does just that. We do not list the code for this program here, but the interested reader can find it with the rest of the textbook code on the website. It uses the `Border` layout with nested containers.

Here are a few screenshots from the running program. The first shows the interface as originally presented to the user:

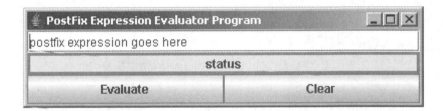

Here's the result of a successful evaluation:

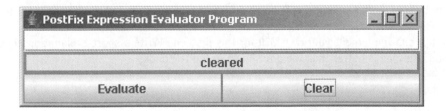

Next, the Clear button is clicked:

Here's what happens when the user enters an expression with too many operands:

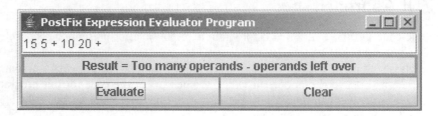

And finally, here's what happens when an illegal operand is used:

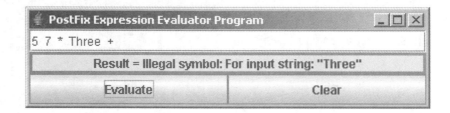

Exercises

1. Revise and test the `PFixGUI` application to meet these specifications:

   a. Use `Flow` layout exclusively.
   b. Keep track of statistics about the numbers pushed onto the stack during the evaluation of an expression. The program should output the largest and smallest numbers pushed, how many numbers were pushed, and the average value of pushed numbers.

2. Revise and test the `PFixGUI` application so that it will step through the evaluation of a postfix expression one step at a time, showing the intermediate results as it goes. Include a Step button on the interface so the user can control when a step is taken. For example, if the original expression is 2 3 4 + + 5 -, clicking Step once will display in the expression box 2 7 + 5 -, clicking it again will display 9 5 -, and clicking it one last time will display 4.

3. Design and implement your own GUI for this problem. Write a short explanation about why your interface is better than the one shown in the textbook.

Figure 3.16 is a UML diagram showing the "uses" relationships among the stack implementation class, the postfix expression evaluation class, and the two main driver classes (one console-based and one GUI-based).

Figure 3.16 *UML diagram for postfix program*

Summary

We have defined a stack at the logical level as an abstract data type, used a stack in two applications, and presented three implementations (array-based, link-based, and `ArrayList`-based). We have also seen how to use Java's generics to enable our stack implementations to work with different kinds of objects.

Although our logical picture of a stack is a linear collection of data elements with the newest element (the top) at one end and the oldest element at the other end, the physical representation of the stack class does not have to re-create our mental image. The implementation of the stack class must always support the last in, first out (LIFO) property; how this property is supported, however, is another matter.

Usually more than one functionally correct design is possible for the same data structure. When multiple correct solutions exist, the requirements and specifications of the application may determine which solution represents the best design.

We have seen how a hierarchy of interfaces can be used to represent the essential features of a data structure ADT and then extend it with different properties, such as being bounded or unbounded in size. We have also seen three different approaches to dealing with exceptional situations that are encountered within an ADT.

In this chapter we developed algorithms for two important applications of stacks in computer science. We can now check whether the grouping symbols in a string are balanced, and we can evaluate a postfix arithmetic expression.

Figure 3.17 is a UML diagram showing the stack-related interfaces and classes developed in this chapter, along with a few other supporting classes, and their relationships.

Exercises

3.1 Stacks

1. True or False?

    a. A stack is a first in, first out structure.

    b. The item that has been in a stack the longest is at the "bottom" of the stack.

    c. If you `push` five items onto an empty stack and then `pop` the stack five times, the stack will be empty again.

    d. If you `push` five items onto an empty stack and then perform the `top` operation five times, the stack will be empty again.

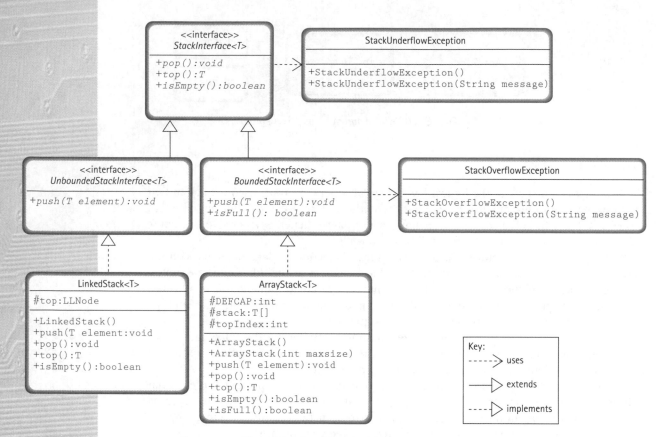

Figure 3.17 *The stack-related interfaces and classes developed in Chapter 3*

    e. The `push` operation should be classified as a "transformer."

    f. The `top` operation should be classified as a "transformer."

    g. The `pop` operation should be classified as an "observer."

    h. If we first `push itemA` onto a stack and then `push itemB`, then the `top` of the stack is `itemB`.

2. Following the style of Figure 3.2, show the effects of the following stack operations, assuming you begin with an empty stack:

        push block5

        push block7

        pop

        pop

        push block2

        push block1

pop
push block8

3.2 Collection Elements

3. In Section 3.2 we looked at four approaches to defining the types of elements we can hold in a collection ADT. Briefly describe each of the four approaches.

4. For each of the following programs that involve casting, predict the result of compiling and running the program. Potential answers include "there is a syntax error because . . . ," "there is a run-time error because . . . ," and "the output of the program would be . . . ."

   a.
   ```java
   public class test1
   {
       public static void main(String[] args)
       {
           String s1, s2;
           Object o1;
           s2 = "E. E. Cummings";
           o1 = s2;
           s1 = o1;
           System.out.println(s1.toLowerCase());
       }
   }
   ```

   b.
   ```java
   public class test2
   {
       public static void main(String[] args)
       {
           String s1, s2;
           Object o1;
           s2 = "E. E. Cummings";
           o1 = s2;
           s1 = (String) o1;
           System.out.println(s1.toLowerCase());
       }
   }
   ```

5. In Chapter 2 we developed a `StringLog` ADT. It represents a "log" that holds objects of class `String`. Suppose that instead of restricting ourselves to strings, we decided to create a "log" that holds objects of type `Object`. Describe the changes you would have to make to each of the following classes to implement such a change.

   a. Change `StringLogInterface` to `ObjectLogInterface`.

   b. Change `ArrayStringLog` to `ArrayObjectLog`.

    c. Change `ITDArrayStringLog` to `ITDArrayObjectLog`.

    d. Change `LLStringNode` to `LLObjectNode`.

    e. Change `LinkedStringLog` to `LinkedObjectLog`.

6. Create a generic array-based log class that features all the functionality of the `StringLog` class, as specified in Section 2.2. Create a driver application that demonstrates that your implementation works correctly.

7. Create a generic link-based `bag` class that features all the functionality of the `Bag` class specified in Exercise 29 of Chapter 2. Create a driver application that demonstrates that your implementation works correctly.

3.3 Exceptional Situations

8. Explain the difference between a programmer-defined exception that extends the Java `Exception` class and one that extends the Java `RunTimeException` class.

9. Expand your solution to Exercise 29 of Chapter 1, where you implemented the `Date` class, to include the appropriate throwing of the `DateOutOfBoundsException` by the class constructor, as described in this chapter. Don't forget to check for legal days, in addition to months and years.

10. Let's assume you have correctly implemented the `Date` class, as requested in Exercise 9. Recall that the `IncDate` class extends `Date`, adding a method called `increment` that adds one day to the date represented by the `Date` object. Consider exceptional situations that might be related to the `increment` method.

    a. Should the `increment` method test the current date values to make sure they are legal before incrementing the date?

    b. How about after incrementing the date? Would it be a good idea for the `increment` method to test the new date to make sure it is legal, perhaps raising the `DateOutOfBoundsException` if it is not?

11. Describe three ways to "handle" error situations within our ADT specification/implementation. For each approach, include a brief description of when it is most appropriate to use it.

12. What is wrong with the following method, based on our conventions for handling error situations?

```
public void method10(int number)
// Precondition:  number is > 0.
// Throws NotPositiveException if number is not > 0,
// otherwise ...
```

13. There are three parts to this exercise:

    a. Create a "standard" exception class called `ThirteenException`.

    b. Write a program that repeatedly prompts the user to enter a string. After each string is entered the program outputs the length of the string, unless the length of the string is 13, in which case the ThirteenException is thrown with the message "Use thirteen letter words and stainless steel to protect yourself!" Your main method should simply throw the ThirteenException exception out to the run-time environment. A sample run of the program might be:

```
Input a string > Villanova University
That string has length 20.
Input a string > Triscadecaphobia
That string has length 16.
Input a string > misprogrammed
```

At this point the program bombs and the system provides some information, including the "Use thirteen letter words and stainless steel to protect yourself!" message.

c. Create another program similar to the one you created for part b, except this time, within your code, include a try-catch clause so that you catch the exception when it is thrown. If it is thrown, then catch it, print its message, and end the program "normally."

14. Write a class Array that encapsulates an array and provides bounds-checked access. The private instance variables should be int index and int array[10]. The public members should be a default constructor and methods (signatures shown below) to provide read and write access to the array.

```
void insert(int location, int value);
int retrieve(int location);
```

If the location is within the correct range for the array, the insert method should set that location of the array to the value. Likewise, if the location is within the correct range for the array, the retrieve method should return the value at that location—the approach taken by the library before Java 5.0. In either case, if location is not within the correct range, the method should throw an exception of class ArrayOutOfBoundsException. Write an application that helps you test your implementation. Your application should assign values to the array by using the insert method, then use the retrieve method to read these values back from the array. It should also try calling both methods with illegal location values. Catch any exceptions thrown by placing the "illegal" calls in a try block with an appropriate catch.

3.4 Formal Specification

15. Based on our Stack ADT specification, an application programmer has two ways to check for an empty stack. Describe them and discuss when one approach might be preferable to the other approach.

16. Show what is written by the following segments of code, given that item1, item2, and item3 are int variables, and stack is an object that fits the

abstract description of a stack as given in the section. Assume that you can store and retrieve variables of type int on stack.

a.
```
item1 = 1;
item2 = 0;
item3 = 4;
stack.push(item2);
stack.push(item1);
stack.push(item1 + item3);
item2 = stack.top();
stack.push (item3*item3);
stack.push(item2);
stack.push(3);
item1 = stack.top();
stack.pop();
System.out.println(item1 + " " + item2 + " " + item3);
while (!stack.isEmpty())
{
   item1 = stack.top();
   stack.pop();
   System.out.println(item1);
}
```

b.
```
item1 = 4;
item3 = 0;
item2 = item1 + 1;
stack.push(item2);
stack.push(item2 + 1);
stack.push(item1);
item2 = stack.top();
stack.pop();
item1 = item2 + 1;
stack.push(item1);
stack.push(item3);
while (!stack.isEmpty())
{
   item3 = stack.top();
   stack.pop();
   System.out.println(item3);
}
System.out.println(item1 + " " + item2 + " " + item3);
```

17. Your friend Bill says, "The push and pop stack operations are inverses of each other. Therefore performing a push followed by a pop is always equivalent to performing a pop followed by a push. You get the same result!" How would you respond to that? Do you agree?

18. The following code segment is a count-controlled loop going from 1 through 5. At each iteration, the loop counter is either printed or put on a stack depending on the `boolean` result returned by the method `random`. (Assume that `random` randomly returns either `true` or `false`.) At the end of the loop, the items on the stack are removed and printed. Because of the logical properties of a stack, this code segment cannot print certain sequences of the values of the loop counter. You are given an output and asked to determine whether the code segment could generate the output.

```
for (count = 1; count <= 5; count++)
{
  if (random())
    System.out.println(count);
  else
    stack.push(count);
}
while (!stack.isEmpty())
{
  number = stack.top();
  stack.pop();
  System.out.println(number);
}
```

   a. The following output is possible: 1 3 5 2 4

      i. True   ii. False   iii. Not enough information

   b. The following output is possible: 1 3 5 4 2

      i. True   ii. False   iii. Not enough information

   c. The following output is possible: 1 2 3 4 5

      i. True   ii. False   iii. Not enough information

   d. The following output is possible: 5 4 3 2 1

      i. True   ii. False   iii. Not enough information

19. In compiler construction, we need an observer method to examine stack elements based on their location in the stack (the top of the stack is considered location 1, the second element from the top is location 2, and so on). This is sometimes called (colloquially) a "glass stack" or (more formally) a "traversable stack." The definition of the stack is exactly as we specify in this chapter, except we add a public method named `inspector` that accepts an `int` argument indicating the location to be returned. The method should return `null` if the argument indicates an unused location. Describe explicitly what you would add to the `StackInterface` interface to include this method.

20. In compiler construction, we need to be able to pop more than one element at a time, discarding the items popped. To do so, we provide an `int` parameter `count` for a `popSome` method that removes the top `count` items from the stack. The new method should throw `StackUnderflowException` as needed.

Write the `popSome` method at the application level, using operations from `StackInterface`.

21. In each plastic container of Pez candy, the colors are stored in random order. Your little brother Phil likes only the yellow ones, so he painstakingly takes out all the candies one by one, eats the yellow ones, and keeps the others in order, so that he can return them to the container in exactly the same order as before—minus the yellow candies, of course. Write the algorithm to simulate this process. (You may use any of the stack operations defined in the Stack ADT, but may not assume any knowledge of how the stack is implemented.)

22. Describe inheritance of interfaces and explain why it was used in Section 3.4.

Exercises 23–26 require "outside" research.

23. Describe the major differences between the Java library's `Vector` and `ArrayList` classes.

24. Explain how the iterators in the Java Collections Framework are used.

25. What is the defining feature of the Java library's `Set` class?

26. Which classes of the Java library implement the `Collection` interface?

3.5   Array-Based Implementations

27. Explain why an array is a good implementation structure for a bounded stack.

28. Describe the effects each of the following changes would have on the `ArrayStack` class.

  a. Remove the `final` attribute from the `DEFCAP` instance variable.

  b. Change the value assigned to `DEFCAP` to 10.

  c. Change the value assigned to `DEFCAP` to −10.

  d. In the first constructor change the statement to `stack = (T[]) new Object[100];`

  e. In `isEmpty`, change "`topIndex == -1`" to "`topIndex < 0`".

  f. Reverse the order of the two statements in the `if` clause of the `push` method.

  g. Reverse the order of the two statements in the `if` clause of the `pop` method.

  h. In the `throws` statement of the `top` method change the argument string from "Top attempted on an empty stack" to "Pop attempted on an empty stack."

29. Create a `toString` method for the `ArrayStack` class. This method should create and return a string that correctly represents the current stack. Such a method could prove useful for testing and debugging the `ArrayStack` class and for testing and debugging applications that use the `ArrayStack` class.

30. Write a segment of code (application level) to perform each of the following operations. Assume `myStack` is an object of the class `ArrayStack`. You may call any of the public methods of `ArrayStack`. You may declare additional stack objects.

  a. Set `secondElement` to the second element from the top of `myStack`, leaving `myStack` without its original top two elements.

b. Set `bottom` equal to the bottom element in `myStack`, leaving `myStack` empty.

c. Set `bottom` equal to the bottom element in `myStack`, leaving `myStack` unchanged.

d. Print out the contents of `myStack`, leaving `myStack` unchanged.

31. Explain the differences between arrays and array lists.

32. Explain why we use a comparison to −1 for the `isEmpty` method of `ArrayStack`, yet in the `isEmpty` method for `ArrayListStack` we use a comparison to 0.

33. Exercise 19 described an `inspector` method for a stack.

a. Implement `inspector` for the `ArrayStack` class.

b. Implement `inspector` for the `ArrayListStack` class.

34. Exercise 20 described a `popSome` method for a stack.

a. Implement `popSome` for the `ArrayStack` class.

b. Implement `popSome` for the `ArrayListStack` class.

35. Two stacks of positive integers are needed, both containing integers with values less than or equal to 1000. One stack contains even integers; the other contains odd integers. The total number of elements in the combined stacks is never more than 200 at any time, but we cannot predict how many are in each stack. (All of the elements could be in one stack, they could be evenly divided, both stacks could be empty, and so on.) Can you think of a way to implement both stacks in one array?

a. Draw a diagram of how the stacks might look.

b. Write the definitions for such a double-stack structure.

c. Implement the `push` operation; it should store the new item into the correct stack according to its value (even or odd).

3.6 Application: Well-Formed Expressions

36. For each of the following programs that involve casting and Autoboxing, predict the result of compiling and running the program. Potential answers include "there is a syntax error because . . . ," "there is a run-time error because . . . ," and "the output of the program would be . . . ."

a.
```
public class test3
{
  public static void main(String[] args)
  {
    String s1;
    int i1;
    Object o1;
    i1 = 35;
    o1 = i1;
    s1 = (String) o1;
```

```
            System.out.println(s1.toLowerCase());
      }
   }
```

b.
```
public class test4
{
   public static void main(String[] args)
   {
      Integer I1;
      int i1;
      Object o1;
      i1 = 35;
      o1 = i1;
      I1 = (Integer) o1;
      System.out.println(I1);
   }
}
```

37. Answer the following questions about the `Balanced` class:

   a. Is there any functional difference between the class being instantiated in the following two ways?

   ```
   Balanced bal = new Balanced ("abc", "xyz");
   Balanced bal = new Balanced ("cab", "zxy");
   ```

   b. Is there any functional difference between the class being instantiated in the following two ways?

   ```
   Balanced bal = new Balanced ("abc", "xyz");
   Balanced bal = new Balanced ("abc", "zxy");
   ```

   c. Is there any functional difference between the class being instantiated in the following two ways?

   ```
   Balanced bal = new Balanced ("abc", "xyz");
   Balanced bal = new Balanced ("xyz", "abc");
   ```

   d. Which type is pushed onto the `stack`? A `char`? An `int`? An `Integer`? Explain.

   e. Under which circumstances is the first operation performed on the `stack` (not counting the `new` operation) the `top` operation?

   f. What happens if the string `s`, which is passed to the `test` method, is an empty string?

38. Suppose we want to change our application so that it reports more information about an unbalanced string—namely, the location and value of the first unbalanced character. To report character locations to the user, we number the char-

acters starting with 1. For example, if the user enters the string "(xxx[x}]xx)x" the output would be "Unbalanced symbol } at location 7."

a. Describe how you would change the classes to implement this change.

b. Make the changes to the application and test the result.

3.7 Link–Based Implementation

39. What are the main differences, in terms of memory allocation, between using an array-based stack and using a reference-based stack?

40. Consider the code for the push method of the LinkedStack class. What would be the effect of the following changes to that code?

a. Switch the first and second lines.

b. Switch the second and third lines.

41. Draw a sequence of diagrams, of the style used in Section 3.7, to depict what happens from the inside view with the dynamic allocation of space for the references to the stack elements. Assume A, B, and C represent objects of class String.

a.
```
UnboundedStackInterface<String> myStack;
myStack = new LinkedStack<String>();
myStack.push(A);
myStack.pop();
myStack.push(B);
myStack.push(C);
```

b.
```
UnboundedStackInterface<String> myStack;
myStack = new LinkedStack<String>();
myStack.push(A);
myStack.push(B);
myStack.push(A);
```

c.
```
UnboundedStackInterface<String> myStack;
myStack = new LinkedStack<String>();
myStack.push(A);
myStack.push(C);
myStack.push(B);
myStack.pop();
```

42. Create a toString method for the LinkedStack class. This method should create and return a string that correctly represents the current stack. Such a method could prove useful for testing and debugging the LinkedStack class and for testing and debugging applications that use the LinkedStack class.

43. Exercise 19 described an inspector method for a stack. Implement inspector for the LinkedStack class.

44. Exercise 20 described a popSome method for a stack. Implement popSome for the LinkedStack class.

45. We decide to add a new operation to our Stack ADT called `popTop`. We add the following code to our `StackInterface` interface:

```
public T popTop() throws StackUnderflowException;
// Throws StackUnderflowException if this stack is empty,
// otherwise removes and returns top element from this stack.
```

An operation like this is often included for stacks. Implement the `popTop` method for the `LinkedStack` class.

46. Suppose we decide to add a new operation to our Stack ADT called `sizeIs`, which returns a value of primitive type `int` equal to the number of items on the stack. The method signature for `sizeIs` is

```
public int sizeIs()
```

a. Write the code for `sizeIs` for the `ArrayStack` class.

b. Write the code for `sizeIs` for the `LinkedStack` class (do not add any instance variables to the class; each time `sizeIs` is called you must "walk" through the stack and count the nodes).

c. Suppose you decide to augment the `LinkedStack` class with an instance variable `size` that always holds the current size of the stack. Now you can implement the `sizeIs` operation by just returning the value of `size`. Identify all of the methods of `LinkedStack` that you need to modify to maintain the correct value in the `size` variable and describe how you would change them.

d. Analyze the methods created/changed in parts a, b, and c in terms of Big-O efficiency.

47. Use the `LinkedStack` class to support an application that tracks the status of an online auction. Bidding begins at 1 (dollars, pounds, euros, or whatever) and proceeds in increments of at least 1. If a bid arrives that is less than the current bid, it is discarded. If a bid arrives that is more than the current bid, but less than the maximum bid by the current high bidder, then the current bid for the current high bidder is increased to match it and the new bid is discarded. If a bid arrives that is more than the maximum bid for the current high bidder, then the new bidder becomes the current high bidder, at a bid of one more than the previous high bidder's maximum. When the auction is over (the end of the input is reached), a history of the actual bids (the ones not discarded), from high bid to low bid, should be displayed. For example:

New Bid	Result	High Bidder	High Bid	Maximum Bid
7 John	New high bidder	John	1	7
5 Hank	High bid increased	John	5	7
10 Jill	New high bidder	Jill	8	10
8 Thad	No change	Jill	8	10
15 Joey	New high bidder	Joey	11	15

The bid history for this auction would be

Joey	11
Jill	8
John	5
John	1

Input/output details can be determined by you or your instructor. In any case, as input proceeds the current status of the auction should be displayed. The final output should include the bid history as described above.

3.8 Case Study: Postfix Expression Evaluator

48. Evaluate the following postfix expressions.

   a. 5 7 8 * +

   b. 5 7 8 + *

   c. 5 7 + 8 *

   d. 1 2 + 3 4 + 5 6 * 2 *

49. Evaluate the following postfix expressions. Some of them may be ill-formed expressions—in that case, identify the appropriate error message (e.g., too many operands, too few operands).

   a. 1 2 3 4 5 + + +

   b. 1 2 + + 5

   c. 1 2 * 5 6 *

   d. / 23 * 87

   e. 4567 234 / 45372 231 * + 34526 342 / + 0 *

50. Revise and test the postfix expression evaluator program as specified here.

   a. Use the `ArrayListStack` class instead of the `ArrayStack` class—do not worry about stack overflow.

   b. Catch and handle the divide-by-zero situation that was assumed not to happen. For example, if the input expression is 5 3 3 - /, the result would be the message "illegal divide by zero."

   c. Support a new operation indicated by "^" that returns the larger of its operands. For example, 5 7 ^ = 7.

   d. Keep track of statistics about the numbers pushed onto the stack during the evaluation of an expression. The program should output the largest and smallest numbers pushed, the total numbers pushed, and the average value of pushed numbers.

Recursion

Knowledge Goals

You should be able to
- define recursion
- discuss recursion as a problem solving technique
- describe the three questions used to analyze a recursive approach
- do the following, given a recursive method:
  - determine whether the method halts
  - determine the base cases
  - determine the general cases
  - determine what the method does
  - determine whether the method is correct and, if it is not, correct it
- compare and contrast dynamic storage allocation and static storage allocation in relation to using recursion
- explain how recursion works internally by showing the contents of the run-time stack
- explain why recursion may or may not be a good choice to implement the solution of a problem

Skill Goals

You should be able to
- do the following, given a recursive-problem description:
  - determine the base cases
  - determine the general cases
  - design and code the solution using recursion
- verify a recursive method, using the Three-Question Approach
- decide whether a recursive solution is appropriate for a problem
- solve the Towers of Hanoi problem recursively
- count the number of blobs on a grid using a recursive approach
- visit the nodes of a linked list in reverse order using recursion
- create an iterative version of a program that uses tail recursion
- replace a recursive solution with a solution based on a stack
- design and implement a recursive solution to a problem

This chapter introduces the topic of recursion—a distinct algorithmic problem-solving approach supported by many computer languages (Java included). What's recursion? Let's look first at a visual analogy.

You may have seen a set of brightly painted Russian dolls that fit inside one another. Inside the first doll is a smaller doll, inside of which is an even smaller doll, inside of which is yet a smaller doll, and so on. Solving a problem recursively is like taking apart such a set of Russian dolls. You first create smaller and smaller versions of the same problem until a version is reached that can no longer be subdivided (and that is easily solved)—that is, until the smallest doll is reached. Determining the overall solution often requires combining the smaller solutions, analogous to putting the dolls back together again.

Recursion, when applied properly, is an extremely powerful and useful problem-solving tool. We will use it many times in upcoming chapters to support our work.

4.1 Recursive Definitions, Algorithms, and Programs

Recursive Definitions

You are already familiar with recursive definitions. Consider the following definition of the directories (or catalogs, or folders) you use to organize files on a computer:

A *directory* is an entity in a file system that contains a group of files and other *directories*.

This is a recursive definition because it expresses *directory* in terms of itself.
Here's another example:

A *compound sentence* is a *sentence* that consists of two *sentences* joined together by a coordinating conjunction.

Recursive definition   A definition in which something is defined in terms of smaller versions of itself

Do you see the recursiveness here? Based on the recursive nature of this definition you can make compound sentences of any length.

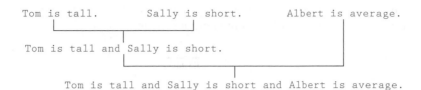

Mathematicians regularly define concepts in terms of themselves. For instance, $n!$ (read "n factorial") is used to calculate the number of permutations of n elements. A nonrecursive definition of $n!$ is

$$n! = \begin{cases} 1 & \text{if } n = 0 \\ n \times (n-1) \times (n-2) \times \quad \times 1 & \text{if } n > 0 \end{cases}$$

Consider the case of 4!. Because $n > 0$, we use the second part of the definition:

$$4! = 4 \times 3 \times 2 \times 1 = 24$$

This definition of $n!$ is not mathematically rigorous. It uses the three dots, rather informally, to stand for intermediate factors. For example, the definition of 8! is $8 \times 7 \times 6 \times \cdots \times 1$, with the $\cdots$ in this case standing for $5 \times 4 \times 3 \times 2$.

We can express $n!$ more elegantly, without using the three dots, by using recursion:

$$n! = \begin{cases} 1 & \text{if } n = 0 \\ n \times (n-1)! & \text{if } n > 0 \end{cases}$$

This is a recursive definition because we express the factorial function in terms of itself. The definition of 8! is now $8 \times 7!$.

Recursive Algorithms

Let's walk through the calculation of 4! using our recursive definition. We can use a set of index cards to help track our work—not only does this demonstrate how we use a recursive definition, but it also models the actions of a computer system executing a recursive program.

We take out an index card and write on it:

```
Calculate 4!
4! =
```

Looking at our recursive definition we determine that 4 is greater than 0, so we use the second part of the definition and continue writing:

```
Calculate 4!
4! = 4 × (4 −1)!
4! = 4 × 3!
4! = 4 × ☐
```

Of course, we can't complete the third line because we don't know the value of 3!. Before continuing with our original problem (calculating 4!), we have to solve this new problem (calculating 3!). So we take out another index card, stack it on top of our original card, and write down our new problem:

```
Calculate 4!
4! Calculate 3!
4! 3! =
4!
```

Again we look at our recursive definition. We determine that 3 is greater than 0, so we use the second part of the definition and continue writing:

```
Calculate 4!
4! Calculate 3!
4! 3! = 3 × (3 −1)!
4! 3! = 3 × 2!
   3! = 3 × ☐
```

As before, we can't complete the third line because we don't know the value of 2!. We take out another index card and write down our new problem. Continuing in this way we eventually have five cards stacked on our desk:

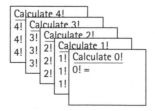

At this point, when we turn to our recursive definition to calculate 0! we find that we can use the first part of the definition: 0! equals 1.

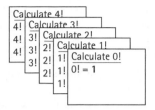

We have finished the problem at the top of our stack of cards. Its result is 1. Remembering that result, we throw away the top card, write the "1" into the empty slot on the card that is now on top (the *Calculate 1!* card), and continue working on that problem. Because we know how to calculate 1×1, we can quickly finish that problem and enter its result.

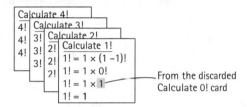

As before, we remember this result, discard the top card, enter the result onto the next card (the *Calculate 2!* card), and continue. In quick succession we determine that

$$2! = 2 \times 1 = 2$$

$$3! = 3 \times 2 = 6$$

$$4! = 4 \times 6 = 24$$

ending with the solution to our original problem:

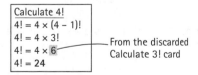

We stop creating new problem cards when we reach a case for which we know the answer without resorting to the recursive part of the definition. In this example, that point occurred when we reached *Calculate 0!*. We know that value is 1 directly from the definition without having to resort to recursion.

When the answer for a case is directly known, without requiring further recursion, it is called a base case. A recursive definition may

> **Base case** The case for which the solution can be stated nonrecursively

General (recursive) case The case for which the solution is expressed in terms of a smaller version of itself

Recursive algorithm A solution that is expressed in terms of (1) smaller instances of itself, and (2) a base case

have more than one base case. The case (or cases) for which the solution is expressed in terms of a smaller version (or versions) of itself is called the recursive or general case. A recursive algorithm is an algorithm that expresses a solution in terms of smaller versions of itself. A recursive algorithm must terminate; that is, it must have a base case, and the recursive cases must eventually lead to a base case.

Here is our recursive algorithm for calculating $n!$ based directly on the recursive definition. It assumes that n is a nonnegative integer.

Factorial (int n)

```
// Precondition: n >= 0
if (n == 0)
  return (1)
else
  return (n * Factorial (n – 1))
```

Recursive Programs

In Java, a method can invoke other methods. A method can even invoke itself! When a method invokes itself, we say it is making a recursive call. It should not come as a surprise that we use recursive method calls to implement recursive-problem solutions.

Recursive call A method call in which the method being called is the same as the one making the call

Here is a Java method that corresponds to our recursive factorial algorithm. It uses a recursive call (<u>emphasized</u>) to calculate the factorial of its integer argument.

```
public static int factorial(int n)[1]
// Precondition: n is nonnegative
//
// Returns the value of "n!"
```

---

1. Normally we do not use single-letter identifiers in our programs. However, several of the examples of this chapter are classically described using single-letter names—and we follow that tradition in our discussions and programs.

```
{
  if (n == 0)
    return 1;          // Base case
  else
    return (n * factorial(n - 1));     // General case
}
```

The argument in the recursive call, n - 1, is different from the argument in the original call, n. This is an important and necessary condition; otherwise, the method would continue calling itself indefinitely.

In our example, the `factorial` method invokes itself. This type of recursion is sometimes called direct recursion, because the method directly calls itself. All of the examples in this chapter involve direct recursion. Indirect recursion occurs when method A calls method B, and method B calls method A; the chain of method calls could be even longer, but if it eventually leads back to method A, then it is indirect recursion.

> **Direct recursion** Recursion in which a method directly calls itself
>
> **Indirect recursion** Recursion in which a chain of two or more method calls returns to the method that originated the chain

Let's augment our recursive `factorial` method with some trace statements that allow us to track its progress toward the solution. We include one `println` statement at the beginning of the method to show that the method was entered, and another one at the end to show the value that is about to be returned. We use a statically defined `String` variable `indent`, initialized to the blank string, to preface every output statement. The length of `indent` is increased (decreased) by two upon entering (leaving) the `factorial` method. This formatting allows us to visually match the entry to the method with the value returned from that method, for each invocation. Note that we need to declare a variable `retValue` to store the return value of the function, as we wish to output the value before actually returning it. The code, with trace-related statements emphasized, follows:

```
private static int factorial(int n)
// Precondition: n is nonnegative
//
// Returns the value of "n!"
{
  int retValue;   // return value
  System.out.println(indent + "Enter factorial " + n);
  indent = indent + "  ";

  if (n == 0)
    retValue = 1;
  else
    retValue = (n * factorial (n - 1));
```

```
    indent = indent.substring(2);
    System.out.println(indent + "Return " + retValue);

    return(retValue);
}
```

Here is the output if we invoke this augmented `factorial` method with an argument of 9. Note that the final result is 362,880. Although the factorial function starts slowly, it grows very quickly.

```
Enter factorial 9
  Enter factorial 8
    Enter factorial 7
      Enter factorial 6
        Enter factorial 5
          Enter factorial 4
            Enter factorial 3
              Enter factorial 2
                Enter factorial 1
                  Enter factorial 0
                  Return 1
                Return 1
              Return 2
            Return 6
          Return 24
        Return 120
      Return 720
    Return 5040
  Return 40320
Return 362880
```

Recursion is a powerful programming technique, but we must be careful when using it. Recursive solutions can be less efficient than iterative solutions to the same problem. In fact, some of the examples presented in this chapter, including `factorial`, are better suited to iterative approaches. We discuss this topic more in Section 4.7.

Iterative Solution for Factorial

We used the factorial algorithm to demonstrate recursion because it is familiar and easy to visualize. In practice, we would never want to solve this problem using recursion, as a straightforward, more efficient iterative solution exists. Let's look at the iterative solution to the problem:

```
// Iterative solution
public static int factorial(int n)
{
    int value = n;
    int retValue = 1;    // return value
    while (value != 0)
```

```
  {
    retValue = retValue * value;
    value = value - 1;
  }
  return(retValue);
}
```

For easy comparison, we repeat the code from the recursive solution:

```
// Recursive solution
public static int factorial(int n)
{
  if (n == 0)
    return 1;              // Base case
  else
    return (n * factorial (n - 1));    // General case
}
```

Iterative solutions tend to employ loops, whereas recursive solutions tend to have selection statements—either an *if* or a *switch* statement. A branching structure is usually the main control structure in a recursive method. A looping structure is the corresponding control structure in an iterative method. The iterative version of factorial has two local variables (`retValue` and `value`), whereas the recursive version has none. There are usually fewer local variables in a recursive method than in an iterative method. The iterative solution is more efficient because starting a new iteration of a loop is a faster operation than calling a method.

4.2 The Three Questions

In this section we present three questions to ask about any recursive algorithm or program. Using these questions helps us verify, design, and debug recursive solutions to problems.

Verifying Recursive Algorithms

The kind of walk-through we did in Section 4.1, using index cards, is useful for understanding the recursive process—but it is not sufficient for validating the correctness of a recursive algorithm. After all, simulating the execution of `factorial(4)` tells us the method works when the argument equals 4, but it doesn't tell us whether the method is valid for other arguments.

We use the Three-Question Approach for verifying recursive algorithms. To verify that a recursive solution works, we must be able to answer yes to all three of these questions:

1. *The Base-Case Question*   Is there a nonrecursive way out of the algorithm, and does the algorithm work correctly for this base case?

2. *The Smaller-Caller Question*   Does each recursive call to the algorithm involve a smaller case of the original problem, leading inescapably to the base case?

3. *The General-Case Question*   Assuming the recursive call(s) to the smaller case(s) works correctly, does the algorithm work correctly for the general case?

Let's apply these three questions to the `factorial` algorithm:

Factorial (int n)

```
// Precondition: n >= 0
if (n == 0)
  return (1)
else
  return (n * Factorial (n – 1))
```

1. *The Base-Case Question*   The base case occurs when *n* is 0. The `Factorial` algorithm then returns the value of 1, which is the correct value of 0!, and no further (recursive) calls to `Factorial` are made. The answer is yes.

2. *The Smaller-Caller Question*   The parameter is *n* and the recursive call passes the argument *n* − 1. Therefore each subsequent recursive call sends a smaller value, until the value sent is finally 0. At this point, as we verified with the base-case question, we have reached the smallest case, and no further recursive calls are made. The answer is yes.

3. *The General-Case Question*   Assuming that the recursive call `Factorial(n - 1)` gives us the correct value of (*n* − 1)!, the *return* statement computes *n* * (*n* − 1)!. This is the definition of a factorial, so we know that the algorithm works in the general case. The answer is yes.

Because the answers to all three questions are yes, we can conclude that the algorithm works. If you are familiar with inductive proofs, you should recognize what we have done. Having made the assumption that the algorithm works for the smaller case, we have shown that the algorithm works for the general case. Because we have also shown that the algorithm works for the base case of 0, we have inductively shown that it works for any integer argument greater than or equal to 0.

For the factorial problem we assumed the original value for *n* is greater than or equal to 0. Note that without this assumption we cannot answer the smaller-caller question affirmatively. For example, if we start with *n* = −5, the recursive call would pass an argument of -6, which is farther from the base case, not closer, as required.

These kinds of constraints often exist on the valid input arguments for a recursive algorithm. We can typically use our three-question analysis to determine these constraints. Simply check whether there are any starting argument values for which the smaller call does not produce a new argument that is closer to the base case. Such starting values are invalid. Constrain your legal input arguments so that these values are not permitted.

Writing Recursive Methods

The questions used for verifying recursive algorithms can also be used as a guide for writing recursive methods. We can take the following approach to write a recursive method:

1. Get an exact definition of the problem to be solved. (This, of course, is the first step in solving any programming problem.)

2. Determine the size of the problem to be solved on this call to the method. On the initial call to the method, the size of the whole problem is expressed in the value(s) of the argument(s).

3. Identify and solve the base case(s) in which the problem can be expressed nonrecursively. This ensures a yes answer to the base-case question.

4. Identify and solve the general case(s) correctly in terms of a smaller case of the same problem—a recursive call. This ensures yes answers to the smaller-caller and general-case questions.

In the case of the factorial problem, the definition of the problem is summarized in the definition of the factorial function. The size of the problem is the number of values to be multiplied: *n*. The base case occurs when *n* is 0, in which case we take the nonrecursive path. The general case occurs when *n* > 0, resulting in a recursive call to `factorial` for a smaller case: `factorial(n - 1)`. We can summarize this information in table form as follows:

Recursive factorial(int n) Method: Returns int

Definition:	Calculates and returns n!
Precondition:	n is nonnegative
Size:	Value of n
Base Case:	If n equals 0, return 1
General Case:	If n > 0, return n*factorial(n − 1)

Debugging Recursive Methods

Because of their nested calls to themselves, recursive methods can be confusing to debug. The most serious problem is the possibility that the method recurses forever. A typical symptom of this problem is an error message telling us that the system has run out of space in the run-time stack, due to the level of recursive calls. (In Section 4.6 we look at how recursion uses the run-time stack.) Using the Three-Question Approach to verify recursive methods and determine argument constraints should help us avoid this problem.

Success with the three questions does not guarantee, however, that the program will not fail due to lack of space. In Section 4.7 we discuss the amount of space overhead required to support recursive method calls. Because a call to a recursive method may generate many, many levels of method calls to itself, the space consumed might be more than the system can handle.

One error that programmers often make when they first start writing recursive methods is to use a looping structure instead of a branching one. Because they tend to think of the problem in terms of a repetitive action, they inadvertently use a *while* statement rather than an *if* statement. The body of a recursive method should always break down into base and recursive cases. Hence, we use a branching statement. It's a good idea to double-check our recursive methods to make sure that we used an *if* or *switch* statement to select the recursive or base case.

Recursive methods are good places to put debug output statements during testing, similar to the trace statements we used with `factorial`. Print out the arguments and local variables, if any, at the beginning and end of the method. Remember to print the values of the arguments on the recursive call(s) so you can check that each call is trying to solve a problem smaller than the previous one.

4.3 Towers of Hanoi

One of your first toys may have been a plastic contraption with pegs holding colored rings of different diameters. If so, you probably spent countless hours moving the rings from one peg to another. If we put some constraints on how they can be moved, we have an adult game called the Towers of Hanoi. When the game begins, all the rings are on the first peg in order by size, with the smallest on the top. The object of the game is to move the rings, one at a time, to the third peg. The catch is that a ring cannot be placed on top of one that is smaller in diameter. The middle peg can be used as an auxiliary peg, but it must be empty at the beginning and at the end of the game. The rings can only be moved one at a time.

The Algorithm

To get a feel for how this might be done, let's look at some sketches of what the configuration must be at certain points for a solution to be possible. We use four rings. The beginning configuration is

To move the largest ring (ring 4) to peg 3, we must move the three smaller rings to peg 2 (this cannot be done with one move). Let's assume we can do this. Then ring 4 can be moved into its final place:

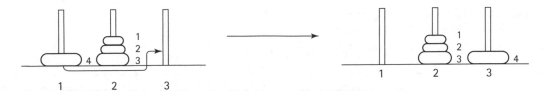

Now, to move the next largest ring (ring 3) into place, we must move the two rings on top of it onto an auxiliary peg (peg 1 in this case). Again we assume we can do this. Then ring 3 can be moved to its final place:

To get ring 2 into place, we must assume we can move ring 1 to another peg, freeing ring 2 to be moved to its final place on peg 3. This is an easy assumption to make:

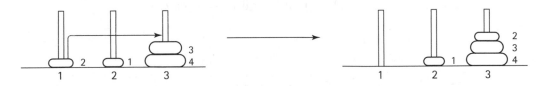

The last ring (ring 1) can now be moved into its final place, and we are finished:

If all of our assumptions are valid, we have solved the problem for four rings. Can you see that all of the assumptions involve solving smaller versions of the problem? We have solved the problem using recursion. The general recursive algorithm for moving n rings from the starting peg to the destination peg is:

Move n Rings from Starting Peg to Destination Peg

Move n - 1 rings from starting peg to auxiliary peg
Move the *n*th ring from starting peg to destination peg
Move n - 1 rings from auxiliary peg to destination peg

The Method

Let's write a recursive method that implements this algorithm. We can see that recursion works well because the first and third steps of the algorithm essentially repeat the overall algorithm, albeit with a smaller number of rings. Notice, however, that the starting peg, the destination peg, and the auxiliary peg are different for the subproblems; they keep changing during the recursive execution of the algorithm. To make the method easier to follow, we call the pegs `startPeg`, `endPeg`, and `auxPeg`. These three pegs, along with the number of rings on the starting peg, are the parameters of the method. We won't actually move any rings but we will print out a message describing the moves.

Our algorithm explicitly defines the recursive or general case, but what about a base case? How do we know when to stop the recursive process? The clue lies in the expression "Move *n* rings." If we don't have any rings to move, we don't have anything to do. We are finished with that stage. Therefore, when the number of rings equals 0, we do nothing (that is, we simply return). That is the base case.

```
public static void doTowers(
    int n,              // Number of rings to move
    int startPeg,       // Peg containing rings to move
    int auxPeg,         // Peg holding rings temporarily
    int endPeg      )   // Peg receiving rings being moved
{
  if (n > 0)
  {
    // Move n - 1 rings from starting peg to auxiliary peg
    doTowers(n - 1, startPeg, endPeg, auxPeg);

    System.out.println("Move ring from peg " + startPeg
            + " to peg " + endPeg);

    // Move n - 1 rings from auxiliary peg to ending peg
    doTowers(n - 1, auxPeg, startPeg, endPeg);
  }
}
```

It's hard to believe that such a simple method actually works, but it does. Let's investigate using the Three-Question Approach:

1. *The Base-Case Question*   Is there a nonrecursive way out of the method, and does the method work correctly for this base case? If the doTowers method is passed an argument equal to 0 for the number of rings (parameter n), it skips the body of the *if* statement and does nothing. This response is appropriate because there are no rings to be moved. This degenerate case does not inspire much confidence. Let's consider the case where the number of rings is 1. One ring must be moved from the startPeg to the endPeg. The doTowers method is invoked with an argument of 1 for the parameter n. In this case the body of the *if* statement is entered. The two recursive calls to doTowers are passed ring count arguments of $n - 1 = 0$ and, as just noted, will do nothing. That leaves only the output statement, which correctly records the movement of a single ring from startPeg to endPeg. The answer to the base-case question is yes.

2. *The Smaller-Caller Question*   Does each recursive call to the method involve a smaller case of the original problem, leading inescapably to the base case? The answer is yes, because the method receives a ring count argument n and in its recursive calls passes the ring count argument n - 1. The subsequent recursive calls also pass a decremented value of the argument, until finally the value sent is 1.

3. *The General-Case Question*   Assuming the recursive calls work correctly, does the method work in the general case? The answer is yes. Our goal is to move *n* rings from the starting peg to the ending peg. The first recursive call within the method moves $n - 1$ rings from the starting peg to the auxiliary peg. Assuming that operation works correctly, we now have one ring left on the starting peg and the ending peg is empty. That ring must be the largest, because all of the other rings were on top of it. We can move that ring directly from the starting peg to the ending peg, as described in the output statement. The second recursive call now moves the $n - 1$ rings that are on the auxiliary peg to the ending peg, placing them on top of the largest ring that was just moved. As we assume this transfer works correctly, we now have all *n* rings on the ending peg.

We have answered all three questions affirmatively.

The Program

We enclose the doTowers method within a driver class called Towers. It prompts the user for the number of rings and then uses doTowers to report the solution.

```
//-------------------------------------------------------------------
// Towers.java          by Dale/Joyce/Weems          Chapter 4
//
// Driver class for doTowers method that gets initial values and
// calls the method.
//-------------------------------------------------------------------

import java.util.Scanner;
```

```java
public class Towers
{
  private static String indent = "";  // indentation for trace

  public static void main(String[] args)
  {
    Scanner conIn = new Scanner(System.in);

    // Number of rings on starting peg.
    int n;
    System.out.print("Input the number of rings: ");
    if (conIn.hasNextInt())
      n = conIn.nextInt();
    else
    {
      System.out.println("Error: you must enter an integer.");
      System.out.println("Terminating program.");
      return;
    }

    System.out.println("Towers of Hanoi with " + n + " rings\n");
    doTowers(n, 1, 2, 3);
  }

  public static void doTowers(
        int n,               // Number of rings to move
        int startPeg,        // Peg containing rings to move
        int auxPeg,          // Peg holding rings temporarily
        int endPeg      )    // Peg receiving rings being moved
  {
    if (n > 0)
    {
      indent = indent + "   ";

      System.out.println(indent + "Get " + n + " rings moved from peg "
                                + startPeg + " to peg " + endPeg);

      // Move n - 1 rings from starting peg to auxiliary peg.
      doTowers(n - 1, startPeg, endPeg, auxPeg);

      // Move nth ring from starting peg to ending peg.
      System.out.println(indent + "Move ring " + n + " from peg "
                                + startPeg + "to peg" + "endPeg"
```

```
        // Move n - 1 rings from auxiliary peg to ending peg.
        doTowers(n - 1, auxPeg, startPeg, endPeg);

        indent = indent.substring(2);
    }
  }
}
```

Within `doTowers` we added an output trace statement to display the subgoal being addressed each time the body of the *if* statement is entered. Indentation of the output statements helps us visualize the depth of each method call. Here is the output from a run with four rings:

```
Input the number of rings: 4
Towers of Hanoi with 4 rings

  Get 4 rings moved from peg 1 to peg 3
    Get 3 rings moved from peg 1 to peg 2
      Get 2 rings moved from peg 1 to peg 3
        Get 1 rings moved from peg 1 to peg 2
        Move ring 1 from peg 1 to peg 2
      Move ring 2 from peg 1 to peg 3
        Get 1 rings moved from peg 2 to peg 3
        Move ring 1 from peg 2 to peg 3
    Move ring 3 from peg 1 to peg 2
      Get 2 rings moved from peg 3 to peg 2
        Get 1 rings moved from peg 3 to peg 1
        Move ring 1 from peg 3 to peg 1
      Move ring 2 from peg 3 to peg 2
        Get 1 rings moved from peg 1 to peg 2
        Move ring 1 from peg 1 to peg 2
  Move ring 4 from peg 1 to peg 3
    Get 3 rings moved from peg 2 to peg 3
      Get 2 rings moved from peg 2 to peg 1
        Get 1 rings moved from peg 2 to peg 3
        Move ring 1 from peg 2 to peg 3
      Move ring 2 from peg 2 to peg 1
        Get 1 rings moved from peg 3 to peg 1
```

```
        Move ring 1 from peg 3 to peg 1
     Move ring 3 from peg 2 to peg 3
    Get 2 rings moved from peg 1 to peg 3
       Get 1 rings moved from peg 1 to peg 2
      Move ring 1 from peg 1 to peg 2
   Move ring 2 from peg 1 to peg 3
      Get 1 rings moved from peg 2 to peg 3
     Move ring 1 from peg 2 to peg 3
```

Here is the output with the trace statements removed:

```
Input the number of rings: 4
Move ring 1 from peg 1 to peg 2
Move ring 2 from peg 1 to peg 3
Move ring 1 from peg 2 to peg 3
Move ring 3 from peg 1 to peg 2
Move ring 1 from peg 3 to peg 1
Move ring 2 from peg 3 to peg 2
Move ring 1 from peg 1 to peg 2
Move ring 4 from peg 1 to peg 3
Move ring 1 from peg 2 to peg 3
Move ring 2 from peg 2 to peg 1
Move ring 1 from peg 3 to peg 1
Move ring 3 from peg 2 to peg 3
Move ring 1 from peg 1 to peg 2
Move ring 2 from peg 1 to peg 3
Move ring 1 from peg 2 to peg 3
```

Try the program for yourself. But be careful—with two recursive calls within the doTowers method, the amount of output generated by the program grows quickly. In fact, every time you add one more ring to the starting peg, you more than double the amount of output from the program. A run of Towers on the author's system, with an input argument indicating 16 rings, generated a 10-megabyte output file.

4.4 Counting Blobs

In this section you learn about blobs—what they are, how to generate a grid of them, and how to count them. This apparently whimsical topic provides a good example of the power of recursion and introduces the important computing technique of marking completed work so that it is not reattempted at a later time. Additionally, the identification of blobs in a grid is related to an important computer imaging problem: labeling connected components. Given an image, it is sometimes important to automatically identify, label, classify, and count the separate items within the image—for example, identifying sun spots on the surface of the sun, separating urban and rural areas on a satellite image, or locating fires in grasslands. All of these problems are related to identifying connected components. The approach we present in this section for marking blobs can also be used to identify connected components in image processing.

For our purposes, blobs are found in grids of characters. A blob is a contiguous collection of X's. Two X's in a grid are considered contiguous if they are beside each other horizontally or vertically. For example, the left grid contains five blobs, as indicated in the corresponding right grid where the blobs are outlined:

```
X - X - - X - - X - -        X - X - - X - - X - -
X X X - - X - - - - -        X X X - - X - - - - -
- - X X - X - - - - -        - - X X - X - - - - -
- - - - - X X - - - -        - - - - - X X - - - -
- - - - X - - - X X X        - - - - X - - - X X X
```

Our goal is to create an application that generates a grid with randomly placed blob characters, displays the grid, and then counts and reports the number of blobs.

Generating Blobs

We will generate our blobs randomly. Each character in a grid is either the blob character "X" or the nonblob character "-". To make things interesting, we allow the user of our application to indicate the percentage of blob characters. The user provides a percentage between 0 and 100 that indicates the probability that any particular character is a blob character. For example, grids with percentages 0, 33, 67, and 100 might appear as follows:

```
- - - - - - - - - -    - X - - X - - - - X -    X - X - X X X - X X -    X X X X X X X X X X
- - - - - - - - - -    X - - - - X - X - - -    X X X X - X X X X X      X X X X X X X X X X
- - - - - - - - - -    - - - X - - - - - X X    X X X X - - - X X -      X X X X X X X X X X
- - - - - - - - - -    X X - X - X - - X - -    - - - X - - - X X X -    X X X X X X X X X X
- - - - - - - - - -    - - - - - - X X—X        X X - - X - X X X X X    X X X X X X X X X X
```

Percentage 0	Percentage 33	Percentage 67	Percentage 100
Blobs 0	Blobs 13	Blobs 3	Blobs 1

Internally we represent a grid as a two-dimensional array of `boolean` values, with `true` indicating a blob character and `false` indicating a nonblob character. Even though we visualize the characters as either "X" or "-", it is easier to manipulate them within our program by representing them with `boolean` values. It is only when a grid is displayed that we have to worry about using the "X" and "-" characters.

Given that the number of rows and columns of a grid are `rows` and `cols`, and that the percentage probability of a character being a blob character is `percentage`, the following code generates a grid:

```
for (int i = 0; i < rows; i++)
   for (int j = 0; j < cols; j++)
   {
      randInt = rand.nextInt(100);  // random number 0 to 99
      if (randInt < percentage)
        grid[i][j] = true;
      else
        grid[i][j] = false;
   }
```

The `rand` variable is an object of the Java library's `Random` class. Its `nextInt` method returns a random integer between 0 and 99. This random integer is compared to `percentage` to determine whether a grid location should hold a blob character.

The Counting Algorithm

Let's consider how we can count the number of blobs on a grid. We can walk through the grid, one row at a time, and each time we see a blob character, increment our count. We "see" a blob character at position `i,j` when the value of `grid[i,j]` is `true`. This reasoning leads to the following code:

```
int count = 0;
for (int i = 0; i < rows; i++)
  for (int j = 0; j < cols; j++)
    if (grid[i][j])
      count++;
```

But there is a problem with this code—do you see it? It counts the number of blob characters, not the number of blobs.

When we encounter a blob character, we need some way of determining whether it is part of a blob that has already been counted. Whenever we encounter and count a blob character, we must somehow mark *all* of the characters within that blob as having been counted. We say that such characters have already been "visited."

To support this approach we create a "parallel" grid called `visited`. This grid is also a two-dimensional array of `boolean` values. Initially all of its entries are `false`, as no blob characters have been visited before we start counting. Let's assume we have a method called `markBlob`, which accepts as arguments the row and column indexes of a blob character, and proceeds to "mark" all characters within that blob as having been visited. In other words, it sets the corresponding values within the `visited` structure to `true`. We'll worry about how to implement `markBlob` in the next section. For now, given that `markBlob` does its job correctly, we can redesign the counting code:

```
int count = 0;
for (int i = 0; i < rows; i++)
  for (int j = 0; j < cols; j++)
    if (grid[i][j] && !visited[i][j])
    {
      count++;
      markBlob(i, j);
    }
```

With our new approach we count a blob character only if it has not already been visited. Once we count it, we proceed to mark it, and all the other characters within its blob, as having been visited using the `markBlob` method.

We use this approach of marking elements as having been visited again, later in the text, when we study trees and graphs.

The Marking Algorithm

All that remains for us to do is to create the method that marks the characters in a blob. As you have probably guessed, we use recursion to simplify the solution to this problem.

The `markBlob` method is passed the location of a blob character that needs to be marked through its two arguments, `row` and `col`. So that is the first thing it does—it marks the location as being visited:

```
visited[row][col] = true;
```

But this method is also responsible for marking all of the other characters in the blob. Thus, in addition to marking the indicated location, it checks the four locations "around" that location to see whether they need to be marked. That is, it checks the locations above, below, to the right of, and to the left of the indicated location.

When should one of those locations be marked? There are three necessary conditions:

1. The location exists; that is, it is not outside the boundaries of the grid.

2. The location contains a blob character.

3. The location has not already been visited.

For example, the following code checks and marks the location above the indicated location:

```
if ((row - 1) >= 0)            // if it's on the grid
  if (grid[row - 1][col])      // and has a blob character
    if (!visited[row - 1][col])  // and has not been visited,
      markBlob(row - 1, col);  // then mark it
```

The code for the remaining three directions (down, left, and right) is similar.

The recursive nature of the markBlob method ensures that all of the blob characters are marked: All of the neighbors of the specified blob character are checked and, if any of them are in the blob, all of their neighbors are checked, and so on. The fact that we mark a character position as visited when it is first encountered guarantees that our method won't recurse forever.

Let's investigate the markBlob method using the Three-Question Approach. Recall that the goal of the method is to mark all blob characters within a blob as having been visited.

1. *The Base-Case Question*   Is there a nonrecursive way out of the method, and does the method work correctly for this base case? If the markBlob method is passed arguments indicating the final unmarked location within a blob, then each check of the four contiguous locations will "fail" for one reason or another and no recursive calls to markBlob will be made. The only action the method takes in this case is to mark the indicated location as having been visited; then it returns. The answer to the base-case question is yes.

2. *The Smaller-Caller Question*   Does each recursive call to the method involve a smaller case of the original problem, leading inescapably to the base case? The answer is yes because every time the method is called, another blob location is marked as being visited. As a consequence, one less blob location needs to be marked. The subsequent recursive calls also mark a location until finally there are no more locations to be marked.

3. *The General-Case Question*   Assuming the recursive calls work correctly, does the method work in the general case? The answer is yes. Our goal is to mark all locations within the blob. Starting with any given location within the blob, we check its four contiguous locations. If any of them are within the blob, they are also marked and we assume that their neighbors are checked and marked as appropriate (we are assuming the recursive calls work correctly). Because each location within the blob is contiguous to some other location within the blob, we eventually check and mark all of the blob locations.

We answered all three questions affirmatively.

The Grid Class

To support our application we create a Grid class. An object of this class, when instantiated, is passed its dimensions and the percentage of blob characters it should contain.

It proceeds to create a grid of characters based on those specifications. Our class exports a `blobCount` method that returns the number of blobs contained in the grid. We use the grid-generation and blob-counting algorithms developed previously in this section. The `Grid` class also exports a `toString` method that transforms the `boolean`-based grid into the appropriate string of characters for display.

```java
//--------------------------------------------------------------------
// Grid.java              by Dale/Joyce/Weems           Chapter 4
//
// Supports grid objects consisting of blob and nonblob characters.
// Allows the number of blobs it contains to be counted.
//--------------------------------------------------------------------

import java.util.Random;

public class Grid
{
  protected int rows;         // number of grid rows
  protected int cols;         // number of grid columns

  protected boolean [][] grid;     // the grid containing blobs
  boolean [][] visited;            // used by blobCount

  public Grid(int rows, int cols, int percentage)
  // Preconditions: rows and cols > 0
  //                0 <= percentage <= 100
  //
  // Instantiates a grid of size rows by cols, where locations are set to
  // indicate blob characters based on the percentage probability.
  {
    this.rows = rows;
    this.cols = cols;
    grid = new boolean [rows][cols];

    // to generate random numbers.
    int randInt;
    Random rand = new Random();

    for (int i = 0; i < rows; i++)
      for (int j = 0; j < cols; j++)
      {
        randInt = rand.nextInt(100);  // random number 0 to 99
        if (randInt < percentage)
          grid[i][j] = true;
```

```
      else
        grid[i][j] = false;
    }
}

public String toString()
{
  String gridString = "";
  for (int i = 0; i < rows; i++)
  {
    for (int j = 0; j < cols; j++)
    {
      if (grid[i][j])
        gridString = gridString + "X";
      else
        gridString = gridString + "-";
    }
    gridString = gridString + "\n";   // end of row
  }
  return gridString;
}

public int blobCount()
// Returns the number of blobs in this grid.
{
  int count = 0;
  visited = new boolean [rows][cols];  // true if location visited

  // initialize visited
  for (int i = 0; i < rows; i++)
    for (int j = 0; j < cols; j++)
      visited[i][j] = false;

  // count blobs
  for (int i = 0; i < rows; i++)
    for (int j = 0; j < cols; j++)
      if (grid[i][j] && !visited[i][j])
      {
        count++;
        markBlob(i, j);
      }
```

```
  return count;
}

private void markBlob(int row, int col)
// Mark position row, col as having been visited.
// Check and if appropriate mark locations above, below, left,
// and right of that position.
{
  visited[row][col] = true;

  // check above
  if ((row - 1) >= 0)              // if it's on the grid
    if (grid[row - 1][col])        // and has a blob character
      if (!visited[row - 1][col])  // and has not been visited,
        markBlob(row - 1, col);    // then mark it

  // check below
  if ((row + 1) < rows)            // if it's on the grid
    if (grid[row + 1][col])        // and has a blob character
      if (!visited[row + 1][col])  // and has not been visited,
        markBlob(row + 1, col);    // then mark it

  // check left
  if ((col - 1) >= 0)              // if it's on the grid
    if (grid[row][col - 1])        // and has a blob character
      if (!visited[row][col - 1])  // and has not been visited,
        markBlob(row, col - 1);    // then mark it

  // check right
  if ((col + 1) < cols)            // if it's on the grid
    if (grid[row][col + 1])        // and has a blob character
      if (!visited[row][col + 1])  // and has not been visited,
        markBlob(row, col + 1);    // then mark it
  }
}
```

The Program

Given the Grid class it is easy to create our application. We assume that a grid should have 10 rows and 40 columns. Our application prompts the user for a percentage probability value, generates the grid based on this value, displays the grid, and then reports the number of blobs.

```
//------------------------------------------------------------------
// BlobApp.java             by Dale/Joyce/Weems             Chapter 4
//
// Instantiates a grid based on a percentage probability provided by the
// user and reports the number of blobs in the grid.
//------------------------------------------------------------------

import java.util.Scanner;

public class BlobApp
{
  public static void main(String[] args)
  {
    Scanner conIn = new Scanner(System.in);

    final int GRIDR = 10;   // number of grid rows
    final int GRIDC = 40;   // number of grid columns

    // Get percentage probability of blob characters.
    int percentage;
    System.out.print("Input percentage probability (0 to 100): ");
    if (conIn.hasNextInt())
      percentage = conIn.nextInt();
    else
    {
      System.out.println("Error: you must enter an integer.");
      System.out.println("Terminating program.");
      return;
    }
    System.out.println();

    // create grid
    Grid grid = new Grid(GRIDR, GRIDC, percentage);

    // display grid and blob count
    System.out.println(grid);
    System.out.println("\nThere are " + grid.blobCount() + " blobs.\n");
  }
}
```

Here is a sample run of the program:

```
Input percentage (0 to 100): 50

        - - - X X - X - - - - X X X - - - X X X X - - X - X - X - - X X - - X X X X X X
        X X X X - - - - - - - X - - - X - X X X X - - - X - - X X X - X X X - X - X - X -
        X X - X X - X X X - X X - - X - - - - - X - X X - X X - X X X X - - X X - X - -
        - - - X X - - - X - - - - X - X - - - - - X - X - X - - - - - X X X - X X - X -
        X X - - X X X - X - X - X X - - X X - - X X X - - - - X - X X - X - - X - X X X
        - X X - X X - X X X - - X - - X - - X - - X - - X X X  X  X  X X X X X X X X
        - X X - X X X X - X - X X - - - - X X - - - X X - X X X - X - X - X - - X X X -
        X X X X - - - - - - - X - - - - - X X - - - X - X - - X - X X - - X X X X X - X
        X X X - - - - - - - - X X - X X - X - X -   X - X X X - - X - X - X X X X - X -
        - X X - - - X X - X X - - X - - X X X - X - X X X X X - - - X - - X - - - - - -
```

There are 36 blobs.

4.5 Recursive Linked-List Processing

In this section we look at a problem that uses a recursive approach for traversing a linked list. In the case of a singly linked list, a recursive approach can sometimes be useful for "backing up" in the list. We use the LLNode class introduced in Section 3.7 to support our list. To simplify our linked list figures in this section, we use a capital letter to stand for a node's information, an arrow to represent the link to the next node (as always), and a slash to represent the null reference.

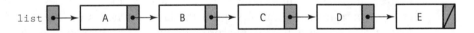

Reverse Printing

Our goal is to print the elements of a linked list. This task is simple to accomplish iteratively, so it does not make any sense to write it recursively. But here's the catch: We want to print the elements in *reverse* order. Now the problem is much more easily and elegantly solved recursively than it is iteratively.

To see why, let's think for a moment about how we could perform this task iteratively. One approach is to use nested loops to repeatedly traverse the list, looking ahead to see if it is time to stop the traversal. The first time through we stop at the node whose next node link is null—that is, when we reach the end of the list. We then print the information of the node where the traversal stopped. We also remember that node. The next time through the list we stop at the node whose next node link is to the remembered node. This is the second from last node. Again we print the information and remember the node. Continuing in this fashion, each time through the list we stop one node earlier than before, printing the information of the node where we stop. Eventually we print out the entire contents of the list, in reverse order.

Here is the algorithm. The `listRef` parameter represents the reference to the first node on the list.

Iterative revPrint (listRef)

```
initialize endTraversal to null                          // the link of the last node on the list is null
while (endTraversal != listRef)
    set currNode to listRef
    while (currNode.getLink() != endTraversal)
        change currNode to point to the next node on the list
    print out the information at currNode                 // the last node
    change endTraversal to point to currNode              // back endTraversal up by one node
```

This approach requires that we scan the list each time we print an element. For a list with N elements, it takes $O(N^2)$ operations. As we see in Section 4.6, using a stack allows us to reduce the number of operations to $O(N)$. But we will still need two loops and a user-defined stack structure for the solution. With recursion, we can avoid all of this complexity.

The key is seeing how a linked list can be viewed recursively. For example, a linked list of five nodes is a node followed by a linked list of four nodes. To print the five nodes in reverse order, we can first print the last four nodes in reverse order and then print the first node. But how do we print the last four nodes in reverse order? That's right, we recurse: We treat the last four nodes as a "first" node followed by a linked list of three nodes, and so on. The algorithm follows and is illustrated in Figure 4.1.

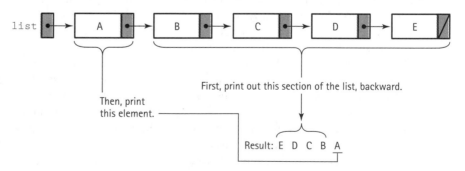

Figure 4.1 *Recursive revPrint*

Recursive revPrint (listRef)

Print out the second through last elements in the list referenced by listRef in reverse order
Then print the first element in the list referenced by listRef

Now let's turn our algorithm into code. The second part of the algorithm is simple. If `listRef` references the first node in the list, we can print out its contents with the statement

```
System.out.println(" " + listRef.getInfo());
```

The first part of the algorithm—printing out all the other nodes in the list in reverse order—is also simple because we have a method that prints out lists in reverse order: We just invoke the method `revPrint` recursively. Of course, we have to adjust the argument so that we are referencing the remaining nodes. The invocation is

```
revPrint(listRef.getLink())
```

This says, "Print, in reverse order, the linked list pointed to by the node referenced by `listRef`." This task, in turn, is accomplished recursively in two steps:

revPrint the rest of the list (third through last elements)
Then print the second element in the list

Of course, the first part of this task is accomplished recursively.

Where does it all end? We need a base case. We can stop calling `revPrint` when we have completed its smallest case: reverse printing a list of one element. Then the value of `listRef.getLink()` is `null`, and we can stop making recursive calls. Let's summarize the problem.

Reverse Print (listRef)

Definition:	Prints out the list referenced by listRef in reverse order.
Size:	Number of elements in the list referenced by listRef.
Base Case:	If the list is empty, do nothing.
General Case:	Reverse print the list referenced by listRef.getLink(), then print listRef.getInfo().

To appreciate how elegant the recursive approach is, compare it to the iterative algorithm. The recursive approach takes only O(*N*) operations to print the list in reverse order, and it doesn't need any loops or a user-defined stack.

To provide a home for our algorithm, we create a `LinkedStack2` class that extends the `LinkedStack`[2] class with a reverse print operation. We are adding an operation that will print the elements of the stack in reverse order—that is, in the order in which they were pushed onto the stack. Recall that the `LinkedStack` class implements a stack as a linked list. Thus, although we are using a stack class for our example, we are actually accessing a linked list. Here is the code:

```
//-------------------------------------------------------------------
// LinkedStack2.java          by Dale/Joyce/Weems          Chapter 4
//
// Extends LinkedStack with a printReversed method.
//-------------------------------------------------------------------

import ch03.stacks.*;
import support.LLNode;

public class LinkedStack2<T> extends LinkedStack<T>
{
  private void revPrint(LLNode<T> listRef)
  {
    if (listRef != null)
    {
      revPrint(listRef.getLink());
      System.out.println(" " + listRef.getInfo());
    }
  }


  public void printReversed()
  {
    revPrint(top);
  }
}
```

Notice that `revPrint` is a private method of the `LinkedStack2` class. Could we make `revPrint` a public method instead? The answer is no. To print the whole linked list, the client's initial call to `revPrint` must pass as an argument the reference to the first node in the list. But in our `LinkedStack` class this reference (`top`) is a protected instance variable of the class, so the following client code is not permitted:

```
myStack2.revPrint(top);      // Not allowed--top is protected
```

---

2. `LinkedStack` is presented in Section 3.7.

Therefore, we must create `revPrint` as an auxiliary, private method and define a public method, `printReversed`, that calls `revPrint`:

```
public void printReversed()
{
  revPrint(top);
}
```

This pattern of defining a private recursive method with a public entry method is used in many of our recursive solutions later in the text. Given this design, the client can now print the entire stack in reverse order:

```
myStack2.printReversed();
```

The public `printReversed()` then invokes `revPrint`, passing it the top of the stack.
Let's verify `revPrint` using the Three-Question Approach.

1. *The Base-Case Question*   When `listRef` is equal to `null`, we skip the *if* body and return. The answer is yes.

2. *The Smaller-Caller Question*   The recursive call passes the list referenced by `listRef.getLink()`, which is one node smaller than the list referenced by `listRef`. Eventually it will pass the empty list; that is, it will pass the `null` reference found in the last node on the original list. That is the base case. The answer is yes.

3. *The General-Case Question*   We assume that `revPrint (listRef.getLink())` correctly prints out the rest of the list in reverse order; this call, followed by the statement printing the value of the first element, gives us the whole list, printed in reverse order. The answer is yes.

We conclude that our approach works correctly. Of course, we still must test the methods using stacks of varying size, including a test with an empty stack.

We will study many other examples of using recursion with linked structures later in the text.

4.6   Removing Recursion

Some languages do not support recursion. Sometimes, even when a language does support recursion, a recursive solution is not desired because it is too costly in terms of space or time. In this section we consider two general techniques that are often substituted for recursion: iteration and stacking. First we take a look at how recursion is implemented. Understanding how recursion works helps us see how to develop nonrecursive solutions.

The Java Programming Model

Java is generally used as an interpreted language. When you compile a Java program, it is translated into a language called Java bytecode. When you run a Java program, your machine's Java interpreter interprets the bytecode version of your program. The interpreter dynamically generates machine code based on the bytecode and then executes the machine code on your computer. You can also use a Java bytecode compiler to translate your bytecode files directly into machine code. In that case, you can run your programs directly on your computer without having to use an interpreter. In either case, your Java programs must be transformed into the machine language of your computer at some point in time.

In this section, we discuss the machine language representation of programs. Programmers working with most other high-level languages typically use compilers that translate programs directly into machine language.

How Recursion Works

The translation of high-level programs into machine language is a complex process. To facilitate our study of recursion, we make several simplifying assumptions about this process. Furthermore, we use a simple program, called Kids, that is not object-oriented; nor is it a good example of program design. It does provide a useful example for the current discussion, however.

Static Storage Allocation

A compiler that translates a high-level language program into machine code for execution on a computer must perform two functions:

1. Reserve space for the program variables.
2. Translate the high-level executable statements into equivalent machine language statements.

Typically a compiler performs these tasks modularly for separate program subunits. Consider the following program:

```java
public class Kids
{
  private static int countKids(int girlCount, int boyCount)
  {
    int totalKids;
    totalKids = girlCount + boyCount;
    return(totalKids);
  }

  public static void main(String[] args)
```

```
    {
        int numGirls;
        int numBoys;
        int numChildren;

        numGirls = 12;
        numBoys = 13;
        numChildren = countKids(numGirls, numBoys);

        System.out.println("Number of children is " + numChildren);
    }
}
```

A compiler could create two separate machine code units for this program: one for the countKids method and one for the main method. Each unit would include space for its variables plus the sequence of machine language statements that implement its high-level code.

In our simple Kids program, the only invocation of the countKids method is from the main program. The flow of control of the program is

The machine code that corresponds to the Kids program might be arranged in memory something like this:

```
  space for the main method variables

main method code that initializes variables
jump to the countKids method
main method code that prints information
exit

  space for the countKids method parameters and local variables

the countKids method code
return to the main program
```

Static allocation like this is the simplest approach possible. But it does not support recursion. Do you see why?

The space for the `countKids` method is assigned to it at compile time. This strategy works well when the method will be called once and then always return, before it is called again. Of course, a recursive method may be called again and again before it returns. Where do the second and subsequent calls find space for their parameters and local variables? Each call requires space to hold its own values. This space cannot be allocated statically because the number of calls is unknown at compile time. A language that uses only static storage allocation cannot support recursion.

Dynamic Storage Allocation

Dynamic storage allocation provides memory space for a method when it is called. Local variables are thus not associated with actual memory addresses until run time.

> **Activation record (stack frame)** Space used at run time to store information about a method call, including the parameters, local variables, and return address

Let's look at a simplified version of how this approach might work in Java. (The actual implementation depends on the particular system.) When a method is invoked, it needs space to keep its parameters, its local variables, and the return address (the address in the calling code to which the computer returns when the method completes its execution). This space is called an activation record or stack frame. Consider our recursive `factorial` method:

```
public static int factorial(int n)
{
  if (n == 0)
    return 1;              // Base case
  else
    return (n * factorial(n - 1));     // General case
}
```

A simplified version of an activation record for method `factorial` might have the following "declaration":

```
class ActivationRecordType
{
  AddressType returnAddr;    // Return address
  int result;                // Returned value
  int n;                     // Parameter
}
```

Each call to a method, including recursive calls, causes the Java run-time system to allocate additional memory space for a new activation record. Within the method, references to the parameters and local variables use the values in the activation record. When the method ends, the activation record space is released.

What happens to the activation record of one method when a second method is invoked? Consider a program whose `main` method calls `proc1`, which then calls `proc2`.

When the program begins executing, the "main" activation record is generated (the `main` method's activation record exists for the entire execution of the program).

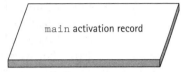

At the first method call, an activation record is generated for `proc1`.

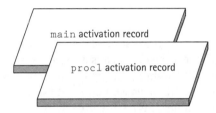

When `proc2` is called from within `proc1`, its activation record is generated. Because `proc1` has not finished executing, its activation record is still around. Just like the index cards we used in Section 4.1, the activation record is stored until needed:

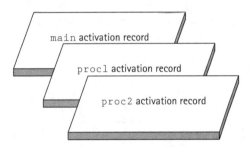

When `proc2` finishes executing, its activation record is released. But which of the other two activation records becomes the active one: `proc1`'s or `main`'s? You can see that `proc1`'s activation record should now be active, of course. The order of activation follows the last in, first out rule. We know of a structure that supports LIFO access—the stack—so it should come as no surprise that the structure that keeps track of activation records at run time is called the run-time or system stack.

> **Run-time (system) stack** A system data structure that keeps track of activation records during the execution of a program

When a method is invoked, its activation record is pushed onto the run-time stack. Each nested level of method invocation adds another activation record to the stack. As each method completes its execution, its activation record is popped from the stack.

Recursive method calls, like calls to any other method, cause a new activation record to be generated.

Depth of the recursion   The number of activation records on the system stack associated with a given recursive method

The number of recursive calls that a method goes through before returning determines how many of its activation records appear on the run-time stack. The number of these calls is the depth of the recursion.

Now that we have an understanding of how recursion works, we turn to the primary topic of this section: how to develop nonrecursive solutions to problems based on recursive solutions.

Iteration

When the recursive call is the last action executed in a recursive method, an interesting situation occurs. The recursive call causes an activation record to be put on the run-time stack; this record will contain the invoked method's arguments and local variables. When the recursive call finishes executing, the run-time stack is popped and the previous values of the variables are restored. Execution continues where it left off before the recursive call was made. Because the recursive call is the last statement in the method, however, there is nothing more to execute and the method terminates without using the restored local variable values. The local variables did not need to be saved. Only the arguments in the call and its return value are actually significant.

In such a case we do not really need recursion. The sequence of recursive calls can be replaced by a loop structure. For instance, for the `factorial` method presented in Section 4.1, the recursive call is the last statement in the method:

```
public static int factorial(int n)
{
  if (n == 0)
    return 1;            // Base case
  else
    return (n * factorial(n - 1));      // General case
}
```

Let's investigate how we could move from the recursive version to an iterative version using a *while* loop.

For the iterative solution we need to declare a variable to hold the intermediate values of our computation. We call it `retValue`, because eventually it holds the final value to be returned.

A look at the base case of the recursive solution shows us the initial value we should assign to `retValue`. We must initialize it to 1, the value that is returned in the base case. This way the iterative method works correctly in the case when the loop body is not entered.

Now let's turn our attention to the body of the *while* loop. Each time through the loop should correspond to the computation performed by one recursive call. Therefore we need to multiply our intermediate value, retValue, by the current value of the n variable. Also, we need to decrement the value of n by 1 each time through the loop—this action corresponds to the smaller-caller aspect of each invocation.

Finally, we need to determine the loop termination conditions. Because the recursive solution has one base case—if the n argument is 0—we have a single termination condition. We continue processing the loop as long as the base case is not met:

```
while (n != 0)
```

Putting everything together we arrive at an iterative version of the method:

```
private static int factorial(int n)
{
  int retValue = 1;   // return value
  while (n != 0)
  {
    retValue = retValue * n;
    n = n - 1;
  }
  return(retValue);
}
```

Cases in which the recursive call is the last statement executed are called tail recursion. Tail recursion can be replaced by iteration to remove recursion from the solution.

> **Tail recursion** The case in which a method contains only a single recursive invocation and it is the last statement to be executed in the method

Stacking

When the recursive call is not the last action executed in a recursive method, we cannot simply substitute a loop for the recursion. For instance, consider the method revPrint, which we developed in Section 4.5 for printing a linked list in reverse order:

```
private void revPrint(LLNode<T> listRef)
{
  if (listRef != null)
  {
    revPrint(listRef.getLink());
    System.out.println(" " + listRef.getInfo());
  }
}
```

Here we make the recursive call and then print the value in the current node. In cases like this one, to remove recursion we must replace the stacking that is done by the system with stacking that is done by the programmer.

For our reverse-printing example, we must traverse the list in a forward direction, saving the information from each node onto a stack, until we reach the end of the list (when our current reference equals null). When we reach the end of the list, we print the information from the last node. Then, using the information we saved on the stack, we back up (pop) and print again, back up and print, and so on, until we have printed the information from the first list element.

The general solution follows:

printReversed (listRef)
Create an empty stack of objects
while listRef is not null
    Push listRef.getInfo( ) onto the stack
    Advance listRef

while the stack is not empty
    Pop the stack to get information
    Print information

To provide a home for our previous reverse-printing example (the recursive example), we created a `LinkedStack2` class that extended the `LinkedStack` class with a reverse print operation. For this iterative example, let's use a similar `LinkedStack3` class.

```
//-------------------------------------------------------------------
// LinkedStack3.java        by Dale/Joyce/Weems            Chapter 4
//
// Extends LinkedStack with a nonrecursive printReversed method.
//-------------------------------------------------------------------

import ch03.stacks.*;
import support.LLNode;

public class LinkedStack3<T> extends LinkedStack<T>
{
  public void printReversed()
```

```
{
  UnboundedStackInterface<T> stack = new LinkedStack<T>();
  LLNode<T> listNode;

  listNode = top;

  while (listNode != null)    // Put references onto the stack
  {
    stack.push(listNode.getInfo());
    listNode = listNode.getLink();
  }

  // Retrieve references in reverse order and print elements
  while (!stack.isEmpty())
  {
    System.out.println(" " + stack.top());
    stack.pop();
  }
}
}
```

The stack we use within this solution to save our information is of the class Linked-Stack. It may appear strange to use a LinkedStack object to implement a method for a class that extends the LinkedStack class. In fact, it is a perfectly reasonable choice. After all, we need a stack to hold information of class T and we do not know ahead of time how large the stack might be.

Notice that the programmer stack version of printReversed is quite a bit longer than its recursive counterpart, especially if we add in the code for the stack methods push, pop, top, and isEmpty. This extra length is caused by our need to stack and unstack the information explicitly. Knowing that recursion uses the system stack, we can see that the recursive algorithm for reverse printing is also using a stack—an invisible stack that is automatically supplied by the system. That's the secret to the elegance of recursive-problem solutions!

4.7 Deciding Whether to Use a Recursive Solution

We might consider several factors when deciding whether to use a recursive solution to a problem. The main issues are the efficiency and the clarity of the solution.

Recursion Overhead

A recursive solution is often more costly in terms of both computer time and space than a nonrecursive solution. (This is not always the case; it really depends on the problem, the computer, and the compiler.) A recursive solution usually requires more "overhead" because of the nested recursive method calls, in terms of both time (each call involves processing to create and dispose of the activation record and to manage the run-time stack) and space (activation records must be stored). Calling a recursive method may generate many layers of recursive calls. For instance, the call to an iterative solution to `factorial` involves a single method invocation, causing one activation record to be put on the run-time stack. Invoking the recursive version of `factorial` requires $n + 1$ method calls and pushes $n + 1$ activation records onto the run-time stack. That is, the depth of recursion is $O(n)$. For some problems, the system just may not have enough space in the run-time stack to run a recursive solution.

Inefficient Algorithms

Another potential problem is that a particular recursive solution might just be inherently inefficient. Such inefficiency is not a reflection of how we choose to implement the algorithm; rather, it is an indictment of the algorithm itself.

Combinations

Consider the problem of determining how many combinations of a certain size can be made out of a group of items. For instance, if we have 20 different books to pass out to four students, we can easily see that—to be equitable—we should give each student five books. But how many combinations of five books can be made from 20 books?

A recursive mathematical formula can be used for solving this problem. Given that C is the total number of combinations, *group* is the total size of the group to pick from, *members* is the size of each subgroup, and *group* $\geq$ *members*,

$$C(group, members) = \begin{cases} group, & \text{if } members = 1 \\ 1, & \text{if } members = group \\ C(group-1, members-1) + C(group-1, members) & \text{if } group > members > 1 \end{cases}$$

Because this definition of C is recursive, it is easy to see how a recursive method can be used to solve the problem.

```
public static int combinations(int group, int members)
{
  if (members == 1)
    return group;                // Base case 1
  else if (members == group)
    return 1;                    // Base case 2
```

```
    else
       return (combinations(group - 1, members - 1) +
                combinations(group - 1, members));
}
```

The recursive calls for this method, given initial arguments (4, 3), are shown in Figure 4.2.

Returning to our original problem, we can now find out how many combinations of five books can be made from the original set of 20 books with the statement

```
System.out.println("Combinations = " + combinations(20, 5));
```

that outputs "Combinations = 15504." Did you guess that it would be that large a number? Recursive definitions can be used to define functions that grow quickly!

Although it may appear elegant, this approach to calculating the number of combinations is extremely inefficient. The example of this method illustrated in Figure 4.2, `combinations(4,3)`, seems straightforward enough. But consider the execution of `combinations(6,4)`, as illustrated in Figure 4.3. The inherent problem with this

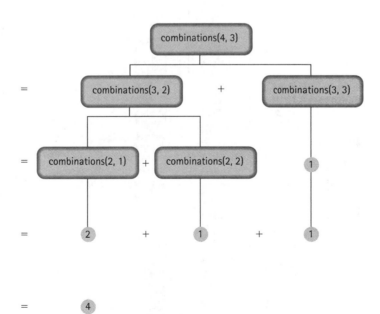

Figure 4.2 *Calculating* `combinations(4,3)`

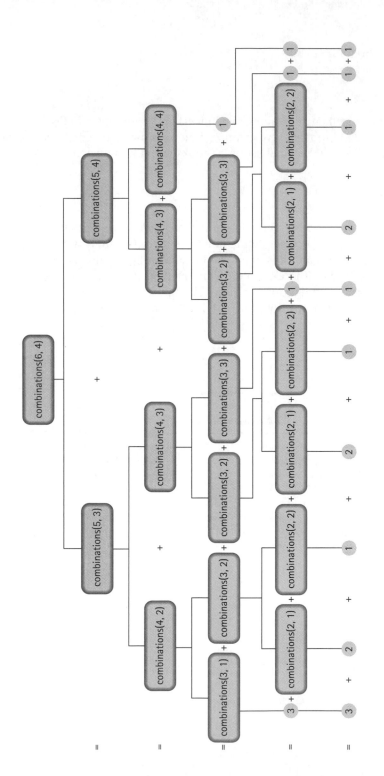

Figure 4.3 *Calculating* `combinations(6,4)`

method is that the same values are calculated over and over. For example, `combinations(4,3)` is calculated in two different places, and `combinations(3,2)` is calculated in three places, as are `combinations(2,1)` and `combinations(2,2)`.

It is unlikely that we could solve a combinatorial problem of any large size using this method. For large problems the program runs "forever"—or until it exhausts the capacity of the computer; it is an exponential-time, $O(2^N)$, solution to the problem.

Although our recursive method is very easy to understand, it is not a practical solution. In such cases, you should seek an alternative solution. A programming approach called *dynamic programming*, where solutions to subproblems that are needed repeatedly are saved in a data structure instead of being recalculated, can often prove useful. Or, even better, you might discover an iterative solution. For the combinations problem an easy (and efficient) iterative solution does exist, as mathematicians can provide us with another definition of the function C:

$$C(\text{group, members}) = \text{group!} / ((\text{members!}) \times (\text{group} - \text{members})!)$$

A carefully constructed iterative program based on this formula is much more efficient than our recursive solution.

Clarity

The issue of the clarity of a problem solution is also an important factor. For many problems, a recursive solution is simpler and more natural for the programmer to write. The total amount of work required to solve a problem can be envisioned as an iceberg. By using recursive programming, the application programmer may limit his or her view to the tip of the iceberg. The system takes care of the great bulk of the work below the surface.

Compare, for example, the recursive and nonrecursive approaches to printing a linked list in reverse order that were developed earlier in this chapter. In the recursive version, the system took care of the stacking that we had to do explicitly in the nonrecursive method. Thus recursion is a tool that can help reduce the complexity of a program by hiding some of the implementation details. With the cost of computer time and memory decreasing and the cost of a programmer's time rising, it is worthwhile to use recursive solutions to such problems.

Summary

Recursion is a very powerful problem-solving technique. Used appropriately, it can simplify the solution of a problem, often resulting in shorter, more easily understood source code. As usual in computing, trade-offs become necessary: Recursive methods are often less efficient in terms of both time and space, due to the overhead of many levels of method calls. The magnitude of this cost depends on the problem, the computer system, and the compiler.

A recursive solution to a problem must have at least one base case—that is, a case in which the solution is derived nonrecursively. Without a base case, the method recurses

forever (or at least until the computer runs out of memory). The recursive solution also has one or more general cases that include recursive calls to the method. These recursive calls must involve a "smaller caller." One (or more) of the argument values must change in each recursive call to redefine the problem to be smaller than it was on the previous call. Thus each recursive call leads the solution of the problem toward the base case.

A typical system implementation of recursion involves the use of a stack. Each call to a method generates an activation record to contain its return address, parameters, and local variables. The activation records are accessed in a last in, first out manner. Thus a stack is the best choice for the data structure. Recursion can be supported by systems and languages that use dynamic storage allocation. The method parameters and local variables do not become bound to addresses until an activation record is created at run time. As a consequence, multiple copies of the intermediate values of recursive calls to the method can be supported, as new activation records are created for them.

With static storage allocation, in contrast, a single location is reserved at compile time for each parameter and local variable of a method. There is no place to store intermediate values calculated by repeated nested calls to the same method. Therefore, systems and languages that provide for only static storage allocation cannot support recursion.

When recursion is not possible or appropriate, a recursive algorithm can be implemented nonrecursively in some cases by using a loop or by pushing and popping relevant values onto a stack. This programmer-controlled stack explicitly replaces the system's run-time stack. Although such nonrecursive solutions are often more efficient in terms of time and space, a trade-off is usually required in terms of the elegance of the solution.

Exercises

The exercises for this chapter are divided into three units: Basics (Sections 4.1 and 4.2), Examples (Sections 4.3, 4.4, and 4.5), and Advanced (Sections 4.6 and 4.7).

Basics (Sections 4.1 and 4.2)

1. Create a recursive factorial program that prompts the user for an integer N and writes out a series of equations representing the calculation of $N!$. For example, if the input is 4, the output could be

```
4! = 4!
   = 4 * 3!
   = 4 * 3 * 2!
   = 4 * 3 * 2 * 1!
   = 4 * 3 * 2 * 1 * 0!
```

Exercises 2–4 use the following three mathematical functions (assume $N \geq 0$):

- $Sum(N) = 1 + 2 + 3 + \cdots + N$

- BiPower(N) = 2^N
- TimesFive(N) = $5N$

2. Define recursively
   a. Sum(N)
   b. BiPower(N)
   c. TimesFive(N)

3. Create a recursive program that prompts the user for a nonnegative integer N and outputs.
   a. Sum(N)
   b. BiPower(N)
   c. TimesFive(N)

   Describe any input constraints in the opening comment of your recursive methods.

4. Use the Three-Question Approach to verify the program(s) you created for Exercise 3.

5. Describe the difference between direct and indirect recursion.

Exercises 6–7 use the following method:

```
int puzzle(int base, int limit)
{
  if (base > limit)
    return -1;
  else
    if (base == limit)
      return 1;
    else
      return base * puzzle(base + 1, limit);
}
```

6. Identify
   a. The base case(s) of the `puzzle` method
   b. The general case(s) of the `puzzle` method
   c. Constraints on the arguments passed to the `puzzle` method

7. Show what would be written by the following calls to the recursive method `puzzle`.
   a. `System.out.println(puzzle (14, 10));`
   b. `System.out.println(puzzle (4, 7));`
   c. `System.out.println(puzzle (0, 0));`

8. Given the following method:

```
int exer(int num)
{
  if (num == 0)
    return 0;
  else
    return num + exer(num + 1);
}
```

a. Is there a constraint on the value that can be passed as an argument for this method to pass the smaller-caller test?

b. Is `exer(7)` a valid call? If so, what is returned from the method?

c. Is `exer(0)` a valid call? If so, what is returned from the method?

d. Is `exer(-5)` a valid call? If so, what is returned from the method?

9. For each of the following recursive methods, identify the base case, the general case, and the constraints on the argument values, and explain what the method does.

a.
```
int power(int base, int exponent)
{
if (exponent == 0)
  return 1;
else
  return (base * power(base, exponent-1));
}
```

b.
```
int factorial (int n)
{
  if (n > 0)
    return (n * factorial (n - 1));
  else
    if (n == 0)
      return 1;
}
```

c.
```
int recur(int n)
{
  if (n < 0)
    return -1;
  else if (n < 10)
    return 1;
  else
    return (1 + recur(n / 10));
}
```

d.
```
int recur2(int n)
{
  if (n < 0)
    return -1;
```

```
        else if (n < 10)
            return n;
        else
            return ((n % 10) + recur2(n / 10));
    }
```

🖥️🖥️ 10. The Fibonacci sequence is the series of integers

0, 1, 1, 2, 3, 5, 8, 13, 21, 34, 55, 89, . . .

See the pattern? Each element in the series is the sum of the preceding two elements. Here is a recursive formula for calculating the *n*th number of the sequence:

$$Fib(N) = \begin{cases} N, & \text{if } N = 0 \text{ or } 1 \\ Fib(N-2) + Fib(N-1), & \text{if } N > 1 \end{cases}$$

   a. Write a recursive method `fibonacci` that returns the *n*th Fibonacci number when passed the argument n.

   b. Write a nonrecursive version of the method `fibonacci`.

   c. Write a driver to test your two versions of the method `fibonacci`.

   d. Compare the recursive and iterative versions for efficiency. (Use words, not Big-O notation.)

Examples (Sections 4.3, 4.4, and 4.5)

   11. What are the constraints on the arguments for parameter n of the `doTowers` method? What happens if the constraints are not met?

🖥️ 12. Change the Towers of Hanoi program so that it does the following:

   a. Prints out only the number of ring moves needed to solve the problem. Use a static variable `count` of type `int` to hold the number of moves.

   b. Repeatedly prompts the user for the number of rings and reports the results, until the user enters a number less than 0.

   13. Using your version of the Towers of Hanoi program from Exercise 12, answer the following:

   a. Fill in the table with the number of moves required to solve the problem, starting with the given number of rings.

Rings	Moves
1	
2	
3	
4	
5	
6	
7	

    b. Describe the pattern you see in the number of moves listed in your table.

    c. Assuming $n > 0$, define the number of moves required to move n rings using a recursive mathematical formula.

    d. Suppose you have a physical Towers of Hanoi puzzle with 11 rings. If it takes one second to move a ring from one peg to another, how long would it take you to "solve" the puzzle?

    e. In Java the data type `int` uses 32 bits and can represent integers in the range $-2,147,483,648$ to $2,147,483,647$. By experimenting with your program from Exercise 12, figure out the largest number of rings that the program can handle before "blowing up"—that is, before the value in `count` overflows.

    f. What is the number of moves reported for that number of rings? How close is that to the maximum `int` value? Explain.

14. What would be the effect of the following changes to the `Grid` class in Section 4.4?

    a. In the constructor, the values assigned to `rows` and `cols` are reversed.

    b. In the constructor, the line

```
if (randInt < percentage)
```

is changed to

```
if (randInt >= percentage)
```

    c. Within the `markBlob` method we drop the line

```
visited[row][col] = true;
```

15. What are the ramifications of the following user responses when the `BlobApp` program prompts for a percentage?

    a. -10

    b. 300

    c. twenty

16. If the blob percentage is 0, there are no blobs. Explain why. If the blob percentage is 100, there is one blob. Explain why. As the blob density changes from 0 to 100, the typical number of blobs increases from 0 to some number and then decreases down to 1. Experiment with the `BlobApp` program to determine approximately what density of blob characters exhibits the greatest number of blobs. If you like, you may modify the program to help your investigation.

17. Modify the blob classes so that the application does the following:

    a. Allows the user to enter the dimensions of the grid.

    b. Outputs the average size of a blob in addition to the number of blobs.

    c. Instead of counting the number of blobs, allows the user to repeatedly enter the coordinates of a grid location and then reports to the user the size of the blob, if any, at that location.

d. A "buffer" of nonblob characters encircles the grid of characters that is being used. The existence of these characters means that the program no longer needs to worry if the location being checked is on the grid.

e. An alternative algorithm is used for markBlob. Rather than marking the indicated location and then checking whether its surrounding locations should be passed to markBlob, it checks whether the indicated location should be marked (Is it on the grid? Does it hold a blob character? Is it currently unvisited?). If so, the algorithm marks it and then "blindly" calls markBlob four times, once for each of its surrounding locations. If the original location does not need to be marked, the method does nothing—it just returns.

18. What are the constraints on the arguments for the revPrint method? What happens if the constraints are not met?

19. Using the recursive method revPrint as a model, write a recursive method printList, which traverses the elements in a linked list in forward order. Does one of these methods constitute a better use of recursion? If so, which one?

20. You must assign the grades for a programming class. Right now the class is studying recursion, and students have been given this simple assignment: Write a recursive method sumSquares that takes a reference to a linked list of Integer elements and returns the sum of the squares of the elements. The list nodes are of class LLNode<Integer>. The objects in the list are all of class Integer.

Example:

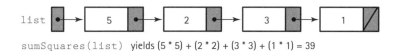

sumSquares(list) yields (5 * 5) + (2 * 2) + (3 * 3) + (1 * 1) = 39

Assume that the list is not empty.

You have received quite a variety of solutions. Grade the methods below, marking errors where you see them.

a.
```
int sumSquares(LLNode<Integer> list)
{
    return 0;
    if (list != null)
        return (list.getInfo()
                    * list.getInfo()
                    + sumSquares(list.getLink())));
}
```

b.
```
int sumSquares(LLNode<Integer> list)
{
    int sum = 0;
```

```
        while (list != null)
        {
          sum = list.getInfo() + sum;
          list = list.getLink();
        }
        return sum;
    }
```

c.
```
   int sumSquares(LLNode<Integer> list)
   {
     if (list == null)
       return 0;
     else
       return list.getInfo() * list.getInfo()
              + sumSquares(list.getLink());
   }
```

d.
```
   int sumSquares(LLNode<Integer> list)
   {
     if (list.getLink() == null)
       return list.getInfo() *
              list.getInfo();
     else
       return list.getInfo() * list.getInfo()
              + sumSquares(list.getLink());
   }
```

e.
```
   int sumSquares(LLNode<Integer> list)
   {
     if (list == null)
       return 0;
     else
       return (sumSquares(list.getLink()) *
               sumSquares(list.getLink()));
   }
```

21. The following defines a function that calculates an approximation of the square root of a number, starting with an approximate answer (approx), within the specified tolerance (tol).

$$
sqrRoot(number, approx, tol) = \begin{cases} approx & \text{if } |\,approx^2 - number\,| \le tol \\ sqrRoot(number, \dfrac{(approx^2 + number)}{(2*approx)}, tol) & \text{if } |\,approx^2 - number\,| > tol \end{cases}
$$

a. What limitations must be placed on the values of the arguments if this function is to work correctly?

b. Write a recursive method `sqrRoot` that implements the function.

c. Write a nonrecursive version of the method `sqrRoot`.

d. Write a driver to test the recursive and iterative versions of the method `sqrRoot`.

22. A palindrome is a string that reads the same forward as well as backward. For example, "otto" and "never odd or even" are palindromes. When determining if a string is a palindrome, we ignore characters that are not letters.

a. Give a recursive definition of a palindrome. (*Hint:* Consider what you get if you remove the first and last letters of a palindrome.)

b. What is the base case of your definition?

c. Write a recursive program based on your definition that repeatedly prompts the user for a string and then reports whether the string is a palindrome.

d. Write an iterative program that does the same thing.

e. Compare your two programs in terms of time and space efficiency.

23. We want to count the number of possible paths to move from row 1, column 1 to row N, column N in a two-dimensional grid. Steps are restricted to going up or to the right, but not diagonally. The illustration shows three of many paths, if $N = 10$:

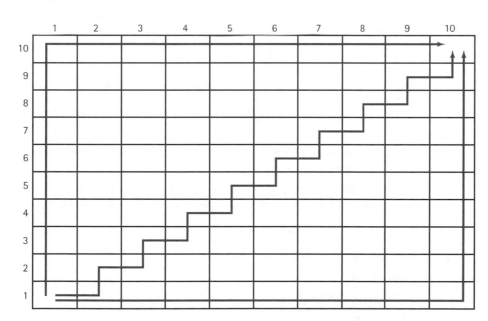

a. The following method, `numPaths`, is supposed to count the number of paths, but it has some problems. Debug the method.

```
int numPaths(int row, int col, int n)
{
```

```
    if (row == n)
      return 1;
    else
      if (col == n)
        return (numPaths + 1);
      else
        return (numPaths(row + 1, col) * numPaths(row, col + 1))
}
```

b. After you have corrected the method, trace the execution of `numPaths` with n = 4 by hand. Why is this algorithm inefficient?

c. The efficiency of this operation can be improved by keeping intermediate values of `numPaths` in a two-dimensional array of integer values. This approach keeps the method from having to recalculate values that it has already done. Design and code a version of `numPaths` that uses this approach.

d. Show an invocation of the version of `numPaths` in part c, including any array initialization necessary.

e. How do the two versions of `numPaths` compare in terms of time efficiency? Space efficiency?

24. Create a program that uses methods provided by the Java class library for exploring files and folders (*Hint:* The `File` class is a good place to start). The path to a specific file folder is provided to your program as a command line argument. Your program should do each of the following tasks:

a. "Print" to standard output a list of all of the files in the argument folder plus their size, along with a list of any folders in the argument folder. Include for each listed folder a list of its files (including sizes) and folders. Do this "recursively" as long as there are subfolders to be listed. Your output should display the hierarchy of folders and files in a visually appealing manner.

b. "Print" to standard output the name, path name, and size of the largest file in the list generated in part a.

c. Create a report about your program that includes a program listing, sample output, and a description of your experience creating the program.

Advanced   (Sections 4.6 and 4.7)

25. Explain what is meant by the following terms:
a. Run-time stack
b. Static storage allocation
c. Dynamic storage allocation
d. Activation record
e. Tail recursion

26. Explain the relationship between dynamic storage allocation and recursion.

27. The greatest common divisor of two positive integers m and n, referred to as gcd(m, n), is the largest divisor common to m and n. For example, gcd(24, 36) = 12, as the divisors common to 24 and 36 are 1, 2, 3, 4, 6, and 12. An efficient approach to calculating the gcd, attributed to the famous ancient Greek mathematician Euclid, is based on the following recursive algorithm:

```
gcd(m, n)

if m < n, then swap the values of m, n
if n is a divisor of m, return n
  else return gcd(n, m % n)
```

   a. Design, implement, and test a program `Euclid` that repeatedly prompts the user for a pair of positive integers and reports the gcd of the entered pair. Your program should use a recursive method `gcd` based on the above algorithm.

   b. Create an iterative version of the same program called `Euclid2`. Use what you learned in Section 4.6 about removing tail recursion to design your iterative approach.

28. Implement a program that repeatedly asks the user to input a positive integer and outputs the factorial of that input integer. Your program should be based on our recursive solution to the factorial problem, but instead of using recursion you should use a stack.

29. True or False? Explain your answers. Recursive methods:

   a. Often have fewer local variables than the equivalent nonrecursive methods

   b. Generally use *while* or *for* statements as their main control structure

   c. Are possible only in languages with static storage allocation

   d. Should be used whenever execution speed is critical

   e. Are always shorter and clearer than the equivalent nonrecursive methods

   f. Must always contain a path that does not contain a recursive call

   g. Are always less efficient in terms of Big-O complexity, than the equivalent nonrecursive methods

30. Using the `combinations` method from Section 4.7:

   a. Create a program that repeatedly prompts the user for two integers, N and M, and outputs the number of combinations of M items that can be made out of N items.

b. Enhance your program so that it also outputs the number of times the `combinations` method is invoked when determining each result.

c. Experiment with your enhanced program, using different variations of input values. Write a short report about the results of your experiment.

31. True or False? Explain your answers. A recursive solution should be used when:

a. Computing time is critical

b. The nonrecursive solution would be longer and more difficult to write

c. Computing space is critical

d. Your instructor says to use recursion

The Queue ADT

Knowledge Goals

You should be able to
- describe a queue and its operations at a logical level
- explain the differences between bounded and unbounded queue interfaces
- describe and compare three approaches for determining whether a string is a palindrome
- describe algorithms for implementing queue operations using an array
- compare fixed- and floating-front approaches to an array-based implementation of a queue
- explain how to implement an unbounded queue using arrays
- describe algorithms for implementing queue operations using a linked list
- use Big-O analysis to describe and compare the efficiency of queue algorithms
- describe an algorithm for simulating the card game of War, using queues and recursion
- explain how concurrent threads can interfere with each other resulting in errors, and how such interference can be prevented
- define inter-arrival time, service time, turnaround time, and waiting time for elements on a queue

Skill Goals

You should be able to
- implement the Bounded Queue ADT using an array
- implement the Unbounded Queue ADT using an array
- implement the Unbounded Queue ADT using a linked list
- draw diagrams showing the effect of queue operations for a particular implementation of a queue
- use a Queue ADT as a component of an application
- expand a queue implementation to define a new class of queue that helps solve a specific problem
- implement a program that properly uses threads to take advantage of parallelism inherent within a problem solution
- calculate turnaround and waiting times for queue elements, given arrival times and service requirements
- use our queue simulation system to investigate properties of real-world queues

In this chapter we consider the queue, which is the logical counterpart of the stack. Whereas the stack is a "last in, first out" (LIFO) structure, a queue is a "first in, first out" (FIFO) structure. Whichever element is in the queue the longest is the next element to be removed. Like the stack, the queue has many important uses related to computer systems software and also offers advantages for many other applications.

We study the queue as an ADT, looking at it from the logical, application, and implementation levels. At the logical level, we formally define our Queue ADT using a Java `interface`. We discuss many applications of queues, looking in particular at how queues are used to determine whether a string is a palindrome and to simulate the card game of War. We investigate the implementation of queues using our two basic approaches: arrays and linked lists. In addition to using an array to implement a bounded queue, we see how to implement an unbounded queue using an array. We discuss how queues are often used to hold tasks targeted for parallel execution and how to indicate that Java can safely exploit such parallelism if it can be used to improve performance. In a case study we design a program that helps us analyze the properties of real-world queues.

5.1   Queues

The stacks we studied in Chapter 3 are structures in which elements are always added to and removed from the same end. But what if we need to represent a collection that operates in a different manner? Suppose we want to simulate cars passing through the stages of a car wash. The cars go in one end and come out the other end. A data structure in which elements enter at one end and are removed from the opposite end is called a queue. The queue data structure, like the car wash, has the property that the first element (car) to go in is the first element (car) to come out.

Several variations on this basic form of queue exist, so to distinguish it we sometimes refer to this version as a FIFO queue. In the rest of this chapter, "queue" refers to a FIFO queue. (Another queue-like data structure, the priority queue, is discussed in Chapter 9.) As we did with the stack, we consider the queue as an ADT from three levels: logical, implementation, and application.

> **Queue**   A structure in which elements are added to the rear and removed from the front; a "first in, first out" (FIFO) structure

A queue is an ordered group of elements in which new elements are added at one end (the "rear") and elements are removed from the other end (the "front"). As another example of a queue, consider a line of students waiting to pay for their textbooks at a university bookstore (see Figure 5.1). In theory, if not in practice, each new student gets in line at the rear. When the cashier is ready for a new customer, the student at the front of the line is served.

To add elements to a queue, we access the rear of the queue; to remove elements, we access the front. The middle elements are logically inaccessible. It is convenient to picture the queue as a linear structure with the front at one end and the rear at the other end. However, we must stress that the "ends" of the queue are abstractions; they may or may not correspond to any physical characteristics of the queue's implementation. The essential property of the queue is its FIFO access.

Figure 5.1   *A FIFO queue*

Like the stack, the queue is a holding structure for data that we plan to use later. We put a data element into the queue; then, when we need it, we remove it from the queue. If we want to change the value of an element, we should take that element from the front of the queue, change its value, and return it to the back of the queue. We usually do not directly manipulate the values of elements that are currently in the queue.

Operations on Queues

The bookstore example suggests two operations that can be applied to a queue. First, new elements can be added to the rear of the queue, an operation that we call *enqueue*. Second, we can remove elements from the front of the queue, an operation that we call *dequeue*. Figure 5.2 shows how a series of these operations would affect a queue, envisioned as a series of blocks.

Unlike the stack operations push and pop, the addition and removal operations for a queue do not have standard names. The *enqueue* operation is sometimes called enq, enque, add, or insert; *dequeue* is also called deq, deque, remove, or serve.

Using Queues

In Chapter 3 we discussed how operating systems and compilers use stacks. Similarly, queues are often used for system programming purposes. For example, an operating system often maintains a queue of processes that are ready to execute or that are waiting for a particular event to occur.

Computer systems must often provide a "holding area" for messages that are being transmitted between two processes, two programs, or even two systems. This holding

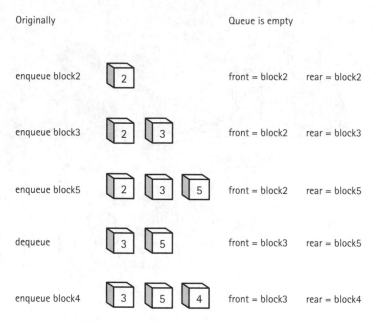

Figure 5.2   *The effects of enqueue and dequeue operations*

area is usually called a "buffer" and is often implemented as a queue. For example, if a large number of mail messages arrive at a mail server at about the same time, the messages are held in a buffer until the mail server can get around to processing them. If it processes the messages in the order they arrived—in "first come, first served" order—then the buffer is a queue.

Many other applications need to store requests before processing. Consider applications that provide services to customers—for example, selling airline or theater tickets. Such applications typically use a queue to manage the requests.

As shown by the bookstore example, our software queues have counterparts in real-world queues. We wait in queues to buy pizza, to enter movie theaters, to drive on a turnpike, and to ride on a roller coaster. Another important application of the queue data structure is to help us simulate and analyze such real-world queues, as we'll see in a case study in Section 5.8.

5.2 Formal Specification

In this section we formally specify our Queue ADT. Other than the fact that we support the operations enqueue and dequeue rather than push, pop, and top, we use the same basic approach as we did for our Stack ADT:

- Our queues are generic—the type of object held by a particular queue is indicated by the client at the time the queue is instantiated.
- The classes defined to support our queues are grouped together in the ch05.queues package.

- We provide observer operations isEmpty and isFull so that an application, when appropriate, can prevent itself from trying to remove an element from an empty queue or insert an element into a full queue.
- We create QueueUnderflowException and QueueOverflowException classes.
- We create a QueueInterface that defines the signatures of the queue methods that do not depend on the boundedness of the queue.
- We create a BoundedQueueInterface and an UnboundedQueueInterface, which extend QueueInterface and define the remaining pertinent method signatures. An implementation of a queue should implement one of these two interfaces.

The code for the two exception classes is essentially the same as that used for the two stack exception classes in Chapter 3, so we do not show it here.

Here is the QueueInterface. As you can see, it defines the signatures of the dequeue and isEmpty methods. These signatures are the same for an unbounded and a bounded queue, so they are included in the general interface.

```
//-------------------------------------------------------------------------
// QueueInterface.java          by Dale/Joyce/Weems          Chapter 5
//
// Interface for a class that implements a queue of T.
// A queue is a "first in, first out" structure.
//-------------------------------------------------------------------------

package ch05.queues;

public interface QueueInterface<T>

{
  T dequeue() throws QueueUnderflowException;
  // Throws QueueUnderflowException if this queue is empty;
  // otherwise, removes front element from this queue and returns it.

  boolean isEmpty();
  // Returns true if this queue is empty; otherwise, returns false.
}
```

The main difference between an unbounded and a bounded queue is the need for the latter to handle the potential of overflow. In the bounded queue interface, we define the signature for an isFull method. Additionally, the signature of enqueue in the bounded queue interface shows it throwing the QueueOverflowException.[1] Here is the BoundedQueueInterface:

---

1. The queue exceptions are unchecked exceptions; therefore including them in the interface has no effect from a syntactic or run-time error-checking standpoint. We show them in the interfaces to describe our expectations for the implementation.

```
//-----------------------------------------------------------------------------
// BoundedQueueInterface.java        by Dale/Joyce/Weems           Chapter 5
//
// Interface for a class that implements a queue of T with a bound
// on the size of the queue. A queue is a "first in, first out" structure.
//-----------------------------------------------------------------------------

package ch05.queues;

public interface BoundedQueueInterface<T> extends QueueInterface<T>
{
  void enqueue(T element) throws QueueOverflowException;
  // Throws QueueOverflowException if this queue is full;
  // otherwise, adds element to the rear of this queue.

  boolean isFull();
  // Returns true if this queue is full; otherwise, returns false.
}
```

And the `UnboundedQueueInterface`:

```
//-----------------------------------------------------------------------------
// UnboundedQueueInterface.java      by Dale/Joyce/Weems           Chapter 5
//
// Interface for a class that implements a queue of T with no bound
// on the size of the queue. A queue is a "first in, first out" structure.
//-----------------------------------------------------------------------------

package ch05.queues;

public interface UnboundedQueueInterface<T> extends QueueInterface<T>

{
  void enqueue(T element);
  // Adds element to the rear of this queue.
}
```

As with stacks, the application programmer can decide to prevent problems by using the `isFull` and `isEmpty` observers before accessing a queue or to "try" the access operations and "catch and handle" any raised exception.

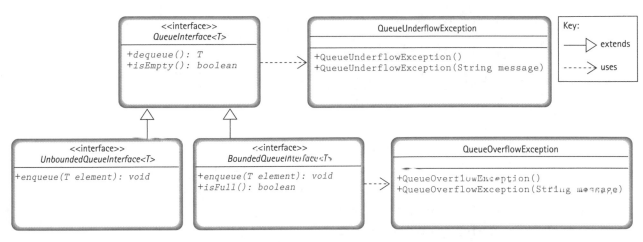

Figure 5.3   *UML diagram of our queue interfaces*

The relationships among our three interfaces and two exception classes are shown in the UML diagram in Figure 5.3. A specific implementation of a queue would implement either the `BoundedQueueInterface` or the `UnboundedQueueInterface`. By virtue of the interface inheritance rules, the implementation must also implement the methods of `QueueInterface`.

Example Use

As we did for stacks we provide a simple example use of a queue to end this section about formal specification. The `RepeatStrings` example shows how we can use a queue to store strings provided by a user and then to output the strings in the same order in which they were entered. The code uses the array-based implementation of a queue we develop in the following section. The parts of the code directly related to the creation and use of the queue are emphasized. We declare the queue to be of type `BoundedQueueInterface<String>` and then instantiate it as an `ArrayBndQueue<String>`. Within the *for* loop, three strings provided by the user are enqueued into the queue. The *while* loop repeatedly dequeues and prints the front string from the queue until the queue is empty.

```
//-------------------------------------------------------------------
// RepeatStrings.java        by Dale/Joyce/Weems          Chapter 5
//
// Sample use of queue. Outputs strings in same order of entry.
//-------------------------------------------------------------------

import ch05.queues.*;
```

```java
import java.util.Scanner;

public class RepeatStrings
{
  public static void main(String[] args)
  {
    Scanner conIn = new Scanner(System.in);

    BoundedQueueInterface<String> queue;
    queue = new ArrayBndQueue<String>(3);

    String line;

    for (int i = 1; i <= 3; i++)
    {
      System.out.print("Enter a line of text > ");
      line = conIn.nextLine();
      queue.enqueue(line);
    }

    System.out.println("\nOrder is:\n");
    while (!queue.isEmpty())
    {
      line = queue.dequeue();
      System.out.println(line);
    }
  }
}
```

Here is the output from a sample run:

```
Enter a line of text > the beginning of a story
Enter a line of text > is often different than
Enter a line of text > the end of a story

Order is:

the beginning of a story
is often different than
the end of a story
```

The Java Library Collection Framework Queue

A `Queue` interface was added to the Java library Collection Framework with Java 5.0. As expected, the library's `Queue` ADT interface is similar to our Queue ADT interfaces in that elements are always removed from the "front" of the queue. However, it also exhibits several important differences:

- It does not require elements to be inserted into the "rear" of the queue. For example, inserted elements might be ordered based on a priority value.
- Because it extends the `Collection` interface, any class that implements it must also implement eight predefined abstract methods. These include methods to observe the size of the queue and to turn the queue into an array.
- No separate interfaces for bounded and unbounded queues exist. Instead, the programmer chooses whether to place a limit on the number of elements a queue holds.
- It provides two operations for enqueuing: `add`, which throws an exception if invoked on a full queue, and `offer`, which returns a `boolean` value of `false` if invoked on a full queue.
- It provides two operations for dequeuing: `remove`, which throws an exception, and `poll`, which returns `false`, when invoked on an empty queue.
- Operations for obtaining the front element, without removing it, are included.

The Java library Collections Framework includes nine classes that implement its `Queue` interface.

5.3 Array-Based Implementations

In this section we study two array-based implementations of the Queue ADT: one that implements a bounded queue and one that implements an unbounded queue. We continue to simplify some of our figures by using a capital letter to represent an element's information.

Note that Figure 5.15, in the chapter's "Summary" section, shows the relationships among all the classes and interfaces created to support our Queue ADT.

The ArrayBndQueue Class

First we develop a Java class that implements the `BoundedQueueInterface`. We call this class `ArrayBndQueue`, in recognition of the fact that it uses an array as the underlying structure. The term `Bnd` in the name distinguishes it from the array-based unbounded queue that we will develop later in this section.

Our first task is to decide how we will store the queue in the array: We need some way of determining the front and rear elements of the queue. Several possible alternatives are available.

Fixed-Front Design Approach

In implementing the stack, we began by inserting an element into the first array position and adjusted the location of `top` with subsequent `push` and `pop` operations. The bottom of the stack, however, was always the first slot in the array. Can we use a similar solution for a queue, keeping the front of the queue fixed in the first array slot and letting the rear move as we add new elements?

Let's see what happens after a few `enqueue` and `dequeue` operations if we insert the first element into the first array position, the second element into the second position, and so on. To simplify our figures in this chapter, we show the element sitting inside its corresponding array slot—keep in mind that, in actuality, the array slot holds a reference to the element. After four calls to `enqueue` with arguments 'A', 'B', 'C', and 'D', the queue would look like this:

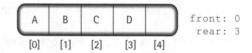

Remember that the front of the queue is fixed at the first slot in the array, whereas the rear of the queue moves down with each enqueue. Now we dequeue the front element from the queue:

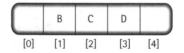

This operation removes the element in the first array slot and leaves a hole. To keep the front of the queue fixed at the top of the array, we need to move every element in the queue up one slot:

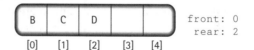

With this design the `enqueue` operation is the same as `push`. The `dequeue` operation is more complicated than `pop`, because the remaining elements of the queue have to shift up toward the front of the array.

Now let's evaluate this design. Its strengths are its simplicity and ease of coding; it is almost as simple as the stack implementation. Although the queue is accessed from both ends rather than one (as in the stack), we just have to keep track of the rear, because the front is fixed. Only the `dequeue` operation is more complicated. What is the weakness of the design? We have to move all of the elements up every time we dequeue, which increases the amount of work done.

How serious is this weakness? To make this judgment, we have to know something about how the queue will be used. If it will hold large numbers of elements, the processing required to move the elements with each dequeue makes this solution a poor one. Conversely, if the queue generally contains only a few elements, the data movement may not be too costly. Although this design can be made to work and has acceptable performance in some situations, in general it isn't the most efficient choice. Let's see if we can develop a design that avoids the need to move the queue elements for each `dequeue` operation.

Floating-Front Design Approach

The need to move the elements in the array was created by our decision to keep the front of the queue fixed in the first array slot and to let only the rear move. What if we allow both the front and the rear to move? As before, an `enqueue` operation adds an element at the rear of the queue and adjusts the location of the rear. But now a `dequeue` operation removes the element at the front and simply adjusts the location of the front. No movement of elements is required. However, we now have to keep track of the array indexes of both the front and the rear of the queue.

Figure 5.4 shows how several `enqueue` and `dequeue` operations would affect a queue that uses this approach.

Letting the queue elements float in the array creates a new problem when the rear indicator gets to the end of the array. In our first design, this situation told us that the queue was full. Now, however, the rear of the queue could potentially reach the end of the (physical) array when the (logical) queue is not yet full (Figure 5.5a).

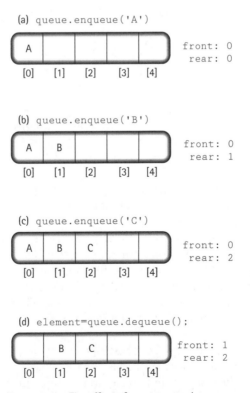

Figure 5.4   *The effect of* enqueue *and* dequeue

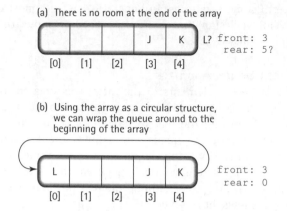

(a) There is no room at the end of the array

| | | | J | K | L? front: 3
                        rear: 5?
[0] [1] [2] [3] [4]

(b) Using the array as a circular structure,
    we can wrap the queue around to the
    beginning of the array

| L | | | J | K | front: 3
                        rear: 0
[0] [1] [2] [3] [4]

Figure 5.5   *Wrapping the queue elements around the array*

Because there may still be space available at the beginning of the array, the obvious solution is to let the queue elements "wrap around" the end of the array. In other words, the array can be treated as a circular structure in which the last slot is followed by the first slot (Figure 5.5b). To get the next position for the rear indicator, for instance, we can use an *if* statement. Assume `capacity` represents the size of the array:

```
if (rear == (capacity - 1))
  rear = 0;
else
  rear = rear + 1;
```

Another way to reset `rear` is to use the modulo (%) operator:

```
rear = (rear + 1) % capacity;
```

Comparing Design Approaches

The circular array (floating-front) solution is not as simple as the fixed-front design. What do we gain by adding this complexity to our design? By using a more efficient `dequeue` operation, we achieve better performance. Because the amount of work needed to move all the remaining elements is proportional to the number of elements, the fixed-front version of `dequeue` is an O(*N*) operation. The floating-front design requires `dequeue` to perform just a few simple operations. The amount of work never exceeds some fixed constant, no matter how many elements are in the queue, so the algorithm's complexity is O(1).

We will use the floating-front approach.

The Instance Variables and Constructors

What instance variables does our implementation need? We need the queue elements themselves; they are held in the underlying array. From our earlier analysis, we know that we must add two instance variables to the class: `front` and `rear`. And we know that to help wrap around the value of `rear` it is useful to know the capacity of the underlying array—that is, the maximum number of elements the queue can hold. The capacity is supplied by the array's length attribute. We are now confident that we can handle the `enqueue` and `dequeue` operations, but what about the remaining operations? To facilitate the `isEmpty` and `isFull` operations we decide to use one more instance variable, `numElements`. The `numElements` variable holds the current number of elements in the queue.

The beginning of the `ArrayBndQueue.java` file is shown here:

```
//-----------------------------------------------------------------------------
// ArrayBndQueue.java          by Dale/Joyce/Weems            Chapter 5
//
// Implements BoundedQueueInterface with an array to hold the queue elements.
//
// Two constructors are provided: one that creates a queue of a default
// capacity and one that allows the calling program to specify the capacity.
//-----------------------------------------------------------------------------

package ch05.queues;

public class ArrayBndQueue<T> implements BoundedQueueInterface<T>
{
  protected final int DEFCAP = 100;  // default capacity
  protected T[] queue;               // array that holds queue elements
  protected int numElements = 0;     // number of elements in the queue
  protected int front = 0;           // index of front of queue
  protected int rear;                // index of rear of queue

  public ArrayBndQueue()
  {
    queue = (T[]) new Object[DEFCAP];²
    rear =  DEFCAP - 1;
  }

  public ArrayBndQueue(int maxSize)
  {
    queue = (T[]) new Object[maxSize];²
    rear =  maxSize - 1;
  }
```

As you can see, we have included the two standard constructors for a bounded structure: one for which the client program specifies a maximum size and one that defaults to a maximum size of `DEFCAP` elements (the default capacity is 100). Recall that

---

2. An unchecked cast warning is generated because the compiler cannot ensure that the array contains objects of class T—the warning can safely be ignored.

because the Java translator will not generate references to a generic type, our code must specify `Object` along with the *new* statement within our constructors. Thus we declare our arrays to be arrays of class `T` but instantiate them to be arrays of class `Object`. Then, to ensure that the desired type checking takes place, we cast array elements into class `T`. Even though this approach is somewhat awkward and typically generates a compiler warning, it is how we must create generic collections using arrays in Java.

The `rear` variable is initialized to the capacity −1. The first time something is enqueued, this value is changed to 0, indicating the array slot that should hold that first element. The `front` variable is initialized to 0, as that is the array index of the first element that is dequeued. Note that when the queue holds just one element, `front` and `rear` will have the same value.

Definitions of Queue Operations

Given the preceding discussion, the implementations of our queue operations are straightforward. Recall that for the bounded queue the `enqueue` method should throw an exception if the queue is full. If the queue is not full, the method should simply increment the `rear` variable, "wrapping it around" if necessary; insert the argument into the `rear` location; and increment the `numElements` variable.

```
public void enqueue(T element)
// Throws QueueOverflowException if this queue is full;
// otherwise, adds element to the rear of this queue.
{
  if (isFull())
    throw new QueueOverflowException("Enqueue attempted on a full queue.");
  else
  {
    rear = (rear + 1) % queue.length;
    queue[rear] = element;
    numElements = numElements + 1;
  }
}
```

The `dequeue` method is essentially the reverse of this operation. It throws an exception if the queue is empty; otherwise, it increments `front`, also wrapping if necessary; decrements `numElements`; and returns the element previously indicated by the `front` variable. Note that this method starts by making a copy of the reference to the object it eventually returns. It does so because during its next few steps, it removes the reference to the object from the array.

```
public T dequeue()
// Throws QueueUnderflowException if this queue is empty;
// otherwise, removes front element from this queue and returns it.
{
  if (isEmpty())
```

```
      throw new QueueUnderflowException("Dequeue attempted on empty queue.");
    else
    {
      T toReturn = queue[front];
      queue[front] = null;
      front = (front + 1) % queue.length;
      numElements = numElements - 1;
      return toReturn;
    }
}
```

Note that dequeue, like the stack pop operation, sets the value of the array location associated with the removed element to null. This allows the Java garbage collection process to work with up-to-date information.

The observer methods are very simple, thanks to the fact that we keep track of the size of the queue in the numElements variable:

```
public boolean isEmpty()
// Returns true if this queue is empty; otherwise, returns false.
{
  return (numElements == 0);
}


public boolean isFull()
// Returns true if this queue is full; otherwise, returns false.
{
  return (numElements == queue.length);
}
```

Test Plan

We should make a comprehensive test plan for our queue implementations, as we did for stacks, listing all of the queue operations and the tests needed for each operation. For example, to test the method isEmpty, we must call it at least five times. We call it in the following scenarios:

- The queue is originally empty.
- The queue is empty after having been nonempty.
- The queue is nonempty.
- The queue has cycled through the empty and nonempty states a few times and is now nonempty.
- The queue is full.

We might enqueue elements until the queue is full and then call methods isEmpty and isFull to see whether they correctly judge the state of the queue. We could then dequeue the elements in the queue, printing them out as we go to make sure that they are correctly removed. At this point we could call the queue status methods again to see whether the empty condition is correctly detected. We must also remember to test the "tricky" part of the array-based algorithm: We `enqueue` until the queue is full; `dequeue` an element; and then `enqueue` again, forcing the operation to circle back to the beginning of the array.

A `toString` method would help us examine the contents of the queue during testing. In the exercises you are asked to create such a method for the various queue implementations.

The ArrayUnbndQueue Class

Here we develop a Java class that uses an array and implements the `Unbounded-QueueInterface`. It may seem surprising to implement an unbounded structure using an array, given that once an array is created its capacity cannot be changed. The trick is to create a new, larger array, when needed, and copy the structure into the new array.

To create the `ArrayUnbndQueue` class we can reuse some of the code from the `ArrayBndQueue` class. Starting with that class, what changes do we need to make so that the queue never becomes full? First, of course, we change the name of the class and indicate that it implements the `UnboundedQueueInterface`:

```
public class ArrayUnbndQueue<T> implements UnboundedQueueInterface<T>
```

We can drop the `isFull` method from the class, as it is not required by the `UnboundedQueueInterface`.

Those are the "easy" changes. Now let's address the issue of making the structure unbounded. We must change the `enqueue` method to increase the capacity of the array if it has run out of space. Because enlarging the array is conceptually a separate operation from enqueuing, we implement it as a separate method named `enlarge`. Now we can begin the `enqueue` method with the following statement

```
if (numElements == queue.length)
  enlarge();
```

Next we need to implement the `enlarge` method. By how much should we increase the size of the array? Several options are possible:

- We could set a constant increment value or multiplying factor within the class.
- We could allow the application to specify an increment value or multiplying factor when the queue is instantiated.
- We could use the original capacity as the increment value.

Because `enlarge` must copy the contents of the entire array, it is a $O(N)$ operation—and therefore we do not want to invoke it too often. This fact implies that we should increment the capacity by a large amount. Of course, if we increment by too large an amount, we waste both time and space.

Let's use the original capacity as the increment value. Our `enlarge` method instantiates an array with a size equal to the current capacity plus the original capacity. In our constructors we remember the value of the original capacity using an instance variable `origCap`.

Within `enlarge`, when copying the contents from the old array into the new array, we must be careful to step through the elements of the old array, beginning at `front`, and properly wrapping around the end of the array on our way to `rear`. In the new array we place the elements at the beginning of the array. After the copy operation, we update instance variables appropriately. Here is the entire `ArrayUnbndQueue` class, with the code changes from the bounded version <u>emphasized</u>.

```
//-------------------------------------------------------------------
// ArrayUnbndQueue.java        by Dale/Joyce/Weems        Chapter 5
//
// Implements UnboundedQueueInterface with an array to hold queue elements.
//
// Two constructors are provided: one that creates a queue of a default
// original capacity and one that allows the calling program to specify the
// original capacity.
//
// If an enqueue is attempted when there is no room available in the array, a
// new array is created, with capacity incremented by the original capacity.
//-------------------------------------------------------------------

package ch05.queues;

public class ArrayUnbndQueue<T> implements UnboundedQueueInterface<T>
{
  protected final int DEFCAP = 100;  // default capacity
  protected T[] queue;               // array that holds queue elements
  protected int origCap;             // original capacity
  protected int numElements = 0;     // number of elements in the queue
  protected int front = 0;           // index of front of queue
  protected int rear = -1;           // index of rear of queue

  public ArrayUnbndQueue()
  {
    queue = (T[]) new Object[DEFCAP];[3]
    rear =  DEFCAP - 1;
    origCap = DEFCAP;
  }

  public ArrayUnbndQueue(int origCap)
  {
```

___
3. An unchecked cast warning is generated because the compiler cannot ensure that the array contains objects of class T—the warning can safely be ignored.

```
    queue = (T[]) new Object[origCap];⁴
    rear = origCap - 1;
    this.origCap = origCap;
}

private void enlarge()
// Increments the capacity of the queue by an amount
// equal to the original capacity.
{
  // create the larger array
  T[] larger = (T[]) new Object[queue.length + origCap];⁴

  // copy the contents from the smaller array into the larger array
  int currSmaller = front;
  for (int currLarger = 0; currLarger < numElements; currLarger++)
  {
    larger[currLarger] = queue[currSmaller];
    currSmaller = (currSmaller + 1) % queue.length;
  }

  // update instance variables
  queue = larger;
  front = 0;
  rear = numElements - 1;
}

public void enqueue(T element)
// Adds element to the rear of this queue.
{
  if (numElements == queue.length)
    enlarge();
  rear = (rear + 1) % queue.length;
  queue[rear] = element;
  numElements = numElements + 1;
}

public T dequeue()
// Throws QueueUnderflowException if this queue is empty;
// otherwise, removes front element from this queue and returns it.
{
```

4. An unchecked cast warning is generated because the compiler cannot ensure that the array contains objects of class T—the warning can safely be ignored.

```
  if (isEmpty())
    throw new QueueUnderflowException("Dequeue attempted on empty queue.");
  else
  {
    T toReturn = queue[front];
    queue[front] = null;
    front = (front + 1) % queue.length;
    numElements = numElements - 1;
    return toReturn;
  }
}
public boolean isEmpty()
// Returns true if this queue is empty; otherwise, returns false
{
  return (numElements == 0);
}
}
```

In Section 3.5 we included a feature about implementing a stack using the Java Library ArrayList class. The ArrayList class is part of the Java Collections Framework. ArrayList can also be used to implement our UnboundedQueueInterface—in fact it's a good choice for the implementation because it provides a structure that grows in size as needed *and* it supports the use of generic types without the generation of any compiler warnings. Exercise 19 asks you to explore this implementation approach.

5.4 Application: Palindromes

To demonstrate the use of queues, we look at the problem of identifying palindromes. A *palindrome* is a string that reads the same forward and backward. While we are not sure of their general usefulness, identifying them provides us with a good example for the use of both queues and stacks. Besides, palindromes can be entertaining. Consider these famous palindromes:

- A tribute to Teddy Roosevelt, who orchestrated the creation of the Panama Canal: "A man, a plan, a canal—Panama!"
- Allegedly muttered by Napoleon Bonaparte upon his exile to the island of Elba (although this is difficult to believe given that Napoleon mostly spoke French!): "Able was I, ere I saw Elba."
- Overheard in a busy Chinese restaurant: "Won ton? Not now!"
- Possibly the world's first palindrome: "Madam, I'm Adam."
- Followed immediately by one of the world's shortest palindromes: "Eve."

As you can see, the rules for what is a palindrome are somewhat lenient. Typically, we do not worry about punctuation, spaces, or matching the case of letters.

The Palindrome Class

As with previous examples, we separate the user interface from the part of the program that does the main processing. First we concentrate on that main processing—identifying a palindrome.

We create a class `Palindrome` with a single exported static method `test`, which takes a candidate string argument and returns a `boolean` value indicating whether the string is a palindrome. Because the method is static, we do not define a constructor for the class. Instead, we invoke the `test` method using the name of the class.

The `test` method, when invoked, creates a new stack of characters and a new queue of characters. It then repeatedly pushes each letter from the input line onto the stack, and also enqueues the letter onto the queue. It discards any nonletter characters, because they are not considered part of a palindrome. To simplify the comparison later, we push and enqueue lowercase versions of the characters.

When all of the characters of the candidate string have been processed, the program repeatedly pops a letter from the stack and dequeues a letter from the queue. As long as these letters match each other the entire way through this process, we have a palindrome. Can you see why? Because the queue is a "first in, first out" structure, the letters are returned from the queue in the same order they appear in the string. But the letters taken from the stack, a "last in, first out" structure, are returned in the opposite order. Thus we are comparing the forward view of the string to the backward view of the string.

Here is the algorithm for determining whether a string is a palindrome:

Test for Palindrome (String candidate)

```
Create a new stack
Create a new queue
for each character in candidate
    if the character is a letter
        Change the character to lowercase
        Push the character onto the stack
        Enqueue the character onto the queue
Set stillPalindrome to true
while (there are still more characters in the structures
        && stillPalindrome)
    Pop character1 from the stack
    Dequeue character2 from the queue
    if (character1 != character2)
        Set stillPalindrome to false
return (stillPalindrome)
```

One part of the algorithm that requires expansion is the determination of when "there are still more characters in the structures." This could be done with the `isEmpty` methods of the `stack` and `queue` classes. But there is another approach: We can count the number of letters in the string as we are storing them. Remember, only letters are placed in the structures. We can use this count to control how many times we remove and compare characters.

We take this second approach. The code for the `Palindrome` class follows. We emphasize the code that involves a queue.

```
//-------------------------------------------------------------------
// Palindrome.java          by Dale/Joyce/Weems          Chapter 5
//
// Provides a method to test whether a string is a palindrome.
// Nonletters are skipped.
//-------------------------------------------------------------------

import ch03.stacks.*;
import ch05.queues.*;

public class Palindrome
{
  public static boolean test(String candidate)
  // Returns true if candidate is a palindrome, false otherwise.
  {
    char ch;                   // current candidate character being processed
    int length;                // length of candidate string
    int numLetters;            // number of letters in candidate string
    int charCount;             // number of characters checked so far

    char fromStack;            // current character popped from stack
    char fromQueue;            // current character dequeued from queue
    boolean stillPalindrome;   // true if string might still be a palindrome

    BoundedStackInterface<Character> stack;    // string characters
    BoundedQueueInterface<Character> queue;    // string characters

    // initialize variables and structures
    length = candidate.length();
    stack = new ArrayStack<Character>(length);
    queue = new ArrayBndQueue<Character>(length);
    numLetters = 0;

    // obtain and handle characters
    for (int i = 0; i < length; i++)
    {
      ch = candidate.charAt(i);
      if (Character.isLetter(ch))
```

```
      {
        numLetters++;
        ch = Character.toLowerCase(ch);
        stack.push(ch);
        queue.enqueue(ch);
      }
    }

    // determine if palindrome
    stillPalindrome = true;
    charCount = 0;
    while (stillPalindrome && (charCount < numLetters))
    {
      fromStack = stack.top();
      stack.pop();
      fromQueue = queue.dequeue();
      if (fromStack != fromQueue)
        stillPalindrome = false;
      charCount++;
    }

    // return result
    return stillPalindrome;
  }
}
```

Note that we use a bounded queue implementation, `ArrayBndQueue`. This implementation was developed in Section 5.3. It is appropriate to use bounded structures because we know the structures need not be larger than the length of the candidate string. Also note that we make use of Java 5.0's autoboxing and unboxing features, when we insert and remove variables of the primitive type `char` to and from the structures. The system automatically wraps the `char` values in a `Character` object before insertion, then unwraps the returned `Character` object back into a `char` value after it is removed.

The Application

The `Palindrome` class does most of the work for us. All that is left to do now is to implement the user I/O. The `PalindromeApp` program is similar to the console-based programs presented in previous chapters. Its basic flow is to prompt the user for a string, use the `Palindrome` class's `test` method to determine whether the string is a palindrome, output the result, and then ask the user if he or she wants to continue. Here is the application:

```
//-------------------------------------------------------------------
// PalindromeApp.java         by Dale/Joyce/Weems            Chapter 5
//
// Checks for strings that are palindromes.
// Input consists of a sequence of strings.
```

```java
// Output consists of whether the input string is a palindrome.
//----------------------------------------------------------------

import java.util.Scanner;

public class PalindromeApp
{
  public static void main(String[] args)
  {
    Scanner conIn = new Scanner(System.in);

    String candidate = null;      // string to be evaluated
    String more = null;           // used to stop or continue processing

    do
    {
      // Get next candidate string to be processed.
      System.out.println("Enter a string to be evaluated: ");
      candidate = conIn.nextLine();

      // Obtain and output result of palindrome testing.
      if (Palindrome.test(candidate))
        System.out.println("is a palindrome.");
      else
        System.out.println("is NOT a palindrome.");

      // Determine if there is another candidate string to process.
      System.out.println();
      System.out.print("Evaluate another string? (Y=Yes): ");
      more = conIn.nextLine();
      System.out.println();
    }
    while (more.equalsIgnoreCase("y"));
  }
}
```

Here is a sample run of the program:

```
Enter a string to be evaluated:
racecar
is a palindrome.

Evaluate another string? (Y=Yes): y

Enter a string to be evaluated:
aaaaaaaaabaaaaaaa
is NOT a palindrome.
```

Evaluate another string? (Y=Yes): y

Enter a string to be evaluated:
fred
is NOT a palindrome.

Evaluate another string? (Y=Yes): y

Enter a string to be evaluated:
Are we not drawn onward, we few? Drawn onward to new era!
is a palindrome.

Evaluate another string? (Y=Yes): n

There are other—probably better—ways of determining whether a string is a palindrome. In fact, in Exercise 22 of Chapter 4 we asked you to consider some other approaches. We included this example application for several reasons: It's interesting but not too complicated, it's fun, and it clearly demonstrates the association between a stack and a queue. Figure 5.6 is a UML diagram showing the relationships among the stack and queue interfaces and classes used in this program.

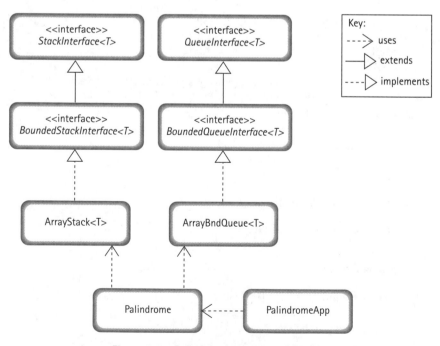

Figure 5.6   *Palindrome program architecture*

5.5 Application: The Card Game of War

In this section we present an application that simulates a popular card game. We use queues for both players' hands and for the pile of cards that is the prize of a card battle. Our solution also provides an interesting example of the use of recursion.

One of the easiest card games to learn is the game of War. A standard deck of playing cards is shuffled and dealt to two players. Each player starts with a hand of 26 cards. The players repeatedly battle with their cards. A battle consists of each player placing the top card from his or her hand face up on the table. Whoever has the higher of the two cards wins the battle prize (the two cards) and places those cards at the bottom of their hands. A tied battle means war!

In a war each player adds three more cards to the prize pile and then turns up another battle card. Whoever wins this battle gets to add the entire prize pile—all 10 cards—to the bottom of his or her hand. What if that battle is also a tie? Then there is another war and the prize pile grows even larger. The card game continues until one of the players runs out of cards, either during a regular battle or during a war. That player loses.

Notice how each player takes cards from the front of his or her hand to put in the prize pile. If a player wins, he or she places the cards from the prize pile at the back of the hand. Thus each hand acts like a queue. In fact, because the cards in the prize pile are kept in order, the prize pile can also be treated as a queue.

The game of War does not require much thought. In fact, the only real decision required is whether to play at all. Our program helps us with that decision. It simulates several games of War and tells us, on average, how many battles are waged in each game. This gives us an idea of how long a game takes, which may influence our decision to play.

To simulate War, we just have to deal cards randomly to the two hands. Then we coordinate the dequeuing and enqueuing operations among the two hands and the prize pile according to the rules of the game.

Our program requires two input values: the number of games to simulate and the maximum number of battles allowed before a game is discontinued. The latter value is needed to ensure that our program doesn't run forever. There is no guarantee that a game of War will ever end! Output from the program consists of statistics about the number of discontinued games, the number of completed games, and the average number of battles waged in completed games.

The RankCardDeck Class

To support our solution we create a class that models a deck of cards. In the game of War we merely need to compare the "rank" of cards; we are not interested in the card suits. This allows us to create a simple card deck class. We call the class `RankCardDeck` to emphasize that it simply models the ranks of the cards. Because we are interested only in gathering statistics and not in displaying cards, we use the integers 0 through 12 to represent the card ranks two through ace. Here is the class:

```
//-------------------------------------------------------------------
// RankCardDeck.java         by Dale/Joyce/Weems            Chapter 5
//
// Models a deck of cards.
// Returns a random card upon request.
// Cards are represented by rank only to an integer between 0 and 12.
//-------------------------------------------------------------------

package support;

import java.util.Random;

public class RankCardDeck
{
  private static final int numCards = 52;

  protected int[] carddeck = new int[numCards];
  protected int curCardPos = 0;        // position of the next card to be dealt

  protected Random rand = new Random();   // to generate random numbers

  public RankCardDeck()
  {
    for (int i = 0; i < numCards; i++)
      carddeck[i] = i / 4;      // there are 4 cards of each rank
  }

  public void shuffle()
  // Randomizes the order of the cards in the deck and resets the
  // position of the current card to card 0.
  {
    int randLoc;  // random location in card deck
    int temp;      // for swap of cards
    for (int i = (numCards - 1); i > 0; i--)
    {
      randLoc = rand.nextInt(i);  // random integer between 0 and i - 1
      temp = carddeck[randLoc];
      carddeck[randLoc] = carddeck[i];
      carddeck[i] = temp;
    }
    curCardPos = 0;
  }
```

```
public boolean hasMoreCards()
// Returns true if there are still cards left to be dealt;
// otherwise, returns false.
{
  return (curCardPos != numCards);
}

public int nextCard()
// Precondition:  curCardPos != numCards
//
// Models a card being dealt by returning an integer representing
// its rank and incrementing the position of the current card.
{
  curCardPos = curCardPos + 1;
  return (carddeck[curCardPos - 1]);
}
}
```

As you can see, the RankCardClass allows an application to create a card deck, shuffle it, check whether there are more cards to be dealt, and deal the next card. The shuffle algorithm is the same one used by the Java library Collections class. It works through the deck (array) backward, selecting a random position from the preceding portion of the deck, and swaps the card at that position with the card at the current position. To select a random position it uses the Java library's Random class. The call to rand.nextInt(i) returns a random integer between 0 and i − 1.

The WarGame Class

This class simulates a game of War. Its constructor requires an argument indicating the maximum number of battles permitted before discontinuing a game. The class exports a play method that simulates a game until it is finished or discontinued, returning true if the game finished normally and false if the game was discontinued. It also exports an observer method that returns the number of battles waged in the most recent game.

The play method, when invoked, creates three queues: one for each player's hand and one for the prize pile of cards. Next the method shuffles the deck of cards and "deals" them to the two players—dealing a card to a player's hand consists of enqueuing the card on the corresponding queue. Once the cards are dealt, the play method repeatedly calls the battle method, which enacts the battle between the two players. This cycle continues until the game is over or discontinued.

The battle method is recursive. Here is the algorithm for battle, using War game terminology:

battle( )

Get player1's card from player1's hand
Put player1's card in the prize pile
Get player2's card from player2's hand
Put player2's card in the prize pile
if (player1's card > player2's card)
{
   remove all the cards from the prize pile
     and put them in player1's hand
}
else
  if (player2's card > player1's card)
  {
    remove all the cards from the prize pile
      and put them in player2's hand
  }
  else // war!
  {
    each player puts three cards in the prize pile
    battle( )
  }

The method models a battle between the two players, obtaining (dequeuing) their battle cards, adding (enqueuing) the cards to the prize pile, and then comparing the cards. Whoever has the higher card gets the cards in the prize pile added to the back of his or her hand (dequeue from prize pile, enqueue to player's hand). If the battle is a tie, there is a war: Three cards from each player's hand are added to the prize pile, and then `battle` recursively calls itself. Whoever wins this recursive battle wins all the cards in the prize pile—unless there is another war, in which case the method calls itself again.

Before we continue the discussion of the `WarGame` class, you should study the code. We have <u>emphasized</u> the parts that involve the Queue ADT.

```
//---------------------------------------------------------------------
// WarGame.java              by Dale/Joyce/Weems           Chapter 5
//
// Models the card game War.
// Tracks how many battles are played.
//---------------------------------------------------------------------

import ch05.queues.*;
```

```
import support.*;        // for RankCardDeck

public class WarGame
{
  BoundedQueueInterface<Integer> player1;   // player 1's hand
  BoundedQueueInterface<Integer> player2;   // player 2's hand

  int maxNumBattles;                // maximum number of battles allowed before
                                    // game is discontinued

  int numBattles = 0;               // number of battles played in current game

  RankCardDeck deck;                // deck of cards

  BoundedQueueInterface<Integer> prize;   // cards for current battle

  static final int numCards = 52;         // number of cards in a deck

  public WarGame(int maxNumBattles)
  {
    this.maxNumBattles = maxNumBattles;
    deck = new RankCardDeck();
  }

  public int getNumBattles()
  {
    return numBattles;
  }

  public boolean play()
  // Simulates one game. If number of battles played
  // reaches maxNumBattles, the game is discontinued.
  // Returns true if game finishes normally; returns false
  // if game is discontinued.
  {
    // instantiate players' hands
    player1 = new ArrayBndQueue<Integer>(numCards);
    player2 = new ArrayBndQueue<Integer>(numCards);

    // instantiate prize pile
    prize = new ArrayBndQueue<Integer>(numCards);

    boolean gameOver = false;   // becomes true when the game is over
    boolean gameOK = true;      // becomes false if game is discontinued
```

```
  // deal original hands
  deck.shuffle();
  while (deck.hasMoreCards())
  {
    player1.enqueue(deck.nextCard());
    if (deck.hasMoreCards())
      player2.enqueue(deck.nextCard());
  }

  // play game until somebody runs out of cards or
  // reach the maximum number of battles
  numBattles = 0;
  while (!gameOver)
  {
    try
    {
      numBattles = numBattles + 1;
      battle();
    }
    catch (QueueUnderflowException exceptionVar)
    {
      gameOver = true;
    }

    if (numBattles == maxNumBattles)
    {
      gameOver = true;
      gameOK = false;
    }
  }
  return gameOK;
}

private void battle()
// Models a battle between player1 and player2. If the battle
// results in a war, three cards from each player are placed
// in the prize queue and the battle is continued recursively.
{
  // cards for this battle
  int p1card;
  int p2card;

  // get cards from players and place in prize queue
  p1card = player1.dequeue();
  prize.enqueue(p1card);
  p2card = player2.dequeue();
```

```
prize.enqueue(p2card);

// determine and handle result of battle
if (p1card > p2card)          // player1 wins
  while (!prize.isEmpty())
    player1.enqueue(prize.dequeue());
else
{
  if (p2card > p1card)        // player2 wins
    while (!prize.isEmpty())
      player2.enqueue(prize.dequeue());
  else
  {
    // it's a war ...
    // each player places 3 cards in prize pile
    for (int i = 0; i < 3; i++)
    {
      prize.enqueue(player1.dequeue());
      prize.enqueue(player2.dequeue());
    }
    // now continue the battle to determine who wins prize
    battle();
  }
}
}
}
```

A few more notes about this class:

- The `player1`, `player2`, and `prize` queues all hold cards—but remember that for this program a card is essentially an `int` value. When an `int` is enqueued, Java 5.0's autoboxing feature wraps it in an `Integer` object, as our queues hold elements of class `Integer`. When we remove a card from a queue, the unboxing feature will let us use it as an `int` value again.
- Recall that a game ends when one of the players runs out of cards. Rather than repeatedly testing whether a player's hand is empty before dequeuing a card from it, we have used the fact that the `dequeue` method throws an underflow exception when invoked on an empty queue. The *try-catch* clause in the `play` method catches the occurrence of the underflow and appropriately stops the simulation.

The WarGameApp Class

The `WarGame` class does most of the work for us. All that is left to do is to implement the user input and present the results. The `WarGameApp` program is similar to our previous console-based programs. It prompts the user for the number of games to simulate and the maximum number of battles to allow before discontinuing a game. It then uses a *for* loop to repeatedly invoke the `WarGame` class's `play` method, and it collects the results. Finally it presents the results to the user. Note that we assume a friendly user—we do not validate input values.

```java
//-----------------------------------------------------------------------
// WarGameApp.java          by Dale/Joyce/Weems            Chapter 5
//
// Interacts with the user through the console.
//
// Simulates a number of instances of the card game War and reports
// the average number of battles required to complete a game.
//
// Input consists of the number of games to simulate and the maximum
// number of battles allowed for a game before it is discontinued.
//
// Output consists of statistics on the number of discontinued games,
// the number of completed games, and the average number of battles
// in the completed games.
//-----------------------------------------------------------------------

import java.util.Scanner;

public class WarGameApp
{
  public static void main(String[] args)
  {
    Scanner conIn = new Scanner(System.in);

    WarGame game;

    int numGames;          // number of games to simulate
    int maxNumBattles;     // maximum number of battles allowed for a game

    int numDiscont = 0;    // number of dicontinued games
    int numCompleted = 0;  // number of completed games

    int totBattles = 0;    // total number of battles in completed games

    System.out.println("How many games should be simulated? ");
    numGames = conIn.nextInt();

    System.out.println("What is the maximum number of battles per game? ");
    maxNumBattles = conIn.nextInt();

    game = new WarGame(maxNumBattles);
```

```
for (int i = 0; i < numGames; i++)
{
  if (game.play())
  {
    numCompleted = numCompleted + 1;
    totBattles = totBattles + game.getNumBattles();
  }
  else
    numDiscont = numDiscont + 1;
}

// Output results
System.out.println("Number of Games Simulated:    "+ numGames);
System.out.println("Number of Discontinued Games: "+ numDiscont);
System.out.println("Number of Completed Games:    "+ numCompleted);
System.out.println();

if (numCompleted > 0)
{
  System.out.println("In the completed games");
  System.out.println("  Total Number of Battles "+ totBattles);
  System.out.println("  Average Number of Battles "
                        + totBattles/numCompleted);
}

System.out.println("\nProgram completed.");
    }
}
```

Testing this program is not easy. One approach is to add testing-related output statements throughout the program to determine whether it correctly represents a game of War. However, the amount of output could be huge, so we may need to reduce the number of opening cards dealt to a player to keep the output reasonable. Another helpful technique is to comment out the part of the code that randomly generates cards and replace it with a sequence of statements that place carefully selected cards in each player's hand— for example, to see whether the program correctly handles multiple levels of nested wars.

Once tested, the program can be used to investigate the game of War. Suppose we put a limit of 300 battles on a game and simulate 1000 games. How many of those games are discontinued? Of the games that are completed, what is the average number of battles per game? Here are our results:

How many games should be simulated?

1000

What is the maximum number of battles per game?

300

Number of Games Simulated: 1000

Number of Discontinued Games: 658
Number of Completed Games: 342

In the completed games
  Total Number of Battles 56138
  Average Number of Battles 164

Program completed.

At least for that run of the program, only about one third of the games were completed when we specified a limit of 300 battles per game. What if we allow more battles—say, 500 or 1000? Just rerun the program with the new input values and see what you discover!

We thought we would investigate how many very short games occurred on average. We ran the program with a maximum battle limit of 7, and we simulated 50,000 games. Only one completed game was recorded. The amazing thing was that the game had only two battles! Each of those battles must have been a multilevel war. It's hard to believe that a game of War could be decided with just two battles. To investigate, you could try playing 50,000 games yourself, by hand. Better yet, study the situation using our simulation program.

Figure 5.7 is a UML diagram showing the relationships among the various interfaces and classes developed in this chapter and used within the War game simulation program.

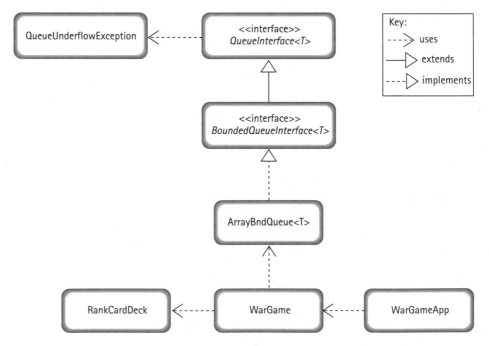

Figure 5.7   *War game simulation program architecture*

5.6 Link-Based Implementations

In this section we implement an unbounded queue using a linked list. We call our class `LinkedUnbndQueue`. As we did for the linked implementation of stacks presented in Chapter 3, we use the `LLNode` class from our `support` package to provide the nodes for the underlying representation.

In the array-based implementation of a queue, we kept track of two indexes that indicated the front and rear boundaries of the data in the queue. In a linked representation, we can use two references, `front` and `rear`, to mark the front and the rear of the queue, respectively. When the queue is empty, both of these references should equal `null`. Therefore, the constructor for the queue must initialize them both accordingly. The beginning of our class definition looks like this:

```
//-------------------------------------------------------------------------
// LinkedUnbndQueue.java          by Dale/Joyce/Weems          Chapter 5
//
// Implements UnboundedQueueInterface using a linked list
//-------------------------------------------------------------------------

package ch05.queues;
import support.LLNode;
public class LinkedUnbndQueue<T> implements UnboundedQueueInterface<T>
{
  protected LLNode<T> front;   // reference to the front of this queue
  protected LLNode<T> rear;    // reference to the rear of this queue

  public LinkedUnbndQueue()
  {
    front = null;
    rear = null;
  }
}
```

Figure 5.8 graphically depicts our queue representation. We often depict queues by showing their instance variables (`front` and `rear`) in different areas of the figure.

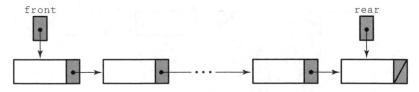

Figure 5.8   *A linked queue representation*

Recall that these variables are actually collected together in a single queue object. Also, recall that dynamically allocated nodes in linked structures exist "somewhere in the system memory" although we show the nodes arranged linearly for clarity.

Note the relative positions of `front` and `rear` in Figure 5.8. Had they been reversed (as in Figure 5.9), we would have difficulty implementing the `dequeue` operation. Recall that we `dequeue` from the front end of the queue. To remove the node that represents the front of the queue, we have to reset the `front` reference to the next node on the chain.

If we implement the queue as in Figure 5.9, we can't easily obtain a reference to the next node in the chain, as it is the preceding node. We would have to either traverse the whole list (an O(N) solution—very inefficient, especially if the queue is long) or keep a linked list with references in both directions. Use of a doubly linked structure is not necessary if we set up our queue references correctly in the first place.

The Enqueue Operation

In our linked implementations of the StringLog and Stack ADTs, we have already seen how to insert and delete a node at the beginning of a linked list. We add new elements to a queue by inserting them at the rear of the structure—we have not yet seen that operation. We need a new algorithm to implement the `enqueue` operation (see Figure 5.10).

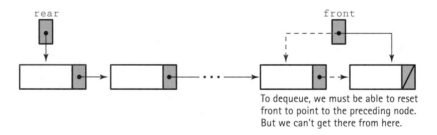

Figure 5.9 *A bad queue design*

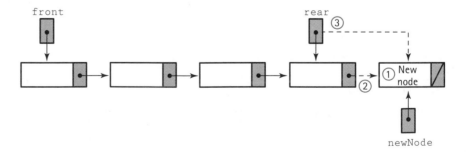

Figure 5.10 *The `enqueue` operation*

Enqueue (element)

Create a node for the new element
Insert the new node at the rear of the queue
Update the reference to the rear of the queue

The first of these tasks is familiar. We create a new node for the `element` by instantiating a new `LLNode` object and passing it the `element` as an argument.

The next part of the `enqueue` algorithm involves inserting our new node at the rear of the queue. We set the link of the current last element to reference the new node, using the `LLNode setLink` method:

```
rear.setLink(newNode);
```

But what happens if the queue is empty when we `enqueue` the element? When using references, you must always be sure to handle the special case of `null`; you cannot use it to access an object. If the queue is empty when we insert the element, the value of `rear` would be `null` and the use of `rear.setLink` would raise a run-time exception. Instead, we must set `front` to point to the new node:

```
if (rear == null)
  front = newNode;
else
  rear.setLink(newNode);
```

The last task in the `enqueue` algorithm, updating the `rear` reference, simply involves the assignment

```
rear = newNode;
```

Does this work if it is the first node in the queue—that is, if we are inserting into an empty queue? Yes, because we always have `rear` pointing to the new node following a call to `enqueue`, regardless of how many elements are in the queue.

Putting this all together, we get the following code for the `enqueue` method:

```
public void enqueue(T element)
// Adds element to the rear of this queue.
{
  LLNode<T> newNode = new LLNode<T>(element);
  if (rear == null)
```

```
      front = newNode;
    else
      rear.setLink(newNode);
    rear = newNode;
  }
```

The Dequeue Operation

The `dequeue` operation is similar to the stack's `pop` operation in that it removes an element from the beginning of the linked list. However, recall that `pop` only removed the top element from the stack, whereas `dequeue` both removes and returns the element. Also, as with the stack's `top` operation, we do not want to return the entire `LLNode`, just the information the node contains.

In writing the `enqueue` algorithm, we noticed that inserting into an empty queue is a special case because we need to make `front` point to the new node. Similarly, in our `dequeue` algorithm we need to allow for the special case of deleting the only node in the queue, leaving it empty. If `front` is `null` after we have reset it, the queue is empty and we need to set `rear` to `null`. The algorithm for removing the front element from a linked queue is illustrated in Figure 5.11.

Dequeue: returns Object

Set element to the information in the front node
Remove the front node from the queue
if the queue is empty
    Set the rear to null
return element

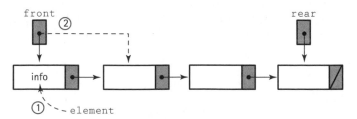

Figure 5.11   *The* `dequeue` *operation*

Let's look at the implementation line by line. We start by "remembering" the information from the first element so that we can return it later. We declare a local T variable `element` and then assign the information (i.e., the reference to the information) from the front queue element to it:

```
T element;
element = front.getInfo();
```

Next we remove the front node from the queue. This step is easy: We just assign the link to the next element to `front` (see Figure 5.11). This approach works even if the resultant queue is empty, because the link would be `null`. If the queue becomes empty, we also set the `rear` of the queue to `null`, as discussed earlier:

```
front = front.getLink();
if (front == null)
  rear = null;
```

Now we just return the information we saved earlier:

```
return element;
```

Finally, we must remember to throw a `QueueUnderflowException` if the `dequeue` operation is attempted on an empty queue. Putting it all together, the code is as shown here:

```
public T dequeue()
// Throws QueueUnderflowException if this queue is empty;
// otherwise, removes front element from this queue and returns it.
{
  if (isEmpty())
    throw new QueueUnderflowException("Dequeue attempted on empty queue.");
  else
  {
    T element;
    element = front.getInfo();
    front = front.getLink();
    if (front == null)
      rear = null;

    return element;
  }
}
```

The Queue Implementation

The remaining operation isEmpty is very straightforward. Here is the code for the entire unbounded FIFO Queue implementation based on the linked approach:

```java
//----------------------------------------------------------------------
// LinkedUnbndQueue.java        by Dale/Joyce/Weems           Chapter 5
//
// Implements UnboundedQueueInterface using a linked list
//----------------------------------------------------------------------

package ch05.queues;

import support.LLNode;

public class LinkedUnbndQueue<T> implements UnboundedQueueInterface<T>
{
  protected LLNode<T> front;    // reference to the front of this queue
  protected LLNode<T> rear;     // reference to the rear of this queue

  public LinkedUnbndQueue()
  {
    front = null;
    rear = null;
  }

  public void enqueue(T element)
  // Adds element to the rear of this queue.
  {
    LLNode<T> newNode = new LLNode<T>(element);
    if (rear == null)
      front = newNode;
    else
      rear.setLink(newNode);
    rear = newNode;
  }

  public T dequeue()
  // Throws QueueUnderflowException if this queue is empty;
  // otherwise, removes front element from this queue and returns it.
  {
    if (isEmpty())
      throw new QueueUnderflowException("Dequeue attempted on empty queue.");
    else
    {
```

```
        T element;
        element = front.getInfo();
        front = front.getLink();
        if (front == null)
          rear = null;

        return element;
    }
}

public boolean isEmpty()
// Returns true if this queue is empty; otherwise, returns false.
{
    if (front == null)
      return true;
    else
      return false;
}
}
```

A Circular Linked Queue Design

Our `LinkedUnbndQueue` class contains two instance variables, one to reference each end of the queue. This design is based on the linear structure of the linked queue. Can we implement the class using only one instance variable? Given only a reference to the front of the queue, we could follow the links to get to the rear of the queue, but this choice makes accessing the rear (to enqueue an element) an O(N) operation. With a reference only to the rear of the queue, we could not access the front because the references only go from front to rear.

However, we could efficiently access both ends of the queue from a single reference if we made the queue circularly linked. That is, the link of the rear node would reference the front node of the queue (see Figure 5.12). Then `LinkedUnbndQueue` would have only one instance variable, rather than two. This queue implementation differs from the logical picture of a queue as a linear structure with two ends. Instead, we have a circular structure with no ends. What makes it a queue is its support of FIFO access.

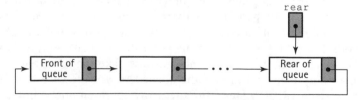

Figure 5.12   *A circular linked queue*

To enqueue an element, we access the "rear" node directly through the reference `rear`. To dequeue an element, we must access the "front" node of the queue. We don't have a reference to this node, but we do have a reference to the node preceding it—`rear`. The reference to the "front" node of the queue is in `rear.getLink()`. For an empty queue, `rear` would be `null`. Designing and coding the queue operations using a circular linked implementation is left for you as an exercise.

Both linked implementations of the Queue ADT can be tested using the same test plan that was discussed for the array-based version.

Comparing Queue Implementations

We have now looked at several different implementations of the Queue ADT. How do they compare? We consider two different factors: the amount of memory required to store the structure and the amount of "work" the solution requires, as expressed in Big-O notation. Let's first compare the `ArrayBndQueue` and `LinkedUnbndQueue` implementations.

The array in the bounded queue consumes the same amount of memory, no matter how many slots are actually used; we need to reserve space for the maximum number of elements. The linked implementation using dynamically allocated storage space requires space only for the number of elements actually in the queue. Note, however, that the node elements are twice as large, because we must store the link (the reference to the next node) as well as the reference to the element.

Figure 5.13 illustrates each queue implementation approach, assuming a current queue size of 5 and a maximum queue size (for the array-based implementation) of 100. Note that the array-based implementation requires space for 4 integers and 101 references (one for `myQueue` and one for each array slot) regardless of the size of the queue. The linked implementation requires space for only 13 references (one for `front`, one for `rear`, two for each of the current queue elements, and one for `myQueue`). However, the required space increases if the size of the queue increases, based on the following formula:

Number of required references = 3 + (2 * size of queue)

A simple analysis reveals that if the queue size is less than half the maximum queue size, then the linked representation uses less space than the array representation. Beyond that size, the linked representation requires more space. In any case, unless the maximum queue size is significantly larger than the average queue size, the difference between the two implementations in terms of space is probably not important.

We can also compare the relative execution "efficiency" of the two implementations in terms of Big-O notation. In both implementations, the complexity of the observer methods (`isFull` for the array implementation and `isEmpty` for both implementations) is clearly $O(1)$. These methods always take the same amount of work regardless of how many elements are on the queue. As was the case for stacks, the queue constructor requires $O(N)$ steps for the array representation, but is $O(1)$ for the linked representation.

Queues with
    Maximum size 100
    Current size 5
    x = null

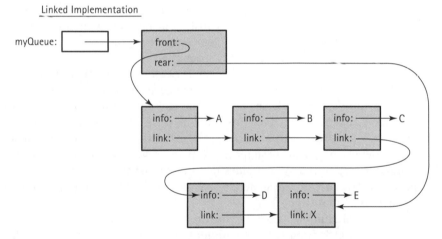

Figure 5.13   *Comparing queue implementations*

What about enqueue and dequeue? Does the number of elements in the queue affect the amount of work done by these operations? No, it does not; in both implementations, we can directly access the front and the rear of the queue. The amount of work done by these operations is independent of the queue size, so these operations also have O(1) complexity. As with the array-based and linked implementations of stacks, both queue implementations are roughly equivalent in terms of the amount of work they do.

Now let's briefly consider our ArrayUnbndQueue approach. The analysis for the bounded approach applies to the unbounded approach. However, with the unbounded approach we can start with an array size that handles an average-size queue; only when the queue becomes larger is the array expanded. Thus we do not pay as big a penalty in terms of extra space. The drawback is the extra time, $O(N)$, required to resize the array. For most applications this operation is not required very often.

5.7 Concurrency, Interference, and Synchronization

The complexities of today require many people to engage in multitasking. For example, right now you may be texting on your phone while watching TV and eating lunch, all at the same time you are doing your data structures homework! Computers also multitask. A computer system can be printing a document, burning a CD, and interacting with a user all at the same time.

Many computer programs require multitasking capabilities. For example, a game program might have separate code sequences to react to changes in user input, to detect collisions between the objects in the game, and to update a scoreboard reflecting the game status. For such a game to be playable each of the code sequences must be active simultaneously and they must interact with each other. Programs that perform this way are called concurrent programs.

> **Multitask** Perform more than one task at a time
>
> **Concurrency** Several interacting code sequences are executing simultaneously, possibly through an interleaving of their statements by a single processor, possibly through execution on distinct processors

Concurrent programs are very common—programs that control systems, provide games, support work productivity, or allow communication are usually concurrent. On a single processor system concurrency is achieved through the interleaving of the instructions of the various code sequences. The computer jumps back and forth among code sequences, executing a "few" instructions from one sequence, and then a "few" from another sequence, and so on. On systems with dual processors, quad processors, or higher levels of physical support for parallelism the concurrency can be "real." The computer's operating system hides the presence or absence of physical concurrency support from the program designer so that as programmers we need not be concerned with the details of that support.

A formal study of program concurrency is typically provided in operating systems, database, or algorithm courses within a computing curriculum and is beyond the scope of this book. However, in this section we introduce the topic by:

- Defining terminology related to concurrency.
- Showing how to indicate that parts of a Java program should be executed concurrently.
- Explaining how concurrent code sequences might interfere with each other.
- Demonstrating how to synchronize the execution of the code sequences so that such interference does not occur.

The Counter Class

To support our investigation of the topics of this section we use the following simple Counter class. It provides an integral attribute that is originally zero, and that can be incremented through calls to an `increment` method. All auxiliary classes created for this section of the text are placed into the `ch05.threads` package.

```java
//-----------------------------------------------------------------------
// Counter.java            by Dale/Joyce/Weems            Chapter 5
//
// Tracks the current value of a counter.
//-----------------------------------------------------------------------

package ch05.threads;

public class Counter
{
  private int count;

  public Counter()
  {
    count = 0;
  }

  public void increment()
  {
    count++;
  }

  public String toString()
  {
    return "Count is:\t" + count;
  }

}
```

The sample program `Demo01` instantiates a `Counter` object, increments it three times, and then prints its status. The sample output is as expected, showing a count of 3. All of the application programs created for this section of the text are placed into the `ch05.concurrency` folder.

```java
import ch05.threads.*;

public class Demo01
{
  public static void main(String[] args)
```

```
      {
        Counter myCounter = new Counter();
        myCounter.increment();
        myCounter.increment();
        myCounter.increment();
        System.out.println(myCounter);
      }
    }
```

The output of the program is:

```
Count is:     3
```

Java Threads

The Java concurrency mechanism we present is the thread. Every Java program that executes has a thread, the "main" thread of the program. The main thread has the ability to generate additional threads. When this occurs the various threads of the program run concurrently. The program terminates when all of its threads terminate.

   We create thread objects by first defining a class that implements the Java library's Runnable interface. Such classes must provide a public run method. As an example see the following Increase class that accepts a Counter object and an integer amount through its constructor, and provides a run method that increments the Counter object the number of times indicated by the value of amount.

```
package ch05.threads;

public class Increase implements Runnable
{
    private Counter c;
    private int amount;

    public Increase (Counter c, int amount)
    {
        this.c = c;   this.amount = amount;
    }

    public void run()
    {
        for (int i = 1; i <= amount; i++)
            c.increment();
    }
}
```

We can then instantiate a `Thread` object by passing its constructor an `Increase` object (or any `Runnable` object). The instantiated `Thread` object can be used to execute the `Increase` object's `run` method in a separate thread from the main program thread. To do this we call the thread object's `start` method. Consider the `Demo02` example:

```
import ch05.threads.*;

public class Demo02
{
  public static void main(String[] args) throws InterruptedException⁵
  {
    Counter  c = new Counter();
    Runnable r = new Increase(c, 10000);
    Thread   t = new Thread(r);

    t.start();

    System.out.println("Count is:    " + c);
  }
}
```

The `Demo02` program instantiates a `Counter` object c, uses c plus the integer literal 10,000 to instantiate a `Runnable` object r, and uses r to instantiate a `Thread` object t. The thread object runs, in a separate thread, after the call to its `start` method. The program displays the value of the counter object before terminating. What value will it display? Considering that the `Increase` object will increment the counter 10,000 times you might expect the output of the program to be the following:

```
Count is:  10000
```

But the increment of the counter and the display of its value occur in different threads, as shown in Figure 5.14. There is no guarantee that the incrementing of the counter by the second thread will finish before its value is displayed by the main thread. In fact, it is very likely that a value other than 10,000 will be output. When run on the author's computer, the `Demo02` program reports values such as 86, 66, and 44.

We can indicate that we want one thread to wait for the completion of another thread by using the `join` command. The following program produces the "correct" output, reporting a count of 10,000, since it indicates that the main thread should wait for completion of the t thread before displaying the value of the counter object. The line of code that accomplishes this is <u>emphasized</u>.

---

5. The `Thread` object can throw the checked run-time `InterruptedException` exception. Therefore we must either catch and handle that exception or throw it out to the execution environment.

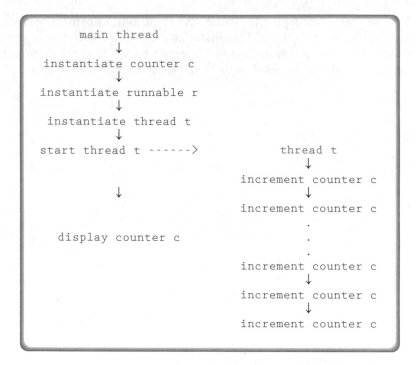

Figure 5.14   *Execution of the Demo02 program*

```
import ch05.threads.*;

public class Demo03
{
  public static void main(String[] args) throws InterruptedException
  {
    Counter  c = new Counter();
    Runnable r = new Increase(c, 10000);
    Thread   t = new Thread(r);

    t.start();
    t.join();

    System.out.println("Count is:    " + c);
  }
}
```

The join command indicates that the main thread should wait until completion of the thread t before continuing. Therefore the counter is incremented completely before its value is output.

Interference

When two or more threads of a program make changes to the same data at the same time they can interfere with each other and create unintended, undesired results. Consider the `Demo04` program that has a total of three threads; the main thread and two others.

```
import ch05.threads.*;

public class Demo04
{
  public static void main(String[] args) throws InterruptedException
  {
    Counter   c = new Counter();
    Runnable r1 = new Increase(c, 5000);
    Runnable r2 = new Increase(c, 5000);
    Thread    t1 = new Thread(r1);
    Thread    t2 = new Thread(r2);

    t1.start();
    t2.start();
    t1.join();
    t2.join();

    System.out.println("Count is:    " + c);
  }
}
```

As you can see, the `Demo04` program runs two separate threads, each of which increments the shared counter object 5000 times. The program uses the `join` method to ensure that all auxiliary threads are finished before it accesses and displays the final values of the counter. Again we ask—what values will this program display? Clearly we would expect the result to be:

```
Count is:  10000
```

However, we would be wrong. This example demonstrates the dangers of working with concurrency. Programmers who use concurrency must be very careful how they wield its power. Three separate runs of the `Demo04` program on the author's computer produce the following three outputs:

```
Count is:  9861
Count is:  9478
Count is:  9203
```

The reason for these unexpected results is that the two incrementing threads interfere with each other. Consider that to increment a counter requires three steps in Java byte code: obtain the current value of the counter, add one to that value, and store the result. If two threads executing simultaneously interleave the execution of these steps, then the resultant value of the counter will be one less than the expected value. For example, consider the following sequence of steps, where the counter begins with the value 12 and both threads increment the counter. Although we would expect the resultant value to be 14, due to the "interference" the final value is only 13:

```
Thread t1                          Thread t2
Step 1: obtains value 12
               ↓                   Step 2: obtains value 12
Step 3: increments value to 13              ↓
Step 4: stores the value 13                 ↓
                                   Step 5: increments value to 13
                                   Step 6: stores the value 13
```

Examining the output from the Demo04 program we conclude that such interference occurs multiple times during the execution of the code. When concurrent threads make changes to shared variables, such as in the Demo04 program, they must synchronize their access of the shared information.

Synchronization

In Java we can force synchronization at either the statement level or the method level. We will use method level synchronization. In the Demo04 example, the method that requires synchronization is the increment method of the Counter class. To demonstrate the use of a synchronized method we create a separate counter class Sync-Counter. Indicating that a method is synchronized simply requires the use of the synchronized keyword as a modifier in the method declaration line, as <u>emphasized</u> in the following code.

```
//-----------------------------------------------------------------------
// SyncCounter.java          by Dale/Joyce/Weems              Chapter 5
//
// Tracks the current value of a counter.
// Provides synchronized access to the increment method.
//-----------------------------------------------------------------------

package ch05.threads;

public class SyncCounter
{
  private int count;
```

```
public SyncCounter()
{
   count = 0;
}

public synchronized void increment()
{
  count++;
}

public String toString()
{
  return "Count is:\t" + count;
}
}
```

Thread access to the `increment` method of the `SyncCounter` class will be executed in a safe fashion. If one thread is in the middle of executing code within the method, no other thread will be given access to the method. No interleaving of Java byte code statements for this method will occur. This prevents the interference that led to the unexpected results in the `Demo04` program.

Whenever the `Demo05` program below is executed it correctly reports the expected value for the counter of 10,000. The `Increase2` class used in the program is identical to the `Increase` class except that it accepts a `SyncCounter` instead of `Counter` as its first parameter.

```
import ch05.threads.*;

public class Demo05
{
  public static void main(String[] args) throws InterruptedException
  {
    SyncCounter  sc = new SyncCounter();
    Runnable r1 = new Increase2(sc, 5000);
    Runnable r2 = new Increase2(sc, 5000);
    Thread    t1 = new Thread(r1);
    Thread    t2 = new Thread(r2);

    t1.start();  t2.start();
    t1.join();   t2.join();

    System.out.println("Count is:    " + sc);
  }
}
```

A Synchronized Queue

Data collections are sometimes at the heart of concurrent programs. The Queue ADT in particular is often used concurrently, for example, to store tasks generated by "producer" threads of a system that need to be handled later by separate "consumer" threads of the system, in essence acting as a repository for unfinished work. When a collection is used by multiple threads, access to it must be synchronized. Otherwise some elements may be mistakenly skipped and others may be erroneously accessed more than once, as threads interfere with each other while manipulating the data structure that underlies the collection.

In this subsection we investigate using a queue as described in the previous paragraph. We use a simple example so that we can concentrate on the synchronization issues. First we look at an unsynchronized version of the program and discuss its potential problems, then we see how to resolve the raised issues. Here is the first version of the program:

```java
import ch05.threads.*;
import ch05.queues.*;

public class Demo06
{
  public static void main(String[] args) throws InterruptedException
  {
    int LIMIT = 100;
    SyncCounter   c = new SyncCounter();
    BoundedQueueInterface<Integer> q;
    q = new ArrayBndQueue<Integer>(LIMIT);

    for (int i = 1; i <= LIMIT; i++)
      q.enqueue(i);

    Runnable r1 = new Increase3(c, q);
    Runnable r2 = new Increase3(c, q);
    Thread   t1 = new Thread(r1);
    Thread   t2 = new Thread(r2);

    t1.start();  t2.start();
    t1.join();   t2.join();

    System.out.println("Count is:    " + c);
  }
}
```

The `Demo06` program above creates a queue of integers and inserts the integers from 1 to 100 into the queue. It then generates and runs two threads: `t1` and `t2`. These threads each contain a copy of an `Increase3` object (see the code below). Therefore each of the threads checks the queue to see whether it is empty, and if not, the thread removes the next number from the queue and increments the shared counter object that number of times. So perhaps the `t1` thread increments the counter once while the `t2` counter is incrementing the counter twice; and then the `t2` thread may increment the counter three times while the `t1` counter is incrementing the counter four times, and so on. Remember that access to the counter is synchronized. After both threads complete, the value of the counter is output.

```
package ch05.threads;

import ch05.queues.*;

public class Increase3 implements Runnable
{
    private SyncCounter c;
    private BoundedQueueInterface<Integer> q;

    public Increase3 (SyncCounter c, BoundedQueueInterface<Integer> q)
    {
        this.c = c;   this.q = q;
    }

    public void run()
    {
        int hold;
        while (!q.isEmpty())
        {
            hold = q.dequeue();
            for (int i = 1; i <= hold; i++)
                c.increment();
        }
    }
}
```

Let's review. The `Demo06` program inserts the numbers from 1 to 100 into a queue. The `t1` and `t2` threads remove numbers from that queue and increment the counter `c` accordingly. The value of the counter is then output. What is that value? It should be 5050, which is equal to the sum of the integers between 1 and 100, correct? When executed on the author's computer the result is 5050. Good. So the program works as expected. Not so fast—when dealing with concurrent programs it is possible for interference errors to occur intermittently. Such errors depend upon the timing of thread interleaving, and so although the program may work as expected on one run, on another run we may get unexpected results.

We ran this program 10 times, and 10 times the result was 5050. But the eleventh test run produced a result of 4980. And the sixteenth test run produced a null pointer exception. Although access to the counter is synchronized, access to the queue itself is not. That is the source of these unexpected results. Interference during access to the dequeue method, perhaps multiple times, would explain both of these unexpected results. Readers are encouraged to try this experiment for themselves and see what happens on their systems.

To create a reliable version of this program we need to create a synchronized queue class. Fortunately this is not difficult. We simply add the synchronized keyword to the qualifiers of each of the exported methods of our queue implementation as emphasized in the SyncArrayBndQueue class below. Adding the synchronized keyword to multiple methods guarantees that if one thread is active in any of those methods, then no other thread will be allowed into the same method or any of the other methods. Using this class in place of the ArrayBndQueue class in the Demo06 program creates a reliable example. We ran that new system over one 100 times and received the expected result of 5050 every time.

```java
//----------------------------------------------------------------------------
// SyncArrayBndQueue.java          by Dale/Joyce/Weems          Chapter 5
//
// Implements BoundedQueueInterface with an array to hold the queue
// elements.
// Operations are synchronized to allow concurrent access.
//
// Two constructors are provided: one that creates a queue of a default
// capacity and one that allows the calling program to specify the
// capacity.
//----------------------------------------------------------------------------

package ch05.queues;

public class SyncArrayBndQueue<T> implements BoundedQueueInterface<T>
{
  protected final int DEFCAP = 100;  // default capacity
  protected T[] queue;               // array that holds queue elements
  protected int numElements = 0;     // number of elements in the queue
  protected int front = 0;           // index of front of queue
  protected int rear;                // index of rear of queue

  public SyncArrayBndQueue()
  {
    queue = (T[]) new Object[DEFCAP];
```

```
    rear = DEFCAP - 1;
  }

  public SyncArrayBndQueue(int maxSize)
  {
    queue = (T[]) new Object[maxSize];
    rear = maxSize - 1;
  }

  public synchronized void enqueue(T element)
  // Throws QueueOverflowException if this queue is full;
  // otherwise, adds element to the rear of this queue.
  {
    if (isFull())
      throw new QueueOverflowException("Enqueue attempted on a full
                                       queue.");
    else
    {
      rear = (rear + 1) % queue.length;
      queue[rear] = element;
      numElements = numElements + 1;
    }
  }

  public synchronized T dequeue()
  // Throws QueueUnderflowException if this queue is empty;
  // otherwise, removes front element from this queue and returns it.
  {
    if (isEmpty())
      throw new QueueUnderflowException("Dequeue attempted on empty
                                        queue.");
    else
    {
      T toReturn = queue[front];
      queue[front] = null;
      front = (front + 1) % queue.length;
      numElements = numElements - 1;
      return toReturn;
    }
  }

  public synchronized boolean isEmpty()
  // Returns true if this queue is empty; otherwise, returns false.
```

```
  {
    return (numElements == 0);
  }


  public synchronized boolean isFull()
  // Returns true if this queue is full; otherwise, returns false.
  {
    return (numElements == queue.length);
  }
}
```

We have avoided the interference problems by making all of the queue access and increment methods synchronized. As a result, every attempt to access the queue waits if the other thread is currently accessing it. Once a thread has the increment value from the queue, it attempts to access the shared counter, but because it too is synchronized, the thread will wait until the other thread is done incrementing the counter. As a result, there are very few concurrent operations taking place. While one thread is incrementing, the other thread can access the queue, and vice versa. If our goal is to make use of two physical processors in the computer to finish the task twice as quickly, the actual speed improvement will be disappointing.

Programmers of concurrent systems often encounter situations such as this. To ensure correctness, they must include so much synchronization that most of the work done by the threads takes place sequentially rather than concurrently. To get greater concurrency, it may be necessary to rethink the solution to the problem.

For example, if each of our threads had its own private counter, they could each get values from the synchronized queue and perform their increments concurrently on their own counters. On completion, each thread would return its counter value, and the main thread would add the two values to get the final result. The threads would only wait on occasions where they interfere in accessing the queue and would no longer need to wait when accessing a counter. Executing this solution on two processors could yield nearly a doubling of performance.

We say, "could," because there are other factors involved in achieving good performance with concurrent processing. For example, creating each new thread requires the run-time system to do some work. If the work to be done by each thread is less than the work required to create the thread, then it actually takes longer to create the threads and do the work concurrently than to do the work in the usual, sequential way. As you can see, concurrency brings many additional considerations to programming.

In every new generation of computer chip, manufacturers add more cores (processors), with each core capable of running multiple threads simultaneously. Taking advantage of these capabilities requires programs to divide their work among multiple threads. Concurrent programming is thus an important future trend in computing, and programmers who learn to do it well will be in great demand.

Concurrency and the Java Library Collection Classes

In Section 5.2 a feature section introduced The Java Library Collection Framework Queue and explained that the library includes a `Queue` interface plus nine classes that implement that interface. As we emphasized in the current section, queues are often used in concurrent programs. Lending credence to this statement is the fact that most of the queue interface implementations in the Java library support concurrent use in one way or another:

- The `ArrayBlockingQueue`, `LinkedBlockingQueue`, `DelayQueue`, `Synchronous-Queue`, and `PriorityBlockingQueue` all share the feature that a thread attempting to put an element into a full queue object will block until such time that the queue object has space available, and that a thread attempting to retrieve an element from an empty queue object will block until an element is available.
- The `ConcurrentLinkedQueue` is thread-safe. This means that like the `SyncArray-BndQueue` we developed in this section, operations on objects of the `Concurrent-LinkedQueue` are synchronized to allow concurrent access.

Originally most of the collection classes in the Collections Framework were thread-safe, just like the `ConcurrentLinkedQueue` class. These include the `Vector`, `Stack`, `Dictionary`, and `HashTable` classes. However, due to the protection code required there is an execution time cost associated with maintaining thread safeness. Furthermore, many users of the collection classes do not need nor want to use concurrent threads, so the built-in cost of thread safeness was considered unnecessary overhead. Therefore, with the release of Java 2, similar classes were included in the library for all of the original collection classes. For example, the `ArrayList` class is a non-thread-safe alternative for the `Vector` class and `HashSet` or `HashMap` are alternatives to `HashTable`.

The original set of collection classes, the thread-safe collection classes, are now known as the "historical" collection classes. Most programmers prefer not to use them; instead, programmers use the collection classes introduced with Java 2 or later. There are facilities in the library for transforming these newer classes into thread-safe classes. For example, you could create a synchronized `Set` collection using the unsynchronized `HashSet` class with the statement

```
Set s = Collection.synchronizedSet(new HashSet());
```

5.8 Case Study: Average Waiting Time

Queues are useful data structures within computer systems: We have process queues, print job queues, and service queues. Queues are also commonly seen in the real world: We have toll-booth queues, ticket-counter queues, and fast-food queues.

The primary function of a queue is to provide a place for a "customer" to wait before receiving a "service." Processes are waiting for a processor, print jobs are waiting for a printer, and hungry people are waiting for their hamburgers. Management is interested in how much time customers spend waiting in queues. For example, a computer system manager wants quick system response time and a fast-food restaurant manager wants to keep his or her customers happy. These goals are achieved by minimizing the time spent in the queues.

One way to minimize queue waiting time is to add more servers, and therefore more queues, to the system.[6] Print jobs spend less time in the print queue if there are 10 printers churning out jobs than they do if there is only one printer. Likewise, a fast-food restaurant with six teller lines can handle more customers, more quickly, than a restaurant with only two lines. However, additional servers are not free—there is usually some cost associated with them. Management must balance the benefits of adding extra servers against the costs when deciding how many servers to provide.

In this case study we create a program that simulates a system of queues. The goal is to help management analyze queuing systems. Computer simulations are a powerful and widely used technique for analysis of complicated real-world problems.

Problem Discussion

Our program simulates a series of customers arriving for service, entering queues, waiting, being served, and finally leaving the queue. It tracks the time the customers spend waiting in queues and outputs the average waiting time.

How do we calculate the waiting time of a customer? To simplify things we assume that time is measured in integer units, and that our simulation starts at time 0. Suppose a customer arrives at time X and leaves at time Y. Is the waiting time for that customer equal to $Y - X$? No, part of that time the customer was being served. The time $Y - X$ is called the *turnaround time*; it is the total time the customer spends in the system, including the service time. Waiting time is turnaround time minus service time.

To calculate waiting time we need to know the arrival time, finish time, and service time. The arrival time and service time depend on the individual customers—when they show up and how much service they need. The finish time depends on the number of queues, the number of other customers in the queues, and the service needs of those other customers.

Generating Arrival and Service Times

A sequence of customers is represented by their arrival times and service requirements. These values can be obtained in several ways. One approach is to read the values from a file. This strategy is great for testing because it allows the programmer to completely control the input values. However, it is awkward if you want to simulate a large number of customers.

Another approach is to generate the values randomly. We will take this approach. It is easy to generate the random service times: The user simply enters the minimum and

---

6. Some systems have several queues feeding into one server. In this section we assume that each queue has its own dedicated server.

maximum expected service times, and using Java's `Random` class our program generates service times between those two values.

We follow a slightly different algorithm with arrival times. Service time measures an amount of time, but arrival time specifies when the customer arrives. For example, customer 1 arrives at 10:00 A.M., customer 2 at 10:05, customer 3 at 10:07, and so on. In our simulation, we simply start the clock at 0 and keep the arrival time as an integer. We cannot directly create a sequence of increasing times by using the random number generator, however. Instead, we randomly generate the times between customer arrivals (the inter-arrival times), and keep a running total of those values.

For example, we might generate a sequence of inter-arrival times of 5, 7, 4, 10, and 7. Given that our simulation starts at time 0, the arrival times are then 5, 12, 16, 26, and 33. To constrain the range of inter-arrival times, we can let the user specify a minimum value and a maximum value.

For each customer our program generates an arrival time and a service time. Through the simulation it then determines the finish time and, based on those values, calculates the waiting time.

The Simulation

In addition to inter-arrival and service time information, our program obtains the number of simulated queues from the user. We index the queues starting at 0; if there are N queues, they are indexed 0 to $N - 1$. The user also provides the total number of customers to be simulated. To ease the input burden, our program will allow the user to enter the sets of minimum and maximum time parameters once, and then run repeated simulations where he or she indicates the number of queues and customers.

Each simulation should take customers in the order they arrive and place them into queues. We assume that a customer always chooses the smallest queue available. In case of a tie, the customer chooses the smaller-numbered queue. The program has to model only two situations: a customer arriving for service and a customer leaving after being served. When a customer leaves, the program must remember the customer's waiting time so that it can calculate the overall average waiting time.

As an example, consider a case with the following four customers:

Customer	Arrival Time	Service Time
1	3	10
2	4	3
3	5	10
4	25	7

Suppose we have two queues. The first customer arrives at time 3 and enters queue 0. We can see that the expected finish time is 13, because the service time is 10. The second customer arrives before the first is finished and enters queue 1. The finish time is 7. This scenario is represented by the following chart:

Time	1 2 3 4 5 6 7 8 9 10 11 12 13 14 15 16 17 18 19 20 21 22 23 24 25
Q0	cust1
Q1	cust2

The third customer arrives at time 5, before either of the preceding customers is finished. So customer 3 enters queue 0, behind customer 1, and has an expected finish time of 23. Do you see why? Customer 1 finishes at time 13 and then customer 3 has a service time of 10.

Time	1 2 3 4 5 6 7 8 9 10 11 12 13 14 15 16 17 18 19 20 21 22 23 24 25
Q0	cust1 cust3
Q1	cust2

If you continue this simulation by hand, you should get the following results, for an average waiting time of $8 \div 4 = 2.0$ time units.

Customer	Arrival Time	Service Time	Finish Time	Wait Time
1	3	10	13	0
2	4	3	7	0
3	5	10	23	8
4	25	7	32	0

Program Design

Let's walk through the process of brainstorming classes, filtering, and scenario analysis. The description below is idealized—the actual design took more head-knocking and backtracking than what is shown here.

Brainstorming

A study of the problem discussion reveals the following nouns, which we have grouped together based on natural relationships. The nouns represent candidate object classes.

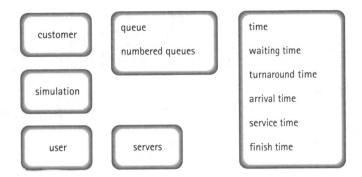

Two of these nouns jump out as good candidate classes: queue and customer. We already have several queue classes that we have developed in this chapter. Perhaps one of them can be used to model the real-world queues. Thinking about the customers, we decide to create a `Customer` class to model customers. It should allow us to create customer objects and place them in the queues. Further reflection reveals that many of the "time" nouns are really just attributes of a customer: A customer has an arrival time, a service time, a finish time, and a wait time. Turnaround time is not needed for the simulation and can be discarded from our list.

Recall that each of the queues has its own dedicated server. As a consequence, we do not really need a separate "server" class. The activity of a server can be bundled with a queue. We no longer need to consider it as a potential class. Thinking further about "numbered queues," we decide they can be represented by an array of queues to be used in the simulation.

Filtering

Continuing with filtering of the candidate classes, we recognize that "user" simply represents the user of the system. Following our conventions for handling I/O, we know that the main driving program will handle all interactions with the user. In a sense, the driving program represents the user. We call the program `SimulationApp`.

Let's see where we stand. Here are the currently identified classes and the remaining candidate classes:

Identified Classes	Candidate Classes
Customer	time
Queue	simulation
SimulationApp	

Should we have a `Time` class? No. We can use a variable to keep track of the time.

What about a `Simulation` class? Because we already have a driver application that interacts with the user, creating a separate class to perform the required work is an excellent idea. A `Simulation` object can be created based on the parameters obtained from the driving program, perform the simulation, and return the average waiting time.

In summation, we have identified three new classes: Customer, Simulation, and SimulationApp. The Simulation class will, in turn, use an array of queues. Next we look at each new class more closely, using scenario analysis to see whether this collection of classes is sufficient for solving the problem.

Scenario Analysis

First we consider the responsibilities of the Customer class. An object of this class represents a single customer. The arrival and service times of the customer can be provided as arguments when a Customer object is instantiated. A Customer must provide observer methods, and it should also provide methods to both set and observe the finish time. Given that the object eventually knows its arrival, service, and finish times, it can be responsible for calculating and returning its own waiting time. Table 5.1 shows our current abstract view of the Customer class. Tables such as this one help us record and organize our evolving design.

We now must ask, "Where do Customer objects originate?" They could be created by the SimulationApp class, but after some consideration we decide that this responsibility should reside elsewhere. We decide to create a CustomerGenerator class. An object of this class is passed the minimum and maximum inter-arrival and service times of the customers upon instantiation. Its primary responsibility is to generate and return the "next" customer when requested, as shown in Table 5.2.

Next we consider the Simulation class. An object of this class performs our simulation. To do so, it gets the simulation setup from the SimulationApp class. Because the

Table 5.1 *Abstract View of the Customer Class*

Class Name: Customer
Primary Responsibility: Model a customer
Responsibilities:
  Allow instantiation with arrival and service time arguments
  Provide a way to set the finish time attribute
  Provide a way to observe the arrival, service, and finish times
  Calculate and return the waiting time

Table 5.2 *Abstract View of the CustomerGenerator Class*

Class Name: CustomerGenerator
Primary Responsibility: Generate a sequence of Customer objects
Responsibilities:
  Allow instantiation with minimum and maximum inter-arrival and service time arguments
  Provide a way to obtain the next customer
  Provide a way to reset the sequence of customers

user must be able to run multiple simulations using the same customer parameters (the time-related parameters), we decide to pass these parameters to the `Simulation` object once, at instantiation—that is, through the constructor of the `Simulation` object. The constructor, in turn, creates a `CustomerGenerator` object to use during the subsequent simulation runs. The application can "ask" the `Simulation` object to run simulations, always using the same `CustomerGenerator` but with differing numbers of queues and customers. We summarize our decisions regarding the `Simulation` class in Table 5.3.

Let's now consider the actual simulation process. As already determined, our program uses an array of queues to hold the customers. It must be able to take the next generated `Customer` object from the `CustomerGenerator` object and insert it into the correct queue. But how can it determine the correct queue? It must pick the smallest queue; therefore it needs to be able to learn the size of the queues. We cannot use any of our previously defined queue classes because they do not provide an observer that returns the queue size. Instead, we must derive a new queue class.

Do we need any other special operations for these queues? After the program determines which queue to use, it must `enqueue` the customer into that queue. Recall that we can determine the finish time of a customer as soon as we know which queue the customer is entering. If the queue is empty, then that customer's finish time is equal to the arrival time plus the service time. If the queue is not empty, then the new customer's finish time is equal to the finish time of the customer at the rear of the queue plus the new customer's own service time. Thus the program can set the finish time of a customer before enqueuing the customer. Note that if the queue is nonempty, the program must be able to peek at the customer at the rear of the queue to set the finish time. For this reason, we add peeking at the rear of a queue to our list of required operations.

To perform the simulation the program must also be able to determine when the "next" customer is ready to leave a queue, and then remove and return that customer. How does it determine when a customer is ready to leave a queue? Because customers in a queue know their finish times, the program just needs to compare the finish times of the customers at the front of each queue and determine which is the earliest. Therefore the program must be able to peek at the customer at the front of a queue. That is one more operation to add to our list.

To provide the necessary queue operations, we extend the `ArrayUnbndQueue` class with a class called `GlassQueue`, which provides `size`, `peekFront`, and `peekRear` methods. Table 5.4 captures these responsibilities.

Table 5.3 *Abstract View of the* `Simulation` *Class*

Class Name: Simulation

Primary Responsibility: Run our simulation and provide access to the results

Responsibilities:

Allow instantiation with customer information

Perform a simulation using its CustomerGenerator object and arguments that indicate the number of queues and customers

Provide a way to obtain the results of the simulation

Table 5.4 *Abstract View of the* `GlassQueue` *Class*

Class Name: GlassQueue

Primary Responsibility: Extend ArrayUnbndQueue with some operations that allow examination of
the queue

Responsibilities:

Return the size of the queue

Return a link to the front element of the queue

Return a link to the rear element of the queue

We have now finished our scenario analysis. We are convinced that we have defined a good set of classes to solve our problem. We are ready to begin coding.

Program Details

In this subsection we look at the code for each class we create to solve our problem. We elaborate when we feel sections of the code require explanation.

We design and create five new classes. The key to understanding a program like this one is to use abstraction. Don't worry about all the details of all the classes at once. Instead, concentrate on one class's responsibilities at a time. When convinced that a class meets its responsibilities, you can move on to the next class.

The Customer Class

Because we may want to use customers in other applications later in the textbook, we decide to place the `Customer` and `CustomerGenerator` classes in the `support` package. The `Customer` class is very straightforward:

```java
//-----------------------------------------------------------------
// Customer.java          by Dale/Joyce/Weems          Chapter 5
//
// Supports customer objects having arrival, service, and finish time
// attributes. Responsible for computing and returning wait time.
//-----------------------------------------------------------------

package support;

public class Customer
{
  protected int arrivalTime;
  protected int serviceTime;
  protected int finishTime;

  public Customer(int arrivalTime, int serviceTime)
  {
    this.arrivalTime = arrivalTime;
```

```
    this.serviceTime = serviceTime;
  }

  public int getArrivalTime()
  {
    return arrivalTime;
  }

  public int getServiceTime()
  {
    return serviceTime;
  }

  public void setFinishTime(int time)
  {
    finishTime = time;
  }

  public int getFinishTime()
  {
    return finishTime;
  }

  public int getWaitTime()
  {
    return (finishTime - arrivalTime - serviceTime);
  }
}
```

The CustomerGenerator Class

This class uses the Java library's `Random` class. Recall that a call to `rand.nextInt(N)` returns a random integer between 0 and N − 1. Note that a `CustomerGenerator` object keeps track of the current time, so it can calculate the next arrival time.

```
//------------------------------------------------------------
// CustomerGenerator.java     by Dale/Joyce/Weems     Chapter 5
//
// Generates a sequence of random Customer objects based on the
// constructor arguments for min and max inter-arrival and service times.
// Assumes a flat distribution of both inter-arrival and service times.
// Assumes time starts at 0.
//------------------------------------------------------------

package support;

import java.util.Random;
```

```
public class CustomerGenerator
{
  protected int minIAT;   // minimum inter-arrival time
  protected int maxIAT;   // maximum inter-arrival time
  protected int minST;    // minimum service time
  protected int maxST;    // maximum service time
  protected int currTime = 0;   // current time
  Random rand = new Random();   // to generate random numbers

  public CustomerGenerator (int minIAT, int maxIAT, int minST, int maxST)
  // Preconditions: all arguments >= 0, minIAT <= maxIAT, minST  <= maxST
  {
    this.minIAT = minIAT;
    this.maxIAT = maxIAT;
    this.minST  = minST;
    this.maxST  = maxST;
  }

  public void reset()
  {
    currTime = 0;
  }

  public Customer nextCustomer()
  // Creates and returns the next random customer.
  {
    int IAT;  // next inter-arrival time
    int ST;   // next service time
    IAT = minIAT + rand.nextInt(maxIAT - minIAT + 1);
    ST  = minST  + rand.nextInt(maxST - minST + 1);
    currTime = currTime + IAT;   // updates current time to the arrival
                                 // time of next customer
    Customer next = new Customer(currTime, ST);
    return next;
  }
}
```

The GlassQueue Class
This class is a straightforward extension of the ArrayUnbndQueue class.

```
//-----------------------------------------------------------------------------
// GlassQueue.java           by Dale/Joyce/Weems                    Chapter 5
//
// Extends ArrayUnbndQueue with operations to determine the size of the queue
```

```
// and to access the front and rear queue elements without removing them.
//-----------------------------------------------------------------------

package ch05.queues;

public class GlassQueue<T> extends ArrayUnbndQueue<T>
{

  public GlassQueue()
  {
    super();
  }

  public GlassQueue(int origCap)
  {
    super(origCap);
  }

  public int size()
  // Returns the number of elements in this queue.
  {
    return numElements;
  }

  public T peekFront()
  // Returns the object at the front of this queue.
  // If the queue is empty, returns null.
  {
    return queue[front];
  }

  public T peekRear()
  // Returns the object at the rear of this queue.
  // If the queue is empty, returns null.
  {
    return queue[rear];
  }
}
```

The Simulation Class
The simulate method works through the simulation until finished. Each time through the *while* loop one of two things is simulated: a new customer is inserted into the queues or a customer is removed from a queue. To decide which of these two actions to simulate, the method determines and compares the next arrival time and the next departure time. The constant MAXTIME is used to simplify the code; an arrival/departure time value of MAXTIME indicates that there are no arrivals/departures.

```
//-----------------------------------------------------------------  -----
// Simulation.java           by Dale/Joyce/Weems           Chapter 5
//
// Models a sequence of customers being serviced
// by a number of queues.
//-----------------------------------------------------------------------

import support.*;        // Customer, CustomerGenerator
import ch05.queues.*;

public class Simulation
{
  final int MAXTIME = Integer.MAX_VALUE;

  CustomerGenerator custGen;    // a customer generator
  float avgWaitTime = 0.0f;     // average wait time for most recent simulation

  public Simulation(int minIAT, int maxIAT, int minST, int maxST)
  {
    custGen = new CustomerGenerator(minIAT, maxIAT, minST, maxST);
  }

  public float getAvgWaitTime()
  {
    return avgWaitTime;
  }

  public void simulate(int numQueues, int numCustomers)
  // Preconditions: numQueues > 0
  //                numCustomers > 0
  //                No time generated during simulation is > MAXTIME
  //
  // Simulates numCustomers customers entering and leaving the
  // a queuing system with numQueues queues
  {

    // the queues
    GlassQueue<Customer>[] queues = new GlassQueue[numQueues];[7]

    Customer nextCust;      // next customer from generator
    Customer cust;          // holds customer for temporary use

    int totWaitTime = 0;    // total wait time
    int custInCount = 0;    // count of customers started so far
```

7. An unchecked cast warning is generated because the compiler cannot ensure that the array actually contains objects of class GlassQueue<Customer>.

```
int custOutCount = 0;    // count of customers finished so far

int nextArrTime;         // next arrival time
int nextDepTime;         // next departure time
int nextQueue;           // index of queue for next departure

int shortest;            // index of shortest queue
int shortestSize;        // size of shortest queue
Customer rearCust;       // customer at rear of shortest queue
int finishTime;          // calculated finish time

// instantiate the queues
for (int i = 0; i < numQueues; i++)
  queues[i] = new GlassQueue<Customer>();

// set customer generator and get first customer
custGen.reset();
nextCust = custGen.nextCustomer();

while (custOutCount < numCustomers)  // while more customers to handle
{
  // get next arrival time
  if (custInCount != numCustomers)
    nextArrTime = nextCust.getArrivalTime();
  else
    nextArrTime = MAXTIME;

  // get next departure time and set nextQueue
  nextDepTime = MAXTIME;
  nextQueue = -1;
  for (int i = 0; i < numQueues; i++)
    if (queues[i].size() != 0)
    {
      cust = queues[i].peekFront();
      if (cust.getFinishTime() < nextDepTime)
      {
        nextDepTime = cust.getFinishTime();
        nextQueue = i;
      }
    }

  if (nextArrTime < nextDepTime)
  // handle customer arriving
  {
    // determine shortest queue
    shortest = 0;
```

```
      shortestSize = queues[0].size();
      for (int i = 1; i < numQueues; i++)
      {
        if (queues[i].size() < shortestSize)
        {
          shortest = i;
          shortestSize = queues[i].size();
        }
      }

      // determine the finish time
      if (shortestSize == 0)
        finishTime = nextCust.getArrivalTime() + nextCust.getServiceTime();
      else
      {
        rearCust = queues[shortest].peekRear();
        finishTime = rearCust.getFinishTime() + nextCust.getServiceTime();
      }

      // set finish time and enqueue customer
      nextCust.setFinishTime(finishTime);
      queues[shortest].enqueue(nextCust);

      custInCount = custInCount + 1;

      // if needed, get next customer to enqueue
      if (custInCount < numCustomers)
        nextCust = custGen.nextCustomer();
    }
    else
    // handle customer leaving
    {
        cust = queues[nextQueue].dequeue();
        totWaitTime = totWaitTime + cust.getWaitTime();
        custOutCount = custOutCount + 1;
    }
  }  // end while

  avgWaitTime = totWaitTime/(float)numCustomers;
  }
}
```

The Application

This application is similar in structure to those presented previously in the text. The primary responsibility of SimulationApp is interacting with the user. We make the simplifying assumption that the user is well behaved—in other words, the user provides valid input data. For example, the minimum service time the user enters is not larger than the maximum service time.

```java
//------------------------------------------------------------------
// SimulationApp.java       by Dale/Joyce/Weems            Chapter 5
//
// Simulates customers waiting in queues. Customers always enter
// the shortest queue.
//
// Input consists of customer information:
//     Minimum and maximum customer inter-arrival time.
//     Minimum and maximum customer service time.
// Followed by a sequence of simulation instance information:
//     Number of queues and customers.
//
// Output includes, for each simulation instance:
//     The average waiting time for a customer.
//------------------------------------------------------------------

import java.util.Scanner;

public class SimulationApp
{
  public static void main(String[] args)
  {
    Scanner conIn = new Scanner(System.in);

    int minIAT;     // minimum inter-arrival time
    int maxIAT;     // maximum inter-arrival time
    int minST;      // minimum service time
    int maxST;      // maximum service time
    int numQueues;  // number of queues
    int numCust;    // number of customers

    String skip;             // skip end of line after reading an integer
    String more = null;      // used to stop or continue processing

    // Get customer information
    System.out.print("Enter minimum inter-arrival time: ");
    minIAT = conIn.nextInt();
    System.out.print("Enter maximum inter-arrival time: ");
    maxIAT = conIn.nextInt();
    System.out.print("Enter minimum service time: ");
    minST = conIn.nextInt();
    System.out.print("Enter maximum service time: ");
    maxST = conIn.nextInt();

    // create object to perform simulation
    Simulation sim = new Simulation(minIAT, maxIAT, minST, maxST);
```

```
do
{
  // Get next simulation instance to be processed.
  System.out.print("Enter number of queues: ");
  numQueues = conIn.nextInt();
  System.out.print("Enter number of customers: ");
  numCust = conIn.nextInt();
  skip = conIn.nextLine();   // skip end of line

  // run simulation and output average waiting time
  sim.simulate(numQueues, numCust);
  System.out.println("Average waiting time is " + sim.getAvgWaitTime());

  // Determine if there is another simulation instance to process.
  System.out.println();
  System.out.print("Evaluate another simulation instance? (Y=Yes): ");
  more = conIn.nextLine();
  System.out.println();
}
while (more.equalsIgnoreCase("y"));

System.out.println("Program completed.");
  }
}
```

Here is an output from a sample run of this program:

Enter minimum inter-arrival time: 0

Enter maximum inter-arrival time: 10

Enter minimum service time: 5

Enter maximum service time: 20

Enter number of queues: 2

Enter number of customers: 2000

Average waiting time is 1185.632

Evaluate another simulation instance? (Y=Yes): y

Enter number of queues: 3

Enter number of customers: 2000

Average waiting time is 5.7245

Evaluate another simulation instance? (Y=Yes): n

Program completed.

As you can see, our program provides us with a powerful analysis tool. Under the conditions of inter-arrival times between 0 and 10 and service times between 5 and 20, with only two queues the waiting time "blows up." But by simply adding one more queue, the expected waiting time becomes very reasonable.

Testing Considerations

How do we know our program works? Besides being careful with the design and coding, we must test it. We should test each of the classes separately as we create it. To do so, we need to create test driver programs that allow us to evaluate the classes under different conditions.

We can test the overall system by carefully selecting the values we enter for input. For example, if we enter the minimum and maximum inter-arrival times both as 5, then we know that a customer should arrive every 5 time units. By controlling the arrival times and service requirements, along with the number of available queues, we can see whether our system provides reasonable answers. Finally, we could tweak the `Cus-tomerGenerator` code slightly, so that it outputs the arrival and service times of each of the customers it generates. Using this information, we can hand-check the results of a simulation to confirm that it is correct.

The GUI Approach

The console-based `SimulationApp` class can easily be replaced by a GUI-based class. Our `SimGUI` class does just that. Like `SimulationApp`, it obtains input from the user, instantiates a `CustomerGenerator` object, uses the `Simulation` class to perform the simulation, and obtains and presents the result. Here is a screenshot of the program in action:

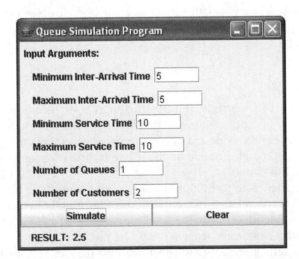

A benefit of the GUI approach is that the user can easily change just one input value and rerun the simulation to see the effect of that change. A drawback of the approach is the previous result is no longer readily available. The `SimGUI` class file is included with the rest of the textbook program files on the website.

Exercises

1. Explain the following:

   a. Some of the text fields, such as `MinIATText`, are declared as class variables.

   b. We use the `Integer` class's `parseInt` method.

   c. The "Clear" action blanks out a number of text values, but sets one text value to a non-empty string.

   d. The effect of changing the following line:

      ```
      JButton simulate   = new JButton("Simulate");
      ```
      to
      ```
      JButton simulate   = new JButton("Evaluate");
      ```
      Would the program still work? Why or why not?

2. Revise and test the `SimGUI` application as described here:

   a. It keeps track of and displays how many simulations have been executed during the current program.

   b. It validates the input arguments. Minimum values must be less than maximum values. The inter-arrival times must be greater than or equal to zero. All other input values must be greater than or equal to one. If invalid input arguments are discovered, an appropriate error message is displayed.

   c. It provides pull-down lists for the input arguments instead of text boxes. Note that this change eliminates the need to validate input arguments.

3. Design and implement your own GUI for this problem. Write a short explanation of why your interface is better than the one shown in the textbook.

Summary

A queue is a "first in, first out" (FIFO) structure. We defined a queue at the logical level as an abstract data type, creating both a bounded queue interface and an unbounded queue interface. For the bounded queue interface, we created an array-based implementation. For the unbounded queue interface, we created two implementations: one array-based and one link-based.

Queues are often used to hold information until it needs to be used or jobs until they can be served. We developed two applications that highlighted this nature of queues. In the palindrome identifier, a queue held a sequence of characters until they could be compared to the characters from a stack. In the card game simulator, queues held a player's cards until it was time to put them into play as well as the pile of prize cards until they were won by a player. We also discussed the use of queues for managing

tasks that can be executed concurrently and looked at some of Java's mechanisms for indicating concurrency and for synchronizing concurrent threads.

In the case study, we developed a tool to analyze queue behavior. Our program allowed us to control the arrival rate and service needs of queue elements, and discover the average amount of time an element spent waiting on a queue. By varying the number of queues, we could determine the suitability of adding new servers to a queuing system. To support the case study, we devised an extension of our standard queue, a "glass" queue that allowed an application to look inside the queue abstraction.

Figure 5.15 is a UML diagram showing the queue-related interfaces and classes developed in this chapter, and their relationships. It includes the GlassQueue class developed to support the case study.

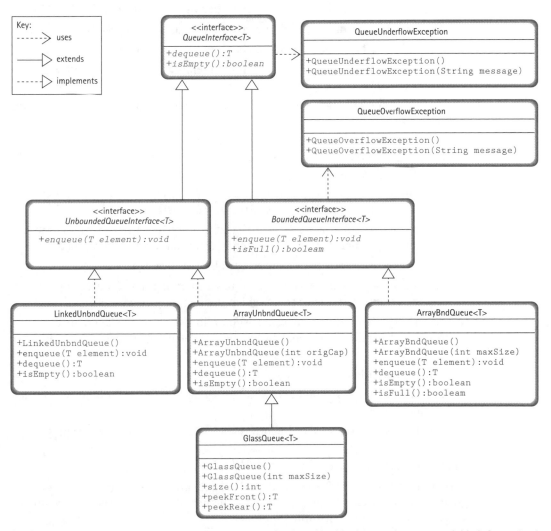

Figure 5.15 *The queue-related interfaces and classes developed in this chapter—instance variable information is omitted*

Exercises

5.1 Queues

1. True or False?

   a. A queue is a "first in, first out" structure.

   b. The element that has been in a queue the longest is at the "rear" of the queue.

   c. If you `enqueue` five elements into an empty queue and then `dequeue` five elements, the queue will be empty again.

   d. If you `enqueue` five elements into an empty queue and then perform the `isEmpty` operation five times, the queue will be empty again.

   e. The `enqueue` operation should be classified as a "transformer."

   f. The `isEmpty` operation should be classified as a "transformer."

   g. The `dequeue` operation should be classified as an "observer."

   h. If we first `enqueue elementA` into an empty queue and then `enqueue elementB`, the `front` of the queue is `elementA`.

2. Indicate whether a queue would be a suitable data structure to use in each of the following applications.

   a. An ailing company wants to evaluate employee records so that it can lay off some workers on the basis of service time (the most recently hired employees are laid off first).

   b. A program is to keep track of patients as they check into a clinic, assigning them to doctors on a "first come, first served" basis.

   c. A program to solve a maze is to backtrack to an earlier position (the last place where a choice was made) when a dead-end position is reached.

   d. An inventory of parts is to be processed by part number.

   e. An operating system is to process requests for computer resources by allocating the resources in the order in which they are requested.

   f. A grocery chain wants to run a simulation to see how average customer wait time would be affected by changing the number of checkout lines in its stores.

   g. A dictionary of words used by a spelling checker is to be initialized.

   h. Customers are to take numbers at a bakery and be served in order when their number comes up.

   i. Gamblers take numbers in the lottery and win if their numbers are picked.

5.2 Formal Specification

3. Based on our Queue ADT specification, an application programmer has two ways to check for an empty queue. Describe them and discuss when one approach might be preferable to the other approach.

4. If we include the abstract `isEmpty` method in the `UnboundedQueueInterface` in addition to the `QueueInterface`, what happens? Is it an error? Does it affect classes that implement the interfaces?

5. In the UML diagram in Figure 5.3, explain the meaning of the following:

   a. Italicized text

   b. A plus sign

   c. A dashed open-head arrow

   d. A solid closed-head arrow

6. Show what is written by the following segments of code, given that `element1`, `element2`, and `element3` are `int` variables, and `queue` is an object that fits the abstract description of a queue as given in Section 5.2. Assume that you can store and retrieve values of type `int` in `queue`.

   a.
```
element1 = 1;
element2 = 0;
element3 = 4
queue.enqueue(element2);
queue.enqueue(element1);
queue.enqueue(element1 + element3);
element2 = queue.dequeue()
qucue.enqueue(element3*element3);
queue.enqueue(element2);
queue.enqueue(3);
element1 = queue.dequeue();
System.out.println(element1 + " " + element2 + " " +
                   element3);
while (!queue.isEmpty())
{
   element1 = queue.dequeue();
   System.out.println(element1);
}
```

   b.
```
element1 = 4;
element3 = 0;
element2 = element1 + 1;
queue.enqueue(element2);
queue.enqueue(element2 + 1);
queue.enqueue(element1);
element2 = queue.dequeue();
element1 = element2 + 1;
queue.enqueue(element1);
queue.enqueue(element3);
while (!queue.IsEmpty())
{
```

```
    element1 = queue.dequeue();
    System.out.println(element1);
  }
  System.out.println(element1 + " " + element2 + " " +
                      element3);
```

7. The following code segment is a count-controlled loop going from 1 through 5. At each iteration, the loop counter is either printed or put on a queue depending on the `boolean` result returned by the method `random`. (Assume that `random` randomly returns either `true` or `false`.) At the end of the loop, the elements in the queue are removed and printed. Because of the logical properties of a queue, this code segment cannot print certain sequences of the values of the loop counter. You are given an output and asked to determine whether the code segment could generate the output.

```
for (count = 1; count <= 5; count++)
{
  if (random())
    System.out.println(count);
  else
    queue.enqueue(count);
}
while (!queue.isEmpty())
{
  number = queue.dequeue();
  System.out.println(number);
}
```

a. The following output is possible: 1 2 3 4 5
   i. True   ii. False   iii. Not enough information
b. The following output is possible: 1 3 5 4 2
   i. True   ii. False   iii. Not enough information
c. The following output is possible: 1 3 5 2 4
   i. True   ii. False   iii. Not enough information

Questions 8–10 require "outside" research.

8. List the Java library classes that implement the Java library `Queue` interface.
9. In the Java library, the `BlockingQueue` interface extends the `Queue` interface. Briefly describe the main differences between a "blocking" queue and a "normal" queue.
10. The informal description provided of the Java library `Queue` suggests that insertion of a `null` object into a queue be disallowed. Why?

5.3 Array-Based Implementations

11. Discuss the relative efficiency of the `enqueue` and `dequeue` operations for fixed-front and floating-front approaches to an array-based implementation of a queue.

12. Draw the "internal" view of memory for each step of the following code sequence:

```
ArrayBndQueue<String> q = new ArrayBndQueue<String>(5);
q.enqueue("X");
q.enqueue("M");
q.dequeue( );
q.enqueue("T");
```

13. Describe the effects each of the following changes would have on the `ArrayBndQueue` class:

    a. Remove the `final` attribute from the `DEFCAP` instance variable.

    b. Change the value assigned to `DEFCAP` to 10.

    c. Change the value assigned to `DEFCAP` to −10.

    d. In the first constructor, change the first statement to

    ```
    queue = (T[]) newObject[100];
    ```

    e. In the first constructor, change the last statement to

    ```
    rear = capacity;
    ```

    f. In the first constructor, change the last statement to

    ```
    rear = -1;
    ```

    g. Reverse the order of the last two statements in the *else* clause of the `enqueue` method.

    h. Reverse the order of the first two statements in the *else* clause of the `dequeue` method.

    i. In `isEmpty`, change "==" to "=."

14. Consider a `toString` method for a queue that would create and return a string that nicely represents the current queue. Assume each `enqueued` object already provides its own reasonable `toString` method that you can invoke from the queue's `toString` method.

    a. Design, code, and test a `toString` method for the `ArrayBndQueue` class.

    b. What changes do you need to make to the method created for part a for it to work with the `ArrayUnbndQueue` class?

15. Write a segment of code (application level) to perform each of the following operations. Assume `myQueue` is an object of the class `ArrayUnbndQueue`. You may call any of the public methods. You may also declare additional queue objects.

a. Set `secondElement` to the second element from the beginning of `myQueue`, leaving `myQueue` without its original two front elements.

b. Set `rear` equal to the rear element in `myQueue`, leaving `myQueue` empty.

c. Set `rear` equal to the rear element in `myQueue`, leaving `myQueue` unchanged.

d. Print out the contents of `myQueue`, leaving `myQueue` unchanged.

16. Consider our array-based unbounded queue implementation.

    a. What would be the effect of starting with a capacity of 1?

    b. What would be the effect of starting with a capacity of 0?

17. Create an interactive test driver for the `ArrayBndQueue` class. See Section 2.4, "Software Testing" for information about interactive test drivers.

18. A "dequeue" is like a queue but it also allows you to insert into the front of the queue and to remove from the rear of the queue. Create an array-based `Dequeue` class.

19. Create an `ArrayListUnbndQueue` class, using an `ArrayList` instead of an array as the underlying storage.

5.4 Application: Palindromes

20. Consider the `test` method of `Palindrome`. What is the effect of:

    a. Switching the order of the `push` and `enqueue` statements in the *for* loop?

    b. Changing "<" to "<=" in the *while* loop termination condition?

    c. Removing the `stack.pop()` statement?

    d. The `candidate` string being `null`?

    e. The `candidate` string having no letters?

21. How would you change the `test` method of the `Palindrome` class so that it considers all characters, not just letters? Identify the statements you would change, and how you would change them.

22. This question deals with palindromic dates—that is, dates that read the same forward and backward.

    a. The year 2002 was a palindromic year. When is the next palindromic year?

    b. If dates are written MMDDYYYY, then May 2, 2050, is a palindromic date. What is the earliest palindromic date of the 21st century?

    c. Create a program that identifies all palindromic dates in a given year. First a user enters a year. Then the program reports the palindromic dates. Finally, the program asks the user if he or she wishes to try again. Note that you need a `Palindrome` class that permits testing "digit" characters.

23. Write a program that repeatedly prompts the user to enter strings, using the string "x done" to indicate when finished. The user is assumed to only enter strings of the form "f name" or "m name." Output the names that had "m" indicated in the same order they were entered, and then do the same for the names that had "f" indicated. Use two `ArrayUnbndQueue` objects in your program.

Sample Run

Input a gender and name (x done to quit) > m Fred

Input a gender and name (x done to quit) > f Wilma

Input a gender and name (x done to quit) > m Barney

Input a gender and name (x done to quit) > m BamBam

Input a gender and name (x done to quit) > f Betty

Input a gender and name (x done to quit) > x done

males: Fred Barney BamBam

females: Wilma Betty

5.5 Application: The Card Game of War

24. Can a game of War end in a tie? If not, why not? If so, explain how, and describe what our War program would do in that case.

25. When you play cards, you normally shuffle the deck several times before playing. Yet the shuffling algorithm used in our program walks through the array of cards only once. Explain the difference between these two situations.

26. Suppose only four cards are dealt in a game of War, two to each player. Describe a deck of four cards, such that when dealt, will result in a game of War that continues forever.

27. In the `play` method of the `WarGame` class, what is the effect of removing the `shuffle` method invocation?

28. The following changes can be assigned separately or in combinations. Change the War game program so that it meets these conditions:

    a. It has a default maximum number of battles of 200.

    b. The user also enters the number of decks to use in the game.

    c. The program also reports the average number of "wars" in a game, where a "war" is defined as any time that a "battle" ends in a tie.

    d. The program also reports the total number of wins for each player.

    e. The user also inputs the number of cards to deal to player 1; player 2 gets all the remaining cards.

    f. `battle` is not recursive (see the information in Chapter 4 about removing tail recursion).

5.6 Link-Based Implementations

29. Draw the "internal" view of memory for each step of the following code sequence:

```
LinkedUnbndQueue<String> q;
q = new LinkedUnbndQueue<String>();
q.enqueue("X");
q.enqueue("M");
q.dequeue( );
q.enqueue("T");
```

30. Describe the effects each of the following changes would have on the `LinkedUnbndQueue` class:

    a. In the constructor, change "`rear = null`" to "`rear = front`."

    b. In the `enqueue` method, move the last statement "`rear = newNode`" to just before the *if* statement.

    c. In the `enqueue` method, change the `boolean` expression "`rear == null`" to "`front == null`."

    d. In the `dequeue` method, switch the second and third statements in the *else* clause.

31. Given the following specification of a `front` operation for a queue:

    Effect: Returns a reference to the front element on the queue.

    Precondition: Queue is not empty.

    a. Write this operation as client code, using operations from the `LinkedUnbndQueue` class. (Remember, the client code has no access to the nonpublic variables of the class.)

    b. Write this operation as a new public method of the `LinkedUnbndQueue` class.

32. Consider a `toString` method for a queue that would create and return a string that nicely represents the current queue. Assume each enqueued object already provides its own reasonable `toString` method that you can invoke from the queue's `toString` method. Design, code, and test a `toString` method for the `LinkedUnbndQueue` class.

33. With the linked implementation of a queue, what are the ramifications of an application enqueuing the same object twice before dequeuing it?

34. Assume that an integer requires 2 bytes of space and a reference requires 4 bytes of space. Also assume the maximum queue size is 200. We define "overhead" space as the space required by the structure that does not include the space used by the elements the structure contains.

    a. How much overhead space is needed for:

        i. Our bounded array-based queue holding 20 elements?

        ii. Our bounded array-based queue holding 100 elements?

        iii. Our bounded array-based queue holding 200 elements?

        iv. Our reference-based queue holding 20 elements?

        v. Our reference-based queue holding 100 elements?

        vi. Our reference-based queue holding 200 elements?

    b. For what size queue do the array-based and reference-based approaches use approximately the same amount of overhead space?

35. A "dequeue" is like a queue but it also allows you to insert into the front of the queue and to remove from the rear of the queue. Create a reference-based `DeQueue` class.

36. Implement the Queue ADT using a circular linked list as discussed at the end of Section 5.6.

5.7 Concurrency, Interference, and Synchronization

37. Seats to events such as concerts are often sold online, at ticket kiosks, and at walk-up ticket booths, simultaneously. Discuss potential interference problems in such situations and options for controlling the interference.

38. What is the output of each of the following code sequences? List all possible results and explain your answers.

    a.
    ```java
    Counter c = new Counter();
    c.increment();
    c.increment();
    System.out.println(c);
    ```

    b.
    ```java
    Counter c  = new Counter();
    Runnable r = new Increase(c, 3);
    Thread   t = new Thread(r);
    t.start();
    System.out.println(c);
    ```

    c.
    ```java
    Counter c  = new Counter();
    Runnable r = new Increase(c, 3);
    Thread   t = new Thread(r);
    c.increment();
    t.start();
    System.out.println(c);
    ```

    d.
    ```java
    Counter c  = new Counter();
    Runnable r = new Increase(c, 3);
    Thread   t = new Thread(r);
    t.start();
    c.increment();
    System.out.println(c);
    ```

    e.
    ```java
    Counter c  = new Counter();
    Runnable r = new Increase(c, 3);
    Thread   t = new Thread(r);
    t.start();
    t.join();
    c.increment();
    System.out.println(c);
    ```

    f.
    ```java
    Counter c  = new Counter();
    Runnable r = new Increase(c, 3);
    Thread   t = new Thread(r);
    t.start();
    c.increment();
    t.join();
    System.out.println(c);
    ```

g.
```
SyncCounter sc = new SyncCounter();
Runnable r = new Increase2(sc, 3);
Thread    t = new Thread(r);
t.start();
sc.increment();
t.join();
System.out.println(sc);
```

39. Create a `PrintChar` class that implements `Runnable`. The constructor should accept a character and an integer as parameters. The `run` method should print the character the number of times indicated by the integer. Create an application that instantiates two `PrintChar` objects, one passed "A" and 200 and one passed "B" and 200. It then instantiates and starts two thread objects, one for each of the two `PrintChar` objects. Experiment with the resulting system, using different numerical parameters for the `PrintChar` objects. Create a report about the results of your experimentation.

40. Create an application that instantiates a 20 × 20 two-dimensional array of integers, populates it with random integers drawn from the range 1 to 100, and then outputs the index of the row with the highest sum among all the rows. To facilitate this create a class from which you can instantiate `Runnable` objects, each of which will sum one row of the two-dimensional array and then place the sum of that row into the appropriate slot of a one-dimensional, 20-element array. To summarize, your application will:

   a. Generate the two-dimensional array of random integers

   b. Start 20 concurrent threads, each of which places the sum of one row of the two-dimensional array into the corresponding slot of a one-dimensional array

   c. Output the index of the maximum value in the one-dimensional array

5.8 Case Study: Average Waiting Time

41. Complete the following table:

Customer	Arrival Time	Service Time	Finish Time	Wait Time
1	0	10		
2	8	3		
3	8	10		
4	20	7		
5	32	18		

a. Assuming one queue—what is the average waiting time?

b. Assuming two queues—what is the average waiting time?

c. Assuming three queues—what is the average waiting time?

42. In the Average Waiting Time program, which class (`Customer`, `CustomerGenerator`, `GlassQueue`, `Simulation`, or `SimulationApp`) is responsible for:

a. Providing the size of a queue?

b. Deciding which queue a customer enters?

c. Obtaining the number of queues from the user?

d. Calculating the arrival time of a customer?

e. Calculating the finish time of a customer?

f. Calculating the waiting time for a customer?

g. Calculating the average waiting time?

43. Use the Average Waiting Time program to determine a reasonable number of queues to use if there are 1000 customers and:

a. The inter-arrival time is 5 and the service time is 5.

b. The inter-arrival time is 1 and the service time is 5.

c. The inter-arrival time ranges from 0 to 20, and the service time ranges from 20 to 100.

d. The inter-arrival time ranges from 0 to 2, and the service time ranges from 20 to 100.

In each case, describe how you arrived at your result.

44. Revise the Average Waiting Time program to do the following:

a. Also output the largest number of customers who were on a queue at the same time.

b. Choose the queue for a customer to enter based on shortest finish time, rather than shortest size. The user should have the ability to choose which approach to use for any simulation run.

45. Solitaire: For this console-based application you should use the `GlassQueue`. Use the `RankCardDeck` class from Section 5.5 to create a deck of cards. Also create three queues of cards (essentially integers); let's call them queues A, B, and C. Shuffle the deck. Deal a card to queue A, then B, then C until 30 cards have been dealt. The user starts with $30. The card values at the front of queues A and C are displayed to the user, with a "?" in between, for example: 5 ? 0. The ? is supposed to represent the card value at the front of queue B. The user must bet anything between $10 and his or her total money that the ? will be "in-between" the other two cards (ties do not count so for example, 3 is not in-between 3 and 5; if the two cards displayed happen to have the same rank value,

then the loser is out of luck). If the ? card is in between the other two cards, he or she wins (e.g., if he or she bets $20 he or she gets back the $20 plus an additional $20). Play continues for 10 rounds or until the player runs out of money. During the game provide appropriate feedback to the user.

46. Do Exercise 45 as a GUI.

The List ADT

Knowledge Goals

You should be able to
- describe different approaches to comparing objects
- describe a list and its operations at a logical level
- explain the ramifications of changing the following assumptions about lists:
  - Lists may have duplicate elements
  - Lists are unbounded
- describe our three kinds of lists and explain their differences
- classify a given list operation as a constructor, iterator, observer, or transformer
- explain the relationships among list interfaces and/or classes
- describe algorithms for list operations using an array
- describe algorithms for list operations using a linked list
- use Big-O analysis to describe and compare the efficiency of list algorithms
- describe and compare algorithms for searching a sorted array
- discuss approaches for saving objects in files

Skill Goals

You should be able to
- create a class that implements the `Comparable` interface
- implement the `ListInterface` using an array and providing an unsorted list
- implement the `ListInterface` using an array and providing a sorted list
- implement the `IndexedListInterface` using an array
- implement the `ListInterface` using a linked list and providing an unsorted list
- implement the `ListInterface` using a linked list and providing a sorted list
- draw diagrams showing the effect of list operations for a particular implementation of a list
- implement nonrecursive and recursive versions of the binary search algorithm
- predict the output of an application that uses a particular list implementation
- use a List ADT as a component of an application
- save an object to a file and then retrieve it

This chapter focuses on the List ADT: its definition, its implementation, and its use in problem solving. Lists are one of the most widely used ADTs in computer science, which is only natural given how often we use them in daily life. We make to-do lists, shopping lists, checklists, party invitation lists, and so on. The list of the kinds of lists that we make is endless!

Fortunately, we need only a few variations of the List ADT to represent the majority of real-world lists. We define, implement, and use three kinds of lists: unsorted, sorted, and indexed. Our list interface and class designs take advantage of the commonality among these three kinds of lists, while supporting their differences. We use both arrays and references to implement our ADT.

Most of the differences in lists relate to the types of values that are stored in them, rather than to their structure or operations. We will see, however, that one significant structural difference is how the values are ordered with respect to one another within each type of list.

Because list operations and organization sometimes depend on the content of the list elements, we begin the chapter with a look at how we compare objects. The chapter concludes with a section on saving objects in files. Armed with this knowledge, we can create a list of objects with one program and use it later, in another program.

6.1 Comparing Objects Revisited

With stacks and queues, we access only the ends of our structures. We push or pop the top element of a stack, or we enqueue a value at the tail of a queue and dequeue it from the head. We do not access elements stored at other places within the structure.

With a list, however, we access elements within the structure. For example, we check whether a given item appears on our to-do list. We insert a name into a list in alphabetical order. We delete the entry with the matching serial number from a parts inventory list. List operations such as these require us to compare the values of objects. For this reason, we need to understand our options for such comparisons.

In Section 1.6, "Basic Structuring Mechanisms," we discussed comparing objects using the comparison operator (==). Recall that when using ==, the comparison is actually made between the contents of the two reference variables that point to the objects, and not between the contents of the objects themselves. This is demonstrated in Figure 6.1 (which replicates Figure 1.7).

The equals Method

The comparison operator doesn't compare the contents of objects. What else can we do? How do we compare the actual objects? One option is to use the `equals` method. Because this method is exported from the `Object` class, which is the root of the Java inheritance tree, it can be used with objects of any Java class. If `c1` and `c2` are objects of the class `Circle`, then we can compare them using

```
c1.equals(c2)
```

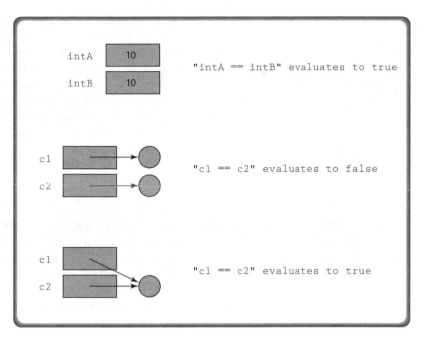

Figure 6.1 *Comparing primitive and nonprimitive variables*

The `equals` method, as defined in the `Object` class, acts in much the same way as the comparison operator. It returns `true` if and only if the two variables reference the same object. To circumvent this problem we can, within a class, redefine the `equals` method to fit the goals of the class.

Suppose we have a `Circle` class that features a `radius` attribute of type `int`. A reasonable definition for equality of `Circle` objects is that they are equal if they have equal radii. To implement this approach, we include the following method in the `Circle` class:

```
public boolean equals(Circle circle)
// Precondition: circle != null
//
// Returns true if the circles have the same radius;
// otherwise, returns false.
{
  if (this.radius == circle.radius)
    return true;
  else
    return false;
}
```

Now when a statement such as

```
c1.equals(c2)
```

is encountered, the customized `equals` method of the `Circle` class is used, rather than the generic `equals` method of the `Object` class. Even though `c1` and `c2` may reference different objects, if those objects have equal radii, the `equals` method returns `true`.

A `Circle` object may have other attributes. For example, it may have a `scale` attribute, as did the circles we defined in Section 2.1. Here, however, we have defined equality of `Circle` objects solely on the basis of their radii. Even though two circles have different scales, as long as they have the same radii, we say they are equal. This is a design choice. When defining the `equals` method, we may compare just one attribute, multiple attributes, all attributes, or some functional combination of the attributes (for example, we could use the "weight" of a circle calculated as the area times the scale).

The Comparable Interface

We can use the `equals` method when checking whether a particular element is on a list. But in addition to checking objects for equality, there is another type of comparison we need. To support a sorted list, we need to be able to tell when one object is less than, equal to, or greater than another object. The Java library provides an interface, called `Comparable`, that can be used to ensure that a class provides this functionality.

The `Comparable` interface consists of exactly one abstract method:

```
public int compareTo(T o);
// Returns a negative integer, zero, or a positive integer as this object
// is less than, equal to, or greater than the specified object.
```

The `compareTo` method returns an integer value that indicates the relative "size" relationship between the object upon which the method is invoked and the object passed to the method as an argument.

We intend to use the `compareTo` method when working with the elements of our sorted lists. To ensure that all such objects support the `compareTo` operation, we require sorted list elements to be objects of a class that implements the `Comparable` interface. We call such objects `Comparable` objects.

Each class that implements the `Comparable` interface defines its own `compareTo` method, with a signature that matches the abstract method defined in the interface. After all, the implementer of the class is in the best position to define how objects of the class should be compared.

As of Java 5.0, the Java `Comparable` interface has been retrofitted to handle generics. Use of generic types with the `compareTo` method helps ensure that comparison takes place only between compatible objects. Let's return to our circle example. A reasonable definition of relative size for `Circle` objects is based on the values of their radii. Here is an example of a `Circle` class that provides its own `equals` method and implements the `Comparable` interface:

```
public class Circle implements Comparable<Circle>
{
  protected float radius;
```

```
    protected static final float PI = 3.14f;


    public Circle(float radius)
    {
      this.radius = radius;
    }


    public boolean equals(Circle circle)
    // Precondition: circle != null
    //
    // Returns true if the circles have the same radius,
    // otherwise, returns false.
    {
      if (this.radius == circle.radius)
        return true;
      else
        return false;
    }


    public int compareTo(Circle circle)
    // Precondition: o != null
    //
    // Returns a negative integer, zero, or a positive integer as this Circle
    // is less than, equal to, or greater than the parameter Circle.
    {
      if (this.radius < circle.radius)
        return -1;
      else
        if (this.radius == circle.radius)
          return 0;
        else
          return 1;
    }


    public float perimeter()
    // Returns perimeter of this figure.
    {
      return(2 * PI * radius);
    }


    public float area()
    // Returns area of this figure.
    {
      return(PI * radius * radius);
    }
}
```

Both the `compareTo` method and the `equals` method accept arguments of class `Circle`. It makes good sense to have circles only compared to other circles.

Notice that the `equals` method and the `compareTo` method are consistent with each other. In other words, the `equals` method returns `true` for two circles if and only if the `compareTo` method returns 0 for the two circles. It is good programming practice to ensure consistency between these two methods.

> **Key** The attributes that are used to determine the logical order of the elements in a collection

To simplify discussion in this text, we sometimes refer to the attribute, or combination of attributes, of an object used by the `compareTo` method to determine the logical order of a collection as the key of the collection. For example, in our `Circle` class the radius of a circle is its key.

6.2 Lists

We all know intuitively what a list is. In our everyday lives, we use lists all the time—grocery lists, lists of assignments, playlists of songs, lists of e-mail addresses, and so on.

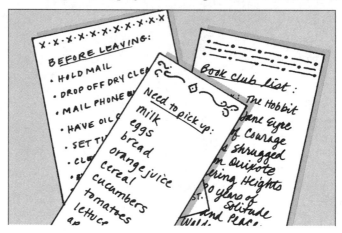

In computer programs, lists are extremely versatile ADTs. Similar to stacks and queues, they provide storage for information. Unlike stacks and queues, however, they do not impose any limitations on how that information is added, accessed, or removed. There are even languages in which the list is a built-in structure. In Lisp, for example, the list is the main data type provided in the language.

From a programming point of view, a list is a collection of elements, with a linear relationship existing among its elements. A linear relationship means that, at the logical level, each element on the list except the first one has a unique predecessor and each element except the last one has a unique successor. The number of elements on the list, which we call the size of the list, is a property of a list. That is, every list has a size.

> **List** A collection that exhibits a linear relationship among its elements
>
> **Linear relationship** Each element except the first has a unique predecessor, and each element except the last has a unique successor
>
> **Size** The number of elements in a list; the size can vary over time

Varieties of Lists

Lists can be unsorted—their elements may be placed into the list in no particular order—or they can be sorted. For instance, a list of numbers can be sorted numerically, a list of strings can be sorted alphabetically, and a list of circles can be sorted by size. We often access a list based on content. For example, we may want to determine whether an element is on the list or we may want to remove an element from the list. To access elements by content, we use the `equals` method, as described in Section 6.1.

> **Unsorted list** A list in which elements are placed in no particular order; the only relationship between data elements is the list predecessor and successor relationships
>
> **Sorted list** A list that is sorted by some property of its elements; there is an ordered relationship among the elements in the list, reflected by their relative positions
>
> **Indexed list** A list in which each element has an index value associated with it

When the elements in a sorted list exhibit several attributes, we can define their logical order in many different ways. As an example, suppose we have a list of student information, with each student represented by his or her first name, last name, identification number, and three test scores. Here are some of the ways we can sort such a list:

- By last name, alphabetically
- By last name, alphabetically, and then by first name, alphabetically (in other words, the first name is used to determine relative ordering if two or more last names are identical)
- By identification number
- By average test score

The sort order for our sorted lists is determined using the `compareTo` operation on the list elements. Therefore we constrain our sorted lists to contain only objects that are `Comparable`, as described in Section 6.1.

Another kind of list is an indexed list, where each element can be accessed by its position, or index, on the list. The indexed lists used in this book allow access in this manner.

Assumptions for Our Lists

Many variations of general list properties are possible. To keep the extent of our coverage manageable, we make the following assumptions:

- Our lists are *unbounded*. When implementing a list with an array, we use the same approach we did with the `ArrayUnbndQueue` class presented in Section 5.3. That is, if an element is added to a "full" list, then the capacity of the underlying array is increased.
- We *allow* duplicate elements on our lists. When an operation involves "finding" such an element, it can "find" any one of the duplicates. We do not specify any distinction among duplicate elements in these cases, with the exception of one indexed list method (`indexOf`).

- We do *not* support `null` elements. As a general precondition for all of our list methods, `null` elements cannot be used as arguments. Rather than stating this precondition for each method, we state it once in the general list interface.
- Other than prohibiting `null` elements, we have *minimal preconditions* for our operations. For example, it is possible to specify a `remove` operation that requires a matching object to be present on the list. We do not do this. Instead, we define a `remove` operation that returns a `boolean` value indicating whether the operation succeeded. This approach provides greater flexibility to applications.
- Our sorted lists are sorted in *increasing* order, as defined by the `compareTo` operation applied to objects on the list.
- We assume consistency between the `equals` and `compareTo` methods of our sorted list elements.
- In our indexed lists, the indexes in use at any given time are *contiguous*, starting at 0. If an indexed list method is passed an index that is outside the current valid range, it will raise an exception.

The exercises at the end of the chapter ask you to investigate the ramifications of changing some of these assumptions.

6.3 Formal Specification

A multitude of operations is possible with lists. For example, the Java library's `List` interface defines about 25 operations (see the feature on the library's list at the end of this section). We define a small but useful set of operations that will work with our lists. In general we try not to include redundant operations: If we can get a job done using a combination of two of our operations, we do not bother defining a third operation just for that job.

The ListInterface

As we did with stacks and queues, we capture the formal specifications of our List ADT using the Java `interface` construct. Our lists are generic—the type of object held by any particular list is indicated by the client at the time the list is instantiated. The following operations allow a client to obtain general information about a list:

- `size`   Returns the number of elements on the list.
- `toString`   Returns a nicely formatted string representing the list.

Here are the operations for dealing with specifically identified list elements—for adding and removing them, checking to see whether they are on the list, and obtaining their information:

- `add`   Passed an object argument, adds the object to the list. This operation's behavior must be clarified for each variety of list we implement.
- `contains`   Passed an object argument and returns a `boolean` value indicating whether the list contains an equivalent element, as determined using the object's `equals` method.

- remove   Passed an object argument and, if an equivalent element exists on the list, removes one instance of that element. Returns a boolean value indicating whether an object was actually removed.
- get   Passed an object argument and returns an equivalent object if one exists on the list. If no such object exists, returns null. Remember that equivalency of objects is defined by their equals method, and that two objects can be equivalent but not identical.

The next two operations require some explanation. Because a list has a linear relationship among its elements, we can support *iteration* through the list. Iteration means that we provide a mechanism to process the entire list, element by element, from the first element to the last element. Each of our list variations provides the operations reset and getNext to support this activity.

- reset   Sets the current position (the position of the next element to be processed) to the first element on the list.
- getNext   Returns the next element and updates the current position.

At any point in time there is a current position within the list. The reset method sets this current position to the beginning of the list. Then each subsequent call to the getNext operation advances the current position to the next position. Thus the current position always indicates the *next* element to be processed. We reset it automatically to the beginning of the list when the last element is returned by getNext.

We call this mechanism iteration because we typically place the getNext method in a loop that processes one list element per loop *iteration*. We refer to getNext as an iterator method.

> **Iteration**   A mechanism that allows us to process the elements of a data structure one at a time in a given sequence
>
> **Iterator method**   A method that returns an element of a data structure and advances the current position to the next element

Consider how the application programmer might use the list iteration methods. The size of the list can help control the loop that looks at each element in turn:

```
listSize = myList.size();
myList.reset();
for (int i = 0; i < listSize; i++)
{
  myElement = myList.getNext();
  // do something with myElement
}
```

What happens if the program inserts or removes an element in the middle of iterating through the structure? Nothing good, you can be sure! Adding and deleting elements changes the size of the list, making the termination condition of the iteration-counting loop invalid. Depending on whether an addition or deletion occurs before or after the current position, our iteration loop could end up skipping or repeating elements.

We have several choices of how to handle this possibly dangerous situation. We can throw an exception, reset the current position whenever an insertion or deletion occurs, or just disallow transformer operations while iteration is taking place. We use the latter approach by mandating a precondition in the documentation of getNext.

Here is the code for our ListInterface. Study the comments and method signatures to learn more about the details of our List ADT.

```java
//-------------------------------------------------------------------------
// ListInterface.java          by Dale/Joyce/Weems          Chapter 6
//
// The lists are unbounded and allow duplicate elements, but do not allow null
// elements. As a general precondition, null elements are not passed as
// arguments to any of the methods.
//
// The list has a property called the current position - the position
// of the next element to be accessed by getNext during an iteration
// through the list. Only reset and getNext affect the current position.
//-------------------------------------------------------------------------

package ch06.lists;

public interface ListInterface<T>
{
  int size();
  // Returns the number of elements on this list.

  void add(T element);
  // Adds element to this list.

  boolean contains (T element);
  // Returns true if this list contains an element e such that
  // e.equals(element); otherwise, returns false.

  boolean remove (T element);
  // Removes an element e from this list such that e.equals(element)
  // and returns true; if no such element exists, returns false.

  T get(T element);
  // Returns an element e from this list such that e.equals(element);
  // if no such element exists, returns null.

  String toString();
  // Returns a nicely formatted string that represents this list.
```

```
void reset();
// Initializes current position for an iteration through this list,
// to the first element on this list.

T getNext();
// Preconditions: The list is not empty
//                The list has been reset
//                The list has not been modified since most recent reset
//
// Returns the element at the current position on this list.
// If the current position is the last element, then it advances the value
// of the current position to the first element; otherwise, it advances
// the value of the current position to the next element.
}
```

The Indexed List Interface

The `ListInterface` suffices for use with our unsorted and sorted lists. Indexed lists, however, require several additional operations—all of the operations involving indexes. We extend the `ListInterface` with a separate interface for indexed lists. Classes that implement the `IndexedListInterface` must, by virtue of the extension, also implement the `ListInterface`.

The elements of an indexed list are indexed sequentially, from zero to one less than the size of the list. For example, if a list has five elements, they are indexed 0, 1, 2, 3, and 4. No "holes" are allowed in the indexing scheme. The interface defines methods for adding, retrieving, changing, and removing an element at an indicated index, as well as a method for determining the index of an element. Details of the operations are included in the comments.

```
//-------------------------------------------------------------------
// IndexedListInterface.java    by Dale/Joyce/Weems        Chapter 6
//
// Extends the ListInterface with methods specific to indexed lists.
//-------------------------------------------------------------------

package ch06.lists;

public interface IndexedListInterface<T> extends ListInterface<T>
{
  void add(int index, T element);
  // Throws IndexOutOfBoundsException if passed an index argument
  // such that index < 0 or index > size().
  // Otherwise, adds element to list at position index; all current
  // elements at that position or higher have 1 added to their index.
```

```
    T set(int index, T element);
    // Throws IndexOutOfBoundsException if passed an index argument
    // such that index < 0 or index >= size().
    // Otherwise, replaces element on this list at position index and
    // returns the replaced element.

    T get(int index);
    // Throws IndexOutOfBoundsException if passed an index argument
    // such that index < 0 or index >= size().
    // Otherwise, returns the element on this list at position index.

    int indexOf(T element);
    // If this list contains an element e such that e.equals(element),
    // then returns the index of the first such element.
    // Otherwise, returns -1.

    T remove(int index);
    // Throws IndexOutOfBoundsException if passed an index argument
    // such that index < 0 or index >= size().
    // Otherwise, removes element on this list at position index and
    // returns the removed element; all current elements at positions
    // higher than that position have 1 subtracted from their index.
}
```

Each method that accepts an index as an argument throws an exception if the index is invalid. Applications must use valid indexes—they can determine the range of valid indexes by using the `size` method. Indexes go from 0 to (`size()` - 1). To allow addition of an element to the end of the list, the valid range for `add` includes `size()`.

We do not define our own exception class to use with the indexed list, because the Java library provides an appropriate exception called `IndexOutOfBoundsException`. This class extends `RunTimeException`, so it is unchecked.

The relationship of our two list interfaces is shown in the UML diagram in Figure 6.2.

Example Use

Studying the output from the following code helps us appreciate the differences among our three types of lists. The code uses the array-based list implementations developed later in this chapter. As you can see, the data and insertion order for each list is identical, but when the list is printed, the ordering of the elements is different for each type of list.

Code Section

```
ListInterface<String> list1 = new ArrayUnsortedList<String>(3);
list1.add("Wirth");
list1.add("Dykstra");
list1.add("DePasquale");
```

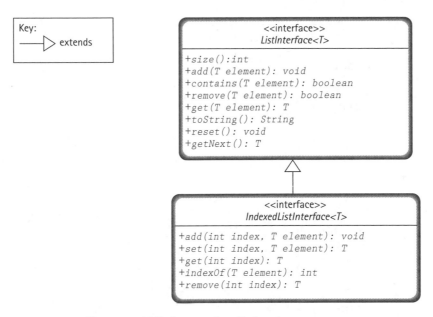

Figure 6.2 *UML diagram of our list interfaces*

```
list1.add("Dahl");
list1.add("Nygaard");
list1.remove("DePasquale");

ListInterface<String> list2 = new ArraySortedList<String>(3);
list2.add("Wirth");
list2.add("Dykstra");
list2.add("DePasquale");
list2.add("Dahl");
list2.add("Nygaard");
list2.remove("DePasquale");

IndexedListInterface<String> list3 = new
ArrayIndexedList<String>(3);
list3.add(0, "Wirth");
list3.add(0, "Dykstra");
list3.add(0, "DePasquale");
list3.add(3, "Dahl");
list3.add(2, "Nygaard");
list3.remove("DePasquale");

System.out.print("Unsorted ");
System.out.println(list1);
System.out.print("Sorted ");
System.out.println(list2);
```

```
        System.out.print("Indexed ");
        System.out.println(list3);
```

Output

```
Unsorted List:
  Wirth
  Dykstra
  Nygaard
  Dahl

Sorted List:
  Dahl
  Dykstra
  Nygaard
  Wirth

Indexed List:
[0] Dykstra
[1] Nygaard
[2] Wirth
[3] Dahl
```

For the unsorted list, the elements are held in an arbitrary order. For the sorted list, the elements are displayed in alphabetical order. For the indexed list, the indexes passed as arguments to the `add` command determine the order.

The specifications of our lists are somewhat arbitrary. We could change our definitions of specific operations or even change our basic assumptions underlying the entire list structure. For instance, we could require that the `remove` method always be invoked with an argument equal to an element already on the list. In that case, `remove` would not need to return a `boolean` value. On a broader scale, we could require our list elements to be unique—that is, we could disallow duplicate elements on the list. Prohibiting duplicates in this ADT implies changes in several operations. For example, each `add` operation must handle the case of being passed an element that is already on the list. Our assumptions are really examples of design choices. For a specific application, design choices are based on the requirements of the problem. In the exercises you are asked to explore some potential changes to our design choices.

The Java Collections Framework Lists

The lists defined by the Java library's `List` interface are quite similar to our indexed lists. They are unbounded, allow duplicate elements, and provide positional access. Because the `List` interface extends the `Collection` interface, however, any class that implements `List` must also implement the 15 standard methods defined in `Collection`—methods such as `size`, `equals`, and `isEmpty`. Additionally, the `List` interface itself requires 11 methods, most of which are index-related counterparts of the standard operations.

The Java Library Collections Framework includes two full implementations of the `List` interface. We used one of these implementations, `ArrayList`, in Chapter 3 to implement a stack. Because a stack is a specialized list, one with access restricted to a single end of the list, we were able to implement it on top of a list structure. The library's `ArrayList` class implements the `List` interface using an underlying array. The other library class that implements `List` is called `LinkedList`. As you would expect, it uses a reference-based approach to provide the list structure.

The Iterator Interface

Unlike our lists, the library lists do not provide `reset` and `getNext` operations. Instead, they provide an operation called `listIterator`, which returns an object that implements the library's `Iterator` interface. This `Iterator` object provides the means to iterate through the list. `Iterator` objects provide three operations: `hasNext`, `next`, and `remove`. The `hasNext` method returns `true` if the iterator has not yet reached the end of the list. Rather than return to the beginning of the list when the end is reached as we did with our own lists, applications are expected to use `hasNext` to prevent going past the end of the list. The `remove` method removes the element that was just visited by the iterator. The implementation keeps track of that element, to allow efficient removal if requested.

As noted, there is no `reset` method. With the library's approach, `reset` is not necessary. If an application wants to start at the beginning of a list, it simply instantiates a new `Iterator` object. In fact, an application can iterate through a list at several different points at the same time, using different `Iterator` objects.

The Iterable Interface

The Java library includes another interface related to iterating through a collection. The `Iterable` interface requires a single method, `iterator()`, which returns an `Iterator` object. Java provides an enhanced *for* loop for use with array or `Iterable` objects. Referred to as a *for-each* loop, this version of the *for* loop allows programmers to indicate that a block of instructions should be executed "for each" of the objects in the array or `Iterable` object.

6.4 Array-Based Implementations

In this section we study array-based implementations of our unsorted, sorted, and indexed lists. We look at reference-based approaches in Section 6.7.

Our basic approach is simple: If a list has N elements, we hold the elements in the first N locations of the array (i.e., in array locations 0 to $N - 1$). We maintain an instance variable, `numElements`, to hold the current number of elements in the list. This example shows how we would represent a sorted list of South American country abbreviations:

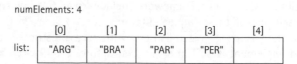

If an element is added to the "middle" of the list, the remaining elements must be shifted up in the array to make room for the new element:

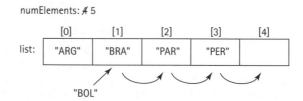

Likewise, if an element is removed from the "middle," the remaining elements must be shifted down to close the hole:

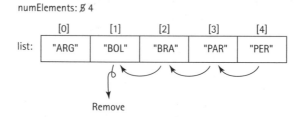

We use this same overall approach for each of our array-based lists—for unsorted, sorted, and indexed lists.

The ArrayUnsortedList Class

The `ArrayUnsortedList` class implements the `ListInterface` using an array. We are not concerned about the order in which elements are stored. The implementation of the `ArrayUnsortedList` class is straightforward, especially if you are familiar with the array-based implementations of the StringLog ADT from Chapter 2 and of the Unbounded Queue ADT from Chapter 5. Figure 6.10, in this chapter's summary, shows the relationships among the primary classes and interfaces created to support our List ADT, including those developed in this subsection.

As was the case with our array-based generic stacks and queues, the instantiation of an array as an array of `Object`, and subsequent casting of it as an array of `T`, typically generates a compiler warning. Even though this approach is somewhat awkward and results in a compiler warning, it is how we must create generic collections using arrays in Java.

For our `ArrayUnsortedList` class we place the code for the array search in a protected helper method, called `find`, which is invoked by each method that needs to search for an element. The `find` method sets the values of the protected instance variables `found` and `location`, thereby indicating the results of the search. The algorithm used here for searching the array for an element is the same one we used for the StringLog `contains` method. We discussed the algorithm extensively in the feature section on stepwise refinement in Chapter 2.

The `ArrayUnsortedList` constructors should remind you of the constructors created for the array-based unbounded queue in Chapter 5. After all, `List` also implements an unbounded structure using the array construct. We use the same protocol as in Chapter 5, allowing an application to indicate an original capacity or to just use the default capacity.

As we did for queues, if the list runs out of room, the capacity of the current array is increased by the original capacity through a helper method called `enlarge`.

In the remove method we take advantage of the unsorted nature of the array. In the general case for a list, when an element is removed, all of the remaining elements are shifted over to fill the gap. Shifting maintains the relative ordering of the list elements, as required for sorted and indexed lists. Of course, ordering is not necessary for unsorted lists. Instead, we can simply move the element at the end of the list into the position occupied by the element to be removed:

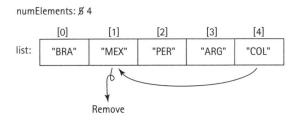

Here is the code for the `ArrayUnsortedList` class:

```
//---------------------------------------------------------------------------
// ArrayUnsortedList.java          by Dale/Joyce/Weems          Chapter 6
//
// Implements the ListInterface using an array.
//
// Null elements are not permitted on a list.
//
// Two constructors are provided: one that creates a list of a default
// original capacity, and one that allows the calling program to specify
// the original capacity.
//---------------------------------------------------------------------------

package ch06.lists;
```

```
public class ArrayUnsortedList<T> implements UnsortedListInterface<T>

{
  protected final int DEFCAP = 100; // default capacity
  protected int origCap;             // original capacity
  protected T[] list;                // array to hold this list's elements
  protected int numElements = 0;     // number of elements in this list
  protected int currentPos;          // current position for iteration

  // set by find method
  protected boolean found;  // true if element found, otherwise false
  protected int location;   // indicates location of element if found

  public ArrayUnsortedList()
  {
    list = (T[]) new Object[DEFCAP];[1]
    origCap = DEFCAP;
  }

  public ArrayUnsortedList(int origCap)
  {
    list = (T[]) new Object[origCap];[1]
    this.origCap = origCap;
  }

  protected void enlarge()
  // Increments the capacity of the list by an amount
  // equal to the original capacity.
  {
    // Create the larger array.
    T[] larger = (T[]) new Object[list.length + origCap];[1]

    // Copy the contents from the smaller array into the larger array.
    for (int i = 0; i < numElements; i++)
    {
      larger[i] = list[i];
    }

    // Reassign list reference.
    list = larger;
  }
```

1. An unchecked cast warning is generated because of the way Java implements generics–the warning can safely be ignored.

```java
protected void find(T target)
// Searches list for an occurence of an element e such that
// e.equals(target). If successful, sets instance variables
// found to true and location to the array index of e. If
// not successful, sets found to false.
{
  location = 0;
  found = false;

  while (location < numElements)
  {
    if (list[location].equals(target))
    {
      found = true;
      return;
    }
    else
      location++;
  }
}

public void add(T element)
// Adds element to this list.
{
  if (numElements == list.length)
    enlarge();
  list[numElements] = element;
  numElements++;
}

public boolean remove (T element)
// Removes an element e from this list such that e.equals(element)
// and returns true; if no such element exists, returns false.
{
  find(element);
  if (found)
  {
    list[location] = list[numElements - 1];
    list[numElements - 1] = null;
    numElements--;
  }
  return found;
}

public int size()
```

```
// Returns the number of elements on this list.
{
  return numElements;
}

public boolean contains (T element)
// Returns true if this list contains an element e such that
// e.equals(element); otherwise, returns false.
{
  find(element);
  return found;
}

public T get(T element)
// Returns an element e from this list such that e.equals(element);
// if no such element exists, returns null.
{
  find(element);
  if (found)
    return list[location];
  else
    return null;
}

public String toString()
// Returns a nicely formatted string that represents this list.
{
  String listString = "List:\n";
  for (int i = 0; i < numElements; i++)
    listString = listString + "  " + list[i] + "\n";
  return listString;
}

public void reset()
// Initializes current position for an iteration through this list,
// to the first element on this list.
{
  currentPos = 0;
}

public T getNext()
// Preconditions: The list is not empty
//                The list has been reset
//                The list has not been modified since the most recent
//                reset
```

```
//
// Returns the element at the current position on this list.
// If the current position is the last element, it advances the value
// of the current position to the first element; otherwise, it advances
// the value of the current position to the next element.
{
  T next = list[currentPos];
  if (currentPos == (numElements - 1))
    currentPos = 0;
  else
    currentPos++;
  return next;
}
}
```

The ArraySortedList Class

The `ArraySortedList` class implements the `ListInterface` using an array. For this class we *are* concerned about the order in which we keep elements stored—the array must be kept sorted. Nevertheless, the implementation of the `ArraySortedList` class has much in common with the implementation of the `ArrayUnsortedList` class. The only required differences are in the `add` and `remove` methods, because these are the only methods that affect the ordering of the elements. To take advantage of the similarities, the `ArraySortedList` class extends the `ArrayUnsortedList` class. Figure 6.10, in the chapter summary, shows the relationships among the primary classes and interfaces created to support our List ADT, including those developed in this subsection.

First let's consider the `add` method. We must override the `add` method of the `ArrayUnsortedList` class. We specify as a precondition of the new `add` method that its argument is an object of class `Comparable`. This ensures us that only `Comparable` objects are contained on a sorted list, because the `add` method is the only way for an element to get onto the list. Therefore, we are guaranteed that all elements of a sorted list support a `compareTo` operation.

As objects are added to the list, their `compareTo` operation is used to determine the correct location for insertion, to keep the list sorted. Within the `add` method we must cast list elements as `Comparable`, so that the Java complier will accept our use of the `compareTo` method.[2] Some compilers will generate a warning message regarding an unchecked call to `compareTo`, because there is no way for the compiler to verify that the generic type `T` will actually implement `Comparable`. Because we understand the reason for the warning message and because our precondition prohibits the use of elements that do not implement `Comparable`, we can safely ignore the compiler warning. An application that ignores the precondition and adds elements to a sorted list that are

---

2. Due to restrictions imposed by Java generics, we are not able, in this case, to use a generic type `T` that extends `Comparable`. If we could do so, it would remove the need for casting and prevent the compiler warning message.

not `Comparable` will cause a type mismatch exception to be thrown—which is exactly the result we desire because incomparable elements should not be added to a sorted list.

To add an element to a sorted list, we first check whether there is room for it, invoking our `enlarge` method if there is not.

Next we must discover where the new element belongs. We use an example to illustrate how this works. Suppose we want to add "CHI" to the list of abbreviations "ARG," "BOL," "BRA," "COL," and "ECU." To maintain the alphabetic ordering of the list, we must accomplish three tasks:

1. Find the place where the new element belongs.

2. Create space for the new element.

3. Put the new element in the created space.

We first traverse the list, comparing the new element to each element on the list, until we find an element that is greater than or equal to it. In our example, this occurs when we reach the fourth element, "COL." To create space we then shift all of the remaining elements starting with "COL" one array location higher. The best way to accomplish this is to start at the end of the list, copying the object references one at a time to the next higher array location, until we have worked our way backward to "COL." Finally, we insert "CHI" into the created space.

This approach is pictured in Figure 6.3. An alternative approach that combines searching and shifting, starting from the back of the list, is investigated in Exercise 29. The code for the `add` method can be found in the listing at the end of this subsection.

Once an element has been added to the list, we assume the element is not changed in any way that might affect where it belongs on the list. We investigate this issue further in the feature section "Implementing ADTs 'by Copy' or 'by Reference.'"

In the *remove* method for the unsorted list we took advantage of the unsorted nature of the array and simply moved the element at the end of the list into the position occupied by the element to be removed. For our sorted lists when an element is removed, all of the remaining elements are shifted over to fill the gap. Shifting maintains the relative ordering of the list elements.

The code for our `ArraySortedList` class is shown below. There are significantly more efficient approaches to finding an element in a sorted array than just looking through the array sequentially, as the inherited `find` method used by the class does. Discussion of those approaches is deferred until Section 6.6.

```
//-------------------------------------------------------------------------------
// ArraySortedList.java          by Dale/Joyce/Weems          Chapter 6
//
// Implements the ListInterface using an array. It is kept in increasing
// order as defined by the compareTo method of the added elements. Only
// Comparable elements may be added to a list.
//
// Null elements are not permitted on a list.
//
```

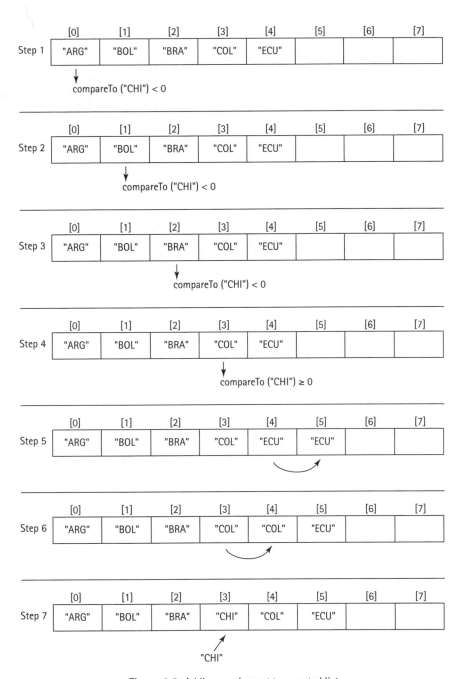

Figure 6.3 *Adding an element to a sorted list*

```
// Two constructors are provided: one that creates a list of a default
// original capacity, and one that allows the calling program to specify
// the original capacity.
//-------------------------------------------------------------------------

package ch06.lists;

public class ArraySortedList<T> extends ArrayUnsortedList<T>
                                 implements ListInterface<T>
{
  public ArraySortedList()
  {
    super();
  }

  public ArraySortedList(int origCap)
  {
    super(origCap);
  }

  public void add(T element)
  // Precondition:  element is Comparable.
  //
  // Adds element to this list.
  {
    T listElement;
    int location = 0;

    if (numElements == list.length)
      enlarge();

    while (location < numElements)
    {
      listElement = (T)list[location];
      if (((Comparable)listElement).compareTo(element) < 0)³
      // list element < add element
        location++;
      else
        break;   // list element >= add element
    }
```

---

3. Some compilers will generate a warning message regarding an unchecked call to `compareTo`, because there is no way for the compiler to verify that the generic type `T` will actually implement `Comparable`.

```
    for (int index = numElements; index > location; index--)
      list[index] = list[index - 1];

    list[location] = element;
    numElements++;
  }

public boolean remove (T element)
// Removes an element e from this list such that e.equals(element)
// and returns true; if no such element exists, returns false.
{
    find(element);
    if (found)
    {
      for (int i = location; i <= numElements - 2; i++)
        list[i] = list[i+1];
      list[numElements - 1] = null;
      numElements--;
    }
    return found;
  }
}
```

Implementing ADTs "by Copy" or "by Reference"

When designing an ADT, such as for a stack, queue, or list, we have a choice about how to handle the elements—"by copy" or "by reference."

By Copy

With this approach, the ADT manipulates copies of the data used in the client program. When the ADT is presented with data element to store, it makes a copy of the element and stores that copy. Making a valid copy of an object can be a complicated process, especially if the object is composed of other objects. Valid copies of an object are typically created using the object's `clone` method. Classes that provide a `clone` method must indicate this fact to the run-time system by implementing the `Cloneable` interface. In the examples that follow, we assume the object classes provide a rigorous `clone` method and implement the `Cloneable` interface. In that case, code for a list `add` operation might be

```
public void add (T element)
// Adds a copy of the element to this list
{
```

```
    list[numElements] = element.clone();
    numElements++;
}
```

In Java, of course, if the list elements are objects, then it is really a reference to a copy of the element that is stored—because all Java objects are manipulated by reference. The key distinction here is that it is a reference to a copy of the element, and not a reference to the element itself, that is stored.

Similarly, when an ADT returns an element using the "by copy" approach, it actually returns a reference to a copy of the element. As an example, consider the code for a list `getNextElement` operation:

```
public T getNextElement ()
// Returns a copy of the next element on this list
{
  T next = list[currentPos];
  if (currentPos == (numElements-1))
    currentPos = 0;
  else
    currentPos++;
  return next.clone();
}
```

This approach provides strong information hiding. In effect, the ADT is providing a separate repository for a copy of the client's data.

By Reference

In this approach, an ADT manipulates references to the actual elements passed to it by the client program. For example, code for a list `add` operation might be

```
public void add (T element)
// Adds an element to this list
{
  list[numElements] = element;
  numElements++;
}
```

Because the client program retains a reference to the element, we have exposed the contents of the collection ADT to the client program. The ADT still hides the way the data is organized—for example, the use of an array of objects—but it allows direct access to the individual elements of the collection by the client program through the client program's own references. In effect, the ADT provides an organization for the original client data.

The "by reference" method is the most commonly used approach and the one we use throughout this textbook. It has the advantage that it takes less time and space than the "by copy" method. Copying objects takes time, especially if the objects are large and require complicated deep-copying methods. Storing extra copies of objects also requires extra memory. Thus the "by reference" approach is an attractive strategy.

When we use the "by reference" approach, we create aliases of our elements, so we must deal with the potential problems associated with aliases. If our data elements are immutable, then no problems will occur. If the elements can be changed, however, problems can arise.

If an element is accessed and changed through one alias, it could disrupt the status of the element when it is accessed through the other alias. This situation is especially dangerous if the client program can change an attribute that the ADT uses to determine the underlying organization of the elements. For example, if the client changes an attribute that determines an object's position on a sorted list, then the object may no longer be in the proper place. Because the change did not go through a method of the sorted list class, the class has no way of knowing that it should correct this situation. A subsequent `get` operation on this list would likely fail.

An Example

The diagrams in Figure 6.4 show the ramifications of both approaches. Suppose we have objects that hold a person's `name` and `weight`. Further suppose that we have a list of these objects sorted by the variable `weight`. We add three objects onto the list, and then transform one of the objects with a `diet` method, which changes the `weight` of the object. The left side of the figure models the approach of storing references to copies of the objects—the "by copy" approach. The right side models the approach of storing references to the original objects—the "by reference" approach.

The middle section of the figure, showing the state of things after the objects have been inserted into the lists, clearly demonstrates the differences in the underlying implementations. The "by copy" approach creates copies and the list elements reference them; these copies take up space that is not required in the "by reference" approach. It is also clear from the right side of the figure that the "by reference" approach creates aliases for the objects, as we can see more than one reference to an object. In both approaches, the list elements are kept sorted by weight.

The situation becomes more interesting when we modify one of the objects. When the person represented by the `S1` object loses some weight, the `diet` method is invoked to decrease the `weight` of the object. In this scenario, both approaches display problems. In the "by copy" approach, we see that the `S1` object has been updated. The copy of the `S1` object maintained on the list is clearly out-of-date. It holds the old weight value. A programmer must remember that such a list stores only the values of objects as they existed at the time of the `add` operation and that changes to those objects are not reflected in the objects stored on the list. The programmer must design the code to update the list, if appropriate.

In the "by reference" approach, the object referred to by the list contains the up-to-date weight information, because it is the same object referred to by the `S1` variable. The list, however, is no longer sorted by the `weight` attribute. Because the update to `weight` took place without any list activity, the list objects remain in the same order as before. The list structure is now corrupt, and calls to the list methods may behave unpredictably. Instead of directly updating the `S1` object, the program should have removed the object from the list, updated the object, and then reinserted it onto the list.

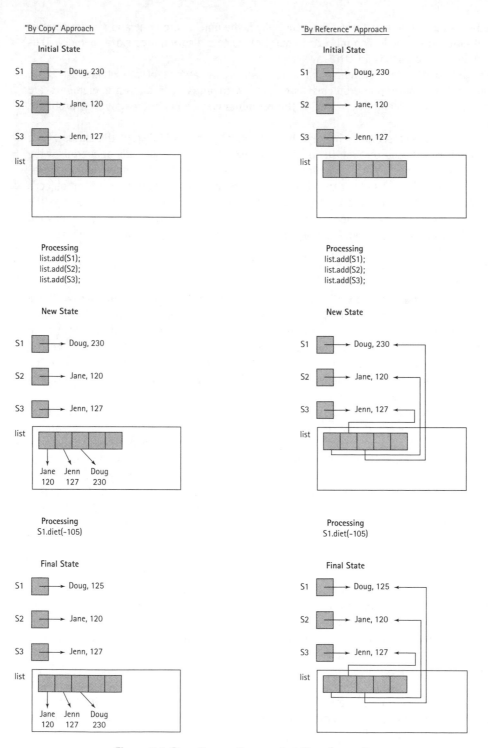

Figure 6.4 *Store "by copy" versus store "by reference"*

Summation

Which approach is better? That depends. If processing time and space are issues, and if we are comfortable counting on the application programs to behave properly, then the "by reference" approach is probably the best choice. If we are not overly concerned about time and space usage (maybe our list objects are not too large), but we are concerned with maintaining careful control over the access to and integrity of our lists, then the "by copy" approach is probably the best choice. The suitability of either approach depends on what the list is used for.

The ArrayIndexedList Class

The `ArrayIndexedList` class also extends the `ArrayUnsortedList` class in order to reuse code. It implements the `IndexedListInterface`. Figure 6.10, in the chapter summary, shows the relationships among the primary classes and interfaces created to support our List ADT, including those developed in this subsection.

The `ArrayUnsortedList` class does not include any methods involving the use of indexes. We must implement all of those methods within `ArrayIndexedList`. Recall that the elements of a list are indexed sequentially, from zero to one less than the size of the list. Because that is exactly the same way the underlying array is indexed, our programming task is very easy.

Consider, for example, the `get` operation. It is passed an integer argument through its `index` parameter and must return the list element that is associated with that index. This is trivial:

```
return list[index];
```

Although implementing the other index-related operations is not quite so easy, they are all straightforward.

Whenever an application provides an index argument, it is tested for legality, and an `IndexOutOfBoundsException` is thrown if the argument fails the test. Because this error is an unchecked exception, we do not need to include a `throws` clause in the method headers.

The only method from `ArrayUnsortedList` that we override is the `toString` method. Instead of just returning a string containing representations of the list elements, the indexed list `toString` method also includes the indexes of the elements within the string.

```
//-----------------------------------------------------------------------
// ArrayIndexedList.java        by Dale/Joyce/Weems         Chapter 6
//
// Implements the IndexedListInterface using an array.
//
// Null elements are not permitted on a list.
//
// Two constructors are provided: one that creates a list of a default
```

```java
// original capacity, and one that allows the calling program to specify
// the original capacity.
//-------------------------------------------------------------------------

package ch06.lists;

public class ArrayIndexedList<T> extends ArrayUnsortedList<T>
                                 implements IndexedListInterface<T>
{
  public ArrayIndexedList()
  {
    super();
  }

  public ArrayIndexedList(int origCap)
  {
    super(origCap);
  }

  public void add(int index, T element)
  // Throws IndexOutOfBoundsException if passed an index argument
  // such that index < 0 or index > size().
  // Otherwise, adds element to this list at position index; all current
  // elements at that index or higher have 1 added to their index.
  {
    if ((index < 0) || (index > size()))
      throw new IndexOutOfBoundsException("illegal index of " + index +
                          " passed to ArrayIndexedList add method.\n");

    if (numElements == list.length)
      enlarge();

    for (int i = numElements; i > index; i--)
      list[i] = list[i - 1];

    list[index] = element;
    numElements++;
  }

  public T set(int index, T element)
  // Throws IndexOutOfBoundsException if passed an index argument
  // such that index < 0 or index >= size().
  // Otherwise, replaces element on this list at position index and
  // returns the replaced element.
  {
```

```
    if ((index < 0) || (index >= size()))
      throw new IndexOutOfBoundsException("illegal index of " + index +
                            " passed to ArrayIndexedList set method.\n");

  T hold = list[index];
  list[index] = element;
  return hold;
}

public T get(int index)
// Throws IndexOutOfBoundsException if passed an index argument
// such that index < 0 or index >= size().
// Otherwise, returns the element on this list at position index.
{
  if ((index < 0) || (index >= size()))
    throw new IndexOutOfBoundsException("illegal index of " + index +
                          " passed to ArrayIndexedList set method.\n");

  return list[index];
}

public int indexOf(T element)
// If this list contains an element e such that e.equals(element),
// then returns the index of the first such element.
// Otherwise, returns -1.
{
  find(element);
  if (found)
    return location;
  else
    return -1;
}

public T remove(int index)
// Throws IndexOutOfBoundsException if passed an index argument
// such that index < 0 or index >= size().
// Otherwise, removes element on this list at position index and
// returns the removed element; all current elements at positions
// higher than that index have 1 subtracted from their index.
{
  if ((index < 0) || (index >= size()))
    throw new IndexOutOfBoundsException("illegal index of " + index +
                          " passed to ArrayIndexedList remove method.\n");

  T hold = list[index];
```

```
    for (int i = index; i < (numElements - 1); i++)
      list[i] = list[i + 1];

    list[numElements - 1] = null;
    numElements--;
    return hold;
  }

  public String toString()
  // Returns a nicely formatted string that represents this list.
  {
    String listString = "List:\n";
    for (int i = 0; i < numElements; i++)
      listString = listString + "[" + i + "] " + list[i] + "\n";
    return listString;
  }
}
```

This completes our development of the three array-based list implementations, at least for now. As with our previous ADT implementations, we must test all of our classes carefully to ensure that they fulfill the ADT specifications. In particular, when testing lists we should remember that it can make a difference if an element is in the first position on the list, in the last position on the list, or somewhere else on the list. Thus we need to include several test cases for each operation being tested.

In the next section we create three applications that use lists, one for each of our list varieties. In Section 6.6, we expand on our approach for the sorted list, making some of the operations more efficient.

6.5 Applications: Poker, Golf, and Music

In this section we look at three applications to see how our list implementations can be used to help solve problems.

Poker

This example shows how we can use program simulation to help verify formal analysis, and vice versa.

Seven-Card Stud is a popular poker game. Each player is dealt seven cards from a standard 52-card playing deck. From those seven cards the participants play their best five-card poker hand. The player with the best hand wins. Keep in mind that the playing cards have two qualities: suit (spades, hearts, clubs, and diamonds) and rank (two through ace). Hands are rated, from best to worst, as follows:

- *Royal Flush*   All cards of the same suit. Ranks from 10 through ace.
- *Straight Flush*   All cards of the same suit. Rank in sequence.

- *Four of a Kind*   Four cards with the same rank.
- *Full House*   Three cards of one rank, and two cards of a second rank.
- *Flush*   All cards of the same suit.
- *Straight*   All cards with ranks in sequence (e.g., 4-5-6-7-8).
- *Three of a Kind*   Three cards with the same rank.
- *Two Pair*   Two sets of cards of the same rank (e.g., 8-8-3-3-9).
- *One Pair*   Two cards of the same rank.
- *High Card*   If we have none of the above, the highest-ranking card in our hand is the "high card."

To help us understand the game of poker, we want to know the probability, when dealt a random seven-card hand, that we get at least two cards of the same rank. We are not concerned with straights and flushes; we are only concerned with getting cards of the same rank.

There are two approaches to investigate this question: We can analyze the situation mathematically or we can write a program that simulates the situation. Let's do both. We can then compare and verify our results.

Numerical Analysis

The analysis is simplified if we turn the question around. We figure out the probability (a real number in the range from 0 to 1) that we do *not* get two cards of the same rank, and then subtract that probability from 1 (which represents absolute certainty).

We proceed one card at a time. When we are dealt the first card, what is the probability we do not have two cards of the same rank? With only one card, it's certain that we don't have a matching pair! We calculate this fact mathematically by using the classic probability formula of *number of favorable events* ÷ *total number of possible events*:

$$\frac{52}{52} = 1$$

There are 52 total possible cards to choose from, and picking any of the 52 has the desired "favorable" result (no matches). The probability we have a pair of matching cards is thus $1 - 1 = 0$ (impossible). It's impossible to have a pair of matching cards when we have only one card. Why do we need this mathematical complexity to say something that's so obvious? Because it acts as a foundation for our continuing analysis.

Now we are dealt the second card. The first card has some rank between 2 and ace. Of the 51 cards that are still in the deck, 48 of them do not have the same rank as the first card. Thus there are 48 chances out of 51 that this second card will not match the first card. To calculate the overall probability of two sequential events occurring, we multiply their individual probabilities. Therefore, after two cards the probability that we do not have a pair is

$$\frac{52}{52} \times \frac{48}{51} \approx 0.941$$

At this point, the probability that we do have a pair is approximately $1 - 0.941 = 0.059$.

For the third card dealt, there are 50 cards left in the deck. Six of those cards match one or the other of the two cards previously dealt, because we are assuming we do not have a pair already. Thus there are 44 chances out of 50 that we do not get a pair with the third card, giving us the probability

$$\frac{52}{52} \times \frac{48}{51} \times \frac{44}{50} \approx 0.828$$

Continuing in this way we get the following probability that we do not have a pair of matching cards after seven cards are dealt:

$$\frac{52}{52} \times \frac{48}{51} \times \frac{44}{50} \times \frac{40}{49} \times \frac{36}{48} \times \frac{32}{47} \times \frac{28}{46} \approx 0.210$$

Therefore the probability that we get at least two matching cards is approximately $1 - 0.210 = 0.790$. We should expect to get at least one pair about eight times out of ten.

Simulation Analysis

Now we address the same problem using simulation. Not only does this endeavor help us double-check our theoretical results, but it also helps validate our programming and the random number generator used to simulate shuffling the cards.

We create a program that deals 1 million seven-card poker hands and tracks how many of them have at least one pair of identical cards.

We use the RankCardDeck class developed for the game of War application in Chapter 5. Recall that this class has a nextCard method that returns the rank of the next card in a 52-card deck. It also provides a shuffle method that reorders the cards in the deck.

Our approach is to reshuffle the cards for every new hand. As cards are dealt, they are placed in an unsorted list called hand. For each new card, we check the list to see whether a card with the same rank is already in hand. The cards themselves are represented as integers—that is, variables of type int. When they are added to the list, they are automatically boxed as Integer objects.

```
//----------------------------------------------------------------------------
// PokerApp.java              by Dale/Joyce/Weems              Chapter 6
//
// Simulates dealing poker hands to calculate the probability of
// getting at least one pair of matching cards.
//----------------------------------------------------------------------------
```

```
import ch06.lists.*;
import support.*;          // RankCardDeck

public class PokerApp
{
  public static void main(String[] args)
  {
    final int HANDSIZE = 7;          // number of cards per hand
    final int NUMHANDS = 1000000;    // total number of hands
    int numPairs = 0;                // number of hands with pairs
    boolean isPair;                  // status of current hand
    float probability;               // calculated probability

    ListInterface<Integer> hand;
    RankCardDeck deck = new RankCardDeck();
    int card;
    for (int i = 0; i < NUMHANDS i++)
    {
      deck.shuffle();
      hand = new ArrayUnsortedList<Integer>(HANDSIZE);
      isPair = false;
      for (int j = 0; j < HANDSIZE; j++)
      {
        card = deck.nextCard();
        if (hand.contains(card))
          isPair = true;
        hand.add(card);
      }
      if (isPair)
        numPairs = numPairs + 1;
    }

    probability = numPairs/(float)NUMHANDS;

    System.out.println();
    System.out.print("There were " + numPairs + " hands out of " + NUMHANDS);
    System.out.println(" that had at least one pair of matched cards.");
    System.out.print("The probability of getting at least one pair,");
    System.out.print(" based on this simulation, is ");
    System.out.println(probability);
  }
}
```

As we have seen several times before, the use of predefined classes, such as our
ArrayUnsortedList class and our RankCardDeck class, makes programming much

easier. Here is the result of one run of this program (which took about 20 seconds to execute on the author's machine):

There were 790291 hands out of 1000000 that had at least one pair of matched cards.

The probability of getting at least one pair, based on this simulation, is 0.790291.

This result is very close to our theoretical result. Additional program runs also produced acceptably close results.

Golf

This application demonstrates how to create classes that implement the `Comparable` interface and how to use them with our sorted list class, to help solve a problem.

Golf is a wonderful sport, enjoyed by all kinds of people—young and old, male and female. At the end of the day we may want to compare results and rank the players based on their scores. Our application accepts golfers' names and scores, creating a sorted list of results, ordered from best to worst score.

Recall that our sorted list class only permits `Comparable` objects. Therefore, we first create a `Golfer` class that implements the `Comparable<Golfer>` interface. By passing the `Golfer` type itself as a parameter to the `Comparable` interface we guarantee that golfers will only be compared to other golfers. Golfers have two attributes: their names and their scores. We sort only on the score, making it the sorting key for the list. The implementation of the `Golfer` class is straightforward.

```
//-------------------------------------------------------------------------
// Golfer.java            by Dale/Joyce/Weems              Chapter 6
//
// Supports golfer objects having a name and a score.
// Allows golfers to be compared based on their scores.
//-------------------------------------------------------------------------

package support;

public class Golfer implements Comparable<Golfer>
{
  protected String name;
  protected int score;

  public Golfer(String name, int score)
  {
    this.name = name;
    this.score = score;
  }

  public String getName()
  {
```

```
    return name;
  }

  public int getScore()
  {
    return score;
  }

  public int compareTo(Golfer other)
  {
    if (this.score < other.score)
      return -1;
    else
      if (this.score == other.score)
        return 0;
      else
        return +1;
  }

  public String toString()
  {
    return (score + ": " + name);
  }
}
```

The application is also straightforward. Because we are mainly interested in demonstrating the use of the sorted list, we did not include input validation. (We ask you to rectify this shortcoming in Exercise 37.) The application asks the user to enter golfer names and scores and then displays the sorted list of golfers. The end of the input is indicated when the user enters a blank golfer name. Here is the program:

```
//---------------------------------------------------------------------
// GolfApp.java          by Dale/Joyce/Weems          Chapter 6
//
// Allows user to enter golfer name and score information.
// Displays information ordered by score.
//---------------------------------------------------------------------

import java.util.Scanner;
import ch06.lists.*;
import support.*;        // Golfer

public class GolfApp
{
  public static void main(String[] args)
```

```
{
  Scanner conIn = new Scanner(System.in);

  String name;           // golfer's name
  int score;             // golfer's score

  ListInterface<Golfer> golfers = new ArraySortedList<Golfer>(20);
  Golfer golfer;
  String skip;  // Used to skip rest of input line after reading integer

  System.out.print("Golfer name (press Enter to end): ");
  name = conIn.nextLine();
  while (!name.equals(""))
  {
    System.out.print("Score: ");
    score = conIn.nextInt();
    skip = conIn.nextLine();

    golfer = new Golfer(name, score);
    golfers.add(golfer);

    System.out.print("Golfer name (press Enter to end): ");
    name = conIn.nextLine();
  }
  System.out.println();
  System.out.println("The final results are");
  System.out.println(golfers);
}
}
```

The sample run is

Golfer name (press Enter to end): Annika
Score: 72
Golfer name (press Enter to end): Tiger
Score: 74
Golfer name (press Enter to end): Grace
Score: 75
Golfer name (press Enter to end): Arnold
Score: 68
Golfer name (press Enter to end): Vijay
Score: 72

Golfer name (press Enter to end): Cristie

Score: 70

Golfer name (press Enter to end):

The final results are

List:

  68: Arnold

  70: Cristie

  72: Vijay

  72: Annika

  74: Tiger

  75: Grace

Music

We round out our set of examples with an application that uses our indexed list. This application takes advantage of the indexing capabilities of the list to allow the user to organize a collection of songs.

Whether someone is creating a cassette, burning a CD, or just organizing a playlist on an MP3 player, a common task is to create an indexed collection of songs and to calculate the total length of the collection. Our application allows a user to enter songs and their lengths. The user indicates where—that is, at what index—in the list of songs to place the current song. The user also enters the length of each song so that the application can keep track of the total amount of time for the entire list.

This example is similar to our earlier golf application. We create a support class called `Song`. Objects of the `Song` class represent a specific song by its name and duration. Unlike the `Golfer` class, however, the `Song` class need not support a `compareTo` method, because objects on our indexed list do not need to be `Comparable`. Within the `Song` class we use a `DecimalFormat` object, from the `java.text` library package, to format seconds for the `toString` method. For example, we want 5 seconds to appear as "05," not "5." Here is the `Song` class:

```
//-----------------------------------------------------------
// Song.java           by Dale/Joyce/Weems           Chapter 6
//
// Supports song objects having a name and a duration.
//-----------------------------------------------------------

package support;

import java.text.*;

public class Song
{
```

```
  protected String name;
  protected int duration;    // in seconds

  DecimalFormat fmt = new DecimalFormat("00");   // to format seconds

  public Song(String name, int seconds)
  {
    this.name = name;
    duration = seconds;
  }

  public Song(String name, int minutes, int seconds)
  {
    this.name = name;
    duration = (60 * minutes) + seconds;
  }

  public String getName()
  {
    return name;
  }

  public int getDuration()
  {
    return duration;
  }

  public String toString()
  {
    return (name + " " + (duration / 60) + ":"
            + fmt.format(duration % 60));
  }
}
```

As with the golfer application, the song organizer repeatedly asks the user for information, uses a list implementation to keep the information organized, and presents the information to the user when required.

```
//-------------------------------------------------------------------
// SongsApp.java           by Dale/Joyce/Weems             Chapter 6
//
// Allows user to enter a collection of songs.
// Keeps track of order and total time.
//-------------------------------------------------------------------
```

```java
import java.util.Scanner;
import java.text.*;
import ch06.lists.*;
import support.*;   // Song
public class SongsApp
{

  public static void main(String[] args)
  {
    Scanner conIn = new Scanner(System.in);

    String name;         // song name
    int minutes;         // song duration
    int seconds;         // song duration
    int number;          // song number
    int numSongs = 0;    // number of songs entered
    int totTime = 0;     // total duration of songs entered so far

    DecimalFormat fmt = new DecimalFormat("00");   // to format seconds

    ArrayIndexedList<Song> songList = new ArrayIndexedList<Song>(20);
    Song song;

    String skip;  // Used to skip rest of input line after reading integer

    System.out.print("Song name (press Enter to end): ");
    name = conIn.nextLine();
    while (!name.equals(""))
    {
      System.out.print("Minutes: ");
      minutes = conIn.nextInt();
      skip = conIn.nextLine();
      System.out.print("Seconds: ");
      seconds = conIn.nextInt();
      skip = conIn.nextLine();
      totTime = totTime + (minutes * 60) + seconds;

      song = new Song(name, minutes, seconds);

      System.out.print("Song number between 0 and " + songList.size() + ": ");
      number = conIn.nextInt();
      skip = conIn.nextLine();
      songList.add(number, song);
      System.out.println();
      System.out.println(songList);
```

```
        System.out.println("Total Time: " + (totTime / 60) +":"
                        + fmt.format(totTime % 60));
        System.out.println();

        System.out.print("Song name (press Enter to end): ");
        name = conIn.nextLine();
      }
    System.out.println();
    System.out.println("The final result is \n");
    System.out.println(songList);
    System.out.println("Total Time: " + (totTime / 60) +":"
                    + fmt.format(totTime % 60));
    System.out.println();
    }
  }
```

Here is a sample run:

Song name (press Enter to end): Cheeseburger in Paradise
Minutes: 2
Seconds: 51
Song number between 0 and 0: 0

List:
[0] Cheeseburger in Paradise 2:51

Total Time: 2:51
Song name (press Enter to end): Growing older but not up
Minutes: 3
Seconds: 7
Song number between 0 and 1: 0

List:
[0] Growing older but not up 3:07
[1] Cheeseburger in Paradise 2:51

Total Time: 5:58

Song name (press Enter to end): Captain America
Minutes: 3

Seconds: 17

Song number between 0 and 2: 1

List:

[0] Growing older but not up 3:07

[1] Captain America 3:17

[2] Cheeseburger in Paradise 2:51

Total Time: 9:15

Song name (press Enter to end):

The final result is

List:

[0] Growing older but not up 3:23

[1] Captain America 3:17

[2] Cheeseburger in Paradise 2:51

Total Time: 9:15

6.6 The Binary Search Algorithm

In Section 6.4 we developed `ArraySortedList`, an array-based implementation of our Sorted List ADT. The `ArraySortedList` class inherits the public methods `contains`, `remove`, and `get` from the `ArrayUnsortedList` class. All three of these methods use the protected method `find`, also defined within the `ArrayUnsortedList` class, which searches the list sequentially (a linear search), looking for a matching object. The `find` method sets the instance variables, `found` and `location`, to indicate the results of the search. These variables are then used by the three calling methods.

In the case of an array-based sorted list, a more efficient approach is available for searching the list: the binary search algorithm. We discussed this algorithm briefly when we considered the problem of finding a number in a phone book in Chapter 1. Now we look at the algorithm more carefully, learning how to use it to improve the efficiency of the `find` method for the sorted list. Before doing so, we discuss a simple improvement that can be made to the linear search approach when the list is already sorted.

Throughout this section, remember that we assume the `equals` and `compareTo` methods of the list elements are consistent, as discussed at the end of Section 6.1.

Improving a Linear Search in a Sorted List

If a list is not sorted, the normal way to search for a target element is to start at the beginning and compare the target element to each element in the list sequentially. This linear search algorithm is used by `find` in the `ArrayUnsortedList` class.

If the list is sorted, however, there is an obvious way to improve the linear searching algorithm: Simply stop searching when we find an element larger than the target element. At that point we know the target element is not on the list. We used this approach in the `add` method of the `ArraySortedList` class to find the location in the array to add the new element.

Consider the following sorted list:

numElements: 6

	[0]	[1]	[2]	[3]	[4]	[5]	
list:	"ARG"	"BRA"	"PAR"	"PER"	"URU"	"VEN"	

If we are searching for "BOL," we first compare it to "ARG" and then to "BRA." The comparison with "BRA" would show that "BRA" is larger. At this point we can stop and set `found` to `false`. This strategy is an improvement over the general linear search approach because we do not have to look through the entire list, but it provides minimal benefits:

- If the target element is on the list, we do the same amount of work as we would using the unimproved approach, examining each element between the start of the list and the target element.
- If the target element is not on the list and its expected location is toward the end of the list, as is the case with "USA," then we still have to examine most of the elements on the list.

The original linear search algorithm and the improved linear search algorithm are both $O(N)$, where N is the size of the list. The improvement described here does not change the Big-O efficiency of the operation. We do not implement the improved linear search algorithm, because we can do much better, as we see next.

Binary Search Algorithm

Let's revisit our phone book example from Chapter 1. Think of how you might go about finding a name in a phone book, and you can get an idea of a faster way to search. Let's look for the name "David." We open the phone book to the middle and see that the names there begin with M. M is larger than (comes after) D, so we can now limit our search to the first half of the phone book, the section that contains A to M.

We turn to the middle of the first half and see that the names there begin with G. G is larger than D, so we search the first half of this section, from A to G. We turn to the middle page of this section and find that the names there begin with C. C is smaller than D, so we search the second half of this section—that is, from C to G—and so on, until we are down to the single page that contains the name "David." This algorithm is illustrated in Figure 6.5.

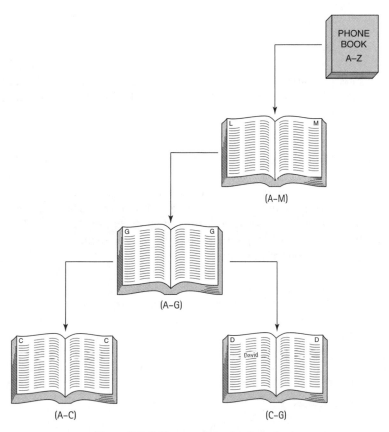

Figure 6.5 *A binary search of a phone book*

Let's now analyze this same approach when applied to the problem of searching an array-based sorted list for a target element. The code for our improved `find` method is shown below. We begin our search with the whole list, by setting the first and last variables as follows:

```
int first = list[0];
int last = list[numElements - 1];
```

In each iteration of the *while* loop, we set `location` to the midpoint of `first` and `last`:

```
location = (first + last) / 2;
```

If the target element is not found at `location`, we split the current search area in half at the midpoint,[4] by either changing the value of `first` to just past `location`,

```
first = location + 1;
```

---

4. The term "binary" is associated with this search approach because the search area is divided by 2 after each iteration.

or by changing the value of `last` to just before `location`,

```
last = location - 1;
```

In the next iteration of the *while* loop, we search the appropriate part of the array. We compute a new value for `location`, at the midpoint of the new search area:

```
location = (first + last) / 2;
```

Each time through the loop, the size of the search area is cut in half.

How do we know when to quit searching? Two terminating conditions are possible: the target element is not on the list, and the target element has been found. The first terminating condition occurs when there is no more to search in the current search area. Therefore we continue searching only if (`first <= last`). The second terminating condition occurs when we actually find the target element. In that case we set `found` to `true` and break out of the loop.

```
protected void find(T target)
// Searches list for an occurrence of an element e such that
// target.equals(e). If successful, sets instance variables
// found to true and location to the array index of e. If
// not successful, sets found to false.
{
  int first = 0;
  int last = numElements - 1;
  int compareResult;
  Comparable targetElement = (Comparable) target;

  found = false;

  while (first <= last)
  {
    location = (first + last) / 2;
    compareResult = targetElement.compareTo(list[location]);5
    if (compareResult == 0)
    {
      found = true;
      break;
    }
    else if (compareResult < 0)
```

---

5. Some compilers generate a warning message regarding an unchecked call to `compareTo`, because there is no way for the compiler to verify that the generic type `T` will actually implement `Comparable`.

```
    // target element is less than element at location
      last = location - 1;
    else    // target element is greater than element at location
      first = location + 1;
  }
}
```

Let's do a walk-through. The element being searched for is "bat." Figure 6.6(a) shows the values of first, last, and location during the first iteration. In this iteration, "bat" is compared with "dog," the value in list[location]. Because "bat" is less than (comes before) "dog," last becomes location - 1 and first stays the same. Figure 6.6(b) shows the situation during the second iteration. This time, "bat" is compared with "chicken," the value in list[location]. Because "bat" is less than (comes before) "chicken," last becomes location - 1 and first again stays the same.

In the third iteration (Figure 6.6c), location and first are both 0. The element "bat" is compared with "ant," the element in list[location]. Because "bat" is greater than (comes after) "ant," first becomes location + 1. In the fourth iteration (Figure 6.6d), first, last, and location are all the same. Again, "bat" is compared with the element in list[location]. Because "bat" is less than "cat," last becomes location - 1. Now that last is less than first, the process stops; found is false.

Table 6.1 shows first, last, location, and list[location] for searches of the elements "fish," "snake," and "zebra" using the same data as in the previous example. Examine the results in Table 6.1 carefully. Trace the code yourself to see whether you get the same values.

Table 6.1   *Trace Results Using the Binary Search Algorithm*

Iteration	first	last	location	list[location]	Terminating Condition
item: fish					
First	0	10	5	dog	
Second	6	10	8	horse	
Third	6	7	6	fish	found is true
item: snake					
First	0	10	5	dog	
Second	6	10	8	horse	
Third	9	10	9	monkey	
Fourth	10	10	10	snake	found is true
item: zebra					
First	0	10	5	dog	
Second	6	10	8	horse	
Third	9	10	9	monkey	
Fourth	10	10	10	snake	
Fifth	11	10			last < first

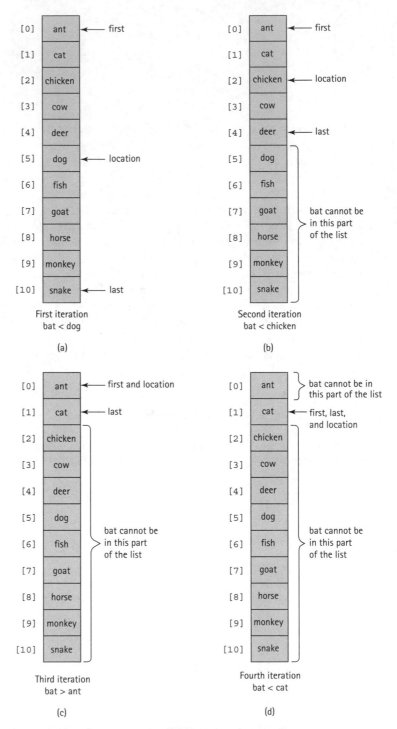

Figure 6.6 *Trace of the binary search algorithm*

Where do we put our new version of `find`? We can't place it in the `Array-UnsortedList` class, because it doesn't work for unsorted lists. We must place it in our sorted list implementation class. To ensure that we don't invalidate our previous coverage of the sorted list, we create a completely new sorted list implementation, called `ArraySortedList2`. It implements `ListInterface` and extends `ArrayUnsortedList`, the same as `ArraySortedList`. The only difference between the two classes is that the new class includes our improved `find` method.

If we instantiate an object of class `ArraySortedList2` and invoke any of its methods `contains`, `remove`, or `get`, those methods in turn invoke the protected method `find`. When they do so, they activate the more efficient `find` contained in `ArraySortedList2`, rather than the `find` contained in `ArrayUnsortedList`. The rules of inheritance dictate that they use the overriding method, even though those three methods are defined themselves in the `ArrayUnsortedList` class.

The `ArraySortedList2` class can be found in this book's `ch06.lists` package.

Recursive Binary Search

Consider this informal description of the binary search algorithm:

To search a list, check the middle element on the list. If it's the target element, you are done; if it's less than the target element, search the second half of the list; otherwise, search the first half of the list.

There is something inherently recursive about this description. We search the list by searching half the list. The solution is expressed in smaller versions of the original problem: If the answer isn't found in the middle position, perform a binary search (a recursive call) to search the appropriate half of the list (a smaller problem). Here we show a `find` method that uses recursion.

In the iterative version, we kept track of the bounds of the current search area with two local variables: `first` and `last`. In the recursive version, we call the recursive method with these two values as parameters. In the iterative version, we used a *while* loop. In the recursive version, we use recursive calls embedded in a selection structure.

We create a third array-based sorted list class, `ArraySortedList3`, in which we implement the recursive approach. It is also found in the `ch06.lists` package, along with the other list-related classes. The `ArraySortedList3` class fits with the other list classes and interfaces exactly the same as `ArraySortedList2`.

The `find` method itself is not recursive, but it does make use of a recursive "helper" method called `recFind`, which does the actual searching. Although a single recursive method might solve our problem, we want to keep the signature of `find` the same as it was before, so that we do not have to change the three public methods of the `Array-UnsortedList` class that use it.

```
protected void recFind(Comparable target, int fromLocation, int
toLocation)
// Searches list between fromLocation and toLocation
// for an occurrence of an element e such that
```

```
// target.equals(e). If successful, sets instance variables
// found to true and location to the array index of e. If
// not successful, sets found to false.
{
  if (fromLocation > toLocation)              // Base case 1
    found = false;
  else
  {
    int compareResult;
    location = (fromLocation + toLocation) / 2;
    compareResult = target.compareTo⁶ (list[location]);

    if (compareResult == 0)                   // Base case 2
      found = true;
    else if (compareResult < 0)
      // target is less than element at location
      recFind (target, fromLocation, location - 1);
    else
     , // target is greater than element at location
      recFind (target, location + 1, toLocation);
  }
}

protected void find(T target)
// Searches list for an occurrence of an element e such that
// target.equals(e). If successful, sets instance variables
// found to true and location to the array index of e. If
// not successful, sets found to false.
{
  Comparable targetElement = (Comparable)target;
  found = false;
  recFind(targetElement, 0, numElements - 1);
}
```

Efficiency Analysis

Did you notice that for all the examples dealing with the binary search algorithm, we never had to do more than four comparisons, even though the list had 11 elements? This is because the list is cut in half each time through the main part of the algorithm. The binary search algorithm is $O(\log_2 N)$, a significant improvement over the $O(N)$ linear search algorithm. Table 6.2 compares a linear search and a binary search in terms of the maximum number of iterations needed to find an element.

---

6. Some compilers generate a warning message regarding an unchecked call to compareTo, because we have declared Comparable objects without specifying a generic type. Because we understand the reason for the warning message, we can safely ignore it. The code will still compile.

Table 6.2   *Comparison of Linear and Binary Searches*

	Maximum Number of Iterations	
Length	Linear Search	Binary Search
10	10	4
100	100	7
1,000	1,000	10
10,000	10,000	14
100,000	100,000	17
1,000,000	1,000,000	20

If the binary search is so much faster, why not use it all the time? It is certainly faster in terms of the number of list comparisons, but more work is needed each time through a stage of the binary search than through a stage of the linear search algorithm. If the number of components on the list is small (say, less than 20), linear search algorithms are faster because they perform less work during each iteration. As the number of components on the list increases, however, the binary search algorithm becomes much more efficient. Of course, the binary search requires the list to be sorted in the first place, and sorting also takes time.

6.7   Reference–Based Implementations

In this section we develop list implementations using references (links). We follow the same basic pattern of development here that we employed in Section 6.4, where we developed list implementations using arrays. Our reference-based implementations fulfill the interfaces we developed in Section 6.3. As we did for arrays, first we implement an unsorted version and then we extend it with a sorted version. Figure 6.10, in the chapter summary, shows the relationships among the primary classes and interfaces created to support our List ADT, including those developed in this section.

We'll implement both unsorted and sorted lists using the linked approach, but we do not implement indexed lists in this way. Why not? The indexed list features four operations (add, set, get, remove) involving index arguments. There is no simple way to implement those operations efficiently using a linked approach. Consider the get operation. In the array-based implementation, it is a simple matter: Return the array element located at the index. It's an $O(1)$ operation. With our linked approach we would need to traverse the list, counting nodes until we reach the requested node. This is an $O(N)$ operation.

Certain linked structures do enable efficient indexed access to a collection of elements, but they are not simple lists. Thus we do not cover a linked indexed list here.

There do exist linked structures that enable efficient indexed access to a collection of elements, but they are not simple lists. Remember, a list is an abstraction. Just because we envision it as being written down like a series of lines on a page, we don't have to implement it that way. For example, a room full of filing cabinets with folders arranged by date is effectively a very long list. Each drawer has a range of dates on the front that we can use to jump into the list near our desired index. As you can imagine, implementing a similar approach to obtain an efficient linked indexed list would result in a different kind of data structure than the linear linked list we have been using, and would use much different algorithms.

As we did for our reference-based stacks and queues, we again use the `LLNode` class from the `support` package to provide our nodes. The information attribute of a node contains the list element; the link attribute contains a reference to the node holding the next list element. We maintain a variable, `list`, that references the first node on the list.

The RefUnsortedList Class

If we followed our established naming protocol, we would probably give the linked classes names such as `LinkedList`. The Java library, however, already has a `LinkedList` class, and we have been using the standard term "linked list" to refer to an implementation-dependent structure. So as not to confuse things, we use the term "Ref" (reference) when naming classes in this section.

We discuss each of the methods required for the `RefUnsortedList` class here. The code for the class is included at the end of this subsection.

- `size` Returns the number of elements on the list.

  In the array-based approach, an instance variable `numElements` held the number of elements in the array and was used to indicate the first empty array location. Because we are now using a linked list, we do not have array locations. Nevertheless, to support the `size` operation we still maintain `numElements`, incrementing it whenever an element is added to the list and decrementing it whenever an element is removed. For both the unsorted and sorted versions, `size` simply returns the value of `numElements`.

- `add` Passed an `object` argument and adds it to the list.

  Because the list is unsorted, and order of the elements is not important, we can just add new elements to the front of the list. This is the easiest, most efficient approach, because `list` already provides a reference to the front of the list. We used this same approach for the StringLogs in Chapter 2.

- `contains` Passed an `object` argument and returns a `boolean` indicating whether the list contains an equivalent element.

  This operation is implemented by traversing the linked list from the first element to the last element, stopping when the argument is found or the end of the list is reached. As was discussed in Section 6.6, when searching a sorted list in this manner, we can stop searching if we reach an element larger than the target element. The implementers of the sorted list class can override this method to use that slightly more efficient approach. This same situation exists for the `remove` and `get` methods.

- `remove` Passed an `object` argument and, if an equivalent element exists on the list, removes one instance of that element from the list. Returns a `boolean` value indicating whether an object was actually removed.

  The element being removed can be found using the approach described for `contains`. Once found, it can be removed by "jumping over" it. This is discussed in more detail below.

- `get` Passed an `object` argument. Returns an equivalent object if one exists on the list. If not, returns `null`.

  The approach described for `contains` to find the required element works here. Once found, the element is returned.

- `toString` Returns a nicely formatted string representing the list.

  This requires a traversal of the underlying linked list, saving elements to a string variable as the traversal proceeds.

- `reset` Initializes the list for an iteration.

  This only requires setting the current position to the beginning of the list.

- `getNext` Returns the next element of an iteration, and updates the current position.

  This only requires returning the element at the current position and correctly updating the value of the current position. Remember that if the current position is the end of the list, then it is set back to the beginning of the list.

The implementations of the `size`, `contains`, `get`, `toString`, `reset`, and `getNext` methods do not need further explanation. We discuss the remaining methods (the constructor and the `find` and `remove` methods) next.

There is only one constructor provided for `RefUnsortedList`, because there is no need to deal with capacity as there was with the array-based implementation. The constructor sets the instance variables `numElements`, `list`, and `currentPos` to their initial values, essentially constructing an empty list.

The protected `find` method is used by the public methods `contains`, `remove`, and `get`. It follows the same algorithm as the `find` method of the array-based implementation: Walk through the list until the target element is found or the end of the list is reached. The only difference is the use of linked list statements instead of array-related statements. Here is the code for both methods, for comparison. In the array-based approach, `location` is of type `int`, indicating the array index of the target element; in the reference-based approach, `location` is an `LLNode`, indicating the node containing the target element.

Array Based

```
protected void find(T target)
{
  location = 0; found = false;
  while (location < numElements)
  {
    if (list[location].equals(target))
    {
      found = true;
      return;
    }
    else
      location++;
  }
}
```

Reference Based

```
protected void find(T target)
{
  location = list; found = false;
  while (location != null)
  {
    if (location.getInfo().equals(target))
    {
      found = true;
      return;
    }
    else
    {
      previous = location;
      location = location.getLink();
    }
  }
}
```

Actually, we lied. There is another difference between the two `find` implementations. Do you see it? The reference-based implementation assigns a value to a variable named `previous` that is not mentioned in the array-based implementation. This variable is used by the `RefList remove` method. Let's take a closer look at this method.

To remove an element, we must first find it. We do so by using the `find` method, which sets the `location` variable to indicate the target element. As shown in Figure 6.7, however, to actually remove the node referenced by `location`, we must change the reference in the previous node. That is, we must change the link of the previous node to reference the node following the one being removed. We "jump over" the removed node. This is where we use the `previous` variable.

Remove Lila

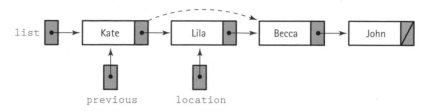

Figure 6.7 *Removing an element from a linked list*

Not only does `find` set `location`, but it also sets `previous` so that the `remove` method has access to the previous node and can implement the "jump over" step.

Removing the first node must be treated as a special case because the main reference to the list (`list`) must be changed. We handle that special case with an *if* statement at the beginning of the code for `remove`. Is removing the last node a special case? No. The link of the last node, referenced by `location`, is `null`. Therefore, in the case of removing the last node the statement

```
previous.setLink(location.getLink());
```

correctly sets the value of the link of the previous node to `null`, indicating that it is now the end of the list.

```
//---------------------------------------------------------------------------
// RefUnsortedList.java          by Dale/Joyce/Weems          Chapter 6
//
// Implements the ListInterface using references (a linked list).
//
// Null elements are not permitted on a list.
//
// One constructor is provided; one that creates an empty list.
//---------------------------------------------------------------------------

package ch06.lists;

import support.LLNode;

public class RefUnsortedList<T> implements ListInterface<T>
{

  protected int numElements;      // number of elements in this list
  protected LLNode<T> currentPos; // current position for iteration

  // set by find method
```

```java
protected boolean found;         // true if element found, else false
protected LLNode<T> location;    // node containing element, if found
protected LLNode<T> previous;    // node preceeding location

protected LLNode<T> list;        // first node on the list

public RefUnsortedList()
{
  numElements = 0;
  list = null;
  currentPos = null;
}

public void add(T element)
// Adds element to this list.
{
  LLNode<T> newNode = new LLNode<T>(element);
  newNode.setLink(list);
  list = newNode;
  numElements++;
}

protected void find(T target)
// Searches list for an occurrence of an element e such that
// e.equals(target). If successful, sets instance variables
// found to true, location to node containing e, and previous
// to the node that links to location. If not successful, sets
// found to false.
{
  location = list;
  found = false;

  while (location != null)
  {
    if (location.getInfo().equals(target))  // if they match
    {
     found = true;
     return;
    }
    else
    {
      previous = location;
      location = location.getLink();
    }
  }
}
```

```
public int size()
// Returns the number of elements on this list.
{
  return numElements;
}

public boolean contains (T element)
// Returns true if this list contains an element e such that
// e.equals(element); otherwise, returns false.
{
  find(element);
  return found;
}

public boolean remove (T element)
// Removes an element e from this list such that e.equals(element)
// and returns true; if no such element exists, returns false.
{
  find(element);
  if (found)
  {
    if (list == location)
      list = list.getLink();    // remove first node
    else
      previous.setLink(location.getLink());  // remove node at location

    numElements--;
  }
  return found;
}

public T get(T element)
// Returns an element e from this list such that e.equals(element);
// if no such element exists, returns null.
{
  find(element);
  if (found)
    return location.getInfo();
  else
    return null;
}

public String toString()
// Returns a nicely formatted string that represents this list.
```

```
{
  LLNode<T> currNode = list;
  String listString = "List:\n";
  while (currNode != null)
  {
    listString = listString + "  " + currNode.getInfo() + "\n";
    currNode = currNode.getLink();
  }
  return listString;
}

public void reset()
// Initializes current position for an iteration through this list,
// to the first element on this list.
{
  currentPos  = list;
}

public T getNext()
// Preconditions: The list is not empty
//                The list has been reset
//                The list has not been modified since most recent reset
//
// Returns the element at the current position on this list.
// If the current position is the last element, then it advances the value
// of the current position to the first element; otherwise, it advances
// the value of the current position to the next element.
{
  T next = currentPos.getInfo();
  if (currentPos.getLink() == null)
    currentPos = list;
  else
    currentPos = currentPos.getLink();
  return next;
}
}
```

The RefSortedList Class

The RefSortedList class implements the ListInterface. We take advantage of similarities between the unsorted and sorted lists by having RefSortedList extend RefUnsortedList. The only method we need to override is the add method. The new add method must insert an element into the correct position on the list. When we implemented stacks, we inserted elements at the front of a linked list. When we implemented queues, we inserted elements at the end of a linked list. This is the first time we have implemented a general insert method for a linked list.

Adding an element to a reference-based sorted list requires three steps:

1. Find the location where the new element belongs.
2. Create a node for the new element.
3. Correctly link the new node into the identified location.

We are already familiar with how to do step 1: Walk through the list until we reach an element that is greater than or equal to our insertion element or we reach the end of the list. By now we have a lot of experience traversing a linked list, so it is not difficult to create code that sets a `location` variable to reference the node on the list that is to follow our new node.

Our experience in coding the `remove` method for the `RefUnsortedList` class, however, tells us that it is not enough to know the location that will follow the new node. To link the new node into the identified location, we also need a reference to the previous node. Therefore, while traversing the list during the search, each time we update the `location` variable, we first save its value in a `prevLoc` variable:

```
prevLoc = location;
location = location.getLink();
```

As an example, Figure 6.8(a) shows the result of searching a list to add "cow."

For the array-based approach, to create space for the new element we had to shift array elements over one location. With the linked approach, no shifting is necessary. To create space for the new element (step 2), we simply instantiate a new `LLNode` object called `newNode`, passing its constructor the new element for use as the information attribute of the node. See Figure 6.8(b).

Now we just have to complete the third step: Correctly link the new node into the identified location. We change the link in the `newNode` to reference the node indicated by `location` and change the link in our `prevLoc` node to reference the `newNode`:

```
newNode.setLink(location);
prevLoc.setLink(newNode);
```

See Figure 6.8(c).

Just as with the `remove` method in the `RefUnsortedList` class, dealing with the situation when `location` indicates the first node of the list is a special case. In this case we do not have a previous node. Instead, we must change the main reference to the list (`list`). We handle the special case using an *if* statement that checks whether the value of `prevLoc` is `null`:

```
if (prevLoc == null)
{
  // Insert as first node.
  newNode.setLink(list);
  list = newNode;
}
```

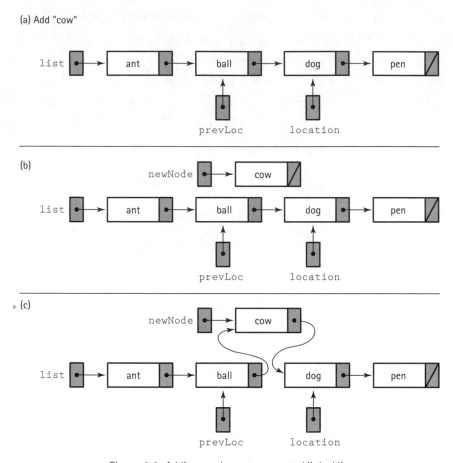

Figure 6.8 *Adding an element to a sorted linked list*

Figure 6.9 depicts the required sequence of steps.

Are there any more special cases to consider? Yes, two: adding an element to the end of the list, and adding an element to an empty list. Both of these cases are handled correctly by the code that is already in place; we leave verification of this to you. The entire `RefSortedList` class is listed below.

Since we are not using arrays within this implementation (because they are not "first-class" objects Java arrays do not work well with Java generics) we *are* able to use a generic-type T that extends `Comparable` in the header for our `RefSortedList`. This ensures that only comparable elements are added to our list and removes any need to cast elements as `Comparable`, as we had to do within `ArraySortedList`.

```
//-------------------------------------------------------------------------
// RefSortedList.java          by Dale/Joyce/Weems          Chapter 6
//
// Implements the ListInterface using a linked list. It is kept in increasing
// order as defined by the compareTo method of the added elements.
```

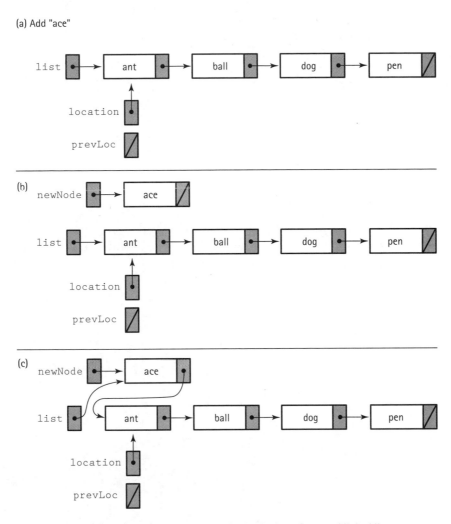

Figure 6.9 *Adding an element to the beginning of a sorted linked list*

```
// Only comparable elements may be added to a list.
//
// Null elements are not permitted on a list.
//
// One constructor is provided; one that creates an empty list.
//-----------------------------------------------------------------------

package ch06.lists;

import support.LLNode;

public class RefSortedList<T extends Comparable<T>>
```

```
            extends RefUnsortedList<T>
            implements ListInterface<T>
{
  public RefSortedList()
  {
    super();
  }

  public void add(T element)
  // Adds element to this list.
  {
    LLNode<T> prevLoc;          // trailing reference
    LLNode<T> location;         // traveling reference
    T listElement;              // current list element being compared

    // Set up search for insertion point.
    location = list;
    prevLoc = null;

    // Find insertion point.
    while (location != null)
    {
      listElement = location.getInfo();
      if (listElement.compareTo(element) < 0)  // list element < add element
      {
        prevLoc = location;
        location = location.getLink();
      }
      else
        break;
    }

    // Prepare node for insertion.
    LLNode<T> newNode = new LLNode<T>(element);

    // Insert node into list.
    if (prevLoc == null)
    {
      // Insert as first node.
      newNode.setLink(list);
      list = newNode;
    }
    else
```

```
  {
    // Insert elsewhere.
    newNode.setLink(location);
    prevLoc.setLink(newNode);
  }
  numElements++;
  }
}
```

We could develop an improved version of the `find` method for the `RefSorted-List` class, but that is left for you as an exercise.

That wraps up our development of the two reference-based list implementations. Both implementations should be carefully tested. It is possible to develop test drivers that work well with all of our list implementations—the unsorted, sorted, and indexed varieties as well as the array- and reference-based implementations. Of course, additional test cases would be required for the sorted and indexed cases because they provide additional functionality.

6.8 Storing Objects and Structures in Files

Suppose we want to save a stack, queue, or list between program runs. Our current programs can build structures and use them for processing information, but the structures are lost when the program terminates. The memory space occupied by the structures, along with all the other memory space used by the program, is returned to the operating system for use by other programs.

Many programs need to save information between program runs. Alternatively, we may want one program to save information for later use by another program. In either case, this information is stored in files, which are the mechanism for permanently storing information on computers. In this subsection we investigate approaches, including Java's serialization facilities, for saving and retrieving objects and structures using files.

Saving Object Data in Text Files

Any information we need to save can be represented by its primitive parts. Consider the `Song` class we defined in Section 6.5. A `Song` object had two instance variables:

```
protected String name;
protected int duration;
```

A song is not a "primitive" object, but when broken into its constituent parts its information consists of a `String` and an `int`. Both of these components can be saved as strings. We can save a `Song` object by breaking it into its constituent parts and writing the strings that represent both parts to a text file. Here's an example:[7]

```java
import java.io.*;
import support.*;

public class SaveSong
{
  private static PrintWriter outFile;

  public static void main(String[] args) throws IOException
  {
    Song song1 = new Song("Penny Lane", 2, 57);

    outFile = new PrintWriter(new FileWriter("song.txt"));
    outFile.println(song1.getName());
    outFile.println(song1.getDuration());
    outFile.close();
  }
}
```

When this program is executed, it creates the `song.txt` file:

```
Penny Lane
177
```

When we need to retrieve the `Song` object, we just reverse the process: Read the strings, and reconstruct the song. We can use the familiar `Scanner` class to help with this task.

```java
import java.io.*;
import java.util.*;
import support.*;

public class GetSong
{
  public static void main(String[] args) throws IOException
  {
    String name;
    int duration;
```

---

7. Appendix E includes a brief introduction to the `FileWriter`, `FileReader`, and `PrintWriter` classes.

```
            FileReader fin = new FileReader("song.txt");
            Scanner songIn = new Scanner(fin);

            name = songIn.nextLine();
            duration = songIn.nextInt();

            Song song2 = new Song(name, duration);

            System.out.println("The name of the song is " + song2.getName());
            System.out.println("The duration of the song is  " +
                                song2.getDuration());
    }
}
```

When these two programs are executed back to back, the second program produces this output:

> The name of the song is Penny Lane
>
> The duration of the song is 177

As you can see, the `Song` object created and saved as text strings by the first program was successfully retrieved, recreated, and used by the second program.

Serialization of Objects

Transforming objects into strings and back again is a lot of work for the programmer. Fortunately, Java provides another way to save objects, called *serializing* the object.

Support Constructs

Before seeing how to serialize objects, we must learn about a new interface and two support classes.

We can write objects using the `writeObject` method of the `ObjectOutputStream` class. We can read objects using the `readObject` method of the `ObjectInputStream` class. To prepare for the output of serialized objects to the file `objects.dat` using the stream variable `out`, we write

```
ObjectOutputStream out = new ObjectOutputStream(new
    FileOutputStream("objects.dat"));
```

Similarly, to prepare for reading from the same file, but this time using the variable `in`, we write

```
ObjectInputStream in = new ObjectInputStream(new
    FileInputStream("objects.dat"));
```

Finally, any class whose objects we plan to serialize must implement the `Serial-izable` interface. This interface has no methods! It is merely a way of marking a class as potentially being serialized for I/O, so that the Java run-time engine knows to convert references as needed on output or input of class instances. Thus, to make our objects serializable, we simply have to state that their class implements this interface. The `Serializable` interface is part of the Java `io` package.

Serializing Objects

Here's the code for a serializable version of our song class, called `SerSong`:

```java
//-------------------------------------------------------------------------
// SerSong.java            by Dale/Joyce/Weems            Chapter 6
//
// Supports song objects having a name and a duration.
// Implements Serializable.
//-------------------------------------------------------------------------

package support;

import java.io.*;
import java.text.*;

public class SerSong implements Serializable
{
  protected String name;
  protected int duration;    // in seconds

  DecimalFormat fmt = new DecimalFormat("00");  // to format seconds

  public SerSong(String name, int seconds)
  {
    this.name = name;
    duration = seconds;
  }

  public SerSong(String name, int minutes, int seconds)
  {
    this.name = name;
    duration = (60 * minutes) + seconds;
  }

  public String getName()
  {
    return name;
  }

  public int getDuration()
  {
```

```
      return duration;
  }

  public String toString()
  {

      return (name + " " + (duration / 60) + ":"
              + fmt.format(duration % 60));

  }
}
```

We have emphasized the differences between this class and our previous Song class—the name of the class, the statement that it implements Serializable, and some updated comments. Additionally, this class must import the java.io package because the Serializable interface is defined there.

Now let's look at a program that creates and saves a SerSong object:

```
import java.io.*;
import support.*;

public class SaveSerSong
{
  private static PrintWriter outFile;
  public static void main(String[] args) throws IOException
  {
    SerSong song1 = new SerSong("Penny Lane", 2, 57);

    ObjectOutputStream out = new ObjectOutputStream(new
                                  FileOutputStream("song.dat"));
    out.writeObject(song1);
    out.close();
  }
}
```

As you can see, to save the SerSong object we simply write the object to the out stream. We do not have to handle the individual attributes separately.

Let's see the corresponding version of retrieving a song:

```
import java.io.*;
import support.*;

public class GetSerSong
{
  public static void main(String[] args) throws IOException
  {
```

```
        SerSong song2;
        ObjectInputStream in = new ObjectInputStream(new
                    FileInputStream("song.dat"));

        try
        {
          song2 = (SerSong)in.readObject();
          System.out.println("The name of the song is " +
                            song2.getName());
          System.out.println("The duration of the song is  "
                            + song2.getDuration());
        }
        catch (Exception e)
        {
          System.out.println("Error in readObject: " + e);
          System.exit(1);
        }
      }
    }
```

The object read from the file must be cast into a SerSong object before being assigned to the song2 variable. Essentially, we promise the compiler that the object retrieved is a SerSong object. Also notice that the readObject method throws several checked exceptions, so we must enclose it in a *try-catch* statement. Other than that, it is a simple matter to read in our SerSong object. Java takes care of all the work of rebuilding the object.

Serializing Structures

The power of Java's serialization tools really becomes evident when we are dealing with data structures. For example, we can save or restore an entire array of SerSong objects with a single statement. To save the array:

```
SerSong[] songs = new SerSong[100];
...
out.writeObject(songs);
```

To retrieve it later, perhaps from another program:

```
SerSong[] laterSongs = (SerSong[])in.readObject();
```

Even more impressive, Java's serialization works for linked structures. We can save an entire linked list using a single writeObject statement, and later restore it using a single readObject statement. For example, if the writeObject statement is invoked on an object list, Java follows all references that start with list and lead to other objects, and it saves those objects along with the `list` object. Of course, all of the objects involved and their constituent parts, including the original `list` object, must implement the `Serializable` interface.

This approach works even for the nonlinear reference-based structures we will study in later chapters. The tree and graph structures retain both their information and their structure when we use serialization.

Application: Song Lists

For an example of serialization of a structure, let's revisit our music application that used indexed lists. Our program allowed us to enter song titles and lengths; it then displayed the song information. Wouldn't it be more useful if the song information we entered could be saved for later use?

Our new program uses Java serialization to accomplish this task. For serialization to work, all of the objects involved must be `Serializable`. Therefore, we created serialized versions of the interfaces and classes needed to support our indexed list, and we placed them in a new package called `ch06.serLists`.

In addition to saving information between runs, the new program includes a few more enhancements:

- The original program forced the user to deal with song indexes starting at 0. This is unnatural for most users. The new program presents the user with song indexes that start at 1.
- If the user provides an illegal index for a song, the program inserts the song at the end of the song list instead of throwing an exception.
- The user can now provide a name for the list of songs, such as "Favorite Rap Oldies" or "New Disco Hits." This provision is a nice feature, considering that a user can now retrieve a song list long after it was created.
- If the data file `songs.dat` does not exist, then the program prompts the user for a song list name and creates a brand new song list. If `songs.dat` does exist, the program retrieves all of the previously entered song data from the file and the user continues working with it wherever he or she left off the last time the program was run.

The SerSongList Class

To support the new functionality, we create a `SerSongList` class. Objects of this class maintain a list of songs in an array-based indexed list. They also maintain, and allow access to, information about the name of the song list and the total duration of the song list. This information is serializable, so that an application can easily save song list data for later use, by writing the entire `SerSongList` object to an `ObjectOutputStream`.

`SerSongList` objects are provided with a name—the name associated with the list of songs—when they are instantiated. Applications can add songs to the list at a specified index through the `add` method. The `SerSongList` class hides the fact that the underlying array-based list uses indexes starting at 0 from the application, allowing the application to assume indexing starts at 1. When a song is added, the program auto-matically updates the total duration of the songs on the list. Applications can use observer methods to get the name, size, and total duration of the song list. Finally, a `toString` method returns a nicely formatted string representing the entire list of songs.

Recall from Chapter 3 that one option for handling error situations within our ADT methods is "detect and handle the error within the method itself." We have not seen many examples of this approach, but the `SerSongList add` method provides a good example. If the `add` method is passed an invalid index—for example, a negative number or a number past the end of the list—instead of raising an exception or ignoring the error it inserts the specified song at the end of the list. This approach is reasonable because the end of the list is the most common place for us to add songs onto a song list. Any application that uses `SerSongList` can override this behavior by catching the erroneous input list index itself, before the index is passed to `add`.

```
//-------------------------------------------------------------------
// SerSongList.java          by Dale/Joyce/Weems          Chapter 6
//
// Supports a list of song objects having a name and a total duration.
// Allows application to view indexing as starting at 1.
// Implements Serializable.
//-------------------------------------------------------------------

package ch06.serLists;

import java.io.*;     // Serializable interface
import java.text.*;   // DecimalFormat
import support.*;     // SerSong

public class SerSongList implements Serializable
{
  protected String listName;         // name of song list
  protected int totDuration = 0;     // total duration of songs in seconds

  protected SArrayIndexedList songList;

  DecimalFormat fmt = new DecimalFormat("00");   // to format seconds

  public SerSongList(String listName)
  {
    this.listName = listName;
    songList = new SArrayIndexedList(10);
  }

  public String getListName()
  {
    return listName;
```

```
  }

  public int getTotDuration()
  {
    return totDuration;
  }

  public int getSize()
  {
    return songList.size();
  }

  public void add(int number, SerSong song)
  // If number is a legal position, then adds song onto the
  // indexed songList at position (number - 1).
  // Otherwise, adds song at the end of the songList.
  {
    totDuration = totDuration + song.getDuration();
    if ((number <= 0) || (number > (songList.size() + 1)))
      songList.add(songList.size(), song);
    else
      songList.add(number - 1, song);
  }

  public String toString()
  {
    // Returns a nicely formatted string that represents this SerSongList.
    SerSong song;
    int duration;
    int numSongs = songList.size();

    String hold = listName + ":\n";
    for (int i = 0; i < numSongs; i++)
    {
      song = (SerSong)songList.get(i);
      duration = song.getDuration();
      hold = hold + (i + 1) + ": " + song.getName() + "   ["
             + (duration / 60) + ":" + fmt.format(duration % 60) + "]\n";
    }
    hold = hold + "\n";
    hold = hold + "Total Time: " + (totDuration / 60) +" minutes, "
               + fmt.format(totDuration % 60) + " seconds\n";
    return hold;
  }
}
```

The Application

The application `SerSongsApp` can be viewed as having three stages:

1. *Initializing the song list* First the application tries to obtain the serialized song list information from the `songs.dat` file. This is accomplished with a single `readObject` command. If this attempt is successful, the `SerSongList` object `songs` is an exact copy of the `songs` object saved the last time the application was executed. If it fails, as indicated by a thrown exception, then the application creates a new song list.

2. *Updating the song list* Next the application repeatedly prompts the user for song name, duration, and index information. It saves that information on the song list through the `SerSongList add` method. The user indicates that he or she is finished entering song information by entering a blank song name.

3. *Saving the song list* Finally, the application saves the entire `SerSongList` object `songs` in the `songs.dat` file for later use, using a single `writeObject` command.

Serialization has allowed us to easily save and retrieve a nontrivial object.

```java
//------------------------------------------------------------------------
// SerSongsApp.java          by Dale/Joyce/Weems          Chapter 6
//
// Allows user to manage a song list.
// Uses the file songs.dat to store and retrieve song list info.
//------------------------------------------------------------------------

import java.util.*;        // Scanner
import java.io.*;          // streams
import ch06.serLists.*;    // SerSongList
import support.*;          // SerSong

public class SerSongsApp
{
  public static void main(String[] args)
  {
    Scanner conIn = new Scanner(System.in);
    final String FILENAME = "songs.dat";

    String name;            // song name
    String listName;        // name of the song list
    int minutes;            // song duration
    int seconds;            // song duration
    int number;             // song number

    SerSongList songs;      // list of songs
    SerSong song;           // a single song
```

```
String skip;  // skip rest of input line after reading integer

try
{
  // Obtain song information from file and display it.
  ObjectInputStream in = new ObjectInputStream(new
                                    FileInputStream(FILENAME));
  songs = (SerSongList)in.readObject();
  System.out.println(songs);
}
catch (Exception e)
{
  // Create a new song list.
  System.out.println("Because the " + FILENAME + " file does not exist ");
  System.out.println("or can't be used, a new song list will be ");
  System.out.println("created.\n");
  System.out.print("Song list name: ");
  listName = conIn.nextLine();
  songs = new SerSongList(listName);
}

// Get song information from user.
System.out.print("\nSong name (press Enter to end): ");
name = conIn.nextLine();
while (!name.equals(""))
{
  System.out.print("Minutes: ");
  minutes = conIn.nextInt();
  skip = conIn.nextLine();
  System.out.print("Seconds: ");
  seconds = conIn.nextInt();
  skip = conIn.nextLine();

  song = new SerSong(name, minutes, seconds);

  System.out.print("Song number between 1 and "
                    + (songs.getSize() + 1) + ": ");
  number = conIn.nextInt();
  skip = conIn.nextLine();
  songs.add(number, song);

  System.out.println();
  System.out.println(songs);
  System.out.println();
```

```java
      System.out.print("Song name (press Enter to end): ");
      name = conIn.nextLine();
    }

    // Display results.
    System.out.println();
    System.out.println("This song list will be saved in " + FILENAME +
                       ":\n");
    System.out.println(songs);
    System.out.println();

    // Save list.
    try
    {
      ObjectOutputStream out = new ObjectOutputStream(new
             FileOutputStream(FILENAME));
      out.writeObject(songs);
      out.close();
    }
    catch (Exception e)
    {
      System.out.println("Unable to save song information.");
    }
  }
}
```

What follows is a trace of two consecutive program runs. For the first run the `songs.dat` file is not found, so a new song list is created.

Run 1

Because the songs.dat file does not exist
or can't be used, a new song list will be created.

Song list name: My Favorites

Song name (press Enter to end): Hey Jude
Minutes: 7
Seconds: 6
Song number between 1 and 1: 1

My Favorites:
1: Hey Jude [7:06]

Total Time: 7 minutes, 06 seconds

Song name (press Enter to end): Let It Be
Minutes: 4
Seconds: 1
Song number between 1 and 2: 2

My Favorites:
1: Hey Jude [7.06]
2: Let It Be [4:01]

Total Time: 11 minutes, 07 seconds

Song name (press Enter to end):

This song list will be saved in songs.dat:

My Favorites:
1: Hey Jude [7:06]
2: Let It Be [4:01]

Total Time: 11 minutes, 07 seconds

Run 2

My Favorites:
1: Hey Jude [7:06]
2: Let It Be [4:01]

Total Time: 11 minutes, 07 seconds

Song name (press Enter to end): Penny Lane
Minutes: 2
Seconds: 57
Song number between 1 and 3: 2

My Favorites:
1: Hey Jude [7:06]
2: Penny Lane [2:57]
3: Let It Be [4:01]

Total Time: 14 minutes, 04 seconds
Song name (press Enter to end):

This song list will be saved in songs.dat:
My Favorites:

1: Hey Jude [7:06]
2: Penny Lane [2:57]
3: Let It Be [4:01]

Total Time: 14 minutes, 04 seconds

Many other improvements can be made to this program. Some of them are suggested in the exercises.

Summary

This chapter examined lists. To support lists, we first had to consider how objects are compared to each other. We need to be able to tell whether a given object appears on a list. For sorted lists, we need to know where to insert a new object.

We explored three variations of lists. The Unsorted List ADT makes no assumptions about the ordering of the list elements. The Sorted List ADT maintains an order among the elements. The Indexed List ADT allows applications to access list elements based on an index value. We viewed each of these ADTs from three perspectives: the logical level, the application level, and the implementation level.

By carefully studying the relationships among our list variations we were able to reuse interfaces and implementations by taking advantage of the Java inheritance mechanism. We created both array-based and reference-based implementations of our lists. Figure 6.10 shows the relationships among the primary classes and interfaces created to support our List ADT in this chapter.

We saw an example application for each type of list. The poker application used an unsorted list to study the probability of obtaining a particular poker hand. The golf application used a sorted list to keep track of golfers ordered by score. The music application used the indexed list to organize a collection of songs. It is important to choose the best abstraction/structure to support a particular application.

We learned how to improve the efficiency of several of the sorted list operations by using the binary search algorithm. We created both nonrecursive and recursive implementations of this algorithm.

The chapter concluded by examining ways of storing object and structure information between runs of a program.

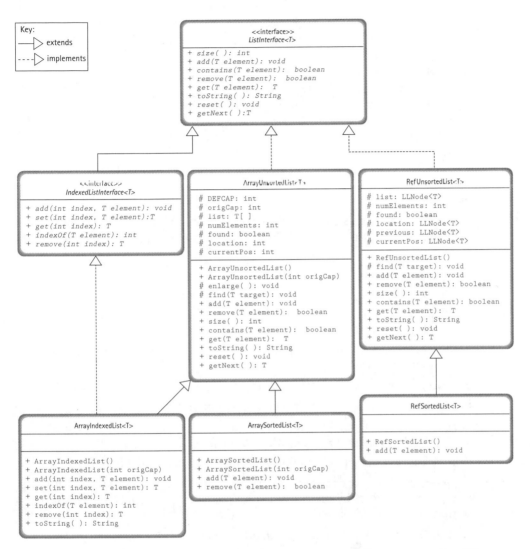

Figure 6.10   *The primary classes and interfaces created to support our List ADT*

Exercises

6.1   Comparing Objects Revisited

1. Based on the `equals` method for `Circle` objects defined in Section 6.1, what is the output of the following code sequence?

```
Circle c1 = new Circle(5);
Circle c2 = new Circle(5);
Circle c3 = new Circle(15);
```

```
Circle c4 = null;
System.out.println(c1 == c1);
System.out.println(c1 == c2);
System.out.println(c1 == c3);
System.out.println(c1 == c4);
System.out.println(c1.equals(c1));
System.out.println(c1.equals(c2));
System.out.println(c1.equals(c3));
System.out.println(c1.equals(c4));
```

2. Rewrite the `Circle` class's `equals` method so that if it is passed a `null` parameter it returns the value `false`. How would this new definition of `equals` affect your answer to Exercise 1?

3. An `equals` method is supposed to provide an equivalence relation among the objects of a class. This means that if a, b, and c are non-null objects of the class, then

    i. `a.equals(a)` is `true`.

    ii. `a.equals(b)` has the same value as `b.equals(a)`.

    iii. If `a.equals(b)` is `true` and `b.equals(c)` is `true`, then `a.equals(c)` is `true`.

State whether the following definitions of `equals` are valid. If they are not, explain why not.

  a. Two circles are equal if they have the same area.

  b. Two circles are equal if their radii are within 10% of each other.

  c. Two integers are equal if they have the same remainder when divided by a specific integer—for example, when divided by 3.

  d. Two integers are equal if the second integer is a multiple of the first.

4. Suppose we have a `Rectangle` class that includes `length` and `width` attributes, of type `int`, both set by the constructor. Create an `equals` method for this class so that two rectangle objects are considered equal if

  a. They have the exact same `length` and `width`.

  b. They have the same dimensions—that is, they are congruent.

  c. They have the same shape—that is, they are similar.

  d. They have the same perimeter.

  e. They have the same area.

Are all of these definitions of `equals` valid, based on the criteria listed in Exercise 3?

5. Create an `equals` method for the `ArrayStringLog` class from Chapter 2 such that two StringLogs are considered equal if

  a. They contain the same number of strings.

b. They contain the same strings (case-insensitive comparison) in the same order.

c. They contain the same strings (case-insensitive comparison) in any order.

Are all of these definitions of `equals` valid, based on the criteria listed in Exercise 3?

6. Based on the `compareTo` method for `Circle` objects defined in Section 6.1, what is the output of the following code sequence?

```
Circle c1 = new Circle(5);
Circle c2 = new Circle(5);
Circle c3 = new Circle(15);
System.out.println(c1.compareTo(c1));
System.out.println(c1.compareTo(c2));
System.out.println(c2.compareTo(c3));
System.out.println(c3.compareTo(c2));
```

7. In Exercise 3 we stated some rules for the behavior of the `equals` method. What similar rule or rules should the `compareTo` method follow?

8. Suppose we have a `Rectangle` class that includes `length` and `width` attributes of type `int`, both set by the constructor. Create a `compareTo` method for this class so that rectangle objects are ordered based on their

a. Perimeter.

b. Area.

9. a. How many "known" classes in the Java library implement the `Comparable` interface?

b. List five such classes that you have used before, or at least have studied.

6.2 Lists

10. Give examples from the "real world" of unsorted lists, sorted lists, indexed lists, lists that permit duplicate elements, and lists that do not permit duplicate elements.

11. Besides unsorted lists, sorted lists, and indexed lists, are there other potential varieties of lists? Describe a few of them informally.

12. We do not allow `null` elements on our lists. Why not? Describe some of the ramifications of removing this restriction—that is, of allowing `null` elements. You should include the potential effects on implementation details.

6.3 Formal Specification

13. Classify each of the List ADT operations according to operation type (constructor, iterator, observer, transformer).

14. Explain the purpose of each of the preconditions listed in the `getNext` method definition.

15. Suppose `indList` is an indexed list that contains seven elements. Suppose `element` is an `Object` that is not already on the list. For each of the following

method invocations, indicate whether they would result in the `IndexOutOf-BoundsException` being thrown. Each part of this question is independent.

a. `indList.add(6, element)`

b. `indList.add(7, element)`

c. `indList.set(6, element)`

d. `indList.set(7, element)`

e. `indList.remove(element)`

f. `indList.get(element)`

g. `indList.remove(-1)`

h. `indList.remove(0)`

16. Our List ADT specifications apply to unbounded lists. How would you change the specifications to address the issues related to placing a bound on the size of the lists?

17. The specifications for our List ADT allow lists to contain duplicate elements. Describe how you would change the specifications if duplicate elements were not permitted.

6.4 Array-Based Implementations

18. Show the output of the following program:

```
import ch06.lists.*;
public class ListExer
{
    public static void main(String[] args)
    {
        ListInterface<String> list1
            = new ArrayUnsortedList<String>();
        list1.add("apple");
        list1.add("peach");
        list1.add("orange");
        list1.add("pear");
        list1.remove("peach");

        ListInterface<String> list2
            = new ArraySortedList<String>();
        list2.add("apple");
        list2.add("peach");
        list2.add("orange");
        list2.add("pear");
        list2.remove("peach");

        IndexedListInterface<String> list3
            = new ArrayIndexedList<String>();
        list3.add(0, "apple");
```

```
        list3.add(0, "peach");
        list3.add(1, "orange");
        list3.add(0, "pear");
        list3.add(2, "plum");
        list3.remove("peach");

        System.out.print("Unsorted");
        System.out.println(list1);
        System.out.print("Sorted");
        System.out.println(list2);
        System.out.print("Indexed");
        System.out.println(list3);
    }
}
```

19. Exercise 17 asked you to describe how the decision to disallow duplicate list elements would affect the list specifications. Now describe how this decision would affect the array-based implementations.

20. What happens if the second constructor for `ArrayUnsortedList` is passed a negative argument? How could this situation be handled by redesigning the constructor?

21. Describe the ramifications of each of the following changes to the chapter's code for the `ArrayUnsortedList` class:

    a. In the first line of `enlarge`, change "+" to "*".

    b. In the boolean expression of `find`, change the second "<" to "<=".

    c. In `size`, change "return numElements;" to "return list.length;".

    d. In `remove`, drop the statement "numElements--".

22. Someone suggests that, instead of shifting list elements to the left when an object is removed, the array location holding that object should just be set to `null`. Discuss the ramifications of such an approach for each of our three list types.

23. Consider the operation: *isEmpty*—returns `true` if the list is empty, otherwise returns `false`. Design a method to be added to the `ArrayUnsortedList` class that implements the operation. Code and test your method.

24. Consider the operation: *removeAll*—removes all elements from the list that are equal to the argument element and returns an `int` indicating how many elements were removed. Design a method to be added to the `ArrayUnsortedList` class that implements the operation. Code and test your method.

25. This chapter specifies and implements an Unsorted List ADT.

    a. Design an algorithm for an application-level method `last` that accepts an unsorted `Circle` list as an argument and returns a `Circle`. If the list is empty, the method returns `null`. Otherwise, it returns the last element of the list. The signature for the routine should be

    ```
    Circle last(ListInterface list)
    ```

    b. Devise a test plan for your algorithm.

c. Implement and test your algorithm.

💻 26. This chapter specifies and implements an Unsorted List ADT.

a. Design an algorithm for an application-level routine that accepts two `Circle` lists as arguments, and returns a count of how many elements from the first list are also on the second list (using the `equals` method to determine equality). The signature for the method should be

```
int compareLists(ListInterface<Circle> list1,
                 ListInterface<Circle> list2)
```

b. Devise a test plan for your algorithm.

c. Implement and test your algorithm.

💻 27. Our implementation of the `remove` operation for the Unsorted List ADT (`ArrayUnsortedList`) does not maintain the order of insertions because the algorithm swaps the last element into the location of the element being removed.

a. Would there be any advantage to having `remove` maintain the insertion order? Justify your answer.

b. Modify `remove` so that the insertion order is maintained. Code your algorithm, and then test it.

💻 28. This chapter specifies and implements a Sorted List ADT.

a. Design an algorithm for an application level routine that accepts two `Circle` lists as arguments and returns a count of how many elements from the first list are also on the second list (using the `equals` method to determine equality). The signature for the routine should be

```
int compareLists(ArraySortedList<Circle> list1,
                 ArraySortedList<Circle> list2)
```

b. Devise a test plan for your algorithm.

c. Implement and test your algorithm.

💻 29. The algorithm for the Sorted List ADT's `add` operation starts at the beginning of the list and looks at each element so as to determine where the insertion should take place. Once the insertion location is determined, the algorithm moves each list element between that location and the end of the list, starting at the end of the list, over to the next location. This operation creates space for the new element to be inserted.

Another approach to this problem is just to start at the last location, examine the element there to see whether the new element should be placed before it or after it, and shift the element in that location to the next location if the answer is "before." Repeating this procedure with the next-to-last element, then the one next to that, and so on, will eventually move all of the elements that need to be moved. When the answer is finally "after" (or the beginning of the list is reached), the needed location is available for the new element.

a. Formalize this new algorithm with a pseudocode description, such as the algorithms presented in the text.

b. Rewrite the `add` method of the `ArraySortedList` class to use the new algorithm.

c. Test the new method.

30. The Sorted List ADT (`ArraySortedList`) is to be extended with an operation called `merge`, which adds the contents of a sorted list argument to the current list.

    a. Write the specifications for this operation. The signature for the routine should be

    ```
    void merge(ArraySortedList<T> list)
    ```

    b. Design an algorithm for this operation.

    c. Devise a test plan for your algorithm.

    d. Implement and test your algorithm.

31. Describe the ramifications of each of the following changes to the chapter's code for the `ArrayIndexedList` class:

    a. In the first line of `add`, change ">" to ">=".

    b. In the first line of `set`, change ">=" to ">".

    c. In `set`, change the order of the two statements immediately before the *return* statement.

    d. Rewrite `indexOf` to invoke `find`, as it currently does, but then just "`return location`".

    e. Remove the statement "`list[numElements] = null;`" from the `remove` method.

6.5 Applications: Poker, Golf, and Music

32. In this exercise you investigate potential improvements to the `PokerApp` program.

    a. Run the program five times on your machine. Record how long it takes. Create a table and record both the reported probability and the number of seconds taken for each run.

    b. Redesign and recode the program so that instead of always dealing out seven cards to a hand, it stops dealing whenever a pair is discovered. Run the program five times, and record both the results and the execution time. Compare your findings to the data gathered in part a, and discuss the differences.

    c. Starting again with the original program, redesign and recode it so that instead of reshuffling after every hand, the deck is reshuffled after every seven hands. Run the program five times, recording both the results and the execution time. Compare your findings to the data gathered in parts a and b, and discuss the differences.

33. Change the `PokerApp` program so that it asks the user how many hands to simulate and how many cards should be in a single hand. Use the new program to investigate the probability of getting a pair in a five-card hand.

34. You need to change the `PokerApp` program so that instead of reporting the probability of getting a pair of identical ranks, it reports the probability of getting three cards of the same rank.

    a. Describe how you would achieve this using the `ArrayUnsortedList` class as defined in Section 6.4.

    b. Suppose you include a `count` method in the `ArrayUnsortedList` class, which returns the number of elements on the list that are equal to its argument element. Describe how you would use this functionality to help solve our new problem.

    c. Choose one of two approaches to solve the new problem and implement it. What is the reported probability?

35. In the `GolfApp` program, a sorted list of size 20 is instantiated. What happens if more than 20 golfers are entered by the user?

36. Describe how you would change our golf application so that

    a. It lists golfers from worst score to best score.

    b. It lists golfers in alphabetical order.

37. Upgrade the `GolfApp` program so that if a user enters anything except a positive integer when asked to enter a score, he or she is reprompted for new input.

38. Explain the difference between the two constructors of the `Song` class.

39. Update the `SongsApp` program so that

    a. It is more robust. It should check any numerical input for legality and reprompt the user if the input values are illegal.

    b. After the user is finished entering songs, he or she is given the option to remove songs. The user can be asked to repeatedly enter the index of a song to remove. Input of −1 can indicate that the user does not wish to remove any more songs.

40. Suppose we have a class called `Car` that models cars. This class has instance variables `year`, `make`, `model`, and `price`. It also provides appropriate observer methods, including one called `getPrice` that returns a value of type `int` indicating the price of "this" car. Implement a client method `totalPrice`, which accepts a list (`ArrayUnsortedList carList`) of cars and returns an integer equal to the total cost of the cars on the list.

41. Use one of our three array-based list implementations to support an application that does the following:

    a. Allows a user to enter a list of the countries he or she has visited and then displays the list in alphabetical order, plus a count of how many countries are on the list. If the user mistakenly enters the same country twice, the program should include it on the list only once.

    b. Allows a user to enter information about university courses: an identification number, a name, and the name of the professor. Once the information is entered, the user can request information based on a course number. The program should handle any input "problems" in a reasonable way.

c. Allows a user to enter a sequence of product information—namely, a product's description and cost. After the information is entered, the user can repeatedly enter a price range, and it displays all of the products in that price range, ordered from the cheapest to the most expensive.

6.6 The Binary Search Algorithm

Exercises 42–45 use the following sorted list of 15 elements, indexed from 0 to 14:

[0] algorithm   [5] formula   [10] kilo
[1] binary   [6] graph   [11] log
[2] computer   [7] heap   [12] mega
[3] digital   [8] int   [13] nano
[4] efficiency   [9] java   [14] open

42. Fill in the table to show how many comparisons of the target element to a list element would be made when searching for the given target element using the algorithm shown at the top of the column.

Target	Linear Search	Improved Linear Search	Binary Search
algorithm			
computer			
heap			
int			
open			
bit			
stack			
queue			

43. Trace the `find` algorithm of the `ArraySortedList2` class and create a table similar to Table 6.1, assuming you are searching for "computer."

44. Trace the `find` algorithm of the `ArraySortedList2` class and create a table similar to Table 6.1, assuming you are searching for "open."

45. How many calls to the `recFind` method of the `ArraySortedList3` class are made when the `find` method of the class is passed each of the following targets?

a. algorithm

b. heap

c. mega

d. dynamic

e. zebra

46. Can the linear search algorithm be encoded using recursion? If not, why not? If so, outline an approach and discuss its advantages and disadvantages.

6.7 Reference-Based Implementations

47. Following the style of the figures in this chapter, draw the list that would result from each of the following code sequences:

    a. ```
    RefUnsortedList<Integer> myList
        = new RefUnsortedList<Integer>();
    myList.add(5);
    myList.add(9);
    myList.add(3);
    ```

    b. ```
    RefUnsortedList<Integer> myList
        = new RefUnsortedList<Integer>();
    myList.add(5);
    myList.add(9);
    myList.add(3);
    myList.remove(9);
    ```

    c. ```
    RefSortedList<Integer> myList
        = new RefSortedList<Integer>();
    myList.add(5);
    myList.add(9);
    myList.add(3);
    ```

    d. ```
    RefSortedList<Integer> myList
        = new RefSortedList<Integer>();
    myList.add(5);
    myList.add(9);
    myList.add(3);
    myList.remove(9);
    ```

48. Show the output of the following program:

```java
import ch06.lists.*;
public class ListExer2
{
    public static void main(String[] args)
    {
        ListInterface<String> list1
            = new RefUnsortedList<String>();
        list1.add("apple");
        list1.add("peach");
        list1.add("orange");
        list1.add("pear");
        list1.remove("peach");

        ListInterface<String> list2
            = new RefSortedList<String>();
```

```
        list2.add("apple");
        list2.add("peach");
        list2.add("orange");
        list2.add("pear");
        list2.remove("peach");

        System.out.print("Unsorted");
        System.out.println(list1);
        System.out.print("Sorted");
        System.out.println(list2);
    }
}
```

49. Exercise 17 asked you to describe how the decision to disallow duplicate list elements would affect the list specifications. Now describe how this decision would affect the reference-based implementations.

50. Describe the ramifications of each of the following changes to the chapter's code for the RefUnsortedList class:
    a. In the if condition of find, use "==" instead of "equals."
    b. In the else clause of find, switch the order of the two statements.
    c. In toString, drop " currNode = currNode.getLink();."

51. Consider the operation: removeAll, which removes all elements from the list that are equal to the argument element and returns an int indicating the number of elements removed. Design a method to be added to the RefUnsortedList class that implements the operation. Code and test your method.

52. The algorithm for the reference-based sorted list's find operation starts at the beginning of the list and looks at each element so as to determine whether the target element is on the list. Another approach to this algorithm is to stop searching once a point in the list is reached that contains an element larger than the target element, because it is then known that the element is not on the list.

    a. Create this new find method and add it to the RefSortedList class.
    b. Test the new method. Describe how you tested it.

53. You are discussing Exercise 52 with a friend. Your friend suggests that you use the binary search algorithm to improve the find method. How do you respond?

54. Describe how you would change the PokerApp program, presented in Section 6.5, so that it uses the RefUnsortedList class instead of the ArrayUnsortedList class.

55. Expand our RefUnsortedList class with a public method endInsert, which inserts an element at the end of the list. Do not add any instance variables to the class. The method signature is

```
public void endInsert(T element)
```

56. Expand our `RefSortedList` class with a public method `ceilingList`, which returns a new list that contains all elements of the current list that are less than or equal to the element argument. The method signature is

```
public RefSortedList<T> ceilingList(T element)
```

57. Consider the operation of merging together two reference-based sorted lists, `list1` and `list2`, into a single reference-based sorted list, `list3`. Suppose `list1` is size *M*, and `list2` is size *N*.

   a. Suppose you implemented this operation at the application level by using the iteration operations to first obtain each element of `list1`, adding all of them to `list3`, and then to obtain each element of `list2`, also adding all of them to `list3`. What is the Big-O complexity of this approach? (Remember to count the time taken by the list methods.)

   b. Another approach is to implement the operation as a public method `merge` of the `RefSortedList` class. The `merge` method would create and return a new reference-based sorted list that consists of the merger of the current list and an argument list.

```
public RefSortedList<T> merge (RefSortedList<T> inList)
// Returns a new list consisting of a merge of
// this list with inList.
```

   Describe an algorithm for implementing this method. What is the Big-O complexity of your algorithm?

   c. Discuss the difference between your answers to parts a and b. What can you conclude from the difference?

58. Fill in the following table with the Big-O efficiency values of the operations as implemented in this chapter within the classes.

	Array-Based				Reference-Based	
	unsorted	sorted	sorted2	indexed	unsorted	sorted
size						
contains						
remove						
get						
getNext						
add						

6.8   Storing Objects and Structures in Files

59. Investigate how information is stored between program runs.

a. Run the SaveSong application. It creates a file named song.txt. Look at that file using a text editor. Describe what you see.

b. Run the SaveSerSong application. It creates a file named song.dat. Look at that file using a text editor. Describe what you see.

c. Explain the difference between what you saw for parts a and b.

60. Create programs similar to SaveSong and GetSong that save and retrieve a Customer object. See the support package for the Customer class.

61. Improve the SerSongApp program so that

a. It is more robust in terms of checking user input and reprompting in case of illegal input.

b. When a user is prompted for the index of a new song, he or she can just press Enter and the song will go on the end of the list. Remember to describe this option clearly in the user interface.

c. On a menu-driven interface, the user can choose among four options:

1. Add a song to the list.

2. Remove a song from the list.

3. Change the index of a song.

4. Change the name of the list.

To implement this improvement, you must update both the SerSongList and SerSongsApp classes.

d. Instead of just maintaining a single song list, it maintains several song lists, allowing the user to choose among them.

62. Create a program that works similarly to SerSongApp with regard to storing and retrieving information between program runs and allows users to

a. Enter information about golfers (their names and scores), and provides a list of golfers sorted by score. Note that the Golfer class is already defined in the support package. You will need to create a Serializable version of it.

b. Keep track of test scores, and report an average. A test score consists of two values: the weight of the test and the points earned.

c. Enter information about movies they want to watch; they can provide a movie rating between 1 and 10, with a higher number meaning a higher priority for watching the movie. Users must be able to remove movies from the list after they have watched them.

More Lists

Knowledge Goals

You should be able to

- describe the benefits and limitations of
  - circular linked lists
  - doubly linked lists
  - linked lists with headers and trailers
  - array-based linked lists
- discuss options, in terms of reuse of existing classes, for implementing new list approaches
- choose a reasonable list approach based on a set of list requirements
- if needed, define a new list approach to help solve a specified problem
- describe an approach for implementing large integers using a linked list

Skill Goals

You should be able to

- implement an unsorted circular linked list
- implement a sorted circular linked list
- implement an unsorted doubly linked list
- implement a sorted doubly linked list
- implement a linked list with a header node, a trailer node, or both
- implement a linked list as an array of nodes
- use one of the new list approaches to help solve a problem

This chapter introduces three new varieties of reference-based lists: circular linked lists, doubly linked lists, and lists with headers and trailers. It also describes an array-based approach to implementing a linked list, which is widely used in operating systems.

All of the lists presented to this point have been general; that is, they are designed to be useful for many applications. At the end of this chapter, we design a List ADT with unique properties targeted for a specific application. In the case study, we design and implement a calculator for working with large integers.

We simplify many of the figures of this chapter by using a capital letter to represent an object, rather than showing a reference to the object using an arrow.

7.1 Circular Linked Lists

The lists that we implemented in Chapter 6 are characterized by a linear relationship between the elements: Each element (except the first one) has a unique predecessor, and each element (except the last one) has a unique successor.

Let's consider a small change to our reference-based approach and see how it would affect our implementation and use of the List ADT. Suppose we change the link of the last node so that it points back to the first node instead of containing null (Figure 7.1). Now our list is a circular linked list rather than a linear linked list. We can start at any node in the list and traverse the whole list.

> **Circular linked list** A list in which every node has a successor; the "last" element is succeeded by the "first" element

Of course, we must now ensure that all of our list operations maintain this new property of the list: After the execution of any list operation, the last node should continue to point to the front node. A quick consideration of each of the operations convinces us that we can efficiently support almost all of them. The one exception is when an operation changes the first element on the list. Consider, for example, if we try to remove the first element. Our previous approach simply changes the list reference to point to the second element on the list. Now, however, we must also update the reference in the last element so that it points to the new first element. To do so, we must traverse the list until we reach the last element and then make the change. A similar problem arises if we add an element to the front of the list.

Adding and removing elements at the front of a list might be a common operation for some applications. Our linear linked list approach supported these operations very

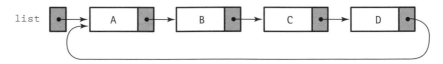

Figure 7.1 *A circular linked list*

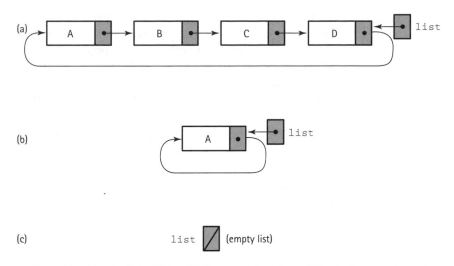

Figure 7.2 *Circular linked lists with the external pointer pointing to the rear element*

efficiently, but our circular linked list approach does not. We can fix this problem by letting our `list` reference point to the last element in the list rather than the first; now we have direct access to both the first and the last elements in the list. Figure 7.2 displays three examples of this approach. When the list is not empty, `list` references its last node, and `list.getLink()` references its first node.

An Unsorted Circular List

Let's implement an unsorted list using our new approach. We must first decide where this class fits in our list framework. Certainly, we expect the new class to implement the `ListInterface`. The question is whether it should implement the interface directly or extend our current `RefUnsortedList` class that already implements the interface. To resolve these issues, let's consider more carefully how the new approach affects our implementation:

- There is no need to change the basic underlying structure of the list. We can still use the `LLNode` class to supply the nodes for the structure. After all, the design of the nodes is the same; only the value of the `link` reference of the last node has changed.
- We can continue to use the same instance variables as before, because we still need a reference into the list, a count of the number of elements on the list, and a current position indicator for list iterations.
- The list constructor does not change—the reference variables are still initialized to `null`—and the number of elements on the original empty list is still zero.
- The `size` method still needs to just return the value of `numElements`.

- We can continue to use our same rules for the find method, having it set the instance variables found, location, and previous to indicate the results of its search. However, we do have to change the find implementation.
- We must change the search termination condition used by find, because the end of the list is no longer marked by null.
- The add and remove methods change the structure of the list, so we must make sure they maintain the circular nature of the list.
- The iterator and toString methods both need to be updated.

Given that so many of our methods are affected by the structure change, we decide not to use inheritance with any of our existing classes, but rather to start over with a new set of classes. It is important to understand that our design decision is just that—a decision. We could have taken other approaches, such as extending the current list classes, and still succeeded in implementing our new list.

The CRefUnsortedList Class

The CRefUnsortedList class will be similar to its linear list counterpart Ref-UnsortedList. The instance variables and constructor are unchanged. As we've noted, the size method need not be changed. Also, if we provide a revised find helper method with functionality that corresponds to the find in RefUnsortedList, we can reuse both the contains and get methods. Here we develop the remaining methods.

The Iterator Methods List

The required changes here are interesting in that the reset method becomes more complicated and the getNext method becomes simpler. Here's the code for the linear linked list and circular linked list, presented side by side for easy comparison:

Linear

```
public void reset()
{
  currentPos = list;
}

public T getNext()
{
  T next = currentPos.getInfo();
  if (currentPos.getLink() == null)
   currentPos = list;
  else
   currentPos = currentPos.getLink();

  return next;
}
```

Circular

```
public void reset()
{
  if (list != null)
    currentPos = list.getLink();
}

public T getNext()
{
  T next = currentPos.getInfo();
  currentPos = currentPos.getLink();
  return next;
}
```

Because we want the `reset` method to set the current position to the beginning of the list and our `list` reference variable points to the last list element, we must access the beginning of the list using `list.getLink()`. If the list is empty, however, this reference does not exist. In that case, the `list` variable itself holds the value `null`. Therefore, we must protect the assignment statement

```
currentPos = list.getLink();
```

with the test for the empty list.

As noted earlier, the `getNext` method has become simpler. For the linear list, this method had to explicitly test for the end of the list condition and handle it as a special case. For the circular list, this step is no longer necessary. When an iteration reaches the end of the list, the circular nature of the list ensures that it is redirected to the beginning of the list, as we wish.

The toString Method

Within the `toString` method, we use a little trick to simplify the code. We want to start the string with the first element on the list. The temporary `prevNode` variable is originally set to the value of `list`. It references the last node on the list. As a consequence, the information in the first node on the list is accessed through the expression

```
prevNode.getLink().getInfo()
```

That expression is used over and over again within the *do-while* loop, as the `prevNode` variable is updated to walk through the list. We are always accessing one node past where `prevNode` is currently pointing. The loop is exited as soon as `prevNode` equals `list`, that is, when `prevNode` becomes the last node in the structure. At that time we know that the information in the last node in the structure has already been added to the string—it was added in the previous step when `prevNode` referenced the next-to-last node.

```
public String toString()
// Returns a nicely formatted String that represents this list.
{
  String listString = "List:\n";
  if (list != null)
  {
    LLNode<T> prevNode = list;
    do
    {
      listString = listString + "  " + prevNode.getLink().getInfo() + "\n";
      prevNode = prevNode.getLink();
    }
    while (prevNode != list);
```

```
      }
      return listString;
  }
```

You should trace the `toString` method to convince yourself that it works for lists of size zero, one, or more elements.

The find Method

Recall that we wish to start our search at the beginning of the list, then continue searching sequentially until we find an element equal to the targeted element or we reach the end of the list. We must make sure that we start searching at the beginning of the list. An easy way to do so is to change the comparison so that instead of looking at `location` we look at `location.getLink()`. Thus, rather than updating `location` at the end of the search loop, we update it at the beginning of the loop, before the comparison is made.

```
protected void find(T target)
// Searches list for an occurrence of an element e such that
// e.equals(target). If successful sets instance variables
// found to true, location to node containing e, and previous
// to the node that links to location. If not successful sets
// found to false.
{
   location = list;
   found = false;

if (list != null)
   do
   {
     // move search to the next node
     previous = location;
     location = location.getLink();

     // check for a match
     if (location.getInfo().equals(target))
       found = true;
   }
   while ((location != list) && !found);
}
```

We also have to revise our method of determining when we reach the end of the list. We use an if statement to prevent attempting to access an empty list. For a nonempty list, the `find` implementation in the `RefUnsortedList` class terminates its search when `location` becomes `null`, indicating that the search has exhausted the entire list:

```
while (location != null)
```

With the circular list, this test no longer works—the list loops back on itself rather than terminating with `null`. The goal is to stop searching when the end of the list is reached. With the circular list, we know we have reached the end of the list when `location` references the same node as the `list` variable (recall that `list` always indicates the last node on the list for the circular approach). Thus the terminating condition is set appropriately:

```
while = (location != list)...
```

This is one of the rare occasions when we really do want to compare the references, rather than comparing the contents of the objects they refer to!

The contains and get Methods
Because the `contains` and `gets` methods access the structure of the list only through the `find` method, updating the `find` method as we have done allows us to leave those two methods unchanged.

The remove Method
We can use the same basic approach for removing an element from a circular list as we used for a linear list. First, we use the `find` method to determine whether any element matches the targeted element and, if so, to set the values of `location` and `previous`. To remove the identified element, we unlink it from the chain of elements by setting the `link` reference of the element immediately prior to the identified element to reference the element after the identified element:

```
previous.setLink(location.getLink());  // remove node at location
```

That approach still works for the general case, at least (see Figure 7.3a).

Which special cases do we have to consider? In the linear list version, we had to check whether we were removing the first (or first-and-only) element. The primary reason that this was a special case was that the overall list reference pointed to the first list element and had to be updated if that element was removed. In the circular version, the overall list reference points to the last list element, so removing the first element is not a special case; Figure 7.3(b) shows why. Removing the only node in a circular list is a special case, however, as we see in Figure 7.3(c). The reference to the list must be set to `null` to indicate that the list is now empty. We can detect this situation by checking whether `list` is equal to `list.getLink()`—in other words, if the node pointed to by `list` points to itself.

We might also guess that removing the last list element (the last node) from a circular list is a special case. After all, `list` points to the last element, so if we remove it, we

(a) The general case (remove B)

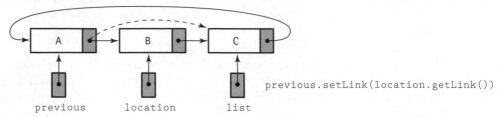

previous.setLink(location.getLink())

(b) Special case (?): Removing the first element (remove A)

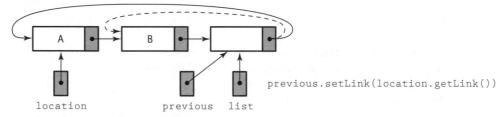

previous.setLink(location.getLink())

(c) Special case: Removing the only element (remove A)

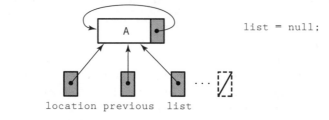

list = null;

(d) Special case: Removing the last element (remove C)

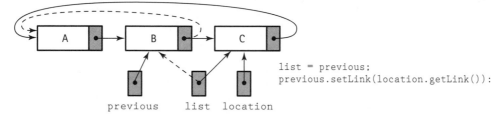

list = previous;
previous.setLink(location.getLink());

Figure 7.3 *Removing a node from a circular linked list*

must change the value in list. As Figure 7.3(d) illustrates, when we remove the last node, we must first update the overall list reference to point to the preceding element. We can detect this situation by checking whether previous.getLink() equals list after the search phase.

You should trace through the remove code and convince yourself that it handles the general case as well as all of the special cases properly.

```
public boolean remove (T element)
// Removes an element e from this list such that e.equals(element)
// and returns true; if no such element exists, returns false.
{
  find(element);
  if (found)
  {
    if (list == list.getLink())      // if single-element list
      list = null;
    else
      if (previous.getLink() == list)  // if removing last node
        list = previous;
      previous.setLink(location.getLink());  // remove node
    numElements--;
  }
  return found;
}
```

The add Method

The implementation of the `add` method is relatively straightforward. First we create the new node using the `LLNode` constructor. Because our list is unsorted, the only special case we need to consider is adding an element to an empty list. In that case we set the `list` variable to reference the new element and link the new element to itself. Otherwise, we simply add the element to the list in the most convenient place—at the location referenced by `list`. In either case we increment `numElements`. See Figure 7.4.

(a) The general case (add H)

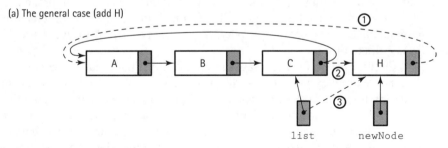

(b) Special case: The empty list (add A)

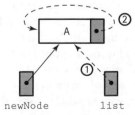

Figure 7.4 *Adding a node to a circular linked list*

```
public void add(T element)
// Adds element to this list.
{
  LLNode<T> newNode = new LLNode<T>(element);
  if (list == null)
  {
    // add element to an empty list
    list = newNode;
    newNode.setLink(list);
  }
  else
  {
    // add element to a nonempty list
    newNode.setLink(list.getLink());
    list.setLink(newNode);
    list = newNode;
  }
  numElements++;
}
```

Circular Versus Linear Linked Lists

Studying circular linked lists provided us with good practice in using references and self-referential structures. Are circular lists good for anything else? You may have noticed that the only operation that is simpler for the circular approach, as compared to the linear approach, is `getNext`; that minimal advantage is counterbalanced by a more complicated `reset` operation. Why, then, might we want to use a circular—rather than linear—linked list?

Circular lists offer advantages in applications that require access to both ends of the list. For example, a circular sorted list class could provide additional operations that take advantage of the new implementation. Perhaps we need an operation `inBetween` that returns a boolean value indicating whether an argument is "in between" the largest and smallest elements of the list; with the circular approach, we have easy access to both the largest element (through `list`) and the smallest element (through `list.getLink()`). Therefore, with the circular list we could implement `inBetween` as an O(1) operation, whereas with our linear approach it would be an O(N) operation.

On many occasions, the data we want to add to a sorted list will already be in order. Sometimes people manually sort raw data before turning the information over to a data entry clerk. Data produced by other programs are often in sorted order. Given a Sorted List ADT and sorted input data, we always add at the end of the list—the most expensive place to add in terms of machine time. A circular sorted list, with the list reference to the end of the list, can avoid this execution overhead.

You may have realized that many of the benefits described here for circular lists could also be obtained by using the linear linked list defined in Chapter 6 augmented with a reference to the last element of the list. This is yet another list variation; as with the circular list, it requires changes to some of the linear list methods. We ask you to explore this variation in the exercises.

Some objects truly are more naturally implemented with a circular list—for example, a slide show that repeats continuously or a repeating playlist of songs. In an operating system, the list of tasks being processed may be stored in a circular list. The system runs through the list, giving each task a little bit of processing time before moving on to the next task, thus allowing multiple tasks to seemingly proceed at the same time. When the operating system reaches the end of the list, it goes back to the first task and repeats the process.

In Section 7.2, we look at another important list structure, doubly linked lists. In this case, the major advantage of the new approach is obvious—it lets us easily traverse a list in either direction.

7.2 Doubly Linked Lists

As discussed previously, circular linked lists enable us to reach any node in the list from any starting point. Although this structure offers advantages over a linear linked list for some applications, it is still too limited for others. Suppose we want to remove a particular node in a list, given only a reference to that node. This task involves changing the `link` reference of the preceding node. Given only a reference to a node, however, it is not easy to access its predecessor in the list.

Another task that is difficult to perform on a linear linked list (or even a circular linked list) is traversing the list in reverse. For instance, suppose we have a list of student records, sorted by grade point average (GPA) from lowest to highest. The Dean of Students might want a printout of the records, ordered from highest to lowest, to use in preparing the dean's list.

In cases where we need to access the node that precedes a given node, a doubly linked list is useful. In a doubly linked list, the nodes are linked in both directions. Each node of a doubly linked list contains three parts:

> **Doubly linked list**   A linked list in which each node is linked to both its successor and its predecessor

`info`:   the element stored in the node
`link`:   the reference to the following node
`back`:   the reference to the preceding node

A linear doubly linked list is pictured in Figure 7.5. The `back` reference of the first node, as well as the `link` reference of the last node, contains `null`. Nodes for such a list could be provided by the following `DLLNode` class, which extends our previously defined `LLNode` class with the required functionality:

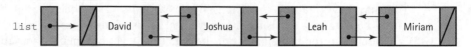

Figure 7.5 *A linear doubly linked list*

```
//-------------------------------------------------------------------------
// DLLNode.java              by Dale/Joyce/Weems                Chapter 7
//
// Implements <T> nodes for a Doubly Linked List.
//-------------------------------------------------------------------------

package support;

public class DLLNode<T> extends LLNode<T>
{
  private DLLNode<T> back;

  public DLLNode(T info)
  {
    super(info);
    back = null;
  }

  public void setBack(DLLNode<T> back)
  // Sets back link of this DLLNode.
  {
    this.back = back;
  }

  public DLLNode<T> getBack()
  // Returns back link of this DLLNode.
  {
    return back;
  }
}
```

The Add and Remove Operations

Using the definition of DLLNode, let's discuss the corresponding add and remove methods for a doubly linked sorted list. The first step for both is to find the location at which to perform the addition or removal. This step was complicated in the singly linked list situation by the need to hold on to a reference to the previous location during the search. That reference is no longer needed; instead, we can get the predecessor to any node through its back reference.

Although our search phase is simpler, the algorithms for the addition and removal operations on a doubly linked list are somewhat more complicated than their counterparts for a singly linked list. The reason is clear: Each node has an extra reference to manipulate with a doubly linked list.

As an example, consider `add`. To link a new node `newNode`, after a given node referenced by `previous`, in a singly linked list, we need to change two references: `newNode.link` and `previous.link` (see Figure 7.6a). The same operation on a doubly linked list requires four reference changes (see Figure 7.6b).

(a) Inserting into a singly linked list

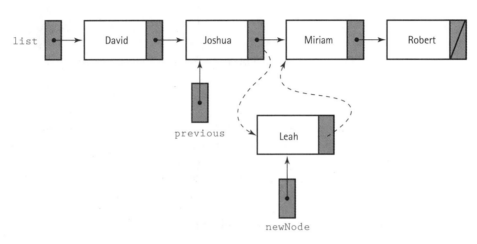

(b) Inserting into a doubly linked list

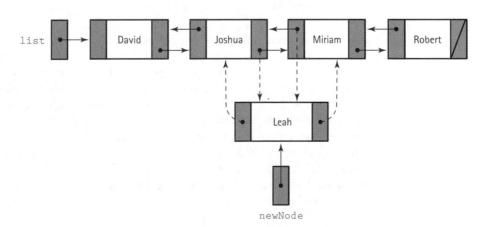

Figure 7.6 *Additions to single and doubly linked lists*

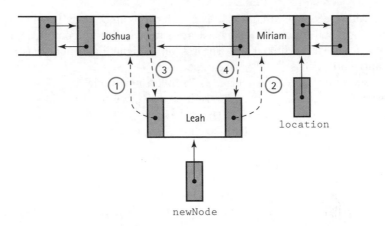

Figure 7.7 *Adding a node to a doubly linked list*

To add a new node, we allocate space for the new node and search the list to find the insertion point. When our search is complete, location references the node that should follow the new node. Now we are ready to link the new node into the list. Because of the complexity of the operation, we must be careful about the order in which we change the references. For instance, when adding the new node before location, if we change the reference in location.back first, we lose our reference to the node that is to precede the new node. The correct order for the reference changes is illustrated in Figure 7.7. The corresponding code would be

```
newNode.setBack(location.getBack());
newNode.setLink(location);
location.getBack().setLink(newNode);
location.setBack(newNode);
```

We do have to be careful about adding into an empty list, as it is a special case.

Now let's consider the remove method. One useful feature of a doubly linked list is that we don't need a reference to a node's predecessor to remove the node. Through the back reference, we can alter the link variable of the preceding node to make it "jump over" the unwanted node. Then we make the back reference of the succeeding node point to the preceding node. This operation is depicted in Figure 7.8.

We do, however, have to be careful about the end cases. If location.getBack() is null, we are removing the first node; if location.getLink() is null, we are removing the last node. If both location.getBack() and location.getLink() are null, we are removing the only node. We leave the complete coding of the doubly linked list for you as an exercise.

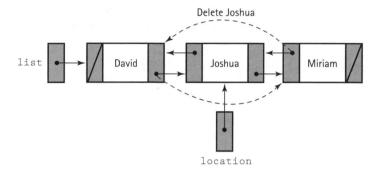

Figure 7.8 *Removing a node from a doubly linked list*

7.3 Linked Lists with Headers and Trailers

In writing the `add` and `remove` methods for the sorted linked list, we see that special cases arise for the first and the last nodes on the list. One way to simplify these methods is to make sure that we never add or remove elements at the ends of the list.

How can we do this? Recall that the elements in the sorted linked list are arranged according to the value in some key—for example, alphabetically by name. If we can identify the range of possible values for the key, it is often a simple matter to set up dummy nodes with values outside of this range. A header node, containing a value smaller than any possible list element key, can be placed at the beginning of the list. A trailer node, containing a value larger than any legitimate element key, can be placed at the end of the list.

> **Header node**   A placeholder node at the beginning of a list; used to simplify list processing
>
> **Trailer node**   A placeholder node at the end of a list; used to simplify list processing

The header and the trailer are regular nodes of the same type as the real data nodes in the list. They have a different purpose, however: Instead of storing list data, they act as placeholders.

If a list of students is sorted by last name, for example, we might assume that no students are named "AAAAAAAAAA" or "ZZZZZZZZZZ." We could therefore initialize our linked list to contain header and trailer nodes with these values as the keys. (See Figure 7.9.) How can we implement a general list ADT if we must know the minimum

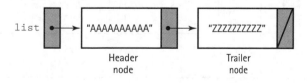

Figure 7.9 *An "empty" list with a header and a trailer*

and maximum key values? We can use a parameterized class constructor and let the user pass elements containing the dummy keys as arguments.

7.4 A Linked List as an Array of Nodes

We tend to think of linked structures as consisting of self-referential nodes that are dynamically allocated as needed, as illustrated in Figure 7.10(a), but this is not a requirement. A linked list could be implemented in an array; the elements might be stored in the array in any order and "linked" by their indexes (see Figure 7.10b). In this section, we develop an array-based linked list implementation.

In our previous reference-based implementations of lists, we used Java's built-in memory management services when we needed a new node for addition or when we were finished with a node and wanted to remove it. Obtaining a new node is easy in Java; we just use the familiar `new` operation. Releasing a node from use is also easy; we just remove our references to it and depend on the Java run-time system's garbage collector to reclaim the space used by the node.

For the array-based linked representation, we must predetermine the maximum list size and instantiate an array of nodes of that size. We then directly manage the nodes in the array. We keep a separate list of the available nodes, and we write routines to allocate nodes to and deallocate nodes from this free list.

Why Use an Array?

We have seen that dynamic allocation of list nodes has many advantages, so why would we even consider using an array-of-nodes implementation? Recall that dynamic alloca-

(a) A linked list in dynamic storage

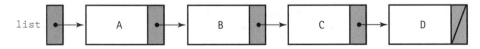

(b) A linked list in static storage

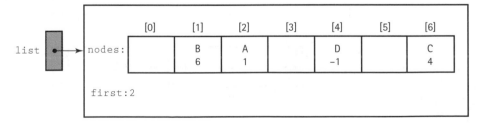

Figure 7.10 *Linked lists in dynamic and static storage*

List as Array of Nodes

tion is just one advantage of choosing a linked implementation; another advantage is the greater efficiency of the add and remove algorithms. Most of the algorithms for operations on a linked structure can be used for either an array-based or a reference-based implementation. The main difference arises from the requirement that we manage our own free space in an array-based implementation. Sometimes managing the free space ourselves gives us greater flexibility.

Another reason to use an array of nodes is that some programming languages do not support dynamic allocation or reference types. You can still use linked structures if you are programming in one of these languages, using the techniques presented in this section.

Finally, sometimes dynamic allocation of each node, one at a time, is too costly in terms of time—especially in real-time system software such as operating systems, air traffic controllers, and automotive systems. In such situations, an array-based linked approach provides the benefits of linked structures without the same run-time costs.

A desire for static allocation is one of the primary motivations driving the array-based linked approach, so we drop our assumption that our lists are of unlimited size in this section. Here, our lists will not grow as needed. Applications should not add elements to a full list. To support this approach, our list will export an isFull operation, in addition to the other standard list operations.

How Is an Array Used?

Let's return to our discussion of how a linked list can be implemented in an array. We can associate a next variable with each array node to indicate the array index of the succeeding node. The beginning of the list is accessed through a "reference" that contains the array index of the first element in the list. Figure 7.11 shows how a sorted list containing the elements "David," "Joshua," "Leah," "Miriam," and "Robert" might be stored in an array of nodes. Do you see how the order of the elements in the list is explicitly indicated by the chain of next indexes?

What goes in the next index of the last list element? Its "null" value must be an invalid address for a real list element. Because the nodes array indexes begin at 0, the value −1 is not a valid index into the array; that is, there is no nodes[-1]. Therefore, −1 makes an ideal value to use as a "null" address. We could use the literal value -1 in our programs:

```
while (location != -1)
```

It is better programming style to declare a named constant, however. We use the identifier NUL and define it to be −1:

```
private static final int NUL = -1;
```

When an array-of-nodes implementation is used to represent a linked list, the programmer must write routines to manage the free space available for new list elements. Where is this free space? Look again at Figure 7.11. All of the array elements that do

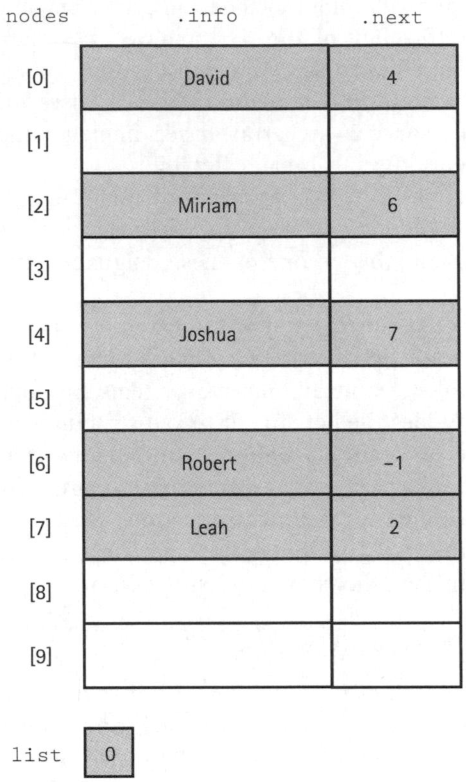

nodes	.info	.next
[0]	David	4
[1]		
[2]	Miriam	6
[3]		
[4]	Joshua	7
[5]		
[6]	Robert	−1
[7]	Leah	2
[8]		
[9]		

list   0

Figure 7.11 *A sorted list stored in an array of nodes*

not contain values in the list constitute free space. Instead of the built-in allocator `new`, which allocates memory dynamically, we must write our own method to allocate nodes from the free space. We call this method `getNode`. We use `getNode` when we add new elements to the list.

When we remove an element from the list, we need to reclaim its space—that is, we need to return the removed node to the free space so it can be used again later. We can not depend on a garbage collector; the node we remove remains in the allocated array so it is not reclaimed by the run-time engine. We write our own method, `freeNode`, to put a node back into the pool of free space.

Of course, we need a way to track the collection of nodes that are not being used to hold list elements. We can link this collection of unused array elements together into a second list, a linked list of free nodes. Figure 7.12 shows the array nodes with both the list of elements and the list of free space linked through their `next` values. The `list` variable is a reference to a list that begins at index 0 (containing the value "David"). Following the links in `next`, we see that the list continues with the array slots at index 4 ("Joshua"), 7 ("Leah"), 2 ("Miriam"), and 6 ("Robert"), in that order. The free list begins

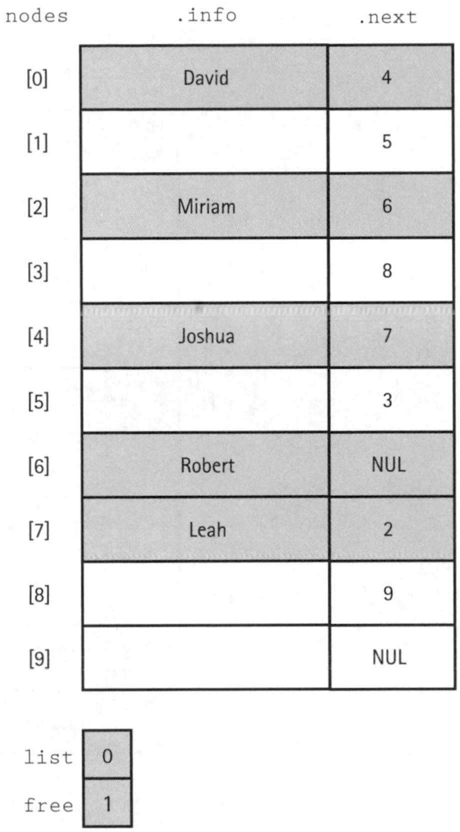

nodes	.info	.next
[0]	David	4
[1]		5
[2]	Miriam	6
[3]		8
[4]	Joshua	7
[5]		3
[6]	Robert	NUL
[7]	Leah	2
[8]		9
[9]		NUL

list	0
free	1

Figure 7.12 *An array with a linked list of values and free space*

at free, at index 1. Following the next links, we see that the free list also includes the array slots at indexes 5, 3, 8, and 9. We see two NUL values in the next column because there are two linked lists contained in the nodes array; thus the array includes two end-of-list values.

There are two approaches to using an array-of-nodes implementation for linked structures. First, we can simulate dynamic memory with a single array. One array is used to store many different linked lists, just as the computer's free space can be dynamically allocated to hold different lists. In this approach, the references to the lists are not part of the storage structure, but the reference to the list of free nodes is part of the structure.

Figure 7.13 shows an array that contains two different lists. The list indicated by list1 contains the values "John," "Nell," "Susan," and "Susanne"; the list indicated by list2 contains the values "Mark," "Naomi," and "Robert." The remaining three array slots in Figure 7.13 are linked together in the free list.

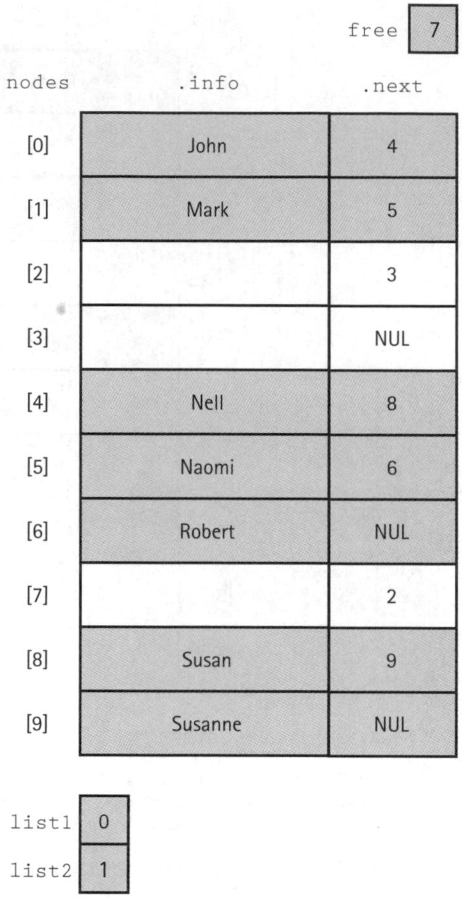

free 7

nodes	.info	.next
[0]	John	4
[1]	Mark	5
[2]		3
[3]		NUL
[4]	Nell	8
[5]	Naomi	6
[6]	Robert	NUL
[7]		2
[8]	Susan	9
[9]	Susanne	NUL

list1 0

list2 1

Figure 7.13 *An array with three lists (including the free list)*

The second approach is to create one array of nodes for each list. In this approach, the reference to the list is part of the storage structure itself (see Figure 7.14). This strategy works because there is only one list. The list constructor has a parameter that specifies the maximum number of elements in the list. This parameter is used to dynamically allocate an array of the appropriate size.

In this section, we implement this second approach. As with the examples we have been using in this section, we implement a sorted list of strings. This nongeneric approach allows us to avoid the problems associated with mixing Java's arrays and generics, with the related need for casts and compiler warnings. It simplifies the code, allowing you to concentrate on the primary topic of this section—implementing a linked-list using an underlying array.

We call our new class `ArrayRefSortedStringList`. In implementing our class methods, we need to keep in mind that there are two distinct processes going on within the array of nodes: bookkeeping relating to the space (such as initializing the array of

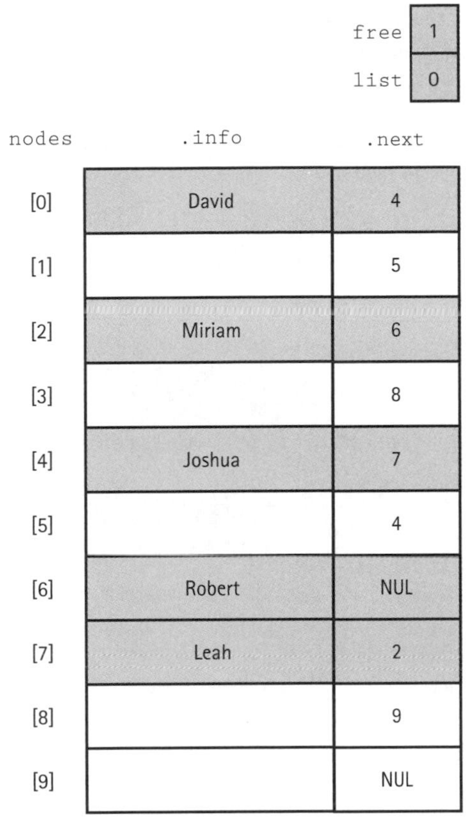

| | free | 1 |
| | list | 0 |

nodes	.info	.next
[0]	David	4
[1]		5
[2]	Miriam	6
[3]		8
[4]	Joshua	7
[5]		4
[6]	Robert	NUL
[7]	Leah	2
[8]		9
[9]		NUL

Figure 7.14 *List and link structure are together*

nodes, getting a new node, and freeing a node) and the operations on the list that contain the user's data. The bookkeeping operations are transparent to the user. Our list interface does not change. In fact, our new class implements the List-Interface<String> interface. The private data, however, changes.

Our class must include the array of nodes. Let's call this array nodes and have it hold elements of the class AListNode. Objects of the AListNode class contain two attributes: info, of class String, which holds a reference to a copy of the user's data; and next, of the primitive type int, which holds the index of the next element on the list. We define AListNode as a protected class within our ArrayRefSortedString-List class. This tactic provides reasonable protection, while allowing us to directly access the instance variables info and next from within the ArrayRefSortedString-List class.

In addition to the array of nodes, we need one integer "reference" to the first node of the list (that we call list) and another to the first free node (that we call free). Of course, we still need our numElements and currentPos variables, as well as the variables set by the `find` method and used by `contains`, `get`, and `remove`. Here is the beginning of our class file:

```
//-------------------------------------------------------------------------
// ArrayRefSortedStringList.java      by Dale/Joyce/Weems          Chapter 7
//
// Implements an array-based sorted linked list of strings
//-------------------------------------------------------------------------

package ch07.array;

import ch06.lists.*;

public class ArrayRefSortedStringList implements ListInterface<String>
{
  protected static final int NUL = -1;    // End of list symbol

  protected class AListNode
  {
    private String info;       // The info in a list node
    private int next;          // A link to the next node on the list
  }

  protected AListNode[] nodes;  // Array of AListNode holds the linked list

  protected int list;           // Reference to first node on the list
  protected int free;           // Reference to first node on the free list

  protected int numElements;    // Number of elements in the list
  protected int currentPos;     // Current position for iteration

  // set by find method
  protected boolean found;      // true if element found, else false
  protected int location;       // node containing element, if found
  protected int previous;       // node preceding location
```

The class constructors for class `ArrayRefSortedStringList` allocate the storage for the array of nodes and initialize the instance variables. They also set up the initial free list of nodes. At the time of instantiation, all of the nodes are on the free list. Thus the variable `free` is set to 0 to "reference" the first array node, the `next` value of that node is set to 1, and so on, until all of the nodes are chained together. This initialization can be handled by a *for* loop, followed by a single assignment statement to set the last `next` value to `NUL`. To be consistent with our past array-based implementations, we provide two constructors: one that accepts a size parameter and one that uses a default maximum size. Here is the code for the constructor that takes a parameter:

```
public ArrayRefSortedStringList(int maxElements)
//  Instantiates and returns a reference to an empty list object with
//  room for maxElements elements.
{
  nodes = new AListNode[maxElements];
  for (int index = 0; index < maxElements; index++)
    nodes[index] = new AListNode();

  // Link together the free nodes.
  for (int index = 1; index < maxElements; index++)
    nodes[index - 1].next = index;
  nodes[maxElements - 1].next = NUL;

  list = NUL;
  free = 0;
  numElements = 0;
  currentPos = NUL;
}
```

The methods that do the bookkeeping, getNode and freeNode, are auxiliary ("helper") methods and, therefore, are protected methods. The getNode method returns the index of the next free node. The easiest node to use is the one at the beginning of the free list, so getNode returns the value of free. In addition, getNode updates the value of free to indicate the next node on the free list. Other than the fact that we must be careful of our order of operations and use a temporary variable to hold the index we need to return, this method is straightforward:

```
protected int getNode()
// Returns the index of the next available node from the free list
// and updates the free list index.
{
  int hold;
  hold = free;
  free = nodes[free].next;
  return hold;
}
```

The freeNode method takes the node index received as an argument and adds the corresponding node into the list of free nodes. The easiest approach is to add the node to the beginning of the list.

```
protected void freeNode(int index)
// Frees the node at array position index by linking it into the
// free list.
{
  nodes[index].next = free;
  free = index;
}
```

Yes, we are keeping the free list as a stack—not because we need the LIFO property, but because it is the most efficient approach.

The public methods are very similar to their reference-based linked list counterparts. From the point of view of the algorithm used, they are identical. The following table shows equivalent expressions for different list implementations. It also shows the expressions for allocating and freeing nodes, where appropriate.

Abstract	Array-Based	Reference-Based	Array Index Links
the node at location	not applicable	location	nodes[location]
the element at location	list[location]	location.getInfo()	nodes[location].info
the next location	list[location+1]	location.getLink()	nodes[location].next
allocate a node	not applicable	new	getNode()
free a node	not applicable	remove links, garbage collector	freeNode(node)

We look here at two of the methods; we leave the rest for you as an exercise. First comes an easy one: isFull. Recall that we are assuming that the size of our list is bounded, so we need to export an isFull operation. We have two ways of determining whether the list is full. First, we can compare the number of elements on the list to the size of the underlying array. If they are equal, then the list is full. But there is a second, even easier way. Can you think of it? If the entire array is being used to hold our list, then the list of free space must be empty. Thus we can just check whether free is equal to NUL.

```
public boolean isFull()
// Returns whether this list is full.
{
  return (free == NUL);
}
```

The remaining methods can be implemented following the same scheme devised for the reference-based approach. We must be careful, however, to correctly transform the implementation. Also, we must remember to handle the memory management ourselves, using our `getNode` and `freeNode` methods. Let's look at the `remove` method. Compare the following code to that developed in Chapter 6:

```
public boolean remove (String element)
// Removes an element e from this list such that e.equals(element)
// and returns true; if no such element exists, returns false
{
  int hold;                     // to remember removed node index
  find(element);
  if (found)
  {
    hold = location;
    if (list == location)
      list = nodes[list].next;   // remove first node
    else
      nodes[previous].next = nodes[location].next;
    freeNode(hold);
    numElements--;
  }
  return found;
}
```

Notice how we carefully store the index of the node being removed, so that we can "free" it before leaving the method.

7.5 A Specialized List ADT

We have defined Unsorted, Sorted, and Indexed List ADTs as well as several implementations of each ADT. Our lists can be used for many applications. There are always some applications, however, that need special-purpose lists. Perhaps they require specific list operations that are not defined by our List ADTs, or perhaps the specific qualities of our lists (for example, allowing duplicate elements) do not fit with the requirements of the application. In such cases, we may be able to extend one of our list classes to create a new list that meets the needs of the application. Alternatively, it may be better just to create a new list class, customized specifically for the application in question.

In the case study in Section 7.6, we need lists with a unique set of properties and operations. The lists must hold elements of the primitive type `byte`; duplicate elements are allowed. The lists need not support `isFull`, `contains`, `get`, or `remove`. In fact, the only list operations that we have been using that are required by this new list construct are the `size` operation and the iterator operations. For the case study, we will need to process elements from left to right and from right to left, so we need to support two iterators. In addition, we will need to add elements at the front and at the back of our lists. The reasons for these requirements are made clear in the case study; for now we just accept the requirements as stated and consider how to implement this new list.

The Specification

Given this unique set of requirements, we decide to start from scratch for our new List ADT. Of course, we can tap into our knowledge of lists and perhaps even reuse (cut and paste) some of the code from the previous list implementations, but we will not implement any of the previously defined interfaces or extend any of our current classes.

Because the new list construct creates a specialized list for a specific application, we call the list class `SpecializedList`, and we specify its behavior in an interface called `SpecializedListInterface`. The new list does not provide a list of generic objects; instead, it provides a list of `byte` elements. Recall that a byte is one of Java's primitive integer types. A byte can hold an integer between –128 and +127. We place the classes related to our new list in a package called `ch07.byteLists`.

Given the requirement that we must be able to iterate through the list in both directions, instead of our standard "current position" property, lists of the class `SpecializedList` have both a "current forward position" and a "current backward position" and provide iterator operations for traversing the list in either direction. This does not mean that an iteration can change directions—it simply means that two separate iterations can be going on at the same time, one forward and one backward.

Here is the formal specification of the new List ADT:

```
//-------------------------------------------------------------------------------
// SpecializedListInterface.java      by Dale/Joyce/Weems          Chapter 7
//
// Interface for a class that implements a list of bytes.
// There can be duplicate elements on the list.
// The list has two special properties called the current forward position
// and the current backward position -- the positions of the next element
// to be accessed by getNextElement and by getPriorElement during an iteration
// through the list. Only resetForward and getNextElement affect the current
// forward position. Only resetBackward and getPriorElement affect the current
// backward position.
//-------------------------------------------------------------------------------

package ch07.byteLists;

public interface SpecializedListInterface
{
  void resetForward();
  // Initializes current forward position for this list to the first
  // byte on the list.

  byte getNextElement ();
```

```
// Preconditions: the list is not empty
//                the list has been resetForward
//                the list has not been modified since most recent reset
//
// Returns the value of the byte at the current forward position on
// this list. If the current forward position is the last element, then
// it advances the value of the current forward position to the first
// element; otherwise, it advances the value of the current forward position
// to the next element.

void resetBackward();
// Initializes current backward position for this list to the last
// byte on the list.

byte getPriorElement ();
// Preconditions: the list is not empty
//                the list has been resetBackward
//                the list has not been modified since most recent reset
//
// Returns the value of the byte at the current backward position on
// this list. If the current backward position is the first element, then
// it advances the value of the current backward position to the last
// element; otherwise it advances the value of the current backward position
// to the previous element.

int size();
// Returns the number of elements on this list.

void addFront (byte element);
// Adds the value of element to the front of this list.

void addEnd (byte element);
// Adds the value of element to the end of this list.
}
```

The Implementation

The unique requirement for the SpecializedList is that we must be able to traverse it by going either forward or backward. Because a doubly linked list is linked in both directions, traversing the list either way is equally simple. Therefore, we use a reference-based doubly linked structure for our implementation.

To begin our backward traversals, and to support the new addEnd operation, it is clear that we need easy access to the end of the list. We have already seen how keeping the list reference pointing to the last element in a circular structure gives direct access

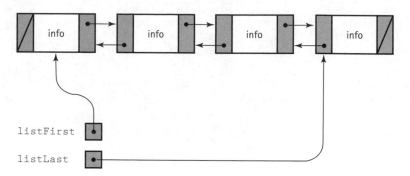

Figure 7.15 *A doubly linked list with two references*

to both the first element and the last element. Thus we could use a doubly linked circular structure. Another approach is also possible, however: We can maintain two list references, one for the front of the list and one for the back of the list. We use this approach as shown in Figure 7.15.

Here is the beginning of the `SpecializedList` class. We follow a doubly linked reference-based approach, using nodes of the `SListNode` class. We use instance variables to track the first list element, the last list element, the number of elements on the list, and the positions for both the forward traversal and the backward traversal. The `info` attribute of the `SListNode` class holds a value of the primitive `byte` type, as discussed earlier. The `SListNode` class is meant to be used only within the `SpecializedList` class, so it is defined within the class. This strategy protects it from misuse but allows it to be easily accessed from within the class itself.

```
//---------------------------------------------------------------------------
// SpecializedList.java          by Dale/Joyce/Weems          Chapter 7
//
// Implements the specialized list ADT using a doubly linked list of nodes
//---------------------------------------------------------------------------

package ch07.byteLists;

public class SpecializedList implements SpecializedListInterface
{
  protected class SListNode
  // List nodes for the specialized list implementation
  {
    protected byte info;          // The info in a list node
    protected SListNode next;     // A link to the next node on the list
    protected SListNode back;     // A link to the previous node on the list
  }

  protected SListNode listFirst;   // Reference to first node on list
```

```
protected SListNode listLast;        // Reference to last node on the list
protected int numElements;           // Number of elements on the list
protected SListNode currentFPos;     // Current forward position for iteration
protected SListNode currentBPos;     // Current backward position for iteration

public SpecializedList()
// Creates an empty list object
{
  numElements = 0;
  listFirst = null;
  listLast = null;
  currentFPos = null;
  currentBPos = null;
}
```

The `size` method is essentially unchanged from previous implementations—it simply returns the value of the `numElements` instance variable.

```
public int size()
// Determines the number of elements on this list
{
   return numElements;
}
```

The iterator methods are straightforward. Resetting an iteration simply requires setting the appropriate instance variable to either the front of the list or the back of the list. The methods that return the next element for an iteration work as they have in the past.

```
public void resetForward()
// Initializes current forward position for an iteration through this list
{
  currentFPos = listFirst;
}

public byte getNextElement ()
// Returns the value of the next element in list in forward iteration
{
  byte nextElementInfo = currentFPos.info;
  if (currentFPos == listLast)
    currentFPos = listFirst;
  else
    currentFPos = currentFPos.next;

  return nextElementInfo;
```

```
  }

  public void resetBackward()
  // Initializes current backward position for an iteration through this list
  {
    currentBPos = listLast;
  }

  public byte getPriorElement ()
  // Returns the value of the next element in list in backward iteration
  {
    byte nextElementInfo = currentBPos.info;
    if (currentBPos == listFirst)
      currentBPos = listLast;
    else
      currentBPos = currentBPos.back;

    return nextElementInfo;
  }
```

The addition methods for our new list are simpler than the addition method for the doubly linked list we used before, because we do not have to handle the general case of addition. The `addFront` method always adds at the beginning of the list and the `addEnd` method always adds at the end of the list. Let's look at `addFront` (see Figure 7.16a).

The method begins by creating the new node and initializing its attributes. The new node is the new front of the list, so we know that its `next` link should reference the current front of the list, and its `back` link should be `null`. An *if* statement guards the case when the addition occurs into an empty list (see Figure 7.16b). In that case, both the `listFirst` and `listLast` instance variables must reference the new node, as it is both the first and last element of the list. Otherwise, the `back` link of the previous first element is set to reference the new element, along with the `listFirst` instance variable. Of course, we must also increment the value of `numElements`.

```
  public void addFront (byte element)
  // Adds the value of element to the front of this list
  {
    SListNode newNode = new SListNode();    // Reference to node being added
    newNode.info = element;
    newNode.next = listFirst;
    newNode.back = null;
    if (listFirst == null)                  // Adding into an empty list
    {
```

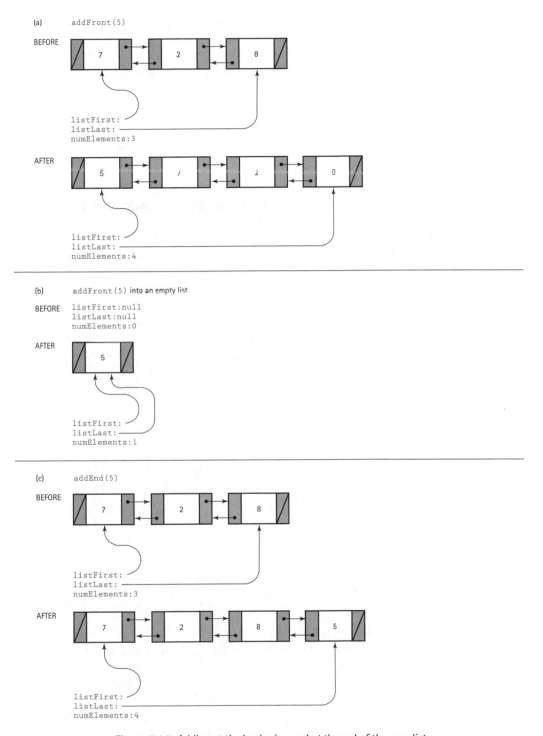

Figure 7.16 *Adding at the beginning and at the end of the new list*

```
    listFirst = newNode;
    listLast = newNode;
  }
  else                                // Adding into a nonempty list
  {
    listFirst.back = newNode;
    listFirst = newNode;
  }
  numElements++;
}
```

The code for the `addEnd` method is similar (see Figure 7.16c):

```
public void addEnd (byte element)
// Adds the value of element to the end of this list
{
  SListNode newNode = new SListNode();    // Reference to node being added
  newNode.info = element;
  newNode.next = null;
  newNode.back = listLast;
  if (listFirst == null)              // Adding into an empty list
  {
    listFirst = newNode;
    listLast = newNode;
  }
  else                                // Adding into a nonempty list
  {
    listLast.next = newNode;
    listLast = newNode;
  }
  numElements++;
}
```

7.6 Case Study: Large Integers

The range of integer values that can be supported in Java varies from one primitive integer type to another. Appendix C contains a table showing the default value, the possible range of values, and the number of bits used to implement each integer type. The largest type, `long`, can represent values between −9,223,372,036,854,775,808 and 9,223,372,036,854,775,807. Wow! That would seem to suffice for most applications. Some programmer, however, is certain to want to represent integers with even larger values. Let's create a class `LargeInt` that allows the programmer to manipulate integers in which the number of digits is limited only by the amount of memory available.[1]

Because we are providing an alternative implementation for a mathematical object, an integer number, the operations are already familiar: addition, subtraction, multiplication, division, assignment, and the relational operators. For this case study, we limit our attention to addition and subtraction. We ask you to enhance this ADT with some of the other operations in the exercises.

In addition to the standard mathematical operations, we need an operation to construct a number digit by digit. This operation cannot be a constructor with an integer parameter, because the desired integer might be too large to represent in Java—after all, that is the idea of this ADT. Thus we must have a special member method, `addDigit`, that can be called within a loop to insert digits one at a time, from most significant digit to least significant digit, as we would normally read a number.

We assume the sign of a large integer is positive, and we provide a way to make it negative. We call the corresponding method `setNegative`. Additionally, we must have an observer operation that returns a string representation of the large integer. We follow the Java convention and call this operation `toString`. It is also convenient to have a constructor that accepts a string argument that represents an integer and instantiates the corresponding `LargeInt` object.

The Underlying Representation

Before we look at the algorithms for these operations, we need to decide on our underlying representation. Because we said earlier that we were designing `SpecializedList` to use in this case study, you know that we will use it to represent our large integers. Nevertheless, let's assume we don't already know about this choice and look at the reasoning behind our design of the `SpecializedList`.

The fact that a large integer can be any size leads us to a dynamic memory-based representation. Also, given that an integer is a list of digits, it is natural to investigate the possibility of representing it as a linked list of digits. Figure 7.17 shows two ways of storing numbers in a singly linked list and an example of addition. Parts (a) and (c) show one digit per node; part (b) shows several digits per node. We develop our Large Integer ADT using a single digit per node. (You are asked in the exercises to explore the changes necessary to include more than one digit in each node.) Thus we have decided to represent our large integers as linked lists of digits. Because a single digit can be represented by Java's smallest integer type, the `byte`, we decide to use linked lists of `byte` values.

Throughout Chapters 6 and 7, we developed several implementations of linked lists. Can we use one of our predefined generic list classes such as `ArrayUnsortedList` or

---

1. Note that the Java library already provides a similar class, `java.math.BigInteger`. We are implementing our own version here because it is a good demonstration of the use of lists, and because it is informative to see how to implement such a class.

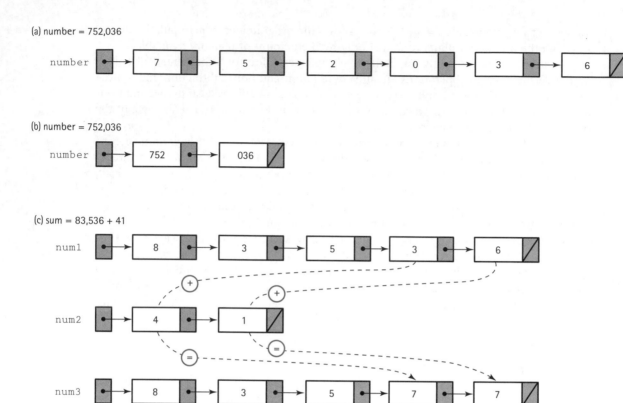

Figure 7.17 *Representing large integers with linked lists*

CRefUnsortedList? No, we cannot, for several reasons. Most importantly, those lists do not guarantee that their contents would be kept in any specific order. We need to know that the representation preserves the order in which we insert digits. None of our generic list implementations can guarantee that property, without extra work by the application. Thus we define a special-purpose list class just for our large integers.

What operations must be supported by this class? The first thing to consider is how large integer objects are to be constructed. We have already decided to build our representation, one digit at a time, from left to right across a particular large integer. That is how we initialize large integers directly. But large integers can also be created as a result of arithmetic operations. Think about how you perform arithmetic operations such as addition—you work from the least significant digit to the most significant digit, obtaining the result as you proceed. Therefore, we also need to create large integers by inserting digits in order from least significant to most significant. Thus our linked list should support insertion of digits at both the beginning and the end of the list.

What type of access do we need? We must be able to access one digit at a time, working from left to right to build a string for display. To support arithmetic operations

Note!! For this case study we are developing a Large Integer ADT that can be used by any application program that requires large integers. This ADT provides operations to build large integers, perform arithmetic operations on large integers, and return strings representing large integers. Now we are discussing using a List ADT to hold the underlying representation of a large integer. In other words, the application program uses the Large Integer ADT since it provides large integers, and the Large Integer ADT uses the List ADT since it provides a list of `byte` values. See Figure 7.18.

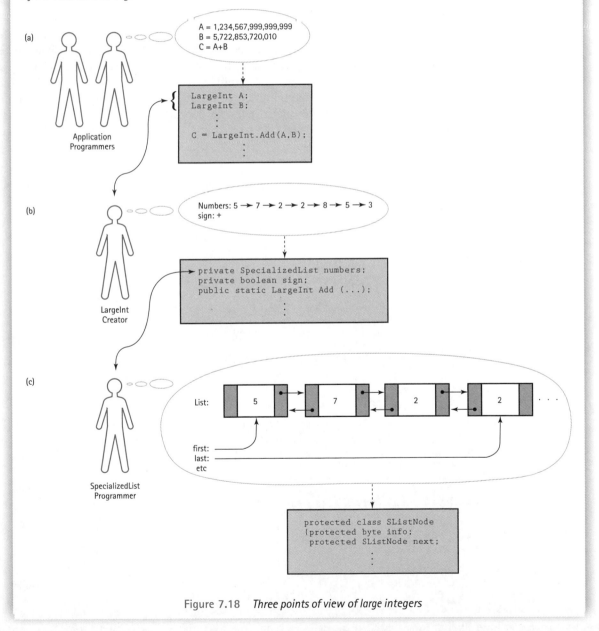

Figure 7.18   *Three points of view of large integers*

on large integers, we must also be able to access the digits from right to left. We conclude that we should use a list that supports both forward and backward iterations. This is beginning to sound familiar! At last we can appreciate the reasoning behind the specification of the SpecializedList class from Section 7.5.

The LargeInt Class

Now we can concentrate on the rest of the definition of the large integer class. In addition to digits, integers have a sign, which indicates whether they are positive or negative. We represent the sign of a large integer with a boolean instance variable sign. Furthermore, we define two boolean constants, PLUS = true and MINUS = false, to use with sign.

Here is the first approximation of the beginning of the class LargeInt. It includes the instance variables, two constructors, and the three methods setNegative (to make a large integer negative), addDigit (to build a large integer digit by digit), and toString (to provide a string representation of a large integer, complete with commas separating every three digits). We place it in the package ch07.largeInts. Our new class uses the SpecializedList class, so it must import the ch07.byteLists package.

```java
//------------------------------------------------------------------------------
// LargeInt.java            by Dale/Joyce/Weems            Chapter 7
//
// Provides a Large Integer ADT. Large integers can consist of any number
// of digits, plus a sign. Supports an add and a subtract operation.
//------------------------------------------------------------------------------
package ch07.largeInts;

import ch07.byteLists.*;

public class LargeInt
{
  private SpecializedList numbers;    // Holds digits

  // Constants for sign variable
  private static final boolean PLUS = true;
  private static final boolean MINUS = false;

  private boolean sign;

  public LargeInt()
  // Instantiates an "empty" large integer.
  {
    numbers = new SpecializedList();
    sign = PLUS;
  }
```

```java
public LargeInt(String intString)
// Precondition: intString contains a well-formatted integer
//
// Instantiates a large integer as indicated by intString
{
  numbers = new SpecializedList();
  sign = PLUS;

  int firstDigitPosition;        // Position of first digit in intString
  int lastDigitPosition;         // Position of last digit in intString

  // Used to translate character to byte
  char digitChar;
  int digitInt;
  byte digitByte;

  firstDigitPosition = 0;
  if (intString.charAt(0) == '+')   //  Skip leading plus sign
    firstDigitPosition = 1;
  else
  if (intString.charAt(0) == '-')   // Handle leading minus sign
  {
    firstDigitPosition = 1;
    sign = MINUS;
  }

  lastDigitPosition = intString.length() - 1;

  for (int count = firstDigitPosition; count <= lastDigitPosition; count++)
  {
    digitChar = intString.charAt(count);
    digitInt = Character.digit(digitChar, 10);
    digitByte = (byte)digitInt;
    addDigit(digitByte);
  }
}

public void setNegative()
{
  sign = MINUS;
}

public void addDigit(byte digit)
{
  numbers.addEnd(digit);
}
```

```
public String toString()
{
  String largeIntString;
  if (sign == PLUS)
    largeIntString = "+";
  else
    largeIntString = "-";

  int length;
  length = numbers.size();
  numbers.resetForward();
  for (int count = length; count >= 1; count--)
  {
    largeIntString = largeIntString + numbers.getNextElement();
    if (((((count - 1) % 3) == 0) && (count != 1))
      largeIntString = largeIntString + ",";
  }
  return(largeIntString);
}
```

Addition and Subtraction

Do you recall when you learned about addition of integers? Remember how special rules applied depending on what the signs of the operands were and which operand had the larger absolute value? For example, to perform the addition (−312) + (+200), what steps would you take? Let's see: The numbers have unlike signs, so we subtract the smaller absolute value (200) from the larger absolute value (312), giving us 112, and use the sign of the larger absolute value (−), giving the final result of (−112). Try a few more additions:

$$(+200) + (+100) = ?$$

$$(-300) + (-134) = ?$$

$$(+34) + (-62) = ?$$

$$(-34) + (+62) = ?$$

Did you get the respective correct answers (+300, −434, −28, +28)?

Did you notice anything about the actual arithmetic operations that you had to perform to calculate the results of the summations listed above? You performed only two kinds of operations: adding two positive numbers and subtracting a smaller positive number from a larger positive number. That's it. In combination with rules about how to handle signs, these operations allow you to do all of your sums.

Helper Methods

In programming, as in mathematics, we also like to reuse common operations. Therefore, to support the addition operation, we first define a few helper operations. These base operations should apply to the absolute values of our numbers, which means we can ignore the `sign` for now. Which common operations do we need? Based on the preceding discussion, we need to be able to add together two lists of digits, and to subtract a smaller list from a larger list. That means we also have to be able to identify which of two lists of digits is larger. Thus we need three operations, which we call `addLists`, `subtractLists`, and `greaterList`.

Let's begin with `greaterList`. We pass `greaterList` two `SpecializedList` arguments; it returns `true` if the first argument represents a larger number than the second argument, and `false` otherwise. When comparing strings, we compare pairs of characters in corresponding positions from left to right. The first characters that do not match determine which number is greater. When comparing positive numbers, we have to compare the numbers digit by digit only if they are the same length. We first compare the lengths; if they are not the same, we return the appropriate result. If the number of digits is the same, we compare the digits from left to right. In the code, we originally set a `boolean` variable `greater` to `false`, and we change this setting if we discover that the first number is larger than the second number. In the end, we return the `boolean` value of `greater`.

```
private static boolean greaterList(SpecializedList first,
                                   SpecializedList second)

// Precondition: no leading zeros
//
// Returns true if first represents a larger number than second:
// otherwise returns false.
{
  boolean greater = false;
  if (first.size() > second.size())
    greater = true;
  else
  if (first.size() < second.size())
    greater = false;
  else
  {
    byte digitFirst;
    byte digitSecond;
    first.resetForward();
    second.resetForward();
```

```
    // Set up loop
    int length = first.size();
    boolean keepChecking = true;
    int count = 1;

    while ((count <= length) && (keepChecking))
    {
      digitFirst = first.getNextElement();
      digitSecond = second.getNextElement();
      if (digitFirst > digitSecond)
      {
        greater = true;
        keepChecking = false;
      }
      else
      if (digitFirst < digitSecond)
      {
        greater = false;
        keepChecking = false;
      }
      count++;
    }
  }
  return greater;
}
```

If we exit the *while* loop without finding a difference, the numbers are equal and we return the original value of `greater`, which is `false` (because `first` is not greater than `second`). Because we blindly look at the lengths of the lists, we must assume that the numbers do not include leading zeros (for example, the method would report that 005 > 14). We make the `greaterList` method private: Helper methods are not intended for use by the client programmer; they are intended for use only within the `LargeInt` class itself.

Let's look at `addLists` next. We pass `addLists` its two operands as `SpecializedList` parameters, and the method returns a new `SpecializedList` as the result. The processing for `addLists` can be simplified if we assume that the first argument is larger than (or equal to) the second argument. We already have access to a `greaterList` method, so we make this assumption.

We begin by adding the two least significant digits (the units position). Next, we add the digits in the tens position (if present) plus the carry from the sum of the least significant digits (if any). This process continues until we finish with the digits of the smaller operand. For the remaining digits of the larger operand, we may need to propagate a carry, but we do not have to add digits from the smaller operand. Finally, if a carry value is left over, we create a new most significant location and place it there. We use integer division and modulus operators to determine the carry value and the value to insert into the result. The algorithm follows:

---

addLists (SpecializedList larger, SpecializedList smaller) returns SpecializedList

Set result to new SpecializedList();
Set carry to 0;
larger.resetBackward( );
smaller.resetBackward( );

for the length of the smaller list
  Set digit1 to larger.getPriorElement( );
  Set digit2 to smaller.getPriorElement( );
  Set temp to digit1 + digit2 + carry
  Set carry to temp/10
  result.addFront(temp % 10)
Finish up digits in larger, adding carries if necessary
if (carry != 0))
  result.addFront(carry)
return result

Apply the algorithm to the following examples to convince yourself that it works. The code follows.

322	388	399	999	3	1	988	0
44	108	1	11	44	99	100	0
366	496	400	1010	47	100	1088	0

```
private static SpecializedList addLists(SpecializedList larger,
                                        SpecializedList smaller)
// Precondition: larger >= smaller
//
// Returns a specialized list that is a byte-by-byte sum of the two
// argument lists
{
  byte digit1;
  byte digit2;
  byte temp;
  byte carry = 0;
```

```
int largerLength = larger.size();
int smallerLength = smaller.size();
int lengthDiff;

SpecializedList result = new SpecializedList();

larger.resetBackward();
smaller.resetBackward();

// Process both lists while both have digits
for (int count = 1; count <= smallerLength; count++)
{
  digit1 = larger.getPriorElement();
  digit2 = smaller.getPriorElement();
  temp = (byte)(digit1 + digit2 + carry);
  carry = (byte)(temp / 10);
  result.addFront((byte)(temp % 10));
}

// Finish processing of leftover digits
lengthDiff = (largerLength - smallerLength);
for (int count = 1; count <= lengthDiff; count++)
{
  digit1 = larger.getPriorElement();
  temp = (byte)(digit1 + carry);
  carry = (byte)(temp / 10);
  result.addFront((byte)(temp % 10));
}
if (carry != 0)
  result.addFront((byte)carry);

return result;
}
```

Now let's examine subtraction. Remember that for our helper method `subtractLists` we are handling only the simplest case: Both integers are positive, and the smaller one is subtracted from the larger one. As with `addLists`, we accept two `SpecializedList` parameters, the first being larger than the second, and we return a new `SpecializedList`.

We begin with the pair of digits in the units position. Let's call the digit in the larger argument `digit1` and the digit in the smaller argument `digit2`. If `digit2` is less than `digit1`, we subtract and insert the resulting digit at the front of the result. If `digit2` is greater than `digit1`, we borrow 10 and subtract. Then we access the digits in the tens position. If we have borrowed, we subtract 1 from the new `larger` and proceed as before. Because we have limited our problem to the case where `larger` is larger than `smaller`, both either run out of digits together or `larger` still contains digits when `smaller` has been

processed. This constraint guarantees that borrowing does not extend beyond the most significant digit of `larger`. See if you can follow the algorithm we just described in the code.

```
private static SpecializedList subtractLists(SpecializedList larger,
                                             SpecializedList smaller)
// Precondition: larger >= smaller
//
// Returns a specialized list that is the difference of the two argument lists
{
  byte digit1;
  byte digit2;
  byte temp;
  boolean borrow = false;

  int largerLength = larger.size();
  int smallerLength = smaller.size();
  int lengthDiff;

  SpecializedList result = new SpecializedList();

  larger.resetBackward();
  smaller.resetBackward();

  // Process both lists while both have digits.
  for (int count = 1; count <= smallerLength; count++)
  {
    digit1 = larger.getPriorElement();
    if (borrow)
    {
      if (digit1 != 0)
      {
        digit1 = (byte)(digit1 - 1);
        borrow = false;
      }
      else
      {
        digit1 = 9;
        borrow = true;
      }
    }

    digit2 = smaller.getPriorElement();

    if (digit2 <= digit1)
      result.addFront((byte)(digit1 - digit2));
```

```
    else
    {
      borrow = true;
      result.addFront((byte)(digit1 + 10 - digit2));
    }
  }


  // Finish processing of leftover digits
  lengthDiff = (largerLength - smallerLength);
  for (int count = 1; count <= lengthDiff; count++)
  {
    digit1 = larger.getPriorElement();
    if (borrow)
    {
      if (digit1 != 0)
      {
        digit1 = (byte)(digit1 - 1);
        borrow = false;
      }
      else
      {
        digit1 = 9;
        borrow = true;
      }
    }
    result.addFront(digit1);
  }

  return result;
}
```

Addition

Now that we have finished the helper methods, we can turn our attention to the public methods provided to clients of the `LargeInt` class. First, let's look at addition. Here are the rules for addition you learned when studying arithmetic:

Addition Rules

1. If both operands are positive, add the absolute values and make the result positive.
2. If both operands are negative, add the absolute values and make the result negative.
3. If one operand is negative and one operand is positive, subtract the smaller absolute value from the larger absolute value and give the result the sign of the larger absolute value.

We use these rules to help us design our add method. We can combine the first two rules as follows: "If the operands have the same sign, add the absolute values and make the sign of the result the same as the sign of the operands." Our code uses the appropriate helper method to generate the new list of digits and then sets the sign based on the rules. Remember that to use our helper methods we pass them the required arguments in the correct order (larger first). Here is the code for add:

```
public static LargeInt add(LargeInt first, LargeInt second)
// Returns a LargeInt that is the sum of the two argument LargeInts
{
  LargeInt sum = new LargeInt();

  if (first.sign == second.sign)
  {
    if (greaterList(first.numbers, second.numbers))
      sum.numbers = addLists(first.numbers, second.numbers);
    else
      sum.numbers = addLists(second.numbers, first.numbers);
    sum.sign = first.sign;
  }
  else    // Signs are different
  {
    if (greaterList(first.numbers, second.numbers))
    {
      sum.numbers = subtractLists(first.numbers, second.numbers);
      sum.sign = first.sign;
    }
    else
    {
      sum.numbers = subtractLists(second.numbers, first.numbers);
      sum.sign = second.sign;
    }
  }

  return sum;
}
```

The add method accepts two LargeInt objects and returns a new LargeInt object equal to their sum. Because it is passed both operands as parameters and returns the result explicitly, it is defined as a static method, which is invoked through the class, rather than through an object. For example, the code

```
LargeInt LI1 = new LargeInt();
LargeInt LI2 = new LargeInt();
LargeInt LI3;
```

```
        LI1.addDigit((byte)9);
        LI1.addDigit((byte)9);
        LI1.addDigit((byte)9);

        LI2.addDigit((byte)9);
        LI2.addDigit((byte)8);
        LI2.addDigit((byte)7);

        LI3 = LargeInt.add(LI1, LI2);

        System.out.println("LI3 is " + LI3);
```

would result in the output of the string "LI3 is +1986."

Subtraction

Remember how subtraction seemed harder than addition when you were learning arithmetic? Not anymore. We need to use only one subtraction rule: "Change the sign of the subtrahend, and add." We do have to be careful about how we "change the sign of the subtrahend," because we do not want to change the sign of the actual argument passed to subtract—that would produce an unwanted side effect of our method. Therefore, we create a new LargeInt object, make it a copy of the second parameter, invert its sign, and then invoke add:

```
public static LargeInt subtract(LargeInt first, LargeInt second)
// Returns a LargeInt that is the difference of the two argument LargeInts
{
  LargeInt diff = new LargeInt();

  // Create an inverse of second
  LargeInt negSecond = new LargeInt();
  negSecond.sign = !second.sign;
  second.numbers.resetForward();
  int length = second.numbers.size();
  for (int count = 1; count <= length; count++)
    negSecond.numbers.addEnd(second.numbers.getNextElement());

  // Add first to inverse of second
  diff = add(first, negSecond);

  return diff;
}
```

Test Plan

Each `LargeInt` operation must be unit tested. We should choose test data that represent all the varieties of possible input. This set of input would involve varying combinations of signs and relative relationships between the absolute values of operands. The examples used in the discussion can serve as test data for those operations. Other test cases should also be included, such as cases in which one or both of the operands are zero, or the expected result is zero. We can use the application developed next as a test driver.

The LargeIntApp Program

The `LargeIntApp` program allows the user to enter two large integers, performs the addition and subtraction of the two integers, and reports the results. Study the code below. You should be able to identify the statements that declare, instantiate and initialize, transform, and observe large integers.

```
//---------------------------------------------------------------
// LargeIntApp.java          by Dale/Joyce/Weems          Chapter 7
//
// Allows user to add or subtract large integers.
//---------------------------------------------------------------

import java.util.Scanner;
import ch07.largeInts.LargeInt;

public class LargeIntApp
{
  public static void main(String[] args)
  {
    Scanner conIn = new Scanner(System.in);

    LargeInt first;
    LargeInt second;

    String intString;
    String more = null;     // used to stop or continue processing

    do
    {
      // Get large integers.
      System.out.println("Enter the first large integer: ");
      intString = conIn.nextLine();
      first = new LargeInt(intString);
```

```
System.out.println("Enter the second large integer: ");
intString = conIn.nextLine();
second = new LargeInt(intString);
System.out.println();

// Perform and report the addition and subtraction.
System.out.print("First number:   ");
System.out.println(first);
System.out.print("Second number: ");
System.out.println(second);
System.out.print("Sum:            ");
System.out.println(LargeInt.add(first,second));
System.out.print("Difference:     ");
System.out.println(LargeInt.subtract(first,second));

// Determine if there is more to process.
System.out.println();
System.out.print("Process another pair of numbers? (Y=Yes): ");
more = conIn.nextLine();
System.out.println();

        }
    while (more.equalsIgnoreCase("y"));
  }
}
```

Here is the result of a sample run of the program:

Enter the first large integer:
1546366374847374837498847777777777777777777

Enter the second large integer:
4536748465999347474948722222222222222223

First number:	+15,463,663,748,473,748,374,988,477,777,777,777,777,777
Second number:	+4,536,748,465,999,347,474,948,722,222,222,222,222,223
Sum:	+20,000,412,214,473,095,849,937,200,000,000,000,000,000
Difference:	+10,926,915,282,474,400,900,039,755,555,555,555,555,554

Process another pair of numbers? (Y=Yes): N

You are encouraged to try the program out for yourself. If you do, you may discover a few problem situations. These situations form the basis for some end-of-chapter exercises.

The GUI Approach: A Large Integer Calculator

The `LargeInt` class can also be used as the basis for an interactive large integer calculator. The interested reader can find the code for this calculator on this book's website. Here are some screenshots, to give you a feeling for the application.

The user first sees this screen:

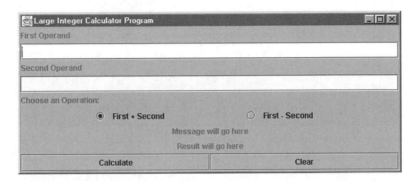

Here is the result of entering two operands, choosing addition, and clicking Calculate:

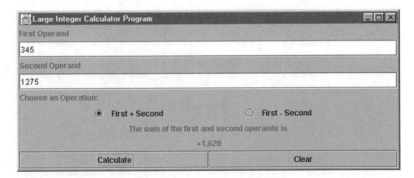

How about subtraction?

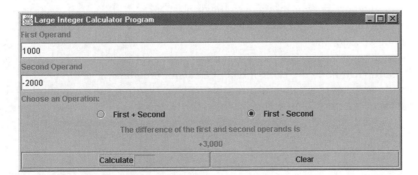

Wait a second, is that answer correct? Of course . . . remember that 1000 − (−2000) = 1000 + 2000. Let's look at an example using really big integers, which is the purpose of the Large Integer ADT:

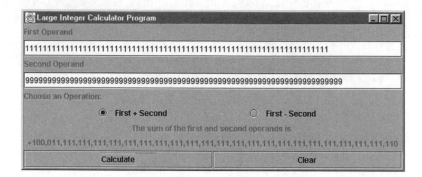

Exercises

1. The Large Integer Calculator program does not "catch" ill-formatted input the way that the Postfix Expression Evaluator program did. For example, consider the following screenshot:

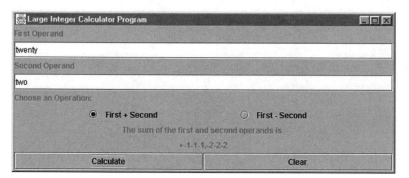

Fix the program so that it is more robust, and so that in situations such as that shown above it writes an appropriate error message to the display.

2. Consider the multiplication of large integers.
   a. Describe an algorithm.
   b. Implement a `multiply` method for the `LargeInt` class.
   c. Add multiplication to the Large Integer Calculator program.

3. Design and implement your own GUI for this problem. Write a short explanation about why your interface is better than the one shown in the textbook.

Summary

This chapter extended the idea of linking the elements in a list to include lists with header and trailer nodes, circular lists, and doubly linked lists. In addition to using dynamically allocated nodes to implement a linked structure, we looked at a technique for implementing linked structures in an array of nodes. With this technique, the links are not references into the free store but rather indexes into the array of nodes. This type of linking is used extensively in systems software.

The case study at the end of the chapter designed a Large Integer ADT, for which the number of digits is bounded only by the size of memory. The Large Integer ADT required a specialized list for its implementation; none of the lists developed so far provided the needed functionality. Thus we created a new class SpecializedList. This case study provided a good example of how one ADT can be implemented with the aid of another ADT, emphasizing the importance of viewing systems as a hierarchy of abstractions.

Exercises

7.1   Circular Linked Lists

1. Describe the differences, if any, between Chapter 6's RefUnsortedList and Chapter 7's CRefUnsortedList versions of the following methods. Also explain the reasons for the differences.

   a. The constructors

   b. find

   c. size

   d. contains

   e. remove

   f. toString

   g. reset

   h. getNext

2. Write a public method printReverse that prints the elements of a CRefUnsortedList object in reverse order. For instance, for the list X Y Z, list.printReverse() would output Z Y X. Assume that the list elements all have an associated toString method. You may use as a precondition that the list is not empty.

3. Using the same approach we used for the unsorted circular list, create a sorted circular list class called CRefSortedList. Be sure to test your final result.

4. Suppose we define an operation on a sorted list called inBetween that accepts an element as a parameter and returns true if the element is "in between" the smallest and largest list elements. That is, based on the compareTo method defined for

list elements, the element is larger than the smallest list element and smaller than the largest list element. Otherwise, the method returns `false` (even if the element "matches" the smallest or largest element).

a. Design and code `inBetween` as client code, using operations of the `ArraySortedList` class (the array-based sorted list class from Chapter 6).

b. Design and code `inBetween` as a public method of the `ArraySortedList` class.

c. Design and code `inBetween` as a public method of the `RefSortedList` class (from Chapter 6).

d. Design and code `inBetween` as a public method of the `CRefSortedList` class (from Exercise 3).

e. State the Big-O complexity of each of your implementations in terms of *N*, the size of the list.

5. We implemented the `CRefUnsortedList` by maintaining a single reference, to the last element of the list. Suppose we changed our approach so that we maintain two references into the linked list, one to the first list element and one to the last list element.

a. Would the new approach necessitate a change in the class constructor? If so, describe the change.

b. Would the new approach necessitate a change in the `getNext` method? If so, describe the change.

c. Would the new approach necessitate a change in the `find` method? If so, describe the change.

d. Would the new approach necessitate a change in the `add` method? If so, describe the change.

6. At the end of the Section 7.1 it was suggested that many of the claimed benefits of circular linked lists could also be obtained by simply augmenting our linear linked list class (from Chapter 6) with a private variable that references the last element of the list. Outline the changes to the public methods of the `RefSortedList` class that should be made to accommodate such a change. For each change, identify whether the change is necessary to support the new implementation or whether it is an improvement made possible by the new implementation.

7.2 Doubly Linked Lists

7. We discussed the add operation for a doubly linked list and showed that the correct order for the reference changes is

```
newNode.setBack(location.getBack());
newNode.setLink(location);
location.getBack().setLink(newNode);
location.setBack(newNode);
```

Describe the ramifications of making the reference changes in a different order as shown here:

a. ```
location.setBack(newNode);
newNode.setBack(location.getBack());
newNode.setLink(location);
location.getBack().setLink(newNode);
```

b. ```
newNode.setBack(location.getBack());
location.getBack().setLink(newNode);
newNode.setLink(location);
location.setBack(newNode);
```

c. ```
newNode.setLink(location);
newNode.setBack(location.getBack());
location.getBack().setLink(newNode);
location.setBack(newNode);
```

8. Consider the `remove` operation for a doubly linked list.

   a. For the situation depicted in Figure 7.8, show the correct order of reference changes so that the node at `location` is removed from the list.

   b. Design and create the code for `remove`. Remember to handle all of the special cases.

9. Using the circular doubly linked list below, give the expression corresponding to each of the following descriptions.

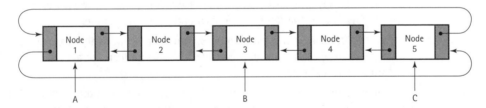

For example, the expression for the `info` value of node 1, referenced from reference A, would be `A.getInfo()`.

a. The `info` value of node 1, referenced from reference C

b. The `info` value of node 2, referenced from reference B

c. The `link` value of node 2, referenced from reference A

d. The `link` value of node 4, referenced from reference C

e. Node 1, referenced from reference B

f. The `back` value of node 4, referenced from reference C

g. The `back` value of node 1, referenced from reference A

10. Design, implement, and test a doubly linked list ADT, using `DLLNode` objects as the nodes. In addition to our standard list operations, your class should provide
```

for backward iteration through the list. To support this operation, it should export a `resetBack` method and a `getPrevious` method. To facilitate this, you may want to include an instance variable `last` that always references the last element on the list.

7.3   Linked Lists with Headers and Trailers

11. Dummy nodes are used to simplify list processing by eliminating some "special cases."

    a. Which special case is eliminated by a header node in a reference-based linked list?

    b. Which special case is eliminated by a trailer node in a reference-based linked list?

    c. Would dummy nodes be useful in implementing a linked stack? That is, would their use eliminate a special case?

    d. Would dummy nodes be useful in implementing a linked queue with a reference to both the header and the trailer elements?

    e. Would dummy nodes be useful in implementing a circular linked queue?

12. Of the three variations of linked lists (circular, with header and trailer nodes, and doubly linked), which would be most appropriate for each of the following applications?

    a. You must search a list for a key and return the keys of the two elements that come before it and the keys of the two elements that come after it.

    b. A text file contains integer elements, one per line, sorted from smallest to largest. You must read the values from the file and create a sorted linked list containing the values.

    c. You need a list that is short and frequently becomes empty. You want the optimal implementation for adding an element into the empty list and removing the last element from the list.

13. John and Mary are programmers for the local school district. One morning John commented to Mary about the funny last name the new family in the district had: "Have you ever heard of a family named Zzuan?" Mary replied, "Uh, oh; we have some work to do. Let's get going." Can you explain Mary's response?

7.4   A Linked List as an Array of Nodes

14. What is the Big-O complexity for initializing the free list in the array-based linked implementation? For the methods `getNode` and `freeNode`?

15. Use the linked lists contained in the array pictured in Figure 7.13 to answer these questions:

    a. Which elements are in the list pointed to by `list1`?

    b. Which elements are in the list pointed to by `list2`?

c. Which array positions (indexes) are part of the free space list?

d. Draw a figure that represents the array after the removal of "Nell" from the first list.

e. Draw a figure that represents the array after the addition of "Anne" to the second list. Assume that before the addition that the array is as pictured in Figure 7.13.

16. An array of nodes is used to hold a doubly linked sorted list, with the `next` and `back` node values indicating the indexes of the linked nodes in each direction.

a. Show how the array would look after it was initialized to an empty state, with all the nodes linked into the free space list. (Free space nodes have to be linked in only one direction.)

nodes	.info	.next	.back
[0]			
[1]			
[2]			
[3]			
[4]			
[5]			

free
list

b. Draw a box-and-arrow picture of an abstract doubly linked list into which the following numbers are added into their proper places: 17, 4, 25.

c. Show how the array in part a would look after the following numbers are added into their proper places in the doubly linked list: 17, 4, 25.

nodes	.info	.next	.back
[0]			
[1]			
[2]			
[3]			
[4]			
[5]			

free
list

d. Show how the array in part c would look after 17 is removed from the doubly linked list.

nodes	.info	.next	.back
[0]			
[1]			
[2]			
[3]			
[4]			
[5]			

free
list

17. We developed code for the constructor and the `getNode`, `freeNode`, `isFull`, and `remove` methods of our `ArrayRefSortedList` class. Develop the code for the following methods:

a. `find`

b. `size`

c. `contains`

d. `get`

e. `toString`

f. `reset`

g. `getNext`

h. `add`

7.5 A Specialized List ADT

18. True or False? The `SpecializedList` class
    a. Uses the "by copy" approach with its elements.
    b. Implements the `ListInterface` interface.
    c. Keeps its data elements sorted.
    d. Allows duplicate elements.
    e. Throws an exception if an iteration "walks off" the end of the list.
    f. Can hold objects of any Java class.
    g. Has only O(1) operations, including its constructor.

19. Describe the difference between the `getPriorElement` method of the `Special-izedList` class and the proposed `getPreviousElement` method of the `DoublyLinkedList` class.

7.6 Case Study: Large Integers

20. Discuss the changes that would be necessary within the `LargeInt` class if more than one digit is stored per node.

21. The Large Integer Application does not "catch" ill-formatted input. For example, consider the following program run:

    Enter the first large integer:
    twenty

    Enter the second large integer:
    two

    First number: +-1-1-1,-1-1-1
    Second number: +-1-1-1
    Sum: +-1-1-1,-2-2-2
    Difference: +-1-1-1,000

    Process another pair of numbers? (Y=Yes): n

Fix the program so that it is more robust, and so that in situations such as that shown above it writes an appropriate error message to the display.

22. Consider the multiplication of large integers.

    a. Describe an algorithm.

    b. Implement a multiply method for the `LargeInt` class.

    c. Add multiplication to the Large Integer Application.

23. The private method `greaterList` of the `LargeInt` class assumes that its arguments have no leading zeros. When this assumption is violated, strange results can occur. Consider the following run of the Large Integer Application that claims $35 - 3$ is -968:

> Enter the first large integer:
> 35
>
> Enter the second large integer:
> 003
>
> First number: +35
> Second number: +003
> Sum: +038
> Difference: -968
>
> Process another pair of numbers? (Y=Yes): n

    a. Why do leading zeros cause a problem?

    b. Identify at least two approaches to correcting this problem.

    c. Describe the benefits and drawbacks of each of your identified approaches.

    d. Choose one of your approaches and implement the solution.

Binary Search Trees

Knowledge Goals

You should be able to
- define and use the following tree terminology:
  - binary tree
  - binary search tree
  - root
  - parent
  - child
  - ancestor
  - descendant
  - level
  - height
  - subtree
  - full
  - complete
- given a binary tree, identify the order the nodes would be visited for preorder, inorder, and postorder traversals
- define a binary search tree at the logical level
- describe an algorithm for balancing a binary search tree
- given a problem description, determine whether a binary search tree is an appropriate structure for solving the problem

Skill Goals

You should be able to
- show how a binary search tree would be structured after a series of insertions and removals
- implement the following binary search tree algorithms in Java:
  - finding an element
  - counting the number of nodes
  - adding an element
  - removing an element
  - retrieving an element
  - traversing a tree in preorder, inorder, and postorder
- discuss the Big-O efficiency of a given binary search tree operation
- use a binary search tree as a component of a problem solution
- show how a binary tree can be represented as an array, with implicit positional links between the elements

We have described some of the advantages of using a linear linked list to store sorted information. One drawback of using a linear linked list is the time it takes to search a long list. A sequential or linear search of (possibly) all the nodes in the entire list is an $O(N)$ operation. In Chapter 6, we saw how a binary search could find an element in a sorted list stored sequentially in an array. The binary search is an $O(\log_2 N)$ operation. It would be nice if we could use a binary search with a linked list, but there is no practical way to find the midpoint of a linked list of nodes. We can, however, reorganize the list's elements into a linked structure that is perfect for binary searching: the binary search tree. The binary search tree provides us with a data structure that retains the flexibility of a linked list while allowing quicker [$O(\log_2 N)$ in the average case] access to any node in the list.

This chapter introduces some basic tree vocabulary and then develops the algorithms and implementations of the operations needed to use a binary search tree. The case study uses a binary search tree to calculate the frequency of words in a text file.

8.1 Trees

Each node in a singly linked list may point to one other node: the one that follows it. Thus a singly linked list is a *linear* structure; each node in the list (except the last) has a unique successor. A tree is a nonlinear structure in which each node is capable of having multiple successor nodes, called *children*. Each of the children, being nodes in a tree, can also have multiple child nodes, and these children can in turn have many children, and so on, giving the tree its branching structure. The "beginning" of the tree is a unique starting node called the root.

> **Tree** A structure with a unique starting node (the root), in which each node is capable of having multiple child nodes, and in which a unique path exists from the root to every other node
>
> **Root** The top node of a tree structure; a node with no parent

Trees are useful for representing hierarchical relationships among data elements. Figure 8.1 shows three example trees. The first represents the chapters, sections, and subsections of this textbook; the second represents the hierarchical inheritance relationship among a set of Java classes, and the third represents a scientific classification of butterflies.

Trees are recursive structures. We can view any tree node as being the root of its own tree; such a tree is called a *subtree* of the original tree. For example, in Figure 8.1(a) the node labeled "1. Getting Organized" is the root of a subtree containing all of the Chapter 1 material. There is one more defining quality of a tree—a tree's subtrees are disjoint; that is, they do not share any nodes. Another way of expressing this property is to say that there is a unique path from the root of a tree to any other node of the tree. As a consequence, every node (except the root) has a unique parent. In the structure at the top of page 534, this rule is violated any way we look at it: The subtrees of A are not disjoint; there are two paths from the root to the node containing D; D has two parents. Therefore, this structure is not a tree.

(a) A textbook

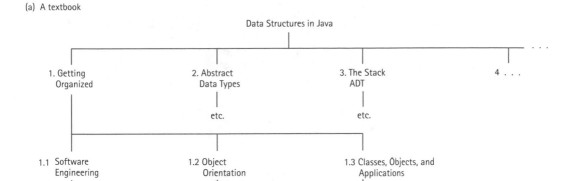

(b) Java classes

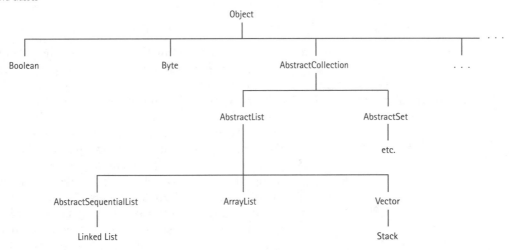

(c) Scientific classification of butterflies and moths

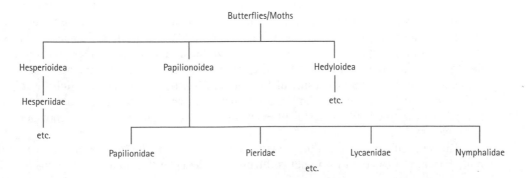

Figure 8.1 *Trees model hierarchical relationships*

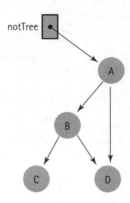

Trees are useful structures. In this chapter, we concentrate on a particular form of tree: the binary tree. In fact, we concentrate on a particular type of binary tree: the binary search tree.

Binary Trees

A binary tree is a tree where each node is capable of having two children. Figure 8.2 depicts such a binary tree. The root node of this binary tree contains the value A. Each node in the tree may have zero, one, or two children. The node to the left of a node, if it exists, is called its *left child*. For instance, the left child of the root node contains the value B. The node to the right of a node, if it exists, is its *right child*. The right child of the root node contains the value C. The root node is the parent of the nodes containing B and C. If a node in the tree has no children, it is called a leaf. For instance, the nodes containing G, H, E, I, and J are leaf nodes.

In Figure 8.2, each of the root node's children is itself the root of a smaller binary tree, or subtree. The root node's left child, containing B, is the root of its *left subtree*, whereas the right child, containing C, is the root of its *right subtree*. In fact, any node in the tree can be considered the root node of a binary subtree.

> **Binary tree**   A tree in which each node is capable of having two child nodes: a left child node and a right child node
>
> **Leaf**   A tree node that has no children
>
> **Descendant**   A child of a node, or a child of a descendant
>
> **Ancestor**   A parent of a node, or a parent of an ancestor

The subtree whose root node has the value B also includes the nodes with values D, G, H, and E. These nodes are the descendants of the node containing B. The descendants of the node containing C are the nodes with the values F, I, and J. The leaf nodes have no descendants. A node is the ancestor of another node if it is the parent of the node, or the parent of some other ancestor of that node. (Yes, this is a recursive definition.) The ancestors of the node with the value G are the nodes containing D, B, and A. Obviously, the root of the tree is the ancestor of every other node in the tree, but the root node has no ancestors itself.

The level of a node refers to its distance from the root. In Figure 8.2, the level of the node containing A (the root node) is 0 (zero), the level of the nodes containing B and C

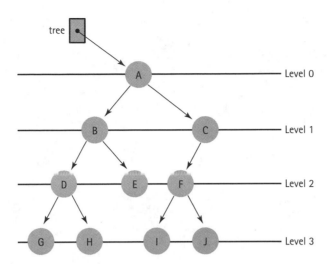

Figure 8.2   *A binary tree*

is 1, the level of the nodes containing D, E, and F is 2, and the level of the nodes containing G, H, I, and J is 3.

The maximum level in a tree determines its height. The maximum number of nodes at any level N is 2^N. Often, however, levels do not contain the maximum number of nodes. For instance, in Figure 8.2, level 2 could contain four nodes, but because the node containing C in level 1 has only one child, level 2 contains only three nodes. Level 3, which could contain eight nodes, has only four. We could make many differently shaped binary trees out of the 10 nodes in this tree. A few variations are illustrated in Figure 8.3. It is easy to see that the maximum number of levels in a binary tree with N nodes is N (counting level 0 as one of the levels). But what is the minimum number of levels? If we fill the tree by giving every node in each level two children until we run out of nodes, the tree has $\log_2 N + 1$ levels (Figure 8.3a). Demonstrate this fact to yourself by drawing "full" trees with 8 [$\log_2(8) = 3$] and 16 [$\log_2(16) = 4$] nodes. What if there are 7, 12, or 18 nodes?

The height of a tree is the critical factor in determining how efficiently we can search for elements. Consider the maximum-height tree shown in Figure 8.3(c). If we begin searching at the root node and follow the references from one node to the next, accessing the node with the value J (the farthest from the root) is an $O(N)$ operation—no better than searching a linear list! Conversely, given the minimum-height tree depicted in Figure 8.3(a), to access the node containing J, we have to look at only three other nodes—the ones containing E, A, and G—before we find J. Thus, if the tree is of minimum height, its structure supports $O(\log_2 N)$ access to any element.

The arrangement of the values in the tree pictured in Figure 8.3(a), however, does not lend itself to quick searching. Suppose we want to find the value G. We begin searching at the root of the tree. This node contains E, not G, so we keep searching. But which of its children should we look at next, the right or the left? There is no special

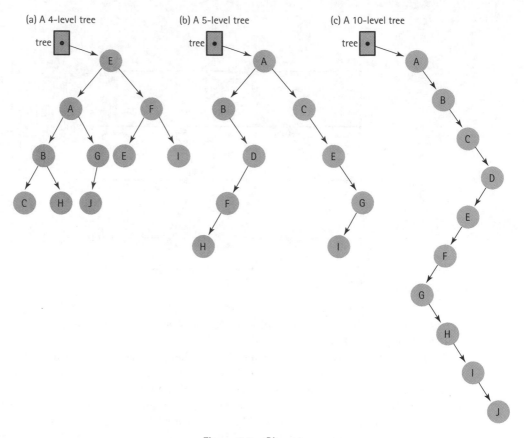

Figure 8.3 *Binary trees*

order to the nodes, so we have to check both subtrees. We could search the tree, level by level, until we come across the value we are searching for. But that is an O(N) search operation, which is no more efficient than searching a linear linked list!

Binary Search Trees

To support $O(\log_2 N)$ searching, we add a special property based on the relationship among the values of the elements in the binary tree. We put all of the nodes with values smaller than or equal to the value in the root into its left subtree, and all of the nodes with values larger than the value in the root into its right subtree. Figure 8.4 shows the nodes from Figure 8.3(a) rearranged to satisfy this property. The root node, which contains E, references two subtrees. The left subtree contains all values smaller than or equal to E and the right subtree contains all values larger than E.

When searching for the value G, we look first in the root node. G is larger than E, so we know that G must be in the root node's right subtree. The right child of the root

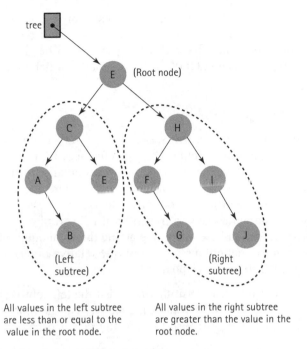

All values in the left subtree are less than or equal to the value in the root node.

All values in the right subtree are greater than the value in the root node.

Figure 8.4 *A binary tree*

node contains H. Now what? Do we go to the right or to the left? This subtree is also arranged according to the binary search property: The nodes with smaller or equal values are to the left and the nodes with larger values are to the right. The value of this node, H, is greater than G, so we search to its left. The left child of this node contains the value F, which is smaller than G, so we reapply the rule and move to the right. The node to the right contains G; we have found the node we were searching for.

A binary tree with this special property is called a binary search tree. As with any binary tree, it gets its branching structure by allowing each node to have a maximum of two child nodes. It gets its easy-to-search structure by maintaining the *binary search property*: The left child of any node (if one exists) is the root of a subtree that contains only values smaller than or equal to the node. The right child of any node (if one exists) is the root of a subtree that contains only values that are larger than the node.

> **Binary search tree** A binary tree in which the value in any node is greater than or equal to the value in its left child and any of its descendants (the nodes in the left subtree) and less than the value in its right child and any of its descendants (the nodes in the right subtree)

Four comparisons instead of a maximum ten doesn't sound like such a big deal, but as the number of elements in the structure increases, the difference becomes impressive. In the worst case—searching for the last node in a linear linked list—we must look at every node in the list; on average, we must search half of the list. If the list contains 1000 nodes, we must make 1000 comparisons to find the last node! If the 1000 nodes were arranged in a binary search tree of minimum height, we would never make more than 10 comparisons [$\log_2(1000) < 10$], no matter which node we were seeking!

Binary Tree Traversals

To traverse a linear linked list, we set a temporary reference to be equal to the beginning of the list and then follow the list references from one node to the other until we reach a node whose reference value is `null`. Similarly, to traverse a binary tree, we initialize our reference to the root of the tree. But where do we go from there—to the left or to the right? Do we visit[1] the root or the leaves first? The answer is "all of these." There are only two standard ways to traverse a list: forward and backward. In contrast, there are many ways to traverse a tree. We define three common ones in this subsection.

Our traversal definitions depend on the relative order in which we visit a root and its subtrees. We define three possibilities here:

- Preorder traversal: Visit the root, visit the left subtree, visit the right subtree
- Inorder traversal: Visit the left subtree, visit the root, visit the right subtree
- Postorder traversal: Visit the left subtree, visit the right subtree, visit the root

Preorder traversal   A systematic way of visiting all the nodes in a binary tree by visiting a node, then visiting the nodes in the left subtree of the node, and then visiting the nodes in the right subtree of the node

Inorder traversal   A systematic way of visiting all the nodes in a binary tree by visiting the nodes in the left subtree of a node, then visiting the node, and then visiting the nodes in the right subtree of the node

Postorder traversal   A systematic way of visiting all the nodes in a binary tree by visiting the nodes in the left subtree of a node, then visiting the nodes in the right subtree of the node, and then visiting the node

The name given to each traversal specifies where the root itself is processed in relation to its subtrees. Also notice that these definitions are recursive.

We can visualize each of these traversal orders by drawing a "loop" around a binary tree as shown in Figure 8.5. Before drawing the loop, extend the nodes of the tree that have fewer than two children with short lines so that every node has two "edges." Then draw the loop from the root of the tree, down the left subtree, and back up again, hugging the shape of the tree as you go. Each node of the tree is "touched" three times by the loop (the touches are numbered in Figure 8.5): once on the way down before the left subtree is reached; once after finishing the left subtree but before starting the right subtree; and once on the way up, after finishing the right subtree. To generate a preorder traversal, follow the loop and visit each node the first time it is touched (before visiting the left subtree). To generate an inorder traversal, follow the loop and visit each node the second time it is touched (in between

---

1. When we say "visit," we mean that the algorithm does whatever it needs to do with the values in the node—print them, sum certain values, or remove them, for example. For this section we assume that a visit means to print out the value of the node.

A binary tree

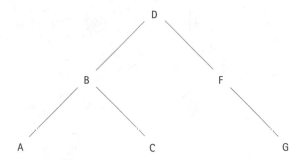

The extended tree

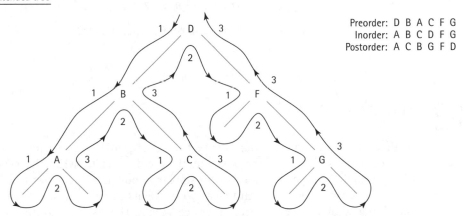

Preorder: D B A C F G
Inorder: A B C D F G
Postorder: A C B G F D

Figure 8.5   *Visualizing binary tree traversals*

visiting the two subtrees). To generate a postorder traversal, follow the loop and visit each node the third time it is touched (after visiting the right subtree). Use this method on the tree in Figure 8.6 and see whether you agree with the listed traversal orders.

You may have noticed that an inorder traversal of a binary search tree visits the nodes in order from the smallest to the largest. Obviously, this type of traversal would be useful when we need to access the elements in ascending key order—for example, to print a sorted list of the elements. There are also useful applications of the other traversal orders. For example, the preorder and postorder traversals can be used to translate infix arithmetic expressions into their prefix and postfix counterparts.

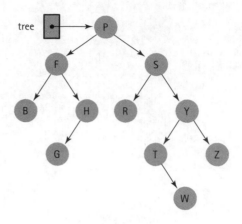

```
Inorder:    B F G H P R S T W Y Z
Preorder:   P F B H G S R Y T W Z
Postorder:  B G H F R W T Z Y S P
```

Figure 8.6   *Three binary tree traversals*

8.2 The Logical Level

In this section, we specify our Binary Search Tree ADT. As we have done for stacks, queues, and lists, we use the Java interface construct to write the specification. Our binary search tree specification is very similar to our sorted list specification. In fact, we could just view a binary search tree as an implementation of a sorted list and not bother specifying a binary search tree interface at all. This is not surprising, because both sorted lists and binary search trees are typically used to store and retrieve sorted data. Of course, the binary search tree can also be treated as a separate ADT. It will be more instructive to see how it can be viewed from the logical, implementation, and application levels, so we'll take the latter approach.

Before proceeding with the specification, we have to decide which kinds of elements we will store in our trees.

Tree Elements

To support a binary search tree we need to be able to tell when one object is less than, equal to, or greater than another object. Recall from Chapter 6 that the Java library provides an interface, called `Comparable`, that can be used to ensure that a class provides this functionality. As we saw there, a class that implements `Comparable` just needs to supply a `compareTo` method.

We will use the `compareTo` method when working with the elements of our binary search trees. To ensure that all such objects support the `compareTo` operation, we require that binary search tree elements be objects of a class that implements the `Comparable` interface. In other words, they must be `Comparable` objects. When we talk about "comparing" the key values of elements of the tree, we really mean using the `compareTo` method to compare the objects. In effect, the `compareTo` method defines the key values used to compare the objects.

As we saw in Chapter 6, the Java library's `Comparable` interface supports generics. This allows us to indicate that our tree elements must be of type `<T extends Comparable<T>>`, ensuring that only objects that can be compared to each other can be inserted into out trees.

The Binary Search Tree Specification

We now know that our binary search trees hold `Comparable` elements. Do we have any other decisions to make before we can formally specify our Binary Search Tree ADT?

First, we must decide whether to allow duplicate elements in our trees. In one sense, we have already made this decision. Our definition of a binary search tree allows duplicate elements. Do you see why? This definition allows the value of a node to be greater than or *equal to* the values in its left subtree. Therefore, two tree nodes can hold the same value, as long as one is not in the right subtree of the other.

Of course, we could change the definition of a binary search tree to state that the key value of a node may only be *greater than* the key values of the nodes in its left subtree. But we don't; instead, we assume that our trees can have duplicate elements. This decision is consistent with our list approach.

As with our lists, we specify that our binary search trees are unbounded and may not hold `null` elements.

In Section 8.1, we defined three types of binary tree traversals. Which one should we use to iterate through our tree? Why not support all three? We define the `reset` and `getNext` operations with a parameter to indicate which of the three traversals to use. As we did with our specialized list in Chapter 7, we allow more than one traversal to be in progress at a time. Within our interface definition we define three constants for use as parameters to `reset` and `getNext`:

```
public static final int INORDER = 1;
public static final int PREORDER = 2;
public static final int POSTORDER = 3;
```

These constants are available to any class that implements the interface. Their use is demonstrated in the next section.

We make one other modification to the definition of the `reset` operation, as compared to the `reset` operation for lists. The binary search tree's `reset` method, in addition to setting up an iteration, returns the current number of nodes in the tree. We explain the reason for this change in the subsection that discusses the implementation of the iteration methods.

Here is the specification of our Binary Search Tree ADT:

```
//---------------------------------------------------------------------------
// BSTInterface.java            by Dale/Joyce/Weems            Chapter 8
//
// Interface for a class that implements a binary search tree (BST).
//
// The trees are unbounded and allow duplicate elements, but do not allow null
// elements. As a general precondition, null elements are not passed as
// arguments to any of the methods.
//
// The tree supports iteration through its elements in INORDER, PREORDER,
// and POSTORDER.
//---------------------------------------------------------------------------

package ch08.trees;

public interface BSTInterface<T extends Comparable<T>>
{
  // used to specify traversal order
  static final int INORDER = 1;
  static final int PREORDER = 2;
  static final int POSTORDER = 3;

  boolean isEmpty();
  // Returns true if this BST is empty; otherwise, returns false.

  int size();
  // Returns the number of elements on this BST.

  boolean contains (T element);
  // Returns true if this BST contains an element e such that
  // e.compareTo(element) == 0; otherwise, returns false.

  boolean remove (T element);
  // Removes an element e from this BST such that e.compareTo(element) == 0
  // and returns true; if no such element exists, returns false.

  T get(T element);
  // Returns an element e from this BST such that e.compareTo(element) == 0;
  // if no such element exists, returns null.
```

```
void add (T element);
// Adds element to this BST. The tree retains its BST property.

int reset(int orderType);
// Initializes current position for an iteration through this BST
// in orderType order. Returns current number of nodes in the BST.

T getNext (int orderType);
// Preconditions: The BST is not empty
//                The BST has been reset for orderType
//                The BST has not been modified since the most recent reset
//                The end of orderType iteration has not been reached
//
// Returns the element at the current position on this BST for orderType
// and advances the value of the current position based on the orderType.
}
```

8.3 The Application Level

As we have already pointed out, our Binary Search Tree ADT is very similar to our Sorted List ADT, from a functional point of view. A comparison of the BSTInterface listed in Section 8.2 to the ListInterface presented in Section 6.3 reveals only a few changes. The biggest difference is that we support three iteration paths through the tree rather than just one, as we do with the list.

Another important difference between our sorted lists and our binary search trees is in the efficiency of some of the operations; we highlight these differences later in this chapter. The similarity between our ADTs means that we can use the binary search tree in many of the same applications where we use lists.

For example, we used the Sorted List ADT in the golf score application in Section 6.5. Let's reimplement that application using a binary search tree. This example shows how a binary search tree client performs tree iteration. The parts of the application that have changed are <u>emphasized</u>. As you can see, there are very few changes.

```
//-------------------------------------------------------------------
// GolfApp2.java          by Dale/Joyce/Weems          Chapter 8
//
// Allows user to enter golfer name and score information.
// Displays information ordered by score.
//-------------------------------------------------------------------

import java.util.Scanner;
import ch08.trees.*;
```

```
import support.*;        // Golfer

public class GolfApp2
{
  public static void main(String[] args)
  {
    Scanner conIn = new Scanner(System.in);

    String name;           // golfer's name
    int score;             // golfer's score

    BSTInterface<Golfer> golfers = new BinarySearchTree<Golfer>();
    Golfer golfer;
    int numGolfers;

    String skip;  // Used to skip rest of input line after reading integer

    System.out.print("Golfer name (press Enter to end): ");
    name = conIn.nextLine();
    while (!name.equals(""))
    {
      System.out.print("Score: ");
      score = conIn.nextInt();
      skip = conIn.nextLine();

      golfer = new Golfer(name, score);
      golfers.add(golfer);

      System.out.print("Golfer name (press Enter to end): ");
      name = conIn.nextLine();
    }
    System.out.println();
    System.out.println("The final results are");

    numGolfers = golfers.reset(BinarySearchTree.INORDER);
    for (int count = 1; count <= numGolfers; count++)
    {
      System.out.println(golfers.getNext(BinarySearchTree.INORDER));
    }
  }
}
```

We use the constant INORDER as an argument to the reset and getNext methods. It is defined in the BSTInterface interface. We access this constant through the BinarySearchTree class, which implements the interface.

We make use of the new functionality of the `reset` operation. It tells us the number of elements in the tree, and we then use that value to control the number of iterations through the *for* loop.

A sample run of the program appears very similar to that shown in Chapter 6:

Golfer name (press Enter to end): Annika
Score: 72
Golfer name (press Enter to end): Grace
Score: 75
Golfer name (press Enter to end): Arnold
Score: 68
Golfer name (press Enter to end): Vijay
Score: 72
Golfer name (press Enter to end): Christie
Score: 70
Golfer name (press Enter to end):

The final results are
68: Arnold
70: Christie
72: Vijay
72: Annika
75: Grace

8.4 The Implementation Level: Basics

We represent a tree as a linked structure whose nodes are allocated dynamically. Before we go on, we need to decide exactly what a node of the tree is. In our earlier discussion of binary trees, we talked about `right` and `left` children. These children are the structural references in the tree; they hold the tree together. We also need a place to store the user's data in the node. We might as well continue to call it `info`. Figure 8.7 shows how we can visualize a node.

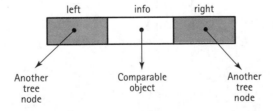

Figure 8.7 *Binary tree nodes*

Here is the definition of a `BSTNode` class that corresponds to the picture in Figure 8.7:

```
//----------------------------------------------------------------------------
// BSTNode.java              by Dale/Joyce/Weems             Chapter 8
//
// Implements Comparable nodes for a binary search tree.
//----------------------------------------------------------------------------

package support;

public class BSTNode<T extends Comparable<T>>
{
  // Used to hold references to BST nodes for the linked implementation
  protected T info;                   // The info in a BST node
  protected BSTNode left;             // A link to the left child node
  protected BSTNode right;            // A link to the right child node

  public BSTNode(T info)
  {
    this.info = info;
    left = null;
    right = null;
  }

  public void setInfo(T info)
  // Sets info of this BSTNode.
  {
    this.info = info;
  }

  public T getInfo()
  // Returns info of this BSTNode.
  {
    return info;
  }

  public void setLeft(BSTNode link)
  // Sets left link of this BSTNode.
  {
    left = link;
  }
```

```
  public void setRight(BSTNode link)
  // Sets right link of this BSTNode.
  {
    right = link;
  }

  public BSTNode getLeft()
  // Returns left link of this BSTNode.
  {
    return left;
  }

  public BSTNode getRight()
  // Returns right link of this BSTNode.
  {
    return right;
  }
}
```

We will call our implementation class `BinarySearchTree`. It implements the `BSTInterface`. The relationships among our binary search tree classes and interfaces are depicted in Figure 8.25 in this chapter's "Summary" section.

The instance variable `root` references the root node of the tree. It is set to `null` by the constructor. The beginning of the class definition follows:

```
//---------------------------------------------------------------------------
// BinarySearchTree.java          by Dale/Joyce/Weems           Chapter 8
//
// Defines all constructs for a reference-based BST
//---------------------------------------------------------------------------

package ch08.trees;

import ch05.queues.*;
import ch03.stacks.*;
import support.BSTNode;

public class BinarySearchTree<T extends Comparable<T>>
          implements BSTInterface<T>
{
  protected BSTNode root;        // reference to the root of this BST
```

```
boolean found;    // used by remove

// for traversals
protected LinkUnbndQueue<T> inOrderQueue;     // queue of info
protected LinkUnbndQueue<T> preOrderQueue;    // queue of info
protected LinkUnbndQueue<T> postOrderQueue;   // queue of info

public BinarySearchTree()
// Creates an empty BST object.
{
   root = null;
}
```

The class is part of the ch08.trees package. The reason for importing queues and stacks will become apparent as we develop the rest of the class. We call the variable that references the actual tree structure root, because it is a link to the root of the tree.

Next let's look at the simple observer method called isEmpty. We could make use of the size method: If it returns 0, isEmpty returns true; otherwise, it returns false. But the size method has to count the nodes on the tree each time it is called. This task takes at least O(N) steps, where N is the number of nodes (as we see in Section 8.5). Is there a more efficient way to determine whether the list is empty? Yes, just see whether the root of the tree is currently null. This approach takes only O(1) steps.

```
public boolean isEmpty()
// Returns true if this BST is empty; otherwise, returns false.
{
   return (root == null);
}
```

We next look at methods that are more complicated. We start with the size method and use it to investigate the differences between iterative and recursive approaches performing tree operations.

8.5 Iterative Versus Recursive Method Implementations

Binary search trees provide us with a good opportunity to compare iterative and recursive approaches to a problem. You may have noticed that trees are inherently recursive: Any node in a tree can be considered the root of a subtree. We even use recursive definitions when talking about properties of trees—for example, "A node is the *ancestor* of another node if it is the parent of the node, or the parent of some other *ancestor* of that node." Of course, the formal definition of a binary tree node, embodied in the class

`BSTNode`, is itself recursive. Thus recursive solutions will likely work well when we are dealing with trees. In this section we address that hypothesis.

First, we develop recursive and iterative implementations of the `size` method. Of course, this method could be implemented by maintaining a running count of tree nodes (incrementing it for every `add` operation and decrementing it for every `remove` operation). In fact, we used that approach for lists. The alternative approach of traversing the tree and counting the nodes each time the number is needed is also viable, and we use it here.

After we look at the two implementations of the `size` method, we discuss the benefits of recursion versus iteration for this problem.

Recursive Approach to the size Method

As we've done in previous cases where we have implemented an ADT operation using recursion, we must use a public method to access the `size` operation and a private recursive method to do all the work. The recursive method requires a reference to a tree node as an argument; because tree nodes remain hidden from the client, the client cannot directly invoke the recursive method. Thus we resort to the public/private pattern.

The public method, `size`, calls the private recursive method, `recSize`, and passes it a reference to the root of the tree. We design the recursive method to return the number of nodes in the subtree referenced by the argument passed to it. Because `size` passes it the root of the tree, `recSize` returns the number of nodes in the entire tree to `size`, which in turn returns it to the client program. The code for `size` is very simple:

```
public int size()
// Returns the number of elements in this BST.
{
   return recSize(root);
}
```

Recall that for function `Factorial` we said that we could determine the factorial of N if we knew the factorial of $N - 1$. The analogous statement here is that we can determine the number of nodes in the tree if we know the number of nodes in its left subtree and the number of nodes in its right subtree. That is, the number of nodes in a tree is

number of nodes in left subtree + number of nodes in right subtree + 1

This is easy. Given a method `recSize` and a reference to a tree node, we know how to calculate the number of nodes in a subtree: We call `recSize` recursively with the reference to the subtree as the argument. Thus we know how to write the general case. What about the base case? A leaf node has no subtrees, so the number of nodes is 1.

How do we determine that a node has no subtrees? The references to its children are `null`. Let's summarize these observations into an algorithm, where `tree` is a reference to a node.

recSize(tree): returns int   Version 1

```
if (tree.getLeft( ) is null) AND (tree.getRight( ) is null)
    return 1
else
    return recSize(tree.getLeft( )) + recSize(tree.getRight( )) + 1
```

Let's try this algorithm on a couple of examples to be sure that it works (see Figure 8.8).

We call `recSize` with the tree in Figure 8.8(a). The left and right children of the root node (M) are not `null`, so we call `recSize` with the node containing A as the root. Because both the left and right children are `null` on this call, we send back the answer 1. Now we call `recSize` with the tree containing Q as the root. Both of its children are `null`, so we send back the answer 1. Now we can calculate the number of nodes in the tree with M in the root:

$$1 + 1 + 1 = 3$$

This seems okay.

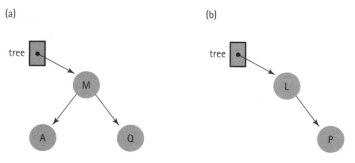

Figure 8.8   *Two binary search trees*

The left subtree of the root of the tree in Figure 8.8(b) is empty; let's see if this condition proves to be a problem. It is not true that both children of the root (L) are null, so recSize is called with the left child as the argument. OOPS! We do have a problem. The left child of L is null, so we just called recSize with a null argument. The first statement checks whether the children of the tree referenced by the argument are null, but the value of tree itself is null. The method crashes when we try to access tree.getLeft() when tree is null. To prevent this outcome, we can check whether a child is null, and not call recSize if it is.

recSize(tree): returns int   Version 2

```
if (tree.getLeft( ) is null) AND (tree.getRight( ) is null)
   return 1
else if tree.getLeft( ) is null
   return recSize(tree.getRight( )) + 1
else if tree.getRight( ) is null
   return recSize(tree.getLeft( )) + 1
else return recSize(tree.getLeft( )) + recSize(tree.getRighl( )) + 1
```

Version 2 works correctly if recSize has a precondition that the tree is not empty. An initially empty tree, however, causes a crash. We must check whether the tree is empty as the first statement in the algorithm and, if it is, return zero.

recSize(tree): returns int   Version 3

```
if tree is null
   return 0
else if (tree.getLeft( ) is null) AND (tree.getRight( ) is null)
   return 1
else if tree.getLeft( ) is null
   return recSize(tree.getRight( )) + 1
else if tree.getRight( ) is null
   return recSize(tree.getLeft( )) + 1
else return recSize(tree.getLeft( )) + recSize(tree.getRight( )) + 1
```

This certainly looks complicated. There must be a simpler solution—and there is. We can collapse the two base cases into one. There is no need to make the leaf node be a special case. We can simply have one base case: An empty tree returns zero. Now we do not have to check the left and right subtrees. If they are `null` and we process them, they just contribute a value of zero.

---

recSize(tree): returns int   Version 4

```
if tree is null
    return 0
else
    return recSize(tree.getLeft( )) + recSize(tree.getRight( )) + 1
```

We have taken the time to work through the versions containing errors and unnecessary complications because they illustrate two important points about recursion with trees: (1) Always check for the empty tree first, and (2) leaf nodes do not need to be treated as separate cases.

Here is the method specification:

Method recSize(tree)

Definition:	Counts and returns the number of nodes in tree
Size:	Number of nodes in tree
Base case:	If tree is null, return 0
General case:	Return recSize(tree.getLeft()) + recSize(tree.getRight()) + 1

Here is the code:

```
private int recSize(BSTNode<T> tree)
// Returns the number of elements in tree.
{
  if (tree == null)
    return 0;
  else
    return recSize(tree.getLeft()) + recSize(tree.getRight()) + 1;
}
```

Iterative Approach to the size Method

An iterative method to count the nodes on a linked list is simple to write:

```
count = 0;
while (list != null)
{
  count++;
  list = list.getLink();
}
return count;
```

However, taking a similar approach to develop an iterative method to count the nodes in a binary tree quickly runs into trouble. We start at the root and increment the count. Now what? Should we count the nodes in the left subtree or the right subtree? Suppose we decide to count the nodes in the left subtree. We must remember to come back later and count the nodes in the right subtree. In fact, every time we make a decision on which subtree to count we must remember to return to that node and count the nodes of its other subtree. How can we remember all of this?

In the recursive version, we did not have to explicitly remember which subtrees we still needed to process. The trail of unfinished business was maintained on the system stack for us automatically. For the iterative version, we must maintain the information explicitly, on our own stack. Whenever we postpone processing a subtree, we can push a reference to that subtree on a stack of references. Then, when we are finished with our current processing, we can remove the reference that is on the top of the stack and continue our processing with it.

We must be careful that we process each node in the tree exactly once. To ensure that we do not process a node twice, we follow these rules:

1. Process a node immediately after removing it from the stack.

2. Do not process nodes at any other time.

3. Once a node is removed from the stack, do not push it back onto the stack.

To ensure that we do not miss any nodes, we begin execution by pushing the root onto the stack. As part of the processing of every node, we push its children onto the stack. This guarantees that all descendants of the root are eventually pushed onto the stack—in other words, it guarantees that we do not miss any nodes.

Finally, we push only references to actual tree nodes; we do not push any `null` references. This way, when we remove a reference from the stack, we can increment the count of nodes and access the left and right links of the referenced node without worrying about `null` reference errors. Here is an algorithm for the iterative `size`:

size: returns int

Set count to 0
if the tree is not empty
    Instantiate a stack
    Push the root of the tree onto the stack
    while the stack is not empty
        Set currNode to top of stack
        Pop the stack
        Increment count
        if currNode has a left child
            Push currNode's left child onto the stack
        if currNode has a right child
            Push currNode's right child onto the stack
return count

The corresponding code, using a stack named `hold`, follows:

```java
public int size()
// Returns the number of elements in this BST.
{
    int count = 0;
    if (root != null)
    {
        LinkedStack<BSTNode<T>> hold = new LinkedStack<BSTNode<T>>();
        BSTNode<T> currNode;
        hold.push(root);
        while (!hold.isEmpty())
        {
            currNode = hold.top();
            hold.pop();
            count++;
            if (currNode.getLeft() != null)
                hold.push(currNode.getLeft());
            if (currNode.getRight() != null)
                hold.push(currNode.getRight());
        }
    }
    return count;
}
```

Recursion or Iteration?

Now that we have examined both the recursive and the iterative versions of counting nodes, can we determine which is a better choice? In Section 4.6 we discussed some guidelines for determining when recursion is appropriate. Let's apply these guidelines to the use of recursion for counting nodes.

Is the depth of recursion relatively shallow?

Yes. The depth of recursion depends on the height of the tree. If the tree is well balanced (relatively short and bushy, not tall and stringy), the depth of recursion is closer to $O(\log_2 N)$ than to $O(N)$.

Is the recursive solution shorter or clearer than the nonrecursive version?

Yes. The recursive solution is shorter than the iterative method, especially if we count the code for implementing the stack against the iterative approach. Is the recursive solution clearer? Although we spent more space discussing the recursive solution, we do believe it is clearer. We used extra space to teach you a little more about recursive design. We believe the recursive version is intuitively obvious. It is very easy to see that the number of nodes in a binary tree that has a root is 1 plus the number of nodes in its two subtrees. The iterative version is not as clear. We need to worry that we did not count any node twice, and that we did not miss any nodes. Compare the code for the two approaches and see what you think.

Is the recursive version much less efficient than the nonrecursive version?

No. Both the recursive and the nonrecursive versions of `size` are $O(N)$ operations. Both have to count every node.

We give the recursive version of the method an "A"; it is a good use of recursion.

8.6 The Implementation Level: Remaining Operations

In this section, we use recursion to implement the remaining Binary Search Tree ADT operations.

The contains and get Operations

At the beginning of this chapter, we demonstrated how to search for an element in a binary search tree. First check whether the element searched for is in the root. If it is not, compare the element with the root and look in either the left or the right subtree. This is a recursive algorithm.

We implement `contains` using a private recursive method called `recContains`. This method is passed the element we are searching for and a reference to a subtree in which to search. It follows the algorithm described above in a straightforward manner.

The only remaining question is how to determine that there is no element with the same key in the tree. If the subtree we are searching is empty, then there cannot be an element with the same key as the element's key. We summarize these observations in a table, which is followed by the code.

Method recContains (element, tree)

Definition:	Searches for an item in tree with the same key as element's key
	If found, return true; otherwise, return false
Size:	Number of nodes in tree (or number of nodes in the path)
Base cases:	(1) If element's key matches key in tree.getInfo( ), return true
	(2) If tree = null, return false
General case:	If element's key is less than key in tree.getInfo( ),
	return recContains(element, tree.getLeft( ));
	otherwise, return recContains(element, tree.getRight( ))

```
private boolean recContains(T element, BSTNode<T> tree)
// Returns true if tree contains an element e such that
// e.compareTo(element) == 0; otherwise, returns false.
{
  if (tree == null)
    return false;        // element is not found
  else if (element.compareTo(tree.getInfo()) < 0)
    return recContains(element, tree.getLeft());   // Search left subtree
  else if (element.compareTo(tree.getInfo()) > 0)
    return recContains(element, tree.getRight());  // Search right subtree
  else
    return true;         // element is found
}

public boolean contains (T element)
// Returns true if this BST contains an element e such that
// e.compareTo(element) == 0; otherwise, returns false.
{
  return recContains(element, root);
}
```

Let's trace this operation using the tree in Figure 8.9. In our trace we substitute actual arguments for the method parameters. We assume we can work with integers. We

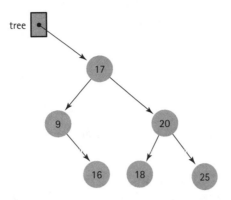

Figure 8.9   *Tracing the* `contains` *operation*

want to search for the element with the key 18 in a tree `myTree`, so the call to the public method is

`myTree.contains(18);`

The `contains` method, in turn, immediately calls the recursive method:

`return recContains(18, root);`

Because `root` is not `null` and 18 `>` `tree.getInfo()`—that is, 18 is greater than 17—we issue the first recursive call:

`return recContains(18, tree.right);`

Now `tree` references the node whose key is 20, so 18 `<` `tree.getInfo()`. The next recursive call is

`return recContains(18, tree.left);`

Now `tree` references the node with the key 18, so processing falls through to the last *else* statement:

`return true;`

This halts the recursive descent, and the value `true` is passed back up the line of recursive calls until it is returned to the original `contains` method and then to the client program.

Next, let's look at an example where the key is not found in the tree. We want to find the element with the key 7. The public method call is

`myTree.contains(7);`

followed immediately by

```
recContains(7, root)
```

Because `tree` is not `null` and 7 < `tree.getInfo()`, the first recursive call is

```
recContains(7, tree.left)
```

Now `tree` is pointing to the node that contains 9; `tree` is not `null`. We issue the second recursive call

```
recContains(7, tree.left)
```

Now tree is `null`, and the return value of `false` makes its way back to the original caller.

The `get` method is very similar to the `contains` operation. In both cases we search the tree recursively to locate the tree element that matches the parameter `element`. However, there is one difference. Instead of returning a `boolean` value, we must return a reference to the tree element that matches `element`. Recall that the actual tree element is the `info` of the tree node; thus we must return a reference to the `info` object. The `info` variable references an object of class `Comparable`. If the element is not in the tree, we return `null`.

```java
private T recGet(T element, BSTNode<T> tree)
// Returns an element e from tree such that e.compareTo(element) == 0;
// if no such element exists, returns null.
{
  if (tree == null)
    return null;              // element is not found
  else if (element.compareTo(tree.getInfo()) < 0)
    return recGet(element, tree.getLeft());     // get from left subtree
  else
  if (element.compareTo(tree.getInfo()) > 0)
    return recGet(element, tree.getRight());    // get from right subtree
  else
    return tree.getInfo();   // element is found
}

public T get(T element)
// Returns an element e from this BST such that e.compareTo(element) == 0;
// if no such element exists, returns null.
{
  return recGet(element, root);
}
```

The add Operation

To create and maintain the information stored in a binary search tree, we must have an operation that inserts new nodes into the tree. We use the following insertion approach: A new node is always inserted into its appropriate position in the tree as a leaf. Figure 8.10 shows a series of insertions into a binary tree.

For the implementation we use the same general approach as we used for contains and get. A public method, add, is passed the element for insertion. The add method

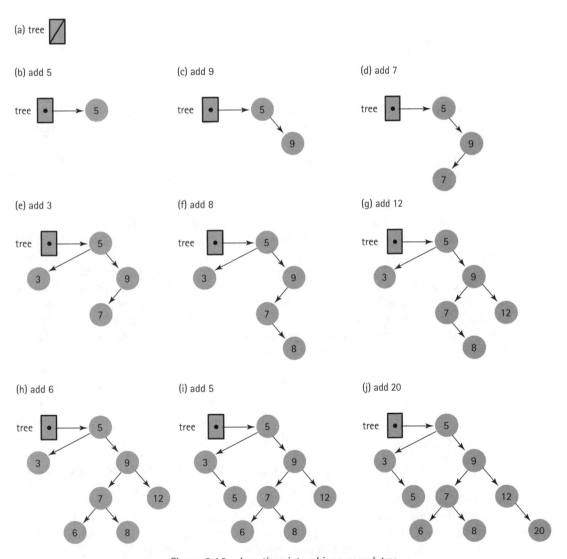

Figure 8.10 *Insertions into a binary search tree*

invokes the recursive method, `recAdd`, and passes it the `element` plus a reference to the `root` of the tree.

```
public void add (T element)
// Adds element to this BST. The tree retains its BST property.
{
   root = recAdd(element, root);
}
```

The call to `recAdd` returns a `BSTNode`. It returns a reference to the new tree—that is, to the tree that includes `element`. The statement

```
root = recAdd(element, root);
```

can be interpreted as "Set the reference of the root of this tree to the root of the tree that is generated when the element is added to this tree." At first this might seem inefficient. We always perform insertions as leaves, so why do we have to change the root of the tree? Look again at the sequence of insertions in Figure 8.10. Do any of the insertions affect the value of the root of the tree? Yes, the original insertion into the empty tree changes the value held in the root. In the case of all the other insertions, the statement in the `add` method just copies the current value of the root onto itself; however, we still need the assignment statement to handle the degenerate case of insertion into an empty tree. When does the assignment statement occur? After all the recursive calls to `recAdd` have been processed and have returned.

Before we begin the development of `recAdd`, we want to reiterate that every node in a binary search tree is the root node of a binary search tree. In Figure 8.11(a) we want to insert a node with the key value 13 into our tree whose root is the node containing 7. Because 13 is greater than 7, we know that the new node belongs in the root node's right subtree. We now have redefined a smaller version of our original problem. We want to insert a node with the key value 13 into the tree whose root is `tree.getRight()` (Figure 8.11b—in the figure we show the actual arguments rather than the formal parameters). Of course, we have a method to insert elements into a binary search tree: `recAdd`. The `recAdd` method is called recursively:

```
tree.getRight() = recAdd(element, tree.right);
```

Of course, `recAdd` still returns a reference to a `BSTNode`; it is the same `recAdd` method that was originally called from `add`, so it must behave in the same way. The above statement says "Set the reference of the right subtree of the tree to the root of the tree that is generated when the element is inserted into the right subtree of tree." Once again, the actual assignment statement does not occur until after the remaining recursive calls to `recAdd` have finished processing and have returned.

The `recAdd` method begins its execution, looking for the place to insert `element` in the tree whose root is the node with the key value 15. We compare the key of `element` (13) to the key of the root node; 13 is less than 15, so we know that the new element

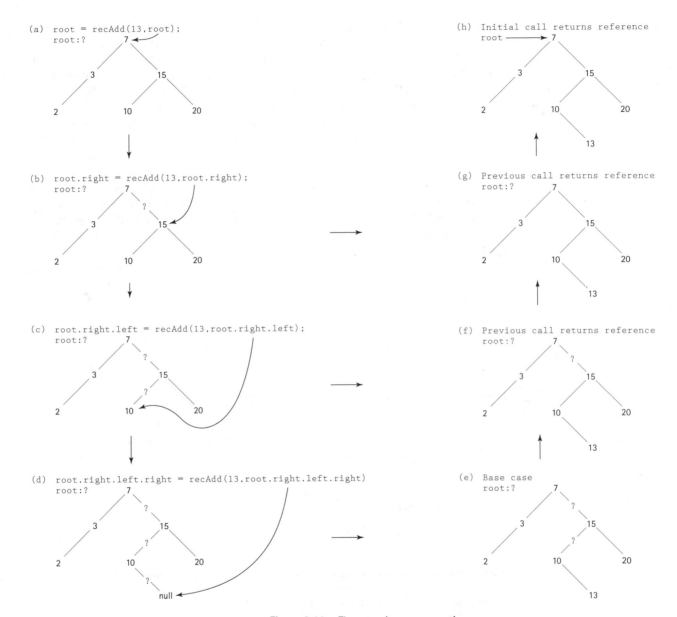

Figure 8.11 *The recursive add operation*

belongs in the tree's left subtree. Again, we have obtained a smaller version of the problem. We want to insert a node with the key value 13 into the tree whose root is `tree.getLeft()` (Figure 8.11c). We call `recAdd` recursively to perform this task. Remember that in this (recursive) execution of `recAdd`, `tree` points to the node whose key is 15, not the original tree root:

```
tree.getLeft() = recInsert(element, tree.left);
```

Now we recursively execute recAdd another time. We compare the key of element to the key of the (current) root node and then call recAdd to insert element into the correct subtree—the left subtree if element's key is less than or equal to the key of the root node, the right subtree if element's key is greater than the key of the root node.

Where does it all end? There must be a base case, in which space for the new element is allocated and the value of element copied into it. This case occurs when tree is null—that is, when the subtree we wish to insert into is empty. (Remember, we plan to add element as a leaf node.) Figure 8.11(d) illustrates the base case. We create the new node and return a reference to it to the most recent invocation of recAdd, where the reference is assigned to the right link of the node containing 10 (see Figure 8.11e). That invocation of recAdd is then finished; it returns a reference to its subtree to the previous invocation (see Figure 8.11f), where the reference is assigned to the left link of the node containing 15. This process continues until a reference to the entire tree is returned to the original add method, which assigns it to root, as shown in Figure 8.11(g) and (h).

While backing out of the recursive calls, the only assignment statement that actually changes a value is the one at the deepest nested level; it changes the right subtree of the node containing 10 from null to a reference to the new node. All of the other assignment statements simply assign a reference to the variable that held that reference previously. This is a typical recursive approach. We do not know ahead of time at which level the crucial assignment takes place, so we perform the assignment at every level.

The recursive method for insertion into a binary search tree is summarized as follows:

Method recAdd(element, tree) returns tree reference

Definition:	Inserts element into the binary search tree
Size:	The number of elements in the path from root to insertion place
Base case:	If tree is null, allocate a new leaf to contain element
General cases:	(1) If element <= tree.getInfo(), then recAdd(element, tree.getLeft())
	(2) If element > tree.getInfo(), then recAdd(element, tree.getRight())

Here is the code that implements this recursive algorithm:

```
private BSTNode<T> recAdd(T element, BSTNode<T> tree)
// Adds element to tree; tree retains its BST property.
{
  if (tree == null)
    // Addition place found
    tree = new BSTNode<T>(element);
  else if (element.compareTo(tree.getInfo()) <= 0)
    tree.setLeft(recAdd(element, tree.getLeft()));    // Add in left subtree
```

```
else
  tree.setRight(recAdd(element, tree.getRight()));   // Add in right subtree
return tree;
}
```

Insertion Order and Tree Shape
Because nodes are always added as leaves, the order in which nodes are inserted determines the shape of the tree. Figure 8.12 illustrates how the same data, inserted in different orders,

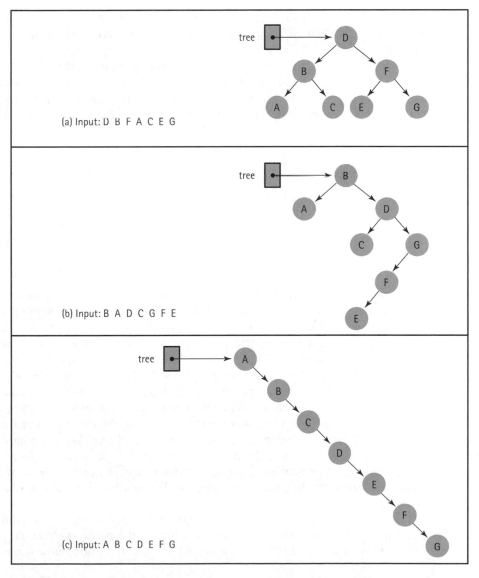

(a) Input: D B F A C E G

(b) Input: B A D C G F E

(c) Input: A B C D E F G

Figure 8.12   *The insertion order determines the shape of the tree*

produce very differently shaped trees. If the values are inserted in order (or in reverse order), the tree is completely *skewed* (a long, "narrow" tree shape). A random mix of the elements produces a shorter, "bushy" tree. Because the height of the tree determines the maximum number of comparisons in a binary search, the tree's shape is very important. Obviously, minimizing the height of the tree maximizes the efficiency of the search. Algorithms have been developed that adjust a tree to make its shape more desirable; one such scheme is presented in Section 8.8.

The remove Operation

The `remove` operation is the most complicated of the binary search tree operations. We must ensure that when we remove an element from the tree, we maintain the binary search tree property.

The setup for the `remove` operation is the same as that for the `add` operation. The private `recRemove` method is invoked from the public `remove` method with arguments equal to the `element` to be removed and the subtree to remove it from. The recursive method returns a reference to the revised tree, just as it did for `add`. Here is the code for `remove`:

```
public boolean remove (T element)
// Removes an element e from this BST such that e.compareTo(element) == 0
// and returns true; if no such element exists, returns false.
{
   root = recRemove(element, root);
   return found;
}
```

In most cases the root of the tree is not affected by the `recRemove` call, in which case the assignment statement is somewhat superfluous, as it is reassigning the current value of `root` to itself. If the node being removed happens to be the root node, however, then this assignment statement is crucial. The `remove` method returns the `boolean` value stored in `found`, indicating the result of the removal. The `recRemove` method sets the value of `found` to indicate whether the element was found in the tree. Obviously, if the element is not originally in the tree, then it cannot be removed.

The `recRemove` method receives an element and the external reference to the binary search tree, finds and removes the node matching the element's key from the tree if possible, and returns a reference to the newly created tree. We know how to determine whether the element is in the tree, and if it is present, how to find its node; we did it for `get`. As with that operation, we use recursive calls to `recRemove` to progressively decrease the size of the tree where the target node could be, until we actually locate the node.

Now we must remove the node and return a reference to the new subtree—this is somewhat complicated. This task varies according to the position of the target node in the tree. Obviously, it is simpler to remove a leaf node than to remove a nonleaf node.

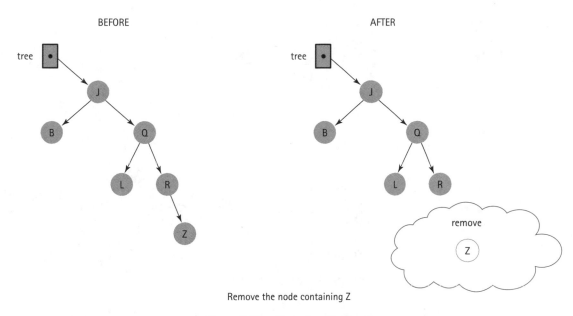

Figure 8.13   *Removing a leaf node*

In fact, we can break down the removal operation into three cases, depending on the number of children linked to the node we want to remove:

1. *Removing a leaf (no children)*   As shown in Figure 8.13, removing a leaf is simply a matter of setting the appropriate link of its parent to `null`.

2. *Removing a node with only one child*   The simple solution for removing a leaf does not suffice for removing a node with a child, because we don't want to lose all of its descendants from the tree. We want to make the reference from the parent skip over the removed node and point instead to the child of the node we intend to remove (see Figure 8.14).

3. *Removing a node with two children*   This case is the most complicated because we cannot make the parent of the removed node point to both of the removed node's children. The tree must remain a binary tree and the search property must remain intact. There are several ways to accomplish this removal. The method we use does not remove the node but rather replaces its `info` with the `info` from another node in the tree so that the search property is retained. We then remove this other node. Hmmm. That also sounds like a candidate for recursion. Let's see how this turns out.

Which element could we replace the removed `element` with that would maintain the search property? The elements whose keys immediately precede or follow the key of `element`—that is, the *logical* predecessor or successor of `element`. We replace the `info` of the node we wish to remove with the `info` of its logical predecessor—the node whose key is closest in value to, but less than or equal to, the key of the node to be removed.

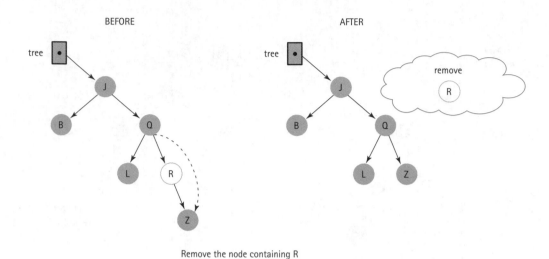

Remove the node containing R

Figure 8.14   *Removing a node with one child*

Look back at Figure 8.10(j) and locate the logical predecessor of the root node 5 and the nodes 9 and 7. Do you see the pattern? The logical predecessor of the root node 5 is the leaf node 5, the largest value in the root's left subtree. The logical predecessor of 9 is 8, the largest value in 9's left subtree. The logical predecessor of 7 is 6, the largest value in 7's left subtree. This replacement value is always in a node with either zero or one child. After copying the replacement value, it is easy to remove the node that the replacement value was in by changing one of its parent's references (see Figure 8.15).

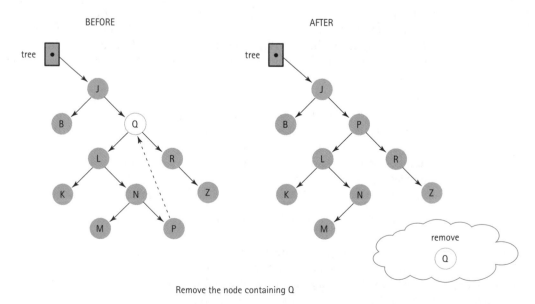

Remove the node containing Q

Figure 8.15   *Removing a node with two children*

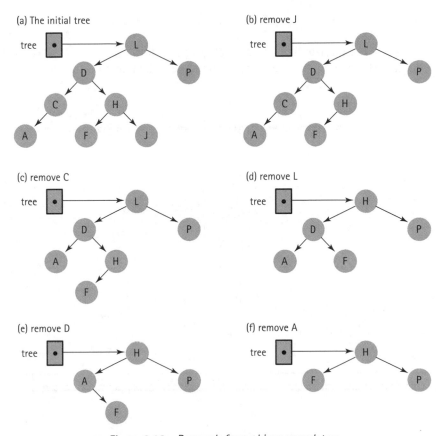

(a) The initial tree

(b) remove J

(c) remove C

(d) remove L

(e) remove D

(f) remove A

Figure 8.16   *Removals from a binary search tree*

Examples of all of these types of removals are shown in Figure 8.16.

It is clear that the removal task involves changing the reference from the parent node to the node to be removed. That explains why the `recRemove` method must return a reference to a `BSTNode`. Let's look at each of the three cases in terms of our implementation.

If both child references of the node to be removed are `null`, the node is a leaf and we just return `null`. The previous reference to this leaf node is replaced by `null` in the calling method, effectively removing the leaf node from the tree.

If one child reference is `null`, we return the other child reference. The previous reference to this node is replaced by a reference to the node's only child, effectively jumping over the node and removing it from the tree (similar to the way we removed a node from a singly linked list).

If neither child reference is `null`, we replace the `info` of the node with the `info` of the node's logical predecessor and remove the node containing the predecessor. The node containing the predecessor came from the left subtree of the current node, so we remove it from that subtree. We then return the original reference to the node (we have not created a new node with a new reference; we have just changed the node's `info` reference).

Let's summarize all of this in algorithmic form as `removeNode`. Within the algorithm and the code, the reference to the node to be removed is `tree`.

removeNode (tree): returns BSTNode

```
if (tree.getLeft( ) is null) AND (tree.getRight( ) is null)
    return null
else if tree.getLeft( ) is null
    return tree.getRight( )
else if tree.getRight( ) is null
    return tree.getLeft( )
else
    Find predecessor
    tree.setInfo(predecessor.getInfo( ))
    tree.setLeft(recRemove(predecessor.getInfo( ), tree.getLeft( )))
    return tree
```

Now we can write the recursive definition and code for `recRemove`.

Method recRemove (element, tree) returns BSTNode

Definition:	Removes element from tree
Size:	The number of nodes in the path from the root to the node to be removed
Base case 1:	If element is not in the tree, set found to false
Base case 2:	If element's key matches key in tree.info, remove node pointed to by tree and set found to true
General case:	If element < tree.getInfo(), recRemove(element, tree.getLeft()); else recRemove(element, tree.getRight())

```
private BSTNode<T> recRemove(T element, BSTNode<T> tree)
// Removes an element e from tree such that e.compareTo(element) == 0
// and returns true; if no such element exists, returns false.
{
  if (tree == null)
    found = false;
  else if (element.compareTo(tree.getInfo()) < 0)
    tree.setLeft(recRemove(element, tree.getLeft()));
  else if (element.compareTo(tree.getInfo()) > 0)
    tree.setRight(recRemove(element, tree.getRight()));
  else
  {
    tree = removeNode(tree);
    found = true;
  }
  return tree;
}
```

Before we code `removeNode`, let's look at its algorithm again. We can eliminate one of the tests if we notice that the action taken when the left child reference is `null` also takes care of the case in which both child references are `null`. When the left child reference is `null`, the right child reference is returned. If the right child reference is also `null`, then `null` is returned, which is what we want if both nodes are `null`.

Let's now write the code for `removeNode` using `getPredecessor` as the name of an operation that returns the `info` reference of the predecessor of the node with two children.

```
private BSTNode<T> removeNode(BSTNode<T> tree)
// Removes the information at the node referenced by tree.
// The user's data in the node referenced by tree is no
// longer in the tree.  If tree is a leaf node or has only
// a non-null child pointer, the node pointed to by tree is
// removed; otherwise, the user's data is replaced by its
// logical predecessor and the predecessor's node is removed.
{
  T data;

  if (tree.getLeft() == null)
    return tree.getRight();
  else if (tree.getRight() == null)
    return tree.getLeft();
  else
  {
    data = getPredecessor(tree.getLeft());
```

```
        tree.setInfo(data);
        tree.setLeft(recRemove(data, tree.getLeft()));
        return tree;
    }
}
```

Now we must look at the operation for finding the logical predecessor. We know that the logical predecessor is the maximum value in tree's left subtree. Where is this node? The maximum value in a binary search tree is in its rightmost node. Therefore, given tree's left subtree, we just keep moving right until the right child is null. When this occurs, we return the info reference of the node. There is no reason to look for the predecessor recursively in this case. A simple iteration until tree.getRight() is null suffices.

```
private T getPredecessor(BSTNode<T> tree)
// Returns the information held in the rightmost node in tree
{
  while (tree.getRight() != null)
    tree = tree.getRight();
  return tree.getInfo();
}
```

That's it. We have used four methods to implement the binary search tree's remove operation! Figure 8.17 illustrates the calling relationships among these four

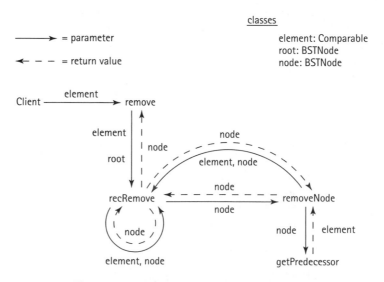

Figure 8.17   *The methods used to remove a node*

methods. Notice that we used both types of recursion in our solution: direct recursion (recRemove invokes itself) and indirect recursion (recRemove invokes removeNode, which in turn may invoke recRemove). Due to the nature of our approach, we are guaranteed that we never go deeper than one level of recursion. Whenever removeNode invokes recRemove, it passes an element and a reference to a subtree such that the element matches the largest element in the subtree. Therefore, the element matches the rightmost element of the subtree, which does not have a right child. This situation is one of the base cases for the recRemove method, so the recursion stops there.

If duplicate copies of the largest element in the subtree are present, the code will stop at the first one it finds—the one closest to the root of the tree. The remaining duplicates must be in that element's left subtree, based on the way we defined binary search trees and the way we implemented the add method. Thus, even in this case, the indirect recursion does not proceed deeper than one level of recursion.

Iteration

For the golf application developed in Section 8.3, we created a program that printed the contents of a binary search tree in order. This program printed the value of a node in between printing the values in its left subtree and the values in its right subtree. Using the inorder traversal resulted in a listing of the values of the binary search tree in ascending key order.

Let's review our traversal definitions:

- *Preorder traversal:* Visit the root, visit the left subtree, visit the right subtree
- *Inorder traversal:* Visit the left subtree, visit the root, visit the right subtree
- *Postorder traversal:* Visit the left subtree, visit the right subtree, visit the root

Recall that the name given to each traversal specifies where the root itself is processed in relation to its subtrees.

Our Binary Search Tree ADT supports all three traversal orders. How can it manage this feat? As we saw in the golf application, the client program passes the reset and getNext methods an argument indicating which of the three traversal orders to use for that particular invocation of the method. Imagine, for example, that reset is called with an INORDER argument, followed by several calls to getNext with INORDER arguments. How does getNext keep track of which tree node to return next? It is not as simple a matter as maintaining an instance variable that references the next element, as we did for linked lists. A simple reference to a node does not capture the status of the traversal. Sure, getNext could return the referenced element, but then how does it update the reference in preparation for the next call? Does it go down the left subtree, or down the right subtree, or back up to the parent? The program could save more information about the indicated traversal, enough to let it find the next element; due to the recursive nature of the traversals it would have to save this information in a stack.

There is a simpler way, however: We let reset generate a queue of node contents in the indicated order and let getNext process the node contents from the queue. Each of the traversal orders is supported by a separate queue. Therefore, the instance variables of our BinarySearchTree class must include three queues:

```
protected LinkedUnbndQueue<T> inOrderQueue;     // Queue of info
protected LinkedUnbndQueue<T> preOrderQueue;    // Queue of info
protected LinkedUnbndQueue<T> postOrderQueue;   // Queue of info
```

The reset method instantiates one of the queues, based on its argument. It then calls one of three recursive methods, depending on the value of its argument. Each of these methods implements a recursive traversal, enqueuing the node contents onto the corresponding queue in the appropriate order.

What happens when getNext reaches the end of the collection of elements? At that point, the corresponding queue is empty, and another call to getNext results in a run-time exception being thrown. Unlike with our List ADT, iterations on binary search trees do not "wrap around." The client must be sure not to call getNext inappropriately.

The code for reset and getNext appears below.

```
public int reset(int orderType)
// Initializes current position for an iteration through this BST
// in orderType order. Returns current number of nodes in the BST.
{
  int numNodes = size();
  if (orderType == INORDER)
  {
    inOrderQueue = new LinkedUnbndQueue<T>(numNodes);
    inOrder(root);
  }
  else
  if (orderType == PREORDER)
  {
    preOrderQueue = new LinkedUnbndQueue<T>(numNodes);
    preOrder(root);
  }
  if (orderType == POSTORDER)
  {
    postOrderQueue = new LinkedUnbndQueue<T>(numNodes);
    postOrder(root);
  }
  return numNodes;
}
```

```
public T getNext (int orderType)
// Preconditions: The BST is not empty
//                The BST has been reset for orderType
//                The BST has not been modified since the most recent reset
//                The end of orderType iteration has not been reached
//
// Returns the element at the current position on this BST for orderType
// and advances the value of the current position based on the orderType.
{
  if (orderType == INORDER)
    return inOrderQueue.dequeue();
  else
  if (orderType == PREORDER)
    return preOrderQueue.dequeue();
  else
  if (orderType == POSTORDER)
    return postOrderQueue.dequeue();
  else return null;
}
```

All that is left to do is to define the three traversal methods to store the required information into the queues in the correct order.

We start with the inorder traversal. We first need to visit the root's left subtree, which contains all the values in the tree that are smaller than or equal to the value in the root node. Then we visit the root node by enqueuing its information in our `inOrderQueue`. Finally, we visit the root's right subtree, which contains all the values in the tree that are larger than the value in the root node (see Figure 8.18).

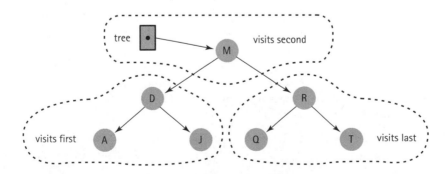

Figure 8.18   *Visiting all the nodes in order*

Let's describe this problem again, developing our algorithm as we proceed. We assume our method is named `inOrder` and is passed a parameter `tree`. We want to visit the elements in the binary search tree rooted at `tree` in order; that is, first we visit the left subtree in order, then we visit the root, and finally we visit the right subtree in order. The call with `tree.getLeft()` references the root of the left subtree. Because the left subtree is also a binary search tree, we can call method `inOrder` to visit it, using `tree.getLeft()` as the argument. When `inOrder` finishes visiting the left subtree, we enqueue the information of the root node. Then we call method `inOrder` to visit the right subtree, using `tree.getRight()` as the argument.

Of course, both of the calls to method `inOrder` use the same approach to visit the subtree: They visit the left subtree with a call to `inOrder`, visit the root, and then visit the right subtree with another call to `inOrder`. What happens if the incoming argument is `null` on one of the recursive calls? The argument is then the root of an empty tree. In this case, we just want to exit the method—clearly there's no point to visiting an empty subtree. That is our base case.

Method inOrder (tree)

Definition:	Enqueues the elements in the binary search tree in order from smallest to largest
Size:	The number of nodes in the tree whose root is tree
Base case:	If tree = null, do nothing
General case:	Traverse the left subtree in order
	Then enqueue tree.getInfo()
	Then traverse the right subtree in order

This is coded as the following recursive method:

```
private void inOrder(BSTNode<T> tree)
// Initializes inOrderQueue with tree elements in inOrder order
{
  if (tree != null)
  {
    inOrder(tree.getLeft());
    inOrderQueue.enqueue(tree.getInfo());
    inOrder(tree.getRight());
  }
}
```

The remaining two traversals are approached in exactly the same way, except that the relative order in which they visit the root and the subtrees is changed. Recursion certainly allows for an elegant solution to the binary tree traversal problem.

```
private void preOrder(BSTNode<T> tree)
// Initializes preOrderQueue with tree elements in preOrder order.
{
  if (tree != null)
  {
    preOrderQueue.enqueue(tree.getInfo());
    preOrder(tree.getLeft());
    preOrder(tree.getRight());
  }
}


private void postOrder(BSTNode<T> tree)
// Initializes postOrderQueue with tree elements in postOrder order.
{
  if (tree != null)
  {
    postOrder(tree.getLeft());
    postOrder(tree.getRight());
    postOrderQueue.enqueue(tree.getInfo());
  }
}
```

Testing Binary Search Tree Operations

Now that we've finished the implementation of the Binary Search Tree ADT we must address testing of our implementation. The code for the entire `BinarySearchTree` class is included with the rest of the files for this book. It provides both the recursive `size` method and the iterative version (`size2`). We have also included an interactive test driver for the ADT called `ITDBinarySearchTree`. This test driver allows the user to create, manipulate, and observe trees containing strings. In addition to directly supporting testing of all the ADT operations, the test driver supports a print operation that allows the user to indicate one of the traversal orders and "prints" the contents of the tree, in that order.

An example of a test run is on the next page. The `printTree` results can be used to help verify the shape of the tree. The repeated display of the operation menu has been replaced with ". . ." in most cases.

What is the name of this test?
Textbook Example

This is test Textbook Example.

Choose an operation:
1: isEmpty
2: size
3: size2
4: contains (string)
5: remove (string)
6: get (string)
7: add (string)
8: print (traversal order)
9: stop Testing

Enter choice: 7
Enter string to add: delta

Choose an operation:
. . .
Enter choice: 7
Enter string to add: alpha

Choose an operation:
. . .
Enter choice: 7
Enter string to add: alpha

Choose an operation:
. . .
Enter choice: 7
Enter string to add: gamma

Choose an operation:
. . .
Enter choice: 7
Enter string to add: beta

Choose an operation:
. . .
Enter choice: 8
Choose a traversal order:
1: Preorder
2: Inorder
3: Postorder
1
The tree in Preorder is:
delta
alpha
alpha
beta
gamma

Choose an operation:
. . .
Enter choice: 5
Enter string to remove: alpha
remove(alpha) returns true

Choose an operation:
. . .
Enter choice: 8
Choose a traversal order:
1: Preorder
2: Inorder
3: Postorder
1
The tree in Preorder is:
delta
alpha
beta
gamma

Choose an operation:
. . .
Enter choice: 9
End of Interactive Test Driver

You are invited to use the test driver to test the various tree operations. Be sure to test all of the operations, in many combinations. In particular, you should test both skewed and balanced trees. Also, don't forget to test trees with duplicate elements.

8.7 Comparing Binary Search Trees and Linear Lists

A binary search tree is an appropriate structure for many of the same applications discussed previously in conjunction with other sorted list structures. The special advantage of using a binary search tree is that it facilitates searching while conferring the benefits of linking the elements. It provides the best features of both the sorted array-based list and the linked list. Similar to a sorted array-based list, it can be searched quickly, using a binary search. Similar to a linked list, it allows insertions and removals without having to move data. Thus a binary search tree is particularly suitable for applications in which search time must be minimized or in which the nodes are not necessarily processed in sequential order.

As usual, there is a trade-off. The binary search tree, with its extra reference in each node, takes up more memory space than a singly linked list. In addition, the algorithms for manipulating the tree are somewhat more complicated. If all of the list's uses involve sequential rather than random processing of the elements, the tree may not be the best choice.

Suppose we have 100,000 customer records in a list. If the main activity in the application is to send out updated monthly statements to the customers, and if the order in which the statements are printed is the same as the order in which the information appears on the list, a linked list would be suitable. But suppose we decide to provide access as part of a pledge to give out account information to the customers whenever they ask. If the data are kept in a linked list, the first customer on the list can be given information almost instantly, but the last customer has to wait while 99,999 nodes are examined and skipped. When direct access to the nodes is a requirement, a binary search tree is a more appropriate structure.

Big-O Comparisons

Finding a node using the `contains` method, as we would expect in a structure dedicated to searching, is the most interesting operation to analyze. In the best case—if the order that the elements were inserted results in a short, bushy tree—we can find any node in the tree with at most $\log_2 N + 1$ comparisons. We would expect to be able to locate a random element in such a tree much faster than we could find an element in a sorted linked list. In the worst case—if the elements were inserted in order from smallest to largest, or vice versa—the tree won't really be a tree at all; it will be a linear list, linked through either the `left` or `right` references. This is called a "degenerate" tree. In this case, the tree operations should perform much the same as the operations on a linked list.

If we were doing a worst-case analysis, we would have to say that the complexity of the tree operations is identical to the comparable linked list operations. In the following analysis, however, we assume that the elements are inserted into the tree in random order, giving a balanced tree.

The `add` and `get` operations are basically finding the node [$O(\log_2 N)$] plus tasks that are $O(1)$—for instance, creating a node or returning references. Thus these operations are all described as $O(\log_2 N)$. The `remove` operation consists of finding the node plus invoking `removeNode`. In the worst case (removing a node with two children), `removeNode` must find the replacement value, an $O(\log_2 N)$ operation. (Actually, the two tasks together add up to $\log_2 N$ comparisons, because if the target node is higher in the tree, fewer comparisons are needed to find it, but more comparisons may be needed to find its replacement node; and vice versa.) Otherwise, if the removed node has zero or one child, `removeNode` is an $O(1)$ operation. Thus `remove` may also be described as an $O(\log_2 N)$ operation.

The `size` and `reset` operations require the tree to be traversed, processing each element once. These are $O(N)$ operations. Of course, iterating through an entire collection of elements takes $O(N)$ steps even if both `reset` and `getNext` are $O(1)$, as `getNext` must be called N times by the client.

Table 8.1 compares the orders of magnitude for the tree and list operations as we have coded them. The binary search tree operations are based on a random insertion order of the elements; the Find operation in the array-based implementation is based on using a binary search. We do not include either the list's or the tree's `size` method in Table 8.1. These methods *can* be implemented with a simple *return* statement if the object maintains an instance variable holding the size of the structure. Of course, this instance variable would have to be updated every time an element is inserted or removed from the structure, so the cost really would depend on how often those operations occur.

8.8 Balancing a Binary Search Tree

In our Big-O analysis of binary search tree operations, we assumed that our tree was balanced. If we drop this assumption and then perform a worst-case analysis assuming a completely skewed tree, the efficiency benefits of the binary search tree disappear. The time required to perform the `contains`, `get`, `add`, and `remove` operations is now $O(N)$, just as it is for the linked list. Therefore, a beneficial enhancement to our Binary Search Tree ADT operations is a `balance` operation that balances the tree. The specification of the operation is

```
public balance();
// Restructures this BST to be optimally balanced
```

Of course, it is up to the client program to use the `balance` method appropriately. It should not be invoked too often, as it also has an execution cost associated with it.

Table 8.1 *Big-O Comparison of List Operations*

	Binary Search Tree	Array-Based Linear List	Linked List
Class constructor	O(1)	O(N)	O(1)
isEmpty	O(1)	O(1)	O(1)
reset	O(N)	O(1)	O(1)
getNext	O(1)	O(1)	O(1)
contains	O(log$_2$N)	O(log$_2$N)	O(N)
get			
Find	O(log$_2$N)	O(log$_2$N)	O(N)
Process	O(1)	O(1)	O(1)
Total	O(log$_2$N)	O(log$_2$N)	O(N)
add			
Find	O(log$_2$N)	O(log$_2$N)	O(N)
Process	O(1)	O(N)	O(1)
Total	O(log$_2$N)	O(N)	O(N)
remove			
Find	O(log$_2$N)	O(log$_2$N)	O(N)
Process	O(1)	O(N)	O(1)
Total	O(log$_2$N)	O(N)	O(N)

There are several ways to restructure a binary search tree. We use a simple approach:

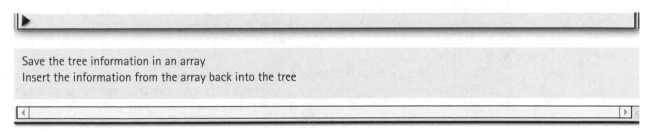

The structure of the new tree depends on the order in which we save the information into the array, the order in which we insert the information back into the tree, or both. Let's start by assuming we insert the array elements back into the tree in "index" order—that is, starting at index 0 and working through the array. We use the following algorithm:

```
Set ORDER to one of the tree traversal orders
Set count to tree.reset(ORDER)
for (int index = 0; index < count; index++)
    array[index] = tree.getNext(ORDER)
tree = new BinarySearchTree()
for (int index = 0; index < count; index++)
    tree.add(array[index])
```

Does that balance the tree? It's impossible to tell what it does without knowing the order of the tree traversal.

Let's consider what happens if we use an inorder traversal. Figure 8.19 provides an example. The results are not very satisfactory, are they? We have taken a perfectly nice bushy tree and turned it into a degenerate skewed tree that does not efficiently support our tree operations. That is the opposite of what we wanted to accomplish. There must be a better approach.

Next we try a preorder traversal, as shown in Figure 8.20. We end up with an exact copy of our tree. Will this always be the case? Yes. Recall our rule for inserting elements into a tree—we always insert at a leaf position. Do you see what this means? Consider the tree in Figure 8.20(a). Assuming it has had no removals, what was the first node inserted into that tree when it was created? It had to be the root node, the node containing the value 10, because the only time the root node is also a leaf is when the tree contains a single element. What was the second element inserted? It was either the node containing 7 or the node containing 15—they are the roots of the left subtree and right subtree. If we re-create the tree based on a pre-order traversal (root first!) of the original tree, we obtain an exact copy of the tree. Because we always insert a node before any of its descendants, we maintain the ancestor–descendant relationships of the original tree and obtain an exact copy. This interesting discovery could be useful if we wanted to duplicate a tree, but it doesn't help us balance a tree.

Using a postorder traversal doesn't help either. Try it out.

How can we do better? One way to ensure a balanced tree is to even out, as much as possible, the number of descendants in each node's left and right subtrees. We insert elements "root first," which means that we should first insert the "middle" element. (If we list the elements from smallest to largest, the "middle" element is the one in the middle of the list—it has as many elements less than or equal to it as it has greater than it, or at least as close as possible.) The middle element becomes the root of the tree. It has about the same number of descendants in its left subtree as it has in its right subtree. Good. Which element do we insert next? Let's work on the left subtree. Its root should be the "middle" element of all the elements that are less than or equal to the root. That element is inserted next. Now, when the remaining elements

(a) The original tree

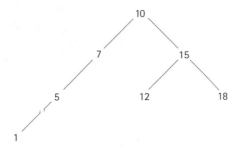

(b) The inorder traversal

	0	1	2	3	4	5	6
array:	1	5	7	10	12	15	18

(c) The resultant tree if linear traversal of array is used

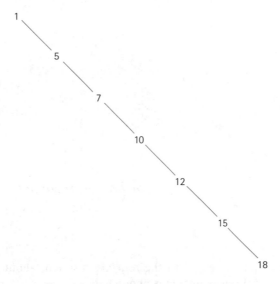

Figure 8.19   *A skewed tree is produced*

(a) The original tree

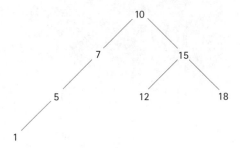

(b) The preorder traversal

	0	1	2	3	4	5	6
array:	10	7	5	1	15	12	18

(c) The resultant tree if linear traversal of array is used

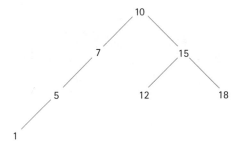

Figure 8.20   *An exact copy is produced*

that are less than or equal to the root are inserted, about half of them will be in the left subtree of the element, and about half will be in its right subtree. Sounds recursive, doesn't it?

Here is an algorithm for balancing a tree based on the approach described above. The algorithm consists of two parts: one iterative, and one recursive. The iterative part, Balance, creates the array and invokes the recursive part, InsertTree, which then rebuilds the tree.

Balance

```
Set count to tree.reset(INORDER)
for (int index = 0; index < count; index++)
    array[index] = tree.getNext(INORDER)
tree = new BinarySearchTree()
tree.InsertTree(0, count - 1)
```

InsertTree(low, high)

```
if (low == high)                    // Base case 1
    tree.add(nodes[low])
else if ((low + 1) == high)         // Base case 2
    tree.add(nodes[low])
    tree.add(nodes[high])
else
    mid = (low + high) / 2
    tree.add(mid)
    tree.InsertTree(low, mid − 1)
    tree.InsertTree(mid + 1, high)
```

We first store the nodes of the tree into our array using an inorder traversal, so that they are stored, in order, from smallest to largest. The algorithm continues by invoking the recursive algorithm InsertTree, passing it the bounds of the array. The InsertTree algorithm checks the array bounds it is passed. If the low and high bounds are the same (base case 1), it inserts the corresponding array element into the tree. If the bounds differ by only one location (base case 2), the algorithm inserts both elements into the tree. Otherwise, it computes the "middle" element of the subarray, inserts it into the tree, and then makes two recursive calls to itself: one to process the elements less than the middle element, and one to process the elements greater than the element.

Trace the InsertTree algorithm using sorted arrays of both even and odd length to convince yourself that it works. The code for `balance` and a helper method `insertTree` follows directly from the algorithm; writing it is left for you as an exercise. Figure 8.21 shows the results of using this approach on the previous example.

(a) The original tree

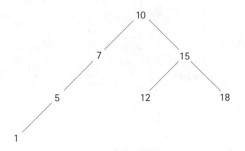

(b) The inorder traversal

	0	1	2	3	4	5	6
array:	1	5	7	10	12	15	18

(c) The resultant tree if InsertTree (0,6) is used

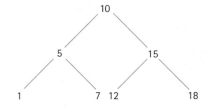

Figure 8.21   *An optimal transformation*

8.9 A Nonlinked Representation of Binary Trees

Our discussion of the implementation of binary trees has so far been limited to a scheme in which the links from parent to children are *explicit* in the implementation structure. In other words, an instance variable was declared in each node for the reference to the left child and the reference to the right child.

A binary tree can be stored in an array in such a way that the relationships in the tree are not physically represented by link members, but rather are *implicit* in the algorithms that manipulate the tree stored in the array. The code is, of course, much less self-documenting and less intuitive, but we might save memory space because no references are required.

Let's take a binary tree and store it in an array in such a way that the parent–child relationships are not lost. We store the tree elements in the array, level by level, from left to right. If the number of nodes in the tree is `numElements`, we can package the array and `numElements` into an object, as illustrated in Figure 8.22. The tree elements are stored with the root in `tree.nodes[0]` and the last node in `tree.nodes[numElements - 1]`.

To implement the algorithms that manipulate the tree, we must be able to find the left and right children of a node in the tree. Comparing the tree and the array in Figure 8.22, we make the following observations:

`tree.nodes[0]`'s children are in `tree.nodes[1]` and `tree.nodes[2]`.

`tree.nodes[1]`'s children are in `tree.nodes[3]` and `tree.nodes[4]`.

`tree.nodes[2]`'s children are in `tree.nodes[5]` and `tree.nodes[6]`.

Do you see the pattern? For any node `tree.nodes[index]`, its left child is in `tree.nodes[index*2 + 1]` and its right child is in `tree.nodes[index*2 + 2]` (provided that these child nodes exist). Notice that the nodes in the array from `tree.nodes[tree.numElements/2]` to `tree.nodes[tree.numElements - 1]` are leaf nodes.

Not only can we easily calculate the location of a node's children, but we can also determine the location of its parent node. This task is not an easy one in a binary tree linked together with references from parent to child nodes, but it is very simple in our implicit link implementation: `tree.nodes[index]`'s parent is in `tree.nodes[(index - 1)/2]`.

Because integer division truncates any remainder, `(index - 1)/2` is the correct parent index for either a left or right child. Thus this implementation of a binary tree is linked in both directions: from parent to child, and from child to parent. We take advantage of this fact in Chapter 9, when we study heaps.

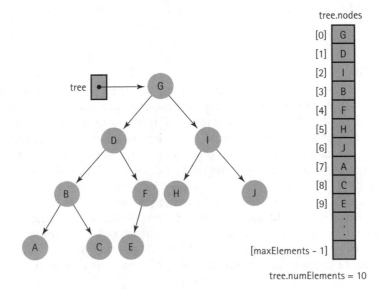

Figure 8.22 *A binary tree and its array representation*

This tree representation works well for any binary tree that is full or complete. A full binary tree is a binary tree in which all of the leaves are on the same level and every nonleaf node has two children. The basic shape of a full binary tree is triangular:

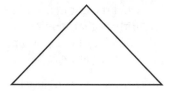

A complete binary tree is a binary tree that is either full or full through the next-to-last level, with the leaves on the last level as far to the left as possible. The shape of a complete binary tree is either triangular (if the tree is full) or something like the following:

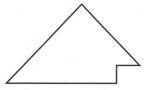

Full binary tree A binary tree in which all of the leaves are on the same level and every nonleaf node has two children

Complete binary tree A binary tree that is either full or full through the next-to-last level, with the leaves on the last level as far to the left as possible

Figure 8.23 shows some examples of different types of binary trees.

The array-based representation is simple to implement for trees that are full or complete, because the elements occupy contiguous array slots. If a tree is not full or complete, however, we must account for the gaps where nodes are missing. To use the array representation, we must store a dummy value in those positions in the array to maintain the proper parent–child relationship. The choice of a dummy value depends on the information that is stored in the tree. For instance, if the elements in the tree are nonnegative integers, a negative value can be stored in the dummy nodes; if the elements are objects, we can use a `null` value.

Figure 8.24 illustrates an incomplete tree and its corresponding array. Some of the array slots do not contain actual tree elements, but rather dummy values. The algorithms to manipulate the tree must reflect this situation. For example, to determine whether the node in `tree.nodes[index]` has a left child, we must check whether `index*2 + 1 < tree.numElements`, and then check whether the value in `tree.nodes[index*2 + 1]` is the dummy value.

Just as with all of our array-based implementations, we must specify the size of the array when we create it, and this size is then fixed. As a consequence, we may waste space if we create an array that is much bigger than needed, and we could potentially run out of space if the tree grows larger than we anticipate. A full implementation of an

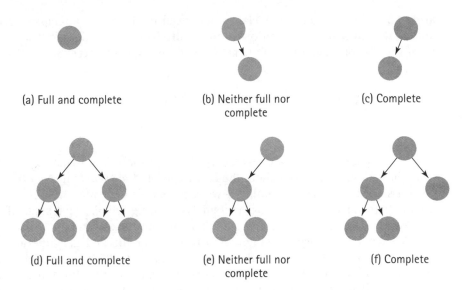

Figure 8.23   *Examples of different types of binary trees*

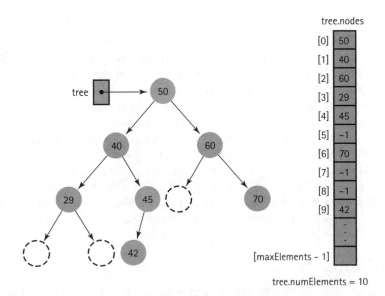

Figure 8.24   *A binary search tree stored in an array with dummy values*

array-based binary search tree class would need to check any attempt to insert a node, and either throw an exception or automatically instantiate a larger array and copy the data from the original array to the new one if more space is needed.

8.10 Case Study: Word Frequency Generator

Problem

Our firm is planning to create several types of text analysis software—for example, software that automatically calculates the reading level of a document. As a first step, we've been assigned the task of creating a word frequency generator. This generator will be used to perform some preliminary text analysis during the planning stage of the project; if it works well, it may be incorporated into the tools developed later.

The word frequency generator is to read a text file and generate an alphabetical listing of the unique words that the file contains, along with a count of how many times each word occurs. To allow users to control the amount of useful output from the generator, based on the particular problem they are studying, the generator must allow users to specify a minimum word size and a minimum frequency count. The generator should skip over words smaller than the minimum word size; it should not include a word on its output list if the word occurs fewer times than the minimum frequency count. Finally, the generator should present a few summary statistics: the total number of words, the number of words whose length is at least the minimum word size, and the number of unique words of the specified size whose frequency is at least the minimum frequency count.

Discussion

The first thing we must do is define a "word." We discuss this question with our manager. What is a tentative definition of a word in this context? How about "something between two blanks"? Or better yet, a "character string between two blanks"? That definition works for most words. All words that immediately precede a period or a comma, however, would have the "." and "," attached. Also, quoted words would cause a problem. Therefore, we settle on the following definition: A word is a string of alphanumeric characters between markers, where markers are whitespace and all punctuation marks.

Although we "lose" some words following this definition (for example, contractions such as "can't" are treated as two words, "can" and "t"), we decide that these small problems do not adversely affect our goals. Finally, our manager points out that all words should be transformed into lowercase characters for processing—"THE" and "the" represent the same word.

Brainstorming

Let's list objects that might be useful in solving the problem. Scanning the problem statement we identify the following "nouns": *word frequency generator, input text file, user, alphabetical listing, unique words, word count, minimum word size, minimum frequency count, output list, summary statistics,* and *word totals.* That's 11 candidate objects. We realize that we need to use a data structure to store words—for now we just call it the *word store* and add that to our list, giving us 12 candidate objects.

Listing the verbs in a problem statement often helps identify the actions our program needs to take. In this case, however, we are clear on the actions needed: Read in the words, determine their frequencies, and output the results. A quick scan of the problem statement reminds us that the results are to be sorted alphabetically and that some pruning of the data is required based on minimum thresholds for word size and word frequency.

Filtering

We have identified 12 candidate objects. A few of them can be discarded immediately: *word frequency generator* is the entire program; *minimum word size* and *minimum frequency count* are input values and can be stored as primitive `int` values. Some of the candidate objects (*input text file*, *user*, *output list*) are related to the user interface. (We discuss the interface in the next subsection.) The remaining candidates are grouped as follows:

- *Summary statistics, word totals* These terms are really the same thing. We decide the statistics can be tracked by the main processing class and presented to the user at the conclusion of processing—this does not require a separate object.
- *Unique words, word count* These two terms are related because we need to have a word count for each unique word. We decide to create a class called `WordFreq` to hold a word frequency pair. A quick analysis tells us that we have to be able to initialize objects of the class, increment the frequency, and observe both the word and the frequency values. We could make this class generic, replacing "word" with a type provided by the client program; however, considering that this is just a preliminary project we decide to simply have the class hide strings (words) and integers (frequency).
- *Alphabetical listing, word store* We can combine these objects by using a container that supports sorted traversals to hold our `WordFreq` objects. We decide to delay our choice of containers until after we perform scenario analysis, but we know it must support insertion, searching, and "in order" traversal. At this point we consider both the Sorted List ADT and the Binary Search Tree ADT as candidates. For now we call this class `Container`.

The User Interface

We do not include an example of a graphical user interface for this case study. According to the problem description, the program is to be used only for preliminary analysis of texts, as an aid in planning full-fledged text analysis tools, and the program is targeted to be embedded in a larger system later, a system that presumably already has a user interface.

For these reasons, we include only a console-based interface. It is easy to create and suits our purposes. We assume that the text file containing the words is named words.dat. The user enters two pieces of information to the program when prompted: the minimum word size and the minimum frequency count. The program reads text from the input file, breaks it into words, generates the word frequency list, displays it, and displays the summary statistics.

Error Handling

For the same reasons we are not creating a graphical interface, we do not worry about checking input arguments for validity. We assume that when our program is embedded in a larger system, this system will ensure valid input. For now, we rely on the user to supply appropriate program arguments and we assume that the input file exists in the correct format and is readable.

Scenario Analysis

There really is only one scenario for this problem: Read a file, break it into words, process the words, and output the results. Let's describe it in algorithmic form:

```
Initialize variables and objects

while there are more words to process
    Get the next word
    Increment numWords
    if current word size is OK
        Increment numValidWords
        Change word to all lowercase
        wordToTry = new WordFreq object based on current word
        if wordToTry is already in the container
            Get the corresponding WordFreq object from the container
            Increment the frequency of the WordFreq object
            Save the WordFreq object back into the container
        else
            Insert a new WordFreq object representing wordToTry into the container

Set up a traversal through the container
while there are more WordFreq elements in the container
    Get the next WordFreq element
    if the frequency of the WordFreq element is large enough
        Increment numValidFreqs
        Display the WordFreq information

Display the summary statistics
```

We need to walk through this algorithm a few times to complete our helper class definitions. At each step, we ask ourselves how we could accomplish that step:

- We can use Java's `Scanner` to break the input file into words. It allows us to know when "there are more words to process" and allows us to "get the next word."
- The `Scanner` class permits us to define the set of delimiters used to separate the tokens found in its input source by invoking its `useDelimiter` method. In our program we can state that the delimiters are "^a-zA-Z0-9"; this regular expression means anything that is not a letter or a digit.
- Checking a word's size and changing it to lowercase can both be accomplished by using methods of the `String` class.
- Iterating through the `WordFreq` elements for output just requires using the iteration tools of whatever data structure we choose for our container. Creating the output does require the output of "`WordFreq` information," so we decide to expand the set of `WordFreq` operations to include a `toString` operation.

That leaves one section of the algorithm for more careful analysis: the section dealing with the container. Let's look at it again and decide exactly which container class to use.

```
if wordToTry is already in the container
    Get the corresponding WordFreq object from the container
    Increment the frequency of the WordFreq object
    Save the WordFreq object back into the container
else
    Insert a new WordFreq object representing wordToTry into the container
```

The first thing we notice is the repeated access to the container required for each word. Potentially we may have to check the container to see whether the word is already there, get the word from the container, and save the word back into the container. Ignoring the fact that we are not sure what "save back" means for now, we realize that we should consider achieving efficient access to the container to be a high priority. Our input files could have thousands of words, so the underlying structure can be large. The need for repeated access and searching in a large structure leads us to choose the binary search tree for our container. This decision means that the `WordFreq` class must implement the `Comparable<WordFreq>` interface, so that we can store `WordFreq` objects on our tree.

Now let's address the "save back" question. The way we "save" information in our tree is to add it. Of course the tree would already have a `WordFreq` object that corresponds to the current word. If we add the revised `WordFreq` object, we would have "identical" copies of that object in the tree. Thus, to "save back" the `WordFreq` object, we would first have to remove the previous version of the object and then insert the new version. But wait a minute: Do we really have to do that? Recall that our tree stores objects "by reference." When we retrieve a `WordFreq` object from the tree, we are actually retrieving a reference to the object. If we use that reference to access the object and increment its frequency count, the frequency count of the object in the tree is incremented. We do not have to "save back" the object at all!

In our discussion of the perils of "store by reference" in the feature section in Chapter 6, we stated that it is dangerous for the client to use a reference to reach into a data structure hidden by an ADT and change a data element. But as we also noted, this practice is dangerous only if the change affects the parts of the element used to determine the underlying physical relationship of the structure. In this case, the structure is based on the word information of a `WordFreq` object; we are changing the frequency information. We can reach into the tree and increment the frequency count of one of its elements without affecting the tree's structure. Thus we can reduce this part of our algorithm to

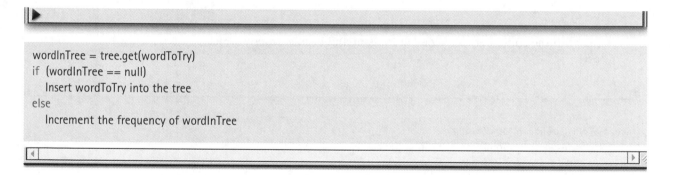

```
wordInTree = tree.get(wordToTry)
if (wordInTree == null)
    Insert wordToTry into the tree
else
    Increment the frequency of wordInTree
```

We have reduced the number of times the tree is "searched" to handle a word that is already in the tree to 1.

The WordFreq Class

The code for the `WordFreq` class is very straightforward. It is placed in the package `ch08.wordFreqs`. A few observations are appropriate:

- The constructor initializes the `freq` variable to 0. As a consequence, the main program must increment a `WordFreq` object before placing it on the tree for the first time. We could have coded the constructor to set the original frequency to 1, but we think it is more natural to begin a frequency count at 0. There may be other applications that can use `WordFreq` where this ability would be important.
- In the `toString` method, we use Java's `DecimalFormat` class to force the string generated from the frequency count to be at least five characters wide. This helps line up output information for applications such as our word frequency generator.

The code corresponding to these points is <u>emphasized</u> in the listing below.

```java
//--------------------------------------------------------------------------
// WordFreq.java              by Dale/Joyce/Weems              Chapter 8
//
// Defines word frequency pairs
//--------------------------------------------------------------------------

package ch08.wordFreqs;

import java.text.DecimalFormat;

public class WordFreq implements Comparable<WordFreq>
{
  private String word;
  private int freq;

  DecimalFormat fmt = new DecimalFormat("00000");

  public WordFreq(String newWord)
  {
    word = newWord;
    freq = 0;
  }

  public void inc()
  {
    freq++;
  }

  public int compareTo(WordFreq other)
  {
    return this.word.compareTo(other.word);
  }

  public String toString()
  {
    return(fmt.format(freq) + " " + word);
  }

  public String wordIs()
  {
    return word;
  }
```

```
public int freqIs()
{
  return freq;
}
}
```

The Word Frequency Generator Program

The main program is provided by the `FrequencyList` class. It implements the algorithm developed in the "Scenario Analysis" section.

```java
//-------------------------------------------------------------------------
// FrequencyList.java          by Dale/Joyce/Weems          Chapter 8
//
// Displays a word frequency list of the words listed in the input file.
// Prompts user for minSize and minFreq.
// Does not process words less than minSize in length.
// Does not output words unless their frequency is at least minFreq.
//-------------------------------------------------------------------------

import java.io.*;
import java.util.*;
import ch08.trees.*;
import ch08.wordFreqs.*;

public class FrequencyList
{
  public static void main(String[] args) throws IOException
  {
    String word;
    WordFreq wordToTry;
    WordFreq wordInTree;
    WordFreq wordFromTree;

    BinarySearchTree<WordFreq> tree = new BinarySearchTree<WordFreq>();
    String skip;          // skip end of line after reading integer

    int numWords = 0;
    int numValidWords = 0;
    int numValidFreqs = 0;
    int minSize;
```

```
int minFreq;
int treeSize;

// Set up file reading
FileReader fin = new FileReader("words.dat");
Scanner wordsIn = new Scanner(fin);
wordsIn.useDelimiter("[^a-zA-Z0-9]");  // delimiters are nonletters-digits

// Set up console reading
Scanner conIn = new Scanner(System.in);

//Get word and frequency limits from user
System.out.print("Minimum word size: ");
minSize = conIn.nextInt();
skip = conIn.nextLine();
System.out.print("Minimum word frequency: ");
minFreq = conIn.nextInt();
skip = conIn.nextLine();

while (wordsIn.hasNext())      // while more words to process
{
  word = wordsIn.next();
  numWords++;
  if (word.length() >= minSize)
  {
    numValidWords++;
    word = word.toLowerCase();
    wordToTry = new WordFreq(word);
    wordInTree = tree.get(wordToTry);
    if (wordInTree == null)
    {
      // insert new word into tree
      wordToTry.inc();                // set frequency to 1
      tree.add(wordToTry);
    }
    else
    {
      // word already in tree, just increment frequency
      wordInTree.inc();
    }
  }
}
```

```
      treeSize = tree.reset(BinarySearchTree.INORDER);
      System.out.println("The words of length " + minSize + " and above,");
      System.out.println("with frequency counts of " + minFreq + " and above:");
      System.out.println();
      System.out.println("Freq  Word");
      System.out.println("----- ----------------");
      for (int count = 1; count <= treeSize; count++)
      {
        wordFromTree = tree.getNext(BinarySearchTree.INORDER);
        if (wordFromTree.freqIs() >= minFreq)
        {
          numValidFreqs++;
          System.out.println(wordFromTree);
        }
      }

      System.out.println();
      System.out.println(numWords + " words in the input file.  ");
      System.out.println(numValidWords + " of them are at least "
                      + minSize + " characters.");
      System.out.println(numValidFreqs + " of these occur at least "
                      + minFreq + " times.");
      System.out.println("Program completed.");
    }
  }
```

Testing

This program should first be tested using small files, where it is easy for us to deter-mine the expected output. It should then be tested on many different files, using varying minimum word sizes and frequency counts. Here we show the results of run-ning the program on a text file version of the Constitution of the United States of America. The minimum word size was set to 7 and the minimum frequency count was set to 6.

> Minimum word size: 7
>
> Minimum word frequency: 6
>
> The words of length 7 and above,
>
> with frequency counts of 6 and above:

Freq	Word
00008	against
00006	another
00008	article
00007	authority
00007	between
00007	citizens
00029	congress
00010	consent
00015	constitution
00006	elected
00007	electors
00007	executive
00009	legislature
00008	members
00006	necessary
00008	officers
00006	persons
00033	president
00008	provide
00015	representatives
00022	section
00008	senators
00006	service
00009	several
00007	supreme
00012	thereof
00007	treason
00007	without

5617 words in the input file.
979 of them are at least 7 characters.
28 of these occur at least 6 times.
Program completed.

Summary

In this chapter we saw how the binary tree may be used to structure sorted information to reduce the search time for any particular element. For applications in which direct access to the elements in a sorted structure is needed, the binary search tree is a very useful data structure. If the tree is balanced, we can access any node in the tree with an $O(\log_2 N)$ operation. The binary search tree combines the advantages of quick random access (like a binary search on a linear list) with the flexibility of a linked structure.

We also saw that the tree operations could be implemented very elegantly and concisely using recursion. This makes sense, because a binary tree is itself a "recursive" structure: Any node in the tree is the root of another binary tree. Each time we moved down a level in the tree, taking either the right or left path from a node, we cut the size of the (current) tree in half, a clear case of the smaller-caller.

We also discussed a tree-balancing approach and a structuring approach that use arrays. Finally, we presented a case study that used our Binary Search Tree ADT.

Figure 8.25 is a UML diagram showing the relationships among the binary search tree classes and interfaces developed in this chapter.

Exercises

8.1 Trees

1. Answer the following questions about binary tree levels.

   a. What does the level of a binary search tree mean in relation to the searching efficiency?

   b. What is the maximum number of levels that a binary search tree with 100 nodes can have?

   c. What is the minimum number of levels that a binary search tree with 100 nodes can have?

2. Which of these formulas gives the maximum total number of nodes in a binary tree that has N levels? (Remember that the root is level 0.)

   a. $N^2 - 1$

   b. 2^N

   c. $2^{N+1} - 1$

   d. 2^{N+1}

3. Which of these formulas gives the maximum number of nodes in the Nth level of a binary tree?

   a. N^2

   b. 2^N

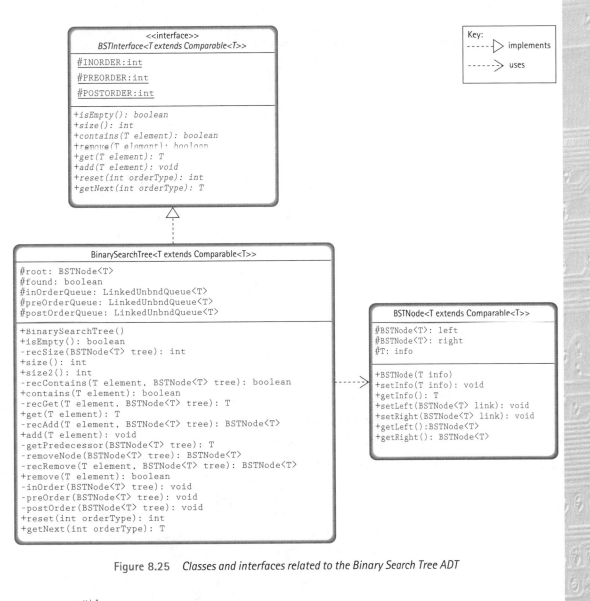

Figure 8.25 *Classes and interfaces related to the Binary Search Tree ADT*

   c. 2^{N+1}

   d. $2^N - 1$

4. How many ancestors does a node in the Nth level of a binary search tree have?

5. How many different *binary trees* can be made from three nodes that contain the key values 1, 2, and 3?

6. How many different *binary search trees* can be made from three nodes that contain the key values 1, 2, and 3?

7. Draw all the possible binary trees (show their shapes) that have four leaves and whose nonleaf nodes all have two children.

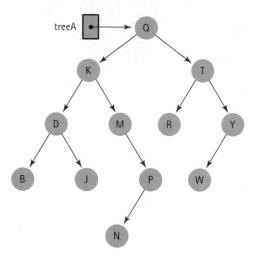

8. Answer the following questions about treeA.
   a. What are the ancestors of node P?
   b. What are the descendants of node K?
   c. What is the maximum possible number of nodes at the level of node W?
   d. What is the maximum possible number of nodes at the level of node N?
   e. What is the order in which the nodes are visited by an inorder traversal?
   f. What is the order in which the nodes are visited by a preorder traversal?
   g. What is the order in which the nodes are visited by a postorder traversal?

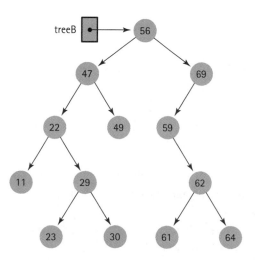

9. Answer the following questions about treeB.

    a. What is the height of the tree?

    b. Which nodes are on level 3?

    c. Which levels have the maximum number of nodes that they could contain?

    d. What is the maximum height of a binary search tree containing these nodes? Draw such a tree.

    e. What is the minimum height of a binary search tree containing these nodes? Draw such a tree.

    f. What is the order in which the nodes are visited by an inorder traversal?

    g. What is the order in which the nodes are visited by a preorder traversal?

    h. What is the order in which the nodes are visited by a postorder traversal?

10. True or False? A preorder traversal of a binary search tree processes the nodes in the tree in the exact reverse order that a postorder traversal processes them.

8.2 The Logical Level

11. Describe the differences between our specifications of the Sorted List ADT and the Binary Search Tree ADT.

12. Suppose you decide to change our Binary Search Tree ADT to not allow duplicate elements. How would you have to change the ADT's specification?

13. At least one of the operations specified in our Binary Search Tree interface is redundant; that is, the functionality it provides is available through another operation or a combination of other operations. Describe the redundant operation or operations and explain the reason for your choices.

8.3 The Application Level

14. Does the order in which golfers and their scores are entered into the golf application have any effect on the outcome of the program? Explain your answer.

For Exercises 15, 16, 17, and 43 we assume the client is working with a tree of Golfer objects. The Golfer class is included in the support package that is included with the textbook code.

15. Write a client method that returns a count of the number of nodes in a binary search tree that contain a value less than or equal to the argument value. The signature of the method is

    ```
    int countLess(BinarySearchTree<Golfer> tree, Golfer maxValue)
    ```

16. Write a client method that returns a reference to the information in the node with the "smallest" value in a binary search tree. The signature of the method is

    ```
    Golfer min(BinarySearchTree<Golfer> tree)
    ```

17. Write a client method that returns a reference to the information in the node with the "largest" value in a binary search tree. The signature of the method is

```
Golfer max(BinarySearchTree<Golfer> tree)
```

8.4 The Implementation Level: Basics

18. Describe the similarities and differences between our `LLNode` and `BSTNode` classes.

19. What changes would you make to the `BSTInterface` and to the basic part of the implementation if our binary search trees were bounded?

20. Extend the Binary Search Tree ADT to include a basic public method `getRoot` that returns a reference to the root of the tree. If the tree is empty, the method should return `null`.

8.5 Iterative Versus Recursive Method Implementations

21. Use the Three-Question Method to verify the recursive version of the `size` method.

22. Extend the Binary Search Tree ADT to include a public method `leafCount` that returns the number of leaf nodes in the tree.

23. Extend the Binary Search Tree ADT to include a public method `singleParent-Count` that returns the number of nodes in the tree that have only one child.

24. The Binary Search Tree ADT is extended to include a `boolean` method `similarTrees` that receives references to two binary trees and determines whether the shapes of the trees are the same. (The nodes do not have to contain the same values, but each node must have the same number of children.)

    a. Write the declaration of the `similarTrees` method. Include adequate comments.

    b. Write the body of the `similarTrees` method.

25. We need a public method for our Binary Search Tree ADT that returns a reference to the information in the node with the "smallest" value in the tree. The signature of the method is

```
public T min()
```

    a. Design an iterative version of the method.

    b. Design a recursive version of the method.

    c. Which approach is better? Explain.

26. We need a public method for our Binary Search Tree ADT that returns a reference to the information in the node with the "largest" value in the tree. The signature of the method is

```
public T max()
```

    a. Design an iterative version of the method.

    b. Design a recursive version of the method.

c. Which approach is better? Explain.

27. We need a public method for our Binary Search Tree ADT that returns a count of the number of nodes of the tree that contain a value equal to the argument value. The signature of the method is

```
public int countLess(T maxValue)
```

a. Design an iterative version of the method.

b. Design a recursive version of the method.

c. Which approach is better? Explain.

8.6 The Implementation Level: Remaining Operations

28. Show how we visualize treeA (page 600) after each of the following changes. Also list the sequence of BinarySearchTree method calls, both public and private, that would be made when executing the change. Use the original tree to answer each part of this question.

a. Add node C.

b. Add node Z.

c. Add node Q.

d. Remove node M.

e. Remove node Q.

f. Remove node R.

29. Draw the binary search tree whose elements are inserted in the following order:

50 72 96 94 107 26 12 11 9 2 10 25 51 16 17 95

30. Draw the binary search tree whose elements are inserted in the following order:

50 72 96 50 107 26 50 72 9 2 10 2 50 107 17 95

Exercises 31–34 use treeB (page 600).

31. Trace the path that would be followed in searching for

a. A node containing 61.

b. A node containing 28.

32. Show how treeB would look after the removal of 29, 59, and 47.

33. Show how the (original) treeB would look after the insertion of nodes containing 63, 77, 76, 48, 9, and 10 (in that order).

34. Show how the (original) treeB would look after the insertion of nodes containing 56, 49, 22, 59, 59, and 59 (in that order).

35. The key of each node in a binary search tree is a short character string.

a. Show how such a tree would look after the following words were inserted (in the order indicated):

"hippopotamus" "canary" "donkey" "deer" "zebra" "yak" "walrus" "vulture" "penguin" "quail"

b. Show how the tree would look if the same words were inserted in this order:

"quail" "walrus" "donkey" "deer" "hippopotamus" "vulture" "yak" "penguin" "zebra" "canary"

c. Show how the tree would look if the same words were inserted in this order:

"zebra" "yak" "walrus" "vulture" "quail" "penguin" "hippopotamus" "donkey" "deer" "canary"

Examine the following binary search tree and answer the questions in Exercises 36–39. The numbers on the nodes are labels so that we can talk about the nodes; they are not key values within the nodes.

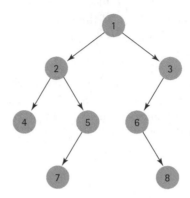

36. If an element is to be inserted whose key value is less than the key value in node 1 but greater than the key value in node 5, where would it be inserted?

37. If node 1 is to be removed, the value in which node could be used to replace it?

38. 4 2 7 5 1 6 8 3 is a traversal of the tree in which order?

39. 1 2 4 5 7 3 6 8 is a traversal of the tree in which order?

40. Devise a set of test cases and use the test driver, developed in Section 8.6, to test our Binary Search Tree ADT and show that the implementation

a. Correctly removes the root of a balanced tree containing the three elements "A," "B," and "C."

b. Correctly builds a skewed tree when the elements "A," "B," "C," "D," and "E" are inserted in alphabetical order.

c. Correctly reports the "contains" value for "B," "C," and "D" in a tree created by adding "C," then "A," and then "E."

Remember that the "print tree" results can be used to help verify the "shape" of the tree.

8.7 Comparing Binary Search Trees and Linear Lists

41. Suppose 100 integer elements are chosen at random and are inserted into a sorted linked list and a binary search tree. Describe the efficiency of searching for an element in each structure, in terms of Big-O.

42. Suppose 100 integer elements are inserted in order, from smallest to largest, into a sorted linked list and a binary search tree. Describe the efficiency of searching for an element in each structure, in terms of Big-O.

🖥 **43.** Write a client `boolean` method `matchingElements` that determines whether a binary search tree of `Golfer` and a sorted list of `Golfer` contain the same values. The signature of the method is

```
boolean matchingElements(BinarySearchTree<Golfer> tree,
                         SortedList<Golfer> list)
```

44. In Chapter 7, we discussed how a linked list could be stored in an array of nodes by using index values as "references" and managing our list of free nodes. We can use these same techniques to store the nodes of a binary search tree in an array, rather than using dynamic storage allocation. Free space is linked through the left member.

  a. Show how the array would look after these elements are inserted in this order:

  Q L W F M R N S

  Be sure to fill in all the spaces. If you do not know the contents of a space, use "?".

nodes	.info	.left	.right
[0]			
[1]			
[2]			
[3]			
[4]			
[5]			
[6]			
[7]			
[8]			
[9]			

free	
root	

b. Show the contents of the array after "B" has been inserted and "R" has been removed.

nodes	.info	.left	.right
[0]			
[1]			
[2]			
[3]			
[4]			
[5]			
[6]			
[7]			
[8]			
[9]			

free	
root	

8.8 Balancing a Binary Search Tree

45. Show the tree that would result from storing the nodes of the tree in Figure 8.19(a) in postorder order into an array, and then traversing the array in index order while inserting the nodes into a new tree.

46. Using the Balance algorithm, show the tree that would be created if the following values represented the inorder traversal of the original tree.

   a. 3 6 9 15 17 19 29

   b. 3 6 9 15 17 19 29 37

   c. 1 2 3 3 3 3 3 3 3 24 37

47. Revise our `BSTInterface` interface and `BinarySearchTree` class to include the `balance` method. How can you test your revision?

8.9 A Nonlinked Representation of Binary Trees

48. Consider the following trees.

   a. Which fulfill the binary search tree property?

   b. Which are complete?

   c. Which are full?

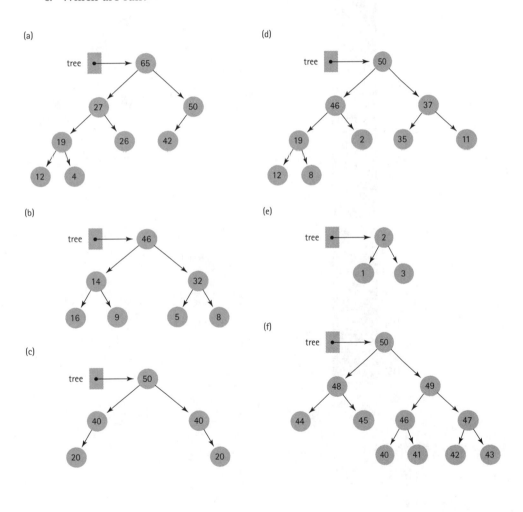

49. The elements in a binary tree are to be stored in an array, as described in Section 8.9. Each element is a nonnegative `int` value.

   a. Which value can you use as the dummy value, if the binary tree is not complete?

   b. Show the contents of the array, given the tree illustrated below.

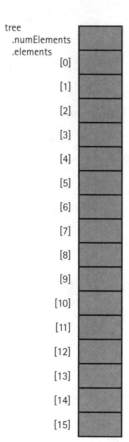

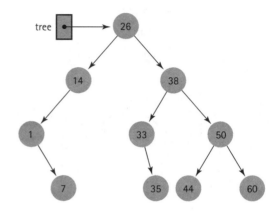

50. The elements in a complete binary tree are to be stored in an array, as described in Section 8.9. Each element is a nonnegative `int` value. Show the contents of the array, given the tree illustrated below.

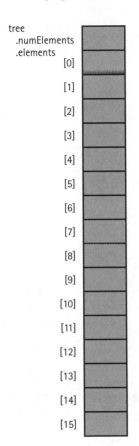

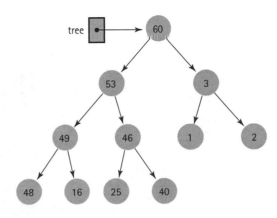

51. Given the array pictured below, draw the binary tree that can be created from its elements. (The elements are arranged in the array as discussed in Section 8.9.)

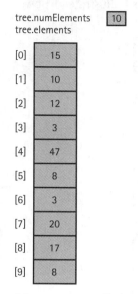

tree.numElements   10
tree.elements

[0]	15
[1]	10
[2]	12
[3]	3
[4]	47
[5]	8
[6]	3
[7]	20
[8]	17
[9]	8

52. A complete binary tree is stored in an array called treeNodes, which is indexed from 0 to 99, as described in Section 8.9. The tree contains 85 elements. Mark each of the following statements as true or false, and explain your answers.

a. treeNodes[42] is a leaf node.

b. treeNodes[41] has only one child.

c. The right child of treeNodes[12] is treeNodes[25].

d. The subtree rooted at treeNodes[7] is a full binary tree with four levels.

e. The tree has seven levels that are full, and one additional level that contains some elements.

8.10 Case Study: Word Frequency Generator

53. List all of the classes used directly by the FrequencyList program.

54. Describe the effect that each of the following changes would have on the FrequencyList program.

a. Remove the call to the useDelimiter method of the Scanner class.

b. Remove the call to the toLowerCase method of the String class.

c. Change the call to the toLowerCase method to a call to the toUpperCase method.

d. In the *else* clause, change the statement wordInTree.inc() to wordToTry.inc().

55. We want the word frequency generator program to output one additional piece of information, the number of unique words in the input file.

   a. Describe two different ways you could solve this problem—that is, two ways to handle the additional words the program now must track.

   b. Which approach do you believe is better? Why?

   c. Implement the change.

Priority Queues, Heaps, and Graphs

Knowledge Goals

You should be able to

- describe a priority queue at the logical level and discuss alternative implementation approaches
- define a heap and the operations reheap up and reheap down
- describe the shape and order properties of a heap
- compare the implementations of a priority queue using a heap, linked list, and binary search tree
- define the following terms related to graphs:
  - directed graph
  - undirected graph
  - vertex
  - edge
  - path
  - complete graph
  - weighted graph
  - adjacency matrix
  - adjacency list
- explain the difference between a depth-first search and a breadth-first search
- describe the shortest-path algorithm for graphs

Skill Goals

You should be able to

- implement a priority queue as a heap
- implement a heap using an array-based nonlinked tree representation
- implement a graph using an adjacency matrix to represent the edges
- implement a graph using adjacency lists
- implement the depth-first searching strategy for a graph using a stack for auxiliary storage
- implement the breadth-first searching strategy for a graph using a queue for auxiliary storage
- implement a shortest-paths operation for a graph, using a priority queue to access the edge with the minimum weight

So far, we have examined several basic data structures in depth, discussing their uses and operations, as well as one or more implementations of each. As we have constructed these programmer-defined data structures out of the built-in types provided by our high-level language, we have noted variations that adapt them to the needs of different applications. In Chapter 8 we looked at how a tree structure—the binary search tree—facilitates searching data stored in a linked structure. In this chapter we see how other branching structures are defined and implemented to support a variety of applications.

9.1 Priority Queues

A priority queue is an abstract data type with an interesting accessing protocol. Only the *highest-priority* element can be accessed. "Highest priority" can mean different things, depending on the application. Consider, for example, a small company with one secretary. When employees leave work on the secretary's desk, which jobs get done first? The jobs are processed in order of the employee's importance in the company; the secretary completes the president's work before starting the vice president's, and does the marketing director's work before beginning the work of the staff programmers. The *priority* of each job relates to the level of the employee who initiated it.

In a telephone answering system, calls are answered in the order that they are received; that is, the highest-priority call is the one that has been waiting the longest. Thus a FIFO queue can be considered a priority queue whose highest-priority element is the one that has been queued the longest time.

Sometimes a printer shared by a number of computers is configured to always print the smallest job in its queue first. This way, someone who is printing only a few pages does not have to wait for large jobs to finish. For such printers, the priority of the jobs relates to the size of the job: Shortest job first.

Priority queues are useful for any application that involves processing elements by priority.

Logical Level

The operations defined for the Priority Queue ADT include enqueuing elements and dequeuing elements, as well as testing for an empty or full priority queue. These operations are very similar to those specified for the FIFO queue discussed in Chapter 5. The `enqueue` operation adds a given element to the priority queue. The `dequeue` operation removes the highest-priority element from the priority queue and returns it to the user. The difference is that the Priority Queue ADT does not follow the "first in, first out" approach; instead, it always returns the highest-priority element from the current set of enqueued elements, no matter when it was enqueued. Here is the specification, as a Java interface named `PriQueueInterface`:

```
//---------------------------------------------------------------------------
// PriQueueInterface.java          by Dale/Joyce/Weems          Chapter 9
//
// Interface for a class that implements a priority queue.
//---------------------------------------------------------------------------

package ch09.priorityQueues;

public interface PriQueueInterface<T extends Comparable<T>>
{
  boolean isEmpty();
  // Returns true if this priority queue is empty; otherwise, returns false.

  boolean isFull();
  // Returns true if this priority queue is full; otherwise, returns false.

  void enqueue(T element);
  // Throws PriQOverflowException if this priority queue is full;
  // otherwise, adds element to this priority queue.

  T dequeue();
  // Throws PriQUnderflowException if this priority queue is empty;
  // otherwise, removes element with highest priority from this
  // priority queue and returns it.
}
```

A few notes on the specification follow:

- Our priority queues hold objects of class T extends Comparable$<T>$. This allows us to compare elements and rank them by priority. We are also assured that only elements that can be compared to each other can be inserted into a specific priority queue.
- Our priority queues are bounded—at least, that is the implication of including an isFull method in the interface. We could, however, create an unbounded priority queue that implements this interface by having its isFull method always return false.
- Our priority queues can hold duplicate elements—that is, elements with the same key value.
- Attempting to enqueue an element into a full priority queue, or dequeue an element from an empty priority queue, causes an unchecked exception to be thrown.

We define the exceptions using the standard approach established in Chapter 3. Here are the definitions of the two exception classes used by our priority queue class:

```
package ch09.priorityQueues;

class PriQUnderflowException extends RuntimeException
{
  public PriQUnderflowException()
  {
    super();
  }

  public PriQUnderflowException(String message)
  {
    super(message);
  }
}

package ch09.priorityQueues;

class PriQOverflowException extends RuntimeException
{
  public PriQOverflowException()
  {
    super();
  }

  public PriQOverflowException(String message)
  {
    super(message);
  }
}
```

Application Level

In discussing FIFO queue applications in Chapter 5, we said that the operating system of a multiuser computer system may use job queues to save user requests in the order in which they are made. Another way such requests may be handled is according to how important the job request is. That is, a request from the head of the company might get higher priority than a request from the junior programmer. Similarly, an interactive program might be designated as a higher priority than a job to print out a report that isn't needed until the next day. To handle these requests efficiently, the operating system may use a priority queue.

Priority queues are also useful in sorting data. Given a set of elements to sort, we can enqueue the elements into a priority queue, and then dequeue them in sorted order (from largest to smallest). We look more at how priority queues can be used in sorting in Chapter 10.

Implementation Level

There are many ways to implement a priority queue. In any implementation, we want to be able to access the element with the highest priority quickly and easily. Let's briefly consider some possible approaches.

An Unsorted List

Enqueuing an element would be very easy with an unsorted list: Simply insert it at the end of the list. Dequeuing, however, would require searching through the entire list to find the largest element.

An Array-Based Sorted List

Dequeuing is very easy with this array-based approach: Simply return the last list element and reduce the size of the list; `dequeue` is a $O(1)$ operation. Enqueuing, however, would be more expensive, because we have to find the place to enqueue the element. This is an $O(\log_2 N)$ step if we use a binary search. Shifting the elements of the list to make room for the new element is an $O(N)$ step.

A Reference-Based Sorted List

Let's assume the linked list is kept sorted from largest to smallest. Dequeuing with this reference-based approach simply requires removing and returning the first list element, an operation that takes only a few steps. But enqueuing again is an $O(N)$ operation, because we must search the list one element at a time to find the insertion location.

A Binary Search Tree

For this approach, the `enqueue` operation is implemented as a standard binary search tree `insert` operation. We know that operation requires $O(\log_2 N)$ steps on average. Assuming we have access to the underlying implementation structure of the tree, we can implement the `dequeue` operation by returning the rightmost tree element. We follow the right subtree references down, maintaining a trailing reference as we go, until we reach a node with an empty right subtree. The trailing reference allows us to "unlink" the node from the tree. We then return the node. This is also a $O(\log_2 N)$ operation, on average.

The binary tree approach is the best—it requires, on average, only $O(\log_2 N)$ steps for both `enqueue` and `dequeue`. If the tree is skewed, however, the performance degenerates to $O(N)$ steps for each operation. In Section 9.2 we present another approach, called the heap, that guarantees $O(\log_2 N)$ steps, even in the worst case.

9.2 Heaps

A heap[1] is an implementation of a priority queue that uses a binary tree that satisfies two properties, one concerning its shape and the other concerning the order of its elements. The *shape property* is simply stated: The tree must be a complete binary tree (see Section 8.9). The *order property* says that, for every node in the tree, the value stored in that node is greater than or equal to the value in each of its children.

> **Heap** An implementation of a priority queue based on a complete binary tree, each of whose elements contains a value that is greater than or equal to the value of each of its children

---

1. "Heap" is also a synonym for the free store of a computer—the area of memory available for dynamically allocated data. The heap as a data structure is not to be confused with this unrelated computer system concept of the same name.

It might be more accurate to call this structure a "maximum heap," because the root node contains the maximum value in the structure. It is also possible to create a "minimum heap," each of whose elements contains a value that is *less* than or equal to the value of each of its children. The term "heap" is used for both the abstract data type—the priority queue implementation—and the underlying structure—the tree that fulfills the shape and order properties.

Figure 9.1 shows two trees containing the letters "A" through "J" that fulfill both the shape and order properties. The placement of the values differs in the two trees, but the shape is the same: a complete binary tree of 10 elements. The two trees have the same root node. A group of values can be stored in a binary tree in many ways and still satisfy the order property of heaps. Because of the shape property, we know that all heap trees with a given number of elements have the same shape. We also know, because of the order property, that the root node always contains the largest value in the tree. This helps us implement an efficient `dequeue` operation. Finally, note that every subtree of a heap is also a heap.

Let's say that we want to dequeue an element from the heap—in other words, we want to remove and return the element with the largest value from the tree. The largest element is in the root node, so we can easily remove it, as illustrated in Figure 9.2(a). Of course, this leaves a hole in the root position. Because the heap's tree must be complete,

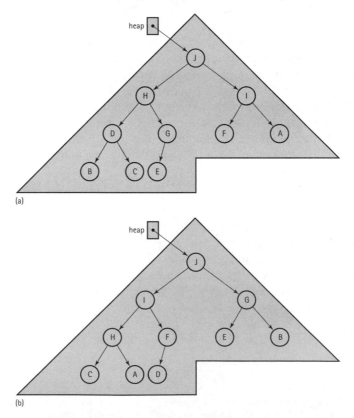

(a)

(b)

Figure 9.1 *Two heaps containing the letters "A" through "J"*

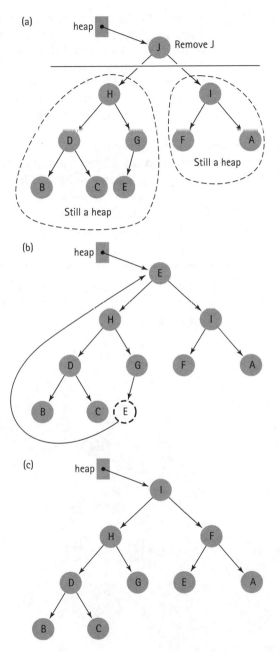

Figure 9.2 *The dequeue operation*

we decide to fill the hole with the bottom rightmost element from the tree; now the structure satisfies the shape property (Figure 9.2b). The replacement value, however, came from the bottom of the tree, where the smaller values are; as a consequence, the tree no longer satisfies the order property of heaps.

This situation suggests one of the standard heap-support operations: Given a binary tree that satisfies the heap properties, *except that the root position is empty*, insert an element into the structure so that it again becomes a heap. This operation, called reheapDown, involves starting at the root position and moving the "hole" (the empty position) down, while moving tree elements up, until we find a position for the hole where the element can be inserted (see Figure 9.2c). We say that we swap the hole with one of its children. The reheapDown operation has the following specification:

reheapDown (element)

Effect:	Adds element to the heap
Precondition:	The root of the tree is empty

To dequeue an element from the heap, we remove and return the root element, remove the bottom rightmost element, and then pass the bottom rightmost element to reheapDown to restore the heap.

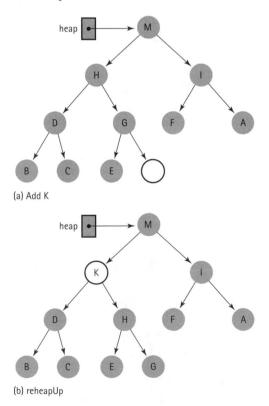

(a) Add K

(b) reheapUp

Figure 9.3 *The* reheapUp *operation*

Now suppose that we want to enqueue an element to the heap—where do we put it? The shape property tells us that the tree must be complete, so we put the new element in the next bottom rightmost place in the tree, as illustrated in Figure 9.3(a). Now the shape property is satisfied, but the order property may be violated. This situation illustrates the need for another heap-support operation: Given a binary tree that satisfies the heap properties, except that the last position is empty, insert a given element into the structure so that it again becomes a heap. Instead of inserting the element in the next bottom rightmost position in the tree, we imagine we have another hole there. We then float the hole position up the tree, while moving tree elements down, until the hole is in a position (see Figure 9.3b) that allows us to legally insert the element. This operation is called reheapUp. Here is the specification:

reheapUp (element)

Effect:	Adds element to the heap
Precondition:	The last index position of the tree is empty

Heap Implementation

Figure 9.17 in the chapter summary section displays a UML class diagram showing our priority queue classes and interfaces.

Although we have graphically depicted heaps as binary trees with nodes and links, it would be very impractical to implement the heap operations using the usual linked tree representation. The shape property of heaps tells us that the binary tree is complete, so we know that it is never unbalanced. Thus we can easily store the tree in an array with implicit links, as discussed in Section 8.9, without wasting any space. Figure 9.4 shows how the values in a heap would be stored in this array representation. If a heap with numElements elements is implemented this way, the shape property says that the heap elements are stored in numElements consecutive slots in the array, with the root element in the first slot (index 0) and the last leaf node in the slot with index numElements - 1.

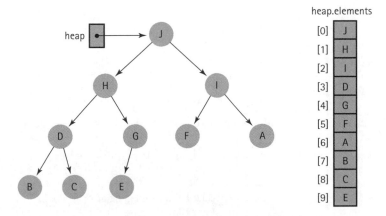

Figure 9.4 *Heap values in an array representation*

Recall that when we use this representation of a binary tree, the following relationships hold for an element at position `index`:

- If the element is not the root, its parent is at position `(index - 1) / 2`.
- If the element has a left child, the child is at position `(index * 2) + 1`.
- If the element has a right child, the child is at position `(index * 2) + 2`.

These relationships allow us to efficiently calculate the parent, left child, or right child of any node. Also, because the tree is complete, we do not waste space using the array representation. Time efficiency *and* space efficiency! We make use of these features in our heap implementation.

Rather than directly use an array to implement our heaps we use the Java library's `ArrayList`[2] class. This provides you with another example of `ArrayList` use (in Chapter 3 we saw how to use it to implement a stack), and allows us to create a generic heap without needing to deal with the troublesome issues surrounding the use of generics and arrays in Java. An `ArrayList` is essentially just a wrapper around an array—therefore the use of an `ArrayList` does not cost much, if anything, in terms of efficiency. This is especially true since we design our heap-based priority queue to be of a fixed capacity, and therefore we prevent the use of the automatic, time-inefficient copying of the underlying array that occurs when an `ArrayList` object needs to be resized. Furthermore, we only ever `add` or `remove` elements at the "end" of the `ArrayList`—adding or removing anywhere else would require costly element shifting.

Here is the beginning of our `Heap` class. As you can see, it implements `PriQueueInterface`. Because it implements a priority queue, we placed it in the `ch09.priorityQueues` package. Also, note that the only constructor requires an integer argument, used to set the size of the underlying `ArrayList`. The `isEmpty` and `isFull` operations are trivial.

```
//-----------------------------------------------------------------------------
// Heap.java              by Dale/Joyce/Weems                    Chapter 9
//
// Defines all constructs for a heap.
// The dequeue method returns the largest element in the heap.
//-----------------------------------------------------------------------------

package ch09.priorityQueues;

import java.util.*;

public class Heap<T extends Comparable<T>> implements PriQueueInterface<T>
{
  private ArrayList<T> elements;  // priority queue elements
```

---

2. The API for the `ArrayList` class is included at the beginning of Appendix E.

```
private int lastIndex;           // index of last element in priority queue
private int maxIndex;            // index of last position in ArrayList

public Heap(int maxSize)
{
  elements = new ArrayList<T>(maxSize);
  lastIndex = -1;
  maxIndex = maxSize - 1;
}

public boolean isEmpty()
// Returns true if this priority queue is empty; otherwise, returns false.
{
  return (lastIndex == -1);
}

public boolean isFull()
// Returns true if this priority queue is full; otherwise, returns false.
{
  return (lastIndex == maxIndex);
}
```

The enqueue Method

We next look at the enqueue method, which is the simpler of the two transformer methods. If we assume the existence of a reheapUp helper method, as specified previously, the enqueue method is

```
public void enqueue(T element) throws PriQOverflowException
// Throws PriQOverflowException if this priority queue is full;
// otherwise, adds element to this priority queue.
{
  if (lastIndex == maxIndex)
    throw new PriQOverflowException("Priority queue is full");
  else
  {
    lastIndex++;
    elements.add(lastIndex, element);
    reheapUp(element);
  }
}
```

If the heap is already full, we throw the appropriate exception. Otherwise, we increase the lastIndex value, add the element to the heap at that location, and call the `reheapUp` method. Of course, the `reheapUp` method is doing all of the interesting work. Let's look at it more closely.

The `reheapUp` algorithm starts with a tree whose last node is empty; we continue to call this empty node the "hole." We swap the hole up the tree until it reaches a spot where the `element` argument can be placed into the hole without violating the order property of the heap. While the hole moves up the tree, the elements it is replacing move down the tree, filling in the previous location of the hole. This situation is illustrated in Figure 9.5.

The sequence of nodes between a leaf and the root of a heap can be viewed as a sorted linked list. This is guaranteed by the heap's order property. The `reheapUp` algorithm is essentially inserting an element into this sorted linked list. As we progress from the leaf to

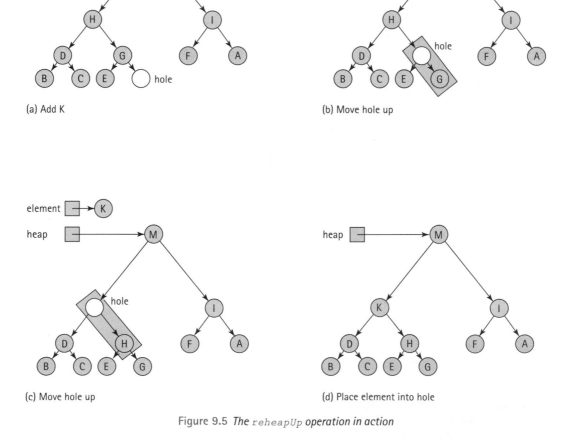

Figure 9.5 *The `reheapUp` operation in action*

the root along this path, we compare the value of `element` with the value in the hole's parent node. If the parent's value is smaller, we cannot place `element` into the current hole, because the order property would be violated, so we move the hole up. Moving the hole up really means copying the value of the hole's parent into the hole's location. Now the parent's location is available and it becomes the new hole. We repeat this process until (1) the hole is the root of the heap or (2) `element`'s value is less than or equal to the value in the hole's parent node. In either case, we can now safely copy `element` into the hole's position.

Here's the algorithm:

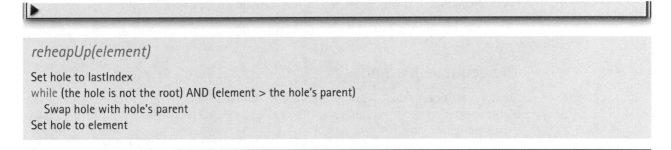

reheapUp(element)

Set hole to lastIndex
while (the hole is not the root) AND (element > the hole's parent)
    Swap hole with hole's parent
Set hole to element

This algorithm requires us to be able to find a given node's parent quickly. This task appears difficult, based on our experiences with references that can be traversed in only one direction. But, as we saw earlier, it is very simple with our implicit link implementation:

- If the element is not the root, its parent is at position `(index - 1) / 2`.

Here is the code for the `reheapUp` method:

```
private void reheapUp(T element)
// Current lastIndex position is "empty".
// Inserts element into the tree and ensures shape and order properties.
{
  int hole = lastIndex;
  while ((hole > 0)    // hole is not root and element > hole's parent
        &&
    (element.compareTo(elements.get((hole - 1) / 2)) > 0))
    {
    // move hole's parent down and then move hole up
    elements.set(hole,elements.get((hole - 1) / 2));
    hole = (hole - 1) / 2;
  }

  elements.set(hole, element);  // place element into final hole
}
```

This method takes advantage of the short-circuit nature of Java's `&&` operator. If the current `hole` is the root of the heap, then the first half of the *while* loop control expression

```
(hole > 0)
```

is `false`, and the second half

```
(element.compareTo(elements.get((hole - 1) / 2)) > 0))
```

is not evaluated. If it was evaluated in that case, it would cause an `IndexOutOfBounds-Exception` to be thrown.

The dequeue Method

Finally, we look at the `dequeue` method. As for `enqueue`, if we assume the existence of the helper method, in this case the `reheapDown` method, the `dequeue` method is very simple:

```
public T dequeue() throws PriQUnderflowException
// Throws PriQUnderflowException if this priority queue is empty;
// otherwise, removes element with highest priority from this
// priority queue and returns it.
{
  T hold;      // element to be dequeued and returned
  T toMove;    // element to move down heap

  if (lastIndex == -1)
    throw new PriQUnderflowException("Priority queue is empty");
  else
  {
    hold = elements.get(0);                  // remember element to be returned
    toMove = elements.remove(lastIndex);     // element to reheap down
    lastIndex--;                             // decrease priority queue size
    if (lastIndex != -1)
      reheapDown(toMove);                    // restore heap properties
    return hold;                             // return largest element
  }
}
```

If the heap is empty, we throw the appropriate exception. Otherwise, we first make a copy of the root element (the maximum element in the tree), so that we can return it to the client program when we are finished. We also make a copy of the element in the "last" position and remove it from the ArrayList. Recall that this is the element we use to move into the hole vacated by the root element, so we call it the toMove element. We decrement the lastIndex variable to reflect the new bounds of the heap and, assuming the heap is not now empty, pass the toMove element to the reheapDown method. The only thing remaining to do is to return the saved value of the previous root element, the hold variable, to the client.

Let's look at the reheapDown algorithm more closely. In many ways, it is similar to the reheapUp algorithm. In both cases, we have a "hole" in the tree and an element to be placed into the tree so that the tree remains a heap. In both cases, we move the hole through the tree (actually moving tree elements into the hole) until it reaches a location where it can legally hold the element. The reheapDown operation, however, is a more complex operation because it is moving the hole down the tree instead of up the tree. When we are moving down, we have more decisions to make.

When reheapDown is first called, the root of the tree can be considered a hole; that position in the tree is available, because the dequeue method has already saved the contents in its hold variable. The job of reheapDown is to "move" the hole down the tree until it reaches a spot where element can replace it. See Figure 9.6.

Before we can move the hole, we need to know where to move it. It should move either to its left child or to its right child, or it should stay where it is. Let's assume the existence of another helper method, called newHole, that provides us this information. The specification for newHole is

```
private int newHole(int hole, T element)
// If either child of hole is larger than element, return the index
// of the larger child; otherwise, return the index of hole.
```

Given the index of the hole, newHole returns the index of the next location for the hole. If newHole returns the same index that is passed to it, we know the hole is at its final location. The reheapDown algorithm repeatedly calls newHole to find the next index for the hole, and then moves the hole down to that location. It does this until newHole returns the same index that is passed to it. The existence of newHole simplifies reheapDown so that we can now create its code:

```
private void reheapDown(T element)
// Current root position is "empty";
// inserts element into the tree and ensures shape and order properties.
{
  int hole = 0;       // current index of hole
  int newhole;        // index where hole should move to

  newhole = newHole(hole, element);   // find next hole
  while (newhole != hole)
```

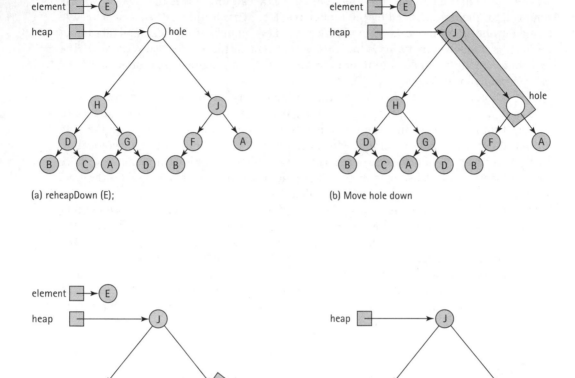

Figure 9.6 *The* `reheapDown` *operation in action*

```
    {
        elements.set(hole,elements.get(newhole));   // move element up
        hole = newhole;                             // move hole down
        newhole = newHole(hole, element);           // find next hole
    }
    elements.set(hole, element);                    // fill in the final hole
}
```

Now the only thing left to do is create the `newHole` method. This method does quite a lot of work for us. Consider Figure 9.6 again. Given the initial configuration, `newHole` should return the index of the node containing J, the right child of the hole node; J is larger than either the element (E) or the left child of the hole node (H). Thus `newHole` must compare three values (the values in `element`, the left child of the hole node, and the right child of the hole node) and return the index of the greatest value. Think about that. It doesn't seem very hard but it does become a little messy when described in algorithmic form:

Greatest(left, right, element) returns index

```
if (left < right)
    if (right <= element)
        return element
    else
        return right
else
if (left <= element)
    return element;
else
    return left;
```

Of course, other approaches to this algorithm are possible, but they all require about the same number of comparisons. One benefit of the preceding algorithm is that if `element` is tied for being the largest of the three arguments, its index is returned. This choice increases the efficiency of our program because in this situation we want the hole to stop moving (`reheapDown` breaks out of its loop when the value of `hole` is returned). Trace the algorithm with various combinations of arguments to convince yourself that it works.

Our algorithm applies only to the case when the hole node has two children. Of course, the `newHole` method must also handle the cases where the hole node is a leaf and where the hole node has only one child. How can we tell if a node is a leaf or if it has only one child? Easily, based on the fact that our tree is complete. First, we calculate the expected position of the left child; if this position is greater than `lastIndex`, then the tree has no node at this position and the hole node is a leaf. (Remember, if it doesn't have a left child, it cannot have a right child because the tree is complete.) In this case `newHole` just returns the index of its hole parameter, because the hole cannot move anymore. If the expected position of the left child is equal to `lastIndex`, then the node has only one child, and `newHole` returns the index of that child if the child's value is larger than the value of `element`.

Here is the code for `newHole`. As you can see, it is a sequence of *if-else* statements that capture the approaches described in the preceding paragraphs.

```
        private int newHole(int hole, T element)
        // If either child of hole is larger than element, return the index
        // of the larger child; otherwise, return the index of hole.
        {
          int left = (hole * 2) + 1;
          int right = (hole * 2) + 2;

          if (left > lastIndex)
            // hole has no children
            return hole;
          else
          if (left == lastIndex)
            // hole has left child only
            if (element.compareTo(elements.get(left)) < 0)
              // element < left child
              return left;
            else
              // element >= left child
              return hole;
          else
          // hole has two children
          if (elements.get(left).compareTo(elements.get(right)) < 0)
            // left child < right child
            if (elements.get(right).compareTo(element) <= 0)
              // right child <= element
              return hole;
            else
              // element < right child
              return right;
          else
          // left child >= right child
          if (elements.get(left).compareTo(element) <= 0)
            // left child <= element
            return hole;
          else
            // element < left child
            return left;
        }
```

A Sample Use

To allow us to test our heap we include the following `toString` method within its implementation:

```
public String toString()
// Returns a string of all the heap elements.
```

```
        {
          String theHeap = new String("the heap is:\n");
          for (int index = 0; index <= lastIndex; index++)
            theHeap = theHeap + index + ". " + elements.get(index) + "\n";
          return theHeap;
        }
```

This toString method simply returns a string indicating each index used in the heap, along with the corresponding element contained at that index. It allows us to devise test programs that create and manipulate heaps, and then displays their structure.

Suppose you enqueue the strings "J," "A," "M," "B," "L," and "E" into a new heap. How would you draw our logical view of the ensuing heap? Which values would be in which ArrayList slots? Suppose you dequeue an element and print it? Which element would be printed, and how would the realigned heap appear?

To demonstrate how you might declare and use a heap in an application we provide a short example of a program that performs those operations, and we show the output from the program. Were your predictions correct?

```
//-------------------------------------------------------------------------
// UseHeap.java              by Dale/Joyce/Weems              Chapter 9
//
// Example of a simple use of the Heap.
//-------------------------------------------------------------------------

import ch09.priorityQueues.*;

public class UseHeap
{
  public static void main(String[] args)
  {
    PriQueueInterface<String> h = new Heap<String>(10);
    h.enqueue("J");
    h.enqueue("A");
    h.enqueue("M");
    h.enqueue("B");
    h.enqueue("L");
    h.enqueue("E");

    System.out.println(h);

    System.out.println(h.dequeue() + "\n");

    System.out.println(h);
  }
}
```

Here is the output from the program, with our logical view of the heap, both before and after dequeing the largest element, drawn to the right:

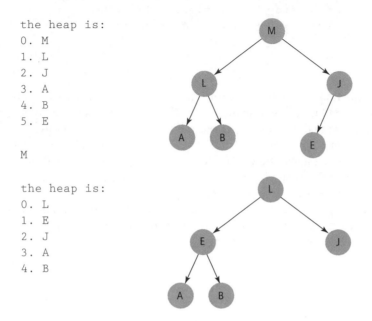

```
the heap is:
0. M
1. L
2. J
3. A
4. B
5. E

M

the heap is:
0. L
1. E
2. J
3. A
4. B
```

Heaps Versus Other Representations of Priority Queues

How efficient is the heap implementation of a priority queue? The constructor `isEmpty` and `isFull` methods are trivial, so we examine only the operations to add and remove elements. The `enqueue` and `dequeue` methods both consist of a few basic operations plus a call to a helper method. The `reheapUp` method creates a slot for a new element by moving a hole up the tree, level by level; because a complete tree is of minimum height, there are at most $\log_2 N$ levels above the leaf level (N = number of elements). Thus `enqueue` is an $O(\log_2 N)$ operation. The `reheapDown` method is invoked to fill the hole in the root created by the `dequeue` method. This operation moves the hole down in the tree, level by level. Again, there are at most $\log_2 N$ levels below the root, so `dequeue` is also an $O(\log_2 N)$ operation.

How does this implementation compare to the others we mentioned in the previous section? If we implement the priority queue with a linked list, sorted from largest to smallest priority, `dequeue` merely removes the first node from the list—an $O(1)$ operation. The `enqueue` operation, by contrast, however, must search up to all the elements in the list to find the appropriate insertion place; thus it is an $O(N)$ operation.

If the priority queue is implemented using a binary search tree, the efficiency of the operations depends on the shape of the tree. When the tree is bushy, both `dequeue` and `enqueue` are $O(\log_2 N)$ operations. In the worst case, if the tree degenerates to a linked

Table 9.1 *Comparison of Priority Queue Implementations*

	enqueue	dequeue
Heap	$O(\log_2 N)$	$O(\log_2 N)$
Linked list	$O(N)$	$O(1)$
Binary search tree		
Balanced	$O(\log_2 N)$	$O(\log_2 N)$
Skewed	$O(N)$	$O(N)$

list, both `enqueue` and `dequeue` have $O(N)$ efficiency. Table 9.1 summarizes the efficiency of the various implementations.

Overall, the binary search tree looks good, if it is balanced. It can, however, become skewed, which reduces the efficiency of the operations. The heap, by contrast, is always a tree of minimum height. It is not a good structure for accessing a randomly selected element, but that is not one of the operations defined for priority queues. The accessing protocol of a priority queue specifies that only the largest (or highest-priority) element can be accessed. The linked list is a good option for this operation (assuming the list is sorted from largest to smallest), but we may have to search the whole list to find the place to add a new element. For the operations specified for priority queues, therefore, the heap is an excellent choice.

9.3 Introduction to Graphs

Binary trees provide a very useful way of representing relationships in which a hierarchy exists. That is, a node is pointed to by at most one other node (its parent), and each node points to at most two other nodes (its children). If we remove the restriction that each node can have at most two children, we have a general tree, as pictured below.

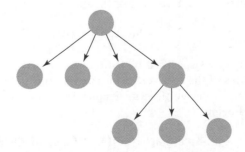

Graph A data structure that consists of a set of nodes and a set of edges that relate the nodes to each other

Vertex A node in a graph

Edge (arc) A pair of vertices representing a connection between two nodes in a graph

Undirected graph A graph in which the edges have no direction

Directed graph (digraph) A graph in which each edge is directed from one vertex to another (or the same) vertex

If we also remove the restriction that each node may have only one parent node, we have a data structure called a graph. A graph is made up of a set of nodes called vertices and a set of lines called edges (or arcs) that connect the nodes.

The set of edges describes relationships among the vertices. For instance, if the vertices are the names of cities, the edges that link the vertices could represent roads between pairs of cities. Because the road that runs between Houston and Austin also runs between Austin and Houston, the edges in this graph have no direction. This is called an undirected graph. If the edges that link the vertices represent flights from one city to another, however, the direction of each edge is important. The existence of a flight (edge) from Houston to Austin does not assure the existence of a flight from Austin to Houston. A graph whose edges are directed from one vertex to another is called a directed graph, or digraph.

From a programmer's perspective, vertices represent whatever is the subject of our study: people, houses, cities, courses, and so on. Mathematically, however, vertices are the abstract concept upon which graph theory rests. In fact, a great deal of formal mathematics is associated with graphs. In other computing courses, you may analyze graphs and prove theorems about them. This textbook introduces the graph as an abstract data type, teaches some basic terminology, discusses how a graph might be implemented, and describes how algorithms that manipulate graphs make use of stacks, queues, and priority queues.

Formally, a graph G is defined as follows:

$$G = (V, E)$$

where

V(G) is a finite, nonempty set of vertices

E(G) is a set of edges (written as pairs of vertices)

The set of vertices is specified by listing them in set notation, within { } braces. The following set defines the four vertices of the graph pictured in Figure 9.7(a):

$$V(Graph1) = \{A, B, C, D\}$$

The set of edges is specified by listing a sequence of edges. Each edge is denoted by writing the names of the two vertices it connects in parentheses, with a comma between them. For instance, the vertices in Graph1 in Figure 9.7(a) are connected by the four edges described below:

$$E(Graph1) = \{(A, B), (A, D), (B, C), (B, D)\}$$

(a) Graph1 is an undirected graph.

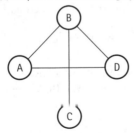

V(Graph1) = {A, B, C, D}
E(Graph1) = {(A, B), (A, D), (B, C), (B, D)}

(b) Graph2 is a directed graph.

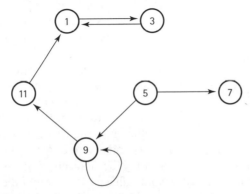

V(Graph2) = {1, 3, 5, 7, 9, 11}
E(Graph2) = {(1, 3), (3, 1), (5, 7), (5, 9), (9, 11), (9, 9), (11, 1)}

(c) Graph3 is a directed graph.

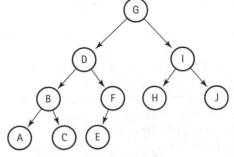

V(Graph3) = {A, B, C, D, E, F, G, H, I, J}
E(Graph3) = {(G, D), (G, I), (D, B), (D, F), (I, H), (I, J), (B, A), (B, C), (F, E)}

Figure 9.7 *Some examples of graphs*

Because Graph1 is an undirected graph, the order of the vertices in each edge is unimportant. The set of edges in Graph1 can also be described as follows:

E(Graph1) = {(B, A), (D, A), (C, B), (D, B)}

If the graph is a digraph, the direction of the edge is indicated by which vertex is listed first. For instance, in Figure 9.7(b), the edge (5, 7) represents a link from vertex 5 to vertex 7. There is no corresponding edge (7, 5) in Graph2. In pictures of digraphs, the arrows indicate the direction of the relationship.

We do not have duplicate vertices or edges in a graph. This point is implied in the definition, because sets do not have repeated elements.

Adjacent vertices Two vertices in a graph that are connected by an edge

Path A sequence of vertices that connects two nodes in a graph

Complete graph A graph in which every vertex is directly connected to every other vertex $N \cdot (N-1) / 2$ edges

Weighted graph A graph in which each edge carries a value

If two vertices in a graph are connected by an edge, they are said to be adjacent. In Graph1 (Figure 9.7a), vertices A and B are adjacent, but vertices A and C are not. If the vertices are connected by a directed edge, then the first vertex is said to be *adjacent to* the second, and the second vertex is said to be *adjacent from* the first. For example, in Graph2 (in Figure 9.7b), vertex 5 is adjacent to vertices 7 and 9, while vertex 1 is adjacent from vertices 3 and 11.

The picture of Graph3 in Figure 9.7(c) may look familiar; it is the tree we looked at earlier in connection with the nonlinked representation of a binary tree. A tree is a special case of a directed graph in which each vertex may only be adjacent from one other vertex (its parent node) and one vertex (the root) is not adjacent from any other vertex.

A path from one vertex to another consists of a sequence of vertices that connect them. For a path to exist, there must be an uninterrupted sequence of edges from the first vertex, through any number of vertices, to the second vertex. For example, in Graph2, there is a path from vertex 5 to vertex 3, but not from vertex 3 to vertex 5. In a tree, such as Graph3 (Figure 9.7c), there is a unique path from the root to every other node in the tree.

A complete graph is one in which every vertex is adjacent to every other vertex. Figure 9.8 shows two complete graphs. If there are N vertices, there are $N * (N - 1)$ edges in a complete directed graph and $N * (N - 1) / 2$ edges in a complete undirected graph.

A weighted graph is a graph in which each edge carries a value. Weighted graphs can be used to represent applications in which the *value* of the connection between the vertices is important, not just the *existence* of a connection. For instance, in the weighted graph pictured in Figure 9.9, the vertices represent cities and the edges indicate the Air Busters Airlines flights that connect the cities. The weights attached to the edges represent the air distances between pairs of cities.

To see whether we can get from Denver to Washington, we look for a path between them. If the total travel distance is determined by the sum of the distances between each pair of cities along the way, we can calculate the travel distance by adding the weights attached to the edges that constitute the path between them. There may be multiple

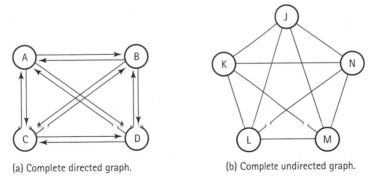

(a) Complete directed graph.

(b) Complete undirected graph.

Figure 9.8 *Two complete graphs*

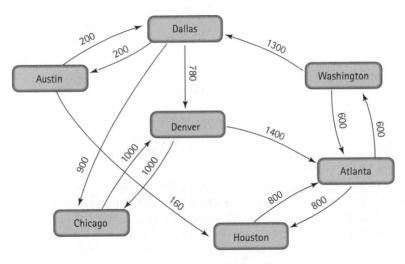

Figure 9.9 *A weighted graph*

paths between two vertices. Later in this chapter, we talk about a way to find the shortest path between two vertices.

9.4 Formal Specification of a Graph ADT

We have described a graph at the abstract level as a set of vertices and a set of edges that connect some or all of the vertices to one another. What kind of operations are defined on a graph? In this chapter we specify and implement a small set of useful graph operations. Many other operations on graphs can be defined as well; we have chosen operations that are useful in the graph applications described later in the chapter.

Our specification for the Graph ADT includes 11 public methods. As expected, it includes methods to check whether the graph is empty or full, and methods to add vertices and edges. Next we describe the remaining, more unusual methods.

The `hasVertex` method can be used to check whether the argument object is used as a vertex in the graph. This issue is important because many of the other methods that accept a vertex as an argument assume, as a precondition, that the given vertex exists within the graph. Equivalence of vertices is determined using the vertices' `equals` method—so if the vertex class has overwritten the `Object` class `equals` method, then equality will be as defined within the vertex class; otherwise it is defined using the default approach of comparing references.

The `weightIs` method can be used to determine whether a given edge is in the graph. It returns the weight of the edge between two given vertices; if there is no such edge, it returns a special value indicating that fact. The special value could vary from one application to another. For example, the value −1 could be used for a graph whose edges represent distances, because there is no such thing as a negative distance. The special value for a specific application could be passed to the Graph constructor.

The most interesting method is `getToVertices`, which returns a queue of vertex objects. The idea is that an application may need to know which vertices are adjacent *to* a given vertex. This method returns the collection of such vertices as a queue. The application can then dequeue the vertices one at a time, as needed. The return value of the method is of "type" `QueueInterface`. The implementation programmer can choose to use any queue class that implements this interface.

Another approach to solving the "get to vertices" problem is to have the method return a Java `Iterator` object. We discussed iterators in the "Java Collections Framework List" feature in Chapter 6.

Often, when an application uses a graph, it must traverse the graph—that is, it must visit the vertices of the graph and perform some operation at each vertex. Because so many paths through a graph are possible, it is not unusual for the traversal algorithm to attempt to visit a vertex more than once. In such cases it is usually important for the application to "know" that it has previously visited the vertex. To facilitate this recognition, our interface includes several methods related to marking vertices as visited. The `markVertex` and `isMarked` methods are used to mark vertices and check for marks, respectively. The `clearMarks` method clears all of the marks throughout the graph; it is used to prepare for a new traversal. Finally, the `getUnmarked` method returns an unmarked vertex. This ability is useful for beginning a traversal or for continuing a traversal, when the application is not sure it has visited every vertex.

```
//----------------------------------------------------------------------------
// WeightedGraphInterface.java       by Dale/Joyce/Weems          Chapter 9
//
// Interface for a class that implements a directed graph with weighted edges.
// Vertices are objects of class T and can be marked as having been visited.
// Edge weights are integers.
// Equivalence of vertices is determined by the vertices' equals method.
//
```

```
// General precondition: Except for the addVertex and hasVertex methods,
// any vertex passed as an argument to a method is in this graph.
//-------------------------------------------------------------------------

package ch09.graphs;

import ch05.queues.*;

public interface WeightedGraphInterface<T>
{
  boolean isEmpty();
  // Returns true if this graph is empty; otherwise, returns false.

  boolean isFull();
  // Returns true if this graph is full; otherwise, returns false.

  void addVertex(T vertex);
  // Preconditions:    This graph is not full.
  //                   Vertex is not already in this graph.
  //                   Vertex is not null.
  //
  // Adds vertex to this graph.

  boolean hasVertex(T vertex);
  // Returns true if this graph contains vertex; otherwise, returns false.

  void addEdge(T fromVertex, T toVertex, int weight);
  // Adds an edge with the specified weight from fromVertex to toVertex.

  int weightIs(T fromVertex, T toVertex);
  // If edge from fromVertex to toVertex exists, returns the weight of edge;
  // otherwise, returns a special "null-edge" value.

  UnboundedQueueInterface<T> getToVertices(T vertex);
  // Returns a queue of the vertices that are adjacent from vertex.

  void clearMarks();
  // Sets marks for all vertices to false.

  void markVertex(T vertex);
  // Sets mark for vertex to true.

  boolean isMarked(T vertex);
  // Returns true if vertex is marked; otherwise, returns false.
```

```
    T getUnmarked();
    // Returns an unmarked vertex if any exist; otherwise, returns null.
}
```

9.5 Implementations of Graphs

Array–Based Implementation

Figure 9.18 in the chapter summary section displays a UML class diagram representing our array-based graph implementation class.

A simple way to represent V(graph), the vertices in the graph, is to use an array where the array elements are the vertices. For example, if the vertices represent city names, the array might hold strings. A simple way to represent E(graph), the edges in a graph, is to use an adjacency matrix, a two-dimensional array of edge values (weights), where the indexes of a weight correspond to the vertices connected by the edge. Thus a graph consists of an integer variable `numVertices`, a one-dimensional array `vertices`, and a two-dimensional array `edges`. Figure 9.10 depicts the implementation of the graph of Air Busters flights between seven cities shown in Figure 9.9. For simplicity, we omit the additional `boolean` data needed to mark vertices as "visited" during a traversal from the figure. Although the city names in Figure 9.10 are in alphabetical order, there is no requirement that the elements in this array be sorted.

> **Adjacency matrix** For a graph with *N* nodes, an *N* by *N* table that shows the existence (and weights) of all edges in the graph

At any time, within this representation of a graph,

- `numVertices` is the number of vertices in the graph.
- V(graph) is contained in `vertices[0]` to `vertices[numVertices - 1]`.
- E(graph) is contained in the square array `edges[0][0]` to `edges[numVertices - 1][numVertices - 1]`.

The names of the cities are contained in `graph.vertices`. The weight of each edge in `graph.edges` represents the air distance between two cities that are connected by a flight. For example, the value in `graph.edges[1][3]` tells us that there is a direct flight between Austin and Dallas, and that the air distance is 200 miles. A `NULL_EDGE` value (0) in `graph.edges[1][6]` tells us that the airline has no direct flights between Austin and Washington. Because this is a weighted graph in which the weights are air distances, we use `int` for the edge value type. If it were not a weighted graph, the edge value type would be `boolean`, and each position in the adjacency matrix would be `true` if an edge exists between the pair of vertices, and `false` if no edge exists.

Here is the beginning of the definition of class `WeightedGraph`. For simplicity, we assume that the edge value type is `int` and that a null edge is indicated by a 0 value.

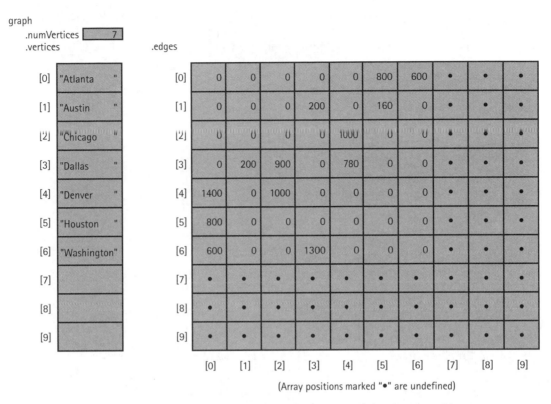

(Array positions marked "•" are undefined)

Figure 9.10 *Matrix representation of graph of flight connections between cities*

```
//--------------------------------------------------------------------------
// WeightedGraph.java           by Dale/Joyce/Weems          Chapter 9
//
// Implements a directed graph with weighted edges.
// Vertices are objects of class T and can be marked as having been visited.
// Edge weights are integers.
// Equivalence of vertices is determined by the vertices' equals method.
//
// General precondition: Except for the addVertex and hasVertex methods,
// any vertex passed as an argument to a method is in this graph.
//--------------------------------------------------------------------------

package ch09.graphs;

import ch05.queues.*;
```

```
public class WeightedGraph<T> implements WeightedGraphInterface<T>
{
  public static final int NULL_EDGE = 0;
  private static final int DEFCAP = 50;  // default capacity
  private int numVertices;
  private int maxVertices;
  private T[] vertices;
  private int[][] edges;
  private boolean[] marks;  // marks[i] is mark for vertices[i]

  public WeightedGraph()
  // Instantiates a graph with capacity DEFCAP vertices.
  {
    numVertices = 0;
    maxVertices = DEFCAP;
    vertices = (T[]) new Object[DEFCAP];³
    marks = new boolean[DEFCAP];
    edges = new int[DEFCAP][DEFCAP];
  }

  public WeightedGraph(int maxV)
  // Instantiates a graph with capacity maxV.
  {
    numVertices = 0;
    maxVertices = maxV;
    vertices = (T[]) new Object[maxV];³
    marks = new boolean[maxV];
    edges = new int[maxV][maxV];
  }
...
}
```

The class constructors have to allocate the space for `vertices` and `marks` (the `boolean` array indicating whether a vertex has been marked). The default constructor sets up space for DEFCAP = 50 `vertices` and `marks`. The parameterized constructor lets the user specify the maximum number of vertices.

The `addVertex` operation puts a vertex into the next free space in the array of vertices. Because the new vertex has no edges defined yet, we also initialize the appropriate row and column of edges to contain NULL_EDGE (0 in this case).

---

3. An unchecked cast warning is generated because the compiler cannot ensure that the array contains objects of class T—the warning can safely be ignored.

```
public void addVertex(T vertex)
// Preconditions:    This graph is not full.
//                   Vertex is not already in this graph.
//                   Vertex is not null.
//
// Adds vertex to this graph.
{
  vertices[numVertices] = vertex;
  for (int index = 0; index < numVertices; index++)
  {
    edges[numVertices][index] = NULL_EDGE;
    edges[index][numVertices] = NULL_EDGE;
  }
  numVertices++;
}
```

To add an edge to the graph, we must first locate the `fromVertex` and `toVertex` that define the edge we want to add. These values become the arguments to `addEdge` and are of the generic `T` class. Of course, the client really passes references to the vertex objects, because that is how we manipulate objects in Java. We are implementing our graphs "by reference" so this strategy should not pose a problem for the client. To index the correct matrix slot, we need the index in the `vertices` array that corresponds to each vertex. Once we know the indexes, it is a simple matter to set the weight of the edge in the matrix. Here is the algorithm:

---

addEdge(fromVertex, toVertex, weight)

Set fromIndex to index of fromVertex in V(graph)
Set toIndex to index of toVertex in V(graph)
Set edges[fromIndex, toIndex] to weight

To find the index of each vertex, let's write a search method that receives a vertex and returns its location (index) in `vertices`. Based on the general precondition stated in the opening comment of the `WeightedGraph` class, we can assume that the `fromVertex` and `toVertex` arguments passed to `addEdge` are already in V(graph). This assumption simplifies the search method, which we code as helper method `indexIs`. Here is the code for `indexIs` and `addEdge`:

```
private int indexIs(T vertex)
// Returns the index of vertex in vertices.
{
  int index = 0;
  while (!vertex.equals(vertices[index]))
    index++;
  return index;
}

public void addEdge(T fromVertex, T toVertex, int weight)
// Adds an edge with the specified weight from fromVertex to toVertex.
{
  int row;
  int column;

  row = indexIs(fromVertex);
  column = indexIs(toVertex);
  edges[row][column] = weight;
}
```

The weightIs operation is the mirror image of addEdge.

```
public int weightIs(T fromVertex, T toVertex)
// If edge from fromVertex to toVertex exists, returns the
// weight of edge; otherwise, returns a special "null-edge" value.
{
  int row;
  int column;

  row = indexIs(fromVertex);
  column = indexIs(toVertex);
  return edges[row][column];
}
```

The last graph operation that we address is getToVertices. This method receives a vertex as an argument, and it returns a queue of vertices that are adjacent from the designated vertex. That is, it returns a queue of all the vertices that we can get to from this vertex in one step. Using an adjacency matrix to represent the edges, it is a simple matter to determine the nodes to which the vertex is adjacent. We merely loop through the appropriate row in edges; whenever a value is found that is not NULL_EDGE, we add another vertex to the queue.

```
public UnboundedQueueInterface<T> getToVertices(T vertex)
// Returns a queue of the vertices that are adjacent from vertex.
{
  UnboundedQueueInterface<T> adjVertices = new LinkedUnbndQueue<T>();
  int fromIndex;
  int toIndex;
  fromIndex = indexIs(vertex);
  for (toIndex = 0; toIndex < numVertices; toIndex++)
    if (edges[fromIndex][toIndex] != NULL_EDGE)
      adjVertices.enqueue(vertices[toIndex]);
  return adjVertices;
}
```

We leave writing `isFull`, `isEmpty`, `hasVertex`, and the marking operations (`clear-Marks`, `markVertex`, `isMarked`, and `getUnmarked`) for you as exercises.

Linked Implementation

The advantages of representing the edges in a graph with an adjacency matrix are twofold: speed and simplicity. Given the indexes of two vertices, determining the existence (or the weight) of an edge between them is an $O(1)$ operation. The problem with adjacency matrices is that their use of space is an $O(N^2)$ operation, where N is the maximum number of vertices in the graph. If the maximum number of vertices is large, adjacency matrices may waste a lot of space. The space used could be minimized by dynamically allocating larger arrays as needed, but that approach can be inefficient in terms of time. We can save space by allocating memory as we need it at run time, using linked structures. Adjacency lists are linked lists, one list per vertex, that identify the vertices to which each vertex is connected. They can be implemented in several different ways. Figure 9.11 shows two different adjacency list representations of the graph in Figure 9.9.

> **Adjacency list**   A linked list that identifies all the vertices to which a particular vertex is connected; each vertex has its own adjacency list

In Figure 9.11(a), the vertices are stored in an array. Each component of this array contains a reference to a linked list of edge nodes. Each node in these linked lists contains an index number, a weight, and a reference to the next node in the adjacency list. Let's look at the adjacency list for Denver. The first node in the list indicates that there is a 1400-mile flight from Denver to Atlanta (the vertex whose index is 0) and a 1000-mile flight from Denver to Chicago (the vertex whose index is 2).

No arrays are used in the implementation illustrated in Figure 9.11(b). Instead, the list of vertices is implemented as a linked list. Now each node in the adjacency list contains a reference to the vertex information rather than the index of the vertex. Because Figure 9.11(b) includes so many of these references, we have used text to describe the vertex that each reference designates rather than draw them as arrows.

(a)

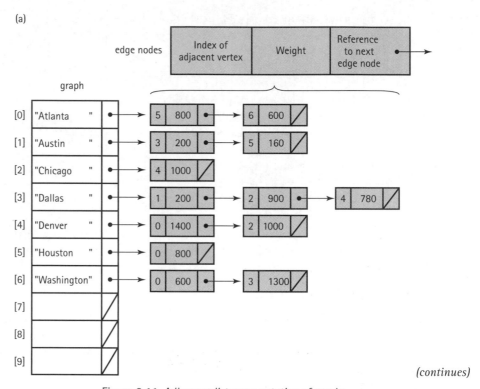

Figure 9.11 *Adjacency list representation of graphs*

(continues)

We leave the implementation of the `Graph` class methods using the linked approach as a programming exercise.

9.6 Graph Applications

The graph specification given in Section 9.4 included only the most basic operations; it did not include any traversal operations. As you might imagine, we can traverse a graph in many different orders. As a result, we treat traversal as a graph application rather than an innate operation. The basic operations given in our specification allow us to implement different traversals *independent* of how the graph itself is implemented. Our graph applications can also be considered graph-related algorithms.

In Chapter 8, we discussed the postorder tree traversal, which goes to the deepest level of the tree and works up. This strategy of going down a branch to its deepest point and moving up is called a *depth-first* strategy. Another systematic way to visit each vertex in a tree is to visit each vertex on level 0 (the root), then each vertex on level 1, then each vertex on level 2, and so on. Visiting each vertex by level in this way is called a *breadth-first* strategy. With graphs, both depth-first and breadth-first strategies are useful. We discuss algorithms for employing both strategies within the context of determining whether two cities are connected in our airline example.

(b)

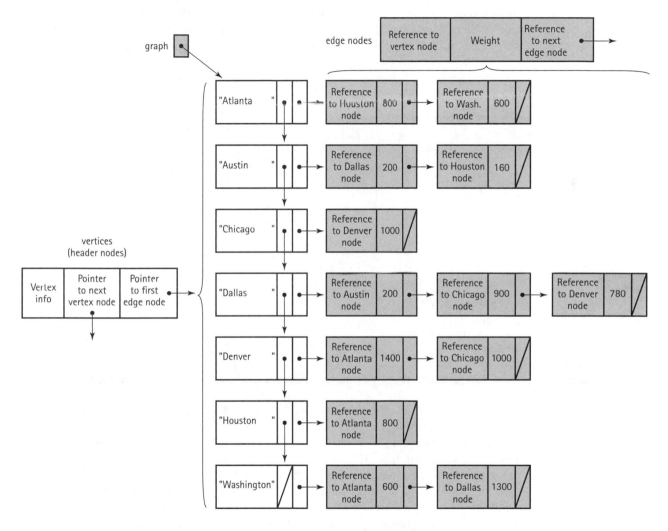

Figure 9.11 *(continued)*

Depth-First Searching

One question we can answer with the graph in Figure 9.9 is "Can I get from city X to city Y on my favorite airline?" This is equivalent to asking, "Does a path exist in the graph from vertex X to vertex Y?" Using a depth-first strategy, let's develop an algorithm IsPath that determines whether a path exists from `startVertex` to `endVertex`.

We need a systematic way to keep track of the cities as we investigate them. With a depth-first search, we examine the first vertex that is adjacent from `startVertex`; if it is `endVertex`, the search is over. Otherwise, we examine all of the vertices that can be reached in one step (are adjacent) from this first vertex. While we examine these vertices, we need to store the remaining vertices adjacent from `startVertex` that have not yet been examined. If a path does not exist from the first vertex, we come back and try the second vertex, third vertex, and so on. Because we want to travel as far as we can down one path, backtracking if the `endVertex` is not found, a stack is a good structure for storing the vertices. Here is the algorithm we use:

IsPath (startVertex, endVertex): returns boolean

```
Set found to false
stack.push(startVertex)
do
    vertex = stack.top( )
    stack.pop( )
    if vertex = endVertex
        Set found to true
    else
        Push all adjacent vertices onto stack
while !stack.isEmpty( ) AND !found
return found
```

Caution:
Contains error

Let's apply this algorithm to the sample airline-route graph in Figure 9.9. We want to fly from Austin to Washington. We initialize our search by pushing our starting city onto the stack (Figure 9.12a). At the beginning of the loop we retrieve the current city, Austin, from the stack using the `top` method and then remove it from the stack using the `pop` method. The places we can reach directly from Austin are Dallas and Houston; we push both of these vertices onto the stack (Figure 9.12b). At the beginning of the second iteration we retrieve and remove the top vertex from the stack—Houston. Houston is not our destination, so we resume our search from there.

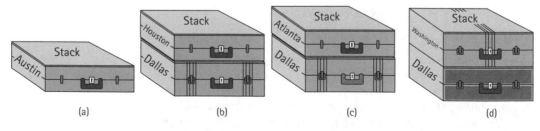

Figure 9.12 *Using a stack to store the routes*

There is only one flight out of Houston, to Atlanta; we push Atlanta onto the stack (Figure 9.12c). Again we retrieve and remove the top vertex from the stack. Atlanta is not our destination, so we continue searching from there. Atlanta has flights to two cities: Houston and Washington.

But we just came from Houston! We don't want to fly back to cities that we have already visited, as it could cause an infinite loop. We have to prevent cycling in this algorithm. We must mark a city as having been visited so that it is not investigated a second time. Here is the corrected version of the algorithm:

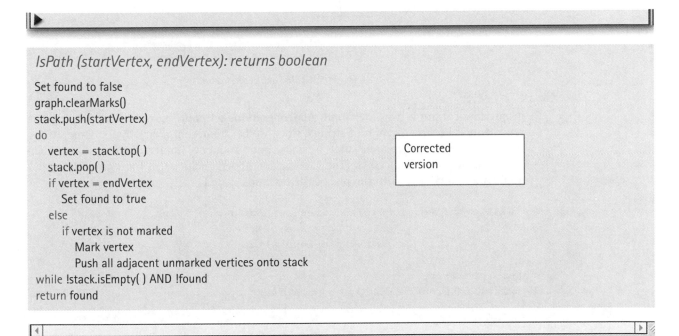

```
IsPath (startVertex, endVertex): returns boolean

Set found to false
graph.clearMarks()
stack.push(startVertex)
do
    vertex = stack.top( )
    stack.pop( )
    if vertex = endVertex
        Set found to true
    else
        if vertex is not marked
            Mark vertex
            Push all adjacent unmarked vertices onto stack
while !stack.isEmpty( ) AND !found
return found
```

Corrected version

Let's assume that we have marked the cities that have already been tried, and continue our example. Houston has already been visited, so we ignore it. The second adjacent vertex, Washington, has not been visited, so we push it onto the stack (Figure 9.12d). Again we retrieve and remove the top vertex from the stack. Washington is our destination, so the search is complete. The examined edges of the graph, using a depth-first search, are illustrated in Figure 9.13.

In the depth-first search, we go to the deepest branch, examining all the paths beginning at Houston, before we come back to search from Dallas. When we have to backtrack, we take the branch closest to where we dead-ended. That is, we go as far as we can down one path before we take alternative choices at earlier branches.

Method `isPath` receives a graph object, a starting vertex, and a target vertex. It uses the depth-first strategy to determine whether a path exists from the starting city to the ending city, displaying the names of all cities visited in the search. Nothing in the method depends on the implementation of the graph. The method is implemented as a

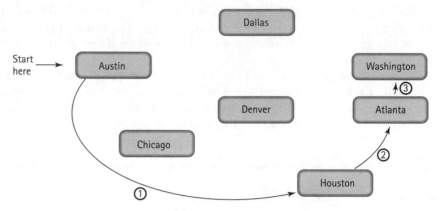

Figure 9.13 *The depth-first search*

graph application; it uses the Graph ADT operations without knowing how the graph is represented. We use a graph of strings, since we can represent a city by its name. In the following code, we assume that a stack and a queue implementation have been imported into the client class. (The `isPath` method is included in the `UseGraph.java` application, available with the rest of the textbook code.)

```
private static boolean isPath(WeightedGraphInterface graph,
                             String startVertex,
                             String endVertex   )

// Returns true if a path exists on graph, from startVertex to endVertex;
// otherwise, returns false. Uses depth-first search algorithm.

{
  UnboundedStackInterface<String> stack = new LinkedStack<String>();
  UnboundedQueueInterface<String> vertexQueue
     = new LinkedUnbndQueue<String>();

  boolean found = false;
  String vertex;
  String item;

  graph.clearMarks();
  stack.push(startVertex);
  do
  {
    vertex = stack.top();
    stack.pop();
    if (vertex == endVertex)
       found = true;
```

```
  else
  {
    if (!graph.isMarked(vertex))
    {
      graph.markVertex(vertex);
      vertexQueue = graph.getToVertices(vertex);

      while (!vertexQueue.isEmpty())
      {
        item = vertexQueue.dequeue();
        if (!graph.isMarked(item))
          stack.push(item);
      }
    }
  }
} while (!stack.isEmpty() && !found);

return found;
}
```

Breadth-First Searching

A breadth-first search looks at all possible paths at the same depth before it goes to a deeper level. In our flight example, a breadth-first search checks all possible one-stop connections before checking any two-stop connections. For most travelers, this strategy is the preferred approach for booking flights.

When we come to a dead end in a depth-first search, we back up as little as possible. We then try another route from a recent vertex—the route on top of our stack. In a breadth-first search, we want to back up as far as possible to find a route originating from the earliest vertices. The stack is not the right structure for finding an early route, because it keeps track of things in the order opposite of their occurrence—the latest route is on top. To keep track of things in the order in which they happened, we use a FIFO queue. The route at the front of this queue is a route from an earlier vertex; the route at the back of the queue is from a later vertex.

To modify the search to use a breadth-first strategy, we change all calls to stack operations to the analogous FIFO queue operations. Searching for a path from Austin to Washington, we first enqueue all the cities that can be reached directly from Austin: Dallas and Houston (Figure 9.14a). Then we dequeue the front queue element. Dallas is not the destination we seek, so we enqueue all the adjacent cities that have not yet been visited: Chicago and Denver (Figure 9.14b). (Austin has been visited already, so it is not enqueued.) Again we dequeue the front element from the queue. This element is the other "one-stop" city: Houston. Houston is not the desired destination, so we continue the search. There is only one flight out of Houston, and it is to Atlanta. Because we haven't visited Atlanta before, it is enqueued (Figure 9.14c).

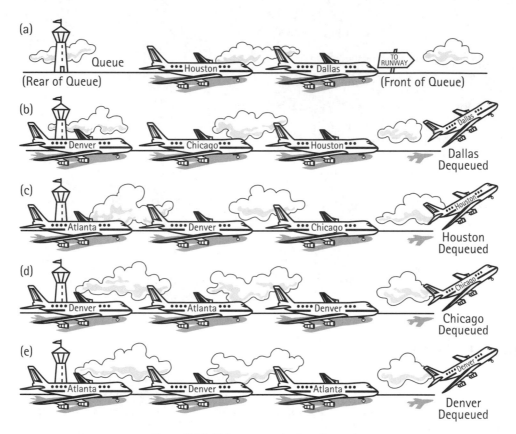

Figure 9.14 *Using a queue to store the routes*

Now we know that we cannot reach Washington with one stop, so we start examining the two-stop connections. We dequeue Chicago; it is not our destination, so we put its adjacent city, Denver, into the queue (Figure 9.14d). Now this is an interesting situation: Denver is in the queue twice. Should we mark a city as having been visited when we put it in the queue or after it has been dequeued, when we are examining its outgoing flights? If we mark it only after it is dequeued, multiple copies of the same vertex may appear in the queue (so we need to check whether a city is marked after it is dequeued).

An alternative approach is to mark the city as having been visited before it is put into the queue. Which is better? It depends on the processing goals. We may want to know whether alternative routes exist, in which case we would want to put a city into the queue more than once.

Back to our example: We have put Denver into the queue in one step and removed its previous entry at the next step. Denver is not our destination, so we put its adjacent cities that we haven't already marked (only Atlanta) into the queue (Figure 9.14e). This processing continues until Washington is put into the queue (from Atlanta), and is finally dequeued. We have found the desired city, and the search is complete. This search is illustrated in Figure 9.15, where the numbers on the edges show the order in which they are investigated.

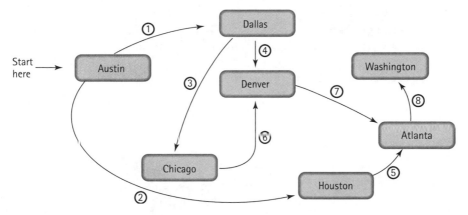

Figure 9.15 *The breadth-first search*

The source code for the breadth-first search approach is identical to the depth-first search code, except for the replacement of the stack with a FIFO queue. It is also included in the UseGraph.java application, as the method isPath2, available with the rest of the textbook code.

```
private static boolean isPath2(WeightedGraphInterface<String> graph,
                         String startVertex,
                         String endVertex    )

// Returns true if a path exists on graph, from startVertex to endVertex;
// otherwise, returns false. Uses breadth-first search algorithm.

{
  UnboundedQueueInterface<String> queue = new LinkedUnbndQueue<String>();
  UnboundedQueueInterface<String> vertexQueue
                            = new LinkedUnbndQueue<String>();

  boolean found = false;
  String vertex;
  String element;

  graph.clearMarks();
  queue.enqueue(startVertex);
  do
  {
    vertex = queue.dequeue();
    if (vertex == endVertex)
      found = true;
    else
    {
      if (!graph.isMarked(vertex))
```

```
    {
      graph.markVertex(vertex);
      vertexQueue = graph.getToVertices(vertex);

      while (!vertexQueue.isEmpty())
      {
        element = vertexQueue.dequeue();
        if (!graph.isMarked(element))
          queue.enqueue(element);
      }
    }
  } while (!queue.isEmpty() && !found);

  return found;
}
```

The Single-Source Shortest-Paths Problem

We know from the two search operations just discussed that there may be multiple paths from one vertex to another. Suppose that we want to find the shortest path from Austin to each of the other cities that Air Busters serves. By "shortest path" we mean the path whose edge values (weights), added together, have the smallest sum. Consider the following two paths from Austin to Washington:

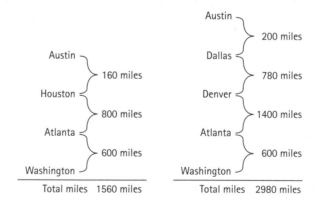

Clearly, the first path is preferable, unless we want to collect extra frequent-flyer miles.

Let's develop an algorithm that displays the shortest path from a designated starting city to *every other city* in the graph—this time we are not searching for a path between a starting city and an ending city. As in the two graph searches described earlier, we need an auxiliary structure for storing cities that we process later. By retrieving the city that was most recently put into the structure, the depth-first search tries to keep going "forward." It tries a one-flight solution, then a two-flight solution, then a three-flight solution, and so on. It backtracks to a fewer-flight solution only when it reaches a dead end. That approach is not suitable for our shortest-paths problem.

By retrieving the city that had been in the structure the longest time, the breadth-first search tries all one-flight solutions, then all two-flight solutions, and so on. The breadth-first search finds a path with a minimum number of flights. But a minimum *number* of flights does not necessarily mean the minimum *total distance*. That approach is also unsuitable for our shortest-paths problem.

Unlike the depth-first and breadth-first searches, this *shortest-path traversal* must use the number of miles (edge weights) between cities. We want to retrieve the vertex that is *closest* to the current vertex—that is, the vertex connected with the minimum edge weight. If we consider minimum distance to be the highest priority, then we know the perfect structure—the priority queue. Our algorithm can use a priority queue whose elements are flights (edges) with the distance from the starting city as the priority. That is, the elements in the priority queue are objects with three attributes: `fromVertex`, `toVertex`, and `distance`. We use a class named `Flight` to define these objects. The class implements the `Comparable<Flight>` interface, using the `distance` attribute to compare two flights (shorter is better). It provides a constructor that accepts three arguments, one for each attribute, and it provides the standard setter and getter methods for the attributes. The code is part of our `support` package. Here is the shortest-path algorithm:

shortestPaths(graph, startVertex)

```
graph.ClearMarks( )
Create flight(startVertex, startVertex, 0)
pq.enqueue(flight)
do
   flight = pq.dequeue( )
   if flight.getToVertex() is not marked
     Mark flight.getToVertex()
     Write flight.getFromVertex, flight.getToVertex, flight.getDistance
     flight.setFromVertex(flight.getToVertex())
     Set minDistance to flight.getDistance()
     Get queue vertexQueue of vertices adjacent from flight.getFromVertex()
     while more vertices in vertexQueue
       Get next vertex from vertexQueue
       if vertex not marked
         flight.setToVertex(vertex)
         flight.setDistance(minDistance + graph.weightIs(flight.getFromVertex(), vertex))
         pq.enqueue(flight)
while !pq.isEmpty( )
```

Caution:
Contains subtle error

The algorithm for the shortest-path traversal is similar to those we used for the depth-first and breadth-first searches, albeit with three major differences:

1. We use a priority queue rather than a FIFO queue or stack.
2. We stop only when there are no more cities to process; there is no destination.
3. It is incorrect if we use a store-by-reference priority queue!

When we code this algorithm, we are likely to make a subtle, but crucial error. This error is related to the fact that our queues store information "by reference" and not "by copy." Take a minute to review the algorithm to see if you can spot the error before continuing.

Recall the feature section in Chapter 6 that discussed the dangers of storing information by reference. In particular, it warned us to be careful when inserting an object into a structure and later making changes to that object. If we use the same reference to the object when we make changes to it, the changes are made to the object that is in the structure. Sometimes this outcome is what we want (see the case study in Chapter 8); at other times it causes problems, as in the current example. Here is the incorrect part of the algorithm:

```
while more vertices in vertexQueue
    Get next vertex from vertexQueue
    if vertex not marked
        flight.setToVertex(vertex)
        flight.setDistance(minDistance + graph.weightIs(flight.getFromVertex(), vertex))
        pq.enqueue(flight)
```

Now can you see the problem? This part of the algorithm walks through the queue of vertices adjacent to the current vertex and enqueues `Flight` objects onto the priority queue `pq` based on the information discovered there. The `flight` variable is actually a reference to a `Flight` object. Suppose the queue of adjacent vertices holds information related to the cities Atlanta and Houston. The first time through this loop, we insert information related to Atlanta in `flight` and enqueue it in `pq`. The next time through the loop, however, we make changes to the `Flight` object referenced by `flight`. We update it to contain information about Houston using the setter methods; and again we enqueue it in `pq`. So now `pq` contains information about Atlanta and Houston, correct? Nope. When we change the information in `flight` to the Houston information, those changes are reflected in the `flight` that is already on `pq`. The `flight` variable still references that object. In reality, the `pq` structure now contains two references to the same `flight`, and that `flight` contains Houston information.

To solve this problem, we must create a new `flight` object before storing on `pq`. Here is the corrected version of that part of the algorithm:

```
while more vertices in vertexQueue
    Get next vertex from vertexQueue
    if vertex not marked
        Set newDistance to minDistance + graph.weightIs(flight.getFromVertex(), vertex)
        Create new Flight(flight.getFromVertex(), vertex, newDistance)
        pq.enqueue(newFlight)
```

Here is the source code for the shortest-path algorithm (also included in the `UseGraph.java` application). As before, the code assumes that a priority queue and a queue implementation have been imported into the client class. For the priority queue, we use our `Heap` class. We want a smaller distance to indicate a higher priority, but our `Heap` class implements a *maximum* heap, returning the *largest* value from the `dequeue` method. To fix this problem, we could define a new heap class, a minimum heap. But there is an easier way. The current `Heap` class bases its decision about what is "larger" on the values returned by the flight's `compareTo` method. Thus we just define the `compareTo` method of the `Flight` class to indicate that the current flight is "larger" than the argument flight if its `distance` is smaller. For every flight in the heap's tree, `flight.distance` is then less than or equal to the `distance` value of each of its children. We can still use our maximum heap.

```java
private static void shortestPaths(WeightedGraphInterface<String> graph,
                                  String startVertex )

// Writes the shortest distance from startVertex to every
// other reachable vertex in graph.
{
  Flight flight;
  Flight saveFlight;          // for saving on priority queue
  int minDistance;
  int newDistance;

  PriQueueInterface<Flight> pq
          = new Heap<Flight>(20);   // Assume at most 20 vertices
  String vertex;
  UnboundedQueueInterface vertexQueue<String>
          = new LinkedUnbndQueue<String>();
```

```
graph.clearMarks();
saveFlight = new Flight(startVertex, startVertex, 0);
pq.enqueue(saveFlight);


System.out.println("Last Vertex   Destination   Distance");
System.out.println("-----------------------------------");

do
{
  flight = pq.dequeue();
  if (!graph.isMarked(flight.getToVertex()))
  {
    graph.markVertex(flight.getToVertex());
    System.out.println(flight);
    flight.setFromVertex(flight.getToVertex());
    minDistance = flight.getDistance();
    vertexQueue = graph.getToVertices(flight.getFromVertex());
    while (!vertexQueue.isEmpty())
    {
      vertex = vertexQueue.dequeue();
      if (!graph.isMarked(vertex))
      {
        newDistance = minDistance
                    + graph.weightIs(flight.getFromVertex(), vertex);
        saveFlight = new Flight(flight.getFromVertex(), vertex,
                                newDistance);
        pq.enqueue(saveFlight);
      }
    }
  }
} while (!pq.isEmpty());
}
```

The output from this method is a table of city pairs (edges) showing the total minimum distance from `startVertex` to each of the other vertices in the graph, as well as the last vertex visited before the destination. We assume that printing a vertex means printing the name of the corresponding city. If `graph` contains the information shown in Figure 9.9, the method call

```
shortestPaths(graph, startVertex);
```

where `startVertex` corresponds to Washington, would print the following:

Last Vertex	Destination	Distance
Washington	Washington	0
Washington	Atlanta	600
Washington	Dallas	1300
Atlanta	Houston	1400
Dallas	Austin	1500
Dallas	Denver	2080
Dallas	Chicago	2200

The shortest-path distance from Washington to each destination is shown in the two columns to the right. For example, our flights from Washington to Chicago total 2200 miles. The left-hand column shows which city immediately preceded the destination in the traversal. Let's figure out the shortest path from Washington to Chicago. We see from the left-hand column that the next-to-last vertex in the path is Dallas. Now we look up Dallas in the Destination (middle) column: The vertex before Dallas is Washington. The whole path is Washington–Dallas–Chicago. (We might want to consider another airline for a more direct route!)

Unreachable Vertices

You may have noticed that in all of our examples so far we have been able to "reach" all of the other vertices in our graphs from our given starting vertex. What if this is not the case? Consider the weighted graph in Figure 9.16, which depicts a new set of

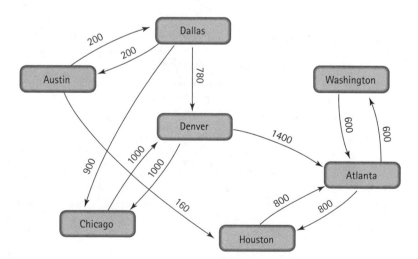

Figure 9.16 *A new set of airline-flight legs*

airline-flight legs. It is identical to Figure 9.9 except that we removed the Washington–Dallas leg. If we invoke our shortestPaths method, passing it this graph and a starting vertex of Washington, we get the following output:

Last Vertex	Destination	Distance
Washington	Washington	0
Washington	Atlanta	600
Atlanta	Houston	1400

A careful study of the new graph confirms that one can reach Atlanta and Houston only when starting in Washington, at least when flying Air Buster Airlines.

Suppose we extend the specification of our shortestPaths method to require that it also print the unreachable vertices. How can we determine the unreachable vertices after we have generated the information about the reachable ones? Easy! The unreachable vertices are the unmarked vertices. We simply need to check whether any vertices remain unmarked. Our Graph ADT provides the operation getUnmarked specifically for this situation.

```
System.out.println("The unreachable vertices are:");
vertex = graph.getUnmarked();
while (vertex != null)
{
  System.out.println(vertex);
  graph.markVertex(vertex);
  vertex = graph.getUnmarked();
}
```

Now the output from the call to shortestPaths would be

Last Vertex	Destination	Distance
Washington	Washington	0
Washington	Atlanta	600
Atlanta	Houston	1400

The unreachable vertices are:

Austin

Chicago

Dallas

Denver

In Exercise 35 we ask you to investigate counting the "connected components" of a graph. This is another interesting application of the getUnmarked method. It is related to the blob-counting problem discussed in Chapter 4. In fact, it is the logical equivalent of that problem.

Summary

In this chapter, we discussed two data structures: priority queues and graphs. For the former, we saw an elegant implementation based on a binary tree with special shape and order properties. The corresponding UML diagram appears in Figure 9.17. For the latter, we saw a time-efficient array-based implementation (see the UML diagram in Figure 9.18) and discussed a space-efficient reference-based implementation. Time and space efficiency tradeoffs are often the key considerations when choosing among alternative implementations of a data structure.

Graphs are the most complex structure we studied. They are very versatile and are a good way to model many real-world objects and situations. Because many different types of applications could potentially use graphs, numerous variations and generalizations of their definitions and implementations exist. In addition, many advanced algorithms for manipulating and traversing graphs have been discovered. They are generally covered in detail in advanced computer science courses on algorithms.

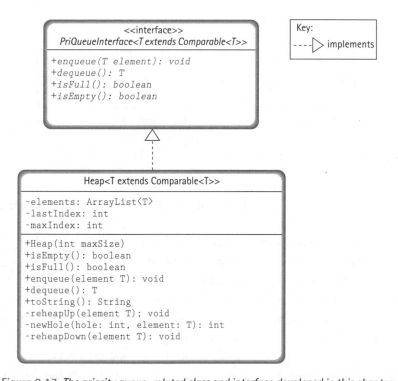

Figure 9.17 *The priority queue–related class and interface developed in this chapter*

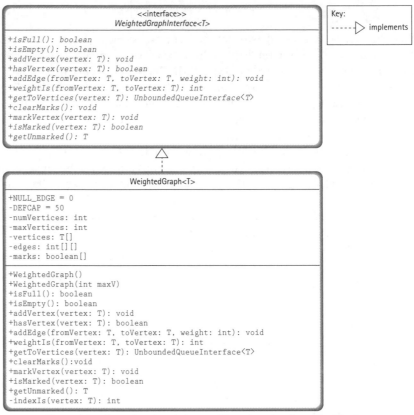

Figure 9.18 *The weighted graph–related class and interface developed in this chapter*

Exercises

9.1 Priority Queues

1. A priority queue is implemented as a linked list, sorted from largest to smallest element.

    a. Write the declarations needed for this implementation.

    b. Write the `enqueue` operation, using this implementation.

    c. Write the `dequeue` operation, using this implementation.

2. A priority queue is implemented as a binary search tree.

    a. Write the declarations needed for this implementation.

    b. Write the `enqueue` operation, using this implementation.

    c. Write the `dequeue` operation, using this implementation.

3. A priority queue is implemented as a sequential array-based list. The highest-priority element is in the first array position, the second-highest priority element is in the second array position, and so on.

    a. Write the declarations needed for this implementation.

b. Write the `enqueue` operation, using this implementation.

c. Write the `dequeue` operation, using this implementation.

4. A stack is implemented using a priority queue. Each element is time-stamped as it is put into the stack. (The time stamp is a number between zero and `Integer.MAX_VALUE`. Each time an element is pushed onto the stack, it is assigned the next largest number.)

   a. What is the highest-priority element?

   b. Describe how the `push`, `top`, and `pop` operations could be implemented.

5. A FIFO queue is implemented using a priority queue. Each element is time-stamped as it is put into the queue. (The time stamp is a number between zero and `Integer.MAX_VALUE`. Each time an element is enqueued, it is assigned the next largest number.)

   a. What is the highest-priority element?

   b. Describe how the `enqueue` and `dequeue` operations could be implemented.

9.2 Heaps

6. Which of the following trees are heaps?

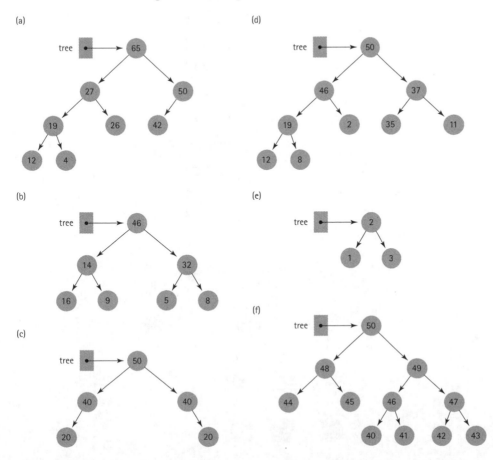

7. Draw a tree that satisfies both the binary search property and the order property of heaps.

8. A minimum heap has the following order property: The value of each element is less than or equal to the value of each of its children. What changes must be made in the heap operations given in this chapter?

9. We created iterative versions of the heap helper methods `reheapDown` and `reheapUp` in this chapter.

   a. Write a recursive version of `reheapDown`.

   b. Write a recursive version of `reheapUp`.

   c. Describe the recursive versions of these operations in terms of Big-O notation.

10. A priority queue containing characters is implemented as a heap stored in an array. The precondition states that this priority queue cannot contain duplicate elements. There are 10 elements currently in the priority queue, as shown below. What values might be stored in array positions 7–9 so that the properties of a heap are satisfied?

[0]	Z
[1]	F
[2]	J
[3]	E
[4]	B
[5]	G
[6]	H
[7]	?
[8]	?
[9]	?

11. A priority queue is implemented as a heap:

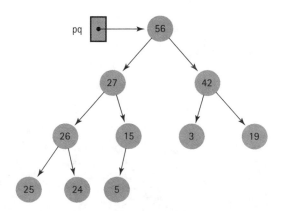

a. Show how this heap would look after the following series of operations:

```
pq.enqueue(28);
pq.enqueue(2);
pq.enqueue(40);
x = pq.dequeue();
y = pq.dequeue();
z = pq.dequeue();
```

b. What would the values of x, y, and z be after the series of operations in part a?

12. Write and compare two implementations of a priority queue whose highest-priority element is the one with the smallest key value. The first implementation uses a minimum heap. You need to modify the heap operations to keep the minimum—rather than maximum—element in the root. The second implementation uses a linear linked list whose elements are ordered by key value. Create a data set that contains 50 elements with priorities generated by a random-number generator. To compare the operations, you must modify the enqueue and dequeue operations to count how many elements are accessed (compared or swapped, in the case of reheaping) during its execution. Write a driver to enqueue and dequeue the 50 test elements and print out the number of elements accessed for the operations. Run your driver once with each implementation.

Deliverables

- A listing of specification and implementation files for both priority queue implementations
- A listing of your driver
- A listing of your test data
- A listing of the output from both runs
- A report comparing the number of elements accessed in executing each operation

9.3 Introduction to Graphs

Use the following description of an undirected graph in Exercises 13 and 14:

EmployeeGraph   = (V, E)

V(EmployeeGraph) = {Susan, Darlene, Mike, Fred, John, Sander, Lance, Jean, Brent, Fran}

E(EmployeeGraph) = {(Susan, Darlene), (Fred, Brent), (Sander, Susan), (Lance, Fran), (Sander, Fran), (Fran, John), (Lance, Jean), (Jean, Susan), (Mike, Darlene), (Brent, Lance), (Susan, John)}

13. Draw a picture of EmployeeGraph.

14. Which one of the following phrases best describes the relationship represented by the edges between the vertices in `EmployeeGraph`?

    a. "works for"

    b. "is the supervisor of"

    c. "is senior to"

    d. "works with"

Use the following specification of a directed graph in Exercises 15–17:

ZooGraph	=	(V, E)
V(ZooGraph)	=	{dog, cat, animal, vertebrate, oyster, shellfish, invertebrate, crab, poodle, monkey, banana, dalmatian, dachshund}
E(ZooGraph)	=	{(vertebrate, animal), (invertebrate, animal), (dog, vertebrate), (cat, vertebrate), (monkey, vertebrate), (shellfish, invertebrate), (crab, shellfish), (oyster, shellfish), (poodle, dog), (dalmatian, dog), (dachshund, dog)}

15. Draw a picture of `ZooGraph`.

16. To tell if one element in `ZooGraph` has relation X to another element, you look for a path between them. Show whether the following statements are true, using the picture or adjacency matrix.

    a. dalmatian X dog

    b. dalmatian X vertebrate

    c. dalmatian X poodle

    d. banana X invertebrate

    e. oyster X invertebrate

    f. monkey X invertebrate

17. Which of the following phrases best describes relation X in Exercise 16?

    a. "has a"

    b. "is an example of"

    c. "is a generalization of"

    d. "eats"

Use the following graph for Exercises 18 and 19:

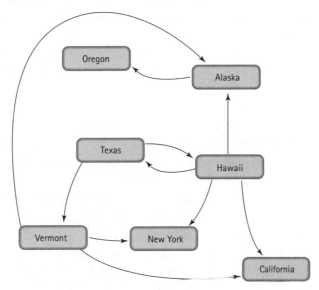

18. Describe the graph pictured above, using the formal graph notation.

    V(StateGraph)   =

    E(StateGraph)   =

19. In the states graph:

    a. Is there a path from Oregon to any other state in the graph?

    b. Is there a path from Hawaii to every other state in the graph?

    c. From which state(s) in the graph is there a path to Hawaii?

9.4 Formal Specification of a Graph ADT

20. Classify the methods defined in the `WeightedGraphInterface` as observers or transformers.

21. It is possible to define more operations for a Graph ADT. Describe two operations that you think would be useful additions to the `WeightedGraphInterface`.

9.5 Implementations of Graphs

22. Draw the adjacency matrix for `EmployeeGraph` (see Exercise 13). Store the vertex values in alphabetical order.

23. Draw the adjacency matrix for `ZooGraph` (see Exercise 15). Store the vertices in alphabetical order.

24. Complete the implementation of the Weighted Graph that we began in this chapter by providing bodies for the methods `isEmpty`, `isFull`, `hasVertex`,

clearMarks, markVertex, isMarked, and getUnmarked in the Weighted-Graph.java file. Test the completed implementation using the UseGraph class. When implementing hasVertex, don't forget to use the equals method to compare vertices.

25. Class WeightedGraph in this chapter is to be extended to include a boolean edgeExists operation, which determines whether two vertices are connected by an edge.

    a. Write the declaration of this method. Include adequate comments.

    b. Using the adjacency matrix implementation developed in this chapter and the declaration from part a, implement the body of the method.

26. Class WeightedGraph in this chapter is to be extended to include a removeEdge operation, which removes a given edge.

    a. Write the declaration of this method. Include adequate comments.

    b. Using the adjacency matrix implementation developed in this chapter and the declaration from part a, implement the body of the method.

27. Class WeightedGraph in this chapter is to be extended to include a removeVertex operation, which removes a vertex from the graph. Deleting a vertex is more complicated than deleting an edge from the graph. Discuss the reasons for this operation's greater complexity.

28. Graphs can be implemented using arrays or references. For the states graph (see Exercise 18):

    a. Show the adjacency matrix that would describe the edges in this graph. Store the vertices in alphabetical order.

    b. Show the array-of-references adjacency lists that would describe the edges in this graph.

29. Design and code a reference-based weighted graph class with the vertices stored in an array as in Figure 9.11(a). Your class should implement our Weighted-GraphInterface.

30. Design and code a reference-based weighted graph class with the vertices stored in a linked list as in Figure 9.11(b). Your class should implement our Weighted-GraphInterface.

9.6 Graph Applications

31. Using the EmployeeGraph (see Exercise 13) describe the path from Susan to Lance

    a. Using a breadth-first strategy.

    b. Using a depth-first strategy.

32. The depth-first search operation can be implemented without a stack by using recursion.

    a. Name the base case(s). Name the general case(s).

    b. Write the algorithm for a recursive depth-first search.

Exercises 33–35 assume completion of Exercise 24, 29, or 30.

33. In our `isPath2` method we use a breadth-first search approach that marks vertices as being visited *after* they are removed from the queue. An alternative approach, discussed in Section 9.6, marks the vertices *before* they are enqueued. Implement another method, `isPath3`, that uses this alternative approach. You can put your new method in our `useGraph` class and use it to test your code.

34. Our `shortestPaths` method is concerned with the minimum *distance* between two vertices of a graph. Create a `minEdges` method that returns the minimum *number of edges* that exist on a path between two given vertices. You can put your new method in our `useGraph` class and use it to test your code.

35. Informally, a connected component of a graph is a subset of the vertices of the graph such that all of the vertices in the subset are connected to each other by a path. For example, the following graph consists of three connected components.

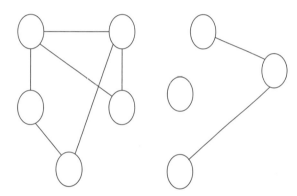

Create a `numComponents` method that returns the number of connected components that exist in a graph. You can put your new method in our `useGraph` class and use it to test your code.

Sorting and Searching Algorithms

Knowledge Goals

You should be able to

- describe the following sorting algorithms:
  - straight selection sort
  - bubble sort (two versions)
  - insertion sort
  - quick sort
  - merge sort
  - heap sort
- analyze the efficiency of the six sorting algorithms in terms of Big-O time and space requirements
- discuss other sorting efficiency considerations: overhead, elimination of method calls, and programmer time
- describe and discuss the performance of the following search algorithms:
  - sequential search of an unsorted list
  - sequential search of a sorted list
  - binary search
  - searching a high-probability sorted list
- define the following terms:
  - hashing
  - rehashing
  - collisions
  - linear probing
  - clustering
  - discuss the efficiency considerations for the searching and hashing algorithms in terms of Big-O complexity

Skill Goals

You should be able to

- implement the following sorting algorithms:
  - straight selection sort
  - bubble sort (two versions)
  - insertion sort
  - quick sort
  - merge sort
  - heap sort
- determine the stability of a specific implementation of a sorting algorithm
- use the Java `Comparator` interface to define multiple sort orders for objects of a class
- design and implement an appropriate hashing function for an application
- design and implement a collision-resolution algorithm for a hash table

At many points in this book, we have gone to great trouble to keep lists of elements in sorted order: golfers sorted by score, airline routes sorted by distance, integers sorted from smallest to largest, and words sorted alphabetically. One goal of keeping sorted lists, of course, is to facilitate searching. Given an appropriate implementation structure, a particular list element can be found faster if the list is sorted.

In this chapter we directly examine strategies for both sorting and searching, two tasks that are fundamental to a variety of computing problems. Section 10.1 introduces the topic of sorting. Section 10.2 discusses the straight selection sort, the bubble sort, and the insertion sort—three simple sorting algorithms that students sometimes study in their first course. Section 10.3 introduces three more complex (but more efficient) sorting algorithms: the merge sort, the quick sort, and the heap sort. So that we can concentrate on the algorithms, during the initial discussions we assume that our goal is to sort a given list of integers that is held in an array. In Section 10.4, we address issues related to sorting objects in general. We introduce the topic of searching in Section 10.5, and in Section 10.6, we discuss in some detail hashing, an approach that allows us to store and retrieve information very quickly under certain conditions.

10.1 Sorting

Putting an unsorted list of data elements into order—*sorting*—is a very common and useful operation. Entire books have been written about sorting algorithms as well as algorithms for searching a sorted list to find a particular element.

Because sorting a large number of elements can be extremely time consuming, an efficient sorting algorithm is very desirable. How do we describe efficiency? List element comparison—that is, the operation that compares two list elements to see which is smaller—is an operation central to most sorting algorithms. We use the number of required element comparisons as a measure of the efficiency of each algorithm. For each algorithm we calculate the number of comparisons relative to the size of the list being sorted. We then use Big-O notation based on the result of our calculation to succinctly describe the efficiency of the algorithm.

In addition to comparing elements, each of our algorithms includes another basic operation: swapping the locations of two elements on the list. The number of element swaps needed to sort a list is another measure of sorting efficiency. In the exercises we ask you to analyze the sorting algorithms developed in this chapter in terms of that alternative measure.

Another efficiency consideration is the amount of memory space required. In general, memory space is not a very important factor when choosing a sorting algorithm. We look at only two sorts in which space would be a consideration. The usual time versus space trade-off applies to sorts—more space often means less time, and vice versa.

A Test Harness

To facilitate our study of sorting we develop a standard test harness, a driver program that we can use to test each of our sorting algorithms. Because we are using this program just to test our implementations and facilitate our study, we keep it simple: It consists of a single class called `Sorts`. This class defines an array that can hold 50 integers. The array is named `values`. Several static methods are defined:

> **Test harness**   A stand-alone program designed to facilitate testing of the implementations of algorithms

- `initValues`   Initializes the `values` array with random numbers between 0 and 99; uses the `abs` method (absolute value) from the Java library's `Math` class and the `nextInt` method from the `Random` class.
- `isSorted`   Returns a `boolean` value indicating whether the `values` array is currently sorted.
- `swap`   Swapping data values between two array locations is common in many sorting algorithms—this method swaps the integers between `values[index1]` and `values[index2]`, where `index1` and `index2` are parameters of the method.
- `printValues`   Prints the contents of the `values` array to the `System.out` stream; the output is arranged evenly in 10 columns.

Here is the code for the test harness:

```
//-------------------------------------------------------------------
// Sorts.java            by Dale/Joyce/Weems           Chapter 10
//
// Test harness used to run sorting algorithms.
//-------------------------------------------------------------------

import java.util.*;
import java.text.DecimalFormat;

public class Sorts
{
  static final int SIZE = 50;          // size of array to be sorted
  static int[] values = new int[SIZE];   // values to be sorted

  static void initValues()
  // Initializes the values array with random integers from 0 to 99.
  {
    Random rand = new Random();
    for (int index = 0; index < SIZE; index++)
      values[index] = Math.abs(rand.nextInt()) % 100;
  }
```

```java
static public boolean isSorted()
// Returns true if the array values are sorted, and false otherwise.
{
  boolean sorted = true;
  for (int index = 0; index < (SIZE - 1); index++)
    if (values[index] > values[index + 1])
      sorted = false;
  return sorted;
}

static public void swap(int index1, int index2)
// Precondition: index1 and index2 are >= 0 and < SIZE.
//
// Swaps the integers at locations index1 and index2 of the values array.
{
  int temp = values[index1];
  values[index1] = values[index2];
  values[index2] = temp;
}

static public void printValues()
// Prints all the values integers.
{
  int value;
  DecimalFormat fmt = new DecimalFormat("00");
  System.out.println("The values array is:");
  for (int index = 0; index < SIZE; index++)
  {
    value = values[index];
    if (((index + 1) % 10) == 0)
      System.out.println(fmt.format(value));
    else
      System.out.print(fmt.format(value) + " ");
  }
  System.out.println();
}

public static void main(String[] args) throws IOException
{
  initValues();
  printValues();
  System.out.println("values is sorted: " + isSorted());
  System.out.println();
```

```
    swap(0, 1);
    printValues();
    System.out.println("values is sorted: " + isSorted());
    System.out.println();
  }
}
```

In this version of Sorts, the main method initializes the values array, prints the array, prints the value of isSorted, swaps the first two values of the array, and again prints information about the array. The output from this class as currently defined would look something like this:

The values array is:
20 49 07 50 45 69 20 07 88 02
89 87 35 98 23 98 61 03 75 48
25 81 97 79 40 78 47 56 24 07
63 39 52 80 11 63 51 45 25 78
35 62 72 05 98 83 05 14 30 23

values is sorted: false

The values array is:
49 20 07 50 45 69 20 07 88 02
89 87 35 98 23 98 61 03 75 48
25 81 97 79 40 78 47 56 24 07
63 39 52 80 11 63 51 45 25 78
35 62 72 05 98 83 05 14 30 23

values is sorted: false

As we proceed in our study of sorting algorithms, we will add methods that implement the algorithms to the Sorts class and change the main method to invoke those methods. We can use the isSorted and printValues methods to help us check the results.

Because our sorting methods are implemented for use with this test harness, they can directly access the static values array. In the general case, we could modify each sorting method to accept a reference to an array-based list to be sorted as an argument.

10.2 Simple Sorts

In this section we present three "simple" sorts, so called because they use an unsophisticated, brute-force approach. They may not be very efficient, but they are easy to understand and to implement.

Straight Selection Sort

If we were handed a list of names on a sheet of paper and asked to put them in alphabetical order, we might use this general approach:

1. *Select* the name that comes first in alphabetical order, and write it on a second sheet of paper.
2. Cross the name out on the original sheet.
3. Repeat steps 1 and 2 for the second name, the third name, and so on, until all the names on the original sheet have been crossed out and written onto the second sheet, at which point the list on the second sheet is sorted.

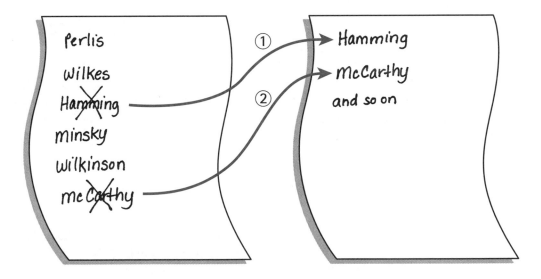

This algorithm is simple to translate into a computer program, but it has one drawback: It requires space in memory to store two complete lists. This duplication is clearly wasteful. A slight adjustment to this manual approach does away with the need to duplicate space. Instead of writing the "first" name onto a separate sheet of paper, we exchange it with the name in the first location on the original sheet.

Repeating this process until finished results in a sorted list on the original sheet of paper.

Within our program, the "by-hand list" is represented in an array. Here is a more formal algorithm:

SelectionSort

for current going from 0 to SIZE − 2
    Find the index in the array of the smallest unsorted element
    Swap the current element with the smallest unsorted one

Figure 10.1 shows the steps taken by the algorithm to sort a five-element array. Each section of the figure represents one iteration of the *for* loop. The first part of a section represents the "find the smallest unsorted array element" step. To do so, we repeatedly examine the unsorted elements, asking if each one is the smallest we have seen so far. The second part of a figure section shows the two array elements to be swapped, and the final part shows the result of the swap.

During the progression, we can view the array as being divided into a sorted part and an unsorted part. Each time we perform the body of the *for* loop, the sorted part grows by one element and the unsorted part shrinks by one element. The exception is the very last step, when the sorted part grows by two elements. Do you see why? When all of the array elements except the last one are in their correct locations, the last one is

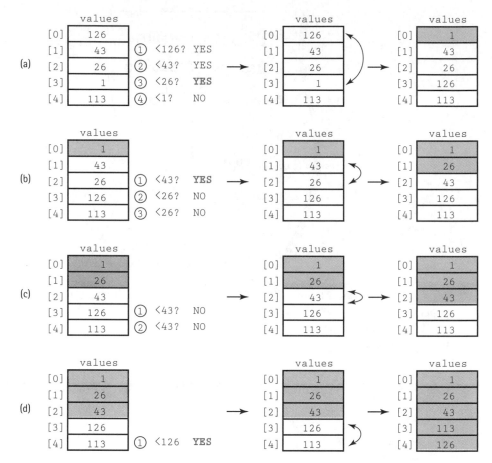

Figure 10.1 *Example of a straight selection sort (sorted elements are shaded)*

in its correct location by default. This is why our *for* loop can stop at index SIZE - 2 instead of at the end of the array, index SIZE - 1.

We implement the algorithm with a method selectionSort that becomes part of our Sorts class. This method sorts the values array, which is declared in that class. It has access to the SIZE constant, which indicates the number of elements in the array. Within the selectionSort method we use a variable, current, to mark the beginning of the unsorted part of the array. Thus the unsorted part of the array goes from index current to index SIZE - 1. We start out by setting current to the index of the first position (0). Figure 10.2 provides a snapshot of the array during the selection sort algorithm.

We use a helper method to find the index of the smallest value in the unsorted part of the array. The minIndex method receives the first and last indexes of the unsorted part, and returns the index of the smallest value in this part of the array. We also use the swap method that is part of our test harness.

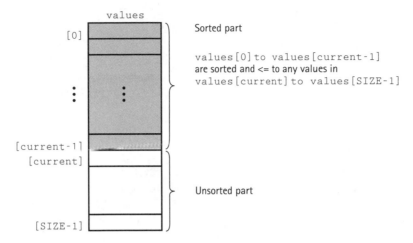

Figure 10.2 *A snapshot of the selection sort algorithm*

Here is the code for the `minIndex` and `selectionSort` methods. Because they are placed directly in our test harness class, a class with a main method, they are declared as static methods.

```
static int minIndex(int startIndex, int endIndex)
// Returns the index of the smallest value in
// values[startIndex]to values[endIndex].
{
  int indexOfMin = startIndex;
  for (int index = startIndex + 1; index <= endIndex; index++)
    if (values[index] < values[indexOfMin])
      indexOfMin = index;
  return indexOfMin;
}

static void selectionSort()
// Sorts the values array using the selection sort algorithm.
{
  int endIndex = SIZE - 1;
  for (int current = 0; current < endIndex; current++)
    swap(current, minIndex(current, endIndex));
}
```

Let's change the main body of the test harness:

```
initValues();
printValues();
System.out.println("values is sorted: " + isSorted());
```

```
System.out.println();

selectionSort();
System.out.println("Selection Sort called\n");
printValues();
System.out.println("values is sorted: " + isSorted());
System.out.println();
```

Now we get an output from the program that looks like this:

The values array is:

92 66 38 17 21 78 10 43 69 19

17 96 29 19 77 24 47 01 97 91

13 33 84 93 49 85 09 54 13 06

21 21 93 49 67 42 25 29 05 74

96 82 26 25 11 74 03 76 29 10

values is sorted: false

Selection Sort called

The values array is:

01 03 05 06 09 10 10 11 13 13

17 17 19 19 21 21 21 24 25 25

26 29 29 29 33 38 42 43 47 49

49 54 66 67 69 74 74 76 77 78

82 84 85 91 92 93 93 96 96 97

values is sorted: true

We can test all of our sorting methods using this same approach.

Analyzing the Selection Sort

Now let's try measuring the amount of "work" required by this algorithm. We describe the number of comparisons as a function of the number of elements in the array—that is, SIZE. To be concise, in this discussion we refer to SIZE as N.

The comparison operation is in the minIndex method. We know from the loop condition in the selectionSort method that minIndex is called $N - 1$ times. Within minIndex, the number of comparisons varies, depending on the values of startIndex and endIndex:

```
for (int index = startIndex + 1; index <= endIndex; index++)
   if (values[index] < values[indexOfMin])
     indexOfMin = index;
```

In the first call to `minIndex`, `startIndex` is 0 and `endIndex` is SIZE - 1, so there are $N - 1$ comparisons; in the next call, there are $N - 2$ comparisons; and so on; until the last call, when there is only one comparison. The total number of comparisons is

$$(N - 1) + (N - 2) + (N - 3) + \cdots + 1 = N(N - 1)/2$$

To accomplish our goal of sorting an array of N elements, the straight selection sort requires $N(N - 1)/2$ comparisons. The particular arrangement of values in the array does not affect the amount of work done at all. Even if the array is in sorted order before the call to `selectionSort`, the method still makes $N(N - 1)/2$ comparisons. Table 10.1 shows the number of comparisons required for arrays of various sizes.

How do we describe this algorithm in terms of Big-O notation? If we express $N(N - 1)/2$ as $\frac{1}{2}N^2 - \frac{1}{2}N$, the complexity is easy to determine. In Big-O notation we consider only the term $\frac{1}{2}N^2$, because it increases fastest relative to N. Further, we ignore the constant, $\frac{1}{2}$, making this algorithm $O(N^2)$. Thus, for large values of N, the computation time is approximately proportional to N^2. Looking at Table 10.1, we see that multiplying the number of elements by 10 increases the number of comparisons by a factor of more than 100; that is, the number of comparisons is multiplied by approximately the square of the increase in the number of elements. Looking at this table makes us appreciate why sorting algorithms are the subject of so much attention: Using `selectionSort` to sort an array of 1,000 elements requires almost a half million comparisons!

The identifying feature of a selection sort is that, on each pass through the loop, one element is put into its proper place. In the straight selection sort, each iteration finds the smallest unsorted element and puts it into its correct place. If we had made the helper method find the largest value instead of the smallest one, the algorithm would

Table 10.1   *Number of Comparisons Required to Sort Arrays of Different Sizes Using Selection Sort*

Number of Elements	Number of Comparisons
10	45
20	190
100	4,950
1,000	499,500
10,000	49,995,000

have sorted in descending order. We could also have made the loop go down from SIZE - 1 to 1, putting the elements into the end of the array first. All of these approaches are variations on the straight selection sort. The variations do not change the basic way that the minimum (or maximum) element is found.

Bubble Sort

The bubble sort uses a different scheme for finding the minimum (or maximum) value. Each iteration puts the smallest unsorted element into its correct place, but it also makes changes in the locations of the other elements in the array. The first iteration puts the smallest element in the array into the first array position. Starting with the last array element, we compare successive pairs of elements, swapping whenever the bottom element of the pair is smaller than the one above it. In this way the smallest element "bubbles up" to the top of the array.

Figure 10.3(a) shows the result of the first iteration through a five-element array. The next iteration puts the smallest element in the unsorted part of the array into the

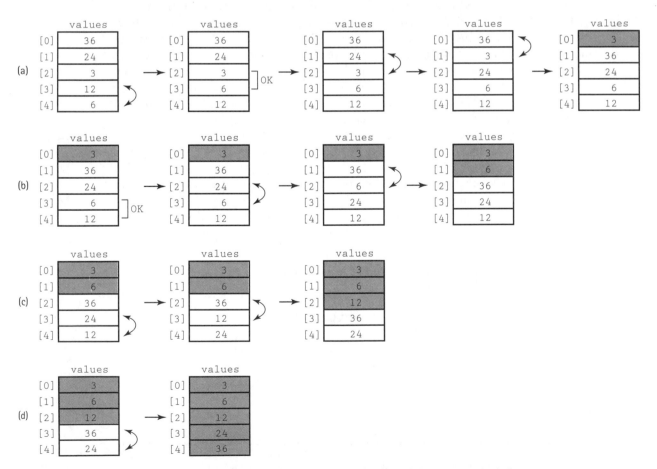

Figure 10.3   *Example of a bubble sort (sorted elements are shaded)*

second array position, using the same technique, as shown in Figure 10.3(b). The rest of the sorting process is represented in Figure 10.3(c) and (d). In addition to putting one element into its proper place, each iteration can cause some intermediate changes in the array. Also note that as with selection sort, the last iteration effectively puts two elements into their correct places.

The basic algorithm for the bubble sort follows:

BubbleSort

Set current to the index of first element in the array
while more elements in unsorted part of array
   "Bubble up" the smallest element in the unsorted part, causing intermediate swaps as needed
   Shrink the unsorted part of the array by incrementing current

The overall approach is similar to that followed in the `selectionSort`. The unsorted part of the array is the area from `values[current]` to `values[SIZE - 1]`. The value of `current` begins at 0, and we loop until `current` reaches `SIZE - 2`, with `current` incremented in each iteration. On entrance to each iteration of the loop body, the first `current` values are already sorted, and all the elements in the unsorted part of the array are greater than or equal to the sorted elements.

The inside of the loop body is different, however. Each iteration of the loop "bubbles up" the smallest value in the unsorted part of the array to the `current` position. The algorithm for the bubbling task is

bubbleUp(startIndex, endIndex)

for index going from endIndex DOWNTO startIndex +1
   if values[index] < values[index − 1]
      Swap the value at index with the value at index − 1

A snapshot of the array during this algorithm is shown in Figure 10.4. We use the `swap` method as before. The code for methods `bubbleUp` and `bubbleSort` follows. The code can be tested using our test harness.

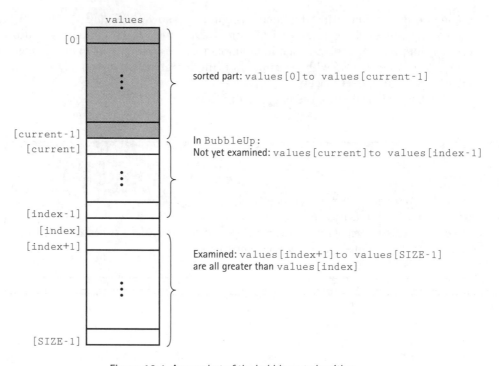

Figure 10.4 *A snapshot of the bubble sort algorithm*

```
static void bubbleUp(int startIndex, int endIndex)
// Switches adjacent pairs that are out of order
// between values[startIndex]to values[endIndex]
// beginning at values[endIndex].
{
  for (int index = endIndex; index > startIndex; index--)
    if (values[index] < values[index - 1])
      swap(index, index - 1);
}

static void bubbleSort()
// Sorts the values array using the bubble sort algorithm.
{
  int current = 0;
  while (current < (SIZE - 1))
  {
    bubbleUp(current, SIZE - 1);
    current++;
  }
}
```

Analyzing the Bubble Sort

Analyzing the work required by `bubbleSort` is easy, because it is the same as for the straight selection sort algorithm. The comparisons are in `bubbleUp`, which is called $N - 1$ times. There are $N - 1$ comparisons the first time, $N - 2$ comparisons the second time, and so on. Therefore, both `bubbleSort` and `selectionSort` require the same amount of work in terms of the number of comparisons. The `bubbleSort` algorithm does more than just make comparisons, however; `selectionSort` has only one data swap per iteration, but `bubbleSort` may do many additional data swaps.

What is the result of these intermediate data swaps? By reversing out-of-order pairs of data as they are noticed, bubble sort can move several elements closer to their final destination during each pass. Its possible that the method will get the array in sorted order before $N - 1$ calls to `bubbleUp`. This version of the bubble sort, however, makes no provision for stopping when the array is completely sorted. Even if the array is already in sorted order when `bubbleSort` is called, this method continues to call `bubbleUp` (which changes nothing) $N - 1$ times.

We could quit before the maximum number of iterations if `bubbleUp` returns a `boolean` flag, telling us when the array is sorted. Within `bubbleUp`, we initially set a variable `sorted` to `true`; then in the loop, if any swaps are made, we reset `sorted` to `false`. If no elements have been swapped, we know that the array is already in order. Now the bubble sort needs to make only one extra call to `bubbleUp` when the array is in order. This version of the bubble sort is as follows:

```
static boolean bubbleUp2(int startIndex, int endIndex)
// Switches adjacent pairs that are out of order
// between values[startIndex]to values[endIndex]
// beginning at values[endIndex].
//
// Returns false if a swap was made; otherwise, returns true.
{
  boolean sorted = true;
  for (int index = endIndex; index > startIndex; index--)
    if (values[index] < values[index - 1])
    {
      swap(index, index - 1);
      sorted = false;
    }
  return sorted;
}

static void shortBubble()
// Sorts the values array using the bubble sort algorithm.
// The process stops as soon as values is sorted.
{
  int current = 0;
```

```
boolean sorted = false;
while ((current < (SIZE - 1)) && !sorted)
{
  sorted = bubbleUp2(current, SIZE - 1);
  current++;
}
}
```

The analysis of `shortBubble` is more difficult. Clearly, if the array is already sorted to begin with, one call to `bubbleUp` tells us so. In this best-case scenario, `shortBubble` is O(N); only $N - 1$ comparisons are required for the sort. But what if the original array was actually sorted in descending order before the call to `shortBubble`? This is the worst possible case: `shortBubble` requires as many comparisons as `bubbleSort` and `selectionSort`, not to mention the "overhead"—all the extra swaps and setting and resetting the `sorted` flag. Can we calculate an average case? In the first call to `bubbleUp`, when `current` is 0, there are SIZE $- 1$ comparisons; on the second call, when `current` is 1, there are SIZE $- 2$ comparisons. The number of comparisons in any call to `bubbleUp` is SIZE $-$ `current` $- 1$. If we let N indicate SIZE and K indicate the number of calls to `bubbleUp` executed before `shortBubble` finishes its work, the total number of comparisons required is

$$\underset{\text{1st call}}{\left(N-1\right)} + \underset{\text{2nd call}}{\left(N-2\right)} + \underset{\text{3rd call}}{\left(N-3\right)} + \cdots + \underset{K\text{th call}}{\left(N-K\right)}$$

A little algebra changes this to

$$(2KN - 2K^2 - K)/2$$

In Big-O notation, the term that is increasing the fastest relative to N is $2KN$. We know that K is between 1 and $N - 1$. On average, over all possible input orders, K is proportional to N. Therefore, $2KN$ is proportional to N^2; that is, the `shortBubble` algorithm is also O(N^2).

Why do we even bother to mention the bubble sort algorithm if it is O(N^2) and requires extra data movements? Due to the extra intermediate swaps performed by the bubble sort, it can quickly sort an array that is "almost" sorted. If the `shortBubble` variation is used, a bubble sort can be very efficient in this situation.

Insertion Sort

In Chapter 6, we created a sorted list by inserting each new element into its appropriate place in an array. We can use a similar approach for sorting an array. The principle of the insertion sort is quite simple: Each successive element in the array to be sorted is inserted into its proper place with respect to the other, already sorted elements. As with the previously mentioned sorting strategies, we divide our array into a sorted part and an unsorted part. (Unlike with the straight selection and bubble sorts, there may be values in the unsorted part that are less than values in the sorted part.) Initially, the sorted portion contains only one element: the first element in the array. Now we take the second element in the array and put it into its correct place in the sorted part; that is, `values[0]` and `values[1]` are in order with respect to each other. Now the value in `values[2]` is put into its proper place, so `values[0]` to `values[2]` are in order with respect to each other. This process continues until all elements have been sorted.

In Chapter 6, our strategy was to search for the insertion point from the beginning of the array and to shift the elements from the insertion point down one slot to make room for the new element. We can combine the searching and shifting by beginning at the end of the sorted part of the array. We compare the element at `values[current]` to the one before it. If it is less than its predecessor, we swap the two elements. We then compare the element at `values[current - 1]` to the one before it, and swap if necessary. The process stops when the comparison shows that the values are in order or we have swapped into the first place in the array.

This approach was investigated in Exercise 29 in Chapter 6. Figure 10.5 illustrates this process, which we describe in the following algorithm, and Figure 10.6 shows a snapshot of the array during the algorithm.

---

insertionSort

for count going from 1 through SIZE − 1
   insertElement(0, count)

InsertElement(startIndex, endIndex)

Set finished to false
Set current to endIndex
Set moreToSearch to true
while moreToSearch AND NOT finished
  if values[current] < values[current − 1]
    swap(values[current], values[current − 1])
    Decrement current
    Set moreToSearch to (current does not equal startIndex)
  else
    Set finished to true

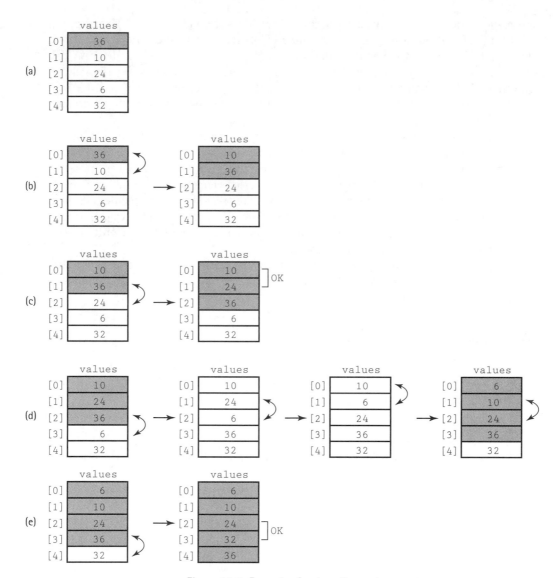

Figure 10.5 *Example of an insertion sort*

Here are the coded versions of `insertElement` and `insertionSort`:

```
static void insertElement(int startIndex, int endIndex)
// Upon completion, values[0]to values[endIndex] are sorted.
{
    boolean finished = false;
    int current = endIndex;
    boolean moreToSearch = true;
```

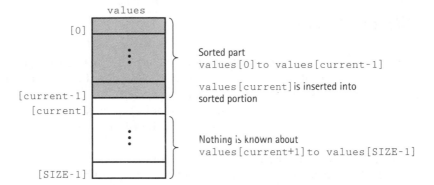

Figure 10.6 *A snapshot of the insertion sort algorithm*

```
while (moreToSearch && !finished)
{
  if (values[current] < values[current - 1])
  {
    swap(current, current - 1);
    current--;
    moreToSearch = (current != startIndex);
  }
  else
    finished = true;
}
}


static void insertionSort()
// Sorts the values array using the insertion sort algorithm.
{
  for (int count = 1; count < SIZE; count++)
    insertElement(0, count);
}
```

Analyzing the Insertion Sort

The general case for this algorithm mirrors the selectionSort and the bubbleSort, so the general case is O(N^2). But as for shortBubble, insertionSort has a best case: The data are already sorted in ascending order. When the data are in ascending order, insertElement is called N times, but only one comparison is made each time and no swaps are necessary. The maximum number of comparisons is made only when the elements in the array are in reverse order.

If we know nothing about the original order of the data to be sorted, selection-Sort, shortBubble, and insertionSort are all O(N^2) sorts and are very time consuming for sorting large arrays. Several sorting methods that work better when N is large are presented in the next section.

10.3 O(N log₂N) Sorts

The sorting algorithms covered in Section 10.2 are all O(N^2). Considering how rapidly N^2 grows as the size of the array increases, can't we do better? We note that N^2 is a lot larger than $(\frac{1}{2}N)^2 + (\frac{1}{2}N)^2$. If we could cut the array into two pieces, sort each segment, and then merge the two back together, we should end up sorting the entire array with a lot less work. An example of this approach is shown in Figure 10.7.

The idea of "divide and conquer" has been applied to the sorting problem in different ways, resulting in a number of algorithms that can do the job much more efficiently than O(N^2). In fact, there is a category of sorting algorithms that are O($N \log_2 N$). We examine three of these algorithms here: `mergeSort`, `quickSort`, and `heapSort`. As you might guess, the efficiency of these algorithms is achieved at the expense of the simplicity seen in the straight selection, bubble, and insertion sorts.

Merge Sort

The merge sort algorithm is taken directly from the idea presented above.

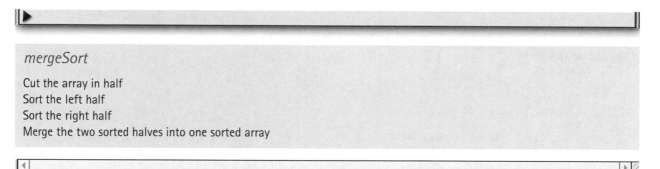

mergeSort

Cut the array in half
Sort the left half
Sort the right half
Merge the two sorted halves into one sorted array

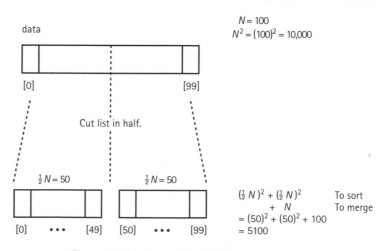

Figure 10.7 *Rationale for divide-and-conquer sorts*

Merging the two halves together is a O(N) task: We merely go through the sorted halves, comparing successive pairs of values (one in each half) and putting the smaller value into the next slot in the final solution. Even if the sorting algorithm used for each half is O(N^2), we should see some improvement over sorting the whole array at once, as indicated in Figure 10.7.

Actually, because mergeSort is itself a sorting algorithm, we might as well use it to sort the two halves. That's right—we can make mergeSort a recursive method and let it call itself to sort each of the two subarrays:

---

mergeSort—Recursive

Cut the array in half
mergeSort the left half
mergeSort the right half
Merge the two sorted halves into one sorted array

This is the general case, of course. What is the base case, the case that does not involve any recursive calls to mergeSort? If the "half" to be sorted doesn't hold more than one element, we can consider it already sorted and just return.

Let's summarize mergeSort in the format we used for other recursive algorithms. The initial method call would be mergeSort(0, SIZE - 1).

Method mergeSort(first, last)

Definition:	Sorts the array elements in ascending order.
Size:	last − first + 1
Base case:	If size less than 2, do nothing.
General case:	Cut the array in half.
	mergeSort the left half.
	mergeSort the right half.
	Merge the sorted halves into one sorted array.

Cutting the array in half is simply a matter of finding the midpoint between the first and last indexes:

```
middle = (first + last) / 2;
```

Then, in the smaller-caller tradition, we can make the recursive calls to mergeSort:

```
mergeSort(first, middle);
mergeSort(middle + 1, last);
```

So far this is simple enough. Now we just have to merge the two halves and we're done.

Merging the Sorted Halves

Obviously, all the serious work takes place in the merge step. Let's first look at the general algorithm for merging two sorted arrays, and then we can look at the specific problem of our subarrays.

To merge two sorted arrays, we compare successive pairs of elements, one from each array, moving the smaller of each pair to the "final" array. We can stop when one array runs out of elements, and then move all of the remaining elements from the other array to the final array. Figure 10.8 illustrates the general algorithm. In our specific problem, the two "arrays" to be merged are actually subarrays of the original array (Figure 10.9). Just as in Figure 10.8, where we merged array1 and array2 into a third array, we need to merge our two subarrays into some auxiliary structure. We need this structure, another array, only temporarily. After the merge step, we can copy the now-sorted elements back into the original array. The entire process is shown in Figure 10.10.

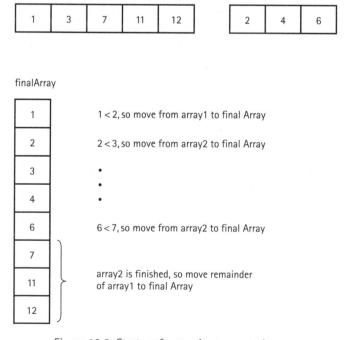

Figure 10.8 *Strategy for merging two sorted arrays*

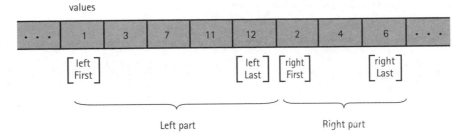

Figure 10.9 *Two subarrays*

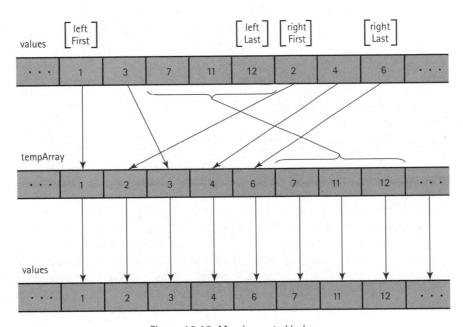

Figure 10.10 *Merging sorted halves*

Let's specify a method, `merge`, to do this task:

---

merge(int leftFirst, int leftLast, int rightFirst, int rightLast)

Method:	Merges two sorted subarrays into a single sorted piece of the array
Preconditions:	values[leftFirst] to values[leftLast] are sorted
	values[rightFirst] to values[rightLast] are sorted
Postcondition:	values[leftFirst] to values[rightLast] are sorted

---

Here is the algorithm for `merge`:

merge (leftFirst, leftLast, rightFirst, rightLast)

(uses a local array, tempArray)

Set index to leftFirst
while more elements in left half AND more elements in right half
  if values[leftFirst] < values[rightFirst]
    Set tempArray[index] to values[leftFirst]
    Increment leftFirst
  else
    Set tempArray[index] to values[rightFirst]
    Increment rightFirst
  Increment index
Copy any remaining elements from left half to tempArray
Copy any remaining elements from right half to tempArray
Copy the sorted elements from tempArray back into values

In the coding of method `merge`, we use `leftFirst` and `rightFirst` to indicate the "current" position in the left and right halves, respectively. Because these variables are values of the primitive type `int` and not objects, copies of these parameters are passed to method `merge`, rather than references to the parameters. These copies are changed in the method; changing the copies does not affect the original values. Both of the "copy any remaining elements" loops are included. During the execution of this method, one of these loops never executes. Can you explain why?

```
static void merge (int leftFirst, int leftLast, int rightFirst, int rightLast)
// Preconditions: values[leftFirst]to values[leftLast] are sorted.
//                values[rightFirst]to values[rightLast] are sorted.
//
// Sorts values[leftFirst]to values[rightLast] by merging the two subarrays.
{
  int[] tempArray = new int [SIZE];
  int index = leftFirst;
  int saveFirst = leftFirst;  // to remember where to copy back

  while ((leftFirst <= leftLast) && (rightFirst <= rightLast))
  {
    if (values[leftFirst] < values[rightFirst])
    {
```

```
      tempArray[index] = values[leftFirst];
      leftFirst++;
    }
    else
    {
      tempArray[index] = values[rightFirst];
      rightFirst++;
    }
    index++;
  }

  while (leftFirst <= leftLast)
  // Copy remaining elements from left half.

  {
    tempArray[index] = values[leftFirst];
    leftFirst++;
    index++;
  }

  while (rightFirst <= rightLast)
  // Copy remaining elements from right half.
  {
    tempArray[index] = values[rightFirst];
    rightFirst++;
    index++;
  }

  for (index = saveFirst; index <= rightLast; index++)
    values[index] = tempArray[index];
}
```

As we said, most of the work occurs in the merge task. The actual mergeSort method is short and simple:

```
static void mergeSort(int first, int last)
// Sorts the values array using the merge sort algorithm.
{
  if (first < last)
  {
    int middle = (first + last) / 2;
    mergeSort(first, middle);
    mergeSort(middle + 1, last);
    merge(first, middle, middle + 1, last);
  }
}
```

Analyzing mergeSort

The `mergeSort` method splits the original array into two halves. It first sorts the first half of the array; it then sorts the second half of the array using the same approach; finally it merges the two halves. To sort the first half of the array, it follows the same approach of splitting and merging. It does likewise for the second half. During the sorting process, the splitting and merging operations all become intermingled. Analysis is simplified if we imagine that all of the splitting occurs first, followed by all of the merging—we can view the process this way without affecting the correctness of the algorithm.

We view the `mergeSort` algorithm as continually dividing the original array (of size N) in two, until it has created N one-element subarrays. Figure 10.11 shows this point of view for an array with an original size of 16. The total work needed to divide the array in half, over and over again until we reach subarrays of size 1, is $O(N)$. After all, we end up with N subarrays of size 1.

Each subarray of size 1 is obviously a sorted subarray. The real work of the algorithm involves merging the smaller sorted subarrays back into the larger sorted subarrays. To merge two sorted subarrays of size X and size Y into a single sorted subarray using the `merge` operation requires $O(X + Y)$ steps. We can see this because each time through the *while* loops of the `merge` method we advance either the `left-First` index or the `rightFirst` index by 1. Because we stop processing when these indexes become greater than their "last" counterparts, we know that we take a total of `(leftLast - leftFirst + 1) + (rightLast - rightFirst + 1)` steps. This expression represents the sum of the lengths of the two subarrays being processed.

How many times must we perform the `merge` operation? And what are the sizes of the subarrays involved? Let's work from the bottom up. The original array of size N is

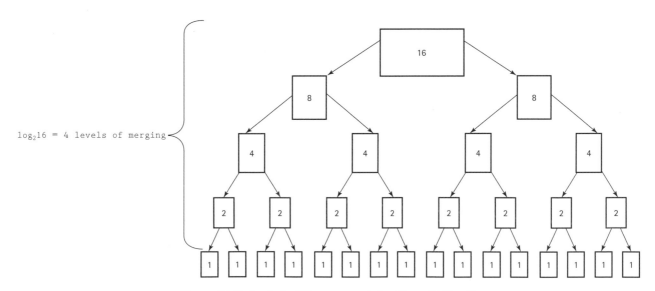

$\log_2 16 = 4$ levels of merging

Figure 10.11 *Analysis of the merge sort algorithm with N = 16*

eventually split into N subarrays of size 1. Merging two of those subarrays into a subarray of size 2 requires O(1 + 1) = O(2) steps, based on the analysis of the preceding paragraph. That is, it requires a small constant number of steps in each case. We must perform this merge operation a total of $\frac{1}{2}N$ times (we have N one-element subarrays and we are merging them two at a time). Thus the total number of steps to create all of the sorted two-element subarrays is O(N) because (2 * $\frac{1}{2}N = N$). Now we repeat this process to create four-element subarrays. It takes four steps to merge two two-element subarrays. We must perform this merge operation a total of $\frac{1}{4}N$ times (we have $\frac{1}{7}N$ two-element subarrays and we are merging them two at a time). Thus the total number of steps to create all of the sorted four-element subarrays is also O(N) because (4 * $\frac{1}{4}N = N$). The same reasoning leads us to conclude that each of the other levels of merging requires O(N) steps—at each level the sizes of the subarrays double, but the number of subarrays is cut in half, balancing them out.

We now know that it takes O(N) total steps to perform merging at each "level" of merging. How many levels are there? The number of levels of merging is equal to the number of times we can split the original array in half. If the original array is size N, we have $\log_2 N$ levels. (This is the same as the analysis of the binary search algorithm in Section 6.6.) For example, in Figure 10.11 the size of the original array is 16 and the number of levels of merging is 4.

Merge Sort

Because we have $\log_2 N$ levels, and we require O(N) steps at each level, the total cost of the merge operation is O($N \log_2 N$). Because the splitting phase was only O(N), we conclude that the merge sort algorithm is O($N \log_2 N$). Table 10.2 illustrates that, for large values of N, O($N \log_2 N$) is a big improvement over O(N^2).

A disadvantage of `mergeSort` is that it requires an auxiliary array that is as large as the original array to be sorted. If the array is large and space is a critical factor, then this sort may not be an appropriate choice. Next we discuss two O($N \log_2 N$) sorts that move elements around in the original array and do not need an auxiliary array.

Table 10.2 *Comparing* N^2 *and* $N \log_2 N$

N	$\log_2 N$	N^2	$N \log_2 N$
32	5	1,024	160
64	6	4,096	384
128	7	16,384	896
256	8	65,536	2,048
512	9	262,144	4,608
1,024	10	1,048,576	10,240
2,048	11	4,194,304	22,528
4,096	12	16,777,216	49,152

Quick Sort

Similar to the merge sort, the quick sort is a divide-and-conquer algorithm, which is inherently recursive. If we were given a large stack of final exams to sort by name, we might use the following approach (see Figure 10.12): Pick a splitting value—say, L—and divide the stack of tests into two piles, A–L and M–Z. (The two piles do not necessarily contain the same number of tests.) Then take the first pile and subdivide it into two piles, A–F and G–L. The A–F pile can be further broken down into A–C and D–F. This division process goes on until the piles are small enough to be easily sorted. The same process is applied to the M–Z pile.

Eventually, all the small sorted piles can be collected one on top of the other to produce a sorted set of tests.

This strategy is recursive: On each attempt to sort the pile of tests, the pile is divided, and then the same approach is used to sort each of the smaller piles (a smaller case). This process continues until the small piles do not need to be further divided (the base case). The parameter list of the quickSort method reflects the part of the list that is currently being processed; we pass the first and last indexes that define the part of the array to be processed on this call. The initial call to quickSort is

```
quickSort(0, SIZE - 1);
```

Method quickSort(first, last)

Definition:	Sorts the elements in subarray values[first] to values[last].
Size:	last − first + 1
Base case:	If size less than 2, do nothing.
General case:	Split the array according to splitting value.
	quickSort the elements <= splitting value.
	quickSort the elements > splitting value.

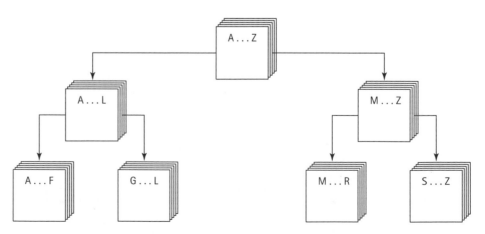

Figure 10.12 *Ordering a list using the quick sort algorithm*

---

quickSort

if there is more than one element in values[first] to values[last]
   Select splitVal
   Split the array so that
      values[first] to values[splitPoint − 1] <= splitVal
      values[splitPoint] = splitVal
      values[splitPoint + 1] to values[last] > splitVal
   quickSort the left subarray
   quickSort the right subarray

As you can see, the algorithm depends on the selection of a "split value," called `splitVal`, that is used to divide the array into two subarrays. How do we select `splitVal`? One simple solution is to use the value in `values[first]` as the splitting value. (We show a better solution later.)

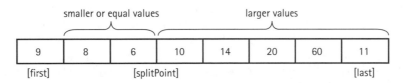

We create a helper method `split`, to rearrange the array elements as planned. After the call to `split`, all of the elements that are less than or equal to `splitVal` appear on the left side of the array and all of the elements that are greater than `splitVal` appear on the right side of the array.

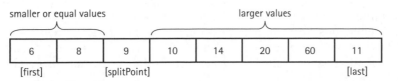

The two subarrays meet at `splitPoint`, the index of the last element that is less than or equal to `splitVal`. We don't know the value of `splitPoint` until the splitting process is complete. Its value is returned by `split`. We can then swap `splitVal` with the value at `splitPoint`.

Our recursive calls to `quickSort` use this index (`splitPoint`) to reduce the size of the problem in the general case.

`quickSort(first, splitPoint - 1)` sorts the left subarray. `quickSort(split-Point + 1, last)` sorts the right subarray. `splitVal` is already in its correct position in `values[splitPoint]`.

What is the base case? When the segment being examined holds fewer than two elements, we do not need to go on. So "there is more than one element in `values[first]` to `values[last]`" can be translated into "`if (first < last)`". We can now code our `quickSort` method.

```
static void quickSort(int first, int last)
{
  if (first < last)
  {
    int splitPoint;

    splitPoint = split(first, last);
    // values[first]to values[splitPoint - 1] <= splitVal
    // values[splitPoint] = splitVal
    // values[splitPoint+1]to values[last] > splitVal

    quickSort(first, splitPoint - 1);
    quickSort(splitPoint + 1, last);
  }
}
```

Now we must develop our splitting algorithm. We must find a way to get all of the elements equal to or less than `splitVal` on one side of `splitVal` and the elements greater than `splitVal` on the other side.

We do so by moving the indexes, `first` and `last`, toward the middle of the array, looking for elements that are on the wrong side of the split point and swapping them (Figure 10.13). While this operation is proceeding, the `splitVal` remains in the `first` position of the subarray being processed. As a final step, we swap it with the value at the `splitPoint`; therefore, we save the original value of `first` in a local variable, `saveF`. (See Figure 10.13a.)

We start out by moving `first` to the right, toward the middle, comparing `values[first]` to `splitVal`. If `values[first]` is less than or equal to `splitVal`, we keep incrementing `first`; otherwise, we leave `first` where it is and begin moving `last` toward the middle. (See Figure 10.13b.)

Now `values[last]` is compared to `splitVal`. If it is greater than `splitVal`, we continue decrementing `last`; otherwise, we leave `last` in place. (See Figure 10.13c.) At this point, it is clear that both `values[last]` and `values[first]` are on the wrong sides of the array. The elements to the left of `values[first]` and to the right of `values[last]` are not necessarily sorted; they are just on the correct side of the array with respect to splitVal. To put values[first] and values[last] into their correct sides, we merely swap them; we then increment first and decrement last. (See Figure 10.13d.)

Now we repeat the whole cycle, incrementing first until we encounter a value that is greater than splitVal, then decrementing last until we encounter a value that is less than or equal to splitVal. (See Figure 10.13e.)

When does the process stop? When first and last meet each other, no further swaps are necessary. Where they meet determines the splitPoint. This is the location

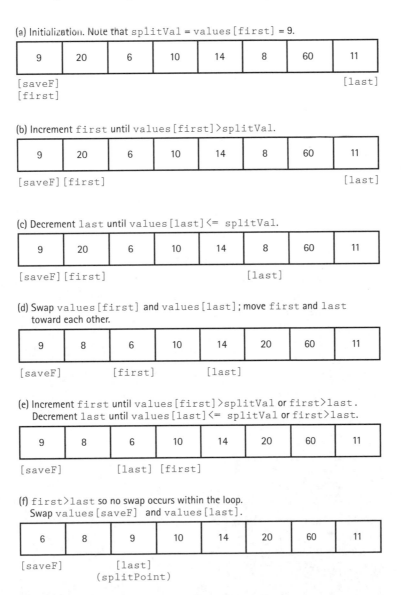

(a) Initialization. Note that splitVal = values[first] = 9.

| 9 | 20 | 6 | 10 | 14 | 8 | 60 | 11 |

[saveF]
[first]   [last]

(b) Increment first until values[first]>splitVal.

| 9 | 20 | 6 | 10 | 14 | 8 | 60 | 11 |

[saveF] [first]   [last]

(c) Decrement last until values[last]<= splitVal.

| 9 | 20 | 6 | 10 | 14 | 8 | 60 | 11 |

[saveF] [first]   [last]

(d) Swap values[first] and values[last]; move first and last
    toward each other.

| 9 | 8 | 6 | 10 | 14 | 20 | 60 | 11 |

[saveF]   [first]   [last]

(e) Increment first until values[first]>splitVal or first>last.
    Decrement last until values[last]<= splitVal or first>last.

| 9 | 8 | 6 | 10 | 14 | 20 | 60 | 11 |

[saveF]   [last] [first]

(f) first>last so no swap occurs within the loop.
    Swap values[saveF] and values[last].

| 6 | 8 | 9 | 10 | 14 | 20 | 60 | 11 |

[saveF]   [last]
                   (splitPoint)

Figure 10.13 *The split operation*

where splitVal belongs, so we swap values[saveF], which contains last, with the element at values[last] (Figure 10.13f). The index last is returned from the method, to be used by quickSort as the splitpoint for the next pair of recursive calls.

```
static int split(int first, int last)
{
  int splitVal = values[first];
  int saveF = first;
  boolean onCorrectSide;

  first++;
  do
  {
    onCorrectSide = true;
    while (onCorrectSide)                // move first toward last
      if (values[first] > splitVal)
        onCorrectSide = false;
      else
      {
        first++;
        onCorrectSide = (first <= last);
      }

    onCorrectSide = (first <= last);
    while (onCorrectSide)                // move last toward first
      if (values[last] <= splitVal)
        onCorrectSide = false;
      else
       {
        last--;
        onCorrectSide = (first <= last);
       }

    if (first < last)
    {
      swap(first, last);
      first++;
      last--;
    }
  } while (first <= last);

  swap(saveF, last);
  return last;
}
```

What happens if our splitting value is the largest value or the smallest value in the segment? The algorithm still works correctly, but because the split is lopsided, it is not so quick.

Is this situation likely to occur? That depends on how we choose our splitting value and on the original order of the data in the array. If we use `values[first]` as the splitting value and the array is already sorted, then *every* split is lopsided. One side contains one element, whereas the other side contains all but one of the elements. Thus our `quickSort` method is not a "quick" sort. Our splitting algorithm works best for an array in random order.

It is not unusual, however, to want to sort an array that is already in nearly sorted order. If this is the case, a better splitting value would be the middle value:

```
values[(first + last) / 2]
```

This value could be swapped with `values[first]` at the beginning of the method.

Analyzing quickSort

The analysis of `quickSort` is very similar to that of `mergeSort`. On the first call, every element in the array is compared to the dividing value (the "split value"), so the work done is O(N). The array is divided into two subarrays (not necessarily halves), which are then examined. *quickSort*

Each of these pieces is then divided in two, and so on. If each piece is split approximately in half, there are O($\log_2 N$) levels of splits. At each level, we make O(N) comparisons. Thus the quick sort is also an O($N \log_2 N$) algorithm, which is quicker than the O(N^2) sorts we discussed at the beginning of this chapter.

But the quick sort isn't always quicker. We have $\log_2 N$ levels of splits if each split divides the segment of the array approximately in half. As we've seen, the array division of the quick sort is sensitive to the order of the data—that is, to the choice of the splitting value. ⇒ *worst case* O(N^2)

What happens if the array is already sorted when our version of `quickSort` is called? The splits are very lopsided, and the subsequent recursive calls to `quickSort` break our data into a segment containing one element and a segment containing all the rest of the array. This situation produces a sort that is not at all quick. In fact, there are $N - 1$ levels; in this case, the complexity of the quick sort is O(N^2).

Such a situation is very unlikely to occur by chance. By way of analogy, consider the odds of shuffling a deck of cards and coming up with a sorted deck. Of course, in some applications we may know that the original array is likely to be sorted or nearly sorted. In such cases we would want to use either a different splitting algorithm or a different sort— maybe even `shortBubble`!

What about space requirements? A quick sort does not require an extra array, as a merge sort does. Are there any extra space requirements, besides the few local variables? Yes—recall that the quick sort uses a recursive approach. Many levels of recursion may be "saved" on the system stack at any time. On average, the algorithm requires O($\log_2 N$) extra space to hold this information and in the worst case requires O(N) extra space, the same as a merge sort.

Heap Sort

In each iteration of the selection sort, we searched the array for the next-smallest element and put it into its correct place in the array. Another way to write a selection sort is to find the maximum value in the array and swap it with the last array element, then find the next-to-largest element and put it into its place, and so on. Most of the work involved in this sorting algorithm comes from searching the remaining part of the array in each iteration, looking for the maximum value.

In Chapter 9, we discussed the *heap*, a data structure with a very special feature: We always know where to find its largest element. Because of the order property of heaps, the maximum value of a heap is in the root node. We can take advantage of this situation by using a heap to help us sort data. The general approach of the heap sort is as follows:

1. Take the root (maximum) element off the heap, and put it into its place.

2. Reheap the remaining elements. (This puts the next-largest element into the root position.)

3. Repeat until there are no more elements.

The first part of this algorithm sounds a lot like the straight selection sort. What makes the heap sort rapid is the second step: finding the next-largest element. Because the shape property of heaps guarantees a binary tree of minimum height, we make only $O(\log_2 N)$ comparisons in each iteration, as compared with $O(N)$ comparisons in each iteration of the selection sort.

Building a Heap

By now you are probably protesting that we are dealing with an unsorted array of elements, not a heap. Where does the original heap come from? Before we go on, we have to convert the unsorted array, `values`, into a heap.

Let's look at how the heap relates to our array of unsorted elements. In Chapter 9, we saw how heaps can be represented in an array with implicit links. Because of the shape property, we know that the heap elements take up consecutive positions in the array. In fact, the unsorted array of data elements already satisfies the shape property of heaps. Figure 10.14 shows an unsorted array and its equivalent tree.

We also need to make the unsorted array elements satisfy the order property of heaps. First, let's discover whether any part of the tree already satisfies the order property. All of the leaf nodes (subtrees with only a single node) are heaps. In Figure 10.15(a), the subtrees whose roots contain the values 19, 7, 3, 100, and 1 are heaps because they consist solely of root nodes.

Now let's look at the first *nonleaf* node, the one containing the value 2 (Figure 10.15b). The subtree rooted at this node is not a heap, but it is *almost* a heap—all of the nodes *except the root node* of this subtree satisfy the order property. We know how to fix this problem. In Chapter 9, we developed a heap utility method, `reheapDown`, that we can use to handle this exact situation. Given a tree whose elements satisfy the order property of heaps, except that the tree has an empty root, and a value to insert into the heap, `reheapDown` rearranges the nodes, leaving the (sub)tree containing the new

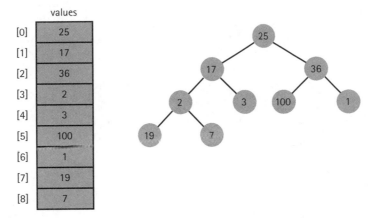

values

[0]	25
[1]	17
[2]	36
[3]	2
[4]	3
[5]	100
[6]	1
[7]	19
[8]	7

Figure 10.14 *An unsorted array and its tree*

element as a heap. We can just invoke `reheapDown` on the subtree, passing it the current root value of the subtree as the element to be inserted.

We apply this method to all the subtrees on this level, and then we move up a level in the tree and continue reheaping until we reach the root node. After `reheapDown` has been called for the root node, the entire tree should satisfy the order property of heaps. Figure 10.15 illustrates this heap-building process; Figure 10.16 shows the changing contents of the array.

In Chapter 9, we defined `reheapDown` as a private method of the `Heap` class. There, the method had only one parameter: the element being inserted into the heap. It always worked on the entire tree; that is, it always started with an empty node at index 0 and assumed that the last tree index of the heap was `lastIndex`. Here, we use a slight variation: `reheapDown` is a static method of our `Sorts` class that takes a second parameter—the index of the node that is the root of the subtree that is to be made into a heap. This is an easy change; if we call the parameter `root`, we simply add the following statement to the beginning of the `reheapDown` method:

```
int hole = root;    // Current index of hole
```

The algorithm for building a heap is summarized here:

buildHeap

```
for index going from first nonleaf node up to the root node
    reheapDown(values[index], index)
```

706 | Chapter 10: Sorting and Searching Algorithms

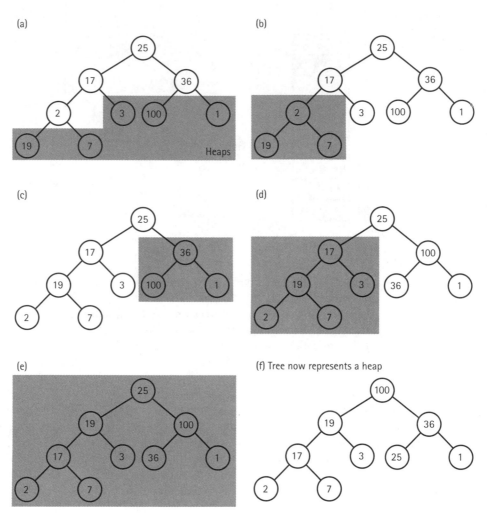

Figure 10.15 *The heap-building process*

	[0]	[1]	[2]	[3]	[4]	[5]	[6]	[7]	[8]
Original values	25	17	36	2	3	100	1	19	7
After reheapDown index = 3	25	17	36	19	3	100	1	2	7
After index = 2	25	17	100	19	3	36	1	2	7
After index = 1	25	19	100	17	3	36	1	2	7
After index = 0	100	19	36	17	3	25	1	2	7

Tree is a heap.

Figure 10.16 *Changing contents of the array*

We know where the root node is stored in our array representation of heaps: `values[0]`. Where is the first nonleaf node? Because half the nodes of a complete binary tree are leaves (prove this yourself), the first nonleaf node is found at position `SIZE/2 - 1`.

Sorting Using the Heap

Now that we are satisfied that we can turn the unsorted array of elements into a heap, let's take another look at the sorting algorithm.

We can easily access the largest element from the original heap—it's in the root node. In our array representation of heaps, the location of the largest element is `values[0]`. This value belongs in the last-used array position `values[SIZE - 1]`, so we can just swap the values in these two positions. Because `values[SIZE - 1]` now contains the largest value in the array (its correct sorted value), we want to leave this position alone. Now we are dealing with a set of elements, from `values[0]` through `values[SIZE - 2]`, that is almost a heap. We know that all of these elements satisfy the order property of heaps, except (perhaps) the root node. To correct this condition, we call our heap utility, `reheapDown`. (But our original `reheapDown` method assumed that the heap's tree ends at position `lastIndex`. We must again redefine `reheapDown`, so that it now accepts three parameters, with the third being the ending index of the heap. Once again the change is easy; the new code for `reheapDown` is included in the `Sorts` class.)

At this point we know that the next-largest element in the array is in the root node of the heap. To put this element in its correct position, we swap it with the element in `values[SIZE - 2]`. Now the two largest elements are in their final correct positions, and the elements in `values[0]` through `values[SIZE - 3]` are almost a heap. We call `reheapDown` again, and now the third-largest element is in the root of the heap.

We repeat this process until all of the elements are in their correct positions—that is, until the heap contains only a single element, which must be the smallest element in the array, in `values[0]`. This is its correct position, so the array is now completely sorted from the smallest to the largest element. At each iteration, the size of the unsorted portion (represented as a heap) gets smaller and the size of the sorted portion gets larger. When the algorithm ends, the size of the sorted portion is the size of the original array.

The heap sort algorithm, as we have described it here, sounds like a recursive process. Each time we swap and reheap a smaller portion of the total array. Because it uses tail recursion, we can code the repetition just as clearly using a simple *for* loop. The node-sorting algorithm is as follows:

Sort Nodes

for index going from last node up to next-to-root node
   Swap data in root node with values[index]
  reheapDown(values[0], 0, index - 1)

Method `heapSort` first builds the heap and then sorts the nodes, using the algorithms just discussed.

```
static void heapSort()
// Post: The elements in the array values are sorted by key
{
  int index;
  // Convert the array of values into a heap
  for (index = SIZE/2 - 1; index >= 0; index--)
    reheapDown(values[index], index, SIZE - 1);

  // Sort the array
  for (index = SIZE - 1; index >=1; index--)
  {
    swap(0, index);
    reheapDown(values[0], 0, index - 1);
  }
}
```

Figure 10.17 shows how each iteration of the sorting loop (the second *for* loop) would change the heap created in Figure 10.16. Each line represents the array after one operation. The sorted elements are shaded.

We entered the `heapSort` method with a simple array of unsorted values and returned with an array of the same values sorted in ascending order. Where did the heap go? The heap in `heapSort` is just a temporary structure, internal to the sorting algorithm. It is created at the beginning of the method to aid in the sorting process, but then is methodically diminished element by element as the sorted part of the array grows. When the method ends, the sorted part fills the array and the heap has completely disappeared. When we used heaps to implement priority queues in Chapter 9, the heap structure stayed around for the duration of the use of the queue. The heap in `heapSort`, by contrast, is not a retained data structure. It exists only temporarily, during the execution of the `heapSort` method.

Analyzing heapSort

The code for method `heapSort` is very short—only a few lines of new code plus the helper method `reheapDown`, which we developed in Chapter 9 (albeit slightly revised). These few

	[0]	[1]	[2]	[3]	[4]	[5]	[6]	[7]	[8]
values	100	19	36	17	3	25	1	2	7
swap	7	19	36	17	3	25	1	2	100
reheapDown	36	19	25	17	3	7	1	2	100
swap	2	19	25	17	3	7	1	36	100
reheapDown	25	19	7	17	3	2	1	36	100
swap	1	19	7	17	3	2	25	36	100
reheapDown	19	17	7	1	3	2	25	36	100
swap	2	17	7	1	3	19	25	36	100
reheapDown	17	3	7	1	2	19	25	36	100
swap	2	3	7	1	17	19	25	36	100
reheapDown	7	3	2	1	17	19	25	36	100
swap	1	3	2	7	17	19	25	36	100
reheapDown	3	1	2	7	17	19	25	36	100
swap	2	1	3	7	17	19	25	36	100
reheapDown	2	1	3	7	17	19	25	36	100
swap	1	2	3	7	17	19	25	36	100
reheapDown	1	2	3	7	17	19	25	36	100
Exit from sorting loop	1	2	3	7	17	19	25	36	100

Figure 10.17 *Effect of* heapSort *on the array*

lines of code, however, do quite a bit of work. All of the elements in the original array are rearranged to satisfy the order property of heaps, moving the largest element up to the top of the array, only to put it immediately into its place at the bottom. It's hard to believe from a small example such as the one in Figure 10.17 that heapSort is very efficient.

In fact, for small arrays, heapSort is not very efficient because of its "overhead." For large arrays, however, heapSort is very efficient. Let's consider the sorting loop. We loop through $N - 1$ times, swapping elements and reheaping. The comparisons occur in reheapDown (actually in its helper method newHole). A complete binary tree with N nodes has O($\log_2(N + 1)$) levels. In the worst case, if the root element had to be bumped down to a leaf position, the reheapDown method would make O($\log_2 N$) comparisons. Thus method reheapDown is O($\log_2 N$). Multiplying this activity by the $N - 1$ iterations shows that the sorting loop is O($N \log_2 N$).

Combining the original heap build, which is O(N), and the sorting loop, we can see that the heap sort requires O($N \log_2 N$) comparisons. Unlike the quick sort, the heap sort's efficiency is not affected by the initial order of the elements. A heap sort is just as efficient in terms of space; only one array is used to store the data. The heap sort requires only constant extra space.

The heap sort is an elegant, fast, robust, space-efficient algorithm!

10.4 More Sorting Considerations

In this section we wrap up our coverage of sorting by revisiting testing and efficiency, considering the "stability" of sorting algorithms, and discussing special concerns involved with sorting objects rather than primitive types.

Testing

All of our sorts were implemented within the test harness presented in Section 10.1. That test harness program, `Sorts`, allows us to generate a random array of size 50, sort it with one of our algorithms, and view the sorted array. It is easy to determine whether the sort was successful. If we do not want to verify success by eyeballing the output, we can always use a call to the `isSorted` method of the `Sorts` class.

The `Sorts` program is a useful tool for helping evaluate the correctness of our sorting methods. To thoroughly test them, however, we should vary the size of the array they are sorting. A small revision to `Sorts`, allowing the user to pass the array size as a command line parameter, would facilitate this process. We should also vary the original order of the array—for example, test an array that is in reverse order, one that is almost sorted, and one that has all identical elements (to make sure we do not generate an "array index out of bounds" error).

Besides validating that our sort methods create a sorted array, we can check their performance. At the start of the sorting phase we can initialize two variables, `numSwaps` and `numCompares`, to 0. By carefully placing statements incrementing these variables throughout our code, we can use them to track how many times the code performs swaps and comparisons. Once we output these values, we can compare them to the predicted theoretical values. Inconsistencies would require further review of the code (or maybe the theory!).

Efficiency

When N Is Small

As we have stressed throughout this chapter, our analysis of efficiency relies on the number of comparisons made by a sorting algorithm. This number gives us a rough estimate of the computation time involved. The other activities that accompany the comparison (swapping, keeping track of `boolean` flags, and so forth) contribute to the "constant of proportionality" of the algorithm.

In comparing Big-O evaluations, we ignored constants and smaller-order terms because we wanted to know how the algorithm would perform for large values of N. In general, an $O(N^2)$ sort requires few extra activities in addition to the comparisons, so its constant of proportionality is fairly small. Conversely, an $O(N \log_2 N)$ sort may be more complex, with more overhead and thus a larger constant of proportionality. This situation may cause anomalies in the relative performances of the algorithms when the value of N is small. In this case, N^2 is not much greater than $N \log_2 N$, and the constants may dominate instead, causing an $O(N^2)$ sort to run faster than an $O(N \log_2 N)$ sort.

We have discussed sorting algorithms that have complexity of either O(N^2) or ($N \log_2 N$). Now we ask an obvious question: Do algorithms that are better than ($N \log_2 N$) exist? No, it has been proven theoretically that we cannot do better than ($N \log_2 N$) for sorting algorithms that are based on comparing keys—that is, on pairwise comparison of elements.

Eliminating Calls to Methods

Sometimes it may be desirable, for efficiency reasons, to streamline the code as much as possible, even at the expense of readability. For instance, we have consistently used

```
swap(index1, index2);
```

when we wanted to swap two elements in the values array. We would achieve slightly better execution efficiency by dropping the method call and directly coding

```
tempValue = values[index1];
values[index1] = values[index2];
values[index2] = tempValue;
```

Coding the swap operation as a method made the code simpler to write and to understand, avoiding a cluttered sort method. Of course, method calls require extra overhead that we may prefer to avoid during a real sort, where the method is called over and over again within a loop.

The recursive sorting methods, mergeSort and quickSort, bring up a similar situation: They require the extra overhead involved in executing the recursive calls. We may want to avoid this overhead by coding nonrecursive versions of these methods.

In some cases, an optimizing compiler replaces method calls with the inline expansion of the code of the method. In that case, we get the benefits of both readability and efficiency.

Programmer Time

If the recursive calls are less efficient, why would anyone ever decide to use a recursive version of a sort? This decision involves a choice between types of efficiency. Until now, we have been concerned only with minimizing computer time. While computers are becoming faster and cheaper, however, it is not at all clear that computer programmers are following that trend. In fact, programmers are becoming more expensive. Therefore, in some situations, programmer time may be an important consideration in choosing an algorithm and its implementation. In this respect, the recursive version of the quick sort is more desirable than its nonrecursive counterpart, which requires the programmer to simulate the recursion explicitly.

Of course, if a programmer is familiar with a language's support library, the programmer can use the sort routines provided there. The Arrays class in the Java library's util package defines a number of sorts for sorting arrays. Likewise, the Java Collections Framework, which was introduced at the end of Section 3.4, provides methods for sorting many of its collection objects.

Space Considerations

Another efficiency consideration is the amount of memory space required. In small applications, memory space is not a very important factor in choosing a sorting algorithm. In large applications, such as a database with many gigabytes of data, space may pose a serious concern. We looked at only two sorts, mergeSort and quickSort, that required more than constant extra space. The usual time versus space tradeoff applies to sorts: More space often means less time, and vice versa.

Because processing time is the factor that applies most often to sorting algorithms, we have considered it in detail here. Of course, as in any application, the programmer must determine the program's goals and requirements before selecting an algorithm and starting to code.

Objects and References

So that we could concentrate on the algorithms, we limited our implementations to sorting arrays of integers. Do the same approaches work for sorting objects? Of course, although a few special considerations apply.

Keep in mind that when we sort an array of objects, we are manipulating references to the objects, not the objects themselves. (See Figure 10.18.) This point does not affect any of our algorithms, but it is still important to understand. For example, if we decide to swap the objects at index 0 and index 1 of an array, it is actually the references to the objects that we swap, not the objects themselves. In one sense, we view objects, and the references to the objects, as identical.

Using the Comparable Interface

When sorting objects, we must have a way to compare two objects and decide which is "larger." Two basic approaches are used when dealing with Java objects.

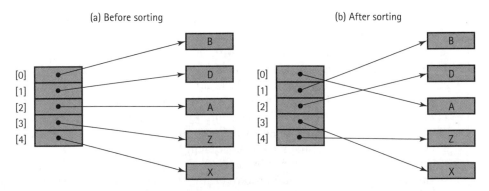

Figure 10.18 *Sorting arrays with references*

The first approach you are familiar with from previous chapters. If the object class exports a `compareTo` operation, or something similar, it can be used to provide the needed comparison. We have used this approach throughout the text. For our sorted lists, binary search trees, and priority queues, we used objects that implemented Java's `Comparable` interface. In fact, the only requirement for a `Comparable` object is that it provides a `compareTo` operation. Indeed, Java programmers, when creating methods that need to compare objects, often insist that all arguments be of type `Comparable`.

For example, here is how we code `bubbleUp` to sort objects of type `Comparable`, rather than just integers:

```
static void bubbleUp(int startIndex, int endIndex)
// Switches adjacent pairs that are out of order
// between values[startIndex]to values[endIndex]
// beginning at values[endIndex].
{
  for (int index = endIndex; index > startIndex; index--)
    if (values[index].compareTo(values[index - 1]) < 0)
      swap(index, index - 1);
}
```

A limitation of this approach is that a class can have only one `compareTo` method. What if we have a class of objects—for example, student records—that we want to sort in many various ways: by name, by grade, by postal code, in increasing order, and in decreasing order? In this case we need to use the approach explained next.

Using the Comparator Interface

The second approach allows more flexibility. The Java library provides another interface related to comparing objects, a generic interface called `Comparator`. This interface defines two abstract methods:

```
public abstract int compare(T o1, T o2);
// Returns a negative integer, zero, or a positive integer to
//  indicate that o1 is less than, equal to, or greater than o2

public abstract boolean equals(Object obj);
// Returns true if this Comparator equals obj; otherwise, false
```

The first method, `compare`, is very similar to the familiar `compareTo` method. It takes two arguments, however, rather than one. The second method, `equals`, is specified in the same way as the `equals` method of the `Object` class, and can be inherited from `Object`. Recall, however, that it usually is important for the `equals` and `compareTo` methods of a class to be consistent. We do not address the `equals` method again in this discussion.

Any sort implementation must compare elements. Our methods so far have used built-in integer comparison operations such as "<" or "<=". If we sort `Comparable` objects instead of integers, we could use the `compareTo` method that is guaranteed to exist by that interface. Alternatively, we could use a versatile approach supported by the `Comparator` interface. If we pass a `Comparator` object `comp` to a sorting method as a parameter, the method can use `comp.compare` to determine the relative order of two objects and base its sort on that relative order. Passing a different `Comparator` object results in a different sorting order. Perhaps one `Comparator` object defines an increasing order, and another defines a decreasing order. Or perhaps the different `Comparator` objects could define order based on different attributes of the objects. Now, with a single sorting method, we can produce many different sort orders.

Let's look at an example. To allow us to concentrate on the topic of discussion, we use a simple circle class, with public instance variables. The fact that the variables are public makes it easy to demonstrate the concepts of this section. We define circles as follows:

```
package ch10.circles;

public class SortCircle
{
  public int xValue;
  public int yValue;
  public int radius;
  public boolean solid;
}
```

Here is the definition of a `Comparator` object that orders `SortCircle` objects based on their `xValue`:

```
Comparator<SortCircle> xComp = new Comparator<SortCircle>()
{
  public int compare(SortCircle a, SortCircle b)
  {
    return (a.xValue - b.xValue);
  }
}
```

Here is a `selectionSort` method, along with its helper method `minIndex`, that accepts and uses a `Comparator` object (the changes from the previous version of selection-Sort are <u>emphasized</u>):

```
      static int minIndex(int startIndex, int endIndex,
                          Comparator<SortCircle>)
      // Returns the index of the smallest value in
      // values[startIndex]to values[endIndex].
      {
        int indexOfMin = startIndex;
        for (int index = startIndex + 1; index <= endIndex; index++)
          if (comp.compare(values[index],values[indexOfMin]) < 0)
            indexOfMin = index;
        return indexOfMin;
      }

      static void selectionSort(Comparator<SortCircle> comp)
      // Sorts the values array using the selection sort algorithm.
      {
        int endIndex = SIZE - 1;
        for (int current = 0; current < endIndex; current++)
          swap(current, minIndex(current, endIndex, comp));
      }
```

Passing a different `Comparator` object to `selectionSort` would result in a different sort order. This makes the sort operation extremely versatile. Just by passing it different `Comparator` objects, it can sort circles in increasing or decreasing order based on any of the circle fields, or even any mathematical combination of circle fields.

The program called `Sorts2` demonstrates our new flexibility. It generates an array of six random `SortCircle` objects, prints them, sorts them by `xValue`, prints them, sorts them by `yValue`, and then prints them again. Study the program carefully.

```
//------------------------------------------------------------------------------
// Sorts2.java              by Dale/Joyce/Weems              Chapter 10
//
// Test harness used to run sorting algorithms that use Comparator.
//------------------------------------------------------------------------------

import java.util.*;
import java.text.DecimalFormat;
import ch10.circles.*;

public class Sorts2
{
  static final int SIZE = 6;                          // size of array to be sorted
  static SortCircle[] values = new SortCircle[SIZE];   // values to be sorted

  static void initValues()
  // Initializes the values array with random circles.
```

```
  {
    Random rand = new Random();
    for (int index = 0; index < SIZE; index++)
    {
      values[index] = new SortCircle();
      values[index].xValue = Math.abs(rand.nextInt()) % 100;
      values[index].yValue = Math.abs(rand.nextInt()) % 100;
      values[index].radius = Math.abs(rand.nextInt()) % 100;
      values[index].solid = ((Math.abs(rand.nextInt()) % 2) == 0);
    }
  }

  static public void swap(int index1, int index2)
  // Swaps the SortCircles at locations index1 and index2 of array values.
  {
    SortCircle temp = values[index1];
    values[index1] = values[index2];
    values[index2] = temp;
  }

  static public void printValues()
  // Prints all the values integers.
  {
    SortCircle value;
    DecimalFormat fmt = new DecimalFormat("00");
    System.out.println("The values array is:");
    System.out.println();
    System.out.println(" x   y   r solid");
    System.out.println("-- -- -- -----");
    for (int index = 0; index < SIZE; index++)
    {
      value = values[index];
      System.out.print(fmt.format(value.xValue) + " ");
      System.out.print(fmt.format(value.yValue) + " ");
      System.out.print(fmt.format(value.radius) + " ");
      System.out.print(value.solid);
      System.out.println();
    }
    System.out.println();
  }

  static int minIndex(int startIndex, int endIndex,
                      Comparator<SortCircle>)
  // Returns the index of the smallest value in
```

```
// values[startIndex] to values[endIndex]
// based on the Comparator comp.
{
  int indexOfMin = startIndex;
  for (int index = startIndex + 1; index <= endIndex; index++)
    if (comp.compare(values[index],values[indexOfMin]) < 0)
      indexOfMin = index;
  return indexOfMin;
}

static void selectionSort(Comparator<SortCircle> comp)
// Sorts the values array using the selection sort algorithm.
{
  int endIndex = SIZE - 1;
  for (int current = 0; current < endIndex; current++)
    swap(current, minIndex(current, endIndex, comp));
}

public static void main(String[] args)
{
  Comparator<SortCircle> xComp = new Comparator<SortCircle>()
  {
    public int compare(SortCircle a, SortCircle b)
    {
      return (a.xValue - b.xValue);
    }
  };

  Comparator<SortCircle> yComp = new Comparator<SortCircle>()
  {
    public int compare(SortCircle a, SortCircle b)
    {
      return (a.yValue - b.yValue);
    }
  };

  initValues();
  printValues();
  selectionSort(xComp);
  printValues();
  selectionSort(yComp);
  printValues();
}
}
```

The output from an execution of the program follows:

```
The values array is:

x  y  r  solid
-- -- -- -----
37 83 82 true
46 25 71 false
43 73 62 true
08 67 40 false
69 68 70 true
20 95 15 false


The values array is:

x  y  r  solid
-- -- -- -----
08 67 40 false
20 95 15 false
37 83 82 true
43 73 62 true
46 25 71 false
69 68 70 true


The values array is:

x  y  r  solid
-- -- -- -----
46 25 71 false
08 67 40 false
69 68 70 true
43 73 62 true
37 83 82 true
20 95 15 false
```

Remember that using the Comparator approach does require revising our sorting routines slightly; they must accept a Comparator as a parameter and use it appropriately. With similar changes, we could use this approach for any of our ADTs that involve comparing elements: our lists, binary search trees, and priority queues. If our goal is to make our ADTs as generally usable as possible, we should certainly consider this approach.

However, the added flexibility of `Comparator` comes at a cost to performance. Just as writing the swap operation within a separate method adds overhead to execution time, so performing the comparison within a method takes more time than a direct comparison. The `Comparable` interface also places the `compareTo` operation within a method, but most optimizing compilers are able to automatically extract the code from the method and place it directly in the sort to avoid this cost. With `Comparator`, different methods are used at different times, so the same optimization can't be applied.

Stability

The stability of a sorting algorithm is based on what it does with duplicate values. Of course, the duplicate values all appear consecutively in the final order. For example, if we sort the list A B B A, we get A A B B. But is the relative order of the duplicates the same in the final order as it was in the original order? If that property is guaranteed, we have a stable sort.

> **Stable sort**   A sorting algorithm that preserves the order of duplicates

In our descriptions of the various sorts, we showed examples of sorting arrays of integers. Stability is not important when sorting primitive types. If we sort objects, however, the stability of a sorting algorithm can become more important. We may want to preserve the original order of unique objects considered identical by the comparison operation.

Suppose the elements in our array are student objects with instance values representing their names, postal codes, and identification numbers. The list may normally be sorted by the unique identification numbers. For some purposes we might want to see a listing in order by name. In this case the comparison would be based on the name variable. To sort by postal code, we would sort on that instance variable.

If the sort is stable, we can get a listing by postal code, with the names in alphabetical order within each postal code, by sorting twice: the first time by name and the second time by postal code. A stable sort preserves the order of the elements when it finds a match. The second sort, by postal code, produces many such matches, but the alphabetical order imposed by the first sort is preserved.

Of the various types of sorts that we have discussed in this book, only `heapSort` and `quickSort` are inherently unstable. The stability of the other sorts depends on how the code handles duplicate values. In some cases, stability depends on whether a < or a <= comparison is used in some crucial comparison statement. In the exercises at the end of this chapter, you are asked to examine the code for the various sorts and determine whether they are stable.

Of course, if we can directly control the comparison operation used by our sort method, we can allow more than one variable to be used in determining a sort order. Thus another, more efficient approach to sorting our students by ZIP code and name is to define an appropriate `compareTo` method for determining sort order as follows (for simplicity, this code assumes we can directly compare the name values):

```
if (postalcode < other.postalcode)
  return -1;
else
if (postalcode > other.postalcode)
  return +1;
else
// Postalcodes are equal
if (name < other.name)
  return -1;
else
if (name > other.name)
  return +1;
else
  return 0;
```

With this approach we need to sort the array only once.

10.5 Searching

Sometimes access to a needed element stored in a structure can be achieved directly. For example, with both our array-based and reference-based stack ADT implementations, we can directly access the top element on the stack; the `top` method is O(1). Access to our array-based indexed lists, given a position on the list, is also direct; O(1) time is needed. Often, however, direct access is not possible, especially when we want to access an element based on its value. For instance, if a list contains student records, we may want to find the record of the student named Suzy Brown or the record of the student whose ID number is 203557. In such cases, some kind of *searching technique* is needed to allow retrieval of the desired record.

In this section we look at some of the basic "search by value" techniques for lists. Some of these techniques (linear and binary search) we have encountered previously in the text. In Section 10.6 we look at an advanced technique, called hashing, that can often provide O(1) searches by value.

Linear Searching

We cannot discuss efficient ways to find an element in a list without considering how the elements were added into the list. Therefore, our discussion of search algorithms is related to the issue of the list's `add` operation. Suppose that we want to add elements as quickly as possible, and we are not overly concerned about how long it takes to find them. We would put the element into the last slot in an array-based list or the first slot in a linked list. Both are O(1) insertion algorithms. The resulting list is sorted according to the time of insertion, not according to key value.

To search this list for the element with a given key, we must use a simple *linear* (or *sequential) search*. For example, we used a linear search for the `find` method of our

`List` class in Chapter 6. Beginning with the first element in the list, we search for the desired element by examining each subsequent element's key until either the search is successful or the list is exhausted.

Based on the number of comparisons, this search is O(N), where N represents the number of elements. In the worst case, in which we are looking for the last element in the list or for a nonexistent element, we will make N key comparisons. On average, assuming that there is an equal probability of searching for any element in the list, we will make $N/2$ comparisons for a successful search; that is, on average we must search half of the list.

High-Probability Ordering

The assumption of equal probability for every element in the list is not always valid. Sometimes certain list elements are in much greater demand than others. This observation suggests a way to improve the search: Put the most-often-desired elements at the beginning of the list.[1] Using this scheme, we are more likely to make a hit in the first few tries, and rarely do we have to search the whole list.

If the elements in the list are not static or if we cannot predict their relative demand, we need some scheme to keep the most frequently used elements at the front of the list. One way to accomplish this goal is to move each element accessed to the front of the list. Of course, there is no guarantee that this element is later frequently used. If the element is not retrieved again, however, it drifts toward the end of the list as other elements move to the front. This scheme is easy to implement for linked lists, requiring only a few pointer changes. It is less desirable for lists kept sequentially in arrays, because we need to move all the other elements down to make room at the front.

An alternative approach, which causes elements to move toward the front of the list gradually, is appropriate for either linked or array-based list representations. As an element is found, it is swapped with the element that precedes it. Over many list retrievals, the most frequently desired elements tend to be grouped at the front of the list. To implement this approach, we need to modify only the end of the algorithm to exchange the found element with the one before it in the list (unless it is the first element). This change should be documented; it is an unexpected side effect of searching the list.

Keeping the most active elements at the front of the list does not affect the worst case; if the search value is the last element or is not in the list, the search still takes N comparisons. It is still an O(N) search. However, the *average* performance on successful searches should improve. Both of these high-probability ordering algorithms depend on the assumption that some elements in the list are used much more often than others. If this assumption is erroneous, a different ordering strategy is needed to improve the efficiency of the search technique.

Lists in which the relative positions of the elements are changed in an attempt to improve search efficiency are called *self-organizing* or *self-adjusting* lists.

---

1. This approach is possible only with our unsorted lists. It could not be used with our sorted or indexed lists, because with those lists the positions of elements is predetermined.

Sorted Lists

As discussed in Section 6.6, "The Binary Search Algorithm," if a list is sorted, we can write more efficient search routines.

If the list is sorted, a sequential search no longer needs to search the whole list to discover that an element does *not* exist. It just needs to search until it has passed the element's logical place in the list—that is, until it encounters an element with a larger key value.

One advantage of linear searching of a sorted list is the ability to stop searching before the list is exhausted if the element does not exist. Again, the search is O(N)—the worst case, searching for the largest element, still requires N comparisons. The average number of comparisons for an unsuccessful search is now $N/2$, however, instead of a guaranteed N.

Another advantage of linear searching is its simplicity. The disadvantage is its performance: In the worst case we have to make N comparisons. If the list is sorted and stored in an array, we can improve the search time to a worst case of O($\log_2 N$) by using a binary search. This improvement in efficiency, however, comes at the expense of simplicity.

The binary search is not guaranteed to be faster for searching very small lists. Even though such a search generally requires fewer comparisons, each comparison involves more computation. When N is very small, this extra work (the constants and smaller terms that we ignore in determining the Big-O approximation) may dominate. For instance, in one assembly-language program, the linear search required 5 time units per comparison, whereas the binary search took 35. For a list size of 16 elements, therefore, the worst-case linear search would require 5 * 16 = 80 time units. The worst-case binary search requires only 4 comparisons, but at 35 time units each, the comparisons take 140 time units. In cases where the number of elements in the list is small, a linear search is certainly adequate and sometimes faster than a binary search.

As the number of elements increases, the magnitude of the difference between the linear search and the binary search grows very quickly. Look back at Table 6.2 to compare the rates of growth for the two algorithms.

The binary search discussed here is appropriate only for list elements stored in a sequential array-based representation. After all, how can we efficiently find the midpoint of a linked list? We already know one structure that allows us to perform a binary search on a linked data representation: the binary search tree. The operations used to search a binary tree were discussed in Chapter 8.

10.6 Hashing

So far, we have succeeded in paring down our O(N) search to a complexity of O($\log_2 N$) by keeping the list sorted sequentially with respect to the key value. That is, the key in the first element is less than (or equal to) the key in the second element, which is less than (or equal to) the key in the third, and so on. Can we do better than that? Is it possible to design a search of O(1)—that is, one with a constant search time, no matter where the element is in the list?

In theory, that is not an impossible dream. Let's look at an example, a list of employees of a fairly small company. Each of the 100 employees has an ID number in the range 0 to 99, and we want to access the employee information by the key idNum. If we store the elements in an array that is indexed from 0 to 99, we can directly access any employee's information through the array index. A one-to-one correspondence exists between the element keys and the array index; in effect, the array index functions as the key of each element.

In practice, this perfect relationship between the key value and the location of an element is not so easy to establish or maintain. Consider a similar small company that uses its employees' five-digit ID numbers as the primary key. Now the range of key values is from 00000 to 99999. It is impractical to set up an array of 100,000 elements, of which only 100 are needed, just to make sure that each employee's element is in a perfectly unique and predictable location.

What if we keep the array size down to the size that we actually need (an array of 100 elements) and use just the last two digits of the key to identify each employee? For instance, the element of employee 53374 is in employeeList[74], and the element of employee 81235 is in employeeList[35]. The elements are not sorted according to the *value* of the key as they were in our earlier discussion; indeed, the position of employee 81235's information precedes that of employee 53374 in the array, even though the value of its key is larger. Instead, the elements are sorted with respect to *some function of the key value.*

> **Hash function**   A function used to manipulate the key of an element in a list to identify its location in the list
>
> **Hashing**   The technique used for ordering and accessing elements in a list in a relatively constant amount of time by manipulating the key to identify its location in the list
>
> **Hash table**   The data structure used to store elements using hashing

This function is called a hash function, and the search technique we are using is called hashing. The underlying data structure is called a hash table.

To simplify our discussion in this chapter, we make three assumptions about the array-based unsorted lists we are searching:

- There is enough room in the underlying array to hold all potential list elements.
- The elements of a list are unique with respect to their key.
- We will not attempt to get or remove an element from the list that is not on the list.

Although these assumptions are not crucial, they do simplify matters somewhat and allow us to focus on hashing itself without worrying about too many special situations. Furthermore, these assumptions are not that unusual for applications where hashing is a good support tool.

Let's return to our discussion of hash functions. In the case of the employee list described earlier, the hash function is (idNum % 100). The key (idNum) is divided by 100, and the remainder is used as an index into the array of employee elements, as illustrated in Figure 10.19. This function assumes that the array is indexed from 0 to 99 (MAX_ELEMENTS = 100). The method to perform the conversion of key values to indexes is very simple:

```
int hash()
// Returns an integer between 0 and MAX_ELEMENTS - 1.
{
   return (idNum % MAX_ELEMENTS);
}
```

Here we assume that hash is a public method of ElementType, the type (class) of the elements in the list, and that idNum is an instance variable of ElementType. To use hashing to facilitate access to a list we can create a new interface Hashable:

```
public interface Hashable
// Objects of classes that implement this interface can be used
// with lists based on hashing.
{
  // A mathematical function is used to manipulate the key of an element
  // in a list to identify its location in the list.
  int hash();
}
```

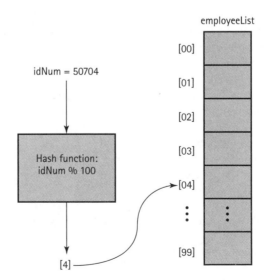

Figure 10.19 *Using a hash function to determine the location of the element in an array*

When we create a class of objects that we intend to store on a hash table we have it implement the Hashable interface, guaranteeing that its objects provide a hash method. For example, consider the following simple Employee class:

```java
//-----------------------------------------------------------------
// Employee.java          by Dale/Joyce/Weems            Chapter 10
//
// Example of a class for use with a hash table.
//-----------------------------------------------------------------

public class Employee implements Hashable
{
  protected String name;
  protected int idNum;
  protected int yearsOfService;

  protected final int MAX_ELEMENTS = 100;

  public Employee(String name, int id, int years)
  {
    this.name = name;
    idNum = id;
    yearsOfService = years;
  }

  public int hash()
  // Returns an integer between 0 and MAX_ELEMENTS - 1.
  {
    return (idNum % MAX_ELEMENTS);
  }
}
```

The hash function has two uses. First, it is used to access a list element. The result of the hash function tells us where to *look* for a particular element—information we need to find the element. Here, for example, is a simple variation of our list method get, which assumes that each potential list element hashes to a unique location in the list:

```java
public Hashable get(Hashable element)
// Returns an element e from this list such that e.equals(element).
{
  int location;
  location = element.hash();
  return (Hashable)list[location];
}
```

The second use of the hash function is to determine where in the array to store the element. If the employee list elements were added into the list using an `add` operation from Chapter 6—into sequential array slots or into slots with their relative order determined by the key value—we could not use the hash function to find them. We have to create a version of the `add` operation that puts each new element into the correct slot according to the hash function. Here is a simple version of `add`, which assumes that the array slot at the index returned from the hash function is not in use:

```
public void add (Hashable element)
// Adds element to this list at position element.hash().
{
  int location;
  location = element.hash();
  list[location] = element;
  numElements++;
}
```

Figure 10.20 shows an array whose elements—information for the employees with the key values (unique ID numbers) 12704, 31300, 49001, 52202, and 65606—were added using `add`. This method does not fill the array positions sequentially. Because we have not yet added any elements whose keys produce the hash values 3 and 5, the array slots [3] and [5] are logically "empty."

Collisions

By now you are probably objecting to this scheme on the grounds that it does not guarantee unique hash locations. Unique ID numbers 01234 and 91234 both "hash" to the same location: `list[34]`. The problem of avoiding such collisions is the biggest challenge in designing a good hash function. A good hash function *minimizes collisions* by spreading the elements uniformly

> **Collision** The condition resulting when two or more keys produce the same hash location

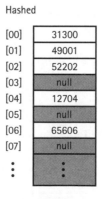

Figure 10.20 *Result of adding elements based on a hash function*

throughout the array. We say "minimizes collisions" because it is extremely difficult to avoid them completely.

Assuming that some collisions occur, where do we store the elements that cause them? We briefly describe several popular collision-handling algorithms next. Of course, the scheme that is used to find the place to store an element determines the approach subsequently used to find it.

Linear Probing

A simple scheme for resolving collisions is to store the colliding element into the next available space. This technique is known as linear probing. In the situation depicted in Figure 10.21, we want to add the employee element with the key ID number 77003. The hash func-

> **Linear probing**   Resolving a hash collision by sequentially searching a hash table beginning at the location returned by the hash function

tion returns 3. But there already is an element stored in this array slot, the record for employee 50003. We increment `location` to 4 and examine the next array slot. Because `list[4]` is also in use, we increment `location` again. This time we find a slot that is empty, so we store the new element into `list[5]`.

What happens if the key hashes to the last index in the array and that space is in use? We can consider the array to be a circular structure and continue looking for an empty slot at the beginning of the array. This situation is similar to our circular array-based queue in Chapter 5. There we used the `%` operator when we incremented our index. We can use similar logic here.

How do we know whether an array slot is "empty"? Assuming we have an array of objects, this is easy—just check whether the value of the array slot is `null`.

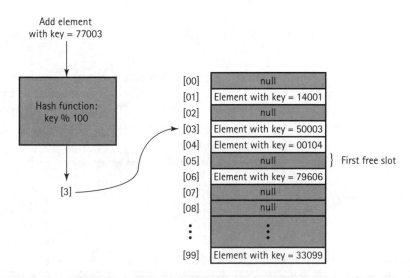

Figure 10.21 *Handling collisions with linear probing*

The following version of add uses linear probing to find a place in which to store a new element. We assume that there is room in the array for another element.

```
public static void add (Hashable element)
// Adds element to this list at position element.hash()
// or the next free array slot.
{
  int location;
  location = element.hash();
  while (list[location] != null)
    location = (location + 1) % list.length;
  list[location] = element;
  numElements++;
}
```

To search for an element using this collision-handling technique, we perform the hash function on the key, then compare the desired key to the actual key in the element at the designated location. If the keys do not match, we use linear probing, beginning at the next slot in the array. Following is a version of the get method that uses this approach. Recall that our get method for hashed lists assumes that the element being retrieved is on the list.

```
public static Hashable get(Hashable element)
// Returns an element e from this list such that e.equals(element).
{
  int location;
  location = element.hash();
  while (!list[location].equals(element))
    location = (location + 1) % list.length;

  return (Hashable)list[location];
}
```

Although we have discussed the insertion and retrieval of elements in a hash table, we have not yet mentioned how to determine whether an element is in the table (contains) or how to remove an element from the table (remove). If we did not need to concern ourselves with collisions, the algorithms would be simple:

contains (element): return boolean

Set location to element.hash( )
Return (list[location] != null)

---

remove (element)

Set location to element.hash( )
Set list[location] to null

Collisions, however, complicate the matter. We cannot be sure that our element is in location `element.hash()`. For `remove`, because we assume the element to be deleted is in the table, we can use the same approach that we used for `get`. We examine every array element, starting with location `element.hash()`, until we find the matching element. For `contains`, we need an extra check to determine whether we have looped all the way back to our starting position without finding a match, in which case we return `false`.

Let's look at an example. In Figure 10.22, suppose we remove the element with the key 77003 by setting the array slot [5] to `null`. A subsequent search for the element with the key 42504 would begin at the hash location [4]. The element in this slot is not the one we are looking for, so we increment the hash location to [5]. This slot, which formerly was occupied by the element that we deleted, is now empty (contains `null`), but we cannot terminate the search—the record that we are looking for is in the next slot.

Not being able to assume that an empty list element indicates the end of a linear probe severely undermines the efficiency of this approach. Even when the hash table is sparsely populated, we must examine every location before determining that an element is not present in the table. This problem illustrates that hash tables, in the forms that we have studied thus far, are not the most effective data structure for implementing lists whose elements may be deleted.

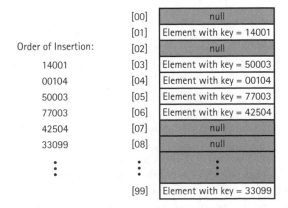

Figure 10.22 *A hash program with linear probing*

Clustering

Clustering The tendency of elements to become unevenly distributed in the hash table, with many elements clustering around a single hash location

One problem with linear probing is that it results in a situation called clustering. A good hash function yields a uniform distribution of indexes throughout the array's index range. Initially, elements are added throughout the array, with each slot being equally likely to be filled. Over time, after a number of collisions have been resolved, the distribution of elements in the array becomes less and less uniform. The elements tend to cluster together, as multiple keys begin to compete for a single hash location.

Consider the hash table in Figure 10.22. Only an element whose key produces the hash value 8 would be inserted into array slot [8]. Any elements with keys that produce a hash value of 3, 4, 5, 6, or 7 would be inserted into array slot [7]. That is, array slot [7] is five times more likely than array slot [8] to be filled. Clustering results in inconsistent efficiency of list operations.

Rehashing

Rehashing Resolving a collision by computing a new hash location from a hash function that manipulates the original location rather than the element's key

The technique of linear probing discussed here is an example of collision resolution by rehashing. If the hash function produces a collision, the hash value is used as the input to a rehash function to compute a new hash value. In the previous section, we added 1 to the hash value to create a new hash value; that is, we used the rehash function:

```
(HashValue + 1) % MAX_ELEMENTS
```

For rehashing with linear probing, we can use any function

```
(HashValue + constant) % array-size
```

as long as `constant` and `array-size` are relatively prime—that is, if the largest number that divides both of them evenly is 1. For instance, given the 100-slot array in Figure 10.23, we might use the constant 3 in the rehash function:

```
(HashValue + 3) % 100
```

(Although 100 is not a prime number, 3 and 100 are relatively prime; they have no common factor larger than 1.)

Suppose that we want to add an element with the key 14001 to the hash table in Figure 10.23. The original hash function (key % 100) returns the hash value 1, but this array slot is in use; it contains the element with the key 44001. To determine the next array slot to try, we apply the rehash function using the results of the first hash function as input: (1 + 3) % 100 = 4. The array slot at index [4] is also in use, so we reapply the rehash function until we find an available slot. Each time, we use the value computed from the previous rehash as input to the rehash function. The second rehash gives

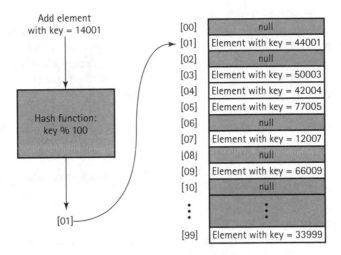

Figure 10.23 *Handling collisions with rehashing*

(4 + 3) % 100 = 7; this slot is in use. The third rehash gives (7 + 3) % 100 = 10; the array slot at index [10] is empty, so the new element is added there.

To understand why the constant and the number of array slots must be relatively prime, consider the rehash function

```
(HashValue + 2) % 100
```

We want to add the element with the key 14001 to the hash table pictured in Figure 10.23. The original hash function, key % 100, returns the hash value 1. This array slot is already occupied. We resolve the collision by applying the rehash function above, examining successive odd-numbered indexes until we find a free slot. What happens if all of the slots with odd-numbered indexes are already in use? The search would fail— even though there are free slots with even-numbered indexes. This rehash function does not cover the full index range of the array. If the constant and the number of array slots are relatively prime (such as 3 and 100), however, the function produces successive rehashes that eventually cover every index in the array.

Rehash functions that use linear probing do not eliminate clustering (although the clusters are not always visually apparent in a figure). For example, in Figure 10.23, any element with a key that produces the hash value 1, 4, 7, or 10 would be inserted into the slot at index [10].

In linear probing, we add a constant (usually 1) in each successive application of the rehash function. Another approach, called quadratic probing, makes the result of rehashing dependent on how many times the rehash function has been applied. The function is:

> **Quadratic probing** Resolving a hash collision by using the rehashing formula (HashValue +/- I^2) % array-size

```
(HashValue +/- I2) % array-size
```

The first rehash adds 1 to `HashValue`, the second rehash subtracts 1, the third rehash adds 4, the fourth subtracts 4, the fifth adds 9, and so on. Quadratic probing reduces clustering, but it does not necessarily examine every slot in the array. For example, if `array-size` is a power of 2 (512 or 1024, for example), relatively few array slots are examined. If `array-size` is a prime number of the form (4 * some-integer + 3), quadratic probing does examine every slot in the array.

> **Random probing**   Resolving a hash collision by generating pseudo-random hash values in successive applications of the rehash function

A third approach uses a pseudo-random-number generator to determine the increment to `HashValue` in each application of the rehash function. Random probing is an excellent choice for eliminating clustering, but it tends to be slower than the other techniques we have discussed.

Buckets and Chaining

Another alternative for handling collisions is to allow multiple element keys to hash to the same location. One solution lets each computed hash location contain slots for multiple elements, rather than just a single element. Each of these multielement locations is called a bucket. Figure 10.24 shows a hash table with buckets that can contain three elements each. Using this approach, we can allow collisions to produce duplicate entries at the same hash location, up to a point. When the bucket becomes full, we must again deal with handling collisions.

> **Bucket**   A collection of elements associated with a particular hash location
>
> **Chain**   A linked list of elements that share the same hash location

Another solution, which avoids this problem, is to use the hash value not as the actual location of the element, but rather as an index identifying a linked list of elements. Each array slot accesses a chain of elements that share the same hash location. Figure 10.25 illustrates this solution to the problem of collisions. Rather than rehashing, we simply allow both elements to share hash location [3]. The entry in the array at this location contains a reference to a linked list that includes both elements.

To search for a given element, we first apply the hash function to the key and then search the chain for the element. Searching is not eliminated, but it is limited to elements that actually share a hash value. By contrast, with linear probing we may have to

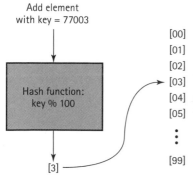

Add element
with key = 77003

Hash function:
key % 100

[3]

[00]	null	null	null
[01]	Element with key = 14001	Element with key = 72101	null
[02]	null	null	null
[03]	Element with key = 50003	Add new element here	null
[04]	Element with key = 00104	Element with key = 30504	Element with key = 56004
[05]	null	null	null
⋮	⋮	⋮	⋮
[99]	Element with key = 56399	Element with key = 32199	null

Figure 10.24 *Handling collisions by hashing with buckets*

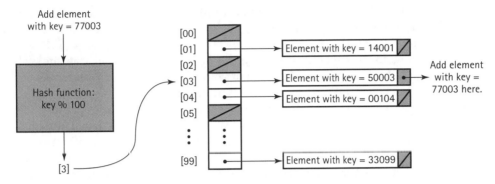

Figure 10.25 *Handling collisions by hashing with chaining*

search through many additional elements if the slots following the hash location are filled with elements from collisions on other hash locations.

Figure 10.26 compares the chaining and hash-and-search schemes. The elements were added in the following order:

45300
20006
50002
40000
25001
13000
65905
30001
95000

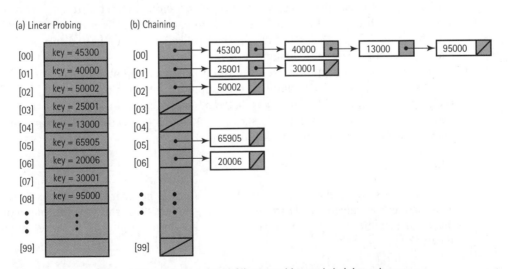

Figure 10.26 *Comparison of linear probing and chaining schemes*

Figure 10.26(a) represents the linear probing approach to collision handling; Figure 10.26(b) shows the result of chaining the colliding elements. Let's search for the element with the key 30001.

Using linear probing, we apply the hash function to get the index [1]. Because list[1] does not contain the element with the key 30001, we search sequentially until we find the element in list[7]. This requires seven steps.

Using the chaining approach, we apply the hash function to get the index [1]. Next, list[1] directs us to a chain of elements whose keys hash to 1. We search this linked list until we find the element with the desired key. This requires only two steps.

Another advantage of chaining is that it simplifies the removal of elements from the hash table. We apply the hash function to obtain the index of the array slot that contains the pointer to the appropriate chain. We can then delete the node from this chain using the linked list algorithm from Chapter 6.

Choosing a Good Hash Function

One way to minimize collisions is to use a data structure that has significantly more space than is actually needed for the number of elements, thereby increasing the range of the hash function. In practice, it is desirable to have the array size be somewhat larger than the number of elements required, so as to reduce the number of collisions. (This approach assumes we are not using a method that requires the contains method to continue searching when it encounters an empty array slot.)

Selecting the table size involves a space versus time trade-off. The larger the range of hash locations, the less likely it is that two keys will hash to the same location. Of course, allocating an array that contains too large a number of empty slots wastes space.

More important, we can design our hash function to minimize collisions. Our goal is to distribute the elements as uniformly as possible throughout the array. Therefore, our hash function should produce unique values as often as possible. Once we admit collisions, we must introduce some sort of searching, either through array or chain searching or through rehashing. The access to each element is no longer direct, and the search is no longer $O(1)$. In fact, if the collisions create very disproportionate-size chains, the worst case may be almost $O(N)$.

To avoid such a situation, we need to know something about the statistical distribution of keys. Imagine a company whose employee information is sorted according to a six-digit ID number. The firm has 500 employees, and we decide to use a chained approach to handle collisions. We set up 100 chains (expecting an average of five elements per chain) and use the hash function

```
idNum % 100
```

That is, we use the last two digits of the six-digit ID number as our index. The planned hash scheme is shown in Figure 10.27(a). Figure 10.27(b) shows what happened when the hash scheme was implemented. How could the distribution of the elements be so skewed?

(a) The plan

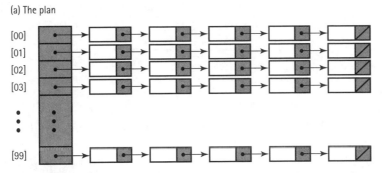

[00]
[01]
[02]
[03]

[99]

Average 5 records/chain
5 records × 100 chains = 500 employees
Expected search — 0(5)

(b) The reality

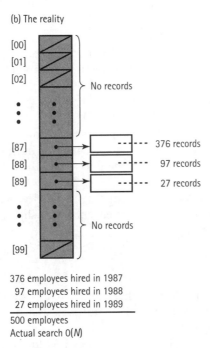

[00]
[01]
[02]

No records

[87]   376 records
[88]   97 records
[89]   27 records

No records

[99]

376 employees hired in 1987
 97 employees hired in 1988
 27 employees hired in 1989

500 employees
Actual search 0(N)

Figure 10.27 *Hash scheme to handle employee elements*

It turns out that the company's ID number is a concatenation of three values:

XXX	X	XX
3 digits, unique number (000–999)	1 digit, dept. number (0–9)	2 digits, year hired (e.g., 89)

The hash scheme depended solely on the year hired to produce hash values. Because the company was founded in 1987, all of the elements were crowded very disproportionately into a small subset of the hash locations. A search for an employee element, in this case, is O(N). Although this is an exaggerated example, it illustrates the need to understand as completely as possible the domain and predicted values of keys in a hash scheme. In the example situation it is much better to use some combination of the first three digits for the hash function.

Division Method
The most common hash functions use division (%) to compute hash values. We used this type of function in the preceding examples. The general function is

```
key % tableSize
```

We have already mentioned the idea of making the table somewhat larger than the number of elements required, thereby increasing the range of hash values. In addition, better results are produced with the division method when the table size is a prime number.

The advantage of the division hash function is its simplicity. Sometimes, however, it is necessary to use a more complicated (or even exotic) hash function to achieve a more uniform distribution of hash values.

Other Hash Methods
How can we use hashing if the element key is a string instead of an integer? One approach uses an arithmetic combination of the internal representations of the string's characters to create a number that can be used as an index. (Each Unicode character is represented in memory as an integer.)

A hash method called folding involves breaking the key into several pieces and then concatenating or exclusive-OR'ing some of those pieces to form the hash value. Another method is to square the key and then use some of the digits (or bits) of the key as a hash value. A number of other techniques are available as well, all of which are intended to make the hash location as unique and random (within the allowed range) as possible.

Folding A hash method that breaks the key into several pieces and then concatenates or exclusive-ORs some of those pieces to form the hash value

When using an exotic hash function, we should keep two considerations in mind. First, we should consider the efficiency of calculating the function. Even if a hash function always produces unique values, it is not a good choice if it takes longer to calculate the hash value than to search half the list. Second, we should consider programmer time. An extremely exotic function that somehow produces unique hash values for all of the known key values may fail if the domain of possible key values changes in a later modification. The programmer who has to modify the program may then waste a lot of time trying to find another hash function that is equally clever.

Finally, note that if we know all of the possible keys ahead of time, it is possible to determine a *perfect* hash function. For example, if we needed a list of elements whose keys were the reserved words in a computer language, we could find a hash function that hashes each word to a unique location. In general, it takes a great deal of work to discover a perfect hash function.

Java's Support for Hashing

The Java library includes a `HashTable` class that uses hash techniques to support storing objects in a table. In fact, the library includes several other collection classes, such as `HashSet`, that provide an ADT whose underlying implementation takes advantage of the approaches described in this section.

The Java `Object` class exports a `hashCode` method that returns an `int` hash code. Because all Java objects ultimately inherit from `Object`, all Java objects have an associated hash code. This is the hash value that Java uses within its hash-based library classes.

The standard Java hash code for an object is a function of the object's memory location. As a consequence, it cannot be used to relate separate objects with identical contents. For example, even if `circleA` and `circleB` have identical field values, it is very unlikely that they have the same hash code. Of course, if `circleA` and `circleB` both reference the same circle object, then their hash codes are identical because they hold the same memory reference.

For most applications, hash codes based on memory locations are not usable. Therefore, many of the Java classes that define commonly used objects (such as `String` and `Integer`) override the `Object` class's `hashCode` method with one that *is* based on the contents of the object. If you plan to use hash tables in your programs, you should do likewise.

Complexity

We began our discussion of hashing by trying to find a list implementation where the addition and removal of elements had a complexity of O(1). If our hash function never produces duplicates and the array size is large compared to the expected number of elements in the list, then we have reached our goal. In general, this is not the case. Clearly, as the number of elements approaches the array size, the efficiency of the algorithms deteriorates. A precise analysis of the complexity of hashing is beyond the scope of this book. Informally, we can say that the larger the array is relative to the expected number of elements and the smaller the number of collisions produced by the hash function, the more time efficient the algorithms are.

Summary

We have not attempted in this chapter to describe every known sorting algorithm. Instead, we have presented a few of the popular sorts, of which many variations exist. It should be clear from this discussion that no single sort is best for all applications. The simpler, generally $O(N^2)$ sorts work as well as, and sometimes better than, the more complicated sorts for fairly small values of N. Because they are simple, these sorts require relatively little programmer time to write and maintain. As we add features to improve sorts, we also increase the complexity of the algorithms, expanding both the work required by the routines and the programmer time needed to maintain them.

Another consideration in choosing a sort algorithm is the order of the original data. If the data are already sorted (or almost sorted), `shortBubble` is $O(N)$, whereas some versions of `quickSort` are $O(N^2)$.

As always, the first step in choosing an algorithm is to determine the goals of the particular application. This effort usually narrows the choice of options considerably. After that, knowledge of the strong and weak points of the various algorithms assists us in selecting a sorting method.

Table 10.3 compares the sorts discussed in this chapter in terms of Big-O notation.

Searching, similar to sorting, is a topic that is closely tied to the goal of efficiency. We speak of a sequential search of a list as an $O(N)$ search, because it may require as many as N comparisons to locate an element. (N refers to the number of elements in the list.) Binary searches are considered to be $O(\log_2 N)$ and are appropriate for array-based lists if they are sorted. A binary search tree may be used to allow binary searches on a linked structure. The goal of hashing is to produce a search that approaches $O(1)$ time efficiency. Because of collisions of hash locations, some searching or rehashing is usually necessary. A good hash function minimizes collisions and distributes the elements randomly throughout the table.

Table 10.3 *Comparison of Sorting Algorithms*

	Order of Magnitude		
Sort	Best Case	Average Case	Worst Case
selectionSort	$O(N^2)$	$O(N^2)$	$O(N^2)$
bubbleSort	$O(N^2)$	$O(N^2)$	$O(N^2)$
shortBubble	$O(N)$*	$O(N^2)$	$O(N^2)$
insertionSort	$O(N)$*	$O(N^2)$	$O(N^2)$
mergeSort	$O(N \log_2 N)$	$O(N \log_2 N)$	$O(N \log_2 N)$
quickSort	$O(N \log_2 N)$	$O(N \log_2 N)$	$O(N^2)$ (depends on split)
heapSort	$O(N \log_2 N)$	$O(N \log_2 N)$	$O(N \log_2 N)$

*Data almost sorted.

It is important that you become familiar with several of the basic sorting and searching techniques. We use these tools over and over again in a programming environment, and we need to know which ones are appropriate solutions to different problems. Our review of sorting and searching techniques has given us another opportunity to examine a measuring tool—the Big-O approximation—that helps us determine how much work is required by a particular algorithm. Both building tools and measuring tools are needed to construct sound program solutions.

Exercises

10.1 Sorting

1. A test harness program for testing sorting methods is provided with the rest of the textbook program files. It is in the file `Sorts.java` in the `ch10` package. The program includes a `swap` method that is used by all of the sorting methods to swap array elements.

   a. Describe an approach to modifying the program so that after calling a sorting method the program prints out the number of swaps needed by the sorting method.

   b. Implement your approach.

   c. Test your new program by running the `selectionSort` method. Your program should report 49 swaps.

10.2 Simple Sorts

2. Multiple choice: How many comparisons would be needed to sort an array containing 100 elements using a selection sort if the original array values were already sorted?

   a. 10,000

   b. 9,900

   c. 4,950

   d. 99

   e. None of these

3. Determine the Big-O complexity for the selection sort based on the number of elements moved rather than on the number of comparisons

   a. For the best case.

   b. For the worst case.

4. In what case(s), if any, is the complexity of the selection sort $O(\log_2 N)$?

5. Write a version of the bubble sort algorithm that sorts a list of integers in descending order.

6. In what case(s), if any, is the complexity of the bubble sort $O(N)$?

7. How many comparisons would be needed to sort an array containing 100 elements using `shortBubble`

    a. In the worst case?

    b. In the best case?

8. Show the contents of the array

43	7	10	23	18	4	19	5	66	14
[0]	[1]	[2]	[3]	[4]	[5]	[6]	[7]	[8]	[9]

after the fourth iteration of

    a. `selectionSort`.

    b. `bubbleSort`.

    c. `insertionSort`.

9. A sorting function is called to sort a list of 100 integers that have been read from a file. If all 100 values are zero, what would the execution costs (in terms of Big-O notation) be if the sort used was

    a. `bubbleSort`?

    b. `shortBubble`?

    c. `selectionSort`?

    d. `insertionSort`?

10. In Exercise 1 you were asked to modify the `Sorts` program so that it would output the number of swaps used by a sorting method. It is a little more difficult to have the program also output the number of comparisons (compares) needed. You must include one or more statements to increment your counter within the sorting methods themselves. For each of the listed methods, make and test the changes needed, and list both the number of swaps and the number of compares needed by the `Sorts` program to sort an array of 50 random integers.

    a. `selectionSort`   swaps: _____   compares: _____

    b. `bubbleSort`   swaps: _____   compares: _____

    c. `shortBubble`   swaps: _____   compares: _____

    d. `insertionSort`   swaps: _____   compares: _____

10.3 $O(N \log_2 N)$ Sorts

11. A merge sort is used to sort an array of 1000 test scores in descending order. Which one of the following statements is true?

    a. The sort is fastest if the original test scores are sorted from smallest to largest.

    b. The sort is fastest if the original test scores are in completely random order.

    c. The sort is fastest if the original test scores are sorted from largest to smallest.

d. The sort is the same, no matter what the order of the original elements.

12. Show how the values in the array in Exercise 8 would be arranged immediately before the execution of method `merge` in the original (nonrecursive) call to `mergeSort`.

13. Determine the Big-O complexity for `mergeSort` based on the number of elements moved rather than on the number of comparisons

    a. For the best case.

    b. For the worst case.

14. Use the Three-Question Method to verify `mergeSort`.

15. In what case(s), if any, is the complexity of the quick sort $O(N^2)$?

16. Which is true about the quick sort?

    a. A recursive version executes faster than a nonrecursive version.

    b. A recursive version has fewer lines of code than a nonrecursive version.

    c. A nonrecursive version takes more space on the run-time stack than a recursive version.

    d. It can be programmed only as a recursive function.

17. Determine the Big-O complexity for `quickSort` based on the number of elements moved rather than on the number of comparisons

    a. For the best case.

    b. For the worst case.

18. Use the Three-Question Method to verify `quickSort`.

19. Using the algorithms for creating a heap and sorting an array using a heap-based approach:

    a. Show how the values in the array in Exercise 8 would have to be rearranged to satisfy the heap property.

    b. Show how the array would look with four values in the sorted portion after reheaping.

20. A sorting function is called to sort a list of 100 integers that have been read from a file. If all 100 values are zero, what would the execution costs (in terms of Big-O notation) be if the sort used was

    a. `mergeSort`?

    b. `quickSort`, with the first element used as the split value?

    c. `heapSort`?

21. Suppose a list is already sorted from smallest to largest when a sort is called. Which of the following sorts would take the longest time to execute and which would take the shortest time?

    a. `quickSort`, with the first element used as the split value

b. `shortBubble`

c. `selectionSort`

d. `heapSort`

e. `insertionSort`

f. `mergeSort`

22. A very large array of elements is to be sorted. The program will be run on a personal computer with limited memory. Which sort would be a better choice: a heap sort or a merge sort? Why?

23. True or False? Explain your answers.

   a. `mergeSort` requires more space to execute than `heapSort`.

   b. `quickSort` (using the first element as the split value) is better for nearly sorted data than `heapSort`.

   c. The efficiency of `heapSort` is not affected by the original order of the elements.

24. In Exercise 1 you were asked to modify the `Sorts` program so that it would output the number of swaps used by a sorting method. It is a little more difficult to have the program also output the number of comparisons needed. You must include one or more statements to increment your counter within the sorting methods themselves. For each of the listed methods, make and test the changes needed, and list the number of comparisons needed by `Sorts` to sort an array of 50 random integers.

   a. `mergeSort`   compares: _____

   b. `quickSort`   compares: _____

   c. `heapSort`   compares: _____

10.4   More Sorting Considerations

25. For small values of N, the number of steps required for an $O(N^2)$ sort might be less than the number of steps required for a sort of a lower degree. For each of the following pairs of mathematical functions f and g below, determine a value N such that if $n > N$, $g(n) > f(n)$. This value represents the cutoff point, above which the $O(n^2)$ function is always larger than the other function.

   a. $f(n) = 4n$ $g(n) = n^2 + 1$

   b. $f(n) = 3n + 20$ $g(n) = \frac{1}{2}n^2 + 2$

   c. $f(n) = 4 \log_2 n + 10$ $g(n) = n^2$

26. Give arguments for and against using methods (such as `swap`) to encapsulate frequently used code in a sorting routine.

27. Many times, to simplify our code, we create recursive methods of the form

```
if condition
   do something
```

If the condition is false, the recursive method does nothing and returns. To avoid the overhead of extra method invocations, it is more efficient to perform the test on the condition before invoking the recursive method. Thus the method becomes

```
do something
```

An example of this is our `quickSort` method. Describe how you would change `quickSort` to avoid the overhead of unneeded invocations. Don't forget to address any needed changes to the original invocation of `quickSort`.

28. What is meant by this statement: "Programmer time is an efficiency consideration." Give an example of a situation in which programmer time is used to justify the choice of an algorithm, possibly at the expense of other efficiency considerations.

29. Modify the `Sorts2` class so that it also sorts the array of `SortCircles`
    a. From smallest to largest.
    b. From right to left, based on the position of the center of the circle. (The coordinate system uses increasing values moving from left to right.)
    c. Based on the distance of the circle from the point 0, 0; shortest distance first.

30. The `Sorts2` class is similar to the `Sorts` class we used to study sorting algorithms. Instead of using integers, the `Sorts2` class generates an array of random `SortCircle` objects, and then sorts them first by `xValue` and then by `yValue`. Create an `isSorted` method for `Sorts2`, similar to the `isSorted` method of `Sorts` except it must accept and use a `Comparator` parameter. Modify `Sorts2` to include this new method; remember to call the method both before and after the calls to the sort routines.

31. Go through the sorting algorithms coded in this chapter and determine which ones are stable as coded. Identify the key statement in the corresponding method that determines the stability. If there are unstable algorithms (other than the quick sort and heap sort), make them stable.

32. We said that the heap sort algorithm is inherently unstable. Explain why.

33. Which sorting algorithm would you *not* use under each of the following conditions?
    a. The sort must be stable.
    b. Space is very limited.

10.5 Searching

34. Fill in the following table, showing the number of comparisons needed either to find the value or to determine that the value is not in the indicated structure based on the given approach and given the following values:

    26, 15, 27, 12, 33, 95, 9, 5, 99, 14

Value	Unsorted Array in the order shown	Sorted Array, Sequential Search	Sorted Array, Binary Search	Binary Search Tree with elements added in the order shown
15				
17				
14				
5				
99				
100				
0				

35. If you know the index of an element stored in an array of N unsorted elements, which of the following best describes the order of the algorithm to find the element?

a. $O(1)$

b. $O(N)$

c. $O(\log_2 N)$

d. $O(N^2)$

e. $O(0.5N)$

36. The element being searched for *is not* in an array of 100 elements. What is the *average* number of comparisons needed in a sequential search to determine that the element is not there

a. If the elements are completely unsorted?

b. If the elements are sorted from smallest to largest?

c. If the elements are sorted from largest to smallest?

37. The element being searched for *is not* in an array of 100 elements. What is the *maximum* number of comparisons needed in a sequential search to determine that the element is not there

a. If the elements are completely unsorted?

b. If the elements are sorted from smallest to largest?

c. If the elements are sorted from largest to smallest?

38. The element being searched for *is* in an array of 100 elements. What is the *average* number of comparisons needed in a sequential search to determine the position of the element

    a. If the elements are completely unsorted?

    b. If the elements are sorted from smallest to largest?

    c. If the elements are sorted from largest to smallest?

39. Choose the answer that correctly completes the following sentence: The elements in an array may be sorted by highest probability of being requested to reduce

    a. The average number of comparisons needed to find an element in the list.

    b. The maximum number of comparisons needed to detect that an element is not in the list.

    c. The average number of comparisons needed to detect that an element is not in the list.

    d. The maximum number of comparisons needed to find an element that is in the list.

40. True or False? Explain your answers.

    a. A binary search of a sorted set of elements in an array is always faster than a sequential search of the elements.

    b. A binary search is an $O(N \log_2 N)$ algorithm.

    c. A binary search of elements in an array requires that the elements be sorted from smallest to largest.

    d. A high-probability ordering scheme would be a poor choice for arranging an array of elements that are equally likely to be requested.

41. How might you order the elements in a list of Java's reserved words to use the idea of high-probability ordering?

10.6   Hashing

For Exercises 42–45, use the following values:

66, 47, 87, 90, 126, 140, 145, 153, 177, 285, 393, 395, 467, 566, 620, 735

42. Store the values into a hash table with 20 positions, using the division method of hashing and the linear probing method of resolving collisions.

43. Store the values into a hash table with 20 positions, using rehashing as the method of collision resolution. Use `key % tableSize` as the hash function, and `(key + 3) % tableSize` as the rehash function.

44. Store the values into a hash table with 10 buckets, each containing three slots. If a bucket is full, use the next (sequential) bucket that contains a free slot.

45. Store the values into a hash table that uses the hash function `key % 10` to determine which of 10 chains to put the value into.

46. Fill in the following table, showing the number of comparisons needed to find each value using the hashing representations given in Exercises 42–45.

Number of Comparisons

Value	Exercise 42	Exercise 43	Exercise 44	Exercise 45
66				
467				
566				
735				
285				
87				

47. True or False? Explain your answers.

a. When a hash function is used to determine the placement of elements in an array, the order in which the elements are added does not affect the resulting array.

b. When hashing is used, increasing the size of the array always reduces the number of collisions.

c. If we use buckets in a hashing scheme, we do not have to worry about collision resolution.

d. If we use chaining in a hashing scheme, we do not have to worry about collision resolution.

e. The goal of a successful hashing scheme is an O(1) search.

48. Choose the answer that correctly completes the following sentence: The number of comparisons required to find an element in a hash table with N buckets, of which M are full,

a. Is always 1.

b. Is usually only slightly less than N.

c. May be large if M is only slightly less than N.

d. Is approximately $\log_2 M$.

e. Is approximately $\log_2 N$.

49. Write a program that repeatedly accepts a string from the user and outputs the hash code for the string, using the String class's predefined hashCode method.

50. Create a data set with 100 integer values. Create a program that uses the division method of hashing to store the data values into hash tables with table sizes of 7, 51, and 151. Use the linear probing method of collision resolution. Print out the tables after the data values have been stored. Search for 10 different values in each of the three hash tables, counting the number of comparisons necessary. Print out the number of comparisons necessary in each case in tabular form. Turn in a listing of your program and a listing of the output.

Appendix A

Java Reserved Words

abstract	continue	for	new	switch
assert	default	goto	package	synchronized
boolean	do	if	private	this
break	double	implements	protected	throw
byte	else	import	public	throws
case	enum	instanceof	return	transient
catch	extends	int	short	try
char	final	interface	static	void
class	finally	long	strictfp	volatile
const	float	native	super	while

Appendix B

Operator Precedence

In the following table, the operators are grouped by precedence level (highest to lowest), and a horizontal line separates each precedence level from the next-lower level.

Precedence (highest to lowest)

Operator	Assoc.*	Operand Type(s)	Operation Performed
.	LR	object, member	object member access
[]	LR	array, int	array element access
(args)	LR	method, arglist	method invocation
++, --	LR	variable	post-increment, decrement
++, --	RL	variable	pre-increment, decrement
+, -	RL	number	unary plus, unary minus
~	RL	integer	bitwise complement
!	RL	boolean	boolean NOT
new	RL	class, arglist	object creation
(type)	RL	type, any	cast (type conversion)
*, /, %	LR	number, number	multiplication, division, remainder
+, -	LR	number, number	addition, subtraction
+	LR	string, any	string concatenation
<<	LR	integer, integer	left shift
>>	LR	integer, integer	right shift with sign extension
>>>	LR	integer, integer	right shift with zero extension
<, <=	LR	number, number	less than, less than or equal
>, >=	LR	number, number	greater than, greater than or equal
instanceof	LR	reference, type	type comparison
==	LR	primitive, primitive	equal (have identical values)
!=	LR	primitive, primitive	not equal (have different values)
==	LR	reference, reference	equal (refer to the same object)
!=	LR	reference, reference	not equal (refer to different objects)
&	LR	integer, integer	bitwise AND
&	LR	boolean, boolean	boolean AND
^	LR	integer, integer	bitwise XOR
^	LR	boolean, boolean	boolean XOR

*LR means left-to-right associativity; RL means right-to-left associativity.

Precedence (highest to lowest)

Operator	Assoc.*	Operand Types(s)	Operation Performed
|	LR	integer, integer	bitwise OR
|	LR	boolean, boolean	boolean OR
&&	LR	boolean, boolean	conditional AND (short circuit evaluation)
||	LR	boolean, boolean	conditional OR (short circuit evaluation)
? :	RL	boolean, any, any	conditional (ternary) operator
=	RL	variable, any	assignment
*=, /=, %=, +=, -=, <<=, >>=, >>>=, &=, ^=, |=	RL	variable, any	assignment with operation

*LR means left-to-right associativity; RL means right-to-left associativity.

Appendix C

Primitive Data Types

Type	Value Stored	Default Value	Size	Range of Values
char	Unicode character	Character code 0	16 bits	0 to 65535
byte	Integer value	0	8 bits	−128 to 127
short	Integer value	0	16 bits	−32768 to 32767
int	Integer value	0	32 bits	−2147483648 to 2147483647
long	Integer value	0	64 bits	−9223372036854775808 to 9223372036854775807
float	Real value	0.0	32 bits	±1.4E-45 to ±3.4028235E+38
double	Real value	0.0	64 bits	±4.9E-324 to ±1.7976931348623157E+308
boolean	true or false	false	1 bit	NA

Appendix D

ASCII Subset of Unicode

The following chart shows the ordering of characters in the ASCII (American Standard Code for Information Interchange) subset of Unicode. The internal representation for each character is shown in decimal. For example, the letter A is represented internally as the integer 65. The space (blank) character is denoted by a "□".

Left Digit(s) \ Right Digit	*ASCII*									
	0	*1*	*2*	*3*	*4*	*5*	*6*	*7*	*8*	*9*
0	NUL	SOH	STX	ETX	EOT	ENQ	ACK	BEL	BS	HT
1	LF	VT	FF	CR	SO	SI	DLE	DC1	DC2	DC3
2	DC4	NAK	SYN	ETB	CAN	EM	SUB	ESC	FS	GS
3	RS	US	□	!	"	#	$	%	&	'
4	(	)	*	+	,	−	.	/	0	1
5	2	3	4	5	6	7	8	9	:	;
6	<	=	>	?	@	A	B	C	D	E
7	F	G	H	I	J	K	L	M	N	O
8	P	Q	R	S	T	U	V	W	X	Y
9	Z	[	\	]	^	_	`	a	b	c
10	d	e	f	g	h	i	j	k	l	m
11	n	o	p	q	r	s	t	u	v	w
12	x	y	z	{	|	}	~	DEL		

Codes 00–31 and 127 are the following nonprintable control characters:

NUL	Null character	VT	Vertical tab	SYN	Synchronous idle
SOH	Start of header	FF	Form feed	ETB	End of transmitted block
STX	Start of text	CR	Carriage return	CAN	Cancel
ETX	End of text	SO	Shift out	EM	End of medium
EOT	End of transmission	SI	Shift in	SUB	Substitute
ENQ	Enquiry	DLE	Data link escape	ESC	Escape
ACK	Acknowledge	DC1	Device control one	FS	File separator
BEL	Bell character (beep)	DC2	Device control two	GS	Group separator
BS	Back space	DC3	Device control three	RS	Record separator
HT	Horizontal tab	DC4	Device control four	US	Unit separator
LF	Line feed	NAK	Negative acknowledge	DEL	Delete

Appendix E

Application Programmer Interfaces for the Java Classes and Interfaces Used in This Book

In this appendix we have listed the application programmer interfaces (APIs) for the Java classes and interfaces, used in this book, plus a few others we believe you may find useful. For each class/interface, the header line shows the name of the class/interface on the left and the name of the library package that contains the class/interface on the right. This is followed by a brief description of the class/interface, plus a selected list of constants, constructors, and methods. There are more constructs for the classes presented here, and there are many more classes and interfaces in the Java class library. You should also explore the robust information about Java APIs at www.java.sun.com.

ArrayList<E>   java.util

Implements a dynamically resizable array of object references that can be treated as a list. The functionality of the `ArrayList` class is similar to that of an array. In fact, the array is the underlying implementation structure used in this class. An `ArrayList` includes a capacity attribute representing the size of this underlying array. The `ArrayList` is a member of the Java Collections Framework. As of Java 5.0, this class supports generics; E indicates the type of element that can be stored in the collection. If no value for E is supplied to the constructor, it defaults to `Object`.

Constructors

```
ArrayList( )
```
Constructs an `ArrayList` object with an initial capacity of 10.

```
ArrayList(int initialCapacity)
```
Constructs an `ArrayList` object with the specified initial capacity. Throws an `IllegalArgumentException` if `initialCapacity` is negative.

Methods

```
boolean add(E element)
```
Appends the specified element to the end of this list. Returns `true`.

```
void add(int index, E element)
```
Inserts the specified element to the specified location of this list. Shifts the remaining elements one position "to the right." Throws the `IndexOutOfBoundsException` if the indicated index is out of the legal range.

```
void clear( )
```
Removes all elements from this list.

```
boolean contains(Object element)
```
Returns `true` if `element` is on this list; otherwise, returns `false`.

```
void ensureCapacity(int minCapacity)
```
If the current capacity of this list is less than `minCapacity`, increases the capacity to `minCapacity`.

```
Object get(int index)
```
Returns the element at the specified `index` position; the element is not removed from this list.

```
int indexOf(Object element)
```
Returns the index of the first occurrence of `element` on this list. If `element` is not on this list, returns −1.

```
boolean isEmpty()
```
Returns `true` if this list is empty; otherwise, returns `false`.

```
Object remove(int index)
```
Returns and removes the element at the specified `index` position.

```
Object set(int index, E newElement)
```
Returns the element at the specified `index` position and replaces that element with `newElement`.

```
int size( )
```
Returns the number of elements in this list.

```
void trimToSize( )
```
Sets the capacity to this list's current size.

Character   java.lang

The Java class library provides a wrapper class for each of the primitive types. The wrapper class allows us to store a primitive value in an `Object` variable. `Character` is the wrapper class that creates an equivalent object for a `char` variable. It also provides useful conversion and utility methods for working with characters. Characters are based on the Unicode standard.

Constructor

`Character(char ch)`

Instantiates a `Character` object that corresponds to a `char` variable having the same value as `ch`.

Methods

`char charValue( )`

Returns the corresponding `char` value of this `Character`.

`int compareTo(Character anotherCharacter)`

Compares this `Character` to the argument `Character` numerically, returning a negative number, zero, or a positive number if this `Character` is less than, equal to, or greater than the argument `Character`, respectively.

`boolean equals(Object obj)`

Returns `true` if `obj` represents the same `char` value as this `Character` object; otherwise, returns `false`.

`int hashCode( )`

Returns a hash code for this `Character`.

`boolean isDigit(char ch)`

Static method that returns `true` if the argument is a digit; otherwise, returns `false`.

`boolean isLetter(char ch)`

Static method that returns `true` if the argument is a letter; otherwise, returns `false`.

`boolean isWhitespace(char ch)`

Static method that returns `true` if the argument is whitespace, according to Java; otherwise, returns `false`.

`char toLowerCase(char c)`

Static method that returns the lowercase version of the `char` argument.

`String toString()`

Returns a `String` object representing this `Character`.

`char toUpperCase(char c)`

Static method that returns the uppercase version of the `char` argument.

```
Character valueOf(char c)
```
Static method that returns an instance of `Character` representing the argument char.

Cloneable (interface) java.lang

The `Cloneable` interface has a unique protocol: Declaring that a class implements `Cloneable` amounts to a promise by the implementer that clients of the class can safely invoke a `clone` method on objects of the class. Either the class provides its own reliable `clone` method or the implementer guarantees that the inherited `Object` class's `clone` method (a bitwise copy operation—that is, an exact copy of the object's memory representation; see `Object`) can be used. If `clone` is invoked on an object of a class that does not implement the `Cloneable` interface, the `CloneNotSupportedException` is thrown.

Comparable<T> (interface) java.lang

The `Comparable` interface consists of exactly one abstract method:

```
int compareTo(T o)
```
Compares this object to the argument object, returning a negative number, zero, or a positive number if this object is less than, equal to, or greater than the argument object, respectively.

See Section 6.1, "Comparing Objects Revisited," for more information.

This interface is a member of the Java Collections Framework. As of Java 5.0, it supports generics; `T` indicates the types of objects that can be compared. A `ClassCastException` is thrown if the argument object's type is not compatible with the object upon which `compareTo` is invoked. If no value for `T` is supplied when a class indicates that it implements `Comparable`, it defaults to `Object`. In that case, however, many compilers will generate an "unchecked warning" wherever the `compareTo` method is invoked.

Comparator<T> (interface) java.util

The `Comparator` interface consists of two abstract methods:

```
int compare(T o1, T o2);
```
Returns a negative integer, zero, or a positive integer to indicate that `o1` is less than, equal to, or greater than `o2`, respectively.

```
boolean equals(Object obj);
```
Returns `true` if this `Object` equals `obj`; otherwise, returns `false`.

See Section 10.4, "More Sorting Considerations," for more information.

This interface is a member of the Java Collections Framework. As of Java 5.0, it supports generics; `T` indicates the types of objects that can be compared. A `ClassCastException` is thrown if the argument types of `compare` are not compatible with each other. If no value for T is supplied when a class indicates that it implements `Comparator`, it defaults to `Object`.

DecimalFormat

java.text

Provides methods for formatting numbers for output.

Constructor

`DecimalFormat(String pattern)`

Instantiates a `DecimalFormat` object with the output `pattern` specified in the argument.

Method

`String format(double number)`

Returns a `String` representation of `number` formatted according to the `DecimalFormat` pattern used to instantiate this object. This method is inherited from the `NumberFormat` class.

Commonly Used Pattern Symbols for a DecimalFormat Object

Symbol	Meaning
0	Required digit. If the value for the digit in this position is 0, print a zero.
#	Digit. Don't print anything if the digit is a leading zero.
.	Decimal point.
,	Comma separator.
%	Multiply by 100 and display a percent sign.

Exception

java.lang

The superclass for all predefined Java exceptions. All subclasses of the `Exception` class inherit these `public` methods. See Section 3.3, "Exceptional Situations," for more information.

Constructors

`Exception( )`

Instantiates an `Exception` object that has the `null` string as its default message.

`Exception(String str)`

Instantiates an `Exception` object that has the `str` string as its default message.

Methods

`String getMessage( )`
　Returns a message indicating the cause of this exception. This method is inherited from the `Throwable` class.

`void printStackTrace( )`
　Prints the line number of the code that caused this exception, along with the sequence of method calls leading up to this exception.

`String toString( )`
　Returns a `String` containing the exception class name and a message indicating the cause of this exception.

FileInputStream   *java.io*

Reads bytes from a file.

Constructor

`FileInputStream(String filename)`
　Constructs a `FileInputStream` object from a `String` representing the name of a file. Throws a `FileNotFoundException` if a corresponding file does not exist or is not readable.

FileOutputStream   *java.io*

Writes bytes to a file.

Constructor

`FileOutputStream(String filename, boolean mode)`
　Constructs a `FileOutputStream` object from a `String` representing the name of a file; if `mode` is false, we will write to the file; if mode is `true`, we will append to the file. Throws a `FileNotFoundException` if the named file cannot be opened for writing.

FileReader   *java.io*

Reads characters from a text file.

Constructor
`FileReader(String filename)`
　Constructs a `FileReader` object from a `String` representing the name of a file. Throws a `FileNotFoundException` if a corresponding file does not exist or is not readable.

FileWriter   *java.io*

Writes characters to a text file.

Constructor
`FileWriter(String fileName, boolean mode)`

Constructs a `FileWriter` object from a `String` representing the name of a file; if `mode` is `false`, we will write to the file; if it is `true`, we will append to the file. Throws an `IOException` if the named file cannot be opened for writing.

Integer   java.lang

The Java class library provides a wrapper class for each of the primitive types. The wrapper class allows us to store a primitive value in an `Object` variable. `Integer` is the wrapper class that creates an equivalent object for an `int` variable. It also provides useful conversion and utility methods for working with integers.

Constructor

`Integer(int i)`
   Instantiates an `Integer` object that corresponds to an `int` variable having the same value as `i`.

Methods

`int compareTo(Integer anotherInteger)`
   Compares this `Integer` to the argument `Integer` numerically, returning a negative number, zero, or a positive number if this `Integer` is less than, equal to, or greater than the argument `Integer`, respectively.

`boolean equals(Object obj)`
   Returns `true` if `obj` represents the same `int` value as this `Integer` object; otherwise, returns `false`.

`int hashCode( )`
   Returns a hash code for this `Integer`.

`int intValue( )`
   Returns the corresponding `int` value of this `Integer`.

`int parseInt(String s)`
   Static method that converts the `String` `s` to an `int` and returns that value.

`String toString()`
   Returns a `String` object representing this `Integer`.

`Integer valueOf(int i)`
   Static method that returns an instance of `Integer` representing the argument `int`.

`Integer valueOf(String s)`
   Static method that converts the `String` `s` to an `Integer` object and returns that object.

Iterable<T> (interface)   java.lang

Objects of a class that implements this interface can be used with the `foreach` statement. The interface consists of one abstract method:

```
Iterator<T> iterator( );
```
Returns an `Iterator` to be used over a collection of elements of type `T`.

This interface is new in Java 5.0. It supports generics; `T` indicates the types of objects that can be iterated through. If no value for `T` is supplied when a class indicates that it implements `Iterable`, it defaults to `Object`.

Iterator<E> (interface) java.util

Objects of a class that implements this interface can be iterated through. That is, the elements that make up the collection represented by the object can be visited, one after the other, using the methods required by the interface. Those methods are described below:

```
boolean hasNext( );
```
Returns `true` if there are more elements to visit during this iteration; otherwise, returns `false`.

```
E next( )
```
Returns the next element, of type `E`, for this iteration.

```
void remove( )
```
Removes the most recent element visited by the iteration from this collection.

This interface is a member of the Java Collections Framework. As of Java 5.0, it supports generics; `E` indicates the types of objects that can be iterated through. If no value for `E` is supplied when a class indicates that it implements `Iterator`, it defaults to `Object`.

Math java.lang

Provides methods for performing common mathematical computations. All methods are static.

Predefined Static Constants

E	double	The base of the natural logarithm. Approximate value is 2.78.
PI	double	Pi, the ratio of the circumference of a circle to its diameter. Approximate value is 3.14.

Static Methods

```
dataTypeOfArg abs(arg)
```
Returns the absolute value of the argument `arg`, which can be a `double`, `float`, `int`, or `long`.

```
double log(double a)
```
Returns the natural logarithm (in base e) of its argument. For example, log(1) returns 0 and log(`Math.E`) returns 1.

`dataTypeOfArgs max(argA, argB)`
Returns the larger of the two arguments. The arguments can be of type `double`, `float`, `int`, or `long`.

`dataTypeOfArgs min(argA, argB)`
Returns the smaller of the two arguments. The arguments can be of type `double`, `float`, `int`, or `long`.

`double pow(double base, double exp)`
Returns the value of `base` raised to the `exp` power.

`double random( )`
Returns a random number greater than or equal to 0 and less than 1.

`int round(float a)`
Returns the closest integer to its argument, `a`.

`double sqrt(double a)`
Returns the positive square root of `a`.

NumberFormat   java.text

Provides methods for formatting numbers in currency, percent, and other formats. There are no constructors for this class.

Methods

`String format(double number)`
Returns a `String` representation of `number` formatted according to the `NumberFormat` object reference used to call the method.

`NumberFormat getCurrencyInstance( )`
This static method creates a format for printing money.

`NumberFormat getPercentInstance( )`
This static method creates a format for printing a percentage.

Object   java.lang

This class is the root of the Java class tree. Every other class inherits from `Object`; it is a superclass of every other class.

Constructor

`Object( )`
Instantiates a new instance of the `Object` class.

Methods

`Object clone( )`
Creates a bit-by-bit copy of this object and returns it. See `Cloneable` for more information.

```
boolean equals(Object obj)
```
Returns `true` if `obj` represents the same object as this `Object`; otherwise, returns `false`.

```
int hashCode( )
```
Returns a hash code for this `Object`.

```
String toString()
```
Returns a `String` object representing this `Object`.

ObjectInputStream   java.io

Reads serialized objects from a file. See Section 6.8, "Storing Objects and Structures in Files," for more information.

Constructor

```
ObjectInputStream(InputStream in)
```
Constructs an `ObjectInputStream` from the `InputStream in`. Throws an `IOException` when appropriate.

Methods

```
void close( )
```
Closes this input stream.

```
Object readObject( )
```
Reads the next object from this input stream and returns it. The object read must be an instance of a class that implements the `Serializable` interface. When the end of the file is reached, an `EOFException` is thrown. Also throws an `IOException` and `ClassNotFoundException` when appropriate.

ObjectOutputStream   java.io

Writes objects in a serialized format to a file. See Section 6.8, "Storing Objects and Structures in Files," for more information.

Constructor

```
ObjectOutputStream(OutputStream out)
```
Creates an `ObjectOutputStream` that writes to the `OutputStream out`. Throws an `IOException`.

Methods

```
void close( )
```
Closes this output stream.

```
void writeObject(Object obj)
```
Writes the object `obj` to this output stream. That object must be an instance of a class that implements the `Serializable` interface. Throws an `InvalidClass-Exception`, `NotSerializableException`, and `IOException` when appropriate.

PrintWriter

Writes primitive data types and `Strings` to a text file.

Constructor

`PrintWriter(OutputStream os)`
 Constructs a `PrintWriter` object from the `OutputStream` object.

Methods

`void close( )`
 Releases the resources associated with this `PrintWriter` object.

`void print(boolean b)`
 Prints the `boolean` b to the `OutputStream`.

`void print(char c)`
 Prints the `char` c to the `OutputStream`.

`void print(double d)`
 Prints the `double` d to the `OutputStream`.

`void print(int i)`
 Prints the `int` i to the `OutputStream`.

`void print(String s)`
 Prints the `String` s to the `OutputStream`.

`void println(boolean b)`
 Prints the `boolean` b to the `OutputStream` and appends a newline.

`void println(char c)`
 Prints the `char` c to the `OutputStream` and appends a newline.

`void println(double d)`
 Prints the `double` d to the `OutputStream` and appends a newline.

`void println(int i)`
 Prints the `int` i to the `OutputStream` and appends a newline.

`void println(String s)`
 Prints the `String` s to the `OutputStream` and appends a newline.

Random

Provides sequences of pseudo-random numbers. A sequence of numbers is based on an initial seed. Two instances created with the same seed will generate the same sequence of numbers. Also see the `random` method of the `Math` class.

Constructors

`Random( )`
　　Creates a new random-number generator, using a seed dependent on the current system status.

`Random(long seed)`
　　Creates a new random-number generator, using a seed equal to `seed`.

Methods

`int nextInt( )`
　　Returns the next pseudo-random number.

`int nextInt(int n)`
　　Returns the next pseudo-random number between 0 (inclusive) and `n` (exclusive).

Scanner   java.util

Provides support for reading from an input stream or file. A `Scanner` object breaks the contents of its input stream into tokens, and returns the tokens one at a time when requested. Unless otherwise indicated, the `Scanner` assumes that standard whitespace separates tokens.

Constructors

`Scanner(InputStream source)`
　　Creates a `Scanner` object for reading from `source`. If `source` is `System.in`, this instantiates a `Scanner` object for reading from the Java console.

`Scanner(File source)`
　　Creates a `Scanner` object for reading from a file.

Methods

`boolean hasNext( )`
　　Returns `true` if there is another token in the input stream; otherwise, returns `false`.

`boolean hasNextBoolean( )`
　　Returns `true` if the next token in the input stream can be read as a `boolean`; otherwise, returns `false`.

`boolean hasNextByte( )`
　　Returns `true` if the next token in the input stream can be read as a `byte`; otherwise, returns `false`.

`boolean hasNextDouble( )`
　　Returns `true` if the next token in the input stream can be read as a `double`; otherwise, returns `false`.

`boolean hasNextFloat( )`
Returns `true` if the next token in the input stream can be read as a `float`; otherwise, returns `false`.

`boolean hasNextInt( )`
Returns `true` if the next token in the input stream can be read as an `int`; otherwise, returns `false`.

`boolean hasNextLong( )`
Returns `true` if the next token in the input stream can be read as a `long`; otherwise, returns `false`.

`boolean hasNextShort( )`
Returns `true` if the next token can be read as a `short`; otherwise, returns `false`.

`String next()`
Returns the next token in the input stream as a `String`.

`boolean nextBoolean()`
Returns the next input token as a `boolean`. Throws an `InputMismatchException` when appropriate.

`byte nextByte( )`
Returns the next input token as a `byte`. Throws an `InputMismatchException` when appropriate.

`double nextDouble()`
Returns the next input token as a `double`. Throws an `InputMismatchException` when appropriate.

`float nextFloat()`
Returns the next input token as a `float`. Throws an `InputMismatchException` when appropriate.

`int nextInt()`
Returns the next input token as an `int`. Throws an `InputMismatchException` when appropriate.

`String nextLine()`
Returns the remainder of the input line as a `String`.

`long nextLong()`
Returns the next input token as a `long`. Throws an `InputMismatchException` when appropriate.

`short nextShort( )`
Returns the next input token as a `short`. Throws an `InputMismatchException` when appropriate.

`Scanner useDelimiter(Pattern pattern)`
Sets up the `Scanner` so that it uses the characters indicated in the argument `pattern` to separate tokens in its stream.

Serializable (interface)   java.io

The `Serializable` interface has no abstract methods. A class implements this interface simply by declaring that it implements the interface. Implementation of this interface enables a class to be serialized. See Section 6.8, "Storing Objects and Structures in Files," for more information.

String   java.lang

Provides support for storing, searching, and manipulating sequences of characters. `String` objects are immutable—once they are created, they are not changed. None of the methods of the `String` class changes the value of a string. Instead, whenever a change is made, a new `String` object is created.

   The Java language provides a few shortcuts for using the `String` class. Just as Java provides literals for all of its primitive types (for example, `-154` is a literal of type `int` and `true` is a literal of type `boolean`), so it provides a literal string mechanism. To indicate a literal string, you simply enclose the sequence of characters within double quotation marks—for example, "`this is a literal string.`" A literal string actually represents an object of the class `String`.

   The second shortcut is the provision of an infix string concatenation operand. The `String` class provides a `concat` method to concatenate two strings together to create a third string. Because this operation is so prevalent, however, the language also provides a shortcut operand, `+`. For example, if `s1`, `s2`, and `s3` are all `String` variables, then these two statements are equivalent:

```
s3 = s1.concat(s2); 2 s3 = s1 + s2;
```

Constructors

`String(String str)`
   Creates a `String` object with the value of `str`, which can be a `String` object or a `String` literal.

`String( )`
   Creates an empty `String` object.

`String(char [ ] charArray)`
   Creates a `String` object containing the characters in the `char` array `charArray`.

Methods

`char charAt(int index)`
   Returns the character at the position in this `String` specified by `index`. The first index is 0.

`int compareTo(String str)`
   Compares the values of the two `String`s. If this `String` object is less than the argument, returns a negative integer. If this `String` object is greater than the `String` argument, returns a positive integer. If the two `String`s are equal, returns 0.

```
String concat(String str)
```
Concatenates the argument to the end of this `String` and returns the result.

```
boolean equals(Object str)
```
Compares the value of two strings. Returns `true` if `str` is a `String`, is not `null`, and is equal to this `String` object; otherwise, returns `false`.

```
boolean equalsIgnoreCase(String str)
```
Compares the values of two strings, treating uppercase and lowercase characters as equal. Returns `true` if the strings are equal; otherwise, returns `false`.

```
int indexOf(char searchChar)
```
Returns the index of the first occurrence of `searchChar` in this `String`.

```
String indexOf(String substring)
```
Returns the index of the first occurrence of `substring` in this `String`.

```
int length( )
```
Returns the length of this `String` (the number of characters).

```
String replace(char oldChar, char newChar)
```
Replaces each occurrence of `oldChar` in this `String` with `newChar` and returns the resultant `String`.

```
String substring(int startIndex, int endIndex)
```
Returns a substring of this `String` beginning at the character at index `startIndex` and ending at the character at index (`endIndex - 1`).

```
String toLowerCase( )
```
Converts all letters in this `String` to lowercase and returns the resultant `String`.

```
String toUpperCase( )
```
Converts all letters in this `String` to uppercase and returns the resultant `String`.

System   java.lang

All of the `System` class's methods and variables are static. The `System` class cannot be instantiated. It includes facilities for accessing the system's standard input, output, and error streams, and for determining various properties of the underlying computer system.

Constants

```
System.out
```
The `out` class constant of the `System` class is a `PrintStream` object, which represents the standard system output device. The following `PrintStream` methods can be called using the object reference `System.out` to print to the Java console.

Methods

`void print(argument)`

Prints argument to the standard output device. The argument is usually any primitive data type or a `String` object.

`void println(argument)`

Prints `argument` to the standard output device, then prints a newline character. The argument is usually any primitive data type or a `String` object.

Likewise, `System.in` and `System.err` represent the standard system input and error streams.

Method

`void exit(int status)`

Static method that exits the currently running Java Virtual Machine.

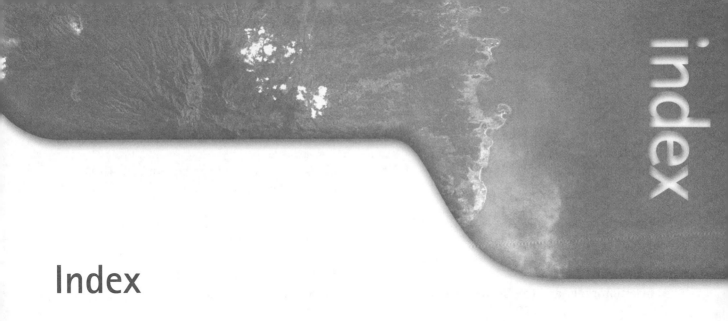

Index

Note: Italicized page locators indicate a figure; tables are noted with a *t*.